Mark Jones and Lance P

BEYOND THE FINAL FRONTIER

An Unauthorised Review of the Trek Universe on Television and Film

SEASON SUMMARIES
CHARACTERS
EPISODES
MOVIES

First published 2003 by Contender Books
Contender Books is a division of
The Contender Entertainment Group
48 Margaret Street
London W1W 8SE
www.contendergroup.com/books

This edition published 2003

1 3 5 7 9 10 8 6 4 2

Text © Contender Ltd 2003

The right of Mark Jones and Lance Parkin to be identified as the authors of this work has been asserted by them in accordance with the Copyright, Designs and Patents Act, 1988.

All rights reserved.

No part of this publication may be reproduced, stored in a retrieval system, or transmitted in any form, or by any means, electrical, mechanical, photocopying, recording or otherwise without the prior permission of the publisher or a licence permitting restricted copying.

ISBN 1 84357 080 7

Images © Science Photo Library
Printed in the UK by Butler & Tanner Ltd, Frome and London
Designed and typeset by Craig Stevens at designsection
Production by Sasha Morton

This is a work of critical review, based on episodes from the television series *Star Trek* which have been broadcast in the UK on terrestrial and satellite channels and also on motion pictures from the *Star Trek* franchise which have been given a UK release.

This is not an official *Star Trek* product and has not been endorsed by the rights owners.

For Lorraine

Thanks to:

Lucy Zinkiewicz, Jim Smith, Mark Clapham and Brie Lewis of Alpha Centauri

Lorraine Jones, Gareth Wigmore and avid Trekkers Lesley Gornall and Alan Challis

And to quatloo: Jon Blum, Graeme Burk, Dave Ford, Donald Gillikin, Michael Lee, Arturo Magidin, Andrew McCaffrey, Greg McElhatton, Eva Palmerton, Trina Short, Robert Smith, Shannon Sullivan, Steve Traylen and Tom Truszkowski

CONTENTS

STAR TREK: THE BASICS

This book is a guide to *Star Trek* on television and in the cinema.

Star Trek is made up of six individual television series and ten movies. These are:

- **STAR TREK (1966-69):** the adventures of Captain Kirk, Mr Spock, Dr McCoy and the crew of the USS Enterprise.
- **STAR TREK (1972-73):**an animated series that's a direct continuation of the adventures of Kirk and his crew.

In 1977 there were plans to make a sequel series, **STAR TREK II**, but these fell through. Instead, *Star Trek* found its way onto the big screen:

- **STAR TREK: THE MOTION PICTURE (1979)**
- **STAR TREK II: THE WRATH OF KHAN (1982)**
- **STAR TREK III: THE SEARCH FOR SPOCK (1984)**
- **STAR TREK IV: THE VOYAGE HOME (1986)**
- **STAR TREK V: THE FINAL FRONTIER (1989)**
- **STAR TREK VI: THE UNDISCOVERED COUNTRY (1991)**

These six movies show an older Kirk.

- **STAR TREK: THE NEXT GENERATION (1987-92):** the adventures of Captain Picard and his crew in the huge USS Enterprise-D, 100 years after Kirk's first missions.

STAR TREK: GENERATIONS (1994)
STAR TREK: FIRST CONTACT (1996)
STAR TREK: INSURRECTION (1998)
STAR TREK: NEMESIS (2002)

These four movies continue the adventures of Picard and his crew (*Star Trek: Generations* also has a lengthy prologue depicting the death of Captain Kirk).

- **STAR TREK: DEEP SPACE NINE (1993-99):** set at the time of *The Next Generation* on a space station that's placed at a strategically vital point on the edge of Federation space.
- **STAR TREK: VOYAGER (1995-2001):** set at the time of *The Next Generation*, about a Federation starship that ends up in a distant corner of the galaxy and is trying to get home to Earth.
- **ENTERPRISE (2001-):** set 100 years *before* Kirk's original missions, the adventures of Captain Archer and the first starship called the Enterprise.

This book has an introductory essay for each individual series which gives a brief history and an overview, and tries to identify its strengths and weaknesses. This is followed by summaries for every episode of that series, broken down into the following categories:

- **TITLE** The title as it appears on screen. The episode number denotes the season and episode – 4.1 would be the first episode of the fourth season of that particular *Star Trek* series. This is in original US broadcast order. The order the episodes were made, the order they are shown in syndication, or released on DVD and video, and therefore the order they appear in other books and reference works, is sometimes slightly different.
- **STRAPLINE** A brief summary of the episode, to act as an *aide memoire*.
- **TX** For the networked *Star Trek* series, animated series, *Voyager* and *Enterprise*, this is the date of the first broadcast in the United States. *The Next Generation* and *Deep Space Nine* were syndicated, and not every station showed the episodes on the same day. The date given for an episode of those series is that of the week of first broadcast in the US.
- **WRITER** Writers' credits in American television and cinema follow a system that's full of byzantine industry rules and subtle but important variations in definition. To simplify this, the 'writer' named in this section is the person who is credited with actually writing the script (usually, in modern *Star Trek*, with a 'written by' or 'teleplay by' credit), and 'story by' covers anyone else who's *credited* with story input ('idea by', 'story by' credits and the like). Where a pseudonym is used, it's noted. *Star Trek* has staff writers, script and story editors and producers, all of whom have input to the scripts. Those responsible for changes to stories while in production, including substantial uncredited work on the story, are noted in the *Trivia* section.
- **DIRECTOR** The credited director of the episode.
- **GUEST CAST** The credited actors, the parts they play (in brackets) and any significant parts played by those who are uncredited. The reason for the lack of credit is listed in *Trivia*.
- **STORY** A brief synopsis of the story, beginning with the stardate of when the episode is set (if known).
- **QUOTES** Dialogue that is notable for summing up a story, making a clever point, being a good joke or being so awful that it's entertaining.
- **TRIVIA** Behind the scenes information.
- **RATING** Our entirely subjective opinion of the episode, which you're free to disagree with.

STAR TREK

THREE SEASONS

One unbroadcast pilot
and 79 x 44-minute episodes
(1966-69)

REGULAR CAST

Captain James T Kirk: William Shatner
Mr Spock: Leonard Nimoy
Dr Leonard 'Bones' McCoy: DeForest Kelley
'Scotty': James Doohan
Sulu: George Takei
Uhura: Nichelle Nichols
Christine Chapel: Majel Barrett
Chekov: Walter Koenig (Seasons 2 and 3)
Janice Rand: Grace Lee Whitney (Season 1)

CREATED BY

Gene Roddenberry

PRODUCER

Gene Roddenberry (Seasons 1-2)
Fred Freiberger (Season 3)

STAR TREK WAS A FAILURE.

It's difficult to believe nearly 40 years on, with five spin-off series, ten feature films, whole companies dedicated to producing spin-off merchandise, and a cult following that has few rivals, but when *Star Trek* was first shown, the network it was shown on, NBC, thought it was too expensive to justify the ratings, seriously considered not renewing it for a second series and only brought it back for a third after a huge letter-writing campaign by viewers. The third season saw radical changes, but *Star Trek* couldn't avoid cancellation.

The real benchmark was *Mission: Impossible. Star Trek* and *Mission: Impossible* started on as level a playing field as possible. The two shows were made on adjacent stages at the Desilu studio, at the same time, the shows' creators both had the same agent (Alden Schwimmer), the studio executives watched the two pilots on the same day, the first episodes were broadcast the same week. *Mission: Impossible* proved cheaper to make – and just as importantly, rarely went over budget – and was a huge critical success, winning Emmys. From the third season onwards, *Mission: Impossible* was a top ten show in the Nielsen ratings – throughout its run, *Star Trek* never got higher than 52 in the same chart. *Mission: Impossible* eventually ran for seven years (with Leonard Nimoy moving over to play Paris in the series, once *Star Trek* had finished).

Star Trek would have been forgotten about or, at best, it would have resurfaced in the late nineties as one of the tranche of sixties television shows revived as a vehicle for Hollywood star names – Bruce Willis as Captain Kirk and John Malkovich as Spock. But shortly after its cancellation, something unprecedented happened: on American TV, once there are enough episodes of a networked show, they are packaged up and sold to smaller, local stations – this is called syndication. Usually, this is simply economic: the smaller stations can't afford to make big shows, but they can afford to buy repeat rights. The network's happy to get more money for, essentially, old rope.

When *Star Trek* was sent into syndication, it found its audience and became a success, then a huge hit. Quite what happened, no-one's sure. Some people involved are convinced that the huge audience had been watching all along, but that the way of collecting ratings was flawed and missed them. The Nielsen system was certainly geared to family audiences, and tended to miss young men, college students and educated young couples. Now, of course, advertisers do everything they can to catch these 'key demographics' and the Nielsens have been adjusted to look for them. But even then, the system wasn't so crude or the networks so blind that they'd miss tens of millions of viewers. All the evidence is that in the sixties the show had a passionate, loyal, literate, vocal following – but a small one.

The surge in organised fan activities, like clubs and conventions, manifestly only came in the early seventies. The first New York convention in January 1972 was the turning point: expecting to attract a couple of hundred people, the organisers stopped counting after three thousand people arrived. *Variety* and *TV Guide* articles reported that there was a *bona fide* phenomenon underway, and it was growing: the 1974 New York convention had 15,000 attendees, with half as many again turned away at the door. Nothing of the sort had happened the first time round – it seems very likely that the syndicated runs picked up new viewers, that a smaller station, far more responsive to a few well-argued letters from local viewers than a national network, was exactly the right environment for a 'cult' to grow. Before long, syndicated stations across America were scheduling *Star Trek* repeats in prime time, against key networked opposition, and it was a huge success.

The obvious question to ask is 'Why did *Star Trek* catch on?'

There are two answers to that, and they contradict each other. Firstly, *Star Trek* had a ferociously loyal and committed fan following, an ever-growing and ever-more-organised body of people who wrote letters and jammed switchboards and let the stations know just how seriously they took *Star Trek*. But *Star Trek* was also a mainstream hit, and the reason for that seems to be because the show didn't take itself too seriously. To this day, there are two interpretations of the original *Star Trek* out there: the first is a series with such a profound philosophy that it's practically a religion for its dedicated followers, and the second is a load of camp, Technicolor nonsense full of over-enthusiastic acting, unconvincing monsters and scantily-clad dolly birds.

The scope of this book is to try to deal with *Star Trek* purely as it appears on screen – you'd need more than one book to discuss the origins, growth, development and influence of its fan following. Those books exist, as do *Trekkies* (1997) and *Trekkies 2* (2003), documentary films on the subject. But it's impossible to tell the story of *Star Trek* without at least mentioning its fans. Sometimes, *Star Trek* fandom is messianic in tone. Fans have tended to exaggerate the impact of their favourite show, to lose a sense of proportion and to treat it as a major social force. It's difficult now to appreciate the context in which *Star Trek* was being made – the Cold War was real, the Vietnam War was underway and racial segregation was still widely practised in some American states. It's true that *Star Trek* tackled all these issues, and because it was science fiction, it could use allegory and analogy to go further than 'real life' shows ever could. But this aspect of the show has been massively overstated by *Star Trek* fans, who often hold up the series as especially radical, somehow intimately connected with the civil rights and peace movements of the sixties, and as somehow inspiring NASA to travel into space. Gene Roddenberry, the creator of *Star Trek,* was seen as some sort of living saint. One website biography asserts:

'He showed us that space is not just for space battles, but for learning new ideas and ways of thinking, and, indirectly, has done more for civil rights and the space program than Martin Luther King Jr and John F Kennedy.'

This is palpable nonsense, actively offensive to the memories of two men who were killed for their beliefs.

It's indisputable that individuals were inspired by *Star Trek*. Some fans' descriptions of how *Star Trek* inspired them to become scientists, engineers, teachers and so on border on the evangelical. It has had a positive effect on many thousands of individual lives, and that's no small achievement. But the wider social or political impact of a little-watched science fiction series was minuscule, and other American shows of the time had far bolder examples of the sort of liberal, optimistic, multicultural social agenda that *Star Trek* fans have long claimed was their unique territory. *Mission: Impossible* had a black character (Barney Collier, played by Greg Morris) – and he was a lead, not just a glorified telephone operator. *The Man From UNCLE* had a Russian character – again, a lead. Viewed now, sixties *Star Trek* looks almost absurdly sexist and in places if it's not actually racist, it's certainly happy to conform to and exaggerate racial stereotypes. And there never was a NASA space shuttle called the Enterprise – the 'shuttle' unveiled in 1977 was a test vehicle with no engines or heat shielding, used for aerodynamic, computer and ground tests, none of which lasted more than six minutes.

The truth is that Gene Roddenberry was no visionary. He was a skilled screenwriter for serial television (see, for example, the *Star Trek* episode *The Menagerie*), albeit one with some serious limitations, and one who – bizarre as it seems – never reached his potential. Before *Star Trek*, he was a jobbing writer on shows like *Dr Kildare* and *Have Gun Will Travel*, and had pitched a couple of ideas for series. He made four pilot episodes: *333 Montgomery Street* (about a defence attorney, with DeForest Kelley), *The Long Hunt of April Savage*, *APO 923* (set in the South Pacific during WW2), *Police Story* (co-starring DeForest Kelley and Grace Lee Whitney) but none of them went to series. During *Star Trek's* first season he pitched a series called *Assignment: Earth*, but again this wasn't picked up and became the *Star Trek* episode of the same name. After *Star Trek* finished, he was keen to move on, but this proved difficult – pilot episodes of *Genesis II*, *The Questor Tapes*, *Planet Earth* and *Spectre* were all filmed, but none of the series were commissioned. A science fiction movie, *The Nine*, was written but couldn't attract funding. Indeed, Roddenberry has proved far more successful at branching out after his death: *Gene Roddenberry's Earth: Final Conflict* and *Gene Roddenberry's Andromeda*, based on formats he created, have proved very popular posthumously.

Roddenberry boiled his original premise down to '*Wagon Train* in space'. The first treatment he submitted to Paramount, dated 11 March 1964, was based on the continuing adventures of Captain Robert April of the cruiser USS Yorktown. April was accompanied by physician Dr Boyce, first officer Number One and the alien Mr Spock. They were explorers and adventurers, and thanks to something called 'the parallel worlds theory', many of the planets they discovered would closely resemble Earth at some point in its history, a concept that allowed the show to use stock sets and costumes. There was, apparently, a move within the studio to call the series *Star Track*, as it was felt 'Trek' sounded too laborious.

Star Trek wasn't startlingly original or unique as a concept – the British comic strip *Dan Dare* and radio series *Journey into Space*, the movies *Destination Moon* (1950) and (particularly) *Forbidden Planet* (1956) all beat *Star Trek* to portraying a future where quasi-military explorers and scientists from a broadly peaceful Earth of the future roamed the galaxy in a spaceship, meeting beautiful women, fighting ugly monsters and asserting Western values.

Star Trek certainly benefited from Gene Roddenberry's insistence that it was more than just a TV show, it represented a philosophy. He was a hands-on producer, and would insist that *Star Trek* articulated his own brand of ultra-secular humanism – the human race is fundamentally good, if subject to base desires; humans are capable of the most incredible achievements, and should never submit to 'gods', greed or dogma; reason is better than violence; a person should strive to constantly improve themself, cherish art and science; men should be rational, but never practise self-denial. *Star Trek*'s future is a place where man has ceased squabbling; where the Earth has been transformed into a garden; where robots ten times stronger and smarter than us strive to be human. It's an optimistic future, a utopian one, and it's not too much of a stretch to imagine that people like watching *Star Trek*, because at some level, they'd like to live in a place like that.

But this also leads to a serious problem with Roddenberry's vision. Utopias are common in science fiction, and they have a common failing – they can be boring, a crude way for an author to present their personal beliefs in the best possible light and ignore the problems with them. The citizens of a utopia are often portrayed as being of one mind, and to have put aside every selfish instinct. Roddenberry's future was an idealised version of Kennedy-era America, one without the assassinations, civil unrest or Vietnam War. It felt like the contemporary United States, but the citizens of the Federation didn't have money or the desire or need for material things... and, if you think about it for the merest moment, that means it's about as far from the real America as it's possible to get.

Sometimes, usually at the start of a *Star Trek* project, we seem to get a pure blast of Roddenberry utopianism, and it can be colourless, preachy and slow – the series pilot *The Cage*, *Star Trek: The Motion Picture* and the first series of *The Next Generation*, while containing flashes of brilliance and vision, are fundamentally rather dull. Non-violent conflict resolution is to be admired in real life, but it rarely makes good drama.

Television shows and movies are never one person's vision – Roddenberry's original pilot, *The Cage*, was rejected by the network (not for being 'too cerebral', as often reported, but because they felt it was too expensive and not very exciting), and a more action-based format developed. It was a recurring pattern – Roddenberry was often forced to water down his vision, or indeed completely lost control of it. Often, you can't help but think the studio was right. Roddenberry hated *Star Trek II: The Wrath of Khan*. Conceding it was 'exciting', he thought there were moments that betrayed the spirit of the original show – he felt, for example, that it was out of character for Kirk to shoot the nasty worm that crawls out of Chekov's ear, rather than make every effort to study it.

Over the years, a lot of the very best *Star Trek* has been the work of people other than Roddenberry, and while they've always acknowledged their debt to him, people like Dorothy ('DC') Fontana, David Gerrold, Gene Coon, Leonard Nimoy, William Shatner, Nicholas Meyer, Patrick Stewart and Rick Berman have often used their weight to push the series away from his vision in favour of a more light-hearted, action-packed and self-referential version of *Star Trek*.

While its fans represent a core audience that means no *Star Trek* film will lose money or series dip too far in the ratings, the true success of *Star Trek* is that it's one of those rare franchises that crosses into the mainstream, one that can sustain Hollywood films that trade on knowledge of the series, like *Galaxy Quest* (1999) and *Jay and Silent Bob Strike Back* (2001), pastiches in shows like *South Park* and *Futurama*, or namechecks in pop songs by everyone from Nena to The Beastie Boys. *Star Trek* phrases like 'beam me up, Scotty' (which, as any fan will tell you, like 'play it again, Sam' and 'elementary, dear Watson' was never *quite* said in the original stories – it's first used in the animated series), 'warp speed', 'to boldly go', 'the final frontier' and 'the next generation' are in common usage. To the mass audience, *Star Trek* is a collection of clichés, catchphrases and iconic visuals, and it wouldn't occur to them that there could be a deeper philosophy at work.

Star Trek fans, particularly in America, have traditionally been repelled by the idea that the original series is camp, even though it's clearly a product of the same period as the Adam West *Batman* or *The Monkees* TV show. The people making *Star Trek* have been happy to embrace the humour and self-parody in the format. Even after nearly 40 years, William Shatner's synonymous with over-acting – one dictionary even lists 'Shatnerian' as 'a clipped, over-enunciated acting style'. He revels in this, and has made a career from either spoofing himself, most memorably in *Airplane II* (1982) and *Miss Congeniality (2000)*, or simply by just playing 'Himself' in films like *Free Enterprise* (1998) or *Showtime* (2002) (in which 'he' gives Robert De Niro's character acting lessons). And it was William Shatner who gave the world a new phrase in a 1986 edition of *Saturday Night Live*:

> *'I've spoken to many of you... and some of you have travelled hundreds of miles to be here. I'd just like to say... get a life, will you people? It was just a TV show. I mean look at you; look at the way you're dressed. You've turned an enjoyable little job I did as a lark for a few years into a colossal waste of time. So, move out of your parents' basements, get your own apartments and grow the hell up!'*

Shatner later got a huge round of applause at a real convention when he suggested it wasn't him saying it, it was his evil double. But one of the great ironies of *Star Trek* fandom has always been that millions of people around the world appreciate the series on a level that many of the most committed fans just don't get: you can be serious about *Star Trek* – but *Star Trek* doesn't take itself too seriously.

The simple answer to the question 'Why did *Star Trek* catch on?' is simple: it's a good show. Not every episode is a classic. It's difficult to argue with Fry's assertion in *Futurama* that the show consists of '79 episodes, about 30 good ones'. It unarguably goes off the boil during the third season, when Roddenberry was sidelined as executive producer, Fred Freiberger took over as line producer and budgets were noticeably lower. But those '30 good ones' are genuinely well-written, exciting, well-acted, memorable and entertaining. Production line television doesn't get any more watchable than *The Devil in the Dark, The Trouble with Tribbles, Amok Time, Arena, Mirror, Mirror, Spectre of the Gun, A Piece of the Action* or the perpetual fan favourite *The City on the Edge of Forever*.

Science fiction scholars may be able to point to various novels and short stories that covered the same sort of ground much earlier, but *Star Trek* got them to the masses. If faster-than-light engines, shuttlecraft, teleportation, androids, time paradoxes, space Federations, evil Empires and parallel universes are clichés, then it's only because of *Star Trek*.

The best *Star Trek* manages to satisfy both the fan and mainstream audiences: it manages to make social commentary within the context of an action adventure, using characters that you really feel for. It's a difficult balancing act and William Shatner deserves far more credit than he usually gets for judging where the line is between integrity and parody. One need only look at Jeffrey Hunter in the pilot for an example of how Captain Kirk could have been pale and dull. To Shatner's intense annoyance, Leonard Nimoy was always seen by fans and the studio as the real star of the show. Again, in other hands, Spock could have been deadly dull, but Nimoy – by all accounts (including his own) a rather serious young actor – made him iconic, helped by writers who fell over themselves to give the character gimmicks, catchphrases and all the best lines. The other members of the cast found themselves in that most invidious position for an actor – worldwide fame without the fortune. With varying degrees of resentment and public acrimony, all of them settled into making a comfortable living on the convention circuit and came back for the movies.

If *Star Trek* is now far more than Kirk and Spock, then it's only because the original series, and the ideas and people behind it, did their job so well. It may not have kick-started the space race or ended segregation in America, but *Star Trek* was the most successful television show of the twentieth century, and that's no small achievement.

STAR TREK
SEASON ONE

1.0 THE CAGE

STARDATE UNKNOWN

Captain Pike is subjected to the mental tricks of the Talosians

TX Unbroadcast pilot (eventually shown on American television 3 October 1988)
WRITER Gene Roddenberry
DIRECTOR Robert Butler
STARRING Majel Barrett (Number One), Peter Duryea (Jose Tyler), Laurel Goodwin (Colt), John Hoyt (Dr Boyce), Jeffrey Hunter (Christopher Pike), Clegg Hoyt (Transporter Chief Pitcairn), Joseph Mell (Trader), Leonard Nimoy (Spock), Susan Oliver (Vina), Malachi Throne (Voice of The Keeper), Meg Wyllie (The Keeper)

Following a disastrous mission to Rigel VII, the Enterprise limps to the Vega colony for repairs. Captain Christopher Pike tells medical officer Dr Boyce of his guilt over the deaths of three crewmen, and considers leaving Starfleet. The Enterprise picks up a distress call from the SS Columbia, a survey ship missing for 18 years. Vulcan science officer Mr Spock urges Pike to check for survivors. Pike takes a landing party to the crash site on Talos IV and encounters Dr Theodore Hask, the leader of the survey team, and a beautiful young woman, Vina. However, they are not the only inhabitants. Pike is transported underground and imprisoned by an alien race called the Talosians, short humanoids with brains three times the size of a human's who have immense mental powers. Their leader, The Keeper, manipulates Pike's thoughts – they want him to mate with Vina in order to produce a new race of obedient servants. Pike experiences a number of scenarios designed to make him bond with Vina, including one where she is a maiden trapped in a beautiful alien castle. The Talosians suspect Pike is not attracted to Vina and instead capture two female crewmembers, the ship's first officer and Yeoman Colt, in between the cage for Pike to choose. Pike manages to overpower the Keeper but the Talosians create new illusions on board the Enterprise that could lead to the ship's destruction. Vina is also revealed to be an old woman. However, the deadlock is broken when the Talosians decide that the human race is too resistant to subjugation to be suitable for their purposes. Pike is freed but reluctant to leave Vina. The Talosians restore Vina's beauty and give her an illusory companion for company, a duplicate of Pike. The crew are allowed to return to the Enterprise, unharmed.

QUOTES

- 'I'm tired of being responsible for 203 lives. I'm tired of deciding which mission is too risky...' – *Pike*

TRIVIA

- Although NBC rejected the *Star Trek* pilot, they were keen not to waste the $630,000 that was spent on the show. A second pilot was commissioned, with a list of alterations: many of the original cast were rejected, including Nimoy, although Gene Roddenbery fought to keep him on board. Roddenbery commissioned three treatments, one from himself (which became *The Omega Glory*), Stephen Kandel's *Mudd's Women*, and a third from Samuel A Peeples that made it to screen as *Where No Man Has Gone Before*. NBC chose Peeples' script, though it was potentially the most expensive. Footage from *The Cage* was reused in the two-parter *The Menagerie*.
- The Talosians were played by women but voiced by male actor, Malachi Throne. When it came to produce *The Menagerie*, Throne had been cast as one of the key protagonists, Commodore Mendez. As a result, the Talosian voices were cypher-dubbed, giving them an echoing, higher pitched sound to disguise Throne's voice. The version of *The Cage* seen in syndication is actually pieced together from the original footage (featuring Throne's voice) and the print for *The Menagerie* (featuring the cypher-dubbed version) and switches between the two.
- *The Cage* was finally broadcast as part of a two-hour Paramount special, *From One Generation to the Next*, in October 1988 as a filler for a *The Next Generation* episode which fell foul of a writers' strike.
- DeForest Kelley turned down the chance to play Spock.

RATING

- Despite their purpose, pilots are rarely the most inspiring of programmes. While *The Cage* manages to communicate some of the show's flavour, it falls short on action and excitement. While these are addressed in the second pilot, there are other interesting elements that go missing between concept and series. Pike's self-doubt reveals a humility we rarely see with Kirk. The female first officer is quickly replaced, as is the elderly doctor. Famously, we see a more emotional side to Mr Spock. But ultimately *The Cage* lacks the pace and drive of the regular episodes.

1.1 THE MAN TRAP

A creature appears as Dr McCoy's former lover

TX 8 September 1966
WRITER George Clayton Johnson
DIRECTOR Marc Daniels
GUEST CAST Jeanne Bal (Nancy Crater), Sharon Gimpel (M-113 Creature), Vince Howard (Crewman), Francine Pyne (Blonde Nancy), Alfred Ryder (Robert Crater), Bruce Watson (Green), Michael Zaslow (Darnell)

STARDATE 1513.1

The Enterprise crew deliver supplies to archaeologists Dr Robert Crater and his wife Nancy, the only inhabitants of planet M-113. Dr McCoy and Nancy were lovers five years previously. McCoy is amazed that Nancy does not appear to have aged, but she appears old to Kirk and youthful to Crewman Darnell. Kirk is surprised when Crater asks only for salt tablets and that he and his wife be left alone. Meanwhile, Darnell is drawn to the beautiful young Nancy and is later found dead. On board the Enterprise, McCoy's autopsy reveals that all the salt was drained from Darnell's body. Kirk discovers that Nancy is the last of an alien race capable of mind control: the creature craves salt and killed Crater's wife for it. Crater continued to give the creature salt in return for companionship. Meanwhile, the creature adopts the form of another crewman and beams aboard the Enterprise. It attacks members of the crew but makes an error when it attacks Spock and cannot stomach his body salts. Found out, the creature appears to McCoy as Nancy to secure protection. Kirk and Spock arrive in time to convince McCoy of the truth. McCoy is forced to gun down the creature, which only then reveals its natural self.

QUOTES

- 'May the Great Bird of the Galaxy bless your planet.' – *Sulu to Rand. A phrase later appropriated by fans as a nickname for Roddenberry*

TRIVIA

- The working title was *Damsel with a Dulcimer*.
- Though the first regular episode to be transmitted, *The Man Trap* was the fifth 50-minute episode to be made. It was felt to be a better introduction to the series, featuring more of the regulars than *Where No Man Has Gone Before*.
- Initially, William Shatner was paid $5,000 an episode, Leonard Nimoy was paid $1,250.
- Nimoy would go on to be nominated for the Supporting Acting Emmy for each of the three years the show ran.

RATING

- A tightly-plotted small scale episode that provides much needed characterisation so early in the series. A terrific performance from DeForest Kelly. The themes of loneliness and need are handled superbly.

1.2 CHARLIE X

STARDATE 1533.6

Kirk grants passage to an orphaned teenager with extraordinary mental powers

TX 15 September 1966
WRITER DC Fontana (story by Gene Roddenberry)
DIRECTOR Lawrence Dobkin
GUEST CAST John Bellah, Gerald Thompson (Crewmen), Don Eitner (Navigator), Patricia McNulty (Tina Lawton), Dallis Mitchell (Nellis), Abraham Sofaer (Thasian), Charles J Stewart (Ramart), Robert Walker, Jr (Charlie Evans)

The Enterprise rendezvous with the USS Antares to collect Charlie Evans, the only survivor of a transport crash on the planet Thasus 14 years previously. Now 17, Charlie is mesmerised by Yeoman Rand, the first woman he has seen. When the captain of the Antares hails the Enterprise to talk about Charlie, the ship is suddenly destroyed. Charlie shows no sign of upset and is keen only keen to be accepted on the Enterprise. However, Charlie is not used to human contact. Quick to anger, he reveals amazing mental powers, injuring crewmen or making them vanish at will. Rand vanishes when she resists his advances. Charlie demands to be taken to the nearest colony, Alpha V, but Kirk refuses, fearing Charlie will cause havoc. Charlie immediately takes over the ship. Kirk quickly retakes the ship but angers Charlie, who moves in to attack. Suddenly, the ship receives a message from a Thasian ship. The Thasians gave Charlie extraordinary mental powers so he could survive alone, but fear he cannot live safely with humans. Charlie pleads to remain on board the Enterprise but the Thasians take him back to their ship. The Thasians restore the Enterprise and her crew to normal.

QUOTES

- 'There's nothing wrong with you that hasn't gone wrong with every other human male since the first model came out.'
  – Kirk to Charlie

TRIVIA

- Dorothy Fontana's first draft script resembled the transmitted version almost exactly, except for a scene in which Uhura does impressions of the crew.
- For several years the scene where a crewman's face becomes featureless was cut from UK transmissions because it was deemed too scary.

RATING

- A tense low-key character story that manages to rise above teenage angst in space. Charlie remains a sympathetic character. Plus there's a strong element of horror that later seasons and series shy away from. However, the Thasians rapidly become a *Star Trek* cliché.

1.3 WHERE NO MAN HAS GONE BEFORE

STARDATE 1312.4

A forcefield at the edge of the galaxy turns one crewmember into a god

TX 22 September 1966
WRITER Samuel A Peeples

The Enterprise recovers the flight recorder of the SS Valiant, a starship missing for 200 years. The databank reveals that the Valiant's captain ordered the ship's destruction after encountering a mysterious forcefield. Soon the Enterprise encounters the same forcefield. Kirk notices changes in his friend Lt Commander Gary Mitchell, who starts to exhibit strong extrasensory powers. The same is shown to a lesser extent by ship's psychiatrist Dr Elizabeth Dehner. Surgeon Dr Piper concludes that

DIRECTOR James Goldstone
GUEST CAST Paul Carr (Lee Kelso), Andrea Dromm (Smith), Paul Fix (Dr Mark Piper), Lloyd Haynes (Alden), Sally Kellerman (Dr Elizabeth Dehner), Gary Lockwood (Gary Mitchell)

Mitchell, now more dangerous, is evolving into an advanced human – a god. Spock realises that this phenomenon was also encountered by the Valiant and that the captain destroyed his ship to prevent the power taking over. Spock convinces Kirk to maroon the two crewmembers on the planet Delta Vega. On the planet, Kirk warns Mitchell that his absolute powers will corrupt him. Mitchell tries to kill Kirk but Dehner intervenes. Dehner is killed and Kirk creates a rockslide that kills Mitchell. Kirk records that both crewmembers gave their lives in the course of their duty. Spock concurs and reveals he felt something approaching human emotion.

TRIVIA

- In June 1965, NBC selected Samuel Peeples' *Where No Man Has Gone Before* as the second pilot episode. When Jeffrey Hunter declined to return, Roddenberry suggested William Shatner, whom he reportedly already had in mind as a potential successor. Paramount were happy with the second pilot and commissioned the series early in 1966.
- Two edits of the pilot were produced. The untransmitted version opened with a view of the galaxy with voice over from Shatner, had no opening titles and was cut into four acts.
- Peeples' original script made reference to an illuminated map table on the bridge that plotted the course of the Enterprise and 'outwarp,' the process of returning from warp speed to impulse engines.
- Gary Lockwood starred in *The Lieutenant*, Roddenberry's first series as producer, made in 1963 for MGM. During the series' 29-episode run, Roddenberry came up with the *Star Trek* concept and discussed it with his secretary on the show, Dorothy Fontana.
- Sally Kellerman later gained stardom as Hotlips Houlihan in the movie *M*A*S*H*.

RATING

- The second pilot after which they replaced Piper with McCoy. Kirk's back story with Mitchell adds gravitas to their final encounter. It's a shame that *Where No Man* was not transmitted first as Dehner and Mitchell are presented as regulars – a later transmission makes it obvious that they are just there for the episode. There's much more promise here, with Kirk making a big impact.

1.4 THE NAKED TIME

The crew behave erratically when exposed to a virus that reduces their inhibitions

TX 29 September 1966
WRITER John DF Black
DIRECTOR Marc Daniels
GUEST CAST John Bellah (Laughing Crewman), Frank da Vinci (Brent), Bruce Hyde (Kevin Riley), William Knight (Amorous Crewman), Stewart Moss (Joe Tormolen)

STARDATE 1704.2

The Enterprise is sent to retrieve a science team from the ice planet Psi 2000 before the planet destroys itself. Spock and Crewman Tormolen beam down but everyone is dead – many froze when their life support was turned off, while others committed suicide. Tormolen contracts a virus and, back on the Enterprise, starts to behave irrationally. Sulu and Riley prevent him from injuring himself but contract the illness. As the virus spreads, crewmembers become uninhibited: Kirk becomes overly amorous with the crew, Chapel reveals her love for Spock and Spock cries over the death of his mother. More seriously, Riley barricades himself in engineering and takes control of the ship. With the engines shut down, the Enterprise is pulled towards Psi 2000 and destruction. As Scotty tries to break into Main Engineering, McCoy realises that the virus is spread by perspiration and develops a cure. Kirk and Scotty retake Main Engineering but they need to escape the planet's pull fast. Kirk risks a controlled antimatter explosion that succeeds in breaking them free of the planet, and unexpectedly takes them 71 hours back in time.

QUOTES

- 'I canna change the laws of physics.' – *Scott to Kirk, shortly before he does*

TRIVIA

- *The Naked Time* tests the limits of the *Star Trek* format by including time travel, an invisible enemy and odd behaviour from the core characters. This is the first time that a Starfleet vessel travels back in time.
- John DF Black would go on to write, among other things, the screenplay for *Shaft*.

RATING

- Light and frothy. The out of character behaviour is fun to watch and handled well, telling us much more about the characters than we had previously known. Unfortunately, *The Next Generation* sequel, *The Naked Now*, takes a far more voyeuristic tack, losing the character points almost entirely. It's fortunate (if unlikely) that McCoy doesn't contract the virus.

1.5 THE ENEMY WITHIN

STARDATE 1672.1

A transporter malfunction splits Kirk into two versions, one good, one evil

TX 6 October 1966
WRITER Richard Matheson
DIRECTOR Leo Penn
GUEST CAST Jim Goodwin (John Farrell), Edward Madden (Fisher), Garland Thompson (Wilson)

While Sulu's landing party collects specimens on the planet Alpha 177, the Enterprise transporter malfunctions, depositing ore on a technician. Scotty can find nothing wrong and allows Kirk to beam aboard, but when they have left the room a second Kirk arrives on the transporter pad. The second Kirk is aggressive and tries to assault Rand in her quarters. Meanwhile, an alien creature is beamed aboard and splits into two versions, one vicious, the other tame. Spock concludes that the transporter may have done the same to Kirk and bans its use, leaving Sulu's landing party stranded and ill-equipped to deal with the freezing night. As the evil Kirk runs amok, the good Kirk is weak and indecisive. Spock realises that Kirk needs both aspects of his personality to function. Kirk tells his evil double that they must be whole to function. Scotty fixes the transporter and beams the two alien creatures back to the planet as a test – the two creatures become one but die in the process. After a further adjustment to the transporter, the two Kirks take their chances and beam down to the planet. Kirk is restored. The landing party are quickly beamed back to the Enterprise.

QUOTES

- 'He's dead, Jim.' – *First use of McCoy's catchphrase (he's referring to a dog)*

TRIVIA

- Richard Matheson's original script called for Spock to pistol-whip the evil Kirk with a phaser. Reports have it that Nimoy objected and, with Shatner, came up with the Vulcan nerve pinch.

RATING

- A little hackneyed by modern standards but with some good ideas. The notion that Kirk's evil side gives him the capacity to command is interesting. Shatner puts in a wonderfully camp performance as both Kirks.

1.6 MUDD'S WOMEN

STARDATE 1329.1

A wanted felon uses his three beautiful female passengers to escape Starfleet justice

TX 31 October 1966
WRITER Stephen Kandel (story by Gene Roddenberry)
DIRECTOR Harvey Hart
GUEST CAST Roger C Carmel (Harry Mudd), Susan Denberg (Magda Kovas), Gene Dynarski (Ben Childress), Jerry Foxworth (Guard), Seamon Glass (Benton), Jim Goodwin (Farrell), Jon Kowal (Herm), Karen Steele (Eve McHuron), Maggie Thrett (Ruth Bonaventure)

The Enterprise pursues an unidentified ship into an asteroid belt and has to rescue the passengers. Harcourt Fenton (Harry) Mudd who is transporting three beautiful women, Ruth, Magda and Eve, to wed settlers on a colony world. Kirk discovers Mudd is a wanted felon and prepares to hand him over to Starfleet but must first replace the Enterprise's lithium crystals. Kirk sets course for the nearest lithium mining planet, Rigel XII, which is inhabited by only three miners. *En route*, Mudd contacts the head miner, Childress, and promises the women in return for lithium crystals and their help to escape Kirk. Meanwhile, the beauty of the women turns out to be the effect of a small pill given to them by Mudd. On arrival at the planet, Childress offers the crystals in return for Mudd and the women, but Kirk refuses. Magda and Ruth marry two of the miners but Eve, in love with Kirk, escapes. Childress brings her back but she has reverted to her natural appearance. Childress is furious. Mudd and Kirk return with the pills, the illegal 'venus drug', and Eve is transformed. Kirk reveals it was actually ineffective – the women can determine their appearance at will. Realising Kirk will never leave the Enterprise, Eve marries Childress. The miners hand over the crystals and Kirk takes Mudd into custody.

QUOTES

- 'Gentlemen, I am simply an honest businessman.'
  'Incorrect.'
  'Blast that tin-plated pot!' – *Mudd is sold out by his computer*

TRIVIA

- *Mudd's Women* was a story floated by Roddenberry as a potential second pilot. The story was later fleshed out by Kandel, who took Roddenberry's concept of an aphrodisiac drug and added Harry Mudd. Drug use in this script seemed to slip through the net, but a drugs sub-plot in Harlan Ellison's first draft of *The City on the Edge of Forever* was immediately cut.

RATING

- The elaborate 'venus drug' sub-plot is an unnecessary inclusion in an otherwise light-hearted romp. The character of Harry Mudd is a delight to watch.

1.7 WHAT ARE LITTLE GIRLS MADE OF?

Kirk and Chapel confront a missing exobiologist who plans to spread androids throughout the galaxy

TX 20 October 1966
WRITER Robert Bloch
DIRECTOR James Goldstone
GUEST CAST Budd Albright (Rayburn), Harry Basch (Dr Brown), Ted Cassidy (Ruk), Vince Deadrick (Matthews), Sherry Jackson (Andrea), Michael Strong (Roger Korby)

STARDATE 2712.4

The Enterprise arrives at Exo III in search of researcher Dr Roger Korby, Nurse Chapel's fiancé. Korby has been missing for five years. Kirk and Chapel beam to the underground tunnels of the planet, built by The Old Ones, the extinct native inhabitants of the planet. They are met by Dr Brown, Korby's assistant, but the man seems oddly aloof. Korby and his two companions, Andrea and an alien giant named Ruk. Korby has discovered alien equipment that can produce androids: his companions are all artificial beings. Korby wants Kirk's help to spread androids across the galaxy, believing humanity will be able to make the perfect society. When Kirk refuses, Korby makes an android duplicate of him and tries to take over the ship. However, Kirk implants false attitudes in the android which draws the suspicion of Spock. Meanwhile, Kirk manages to gain Ruk's help. Kirk and Chapel confront Korby and realise that he too is an android. Unable to accept this truth, Korby grabs Andrea and kills them both with a phaser.

TRIVIA

- Ted Cassidy (Ruk) became famous as Lurch in *The Addams Family*. Roddenberry used him again in the rejected pilots *Genesis II* and *Planet Earth*.
- The episode makes reference to George Samuel Kirk, the captain's brother. In this episode George is said to have three sons, but he has only one in *Operation: Annihilate!*
- Majel Barrett (Nurse Chapel) became the wife of Gene Roddenberry in 1969. Her involvement in *Star Trek* began when she did the first camera tests for the Orion slave girl in *The Cage*. Legend has it that the film technicians kept correcting the colour balance of the prints so that the dancer wasn't green, and were baffled why only one figure was affected by the problem. Barrett also appears in *The Next Generation* as Deanna Troi's mother, Lwaxana Troi, and the voice of Federation computers in this and later *Star Trek* series.

RATING

- Pretty mundane stuff with little to single it out. The interesting idea of the nature of Korby is all too short-lived.

1.8 MIRI

The crew are exposed to a virus that kills adults but prolongs the life of pre-pubescent children

TX 27 October 1966
WRITER Adrian Spies
DIRECTOR Vincent McEveety

STARDATE 2713.5

Following a distress call, the Enterprise arrives at an unnamed planet inhabited by children. Kirk, Spock, Rand and McCoy beam down and are attacked by a deranged man. McCoy concludes that the man aged centuries in minutes. The crew find a young girl, Miri, who is attracted to Kirk. They discover that they have been exposed to a plague that only affects adults. The inhabitants had conducted a project to prolong their lives but had instead created the virus that killed them. The virus slows the ageing process in children, allowing them to live hundreds of years

GUEST CAST Kim Darby (Miri), Jim Goodwin (John Farrell), Steve McEveety (Red Headed Boy), Michael J Pollard (Jahn), David L Ross (Galloway), Keith Taylor (Jahn's Friend)

before they reach puberty. Kirk tries to befriend the children but they are fearful. When Kirk comforts Rand, Miri becomes jealous and helps to steal the crew's communicators. Meanwhile, McCoy thinks he may have found an antidote, but he needs the communicators to access the ship's computer to make sure it is safe. Kirk convinces the children that they will all die without the antidote. He rescues the communicators but McCoy has already taken his chance with the antidote and injected himself. The unconscious McCoy starts to wake, cured. The antidote is dispensed and the Enterprise crew leave, knowing a Federation ship is *en route* to take care of the children.

TRIVIA

- Adrian Spies' draft script featured more of a relationship between Jahn and Miri.
- Roddenberry suggested that the children would use a corrupted language, e.g. 'grups' for 'grown ups.'
- Two of Grace Lee Whitney's children and William Shatner's daughters, Leslie and Elizabeth, were extras in this episode.
- A 1984 early evening showing of this episode on the BBC got so many complaints about the scenes of the children attacking Kirk that the BBC pulled the episode from every repeat run of the show until the mid-nineties, and also took out three other shows with torture scenes or explicit violence: *Whom Gods Destroy*, *Plato's Stepchildren* and *The Empath*.

RATING

- A neat little mystery to be solved. The race for the virus provides some much needed tension. The children's society is intriguingly ritualistic.

1.9 DAGGER OF THE MIND

STARDATE 2715.1

The Enterprise crew are threatened with brainwashing experiments on a penal colony

TX 3 November 1966
WRITER 'S Bar-David' (pseudonym for Shimon Wincelberg)
DIRECTOR Vincent McEveety
GUEST CAST Larry Anthony (Berkeley), John Arndt (First Crewman), James Gregory (Dr Tristan Adams), Marianna Hill (Helen Noel), Suzanne Wasson (Lethe), Morgan Woodward (Dr Simon Van Gelder)

As the Enterprise completes a mission to the Tantalus V penal colony, a stowaway beams on board. The man is Dr Simon Van Gelder, former director of the colony, who exhibits signs of mental instability. On the planet, the new director, Dr Adams, explains that Van Gelder was the victim of a failed experiment with the 'neural neutraliser', a device that relaxes inmates. Kirk and Dr Helen Noel discover that Adams has used the machine on his own staff to ensure their obedience. That night, Noel tests the device on Kirk and finds he will take hypnotic suggestion. Suddenly, Adams overpowers Noel and brainwashes Kirk to forget his mission and order him to fall madly in love with Noel. Meanwhile, Van Gelder warns Spock that Noel and Kirk are in grave danger but can explain no more. Spock attempts a mind-meld and discovers the truth. On the colony, Noel cuts the power, disabling the planet's defensive shield and allowing Spock to beam down a security team. Kirk fights with Adams who falls into the neural neutraliser. With the power reactivated, the machine drains Adams' mind, killing him.

QUOTES

- 'Your Earth people glorified organised violence for 40 centuries, but you imprison those who employ it privately.' – *Spock to Kirk*

TRIVIA

- Before the writers invented the mind-meld, Spock used a hypnosis machine to enter Van Gelder's mind. Another change was the last minute replacement of Rand with Helen Noel. Rand would soon be written out.
- The *South Park* episode *Roger Ebert Should Lay Off The Fatty Foods* is a sustained parody of this episode. It even features a character called Simon Van Gelder who runs a Tantalus V Observatory with its own hypnotic device.

RATING

- Pretty simple stuff with no real examination of Adams' motives. Helen Noel is a welcome addition to the crew – pity we didn't see her again!

1.10 THE CORBOMITE MANEUVER

STARDATE 1512.2

The crew encounter a threatening alien called Balok who tests their aggression and humanity

TX 10 November 1966
WRITER Jerry Sohl
DIRECTOR Joseph Sargent
GUEST CAST Anthony Call (David Bailey), Clint Howard (Balok), Bruce Mars, Stewart Moss (Crewmen)

The Enterprise encounters a mysterious cube-shaped buoy in an uncharted area of space. Kirk orders the buoy destroyed. They are interrupted by the appearance of an alien vessel, the Fesarius. Its captain, Balok of the First Federation, denounces the savagery of the human race and tells the Enterprise crew he will destroy their ship in ten minutes. Kirk bluffs, claiming to have a corbomite device that reflects energy weapons back on the aggressor. Balok rethinks and instead tows the Enterprise with a tractor beam. The Enterprise breaks free, damaging Balok's ship. Balok issues a distress call and Kirk, McCoy and navigator Bailey beam over. They discover that Balok is actually a good-natured childlike creature – the face on the viewscreen was a dummy used to scare away potential enemies. The Fesarius is also fully functional: Balok was testing the crew to see if they were as compassionate as they claimed to be. Balok suggests a diplomatic exchange and Bailey becomes the Federation's cultural ambassador to the alien race.

QUOTES

- 'What am I? A doctor or a moon shuttle conductor?' – *McCoy*

TRIVIA

- Balok was voiced by Vic Perrin, who also narrated the opening credits of *The Outer Limits*.
- A still image of the dummy Balok became the last freeze-frame under the end credits from season two onwards, making it one of the series' most enduring images.

RATING

- A fun take on *The Wizard of Oz*, with the real Balok hiding behind the dummy. There's an unintentionally perverse joke in there, with the dummy-like baddy actually turning out to be a dummy.

1.11 THE MENAGERIE Part 1

STARDATE 3012.4

Spock is court-martialled when he abducts his former captain and takes control of the Enterprise

TX 17 November 1966
WRITER Gene Roddenberry
DIRECTOR Marc Daniels
GUEST CAST Jeffrey Hunter (Christopher Pike), Sean Kenney (Crippled Pike), Julie Parrish (Miss Piper), Malachi Throne (Mendez). See *The Cage* for other cast

Kirk, Spock and McCoy beam down to a starbase to answer a distress call issued by Captain Christopher Pike, the former captain of the Enterprise. Pike who has been crippled by delta rays and could not have sent the message. Spock, however, seems to know more and Kirk begins to suspect his first officer of treachery. Spock takes over the starbase's computer and sends false orders to the Enterprise. He, McCoy and Pike return to the ship and leave at warp speed. McCoy is suspicious when Spock claims that Kirk has placed him in command. Kirk and Commodore Mendez pursue the Enterprise and beam aboard. Spock puts himself under arrest but has locked the ship's controls – they are heading to Talos IV, the only Federation planet to which a visit carries the death penalty. Spock is courtmartialled and in his defence shows his mission with Pike to Talos IV 13 years previously. They watch as Pike is captured by the Talosians. Meanwhile, the Enterprise detects a communication from the planet below. The court martial is adjourned, but Spock tells Kirk that he must watch the rest of the evidence as Pike's life depends on it...

TRIVIA

- To save production costs, Roddenberry came up with a framing story to reuse material from the untransmitted pilot. The production team could not afford Jeffrey Hunter and cast look-alike Sean Kenney instead, disguising him under heavy makeup and a wheelchair.
- Despite the humanitarian pretensions of Starfleet, it still has a death penalty. It is revealed that after Pike's visit the planet Talos IV was placed under General Order 7, which prevents Federation visitors on pain of death.

RATING

- The better of the two parts, *The Menagerie Part 1* manages to tell an interesting story around Spock without getting bogged down in reused footage. The mystery surrounding Spock's behaviour is genuinely intriguing.

1.12 THE MENAGERIE Part 2

STARDATE 3013.1

As Spock's court martial continues, Kirk discovers the secret of Talos IV

TX 24 November 1966
WRITER Gene Roddenberry
DIRECTOR Robert Butler
GUEST CAST Jeffrey Hunter (Christopher Pike), Sean Kenney (Crippled Pike), Julie Parrish (Miss Piper), Malachi Throne (Mendez). See *The Cage* for other cast

Mendez recalls the court martial and the transmission begins again. Kirk watches as the Talosians use their mental powers to make Pike relive a doomed mission to Rigel VII, this time accompanied by a beautiful slave girl, Vina. Spock reveals that the Talosians want Pike back but refuses to say why. The transmission resumes: the Talosians capture two more crew members but Pike gets a gun and escapes. The court finds Spock guilty but the transmissions resume unbidden: the Talosians release Pike and their captives, lamenting the aggression of humanity. Vina, however, was mutilated when she crash landed on Talos IV and decides to live out her years in the fantasy created by the Talosians. The transmission over, Commodore Mendez is revealed to be an illusion, created by the Talosians to keep Kirk occupied. Kirk allows Pike to beam down to the planet where he can live his life free from his disabilities and be reunited with Vina. Kirk realises that Spock risked everything to help his former captain and drops all charges.

TRIVIA

- Pike's wheelchair appears in the *Futurama* episode *Where No Fan Has Gone Before*, which featured the *Star Trek* cast.

RATING

- Clumsy and heavy-handed, *The Menagerie Part 2* fails to build on the strengths of the previous episode and is limited by the reused footage. Spock's need for cloak-and-dagger tactics is completely inexplicable.

1.13 CONSCIENCE OF THE KING

STARDATE 2817.6

Kirk searches for Kodos the Executioner, a colonial governor responsible for a massacre

TX 8 December 1966
WRITER Barry Trivers
DIRECTOR Gerd Oswald
GUEST CAST Marc Adams (Hamlet), Barbara Anderson (Lenore Karidian), Majel Barrett (Computer voice), Karl Bruck (King Duncan), Bruce Hyde (Kevin Riley), Arnold Moss (Anton Karidian), Natalie Norwick (Martha Leighton), Eddie Paskey (Leslie), William Sergeant (Thomas Leighton), David Troy (Larry Matson)

The Enterprise arrives at Planet Q where Kirk is reunited with old friend, actor Dr Thomas Leighton. Leighton believes a fellow actor, Anton Karidian, is actually Kodos the Executioner, a murderous colonial governor who killed thousands of his people to control a famine. Leighton, Kirk and Lieutenant Riley are three of only nine eyewitnesses to the massacre. Kirk tries to find out more about Karidian by getting closer to his daughter, Lenore. They find Leighton murdered. Kirk arranges to transport the troupe to their next venue so he can investigate further. When Riley is poisoned and Kirk is almost killed by a phaser, Spock insists that Karidian is the culprit, but Kirk is unconvinced. Riley, meanwhile, tries to kill Karidian but is disarmed by Kirk. Karidian is upset by the accusation and is innocent – the culprit was Lenore who killed the witnesses to protect her father. Lenore grabs a gun to protect herself but accidentally kills her father. Lenore is driven insane by her actions and Kirk has her arrested.

QUOTES

- 'Worlds may change, galaxies disintegrate, but a woman... always remains a woman.' – *Kirk to Lenore*

TRIVIA

- A scene cut from the final edit sees Karidian return from a walk around the Enterprise and recite to Lenore the passage 'I am thy father's spirit...' from *Hamlet* Act I.
- This episode sees the last appearance of Yeoman Rand in the series. Originally brought in as a love interest for Kirk, the network felt the character cramped the Captain's style. Grace Lee Whitney has also admitted that she had an alcohol problem

around this time. Gene Roddenberry brought her back as the transporter chief in *Star Trek – The Motion Picture.* Rand also serves on Sulu's Excelsior in *Star Trek VI: The Undiscovered Country* and in the *Voyager* episode *Flashback.*

RATING

- A simple little mystery executed well, although the Shakespearean moments are cringe-worthy. Shatner and Moss are notably overblown. Peculiarly, it is still widely regarded by fans as one of the better episodes of the first season.

1.14 THE BALANCE OF TERROR

STARDATE 1709.2

Kirk battles a Romulan commander as the Federation teeters on the verge of war

TX 15 December 1966
WRITER Paul Schneider
DIRECTOR Vincent McEveety
GUEST CAST Barbara Baldavin (Angela Martine), Paul Comi (Stiles), Mark Lenard (Romulan Commander), Stephen Mines (Robert Tomlinson), Lawrence Montaigne (Decius), Gary Waldberg (Hansen), John Warburton (Romulan Centurion)

The Enterprise receives a distress call from a Federation outpost on the edge of Romulan space. Spock explains that a neutral zone demarcates the boundary between the two powers – the Enterprise must not break the terms of the treaty. Uhura hails the outpost but it is destroyed by a Romulan Bird of Prey, a powerful battleship equipped with a device that renders it invisible. The Enterprise pursues the battleship as it races towards Romulan space. The crew realises that the cloaking device prevents the Romulans from firing their weapons or using their sensors to track the Enterprise. The Romulan ship is hailed and the humans see the Vulcan-like appearance of the Romulans for the first time. Lieutenant Stiles, whose family fought the Romulans, is immediately suspicious of Spock. The Romulans decloak and fight. Both ships are damaged. In the phaser room, Stiles and Tomlinson are overcome by fumes from the damage. Spock saves Stiles, who apologises for his bigotry. Spock fires the last operational phaser and disables the Bird of Prey. The Romulan commander destroys his ship rather than be captured.

QUOTES

- 'I regret that we meet in this way. You and I are of a kind. In a different reality, I could have called you friend.' – *Romulan Commander to Kirk*

TRIVIA

- *Balance of Terror* marks the first appearance in *Star Trek* of Mark Lenard, who later appears as Sarek, Spock's father, in *Journey to Babel* and up to *The Next Generation* episode *Unification, Part 1* in 1991.
- We find out a few interesting facts about the Romulans that are later called into question. There are seven Earth outposts along the Neutral Zone in sector Z-6. The Romulan home planet is called Romulus and is close to a second planet called Romh.
- *Balance of Terror* bears a strong resemblance to *The Enemy Below* (1957) in which an American Destroyer captain pits his wits against a German U-Boat commander.

RATING

- A gripping episode with some landmark moments. The battle of wits between Kirk and the Romulan commander draws more on submarine films than sci-fi. Claustrophobic and effective.

1.15 SHORE LEAVE

STARDATE 3025.3

The crew chance upon an alien amusement park where their fantasies come to life

TX 29 December 1966
WRITER Theodore Sturgeon
DIRECTOR Robert Sparr
GUEST CAST Barbara Baldavin (Angela Martine), Emily Banks (Tonia Barrows), Shirley Bonne (Ruth), Marcia Brown (Alice), James Gruzaf (Don Juan), Perry Lopez (Esteban Rodriguez), Bruce Mars (Finnegan), Oliver McGowan (Caretaker), Sebastian Tom (Samurai Warrior)

The Enterprise finds an Earth-like planet and Kirk allows the crew shore leave. McCoy takes a landing party and encounters the large white rabbit from *Alice in Wonderland.* McCoy believes he is hallucinating but the rabbit left unmistakeable tracks. Kirk beams down to investigate. He talks to McCoy about Finnegan, a rival from his days as a cadet, and miraculously meets him. Kirk also encounters Ruth, an old flame. Neither Finnegan nor Ruth has changed since he last saw them. Meanwhile, Lieutenant Barrows is attacked by Don Juan and Sulu fights a Samurai. On the Enterprise, Spock detects energy fluctuations and realises a source on the planet is draining the ship of power. He beams down to warn Kirk, only to see McCoy killed by a knight on horseback. Kirk and Spock realise that somehow their thoughts are coming to life. As Kirk musters the landing party, an elderly man appears and explains that the

Enterprise crew have chanced upon an amusement park, designed by an advanced race. The caretaker explains that the fantasies are harmless and invites them to stay. McCoy reappears, apparently unhurt, accompanied by two cabaret girls! Kirk agrees to let the crew take their shore leave.

QUOTES

- 'Oh, my paws and whiskers! I'll be late.' – *The White Rabbit freaks out McCoy*

TRIVIA

- *Shore Leave* was Theodore Sturgeon's last story outline for the show.
- The animated episode *Once Upon a Planet* is a sequel to this story.

RATING

- Insane rubbish, but worth it for McCoy's expression when the white rabbit appears. There's a lot of fun to be had, and it has a levity that the series needs at this point, but there's very little merit otherwise.

1.16 THE GALILEO SEVEN

STARDATE 2821.5

Spock has to make tough decisions to save the crew of the Galileo shuttlecraft from death

TX 5 January 1967
WRITER Oliver Crawford (story by Oliver Crawford and S Bar-David)
DIRECTOR Robert Gist
GUEST CAST John Crawford (High Commissioner Ferris), Phyllis Douglas (Mears), Buck Maffei (Creature), Peter Marko (Gaetano), Don Marshall (Boma), David L Ross (Transporter Chief), Reese Vaughn (Latimer), Grant Woods (Kelowitz)

En route to Makus III to deliver medical supplies, the Enterprise encounters a strange anomaly named Murasaki 312. Kirk sends Spock, Scott, McCoy and four crewmen to investigate in the Galileo shuttlecraft. However, the Galileo is pulled off course and crashes on Taurus II, an inhospitable planet inhabited by violent primitives. The Enterprise sensors are also affected and cannot trace the shuttlecraft. On the planet, Spock and Scott try to repair their ship, but the fuel line breaks and their hopes are dashed. The Galileo crew have to fend off the primitives with their phasers. Scotty realises he could adapt the phasers to power the shuttlecraft. Spock lets him try, aware that if the repairs do not work he has just sacrificed the crew's only hope of defence. The surviving crew board the Galileo and make a shaky return to orbit. However, the Enterprise is already making for Makus III. In desperation, Spock ignites the remaining fuel as a beacon for the Enterprise. The gamble pays off and the crew are beamed back onto the Enterprise just before the Galileo breaks up. Kirk is bemused by Spock's apparent act of desperation, but Spock insists it was a logical solution to the problem.

TRIVIA

- Oliver Crawford derived the idea for *The Galileo Seven* from a movie, *Five Came Back* (1939), about a plane crash in the Andes in which the survivors are hunted down.

RATING

- An interesting little Spock story that explores his distance from the rest of the crew. The suspense builds right to the final sequence.

1.17 THE SQUIRE OF GOTHOS

STARDATE 2124.5

The Enterprise crew are held captive by an eighteenth century dandy

TX 12 January 1967
WRITER Paul Schneider
DIRECTOR Don McDougall
GUEST CAST Barbara Babcock (Voice of Mother), Michael Barrier (De Salle), William Campbell (Trelane), Richard Carlyle (Karl Jaeger), James Doohan (Voice of Father), Venita Wolf (Teresa Ross)

When the Enterprise chances upon a previously unrecorded planet, Kirk and Sulu disappear from the bridge. Sensors suggest that the planet is uninhabitable, but Uhura soon receives a message from below: 'Hip-Hip-Hoorah Tallyho!' McCoy and Lieutenant Jaeger beam down and find themselves in a bizarre stately home. Their host is Squire Trelane, an eighteenth century dandy with a passion for Earth's military history. Trelane can control matter and, to prove his point, transports Kirk at will. Spock manages to beam the crew up to the ship, but Trelane transports the entire bridge crew to his residence for a banquet. Kirk notices that Trelane never moves far from a mirror in the home and, guessing it is the source of the Squire's power, destroys it. Trelane is furious but repairs the device and is able to prevent the Enterprise from leaving orbit. Kirk offers himself as bait in a hunt in return for the crew's freedom. Trelane agrees and corners Kirk, ready for the kill. He is stopped by the sudden sound of two voices that chastise Trelane. The Squire is actually an errant child and is scolded by his parents. The Enterprise crew are free to leave.

TRIVIA

- James Doohan (Scotty) provides the voice of Trelane's father.
- To keep the budget down, Trelane's mansion was covered with re-used props, many from Cecil B DeMille movies. The M-113 creature costume from *The Man Trap* can be seen displayed on the walls.

RATING

- Fun throwaway nonsense. The errant child is perhaps the ultimate Star Trek cliché. There are strong parallels between the character of the Squire and Q in *The Next Generation.* At one point, the Squire puts Kirk on trial.

1.18 ARENA

STARDATE 3045.6

An alien race forces Kirk and an alien captain to fight each other for the safety of their ships

TX 19 January 1967
WRITER Gene L Coon (story by Fredric Brown)
DIRECTOR Joseph Pevney
GUEST CAST Jerry Ayres (O'Herlihy), Bobby Clark, Gary Combs (Gorn Captain), James Farley (Lang), Sean Kenney (DePaul), Eddie Paskey (Leslie), Vic Perrin (Voice of Metron/Voice of Gorn), Carole Shelyne (Metron), Tom Troupe (Harold), Grant Woods (Kelowitz)

After receiving a distress call, the Enterprise arrives at Cestus III only to find the colony has been destroyed. The landing party is attacked but Kirk manages to defend the crew. A colony survivor reveals that the attack was unprovoked and that the distress message was a trap. The landing party returns to the Enterprise and chases a mysterious alien ship into an uncharted system. Suddenly, both ships draw to a halt. A disembodied voice informs the two crews that Kirk and the alien captain, a Gorn, will fight to decide the fate of their ships. Kirk and the Gorn captain, a tall lizard-like creature, are beamed to the planet's surface where they are given materials to make weapons. The Gorn captain is stronger than Kirk but slower. Kirk is almost killed when the Gorn traps him in a rudimentary snare but narrowly escapes. Kirk manufactures a cannon and incapacitates the Gorn. Although in a position to kill the Gorn, Kirk relents, impressing the Metrons. The Gorn skip is spared and the Metrons transport the two ships outside their part of space.

QUOTES

- 'We feel that there may be hope for your kind, therefore you will not be destroyed. It would not be... civilised.' – *Metron leader to Kirk*

TRIVIA

- Gene Coon's original story was very similar to a short story called 'Arena,' written by Fredric Brown in 1945, that had already been adapted by The Outer Limits in 1964. The episode, Fun and Games, saw an alien kidnap an ex-boxer and a divorcee and pit them against two primitive beasts on his home planet. As a result, Brown was given an on-screen credit.
- The location for the alien battle is probably the most reused location in cinema. Numerous films have parodied the episode, notably Bill and Ted's Excellent Adventure (1991) and Jay and Silent Bob Strike Back (2001)in which a restaurant at the location is called the 'Arena Diner.'

RATING

- Great fun! The lumbering Gorn alone makes it worth watching. Yet there's a more serious message here about prejudice. Kirk comes out on top for sparing the Gorn captain's life.

1.19 TOMORROW IS YESTERDAY

STARDATE 3113.2

The crew travel back to 1960s Earth but must take care not to interfere with history

TX 26 January 1967
WRITER DC Fontana
DIRECTOR Michael O'Herlihy

Close to Earth, the Enterprise is thrown back in time to the twentieth century. The US Air Force sends an interceptor to investigate but it is damaged when Kirk uses a tractor beam to deter it. The pilot, Captain John Christopher, is beamed to safety and Kirk explains all. Spock is concerned that Christopher's knowledge will now change the past and hopes to keep him on the Enterprise. However, Spock discovers that Christopher's unborn son will lead a space mission and Christopher must be returned. Kirk decides to remove the flight recording that proves the existence of the Enterprise but he and Sulu are captured in

GUEST CAST Majel Barrett (Computer Voice), Marc Dempsey (Air Force Captain), Hal Lynch (Air Police Sergeant), Richard Merrifield (Webb), Ed Peck (Colonel Fellini), Roger Perry (Captain John Christopher), Jim Spencer (Air Policeman), Sherri Townsend (Crewman), John Winston (Transporter Chief)

the air force base. Sulu manages to escape with the footage but Kirk is held. Back on the Enterprise, Spock suggests that they can slingshot the ship around the sun to gain the necessary speed to time-travel. For a moment, the ship travels back in time and Christopher is returned to Earth before he left it, repairing the timeline. The Enterprise speeds into the future and narrowly avoids destruction. A message from Starfleet confirms that they have returned to their present.

TRIVIA

- *Tomorrow is Yesterday* was originally conceived as a second part for *The Naked Time*, picking up from the Enterprise's journey back in time. John Black was unable to write a second part and the idea was shelved until Fontana resurrected it for this episode.

RATING

- Meat and potatoes time-paradox stuff but done here in *Star Trek* for the first time. There are still some good moments and some themes that are picked up in *Star Trek IV: The Voyage Home* but it doesn't push the concept particularly far.

1.20 COURT-MARTIAL

STARDATE 2947.3

Kirk is court-martialled over the death of an officer

TX 2 February 1967
WRITER Don M Mankiewicz and Stephen W Carabatsos (story by Don M Mankiewicz)
DIRECTOR Marc Daniels
GUEST CAST Hagan Beggs (Hansen), Bart Conrad (Krasnowsky), Elisha Cook Jr (Samuel T Cogley), Winston DeLugo (Timothy), Reginald Lalsingh (Chandra), Joan Marshall (Areel Shaw), William Meader (Lindstrom), Alice Rawlings (Jamie Finney), Percy Rodriguez (Stone), Richard Webb (Benjamin Finney)

The Enterprise arrives at Starbase 11 after braving an ion storm in which crewman Ben Finney was killed. Finney and Kirk had served together years before but had a disagreement that ruined their friendship. Kirk tells Commodore Stone that Finney entered an ion pod to take readings during a yellow alert but the pod had to be jettisoned when the ship went to red alert. However, the Enterprise's records clearly show that Kirk jettisoned the pod during yellow alert. Kirk is incredulous when the Commodore orders a court martial. Kirk is prosecuted by Areel Shaw, an old flame, and defended by Samuel T Cogley, a somewhat eccentric lawyer. Meanwhile, Spock suspects that the Enterprise's records have been tampered with, and realises that Finney may still be alive. The court moves aboard the Enterprise to follow Mr Spock's investigation. The ship's sensors are used to identify Finney's heartbeat on board. Kirk finds Finney and the two men fight. Kirk wins but Finney has sabotaged the ship's engines. Kirk repairs the damage and the ship is saved. Kirk is cleared of all charges.

TRIVIA

- An episode that fleshes out Kirk's back story a bit more. We hear that Kirk and Finney served together on the USS Republic. Finney named his daughter Jamie after Kirk.

RATING

- A heavy Kirk episode that shows off what William Shatner can do. Also worth mentioning is a scene where McCoy berates Spock for playing chess while the Kirk is on trial. We discover that Spock is actually testing the computer to find out if it has been modified.

1.21 THE RETURN OF THE ARCHONS

STARDATE 3156.2

The crew find the descendants of missing Starfleet officers under the control of a supercomputer

TX 9 February 1967
WRITER Boris Sobelman (story by Gene Roddenberry)
DIRECTOR Joseph Pevney

The Enterprise arrives at Beta III in search of the Archon, a starship that went missing 100 years previously. The planet's inhabitants wear the fashions of the late nineteenth century midwest and appear polite and tranquil, but at six o'clock run berserk in violent revelry called the Festival. An inhabitant, Reger, explains that the citizens are controlled by the Body – the Festival is the only freedom they get from subjugation. Reger is part of an underground movement formed to resist the Body and its leader, Landru. Two lawgivers arrive and the Enterprise crew are knocked unconscious by an alien weapon. McCoy and O'Neil are now controlled by the Body. Kirk and Spock escape with the help of another resistance worker. They find that Landru is actually a computer, programmed with the memories and

GUEST CAST Morgan Farley (Hacom), Brioni Farrell (Tula), Sid Haig (First Lawgiver), Christopher Held (Lindstrom), Jon Lormer (Tamar), Charles Macaulay (Landru), Ralph Maurer (Bilar), Miko Mayama (Tamura), Sean Morgan (O'Neil), Eddie Paskey (Leslie), David L Ross (Guard), Torin Thatcher (Marplon), Harry Townes (Reger)

knowledge of a scientist by the same name who lived thousands of years previously. The computer has sought to create the perfect society but Kirk convinces Landru that it is harming the population. Landru destroys itself, releasing the populace from its mind control.

QUOTES

- 'Without freedom of choice there is no creativity. Without creativity there is no life.' – *Kirk to Landru*

TRIVIA

- The original script included a relationship between Tula and Luster, who became Lindstrom in later drafts.

RATING

- The first of many episodes to demonstrate Kirk's superior skills as a computer destroyer. It's an odd episode with little substance.

1.22 SPACE SEED

STARDATE 3141.9

The Enterprise is taken over by a genetically engineered tyrant from Earth's past

TX 16 February 1967
WRITER Gene L Coon and Carey Wilber (story by Carey Wilber)
DIRECTOR Marc Daniels
GUEST CAST Kathy Ahart (Crewman), Blaisdell Makee (Spinelli), Ricardo Montalban (Khan Noonien Singh), Madlyn Rhue (Marla McGivers), Mark Tobin (Joaquin), John Winston (Kyle)

The Enterprise crew find an old Earth ship floating in space with its crew in suspended animation. Ship's historian Marla McGivers and Spock identify it as the Botany Bay and deduce it was launched during the Eugenics Wars, a violent and bitter struggle that took place during the 1990s. One sleeper is revived, Khan Noonien Singh, a tyrannical genetically engineered superhuman, stronger than a normal man. Khan insists that all his crew be revived but Kirk arrests him. However, McGivers has fallen under Khan's spell and helps him to escape and revive some of his followers. Khan takes control of the Enterprise and threatens to kill Kirk unless the crew help him. McGivers is distressed and helps Kirk on the condition that Khan's life is spared. Khan sets the ship's engines to self-destruct but is overpowered by Kirk. Kirk decides to leave Khan and his followers on a deserted planet, Ceti Alpha V, where they will be able to create a new world. McGivers decides to join Khan. Spock notes it would be interesting to return one day and see what has become of Khan and his people.

QUOTES

'Improve a mechanical device and you may double productivity. But improve man and you gain thousandfold. I am such a man.' – *Khan*

TRIVIA

- Carey Wilber plundered *Odyssey Into Peril*, a script he had written for *Captain Video*, a sci-fi children's serial transmitted between 1949 and 1955. The original story, transmitted in June 1954, featured an evil Greek goddess with superpowers who was brought to the present day.
- Originally Khan was named Harold Ericcson, drawing on the Nordic-Viking tradition, but he was renamed after an army buddy of Gene Roddenberry.
- Khan returns in the second movie, *Star Trek II: The Wrath of Khan.*

RATING

- It all starts here, with a mesmerising performance from Ricardo Montalban. We get a fascinating glimpse of Starfleet's history as we learn more about the Eugenics Wars. You get the sense that there's something dark lurking in the Federation's past that we haven't been told about.

1.23 A TASTE OF ARMAGEDDON

STARDATE 3192.1

The crew find a planet where war is conducted by computer and casualties willingly give themselves up for disintegration

TX 23 February 1967
WRITER Robert Hamner and Gene L Coon (story by Robert Hamner)
DIRECTOR Joseph Pevney
GUEST CAST Barbara Babcock (Mea 3), Sean Kenney (DePaul), Gene Lyons (Robert Fox), Miko Mayama (Tamura), David Opatoshu (Anan 7), David L Ross (Galloway), Robert Sampson (Sar 6)

The Enterprise transports Ambassador Fox to the planet Eminiar VII on a diplomatic mission. They are warned to stay away but Fox insists that the Enterprise continue. Eminiar VII has been at war with its neighbour, Vendikar, for more than 500 years yet looks peaceful. The planet's leader, Anan 7, explains that the two planets conduct their war by computer – when an explosion is recorded, the 'casualties' report to a disintegration chamber and are vapourised. The Enterprise has been designated a casualty and must also be destroyed. Kirk and the landing party are taken prisoner. Anan 7 tries to dupe Scotty into lowering the shields, in an attempt to destroy the Enterprise, but Scotty is unconvinced. Meanwhile, Spock and Kirk escape and destroy the battle computers. Kirk tells the warring peoples that they will now experience the true horrors of war unless they can come to a lasting peace with their neighbours. Ambassador Fox stays behind to negotiate the peace.

TRIVIA

- The first draft had Mea and Sar scheduled to be married. The diplomatic story was added later.

RATING

- An interesting take on the supercomputer where social conditioning rather than mind control (*Return of the Archons*) makes for a nightmarish society. Gene Lyons is wonderful as the frustrating Ambassador Fox.

1.24 THIS SIDE OF PARADISE

STARDATE 3417.3

Spock's emotions are unleashed when he is exposed to a strange alien plant

TX 2 March 1967
WRITER DC Fontana (story by 'Nathan Butler' [pseudonym for Jerry Sohl] and DC Fontana)
DIRECTOR Ralph Senensky
GUEST CAST Michael Barrier (DeSalle), Jill Ireland (Leila Kalomi), Frank Overton (Elias Sandoval), Eddie Paskey (Leslie), Dick Scotter (Painter), Grant Woods (Kelowitz)

The Enterprise crew arrive at Omicron Ceti III expecting to find the colonists dead, but are surprised to find the colony flourishing. Leader Elias Sandoval reintroduces Spock to Leila Kalomi, a beautiful young botanist who had feelings for him at the academy. Leila takes Spock to a secluded spot where he is sprayed with the spores of a strange plant. The spores break down Spock's reserve and he admits his love for Leila and desire to stay on the planet. Meanwhile, Kirk receives orders to evacuate the colony, but Sandoval refuses. A search party finds Spock behaving oddly but they too are sprayed by the plant. Kirk evades the plants but finds McCoy and others beaming plants to the Enterprise. Soon the crew is out of control. On the deserted bridge, Kirk succumbs, but his momentary distress at the thought of leaving the Enterprise and his anger at abandoning his mission breaks the spell. Kirk riles Spock and the two fight. Spock recovers his senses just short of killing Kirk. Spock in turn rejects Leila's advances and she recovers also. Kirk starts a sonic bombardment of the planet that riles the inhabitants, provoking fights. The crew soon return to normal and the colony is evacuated.

QUOTES

- 'I've never understood the female capacity to avoid a direct answer to any question.' – *Spock to Leila*

TRIVIA

- The story, provisionally titled *The Way of the Spores*, was designed around a single question: What would happen if the crew took LSD? An early version had Sulu in love with Leila, with the spores a cure for a medical condition that jeopardises Sulu's career. The spores were a collective intelligence, able to cure and even to restore life.

RATING

- A simple story, only remembered for the breakdown of Spock's reserve. The moment when he tells Leila that he loves her hints at a tragedy in Spock's past.

1.25 THE DEVIL IN THE DARK

STARDATE 3196.1

The crew trace the deaths of miners on the planet Janus VI to a silicon-based life-form

TX 9 March 1967
WRITTENGene L Coon
DIRECTOR Joseph Pevney
GUEST CAST George E Allen (Engineer), John Cavett (Guard), Biff Elliott (Schmitter), Ken Lynch (Vanderberg), Janos Prohaska (Horta), Barry Russo (Giotto), Brad Weston (Ed Appel)

The Enterprise crew arrive at Janus VI where pergium miners are being killed by a mysterious creature. The mine's chief engineer, Vanderberg, explains that the attacks began in the lower levels where they were clearing silicon nodules. The creature is now attacking the upper levels but phasers have no effect. When the creature sabotages the colony's reactor, Spock deduces that it is intelligent and acting with purpose. Kirk and Spock search the lower levels for the creature and find a network of tunnels cut from the rock. Spock suspects the creature is a silicon-based life-form and the last of its kind. The creature traps Kirk but does not attack and instead reveals that it is injured. Spock mind-melds with the creature and discovers it is a Horta. It is in great pain. The Horta shows Kirk and Spock to a chamber containing the reactor pump and broken silicon nodules – they realise these are the Horta's eggs. The miners storm the chamber to kill the Horta but Kirk tells them of their error and convinces them to work with the Horta, the most talented miner among them. McCoy heals the Horta. As the Enterprise crew leave, the baby Horta hatch and begin digging.

TRIVIA

- Gene Coon reportedly based the Horta on an alien organism featured in *The Probe*, the last episode of *The Outer Limits*. Coon came up with the idea that the Horta was misunderstood. The final script, one of the best of the first season, took three days to write.
- The book version uses the working title of the story, *A Thousand Devils in the Dark*.

RATING

- A simple tale of prejudice, and a classic episode of *Star Trek* that everyone remembers, *The Devil in the Dark* manages to make its point without spelling everything out and rises above a simple monster flick. The search of the tunnels is suitably tense.

1.26 ERRAND OF MERCY

STARDATE 3198.4

Inhabitants of a remote planet are caught in war between the Federation and the Klingons

TX 23 March 1967
WRITER Gene L Coon
DIRECTOR John Newland
GUEST CAST Jon Abbott (Ayelborne), Peter Brocco (Claymare), John Colicos (Kor), Walt Davis (Klingon Soldier), David Hillary Hughes (Trefayne), Victor Lundin (Lieutenant), George Sawaya (Second Soldier)

When war breaks out between the Klingon Empire and the Federation, the Enterprise is sent to safeguard the strategically important planet Organia. Its leader, Ayelborne, and the Organian Council of Elders politely refuse Kirk's offer of protection and technological help, preferring to continue their mediaeval existence. However, eight Klingon ships surround the planet and beam down landing parties. The Council of Elders disguise Kirk as an Organian and Spock as a Vulcan merchant. The Klingon leader, Kor, proclaims a military dictatorship and, admiring Kirk's resistance, makes the Captain his official liaison. That night, Kirk and Spock destroy a munitions dump to inspire the Organians to resist, but Ayelborne refuses to condone violence. Kor discovers Kirk's true identity and has Spock and Kirk captured, but they are rescued by Ayelborne. Enraged, Kor orders 200 Organians killed until the prisoners are returned. That night, Kirk and Spock infiltrate Kor's headquarters. They are surrounded but as Kor's guards take aim their guns become white hot and they drop them. The same happens to the ships in orbit. Ayelborne explains that the Organians are a highly advanced race and will not permit a war. They return to their natural state of pure energy. Kor is dismayed that a glorious battle has been prevented.

QUOTES

- 'We are similar as a species. Here we are on a planet of sheep, two tigers, predators, hunters, killers. And it is precisely that which makes us great.' – *Kor to Kirk*

TRIVIA

- Dorothy Fontana reported that the production team were not happy with the name Klingons but didn't think of a better one in time. The Klingons quickly became the favoured stock villain as the Romulan make-up posed more production problems.
- Kor is played by John Colicos, who went on to play Baltar in *Battlestar Galactica.* Colicos would return as Kor in *Deep Space Nine.*

RATING

- If you take out the first appearance of the Klingons there is little to recommend *Errand of Mercy*. Colicos puts in a marvellous performance as Kor, a calculating and devious adversary.

1.27 THE ALTERNATIVE FACTOR

STARDATE 3087.6

Kirk battles two beings, one matter, one antimatter, which will destroy the universe if they meet

TX 30 March 1967
WRITER Don Ingalls
DIRECTOR Gerd Oswald
GUEST CAST Robert Brown (Lazarus), Richard Derr (Barstow), Janet MacLachlan (Charlene Masters), Eddie Paskey (Leslie), Christopher Patrick (Transporter Technician), Arch Whiting (Engineer Assistant)

While scanning a deserted planet, the Enterprise is rocked by a disturbance. Sensors now show a lifesign on the planet. Kirk beams down and finds Lazarus, a badly injured man who claims to have been attacked by an 'evil thing'. Spock discovers radiation on the planet that is coming from a rip in space-time. Lazarus asks for dilithium crystals to help defeat his enemy but Kirk refuses. Lazarus, suffering from mood-swings and convulsions, steals the crystals. Kirk catches him but Lazarus claims it was the work of his enemy. Meanwhile, Spock deduces that the radiation is coming from a parallel universe. Kirk realises that there are two Lazaruses – if they meet they could destroy both universes. Lazarus steals more crystals and Kirk pursues him to the planet's surface. Kirk attacks him and is transported to the other universe. The sane Lazarus tells Kirk to lead the insane Lazarus to the rip in space-time where they can be held together in perpetuity without destroying the universe. Kirk forces the evil Lazarus into the rip and destroys the ship, trapping the two Lazaruses in an eternal struggle between the two universes.

TRIVIA

- The original script had the sane Lazarus fall in love with Charlene Masters. The insane Lazarus used the relationship to obtain the dilithium crystals.
- John Drew Barrymore, son of John and father of Drew, was cast as Lazarus, but had to drop out. The publicity department weren't told, and publicity material credited him for the episode.

RATING

- A highly experimental episode of *Star Trek* that has some success. Gerd Oswald plays up the ambiguity, editing some scenes to force you to question what is going on. It's a gamble but one that pays off.

1.28 THE CITY ON THE EDGE OF FOREVER

STARDATE 3134.0

Kirk must allow his new love, Edith Keeler, to die if he is to prevent history being changed

TX 6 April 1967
WRITER Harlan Ellison
DIRECTOR Joseph Pevney
GUEST CAST Hal Baylor (Policeman), Joan Collins (Edith Keeler), John Harmon (Rodent), Bartell La Rue (Voice of the Guardian of Forever), David L Ross (Galloway), John Winston (Transporter Operator)

The Enterprise tracks some time disturbances to a deserted planet. McCoy accidentally injects himself with cordrazine, a powerful drug that causes paranoia, and beams down to the planet. Kirk and Spock follow and find the remains of a ruined city, some 10,000 centuries old, and a strange arch that pulses with power. It identifies itself as the Guardian of Forever, a time portal that displays images of Earth's past. McCoy breaks past the landing party and dives into the portal. Suddenly, Uhura reports she can no longer contact the Enterprise. The Guardian explains that McCoy has changed history – their world no longer exists. Kirk and Spock pursue McCoy and find themselves in America during the Depression. They are found by Edith Keeler, who offers them work and lodgings at a mission she runs. Kirk and Edith grow closer. Meanwhile. Spock manufactures a computer from his tricorder that shows how history has changed. Edith was meant to die in a motor accident in 1930 but instead lived and created a peace movement that delayed America's entry into the Second World War, allowing the Nazis to develop the atom bomb first and win the war. Spock tells Kirk that Edith must die to save history, but Kirk is in love with her. Edith finds McCoy, who regains consciousness, confused by his surroundings. As McCoy and Kirk are reunited, a van hurtles towards Edith. Kirk stops himself saving Edith and watches as she is knocked down and killed. McCoy is incredulous but Spock knows that Kirk did the right thing. The three men are returned to their own time.

QUOTES

- 'You deliberately stopped me, Jim. I could have saved her. Do you know what you just did?'
  'He knows, doctor. He knows.' – *McCoy and Spock*

TRIVIA

- Ellison's first draft was written in 1966 when only the first two pilots had been produced. In this version, a crewman called Beckwith, suffering from drug addiction, travels back in time. Kirk and crew pursue him, meeting Edith, an innocent who would kill herself if she knew her destiny. Spock prevents Edith's rescue. Ellison's story won the Writer's Guild of America award for Outstanding Dramatic Episode Teleplay in 1967-68. The transmitted episode, which had inclusions from Gene Coon and Steve Carbastos, major changes from Dorothy Fontana and a final rewrite by Roddenberry, won the Hugo Award for Best Dramatic Presentation in 1968.
- The original script was published in 1995 with a new essay by Ellison and a variety of afterwords setting out their position by other people involved, including Leonard Nimoy, Dorothy Fontana and David Gerrold.

RATING

- Rightly regarded as the highlight of original *Star Trek*, this episode takes a time travel story and builds it to a wrought emotional drama. Kirk's decision to let Edith die is horrifying and heart-rending, adding another dimension to his character. This is the epitome of what *Star Trek* does best – taking the sci-fi setting and distilling it into a tight character piece. Wonderful stuff.

1.29 OPERATION: ANNIHILATE!

The Enterprise crew battles insidious alien parasites that have killed Kirk's only brother

TX 13 April 1967
WRITER Stephen W Carabatsos
DIRECTOR Herschel Daugherty
GUEST CAST Dave Armstrong (Kartan), Majel Barrett (Christine Chapel), Fred Carson (First Denevan), Jerry Catron (Second Denevan), Craig Hundley (Peter Kirk), Mauriska Taliferro (Zahra Jamal), Joan Swift (Aurelan Kirk)

STARDATE 3287.2

The Enterprise arrives at the planet Deneva, home to Kirk's brother Sam, where the inhabitants may soon fall victim to an outbreak of mass insanity. In orbit, they hear a Denevan pilot fly his ship into a sun to free himself from an unknown force. Kirk takes a landing party but finds Sam is already dead. Sam's wife, Aurelan, and son Peter are taken back to the ship. Before Aurelan dies, she explains that alien parasites are controlling the inhabitants and forcing them to build ships. Kirk and crew return to the surface and are attacked but phasers prove useless. One parasite infects Spock but he is able to ignore the excruciating pain and captures an alien creature that they can take to the Enterprise for analysis. McCoy can find no answer but Kirk, remembering the pilot, deduces that a large amount of light may kill the parasite. Spock is exposed to a powerful blast of light which kills the parasite but leaves him blind. The Enterprise bombards the planet with ultraviolet light, killing the parasites. Spock regains his sight – his second Vulcan eyelids had protected him from permanent blindness!

TRIVIA

- Kirk's brother was absent from the first draft, entitled *Operation: Destroy*.
- Shatner briefly appears with grey hair and moustache as the body of Kirk's brother.

RATING

- An end-of-season show where you can feel the production team flagging. The story has very little to it and the mystery unfolds painfully slowly.

STAR TREK
SEASON TWO

2.1 AMOK TIME

STARDATE 3372.7

Spock returns to Vulcan to marry and is pushed into a fight to the death with Kirk

TX 15 September 1967
WRITER Theodore Sturgeon
DIRECTOR Joseph Pevney
GUEST CAST Majel Barrett (Christine Chapel), Celia Lovsky (T'Pau), Arlene Martel (T'Pring), Lawrence Montaigne (Stonn), Byran Morrow (Komack)

Spock starts to behave emotionally and requests a leave of absence. Kirk sets course for Vulcan but is diverted by Starfleet to Altair VI. Spock changes the course controls back but cannot remember doing so. McCoy discovers that Spock's body is being flooded with adrenaline – if they do not reach Vulcan in eight days, Spock will die. Spock ashamedly reveals that he is in the Pon farr, an uncontrollable need to mate that all Vulcans experience every seven years. Kirk heads for Vulcan, disobeying Starfleet orders. On Vulcan, Spock meets with T'Pring, his fiancée by arrangement. The wedding party arrives, led by T'Pau, but Spock is in the grip of the *Plak tow*, the blood fever, and must fight for T'Pring. T'Pring names Kirk as her champion but her companion, Stonn, objects. Convinced that Stonn will beat Spock, Kirk agrees to fight for T'Pring. Kirk is horrified to discover it is a fight to the death. Spock and Kirk are equally matched. In the break, McCoy gives Kirk an injection to help him breathe in the Vulcan atmosphere. The fight resumes and Spock strangles Kirk, dropping his limp body to the ground. McCoy reports that Kirk is dead. The shock breaks Spock from his fever. Spock asks T'Pring why she invoked the challenge. T'Pring wants to marry Stonn. The marriage is cancelled. Back on the Enterprise, Spock is delighted to see Kirk alive: McCoy injected him with a paralyser to fake death.

QUOTES

- 'Live long, T'Pau, and prosper.' – *Spock utters the famous words for the first time*

TRIVIA

- *Amok Time* premiered at the World Science Fiction Convention held in New York in 1967.
- From the start of the second season, DeForest Kelley's name appears on the opening credits.
- This story is parodied in the *Futurama* episode *Why Must I Be a Crustacean in Love?*

RATING

- For all its complete Vulcan overload, *Amok Time* has some strong character moments. One notably powerful scene has T'Pau deriding Spock's half-human ancestry. And even people who know very little about *Star Trek* know Spock only has sex once every seven years. A classic episode.

2.2 WHO MOURNS FOR ADONAIS?

STARDATE 3468.1

The Enterprise crew are captured by Apollo, last of the Greek gods

TX 22 September 1967
WRITERS Gilbert Ralston and Gene L Coon (story by Gilbert Ralston)
DIRECTOR Marc Daniels
GUEST CAST Michael Forest (Apollo), Leslie Parrish (Carolyn Palamas), John Winston (Kyle)

As the Enterprise approaches Pollux IV, an enormous hand takes hold of the ship. A being that looks like a Greek god invites the crew to join him on the planet's surface. Kirk asks Lieutenant Carolyn Palamas, an expert in ancient history, to join them. On the surface, the creature claims to be Apollo, the last of the Greek gods from Mount Olympus. He insists that the crew leave the Enterprise and settle on Pollux IV where they will worship him. On the Enterprise, Spock scans the planet and discovers that Apollo draws his energy from a hidden power source. Kirk plans to drain Apollo of his energy, but his idea is jeopardised by Palamas, who has fallen for Apollo. Apollo decides to

take Palamas as his bride and blasts a thunderbolt at Scotty when the engineer objects. Spock discovers that the energy source is Apollo's temple. Kirk orders Palamas to reject Apollo's advances. Palamas is reluctant but finally agrees. Apollo is enraged and uses up much of his energy in the tantrum. Kirk takes the opportunity to order the Enterprise to destroy the temple. Apollo, drained of his energy and aware that mankind has no more need for gods, spreads himself on the wind until he is no more.

TRIVIA

- Several sections of Fred Steiner's original score for the episode are reused in *Requiem for Methuselah*.
- In the original draft (and the novelisation) Palamas is pregnant at the end of the story.
- The title appears to be a misspelling – presumably, it's meant to be *Who Mourns for Adonis?* There's an Adonis in Greek myth, a beautiful man beloved of Venus, but there's no Adonais.
- Gene L Coon did a significant amount of writing work on the episode.

RATING

- An interesting if hokey idea. Michael Forest is brilliant as Apollo, swinging from loneliness to love and rage. Equally strong is Leslie Parrish's performance as Palamas. The scene where Palamas is attacked by the elements is harrowing and suggestive.

2.3 THE CHANGELING

Kirk and crew confront an Earth space probe that is now intent on galactic genocide

TX 29 September 1967
WRITER John Meredyth Lucas
DIRECTOR Marc Daniels
GUEST CAST Majel Barrett (Christine Chapel), Barbara Gates (Crewman), Arnold Lessing (Carlisle), Blaisdell Makee (Singh), Vic Perrin (Voice of Nomad)

STARDATE 3451.9

The Enterprise investigates the deaths of four billion people in the Malurian system and is attacked by a tiny vessel. Kirk hails the ship, which is called Nomad, and beams it aboard. Nomad announces that it is programmed to destroy all imperfect biological life and recognises Kirk as its creator. Spock checks the archives and discovers that Nomad was a probe launched from Earth in the early twenty-first century. It has confused Kirk with its true creator, Jackson Roykirk, who launched Nomad to search for alien life. However, the probe's purpose and capabilities have been altered. While Nomad starts purging the crew, Spock mind-melds with it and discovers that, shortly after its launch, Nomad contacted Tan-Ru, an alien probe sent to collect soil samples and sterilise them. Somehow, their programming merged. Nomad insists that all biological life forms are inferior, but Kirk reminds the probe that he is a biological life form and created Nomad. Nomad is puzzled and investigates Kirk's personnel file. Discovering the truth, Nomad shuts off life support, intent on killing the crew for being imperfect. Kirk tells Nomad that it itself is imperfect – it confused Kirk with its creator. Nomad begins to self-destruct and is hurriedly taken to the transporter room. Moments after being beamed into space, Nomad explodes.

QUOTES

- 'Nomad, it's about time I told you who and what you are. I'm a biological unit and I created you.' – *Kirk confuses Nomad*

TRIVIA

- In the first draft, Kirk jettisons a cloud of gas into space onto which he projects an image of himself to communicate with the probe, then named Altair.

RATING

- An idea so good they used it twice. The deviant Earth probe is reused to great effect in *Star Trek: The Motion Picture*. Nomad is a palpable threat, capable of extinguishing the crew at a moment's notice. Its regard for Spock, as distinct from the rest of the crew, results in a wonderful smugness from the Vulcan.

2.4 MIRROR, MIRROR

Kirk is beamed to a parallel universe where the crew are warmongers intent on domination

STARDATE UNKNOWN

After failing to gain access to dilithium from the Halkans, Kirk, McCoy, Scotty and Uhura beam back to the Enterprise and find themselves in a parallel universe where the Federation is a brutal empire, intent on taking the crystal by force. While Scotty attempts to disable the ship's

TX 6 October 1967
WRITER Jerome Bixby
DIRECTOR Marc Daniels
GUEST CAST Pete Kellett (Farrell), Barbara Luna (Marlena Moreau), Vic Perrin (Tharn), Garth Pillsbury (Wilson), John Winston (Kyle and Computer Voice)

phasers to protect the Halkans, Kirk holds the order to fire until the ship has missed its optimum firing window, drawing Spock's suspicions. Kirk returns to his quarters but has to battle Chekov, who is intent on killing the captain and moving up in rank. The landing party regroups and discovers that the transporter accident can be reproduced. When Kirk realises that Sulu will be aware of what they are doing, he sends Uhura to create a diversion. Kirk returns to his quarters to find Marlene, the 'captain's woman', waiting for him. He tries to fool her into thinking he has other plans for the Halkans, but she becomes suspicious and monitors Kirk with the Tantalus field, a device that allows the captain to watch and kill people from a distance. Uhura's distraction fails and Sulu heads to the transporter room where he sees Spock being overpowered by the landing party. Sulu decides to make it look as though Kirk and Spock killed each other, leaving him in command, but Marlene uses the Tantalus device to kill Sulu's armed guards. Kirk quickly overpowers Sulu and McCoy treats Spock. Spock revives and decides to help Kirk and the landing party leave and return his familiar crewmates to him. Kirk insists that the Federation Empire will one day fall and it is illogical for Spock to be part of that. He offers Spock the Tantalus field, giving him the power to make a change. Spock agrees to consider Kirk's suggestion as the landing party return to their own universe.

QUOTES

- 'If change is inevitable, predictable, beneficial... doesn't logic demand that you be a part of it?' – *Kirk to the parallel universe Spock*

TRIVIA

- Jerome Bixby penned *Mirror, Mirror* in 1967 after his parallel universe short story called *One Way Street*. In Bixby's original script, Kirk found a parallel universe crew suffering defeat at the hands of the Tharn empire. Kirk used his phaser to create weapons to defeat the Tharn. A nice touch had Kirk discovering that his counterpart was married and seeing that woman, a nurse, in sickbay on his return. Bixby's script was nominated for the Hugo Award for Best Dramatic Presentation.
- The Mirror Universe is revisited in *Deep Space Nine*, starting with the episode *Crossover*. It's been pastiched and parodied, not to mention just stolen from, by any number of science fiction shows and comic books (*Doctor Who* had *Inferno*, for example). The Mirror Spock's 'evil beard' has also become useful shorthand – ironically, given that Mirror Spock is a decent man – in shows such as *Futurama* (*The Lesser of Two Evils*), *South Park* (*Spookyfish*) and even *Knight Rider* (any episode with the evil double of Michael, Garth Knight).

RATING

- Hugely effective, *Mirror, Mirror* is widely regarded as one of the finest original *Star Trek* episodes, and it's been hugely influential. It's a busy episode that wisely chooses to focus on Kirk's adventures in the parallel universe rather than split the narrative with the real Enterprise. The glimpse of the Federation that might have been is fascinating and has much more mileage that this single episode can cover.

2.5 THE APPLE

STARDATE 3715.3

The crew battle a powerful supercomputer in control of a paradise world

TX 13 October 1967
WRITER Max Ehrlich and Gene L Coon (story by Max Ehrlich)
DIRECTOR Joseph Pevney
GUEST CAST Keith Andes (Akuta), Jerry Daniels (Marple), Dick Dial (Kaplan), Mal Friedman (Hendorff), Jay Jones (Mallory), Shari Nims (Sayana), David Soul (Makora), John Winston (Kyle), Celeste Yarnall (Martha Landon)

A landing party on Gamma Trianguli VI, a beautiful paradise world like the Garden of Eden, encounters poisonous plants that kill an ensign. When the landing party try to beam back, they discover that the planet interferes with the beam and they cannot return. After more crewmembers die, the landing party captures Akuta, leader of the Feeders of Vaal, who has two small antennae implanted in him. Meanwhile, the Enterprise is caught in a tractor beam and slowly pulled to the planet's atmosphere, where it will burn up. Akuta takes the landing party to Vaal, their god, a large stone head carved into the rocks. Spock realises that inside is a power supply protected by a forcefield. He suspects that Vaal is a large computer that controls the planet's atmosphere. McCoy discovers that the Feeders are innocents, unaware of love or sex, and that they do not age. Their offerings of produce provide the god with power. Akuta receives instructions to destroy the visitors and begins to educate the villagers in killing. The Feeders are quickly overpowered. When Vaal calls for feeding, the villagers do not respond and Vaal's grip on the Enterprise starts to weaken. Kirk orders Scotty to fire on the head from orbit. The phasers eventually breach the forcefield and Vaal is stopped, freeing the villagers from its influence.

TRIVIA

- Makora is played by David Soul, who became better known as Ken Hutchinson in *Starsky and Hutch*.

RATING

- From one extreme to the other – after the excitement and interest of *Mirror, Mirror* comes the ponderous absurdity of *The Apple*. The episode is not helped by some of the worst make up and design work the show ever turned out.

2.6 THE DOOMSDAY MACHINE

STARDATE 4202.9

The crew must stop a planet killer en route to a densely populated part of the galaxy

TX 20 October 1967
WRITER Norman Spinrad
DIRECTOR Marc Daniels
GUEST CAST Tim Burns (Russ) Jerry Catron (Montgomery), Richard Compton (Washburn), John Copage (Elliot), Elizabeth Rogers (Palmer), William Windom (Matthew Decker), John Winston (Kyle)

The Enterprise receives a distress call from the USS Constellation and finds one survivor, Commodore Matt Decker. Decker explains how they came under attack from a mysterious craft found slicing planets with an anti-proton beam. Decker transported the crew to the third planet but watched helplessly as the entity destroyed it. Decker and McCoy beam back to the Enterprise. Checking the ship's logs, Spock discovers that the 'Planet Killer' is a robotic entity from outside the galaxy, *en route* to the most densely populated part of the galaxy. The planet-killer attacks the Enterprise, leaving Kirk and Scotty stranded on the Constellation. Decker takes command of the Enterprise and decides to attack the planet killer, against Spock's advice. When Kirk restores the Constellation's viewscreen, he is horrified to see the Enterprise in combat with the entity and orders Scotty to restore power. The machine slowly drags the Enterprise into its jaws with a tractor beam. Scotty restores power and Kirk uses the Constellation to draw the planet-killer away. A furious Kirk contacts the Enterprise and orders Spock to assume command. Decker is escorted to sickbay but overcomes the guard and steals a shuttlecraft. Guilt-ridden over the loss of his crew, Decker pilots the small craft into the mouth of the entity and is killed. The explosion causes a small drop in the planet killer's power levels. Kirk orders Scotty to rig the Constellation's engines to explode and pilots it into the machine's mouth. Scotty beams back and manages to transport Kirk back to the Enterprise shortly before the Constellation and the planet-killer are destroyed.

QUOTES

- 'You have been relieved of command. Don't force me to relieve you of duty as well.' – *Decker to Kirk*

TRIVIA

- Norman Spinrad adapted a science fiction novel he had not had published that was based on *Moby Dick*.
- The story of the Doomsday Machine was picked up by Peter David in the novel *Vendetta* in which he theorises that the planet-killer was designed by an ancient race to combat the Borg.

RATING

- Combining pace, characterisation and genuine excitement, *The Doomsday Machine* is top ten material. Decker's Ahab works well as a contrast to the more traditional jeopardy facing Kirk. The origin of the threat is left nicely unresolved, with questions that were to be picked up in the novels.

2.7 CATSPAW

STARDATE 3018.2

Kirk, Spock and McCoy battle a witch and wizard to rescue missing officers

The Enterprise loses contact with Scotty, Sulu and the other members of a landing party sent to investigate the planet Pyris VII. A voice warns the rest of the crew to stay away, but Kirk is determined to rescue the others. Kirk, Spock and McCoy find it is night on Pyris VII and the planet

TX 27 October 1967
WRITER Robert Bloch and DC Fontana
DIRECTOR Joseph Pevney
GUEST CAST Michael Barrier (DeSalle), Gail Bonney (Second Witch), Antoinette Bower (Sylvia), Rhodie Cogan (First Witch), Mary Esther Denver (Third Witch), Jimmy Jones (Jackson), Theo Marcuse (Korob), John Winston (Kyle)

is shrouded in fog. They come upon a group of witches and then a castle, but the floor collapses beneath them. They awaken, chained to a dungeon wall. Scotty and Sulu arrive in a trance-like state and take the newcomers to Korob, a powerful conjuror, and his black cat that transforms into a female companion, Sylvia. Korob promises the officers jewels if they leave the planet, but Kirk refuses. Sylvia produces a model of the Enterprise which she holds over a flame, causing the real ship to become very hot. Back in the dungeon, Spock suggests that Korob and Sylvia have created a fantasy world using the human unconscious. Meanwhile, Sylvia makes a play for Kirk, intent on exploring the sensations of her human form. She becomes angry when she realises he is using her to try to escape. Scared by Sylvia's rage, Korob frees the senior officers, who are pursued by Sylvia – now taking the form of a giant cat. Kirk takes Korob's staff and, realising it is the source of their power, destroys it. The castle disappears and the landing party are restored, but Korob and Sylvia revert to their natural form and die.

QUOTES

- 'Where did your race get this ridiculous predeliction for resistance?' – *Korob to Kirk*

TRIVIA

- *Catspaw* was conceived as *Star Trek*'s Halloween episode.
- This was the first episode recorded that featured Chekov but the episodes were transmitted in a different sequence. He first appeared to the public in *Mirror, Mirror*.

RATING

- One of those episodes that is just too silly to stomach. It's an ill thought-out, unbalanced story where the motivations and reasoning are skewed. Two appalling guest star performances make for a story that is best left forgotten.

2.8 I, MUDD

STARDATE 4513.3

Mudd lures the crew to an isolated planet to free himself from an android race

TX 3 November 1967
WRITER Stephen Kandel (uncredited rewrite by David Gerrold)
DIRECTOR Marc Daniels
GUEST CAST Alyce Andrece, Rhae Andrece (Alice series), Roger C Carmel (Harry Mudd), Kay Elliott (Stella series), Mike Howden (Rowe), Ted Legarde, Tom Legarde (Herman series), Richard Tatro (Norman), Colleen Thornton, Maureen Thornton (Barbara series), Starr Wilson, Tamara Wilson (Maisie series), Michael Zaslow (Jordan)

An android, Norman, takes control of the Enterprise and sets course for an uncharted planet. On their arrival, Norman takes Kirk and a landing party to the surface where they find galactic conman Harry Mudd. Although appearing to rule the planet of 200,000 androids, Mudd is actually a captive, held for the purposes of study. To escape, he has promised the androids the entire crew of the Enterprise to study. Harry has learnt something of android technology and has created a replica of his harridan wife, Stella, who obeys his commands. He replaces the crew with android duplicates. Kirk discovers that the androids have no intention of letting Mudd go free – they have deemed humanity too flawed to rule the galaxy. They intend to explore space while the real crew grow dependent on their service. Spock deduces that the androids share one giant mind, centred on Norman. Kirk and the crew unnerve the android by bombarding him with scenes of irrational behaviour. When Kirk tells Norman that Harry is lying and Harry claims that *he* is lying, the logical paradox is too much for the android. The machines seize up, allowing the crew to escape. Before they leave, the crew reprogram the androids to make the planet productive and leave Mudd behind as an example of human failure, accompanied by 500 copies of the old Stella.

QUOTES

- 'Nowhere am I so desperately needed as among a shipload of illogical humans.' – *Spock to McCoy*

TRIVIA

- Kandel and Gerrold's first draft played more on Norman's ruse than events on the planet.

- Stephen Kandel proposed a third outing for Harry in *Deep Mudd*, but actor Roger C Carmel was busy with a feature film. The story saw Harry escape from the android planet by finding a secret cache of highly advanced weapons and offering them to a group of pirates in return for their help, but quickly getting out of his depth.

RATING

- Amusing throwaway stuff with Harry Mudd. The 500 androids is a great idea, topped only by Kay Elliot's Stella, a kind of intergalactic Ethel Merman.

2.9 METAMORPHOSIS

STARDATE 3219.8

Kirk finds Zefram Cochrane, the creator of warp drive, marooned on a planet with a mysterious alien companion

TX 10 November 1967
WRITER Gene L Coon
DIRECTOR Ralph Serensky
GUEST CAST Majel Barrett (Voice of Companion), Glenn Corbett (Zefram Cochrane), Elinor Donahue (Nancy Hedford)

Kirk, Spock and McCoy are transporting Commissioner Nancy Hedford, a diplomat with Sakuro's disease, in the Galileo shuttlecraft when they are enveloped by a mysterious energy cloud and taken to the surface of an isolated planet. The cloud disappears but the shuttle has been disabled. The officers find a shipwrecked human, Zefram Cochrane, who Kirk recognises as the inventor of warp engines. Cochrane tells how he had taken a ship into space to die 150 years previously but was rejuvenated by the energy cloud, which he calls the Companion, and brought to the planet, where he has been cared for ever since. Cochrane believes that the Companion has brought him the Enterprise crewmembers to keep him company. Hedford's condition deteriorates and Cochrane asks the Companion if it can help. The being says it can't. Meanwhile, Spock tries to use the Galileo to call for help but is warned off by an electric shock by the Companion. Spock and McCoy invent a device to scramble the Companion's electrical impulses but it is ineffective and the Companion attacks Kirk and Spock. They are saved only when Cochrane calls the entity off. McCoy suggests that they reason with it. Using the universal translator, Kirk discovers that the Companion is a female and devoted to Cochrane. Kirk tries to convince the Companion to release Cochrane, claiming it will never know how to love as it is not human. When Hedford dies, the Companion merges with her, restoring her to life. The Companion/Hedford has given up its immortal form for a mortal life with Cochrane. Moved, Cochrane decides to stay with the Companion and asks Kirk to keep his life secret.

QUOTES

- 'Fascinating. A totally parochial response.' – *Spock notes Cochrane's bitter refusal to accept that the Companion loves him*

TRIVIA

- Zefram Cochrane was to reappear in *Star Trek: First Contact*, played by a different actor. The man's legendary status is only hinted at here.

RATING

- A complicated situation that is difficult to put across. It is testament to some very good writing and direction that the relationship between Cochrane and the Companion is communicated effectively. If there is a let-down, it is the final scene with the Hedford creature, which somehow lacks the impact of previous scenes.

2.10 JOURNEY TO BABEL

STARDATE 3842.3

Spock's father is implicated in the murder of a Federation conference delegate

TX 17 November 1967
WRITER DC Fontana
DIRECTOR Joseph Pevney

The Enterprise transports delegates to a conference on Babel, among them Vulcan Ambassador Sarek and his human wife, Amanda – Spock's parents. Sarek is cold towards Spock. Amanda explains that Sarek wanted Spock to follow in his footsteps and not join Starfleet. At a reception for the delegates, Sarek refuses to tell Tellarite Ambassador Gav whether the Vulcan government will support Coridan's application to join the Federation. However, after a mysterious ship passes the Enterprise, Sarek announces that the Vulcans will support the application

GUEST CAST Majel Barrett (Christine Chapel), Mark Lenard (Sarek), James X Mitchell (Josephs), Reggie Nalder (Sharas), William O'Connell (Thelev), John Wheeler (Gav), Jane Wyatt (Amanda)

to protect the Federation from the greedy Tellarites. A fight is narrowly averted. Later, Gav is found killed in the manner of the Vulcan execution, *Tal-shaya*. Spock admits that, if Sarek deemed it logical, he could have killed the ambassador. Sarek collapses with a weak heart. Spock is the only match for Sarek's rare blood type, T negative. Meanwhile, Kirk gets into a fight with an Andorian and is stabbed. Spock takes command and refuses to leave until Kirk is better, endangering Sarek's life. Kirk hides his discomfort and takes command. Soon they pick up the mysterious vessel again, in communication with someone in the brig. The Andorian is an impostor, bent on wrecking the conference. The small ship attacks the Enterprise. Kirk shuts down power, pretending that the Enterprise is damaged, but as soon as the inquisitive ship investigates he fires, destroying it. The spy takes poison but is suspected of being an Orion, a race that has been raiding Coridan and hoped to supply both sides in a war. McCoy orders Kirk to join Sarek and Spock in recovery.

TRIVIA

- Fontana was keen to flesh out Spock's back story, and pitched this script which picked up on references to Spock's family in earlier episodes. Fontana introduced the rift between Spock and Sarek. We learn that Sarek was an astrophysicist before becoming a diplomat and that his father was a famous Vulcan ambassador, Shariel, adding another dimension to Sarek's motivation for pressurising his son.
- Mark Lenard was born in 1927, only four years before Leonard Nimoy, his screen 'son'.

RATING

- A popular episode that is rich with colour and texture. The relationship between Spock and Sarek is done extremely well, with Amanda's concern and disappointment adding an absent emotional context that makes the father-son relationship seem more tragic.

2.11 FRIDAY'S CHILD

STARDATE 3497.2

Kirk and crew intervene when a Klingon manipulates the power politics of a primitive planet

TX 1 December 1967
WRITER DC Fontana
DIRECTOR Joseph Pevney
GUEST CAST Tige Andrews (Kras), Cal Bolder (Keel), Robert Bralver (Grant), Michael Dante (Maab), Ben Gage (Akaar), Julie Newmar (Eleen), Kirk Raymone (Duur)

The Enterprise crew arrives at Capella IV to negotiate a mining treaty with the primitive inhabitants but discovers the Klingons have beaten them to it. Kirk negotiates with the Capellan leader, Teer Akaar, but that night Maab, in league with the Klingons, stages a revolt and Akaar is killed. Maab decides to kill Akaar's widow, Eleen, pregnant with the rightful heir, but the landing party take her and escape. Meanwhile, on the Enterprise, Scotty picks up a distress call and leaves orbit to investigate. On the planet, Kirk, Spock and McCoy contact the Enterprise but it is out of range. They head into the mountains with Eleen and create a landslide to slow their pursuers. The officers find a cave where McCoy delivers Eleen's child. On the Enterprise, Scotty realises the distress call was a decoy and sets course for Capella IV. With the pursuers closing, Eleen leaves the cave and tells the men that the Starfleet officers are dead. The Klingon refuses to believe her and heads to the cave but Kirk breaks cover and shoots him with an arrow. Eleen persuades Maab to turn on the Klingons. Maab is killed but the Klingons are repelled, leaving Kirk to sign the treaty with the new regent, Eleen.

TRIVIA

- In an early draft, Eleen is a power-hungry woman who offers her child in return for her own life. Maab has her executed for adultery but is later killed by his people for plotting with the Klingon, Keel.
- Julie Newmar (Eleen) is better known as the original Catwoman in the Adam West *Batman* series.

RATING

- A story that tells the machinations of power politics from the point of view of a single mother. Sadly, the motivations of the inhabitants seem a little flimsy and the Enterprise officers appear as bystanders in a story that could be told equally well without them.

2.12 THE DEADLY YEARS

STARDATE 3478.2

The crew are exposed to radiation that results in rapid ageing

TX 8 December 1967
WRITER David P Harmon
DIRECTOR Joseph Pevney
GUEST CAST Majel Barrett (Christine Chapel), Charles Drake (George Stocker), Felix Locher (Robert Johnson), Sarah Marshall (Janet Wallace), Carolyn Nelson (Doris Atkins), Beverly Washburn (Arlene Galway), Laura Wood (Elaine Johnson)

Kirk, Spock, McCoy and Chekov beam down to Gamma Hydra IV to locate an expedition. Chekov is terrified when he finds four members of a six-man expedition have died of premature old age. The two survivors, Elaine and Robert Johnson, are both dying of old age despite being in their late twenties. Kirk theorises that the colonists may have been the victims of a Romulan weapon. Commodore Stocker, a passenger on the Enterprise, urges Kirk to continue to Starbase 10 so he can take up his post. Soon, the landing party age markedly – Chekov is the only exception. The crew discover that a comet that passed by recently left unusual radiation in the planet's atmosphere. Kirk suffers from the onset of senility and Stocker takes command. Unfamiliar with the command of a starship, Stocker orders a direct course for Starbase 10, taking the Enterprise through the Neutral Zone. Kirk is horrified and, in a moment of clarity, remembers Chekov's fear when discovering the bodies. McCoy realises that adrenaline was once used to treat radiation poisoning and starts developing a treatment. The Enterprise enters the Neutral Zone and is attacked by the Romulans but Kirk is restored by an experimental serum, and, rejuvenated, takes command. He fools the Romulans into thinking he is about to destroy the Enterprise using a corbomite device. The Romulans back off and the crew escape.

TRIVIA

- David Harmon was reportedly inspired to write *The Deadly Years* after musing on the different attitudes to old age in the east and west.

RATING

- An interesting story but the solution is painfully obvious. It's hard to watch the performances of the regulars without thinking about the cast as they now appear today!

2.13 OBSESSION

STARDATE 3619.2

Kirk faces a deadly gaseous entity that he failed to kill as a lieutenant

TX 15 December 1967
WRITER Art Wallace
DIRECTOR Ralph Senensky
GUEST CAST Jerry Ayres (Rizzo), Majel Barrett (Christine Chapel), Stephen Brooks (Garrovick)

While analysing deposits of tritatium on a planet, Kirk recognises a familiar sweet smell. He orders the crew to be on guard for a gaseous cloud but the vapour manages to kill three crewmen. Kirk encountered the cloud 11 years previously when he served on the USS Farragut – he was one of the few survivors. The son of the Farragut's dead captain, Garrovick, accompanies Kirk to the surface. They encounter the cloud again, but phasers have no impact. Kirk is convinced that the cloud is the same one that attacked the Farragut crew. He is furious with Garrovick, who hesitated before firing: Kirk hesitated years previously and blames himself for the death of his crewmates. The cloud heads into space. Kirk fires all weapons but it is futile. The gas enters the ship through an impulse vent. Spock is convinced that the gas is intelligent and tells Kirk and Garrovick that they could do little against it. Scotty succeeds in blowing the gaseous entity into space. It heads to Tycho IV, where it had attacked the Farragut crew. Kirk and Garrovick use themselves as bait to draw the gas to an antimatter bomb. At the last moment, they beam to the Enterprise and the bomb is detonated, destroying the entity. Kirk and Garrovick make their peace.

QUOTES

- 'No man achieves Starfleet command without relying on intuition but have I made a rational decision? Am I letting the horrors of the past distort my judgment of the present?' – *Kirk's handily expository log entry*

TRIVIA

- This episode sees the death of crewman Leslie. He makes repeat appearances later in the season!

RATING

- A great story for Kirk, drawing on the *Star Trek* obsession with Melville's *Moby Dick*, only recently adapted as *The Doomsday Machine*. Still, Kirk's actions are more rational and there's a profound sense of guilt that adds to his character. It's an odd episode for Spock, however, whose attempt to stop the gas is completely illogical. He only survives because Vulcans have copper-based blood. Duh.

2.14 WOLF IN THE FOLD

STARDATE 3614.9

Scotty is implicated in murders committed by the spirit of Jack the Ripper

TX 22 December 1967
WRITER Robert Bloch
DIRECTOR Joseph Pevney
GUEST CAST Virginia Aldridge (Karen Tracy), Joseph Bernard (Tark), Charles Dierkop (Morla), John Fiedler (Mr Hengist), Tania Lemani (Kara), Charles Macaulay (Jaris), Judy McConnell (Tankris), Pilar Seurat (Sybo), Judi Sherven (Nurse), John Winston (Transporter Chief and Argelian Bartender)

In a bar on Argelius II, Kirk, McCoy and Scotty are entertained by a belly dancer, Kara. Scotty and Kara go for a walk, but there is a scream and Kara is found stabbed to death: Scotty is holding the knife. An administrator from Rigel IV, Mr Hengist, questions Scotty, but he cannot remember anything. Later, when Lieutenant Tracy performs tests on Scotty, she too is killed and Scotty left unconscious. Prefect Jaris of Argelius and his wife Sybo prepare an Argelian empathic contact to investigate the crimes. They are joined by Kara's father and her jealous lover. In the dark, Sybo senses a presence, driven by a hatred of women, and cries out some names before screaming. Later she is also found murdered, apparently by Scotty. On the Enterprise, a lie-detector test confirms that Scotty did not kill the woman. Kirk investigates the names Sybo screamed and discovers that one, Redjac, was a nickname for Jack the Ripper. Spock theorises that the Ripper entity may not possess a physical form. They discover that the murder weapon was from Rigel IV and question Hengist. The Redjac entity controlling Hengist is discovered and enters the ship's computer, leaving the administrator dead. Spock ejects Redjac from the computer and it retakes Hengist. He is dragged to the transporter room and beamed with the entity into space.

TRIVIA

- *Wolf in the Fold* was a reworking of a script written by Bloch in 1961 for *Thriller* named *Yours Truly, Jack the Ripper*. The episode, based on a short story by Bloch, had Scotland Yard detectives tracing murders in 1960s America to the infamous serial killer. The Ripper was unmasked as a demon that could take on human form.
- Robert Bloch is better known as the author of *Psycho* (1959), filmed by Hitchcock in 1960.

RATING

- A great idea, so good Bloch used it at least three times! It's good to see Scotty get something to do. The use of the computer is novel, although a large amount of technobabble is required to make the story work.

2.15 THE TROUBLE WITH TRIBBLES

STARDATE 4523.3

As the crew try to protect a cargo of food, the Enterprise is overrun by Tribbles

TX 29 December 1967
WRITER David Gerrold
DIRECTOR Joseph Pevney

The Enterprise receives a distress call from Deep Space Station K-7. On arrival, Nilz Baris and his assistant Arne Darvin order Kirk to guard a shipment of quadrotriticale, a grain needed on Sherman's Planet, that they fear the Klingons want to destroy. Kirk is furious that the distress call was not more serious. Meanwhile, Uhura and Chekov meet trader Cyrano Jones, who is trying to sell a small, furry creature, a Tribble, to the bartender. Uhura is given one as a free sample. The Klingons arrive for shore leave, but Kirk only lets a few on the station at a time. There is much animosity between the two crews and, when Scotty attacks a Klingon who claims the Enterprise is scrap, a fight erupts. The Tribbles seem to show equal animosity towards Klingons. Meanwhile, on the Enterprise, the Tribbles are reproducing at a phenomenal rate and soon the ship is completely overrun. However, when the Tribbles eat the grain,

GUEST CAST Stanley Adams (Cyrano Jones), Paul Baxley (Freeman), Whit Bissell (Mr Lurry), Charlie Brill (Arne Darvin), William Campbell (Koloth), Eddie Paskey (Security Guard), Michael Pataki (Korax), Guy Raymond (Trader/Bartender), Ed Reimers (Admiral Fitzpatrick), David L Ross (Guard), William Schallert (Nilz Baris)

they start dying – the grain was poisoned. Kirk sees the tribbles react badly to Darvin and discovers that the man is a Klingon in disguise. The Klingons are ordered to leave, but not before Scotty beams every Tribble on the Enterprise into the Klingon ship's engine room.

QUOTES

- 'I transported the whole kit and caboodle into their engine room – where they'll be no 'tribble' at all.' – *Scotty, shortly before the crew beat him up, one hopes*

TRIVIA

- Reports have it that there was a lot of resistance internally to an out-and-out comedy episode. Pevney, who had worked in vaudeville and directed episodes of *The Munsters*, was a firm advocate for the lighter approach.
- Footage from this episode was cut into the *Deep Space Nine* episode *Trials and Tribble-ations* in which Arne Darvin travels back in time to destroy Kirk with an exploding Tribble.

RATING

- Fantastic stuff proving that *Star Trek* can do comedy. It's cram-packed full of amusing concepts, from the idea of the Tribble gestation period to Scotty's argument with the Klingons over the Enterprise. A sure-fire hit.

2.16 THE GAMESTERS OF TRISKELION

STARDATE 3211.8

Kirk is forced to fight to fuel the gambling habit of three alien Providers

TX 5 January 1968
WRITER Margaret Armen
DIRECTOR Gene Nelson
GUEST CAST Dick Crockett (Andorian Thrall), Victoria George (Jana Haines), Mickey Morton (Kloog), Angelique Pettyjohn (Shahna), Jane Ross (Tamoon), Joseph Ruskin (Galt), Steve Sandor (Lars)

Kirk, Chekov and Uhura are transported to a strange arena and surrounded by four aliens. Though their attempts to escape are thwarted, they earn the admiration of Galt, Master Thrall of Triskelion, who explains that they are now thralls of the Providers. The three officers are fitted with collars that cause pain when activated by Galt. They are each prepared for combat by their own 'drill thrall', before they are 'vended' to a Provider. Kirk is taken with his trainer, Shahna, but when he compliments the green haired beauty she does not understand his words. The three officers are put through their paces in the arena. When Kirk defeats a large primitive thrall named Kloog, three disembodied voices begin bidding for him. The officers are sold to Provider One. Kirk asks Shahna about the Providers but she is punished by Galt for speaking of them. Kirk intervenes and Shahna is grateful, and responds to his embrace. Kirk sees an opportunity to escape but is stopped by Galt, who now takes control of the Enterprise. Kirk discovers that the Providers are three disembodied brains whose only entertainment is to watch and bet on combat. Kirk wages the Enterprise and its crew on the landing party defeating three thralls. The Providers pit Kirk against three of the largest thralls. He kills two and wounds a third but has to battle the Provider's substitute, Shahna. Eventually, Kirk overpowers Shahna, sparing her life, and the crew are freed.

QUOTES

- 'Provider one bids three hundred quatloos for the newcomers.' – *The 'vending' begins*
- 'Goodbye, Jim Kirk. I will learn... and watch the lights in the sky... and remember.' – *Shahna pines after Kirk, before beginning lessons in astrophysics*

TRIVIA

- The first draft had Sulu visit the planet but the role was given to Chekov as George Takei was filming *The Green Berets* at the time.
- *The Simpsons* parodied the episode in *Deep Space Homer*, in which Homer briefly fights before NASA scientists in an identical arena. As the same incidental music plays, one scientist bets four quatloos on the newcomer.

RATING

- Lumbering alien gladiators, talking brains and a lesson in love for a space vixen with green hair – does *Star Trek* get any more camp than this? Wonderfully over-the-top stuff which has become the focus for much parody, sadly never as amusing or enjoyable as the original. A love it-or-hate it episode that separates true fans from those who take it too seriously.

2.17 A PIECE OF THE ACTION

STARDATE 4598.0

The crew try to bring peace to a planet which has developed a Chicago Mob culture

TX 12 January 1968
WRITER David P Harmon and Gene L Coon (story by David P Harmon)
DIRECTOR James Komack
GUEST CAST William Blackburn (Hadley), Anthony Caruso (Bela Oxmyx), Sheldon Collins (Boy), Lee Delano (Kalo), Buddy Garion (Hood), John Harmon (Tepo), Sharyn Hillyer, Dyanne Thorne (Girls), Jay Jones (Mirt), Steve Marlo (Zabo), Victor Tayback (Jojo Krako)

The Enterprise arrives at Sigma Iotia II, a planet visited by the USS Horizon 100 years previously. They beam down to what appears to be an American street from the 1920s, where the gun culture of the Mafia is rife. They meet Boss Oxmyx, who is at war with a rival gang run by Krako. Spock discovers that a book left behind by the Horizon, *Chicago Mobs of the Twenties*, is the source of the cultural contamination. Oxmyx wants the Enterprise's weapons to use against Krako, but Kirk refuses. The landing party escapes but is soon captured by Krako who makes the same demand. Kirk escapes again and he and Spock decide to take direct action. Disguised as mobsters, they raid Krako's hideout, stunning his men, but are stopped by Krako. Kirk insists that the Federation is taking over and will only help one boss. Krako agrees to help. Kirk manages to pass a coded instruction to beam Krako aboard the Enterprise before he offers Oxmyx the same deal. When Oxmyx tries to contact the other bosses, Scotty has them all beamed to Oxmyx's headquarters. When Krako's men attack, Kirk has Scotty stun the entire block with the Enterprise phasers. The bosses are in awe and agree to co-operate.

QUOTES

- 'Captain, you are an excellent starship commander but as a taxi driver you leave a lot to be desired.' – *Spock derides Kirk's driving abilities*

TRIVIA

- Harmon's original draft, *Mission into Chaos*, explained that the planet is strategically important, based on the border of the Neutral Zone. Kirk and crew are sent to negotiate a treaty but the Romulans have already approached Oxmyx. The Romulans provide Krako with weapons, prompting the Enterprise to send down a security team. Although the Romulans are defeated, Oxmyx is fearful and signs a treaty with Kirk. All 12 bosses elect themselves as representatives of the planet and are beamed aboard the Enterprise to be taken to the Federation Council.

RATING

- A fun but badly structured story with lots of running around in costume for very little gain. *A Piece of the Action* heralds a period when *Star Trek* seems distinctly bored with space. Chicago Mobs would soon be followed by Romans, Nazis and eventually contemporary Earth. Still, there are some amusing slapstick asides, notably Kirk's attempt to drive an antique car.

2.18 THE IMMUNITY SYNDROME

STARDATE 4307.1

The Enterprise must destroy an enormous amoeba that has killed billions

TX 19 January 1968
WRITER Robert Sabaroff
DIRECTOR Joseph Pevney
GUEST CAST Majel Barrett (Christine Chapel), John Winston (Kyle)

When a transmission from the Vulcan-crewed USS Intrepid is cut short, Spock senses the sudden death of the crew. Chekov reports that all life in the Gamma 7A system, which the Intrepid was investigating, has been destroyed. The Enterprise crew find a strange dark patch in space which, when probed, emits a disorientating, high-pitched whine. When the crew recover, they are inside the hole. Spock deduces that the whine was caused when they passed through a membrane and that they are inside a field of energy that is incompatible with their systems. The hole in space begins to drain all energy from the Enterprise. Kirk orders full power to engines to escape but the effort only alerts a single-cell organism 11,000 miles long which is the source of the energy drain. Spock takes a shuttle into the amoeba and discovers that it can be destroyed from the inside, but his transmission breaks up before he can explain. Kirk and McCoy decide to produce antibodies that will destroy the cell. With shields at maximum, the Enterprise passes inside the creature and plants an antimatter charge on the nucleus. On the way out, the Enterprise finds Spock's shuttle. When the creature is destroyed, both ships are thrown to safety.

TRIVIA

- Sabaroff's treatment played more on the uneasy feelings of the crew, caused when the polarity of the ship's equipment is reversed in close proximity to the virus. In this draft, McCoy and Spock don't clash but work together.

RATING

- A fascinating idea that is well handled. The officers speculate that the amoeba is a disease invading the galaxy and that the Enterprise is an aggressive antibody. Sabaroff's original idea was that this was man's place in the universe. The episode is also notable for the McCoy-Spock relationship, as the two study the virus and protect Kirk.

2.19 A PRIVATE LITTLE WAR

STARDATE 4211.4

Kirk intercedes in Klingon power games on a primitive planet

TX 2 February 1968
WRITER Gene Roddenberry (story by 'Judd Crucis' [pen name for Don Ingalls])
DIRECTOR Marc Daniels
GUEST CAST Majel Barrett (Christine Chapel), Paul Baxley (Patrol Leader), Arthur Bernard (Apella), Nancy Kovak (Nona), Booker Marshall (Dr M'Benga), Gary Pillar (Yutan), Janos Prohaska (Mugato), Ned Romero (Krell), Michael Witney (Tyree)

Kirk returns to a planet he once surveyed as a lieutenant and is surprised to discover the primitive villagers now have flintlock rifles. They shoot Spock. While Dr M'Benga struggles to help Spock, the crew discover a Klingon vessel in orbit around the planet. Kirk and McCoy beam back to obtain evidence of Klingon interference, but Kirk is attacked by a white haired ape-like creature called a Mugato. With the Enterprise out of communication range, McCoy contacts Tyree, Kirk's friend from his earlier visit and leader of the hill people. Tyree's wife, Nona, cures Kirk and asks him to give his phaser to Tyree to make her husband a powerful leader. Kirk refuses. Later, Kirk and McCoy investigate Tyree's rivals and find a Klingon assisting them. Kirk teaches Tyree's people how to use the flintlock in order to maintain the status quo. Nona tries to seduce Kirk but Tyree cannot turn the weapon on her. Suddenly, Kirk and Nona are attacked by a mugato. Nona takes Kirk's phaser but runs into a pack of villagers and is killed. Angered, Tyree tells Kirk he needs more weapons. Kirk tells Scotty to make 100 flintlocks for the hill people.

TRIVIA

- The first draft script was penned by Don Ingalls. In this version, Kirk had not met Tyree before but had seen the Klingon, Krell, at the Organian Peace Conference and had disliked him instantly. According to Ingalls, Roddenberry added the Vietnam parallels.
- Gene L Coon did significant writing work on the episode.

RATING

- A peculiar episode that runs counter to much of the spirit of *Star Trek*. Though Kirk's decision to give weapons to Tyree's people is rationalised as maintaining the status quo, the solution could equally have been to destroy the villagers' flintlocks. Nevertheless, it shows more clearly than most the value of the Prime Directive – even if we don't know what the Klingons want out of their warmongering.

2.20 RETURN TO TOMORROW

STARDATE 4768.3

The officers loan their bodies to ephemeral aliens who then refuse to return them

TX
9 February 1968
WRITER
'John Kingsbridge' (pseudonym for John T Dugan)

On a dead planet, the Enterprise crew encounter Sargon, a powerful telepath 100 miles beneath the planet's surface. Sargon is a creature of pure thought housed in a glowing sphere. He tells Kirk, McCoy, Spock and Dr Ann Mulhall that his people were destroyed in a war half a million years previously. He and the two other survivors, his wife Thalassa and enemy Henoch, want to 'borrow' the bodies of Kirk, Spock and Mulhall long enough to produce artificial bodies for them to inhabit. The transfer takes place on the Enterprise under McCoy's observation: Sargon into Kirk, Thalessa into Mulhall and Henoch into Spock. The aliens are overwhelmed by the sensations of touch once more. Henoch convinces Thalassa that they should keep their human

DIRECTOR
Ralph Senensky
GUEST CAST
Majel Barrett (Christine Chapel), James Doohan (Voice of Sargon), Cinoy Lou (Nurse), Diana Muldaur (Dr Ann Mulhall)

bodies for good. Sargon weakens and dies – Kirk's body is kept alive, but his mind is still trapped in the sphere. Thalassa offers to restore Kirk in return for keeping Mulhall's body. When McCoy refuses, Thalassa unleashes a fierce psychic attack, but is quickly remorseful. Suddenly, Sargon speaks to them – he transferred his mind into the ship's computer and has a plan to overcome Henoch, who has now taken control of the ship. Sargon tricks Henoch by manipulating McCoy's thoughts and transferring Spock's mind into Nurse Chapel's body. With Henoch overcome and Spock restored, Sargon and Thalassa take control of Kirk and Mulhall for one last time, and share an embrace before they let their minds die.

QUOTES

- 'Lungs filling with air again. To see again. Heart pumping, arteries surging blood again!' – *Sargon speaks through Kirk*

TRIVIA

- Diana Muldaur would return as Dr Pulaski in season two of *The Next Generation*. Roddenberry also used her in the rejected pilot *Planet Earth*.
- Gene Roddenberry extensively rewrote John T Dugan's script.

RATING

- An interesting exploration of the plight of advanced beings who have lost touch with their humanity. Nimoy relishes the villainy of Henoch but never lets the excesses get the better of him. Good performances all round.

2.21 PATTERNS OF FORCE

STARDATE 2534.0

The Enterprise discovers a Federation historian is responsible for creating a Nazi planet

TX 16 February 1968
WRITER John Meredyth Lucas
DIRECTOR Vincent McEveety
GUEST CAST Paul Baxley (First Trooper), David Brian (John Gill), Peter Canon (Gestapo Lieutenant), Chuck Courtney (Davod), Skip Homeier (Melakon), Richard Evans (Isak), Gilbert Green (SS Major), Patrick Horgan (Eneg), Bart LaRue (Newsreader), Ed McCready (SS Trooper), Ralph Mauer (SS Lieutenant), Valora Norland (Daras), William Wintersole (Abrom)

The Enterprise arrives in orbit around Ekos, a primitive, warlike planet, in search of missing Federation historian John Gill. They are attacked by a thermonuclear probe, too advanced for either Ekos or the peaceful neighbouring planet Zeon that are now mysteriously at war with each other. Kirk and Spock beam down to Ekos and witness a Zeon man captured by the SS: Ekos is a Nazi planet. They view a newscast that reveals, against Kirk's instincts, that Gill is the Führer. Kirk and Spock assume identities as Nazi officers but are captured before they can reach Gill. They are tortured and interrogated. They meet Isak, the man they saw captured, and together escape to the resistance, led by Isak's brother, Abrom. Kirk convinces them to help him reach Gill but Abrom explains that Deputy Führer Melakon is actually in command. Disguised as a Gestapo film crew, Kirk, Spock and Isak infiltrate the Chancellery where they discover Gill is drugged. McCoy is beamed down to verify the assessment, but his sudden appearance almost gives the game away. Spock revives Gill, who explains that he used the example of Nazi Germany to bring order to Ekos. Melakon seized control then declared war on Zeon. Gill makes a public broadcast that recalls his forces and denounces Melakon as a traitor. Melakon is shot – but not before he can kill Gill, who dies having put things right.

QUOTES

- 'Even historians fail to learn from history. They repeat the same mistakes.' – *Gill*

TRIVIA

- The Nazi party chairman is named 'Eneg' – Gene in reverse.

RATING

- Another Prime Directive episode, with some interesting aspects. It's really an exploration, no matter how thin, of how a totalitarian state comes into being. Spock's theoretical defence of Gill's use of the Nazi regime to bring order is nigh-on reprehensible. The Jewish resistance movement is hideously unsubtle.

2.22 BY ANY OTHER NAME

STARDATE 4657.5

The Enterprise is hijacked by aliens from Andromeda who are becoming human

TX 23 February 1968
WRITER DC Fontana and Jerome Bixby (story by Jerome Bixby)
DIRECTOR Marc Daniels
GUEST CAST Majel Barrett (Christine Chapel), Barbara Bouchet (Kelinda), Carol Byrd (Shea), Julie Cobb (Leslie Thompson), Lizlie Dalton (Drea), Robert Fortier (Tomar), Stewart Moss (Hanar), Warren Stevens (Rojan)

A distress call lures Kirk and a landing party to the presence of two Kelvans, Rojan and Kalinda, who demand that the captain surrender the Enterprise. The Kelvans are from Andromeda, a galaxy that has become uninhabitable, and intend to conquer another. The Kelvans are able to paralyse their opponents and within minutes take control of the Enterprise. McCoy believes that the Kelvans are humans but Spock is unconvinced. Spock mind-melds with Kalinda and discovers that the Kelvans are actually immense beings with hundreds of limbs that have merely taken human form to be able to use the Enterprise. The landing party are returned to the ship, which the Kelvans have adapted to cross the galactic barrier. Rojan turns the crew into small cubes, leaving only Kirk, McCoy, Spock and Scotty to operate the ship. The officers realise that the Kelvans are unused to human sensation and use this to their advantage: Scotty gets Tomar drunk, McCoy incapacitates Hanar with injections and Kirk kisses Kalinda, making Rojan jealous. Kirk takes his chance and overpowers Rojan. Kirk explains that the Kelvans are becoming human – by the time they return home they will be alien to their own people. Rojan accepts Kirk's offer of freedom in the Federation.

QUOTES

- 'What is it?'
  'It's... green.' – *Tomar and Scotty, setting to on the alien liquor*

TRIVIA

- Bixby's original story focused on the notion that the 300-year voyage to Andromeda would see the crew's deaths. Fontana added the humour and beefed up the role of the main characters in the script.

RATING

- Another play on the power of human sensations, already seen this season in *Catspaw*, *Return to Tomorrow* and even *The Gamesters of Triskellion.* Although the idea of the Enterprise becoming a prison for the crew is interesting, the execution is pretty mundane – even crossing the galactic barrier is relatively uneventful given *Where No Man Has Gone Before.* At least we get a priceless moment when Scotty, victor of the drinking binge, finds himself incapable of doing anything else.

2.23 THE OMEGA GLORY

STARDATE UNKNOWN

The Enterprise battles a renegade captain on a planet that has evolved like Earth

TX
1 March 1968
WRITER
Gene Roddenberry
DIRECTOR
Vincent McEveety

The Enterprise finds one of its sister ships, the USS Exeter, deserted in orbit around Omega IV. On board, they find the crew were turned into a crystalline substance, although some escaped to the planet's surface. Kirk takes a landing party to the surface and finds the sole survivor, Captain Ron Tracey, intervening in a conflict between the Kohm villagers and their attackers, the brutal Yangs. Tracey reveals that something on the planet is keeping the infected alive. He plans to produce an elixir of life and sell it to the highest bidder. McCoy discovers that the longevity of the inhabitants is down to an immune system that evolved after a biological war – there can be no elixir. Kirk tells Tracey and they fight, only to be captured by Yangs along with Spock and McCoy. Kirk discovers that the Yangs are like the

GUEST CAST
Frank Atienza (Kohm Villager), Morgan Farley (Yang Scholar), Roy Jenson (Cloud William), Irene Kelly (Sirah), Lloyd Kino (Wu), Ed McCready (Dr Carter), Eddie Paskey (Leslie), David L Ross (Galloway), Morgan Woodward (Ronald Tracey)

Yankees while Spock surmises that the Asiatic Kohms are akin to Communists – they have fought a war the twentieth century avoided. Their theory is confirmed when the Yang leader, Cloud William, produces an American flag and recites the pledge of allegiance. Kirk and Tracey are made to fight. Kirk wins but refuses to kill Tracey. Instead Sulu arrives with a security team. Kirk tells Cloud William to share the words of the American constitution with everyone.

QUOTES

- 'Are you grasping all it means? This immunising agent here, once we've found it, is a fountain of youth. Virtual immortality, or as much as any man will ever want.' – *Tracey*

TRIVIA

- *The Omega Glory* began life as one of three draft scripts submitted to NBC for a potential second pilot. The original saw Spock use his powers with women to obtain information. In the final gunfight, Spock was shot twice, but survived because his heart is in his abdomen!

RATING

- Dull nonsense, understandably rejected by NBC. The ludicrous parallel development of American history and the constitution is just plain bad. The Kirk-Tracey relationship is the material that needs bolstering.

2.24 THE ULTIMATE COMPUTER

STARDATE 4729.4

The Enterprise is taken over by an ingenious computer programmed with human instincts

TX 8 March 1968
WRITER DC Fontana (story by Laurence N Wolfe)
DIRECTOR John Meredyth Lucas
GUEST CAST William Marshall (Dr Richard Daystrom), Sean Morgan (Harper), Barry Russo (Robert Wesley)

Commodore Wesley informs Kirk that the Enterprise is to take part in a war game exercise under the control of the M-5 unit, a new computer, designed by Dr Richard Daystrom. Scotty reluctantly hooks the M-5 to the Enterprise. *En route*, the M-5 shuts down systems across the ship to draw more power. It quickly defeats a surprise attack from the USS Excalibur and USS Lexington, under Wesley's command. Spock is impressed but the M-5 soon destroys a harmless ore freighter. Kirk cancels the test but the unit protects itself with a forcefield and Daystrom tries to stop Spock and Scotty restoring manual control. They are successful but M-5 still controls the helm. At the war game site, the M-5 launches a devastating attack, killing 53 on the Lexington, damaging the Potemkin and destroying the Excalibur with the loss of all hands. Spock realises that M-5 shares Daystrom's brain engrams and asks Daystrom to reason with the computer, but he is unsuccessful. Meanwhile, the Lexington is told to destroy the Enterprise. Kirk realises that the M-5 can feel guilt and convinces it of its errors. M-5 shuts down just in time for Kirk to avert the Enterprise's destruction.

QUOTES

- 'Computers make excellent and efficient servants, but I have no wish to serve under them. Captain, a starship also runs on loyalty to one man, and nothing may replace it or him.' – *Spock to Kirk*

TRIVIA

- William Marshall is better known to cult film fans as Blacula in the movie of the same name (1972), and the sequel *Scream! Blacula Scream!* (1973)
- James Doohan certainly earns his fee in this episode. Not only does he provide the voice of the M-5 computer, he is the voice of Commodore Enright, heard in the teaser scene, and the voice of Starfleet Command.

RATING

- *The Ultimate Computer* is one of those episodes that all new *Star Trek* writers should be forced to watch to drum into them that the series is about characters not technology. A tight, no-nonsense episode with a good performance from William Marshall.

2.25 BREAD AND CIRCUSES

STARDATE 4040.7

The crew find a treacherous captain on a planet where Rome never fell

TX 15 March 1968
WRITERS Gene Roddenberry and Gene L Coon (story by John Kneubuhl)
DIRECTOR Ralph Senensky
GUEST CAST William Bramley (Policeman), Max Kelven (Maximus), Bart La Rue (Announcer), Jack Perkins (Master of the Game), Logan Ramsey (Claudius Marcus), Rhodes Reason (Flavius), Lois Sewell (Drusilla), William Smithers (RM Merrick), Ian Wolfe (Septimus)

The Enterprise crew find the wreckage of SS Beagle, a ship lost six years previously, around Planet IV, System 892. Uhura picks up the transmission of a gladiatorial combat on the planet in which the last of the Beagle crew is killed. Kirk, Spock and McCoy beam down and find a culture like Ancient Rome. They are captured by slaves and taken to their leader, Septimus. Kirk discovers that the Beagle's captain, Merrick, is now Merrickus, First Citizen and enemy of the slaves. With their help, Kirk approaches the city but they are captured. Kirk and the officers escape, only to be confronted by Merrick and his proconsul, Claudius Marcus. Marcus persuaded Merrick to stay, and to kill the uncooperative members of his crew, to protect his planet's civilisation. Merrick orders Kirk to have the Enterprise crew beam down but Kirk warns Scotty. Spock and McCoy are ordered to fight slaves in the arena. Spock incapacitates their opponents and is threatened with execution. Kirk is then sent to the arena but Scotty disrupts the power, enabling Kirk to escape. Guilty, Merrick obtains a communicator and throws it to Kirk, enabling the landing party to escape though he is killed for treachery.

QUOTES

- 'Medical men are trained in logic, Mr Spock.'
  'Really, doctor? I had no idea that you were trained. Watching you, I thought it was trial and error.' – *McCoy and Spock*

TRIVIA

- The story went through a number of early renditions. In one, Spock suffers the Vulcan equivalent of appendicitis.
- *Bread and Circuses* is the last of a string of stories that look at different alien cultures that resemble human history. In *A Piece of the Action, Patterns of Force* and *A Private Little War*, 'alien' intervention has resulted in a parallel culture. In *The Omega Glory* and *Bread and Circuses*, the evolution seems to have occurred naturally. It is a theme that is no less resolved by later series.

RATING

- Yet another repeat of the same story with little to add. There's no sense in which the planet has evolved a technologically advanced Roman culture – the technology and the Romans are segregated. One final revelation, that the slaves are worshippers of the Son of God, is rapidly thrown away.

2.26 ASSIGNMENT: EARTH

STARDATE UNKNOWN

Kirk and crew confront a time-traveller who appears to threaten Earth's history

TX 29 March 1968
WRITER Art Wallace (story by Gene Roddenberry and Art Wallace)
DIRECTOR Marc Daniels
GUEST CAST Paul Baxley (Security Chief), Lincoln Demyan (Rawlings), Teri Garr (Roberta Lincoln), Morgan Jones (Nesvig), Jim Keefer (Cromwell), Robert Lansing (Gary Seven)

While the Enterprise orbits twentieth century Earth on a research mission, a man carrying a cat beams onto the transporter pad. The human, Gary Seven, has been living on another planet. He warns Kirk not to interfere in his work or he risks changing Earth's history. Kirk has Gary locked up. Meanwhile, Spock discovers that the US is launching a nuclear warhead platform in retaliation against another power. Gary escapes to Earth where he discovers that his two fellow agents, 201 and 347, are missing and have been unable to reprogram the US rocket. Gary contacts Roberta Lincoln, a secretary used by the missing agents, who detains Kirk and Spock on their arrival while Gary makes for the rocket using a hidden transporter. Scotty tries to beam Gary to the Enterprise but fails. The warhead is launched and armed. Kirk and Spock arrive to intervene but Gary insists that they let him detonate the bomb just above the atmosphere – the close call will convince the nations to oppose nuclear weapons. Kirk relents. Earth's history is protected and the agent's mission is a success. His cat, meanwhile, briefly turns into a beautiful woman to congratulate him.

QUOTES

- 'You've got to let me finish what I've started, or in six minutes World War Three begins!' – *Gary Seven to Kirk*

TRIVIA

- *Assignment: Earth* was a show Gene Roddenberry unsuccessfully pitched to Paramount in 1966. The original idea concerned Gary Seven, a human sent from the future to protect present-day Earth from the Omegans. Seven, disguised as a private investigator and supported by his secretary Roberta Hornblower, would protect Earth's timeline from the threat. In 1966, with *Star Trek* on the verge of cancellation, Roddenberry revived the idea. The show did not generate interest.
- Kirk makes a Captain's Log entry with his mouth closed, no communicator and a gun to his head in one of the more obvious examples of the narrative device not making story sense.

RATING

- Completely absurd if taken out of context, *Assignment: Earth* is best understood as a last ditch attempt to keep the cheques rolling in from Paramount. It isn't *Star Trek* and feels completely parochial and out of place at the end of a season that had shown a great deal of experimentation. But I suppose it's a small price to pay for not having a whole series of Gary Seven's dull adventures looped on satellite TV.

STAR TREK
SEASON THREE

3.1 SPOCK'S BRAIN

A mysterious woman steals Spock's brain to save her advanced civilisation

TX 20 September 1968
WRITER 'Lee Cronin' (pseudonym for Gene L Coon)
DIRECTOR Marc Daniels
GUEST CAST James Daris (Morg), Marj Dusay (Kara), Sheila Leighton (Luma)

STARDATE 5431.4

Kara, leader of an advanced all-female race, the Eymorgs, beams aboard the Enterprise and renders the crew unconscious. When they awake, they discover that Spock's brain has been removed from his body – they have 24 hours to reunite brain and body, or Spock will die. The crew track Kara to Sigma Draconis VI and beam down but are attacked by the primitive Morgs. Kirk descends to an underground city, where they meet Kara and are told that Spock's brain has been used to replace the Controller, which regulated the city: until it recently broke down. It becomes clear that the Eymorgs didn't build the city, it was built for them by a long-dead race. McCoy uses their advanced technology to reconnect Spock's brain – with a little help from Spock, once his vocal cords are reattached! Kirk suggests that the Eymorgs should make peace with the Morgs and learn how to live independently.

QUOTES

- 'Brain and brain! What is brain?' – *Kara*

TRIVIA

- Spock has two brain transplant operations without needing to shave his head. Neither so much as musses up his hair!
- Gene L Coon had served as producer during much of the first and second seasons. He wanted to leave to work on *It Takes a Thief*, but was under contract, and Gene Roddenberry was reluctant to let him go.

RATING

- Long derided as the nadir of *Star Trek*, *Spock's Brain* doesn't trouble itself with scientific accuracy, but it's – ahem – brainless fun and achieves a camp grandeur. Each of the *Star Trek* series has a worse episode than this.

3.2 THE ENTERPRISE INCIDENT

STARDATE 5027.3

Kirk is on a secret mission – and takes the Enterprise to the Romulans

TX 27 September 1968
WRITER D C Fontana
DIRECTOR John Meredyth Lucas
GUEST CAST Gordon Coffey (Soldier), Richard Compton (Technical Officer), Jac Donner (Tal), Robert Gentile (Romulan technician), Mike Howden (Guard), Joanne Linville (Romulan Commander)

McCoy thinks Kirk is at breaking point, an impression confirmed when the captain orders the Enterprise into Romulan space. The Romulans intercept the ship, and the female commander has Kirk and Spock beamed over. Kirk claims the Enterprise is malfunctioning, but he is charged with espionage. Kirk escapes, but Spock apparently kills him with the Vulcan death grip. Kirk is declared dead and beamed back to the Enterprise. It is a ruse – Kirk disguises himself as a Romulan, and with the knowledge of their ship he and Spock have acquired, he steals the Romulan cloaking device. Scotty quickly fits the device to the Enterprise, and they make their escape.

QUOTES

- 'It is unworthy of a Vulcan to resort to subterfuge.'
  'You are being clever, Commander. That is unworthy of a Romulan.' – *Romulan Commander and Spock*

TRIVIA

- Fontana based the story on the USS Pueblo incident (that January, a CIA intelligence ship had been caught in North Korean waters), but wasn't happy with the hints of attraction between Spock and the Romulan commander, feeling that it made the Romulan look foolish.
- Klingon ships and gun props were reused to save money. The Klingon ship had been built for *Elaan of Troyius*, recorded first, but this episode was broadcast before it, meaning that the Romulans are flying the familiar Klingon battlecruisers the first time they are seen. A line added to the script explained that the Klingons had exchanged the ships for cloaking technology. This isn't the only time the writers apparently got the two confused – *Star Trek II: The Wrath of Khan* has a Klingon Neutral Zone, and *Star Trek III: The Search for Spock* begins a long tradition of Klingons using Bird of Prey starships, like the Romulans do in *Balance of Terror.*

RATING

- An action romp, the gimmick of which (Kirk's faked death) is highly reminiscent of the then-most recent Bond film, *You Only Live Twice.* It's entertaining and fast-paced, but it's probably best not to think too hard about Kirk and Spock's plan.

3.3 THE PARADISE SYNDROME

STARDATE 4842.6

A planet of Native Americans is threatened by an asteroid

TX 4 October 1968
WRITER Margaret Armen
DIRECTOR Jud Taylor
GUEST CAST Richard Hale (Goro), Sabrina Scharf (Miramanee), Rudy Solari (Salish)

Kirk, McCoy and Spock beam down to a planet threatened by an asteroid, but Kirk vanishes near a mysterious obelisk. Spock and McCoy have to return to the ship to deal with the pressing problem of the asteroid. Kirk is found by the locals, a race similar to Native Americans, who think the amnesiac Kirk is their god, Kirok. Kirk weds the beautiful Miramanee. Spock has deciphered symbols he found on the obelisk – it was placed there by the Preservers, who also transplanted the tribe, and the device is an asteroid deflector. Kirk is denounced as a false god and he and Miramanee are stoned by the villagers. He is reunited with his crew, Spock restores his memory with a mind meld, and they activate the obelisk to deflect the asteroid, but Miramanee, who was pregnant, has died from her injuries.

QUOTES

- 'Each kiss is as the first' – *Miramanee's dying words to Kirk*

TRIVIA

- In a season where budgets were tight, this was a rare chance for extensive location filming.
- Richard Hale may be oldest person to have appeared in *Star Trek* – he was born in 1893.

RATING

- An episode where Kirk's left to his own devices and lives a quiet life without the Enterprise. It's another peculiar one, but Miramanee's fate is surprisingly poignant.

3.4 AND THE CHILDREN SHALL LEAD

STARDATE 5029.5

A group of children take control of the Enterprise

TX 11 October 1968
WRITER Edward J Lasko
DIRECTOR Marvin Chomsky
GUEST CAST Caesar Belli (Steve), Melvin Belli (Gorgan), Pamela Ferdin (Mary), Craig Hundley (Tommy), Mark Robert Brown (Don), Brian Tochi (Ray), James Wellman (Starnes)

The adult members of the expedition to Triacus are dead, but their children not only survived, they seem unaffected by their parents' deaths. Back on the Enterprise, the children summon a 'friendly angel', Gorgan, who orders them to seize control of the ship and take it to Marcos XII. Spock recalls that Triacus was the home of a legendary gang of marauders. Gorgan, a being capable of mental domination, was clearly their leader. Kirk tries to regain control of the ship, but the children can induce fear in the crew. Kirk and Spock show the children pictures of them playing with their parents, then their parents' bodies – they realise what they've lost, and without their support, Gorgan dies.

TRIVIA

- Kirk's greatest fear is that he could lose command of the Enterprise. Uhura's is that she'll grow old and ugly.
- The title comes from the Bible, Mark 13.
- Gorgan was played by Melvin Belli, a celebrity attorney who had Errol Flynn and Mae West as clients, among others.
- The Enterprise landing party includes two 'redshirt' crewmen who don't beam up with the crew when the children are taken aboard. Hopefully, someone eventually noticed they were missing...

RATING

- Another *Star Trek* with a message: if you're making drama, cast actors, not attorneys. It's the first of a *lot* of stories this season where the guest cast arrive aboard the Enterprise and easily take control of the ship.

3.5 IS THERE IN TRUTH NO BEAUTY?

STARDATE 5630.7

A mission to transport an ambassador leaves the ship stranded

TX 18 October 1968
WRITER Jean Lisette Aroeste
DIRECTED Ralph Senesky
GUEST CAST David Frankham (Marvick), Diana Muldaur (Miranda)

The Enterprise is taking the Medusan ambassador, Kollos, home. The Medusans are skilled navigators, but the mere sight of one can drive a human mad (even Spock needs a special visor). He is escorted by the blind Dr Miranda Jones and Marvick, an engineer. Miranda is jealous of Spock's mind-melding abilities, which means he could communicate with the ambassador far better than her. Marvick attempts to kill Kollos, but seeing the Medusan drives him mad. Before dying, he goes to Engineering and pushes the Enterprise to Warp nine and into a space-time continuum that throws it out of the galaxy. Spock mind-melds with Kollos to get the navigational information to return home, but glimpses the Medusan. Miranda overcomes her jealousy and uses her expertise to save Spock.

TRIVIA

- Diane Muldaur was in *Return to Tomorrow*, and would go on to play Dr Pulaski in the second season of *The Next Generation*.

RATING

- A fairly unremarkable episode, this one isn't sure if it's a murder mystery, a romance or a monster movie.

3.6 SPECTRE OF THE GUN

STARDATE 4385.3

An alien race forces the crew to recreate the Gunfight at the OK Corral

The Melkotians warn the Enterprise away from their planet, but Kirk nonetheless leads a landing party. The planet features a surreal recreation of an old Wild West town – and their phasers have been replaced with six-shooters. They are told to recreate the Gunfight at

TX 25 October 1968
WRITER 'Lee Cronin' (pseudonym for Gene L Coon)
DIRECTOR Vince McEveety
GUEST CAST Richard Anthony (Rider), Bonnie Beacher (Sylvia – incorrectly credited as 'Beecher'), James Doohan (Melkotian voice), Sam Gilman (Doc Holliday), Rex Holman (Morgan Earp), Charles Maxwell (Virgil Earp), Ed McReady (Barber), Gregg Palmer (Rancher), Charles Seel (Ed), Abraham Soafaer (Melkotian), Rob Soble (Wyatt Earp), Bill Zuckert (Sheriff Behan)

the OK Corral, playing the Clantons... the losing side! They try to avoid this by constructing a tranquilliser grenade from local materials. After Chekov is wounded and the tranquilliser grenade fails to work, Spock realises that their minds are being manipulated – the bullets will only kill them if they believe they will. He performs mind melds on the other crew members to protect them. The Melkotians realise the crew are peaceful, and return them to the Enterprise, where they promise to open negotiations.

TRIVIA

- The original story had the crew transported through time to the Wild West, while a second version took the Enterprise to a planet that was modelled after the old West, but these were thought to be retreading old ground, and so a more stylised approach was tried.
- This was the first episode of the season to be filmed. Walter Koenig has claimed that Chekov was to play a larger role, as he was felt to be an identification figure for young viewers, but Fred Freiberger returned the focus to Kirk, Spock and McCoy. This episode certainly does feature Chekov quite heavily.

RATING

- A weird, trippy story that's an interesting and imaginative way to use the spare costumes and props on the studio lot. It's very sixties and a bit like watching a Western show while dropping LSD.

3.7 THE DAY OF THE DOVE

A colony is wiped out, and it looks like the Klingons are to blame

TX 1 November 1968
WRITER Jerome Bixby
DIRECTOR Marvin Chomsky
GUEST CAST Michael Ansara (Kang), Susan Howard (Mara)

STARDATE UNKNOWN

An unidentified ship destroys the human colony of Beta XII-A, and the Enterprise is sent to investigate. A Klingon battle cruiser is orbiting the planet, but the Enterprise detects explosions and radiation on board. They capture the Klingon landing party. Kang, the captain, denies attacking the colony and accuses Kirk of firing on his ship. The Enterprise suddenly enters warp, and the crewmen are locked in the lower decks. Swords and other weapons materialise, and the humans and Klingons begin fighting. Spock detects an energy being, and he and Kirk surmise it is responsible for the increased aggression. Kirk rescues Kang's wife, Mara, but the two captains duel, until they realise the energy being feeds off aggression. They declare a truce and Kirk and Kang laugh. The laughter drives the alien being away.

QUOTES

- 'Look Kang... for the rest of our lives, a thousand lifetimes... senseless violence... fighting' – *Kirk*

TRIVIA

- Determined to make a statement about the Vietnam War, Bixby's original script reportedly ended with Kirk and Kang arm-in-arm at a peace march!
- The Klingon captain was originally Kor (*Errand of Mercy*), but John Colicos had other filming commitments. Kor and Kang (and Koloth from *The Trouble with Tribbles*) went on to appear together in *Deep Space Nine's Blood Oath*, 26 years later. Kang also has a cameo appearance in the *Voyager* episode *Flashback*.

RATING

- An allegory with the less than profound message that peace and laughter are better than fighting and hatred. Luckily, Michael Ansara is an excellent opponent for Kirk, and the two of them make entertaining adversaries.

3.8 FOR THE WORLD IS HOLLOW AND I HAVE TOUCHED THE SKY

STARDATE 5476.3

McCoy is dying, and an inhabited asteroid is heading for a planet

TX 8 November 1968
WRITER Rik Vollaerts
DIRECTOR Tony Leader
GUEST CAST John Lormer (Old Man), Byron Morrow (Westervliet), Kate Woodville (Natira)

McCoy has been diagnosed with terminal xenopolycythemia, and has a year to live. The Enterprise learns that an inhabited asteroid is going to collide with the planet Daran V. Beaming over, Kirk, Spock and McCoy are captured and brought before the Natira, High Priestess of the Yonada, servant of the Oracle which controls the population. Natira wants McCoy as a husband, and shows him a book of knowledge, which McCoy recognises as the flight manual of a spacecraft. The Enterprise crew teach Natira to question the Oracle, discovering that it is a computer. Spock reprograms it and discovers a cure for McCoy's illness in the archives. McCoy and Natira reluctantly go their separate ways.

QUOTES

- 'Is truth not truth for all?' – *Natira asks an important question*

TRIVIA

- Kate Woodville is the ex-wife of *The Avengers* hero Patrick Macnee.

RATING

- *Star Trek*-by-numbers, with the twist that it's a McCoy episode. His terminal illness would be a strong story, if it wasn't painfully obvious that he'll be cured by the end of the episode.

3.9 THE THOLIAN WEB

STARDATE 5693.2

Kirk vanishes and the Enterprise becomes snared in a strange trap

TX 15 November 1968
WRITER Judy Burns and Chet Richards
DIRECTOR Ralph Senesky

The Enterprise discovers that the crew of the missing USS Defiant have all murdered each other. The Defiant begins to dissolve – Scotty beams the landing party back, but Kirk becomes caught in a spatial interphase and doesn't arrive back. The Enterprise crew begin to act violently. A Tholian ship, commanded by Loskene, arrives and demands the Enterprise leaves their territory – Spock decides to stay: it is their only chance of retrieving Kirk. The Tholians begin to spin a web to trap the Enterprise. Reported sightings of Kirk are dismissed by Spock as the hallucinations of a disturbed crew, until Kirk appears in front of him. They use the transporters to retrieve Kirk.

TRIVIA

- A story that started out as a ghost story with a scientific explanation, 'In Essence Nothing', where it was Spock that vanished.
- The Tholians have never been seen again, but have often been mentioned, most recently in *Star Trek: Nemesis* and the *Enterprise* episode *Future Tense.* A later version of the USS Defiant was a regular feature of *Deep Space Nine.*

RATING

- A memorable episode that makes you forget that the last episode where the entire Enterprise crew became irrational and violent was only three weeks before (*The Day of the Dove*).

3.10 PLATO'S STEPCHILDREN

STARDATE 5784.2

The Enterprise crew become the playthings of powerful aliens

TX 22 November 1968
WRITER Meyer Dolinsky

The Enterprise has discovered deposits of a powerful fuel, kironide, on Platonius. Kirk, Spock and McCoy beam down to the planet and are greeted by the midget Alexander, who takes them to his leaders – the immortal Platonians. They are exiles from Sahndara, who have developed powerful psychokinetic abilities on their adopted home. Their leader Parmen demands that McCoy stays – they are vulnerable to injury, so need a doctor. When Kirk refuses, the Platonians use their

DIRECTOR David Alexander
GUEST CAST Barbara Babcock (Philana), Michael Dunn (Alexander), Derek Partridge (Donyd), Ted Scott (Eraclitus), Liam Sullivan (Parmen)

powers to force the Starfleet men to commit humiliating acts. Spock deduces that the kironide has both given the Platonians their powers and driven them mad. Parmen summons Uhura and Chapel, and forces them to join the performance. McCoy injects Kirk with kironide, and Kirk manifests psychic powers which he uses to force Parmen to submit. The crew are free to leave – they take Alexander with them.

QUOTES

- 'We may disappear tomorrow, but at least we're living now. You're half-crazed because you've got nothing inside. Nothing! You have to torture us to convince yourselves you're superior.' – *Kirk turns the tables on Parmen*

TRIVIA

- One of four episodes that the BBC regularly used to drop from their repeats of *Star Trek*, in this case because they felt the sadism wasn't suitable for teatime viewing.
- Michael Dunn was famous at the time as the evil Dr Loveless in *The Wild Wild West*. Gene Roddenberry had thought about casting him as Spock.
- This episode is famous for the 'interracial kiss' between Kirk and Uhura, allegedly the first on American television. This claim has been disputed, and depends on your definition (*I Love Lucy* had a white woman married to an Hispanic man in a show that ran throughout the fifties). It was certainly an issue at the time – the first time a black man kissed a white woman in a major Hollywood film, in the previous year's *Guess Who's Coming to Dinner?*, it had generated a lot of controversy. Conversely, when a white doctor kissed a black patient in a July 1964 edition of *Emergency Ward 10* on British TV, if anyone even noticed they didn't make a fuss. The *Star Trek* production team faced a couple of problems: the first being a reluctance on the part of some at the studio to depict the kiss, the second – paradoxically – being the realisation that by the multi-racial future portrayed in *Star Trek*, such a relationship just wouldn't be an issue. In the end, the 'kiss' is fudged – Kirk and Uhura are forced to kiss by the psychic powers of the Platonians and we barely see it. Whether it's the first or not, it's hardly the powerful civil rights statement that some would have you believe. Another myth, that Martin Luther King phoned Nichelle Nichols to congratulate her on the episode, is more easy to debunk: he was assassinated on April 4 1968, months before the episode was made. This seems to be a garbled version of encouragement Dr King reportedly gave the actress which persuaded her to sign up for the second season.

RATING

- A weird and lurid episode, in which William Shatner's performance reaches an... intensity... that connoisseurs agree has never been bettered, including as it does a spot of toga-wearing, a spirited impersonation of a horse, and – right at the end of the episode – his pulling a communicator out of his bottom.

3.11 WINK OF AN EYE

Super-fast aliens invade the Enterprise

TX 29 November 1968
WRITER Arthur Heinemann (story by 'Lee Cronin', pseudonym for Gene L Coon)
DIRECTOR Jud Taylor
GUEST CAST Geoffrey Binney (Compton), Kathie Browne (Deela), Jason Evers (Rael), Eric Holland (Ekor)

STARDATE 5710.5

The Enterprise responds to a distress call, but finds nothing. Soon, the ship starts to malfunction, and it's clear they've been invaded. Kirk realises everything is moving far more slowly than normal, and Deela, the Scalosian Queen, makes herself known. Her people have been mutated by radiation, and live at a hugely accelerated rate, and need to mate with outsiders. As the Scalosians set up a suspended animation device, Spock accelerates himself and helps Kirk defeat the invaders. At super-speed, Spock quickly repairs the Enterprise.

TRIVIA

- The accelerated Enterprise was filmed at weird angles, in the style of the *Batman* TV series, to make it look suitably unfamiliar.

RATING

- An interesting twist raises this version of the 'small group of aliens takes control of the Enterprise' story so common to this series above the average. It's also surprising that Kirk doesn't just ask if Deela will return him to his normal speed after he mates with her, which would seem to be an ideal solution for all involved.

3.12 THE EMPATH

STARDATE 5121.5

Kirk, Spock and McCoy are experimented upon by a group of sadistic aliens

TX 6 December 1968
WRITER Joyce Muskat
DIRECTOR John Erman
GUEST CAST Alan Berman (Lal), Kathryn Hays (Gem), Davis Roberts (Ozaba), Willard Sage (Thann), Jason Wingreen (Linke)

The Minaran star is about to go nova, and the Enterprise is sent to rescue a scientific team there. Kirk, Spock and McCoy materialise in a dark room, with only a mute woman, who McCoy christens Gem, for company. Two aliens, Vians, appear and Kirk is injured – Gem mysteriously heals the injury, taking the wounds herself. The Vians, who have killed the missing scientists, experiment on the humans. There are two intelligent races in this system. The Vians can only save one of them from the nova, and are trying to see if Gem's people are worthy by engineering a chance for her to show noble qualities. McCoy is tortured to the brink of death – but Gem can't bring herself to sacrifice herself for him. Kirk and Spock demonstrate to the Vians that they are being cruel. The Vians agree to save Gem's people.

TRIVIA

- Another episode pulled by the BBC from its re-runs because of its explicit violence.

RATING

- It's not hard to see why McCoy's torture got the episode 'banned' in the UK – it's really unpleasant. But this is a stronger episode than the synopsis might suggest, with echoes of colonialism, animal and psychology experiments.

3.13 ELAAN OF TROYIUS

STARDATE 4372.5

The Enterprise transports a beautiful woman to an arranged marriage

TX 20 December 1968
WRITER John Meredyth Lucas
DIRECTOR John Meredyth Lucas
GUEST CAST Victor Brandt (Watson), Lee Duncan (Evans), France Nuyen (Elaan), Jay Robinson (Petri), K L Smith (Klingon), Tony Young (Kryton)

The two worlds of Elas and Troyius are on the verge of war, but an arranged marriage between the beautiful but arrogant Elaan of Elas and the Troyian leader will secure peace. The Enterprise is to take Elaan to her new life, but it is approached by a Klingon warship. Elaan needs civilising – she stabs her Troyian tutor Petri. Elaan and Kirk fall for each other – it becomes obvious that her tears contain a chemical that makes men obey her. An Elasian bodyguard, Kryton, has contacted the Klingons in an attempt to prevent Elaan arriving. He's removed the dilithium crystals to sabotage the Enterprise. Elaan's necklace is made of dilithium crystals, and Scotty can rig them up. The Enterprise has enough power to repel the Klingons, and Elaan is delivered to her new life.

QUOTES

- 'Stop trying to kill each other, then worry about being friendly' – *Wise words from Kirk*

TRIVIA

- The first and last story written and directed by the same person, it was a love story, drawn up because the studio felt the show wasn't appealing to women.
- *The Next Generation* story *The Perfect Mate* is very similar to this episode.
- Despite this episodes title, the story doesn't bear any resemblance to that of Helen of Troy. Helen was *abducted*, and that *started* a war – the exact opposite of this story. And Elaan is from Elas, not Troyius – but, then again, Helen of Troy wasn't from Troy and the Trojan horse was Greek, not Trojan.

RATING

- Like *Day of the Dove*, this is another episode saved from a silly premise by some very entertaining sparring between Kirk and a guest star, in this case France Nuyen's Elaan.

3.14 WHOM GODS DESTROY

STARDATE 5718.3

The lunatics take control of an asylum for the criminally insane

TX 3 January 1969
WRITER Lee Erwin
DIRECTOR Herb Wallerstein
GUEST CAST Yvonne Craig (Marta), Steve Ihnat (Garth), Key Luke (Cory)

Kirk and Spock beam down to Elba II, a penal colony for the handful of the Federation's criminally insane. The most recent inmate is Garth of Izar, a hero of Kirk's, who was driven mad and convicted of mutiny after trying to wipe out the Antosians of Antos IV. Kirk and Spock go to his cell – only to be imprisoned by Garth, a shapeshifter who was posing as the warder. Garth wants the Enterprise, and tries to pose as Kirk, but doesn't have the right code to beam up. Garth tortures the captain, after which Kirk is comforted by Marta, an Orion girl. Marta is also insane, and tries to stab Kirk, but Spock saves him. Heading to the transporter room, Kirk realises that this 'Spock' is really Garth. The real Spock escapes, and – able to distinguish him from the real Kirk, despite his disguise – he stuns Garth. A security team restore order, and Garth receives treatment for his illness.

QUOTES

- 'I am the most beautiful woman on this planet.'
  'You're the only woman on this planet, you stupid girl!' – *Marta and Garth*

TRIVIA

- This was another of the four episodes the BBC didn't repeat, presumably because of the torture scene.
- Yvonne Craig played Batgirl in the Adam West *Batman* series which had ended the previous March.
- The title derives from a line from Euripedes: 'Whom gods destroy, they first send mad.'
- As originally scripted, the last fight ended with Spock being hit over the head and knocked unconscious. Leonard Nimoy argued that it would take more to hurt Spock and he was slammed against a wall instead. Unfortunately, Kirk's dialogue wasn't changed and he refers to Spock 'getting hit on the head'.

RATING

- This episode is colourful and fun, even if it doesn't exactly fill you with confidence about the Federation's methods of treating the mentally ill. Yvonne Craig is exuberant and suitably balances her character's vulnerability and barminess. William Shatner's turn as Garth-impersonating-Kirk is a wonder to behold.

3.15 LET THAT BE YOUR LAST BATTLEFIELD

STARDATE 5730.2

The Enterprise deals with two aliens from Cheron, a world ravaged by race hatred

TX 10 October 1969
WRITER Oliver Crawford
DIRECTOR Jud Taylor
GUEST CAST Lou Antonio (Lokai), Frank Gorshin (Bele)

The Enterprise pursues a shuttle stolen from Starbase 4 three weeks before, and brings it onboard with the tractor beam. Lokai of Cheron staggers out – half his face is white, the other is black. Another alien from Cheron, Bele, arrives and tells them Lokai is a criminal he's been pursuing for 50,000 years. Kirk wants to see Lokai charged with theft of the shuttle before he's returned home. Lokai demands asylum, saying Bele oppresses his 'people'. Bele has the power to alter the ship's course, and diverts it to Cheron. Kirk regains control by threatening to self-destruct the ship. Cheron is divided between those like Bele who are white on the left, black on the right, and Lokai's people, white on the right, black on the left. The Enterprise arrives on Cheron, but the hatred has led to one final war, and Bele and Lokai are the only survivors. Lokai escapes to the surface, Bele pursues – even now, there is only mutual hatred.

TRIVIA

- Gene Coon's last contribution to *Star Trek* was to suggest this story, although the original idea was to have an alien that looked like a devil chasing one that looked like an angel.
- Another week, another *Batman* actor – Frank Gorshin was the best-remembered of the Adam West show's Riddlers.

RATING

- An example of a message story that works because it's so purely visual – Kirk (and the audience) can't tell the difference between the aliens until it's pointed out. Frank Gorshin, a seriously under-rated actor, puts in one of *Star Trek's* strongest ever performances as Bele. The downbeat ending is yet more icing on the cake.

3.16 THE MARK OF GIDEON

STARDATE 5423.4

Kirk finds himself alone on the Enterprise

TX 17 January 1969
WRITER George F Slavin and Stanley Adams
DIRECTOR Jud Taylor
GUEST CAST Sharon Acker (Odona), Richard Derr (Fitzgerald), David Hurst (Hodin), Gene Kynarski (Krodack)

Kirk beams down to the planet Gideon, but he materialises on a deserted Enterprise. Ambassador Hodin contacts Spock to ask why Kirk hasn't arrived, but won't let anyone beam down to investigate. Kirk finds a young woman, Odona – she claims to have lost her memory. Kirk is drawn to her, but as they are getting close, Kirk sees a multitude of faces through a viewport. Odona collapses, and Hodin arrives, delighted she is ill. Odona is his daughter. Gideon is a utopia, but it's over-populated – the council have used Kirk to reintroduce sickness to their planet, and they knew Kirk was a carrier of vegan choriomeningitis. They've built an elaborate replica of the Enterprise on the surface of the planet to get Kirk and Odona together. Spock locates Kirk, and they cure Odona in the real Enterprise sickbay – but she's a carrier, like Kirk, now, and she's delighted she'll be able to carry out the council's plan.

TRIVIA

- Fans have noted that John Boorman's 1974 film *Zardoz* has the same idea of bringing an outsider to a utopia to reintroduce death and disease, and have speculated that it was influenced by this episode. It's not an entirely new idea, though: a lot of utopian fiction has a 'savage' outsider disrupting the ordered society (*Brave New World*, for example), and *Zardoz* wears its primary source on its sleeve – *The WiZARD of* OZ.
- On the contrary, this episode is like a number of *Mission: Impossible* episodes where the IMF team drop someone onto an elaborate set and trick them into doing something they wouldn't do otherwise – *The Mind of Stefan Milkos* and *The Freeze*, for example, which had just been shown when this episode was first broadcast.
- Writer Stanley Adams had played Cyrano Jones in *The Trouble with Tribbles.*

RATING

- An episode that starts out spooky and tense, but collapses well before the end under a mass of plot holes – leaving aside *how* the people of Gideon built such an exact replica of the Enterprise that even Kirk is fooled, there's just no reason *why* they build it. And if Kirk's so infectious, why is he allowed to beam down to planets in the first place?

3.17 THAT WHICH SURVIVES

STARDATE UNKNOWN

A mysterious force is at work on a young planet

TX 24 January 1969
WRITER John Meredyth Lucas (story by DC Fontana)
DIRECTOR Herb Wallerstein
GUEST CAST Lee Meriweather (Losira), Arthur Batanides (D'Amato), Lee Meriweather (Losira), Naomi Pollack (Rahada)

The Enterprise investigates a planet which has life, despite being relatively young. A mysterious woman appears in the transporter room and kills the operator with a single touch. The Enterprise is then thrown nearly a thousand light years, marooning the landing party. The woman appears on the planet, killing D'Amato, a geologist. The Enterprise is racing away at dangerous speeds – Scotty manages to regain control as it hits Warp 14. The landing party discover a room where images of the woman appear – she is Losira, an automated defence mechanism created to protect her people, the Kalandans. Only Losira's beauty has survived.

QUOTES

- 'Beauty survives' – *Kirk*

TRIVIA

- Lee Meriweather is yet another *Batman* veteran – she played Catwoman in the movie version (but not in the TV series).

RATING

- An odd and inconsequential episode, but one that works well enough.

3.18 THE LIGHTS OF ZETAR

STARDATE 5725.3

An energy storm takes possession of a young lieutenant

TX 31 January 1969
WRITER Jeremy Tarcher and Shari Lewis
DIRECTOR Herb Kenwith
GUEST CAST Libby Erwin (Rindonian), Jan Shutan (Mira Romaine), John Winston (Kyle)

The Enterprise is transferring equipment to library world Memory Alpha when it is hit by an energy storm. Mira Romaine, a young lieutenant, is hit by the full force. The storm has killed all but one of the staff at Memory Alpha. The storm pursues the Enterprise. Kirk tries firing phasers, but using them causes Romaine pain – McCoy discovers her brainwave now matches the storm's energy pattern. The cloud is alive – they are the last survivors of Zetar, and want to possess bodies. Kirk ejects them into space, where they die. Romaine elects to stay behind to rebuild Memory Alpha.

TRIVIA

- Kyle reappears in the animated series, voiced by James Doohan. John Winston next shows up as a Commander on the USS Reliant in *Star Trek II: The Wrath of Khan.*
- Shari Lewis is better known as the creator of sheep sock puppet Lambchop.

RATING

- A passable episode with an unduly large focus on a character whom we have never met before. There is a bit too much retreading of old ground here.

3.19 REQUIEM FOR METHUSELAH

STARDATE 5843.7

A mysterious man blocks the Enterprise's attempts to cure a fever sweeping the ship

TX 14 February 1969
WRITER Jerome Bixby
DIRECTOR Murray Golden
GUEST CAST James Daly (Flint), Louise Sorel (Rayna Kapec)

A lethal epidemic of Rigellian fever is sweeping the Enterprise. The antidote, ryetalyn, is found on Holberg 917-G in the Omega system, but when Kirk leads a landing party, they are attacked by a floating robot, M4. The planet is owned by the reclusive and clearly wealthy Mr Flint. He agrees to collect the antidote, and while they wait Kirk falls for Flint's ward, Rayna. McCoy stumbles across a lab where androids are built. Flint admits he is really Akharin, from ancient Mesopotamia, an immortal who was also Da Vinci, Brahms and other intellectual giants. He doesn't want his secret revealed, so proposes to keep the Enterprise here. Rayna dies, unable to resolve her divided loyalties, and Flint is also dying as his link with Earth is severed. Kirk returns to the ship with the antidote, and Spock erases his grief with a mind meld.

QUOTES

- 'It is a flower dying in the desert' – *Flint describing what it is to be lonely*

TRIVIA

- Rayna's surname is a homage to Karel Capek, the writer who coined the term 'robot'.

RATING

- An episode that seems to be cobbled together from other episodes lying around, like *The Squire of Gothos* and *Mudd's Women.* It's *Star Trek*-by-numbers again.

3.20 THE WAY TO EDEN

STARDATE 5832.1

The Enterprise is invaded by space hippies

The Enterprise chases the stolen spaceship Aurora, causing the smaller ship to burn out its engines. The six occupants are beamed to the Enterprise, and turn out to be idealistic dropouts – hippies. One,

TX 21 February 1969
WRITER Arthur Heinemann (story by 'Michael Richards' [pseudonym for DC Fontana] and Arthur Heinemann)
DIRECTOR David Alexander
GUEST CAST Victor Brandt (Tongo Rad), Phyllis Douglas (Hippy), Deborah Downey (Hippy), Skip Homeier (Severin), Charles Napier (Adam), Mary Linda Rapelye (Irina)

Tongo Rad, is the Catullan ambassador's son, so Kirk has to treat them more lightly than he'd like – especially as they show him no respect and call him 'Herbert'. Chekov knows one of the women, Irina Galliulin, and disapproves of her decision to drop out of Starfleet Academy. Their leader, Dr Sevrin, says they were looking for Eden, a legendary unspoiled planet. Spock, perhaps surprisingly, is sympathetic to their aim to find a more simple way of life, and secretly helps to locate Eden, but discovers Sevrin is insane. Tongo Rad frees Severin, and they render the Enterprise crew unconscious with ultrasonics then pilot the ship through Romulan space to Eden, taking a shuttle to the surface. The Enterprise crew recover and follow them down – to discover the planet has poisonous plant life and acidic grass. Sevrin dies after eating a toxic fruit. The other travellers are taken to a starbase; Spock hopes that one day they'll find Eden.

QUOTES

- 'They regard themselves as aliens in their own world, a condition with which I am somewhat familiar' – *Spock explains why he's joined the counterculture*

TRIVIA

- In Dorothy Fontana's original story, Irina was McCoy's daughter, Joanna, and the focus was on that father-daughter relationship. She asked for her name to be taken off the story when that aspect was completely dropped. Joanna is mentioned in the animated series episode *Survivor*.

RATING

- A story that must have felt horribly dated before the ink was dry on the script, *The Way to Eden* doesn't quite manage to be so bad it's good. This is not a good argument for a fourth season.

3.21 THE CLOUD MINDERS

STARDATE 5818.4

The planet Ardana is divided between the cloud city dwellers and the miners

TX 28 February 1969
WRITER Margaret Armen (story by David Gerrold and Oliver Crawford)
DIRECTOR Jud Taylor
GUEST CAST Jeff Corey (Plasus), Diana Ewing (Droxine), Jimmy Fields (Cloud Guard #2), Ed Long (Midro), Garth Pillesbury (Prisoner), Charlene Polite (Vanna), Kirk Raymone (Cloud Guard #1), Hary Selsby (Guard), Fred Williamson (Anka)

The antidote to a plague on Merak II, the mineral zenite, is only found on the planet Ardana. Kirk and Spock beam down to acquire supplies and are attacked by Troglytes, the primitive miners. They are rescued by High Advisor Plasus, who takes them to the cloud city, Stratos, where the ruling elite lives in luxury. Kirk discovers that the miners' leader, Vana, is being tortured and objects – and Plasus orders them to leave the planet. Meanwhile McCoy has discovered that the zenite gas in the mines is making the Troglytes violent and regressive – simply wearing filter masks would solve the problem. Kirk frees Vana, but she doesn't believe McCoy's theory. Kirk arranges for himself and Plasus to be beamed to the mines – where they quickly regress. Vana agrees to exchange zenite for protective masks, and hopes that one day all the people of the planet will live in the clouds.

TRIVIA

- David Gerrold's original story, *Castles in the Sky*, ended with McCoy challenging Kirk's assertion that as a result of their actions the two sides would start to talk, with the line 'Right, but how many children are going to die in the meantime?' Fred Freiberger was unhappy with what he saw as a polemical script.

RATING

- One of those *Star Trek* episodes you've seen even if you haven't seen it, *The Cloud Minders* is an allegory of haves and have-nots which has a problem a lot of 'issues' *Star Trek* stories have had over the years. It so simplifies the real-life situation that it stops resembling it and so ends up with nothing very useful to say.

3.22 THE SAVAGE CURTAIN

STARDATE 5906.4

The Enterprise joins history's heroes in a battle against its villains

TX 7 March 1969
WRITER Arthur Heinemann and Gene Roddenberry (story by Gene Roddenberry)
DIRECTOR Herschel Daugherty
GUEST CAST Barry Atwater (Surak), Lee Bergere (Abraham Lincoln), Arell Blanton (Dickerson), Carol Daniels Dement (Zora), Robert Herron (Kahless), Nathan Jung (Genghis Khan), Bart LeRue (Voice of Yarnek), Phillip Pine (Colonel Green), Janos Prohaska (Yarnek)

As the crew finishes charting a lifeless planet, the image of Abraham Lincoln appears on the screen, then beams aboard. Lincoln is amazed by humanity's achievements and asks the crew to beam down. On the planet, Kirk and Spock meet Surak, Vulcan's equivalent of Lincoln. A rock stands up – it is Yarnek, a shapeshifting Excalbian who doesn't understand good or evil, so he's arranged a contest to see the difference. Kirk and his allies have to defeat a group of the most evil beings in history, including Genghis Khan, mad scientist Zora, Colonel Green (the man responsible for World War III) and Kahless (founder of Klingon society). Kirk overcomes the odds, explaining that while evil fights for power, he fights for the lives of his crew. Yarnek releases Kirk and Spock.

TRIVIA

- Arthur Heinemann reports he was handed the first half of the script by Roddenberry and asked to complete it.
- Mark Lenard was originally cast to play Lincoln, but dropped out because of a film role.
- Kahless has frequently been mentioned by Worf in *The Next Generation* and *Deep Space Nine*, and even showed up in *Rightful Heir* (looking nothing like he does here).

RATING

- No, honestly – that *is* what happens in the story. Fantastically simplistic in its morality, and showing something of a cultural bias (Spock reveres Lincoln, Kirk hasn't even heard of Surak), this story is basically an excuse for an *Arena* style fight, but one shot in a tiny studio. The ideas and money are clearly both running out as the end of the series approaches.

3.23 ALL OUR YESTERDAYS

STARDATE 5943.7

Kirk, Spock and McCoy are thrown into the primitive past of a dying planet

TX 14 March 1969
WRITER Jean Lisette Aroeste
DIRECTOR Marvin Chomsky
GUEST CAST Ed Bake (First Fop), Stan Barret (Jailer), Al Cavens (Second Fop), Mariette Harley (Zarabeth), Johnny Haumer (Constable), Anna Karen (Woman), Kermit Murdock (Prosecutor), Ian Wolfe (Atoz)

The star Beta Niobe is going nova, and the planet Sarpeidon will be destroyed in three hours. Kirk, Spock and McCoy beam down to discover that the population of the planet has vanished. They arrive in a library run by Mr Atoz, and they discover he's sent the population back into history via a time machine, the atavachron. The three accidentally end up in the past – Kirk in the equivalent of the seventeenth century, where he's accused of being a witch, and Spock and McCoy in an ice age, where they are sheltered by the alluring Zarabeth, exiled to the past by the tyrant Zor Khan. Spock loses his temper – he's reverting to a more primitive time, and in love with Zarabeth. Kirk gets back to the present, and recovers McCoy and a reluctant Spock. They let Atoz escape into the past, and manage to escape the doomed planet in the nick of time.

QUOTES

- 'I heard the spirit talk to him. He answered and called it 'Bones'' – *McCoy's nickname backfires, as a constable accuses Kirk of communing with the dead*

TRIVIA

- This is a story where the convention of Kirk narrating a captain's log makes no sense – we hear the voiceover when he's in a cave in the distant past.
- 'Atoz' is, of course, a rather charming name for a librarian.

RATING

- Spock becomes emotional and falls in love (again). A solid episode, and an ambitious one for a cash-strapped season, but it's clearly modelled on *The City at the Edge of Forever*, and it's a pale shadow of that.

3.24 TURNABOUT INTRUDER

STARDATE 5928.5

An hysterical woman swaps bodies with Kirk and becomes captain of the Enterprise

TX 28 March 1969
WRITER Arthur M Singer
DIRECTOR Herb Wallerstein
GUEST CAST Harry Lander (Dr Coleman), Sandra Smith (Janice Lester)

The Enterprise receives a distress call from Camus II. The expedition leader, Janice Lester, is suffering from radiation poisoning. Lester gets Kirk alone, then uses an alien device to swap bodies with him – she has been denied the right to be a starship captain, and wants to prove she is up to the job. Her strange behaviour makes the crew suspicious, and Spock performs a mind meld on 'Lester', discovering 'she' is Kirk. 'Kirk' captures Spock and charges him with mutiny. The crew rise up against the impostor, and Kirk is restored to his body.

TRIVIA

- So, does Starfleet allow female starship captains? The earliest we see (barring Uhura taking command in the animated episode *The Lorelei Signal*, when all the men are incapacitated, and Saavik's simulated mission in *Star Trek II: The Wrath of Khan*) is the captain of the USS Saratoga in *Star Trek IV: The Voyage Home*. There are only a dozen starships like the USS Enterprise, according to *Tomorrow is Yesterday*, so there aren't a huge number of job vacancies. But that's still a lame excuse.
- Another crazy Captain's log entry: Janice, posing as Kirk, makes a log entry where she puts on the record that no one suspects that she's swapped bodies with the real Kirk.

RATING

- Hysterical's the word – an absurdly sexist story, with William Shatner camping it up magnificently as the woman-in-Kirk's-body, and Sandra Smith doing a fine Shatner impersonation in turn. Good, but for all the wrong reasons.

STAR TREK: THE ANIMATED SERIES

TWO SEASONS

22 episodes
(1973-74)

REGULAR CAST

Captain James T Kirk: William Shatner
Mr Spock: Leonard Nimoy
Dr Leonard 'Bones' McCoy: DeForest Kelley
'Scotty'/Arex: James Doohan
Sulu: George Takei
Uhura/M'Ress: Nichelle Nichols
Christine Chapel: Majel Barrett

PRODUCERS

Norm Prescott, Lou Scheimer

ASSOCIATE PRODUCER/ STORY EDITOR

DC Fontana

By the early seventies, *Star Trek* was proving popular in syndication, and NBC at least briefly considered reviving the series, before deciding it would be too expensive. An animated show could be done at a fraction of the cost, and a couple of people approached the studio with an eye to producing it. The studio picked Filmation, creators of a number of popular Saturday morning kids shows, including the award-winning *Fat Albert and the Cosby Kids* and, perhaps most pertinently, *The New Adventures of Batman*, voiced by the former live-action Batman and Robin, Adam West and Burt Ward.

Gene Roddenberry retained creative control, vetoing plans that the series would make a direct appeal to the kiddie market by depicting the 'cadet years' of Kirk and Spock, or that the adult crew of the Enterprise would be training a crew of cadets. Reports vary as to how far those two plans got – it was far enough to prepare production sketches showing young crewmen. The two ideas have never quite died a death. *Star Trek II: The Wrath of Khan* showed an Enterprise crewed mostly by cadets, Roddenberry himself created the character of Wesley Crusher for *The Next Generation* (Roddenberry's middle name was Wesley), and Paramount spent much of the eighties apparently contemplating an *Academy Years* film, an idea that has also featured in the spin-off comics and books.

Roddenberry was convinced that the right approach for the cartoon was to recreate the live-action show as closely as possible, with animation simply allowing the writers' imaginations to transcend budgetary restraints. He pushed for it to be shown in the same evening time slot. While *The Flintstones* had proved it was possible to get adults to watch animation, the networks believed that was a unique case and that cartoons were for kids. It would be 20 years before that orthodoxy was overturned with the advent of *The Simpsons*, and the *Star Trek* cartoon became strictly Saturday morning fare, albeit one with a high budget – a reported $75,000 per episode. At the time, parents' groups had succeeded in bowdlerising cartoons, removing any hint of violence. This was the period infamous for the *Tom and Jerry* cartoons where the cat and mouse co-operated instead of fought. While fans often cite this as a reason why the animated *Star Trek* show lacks bite, perhaps this was one of the reasons it was commissioned in the first place – it was one of the few shows that could give kids a science fiction adventure while also emphasising problem-solving over fighting.

As he later would with the *Star Trek II* series and *Star Trek: The Next Generation*, Roddenberry surrounded himself with writers he could trust, about half of them *Star Trek* veterans. Samuel A Peeples was commissioned to write a pilot episode – he had, after all, written *Where No Man Has Gone Before*, the 'second pilot' of the original series. His episode was eventually shown towards the end of the first season. New writers were also recruited, notably Larry Niven, a hot new SF property after his 1970 novel *Ringworld*, who adapted his short story *The Soft Weapon*. The scripts were overseen by DC Fontana, as Associate Producer and Story Editor. A few stories were direct sequels to live-action episodes: David Gerrold resurrected a rejected third-season Tribble story, Stephen Kandel brought back his Harry Mudd character and there was a sequel to *Shore Leave*. Others were almost identical to original episodes – the ageing in *The Lorelei Signal* is reminiscent of *The Deadly Years* and *How Sharper Than a Serpent's Tooth?* pays homage to *Who Mourns for Adonais?* Romulans, Vulcans and Klingons were also to put in an appearance.

Ironically, given the reason for doing an animated series, the budget limitations would prove to be a serious problem. It was possible to create a giant Spock or have the Enterprise come up against powerful magicians and space dragons... but the animation was stiff and inexpressive, and relied on stock shots. The voiceover budget was so limited that the original plan was to have James Doohan double up as Scotty and Sulu, and Majel Barrett to play Chapel and Uhura – the contracts stipulated that actors got paid the same for playing two characters as one. Leonard Nimoy refused to do the series on those terms, and George Takei and Nichelle Nicols were added to the cast. The regular cast were called on to play most of the parts, though. Between them, Nichelle Nicols and Majel Barrett played every female role in the show, not just Uhura and Chapel (a total of 30 parts). That was nothing compared with James Doohan. He played both Scotty and the new bridge officer Arex (a pink three-legged alien), as well as just about every other part – 57 roles over the course of the series. There was no room, though, for Chekov. Walter Koenig was unhappy at his treatment, but wrote a script, *The Infinite Vulcan*, for the series. The cast were grateful for the money – they had seen little or nothing from the syndicated success of the original series – but weren't happy with the cartoon. There was little camaraderie at the recordings. As was the standard practice at the time, roles were often recorded separately, even on different days in different studios (sometimes in different cities), so often the actors didn't meet and their lines were spliced together in post-production.

The series began on 9 September 1973, seven years and a day after the debut of the original series. Response was muted: reviewers that praised it did so only in relation to other Saturday morning cartoons. Fans saw the animated show as vindication of their belief that *Star Trek* was viable, not as anything to get excited about in its own right. *Star Trek Lives!*, a book written at the time by three fans of the show, barely mentions the animated series except in passing, in a book that's never less than breathless about every other aspect of *Star Trek* (one of the authors describes receiving a phone call from Leonard Nimoy in terms that would make a slash writer blush: 'Those deep, resonant tones flowed down the phone lines and into my eager ears... oh bliss, oh frabjous joy...'). It was popular enough that a further six episodes were ordered for a 'second season', but since ending, the animated series has become little more than a footnote in *Star Trek* history. Gene Roddenberry, who fought so hard to maintain control of it, soon declared that he didn't consider it part of the official *Star Trek* 'canon' and blocked attempts to refer to characters from it in the spin-off books and comics, although a couple of references have snuck in over the years (and it was the place that first established that James T Kirk's middle name was Tiberius, in *Bem*). Despite being available on video on both sides of the Atlantic for many years, it's remained resolutely ignored or unloved by most fans.

The animated series has a few moments of interest. It won *Star Trek*'s first creative Emmy (Best Daytime Show) in 1974 for *How Sharper Than a Serpent's Tooth?*, after losing out to *Zoom* the previous year, when *Yesteryear* was nominated. It's going out of its way to recreate the look and sound of the original series, and is surprisingly faithful to Roddenberry's vision. At its worst, though, that means an often slow pace, simplistic philosophical messages and more than a touch of dullness. Apologists have claimed that as the episodes were half the length of the live action ones, the animated series was always going to struggle to match the complexity of the original. But the truth is that many of the cartoons struggle to fill even 22 minutes, and the series has a real problem with repetitious storylines – even with less than two dozen episodes, you almost lose count of energy fields trapping the ship, a new arrival being a bit of a nuisance, Kirk trapped in a zoo or godlike beings setting the crew a simple puzzle. Some stories suffer from the form – *Albatross* is a great idea for a live-action story, but loses most of its bite and nuance as a cartoon.

Three episodes stand out from the pack: *More Tribbles, More Troubles* is fun, *The Slaver Weapon* is a fairly uncompromising burst of real science fiction (and is the first episode without Kirk in it), and both would have made great live-action shows. The undoubted highlight is the first episode to be broadcast, *Yesteryear*, that transcends the limitations of the animation to present a story that's rich, complex and moving, as well as being a fanboy wet dream. Even now, *Yesteryear* ranks as one of the best *Star Trek* episodes.

STAR TREK: THE ANIMATED SERIES

SEASON ONE

(Every episode was directed by Hal Sutherland, apart from *How Sharper Than A Serpent's Tooth?* and *The Counter-Clock Incident*, which were directed by Bill Reed.)

YESTERYEAR

TX 9 September 1973 **WRITER** DC Fontana
GUEST CAST Mark Lenard (Sarek), Billy Simpson (Young Spock), Keith Sutherland (Young Sepek)

STARDATE 5373.4

History has been changed so that Spock was killed as a child. Spock uses the Guardian of Forever to travel back to the Vulcan of his youth and helps him through a rite of passage, and the death of his beloved pet sehlat.

ONE OF OUR PLANETS IS MISSING

TX 22 September 1973 **WRITER** Marc Daniels

STARDATE 5373.4

A huge cloud is eating planets. The Enterprise discovers the cloud is sentient, and Spock persuades it not to destroy the planet Mantilles.

THE LORELEI SIGNAL

TX 29 September 1973 **WRITER** Margaret Armen

STARDATE 5483.7

The men on the Enterprise start acting oddly and Kirk orders the ship to the Taurean system. Kirk, Spock and McCoy are kidnapped by female aliens who drain the life energy of men to stay immortal. The female crewmembers save the ship.

MORE TRIBBLES, MORE TROUBLES

TX 6 October 1973 **WRITER** David Gerrold
GUEST CAST Stanley Adams (Cyrano Jones), David Gerrold (Korax)

STARDATE 5329.4

Cyrano Jones has taken Tribbles to a Klingon planet, and steals the Glommer, a predator the Klingons use to keep down the pests. Jones also has a new type of Tribble that doesn't breed... but he's neglected to mention that the more it eats, the more it grows.

THE SURVIVOR

STARDATE 5143.3

TX 13 October 1973 **WRITER** James Schmerer
GUEST CAST Ted Knight (Carter Winston)

A man claiming to be the explorer Carter Winston is actually a Vendorian – a shapeshifter working for the Romulans. Impersonating Kirk, he flies the Enterprise into the Neutral Zone, where it is surrounded by Romulan warships.

THE INFINITE VULCAN

STARDATE 5554.4

TX 20 October 1973 **WRITER** Walter Koenig
GUEST CAST Mark Lenard (Sarek), Billy Simpson (Young Spock), Keith Sutherland (Young Sepek)

The planet Phylos has intelligent plants and is ruled by a giant clone of Dr Starros Keniclius V, a survivor of the Eugenics Wars. He creates a giant clone of Spock, to act as a galactic peacemaker, although this could mean the death of the original.

THE MAGICKS OF MEGAS-TU

STARDATE 1254.4

TX 27 October 1973 **WRITER** Larry Brody
GUEST CAST Ed Bishop (Megan Prosecutor)

After emerging from a space storm, the Enterprise arrives at a world where magic works and science doesn't. The satanic alien Lucien rules here, and puts the Enterprise crew on trial for witchcraft.

ONCE UPON A PLANET

STARDATE 5591.2

TX 3 November 1973 **WRITER** Len Jenson and Chuck Menville

Kirk arranges shore leave for the crew on the planet seen in *Shore Leave*. As with their previous visit, the illusions become deadly and have to be defeated.

MUDD'S PASSION

STARDATE 4978.5

TX 10 November 1973 **WRITER** Stephen Kandel
GUEST CAST Roger C Carmel (Harry Mudd)

Kirk rescues Harry Mudd from a group of irate miners. Mudd has a love potion, which Chapel uses on Spock. She's furious when it doesn't work, but then Spock falls madly in love with her. Soon, many of the crew are also lovestruck.

THE TERRATIN INCIDENT

STARDATE 5577.3

TX 17 November 1973 **WRITER** Paul Schneider

The Enterprise is struck by lightning and begins to shrink. Kirk beams down to the nearest planet, Cepheus, and discovers a tiny race desperate to escape their exploding homeworld. The transporters return the crew to normal size.

THE TIME TRAP

STARDATE 5267.2

TX 24 November 1973 **WRITER** Joyce Perry

The Enterprise and the Klingon ship Klothos, captained by Kor, end up trapped in the Delta Triangle time warp by aliens who want to force them to work together. Many other races live here, trapped, and loosely governed by the Elysian Council. Spock comes up with a plan that will let the ships escape, but the Klingons have planted a bomb on the Enterprise which will explode if they do.

THE AMBERGRIS ELEMENT

STARDATE 5499.9

TX 1 December 1973 **WRITER** Margaret Armen
GUEST CAST David Gerrold (Nephro)

The Enterprise crew explore the water planet Argo in the aquashuttle, but the ship is damaged by a sea monster. Kirk and Spock are rescued by the local people, the Aquans, who convert them into water-breathers – a process they claim can't be reversed.

THE SLAVER WEAPON

TX 15 December 1973 **WRITER** Larry Niven

STARDATE 4187.3

The Enterprise is taking a stasis box to a nearby starbase for examination. It's the artefact of a lost advanced civilisation, and will contain some advanced technology. It can also be used to locate other stasis boxes. The Enterprise detects another on Beta Lyrae. There, the crew are ambushed by a ferocious cat-like Kzin, who steals the box.

BEYOND THE FARTHEST STAR

TX 22 December 1973 **WRITER** Samuel A Peeples

STARDATE 5521.3

The Enterprise is trapped near the black hole Questar M17 by a formless alien, who boards the ship. Kirk must decide whether to destroy the ship to prevent it from spreading to other planets.

THE EYE OF THE BEHOLDER

TX 6 January 1974 **WRITER** David Harmon

STARDATE 5501.2

The Enterprise crew are captured by the slug-like Lactrans of Lactra VII and placed in a zoo. Spock uses a mind meld to convince a Lactran child that they are intelligent, and they are released.

THE JIHAD

TX 13 January 1974 **WRITER** Stephen Kandel
GUEST CAST David Gerrold (Em/3/Green)

STARDATE 5683.1

The Vedala, the first race to invent space travel, send Kirk on a quest to find a religious relic of Skorr. The Skorr are benevolent, but only because of the influence of the Soul of Alar – unless it is returned, they threaten to begin a holy war across the galaxy.

STAR TREK: THE ANIMATED SERIES
SEASON TWO

THE PIRATES OF ORION

TX 7 September 1974 **WRITER** Howard Weinstein

STARDATE 6334.1

Spock contracts fatal choriocytosis, and the only antidote is strobolin. The SS Huron heads to the Enterprise with supplies, but is raided by pirates *en route*. Kirk has to find the pirates before Spock dies.

BEM

TX 14 September 1974 **WRITER** David Gerrold

STARDATE 7403.6

The operation of the Enterprise is observed by the erratic Ari Ben Bem of Pandro, who makes a nuisance of himself. On a landing mission, he replaces the real phasers with fakes, and everyone is captured. It is all a test to see how the crew respond to pressure – Bem is the emissary of an advanced race that isn't sure whether to ally with the Federation.

THE PRACTICAL JOKER

TX 21 September 1974 **WRITER** Chuck Menville
GUEST CAST Norm Prescott (Romulan), Lou Scheimer (Romulan Commander)

STARDATE 3183.3

An alien practical joker enters the ship's computer, and starts relentlessly playing jokes on the crew. This is a minor annoyance – until the ship starts heading towards Romulan space.

ALBATROSS

STARDATE 5275.6

TX 28 September 1974 **WRITER** Dario Finelli

The rulers of Dramia II accuse McCoy of genocide – 20 years before, a vaccination programme he was in charge of actually helped to spread the Saurian plague, killing millions. McCoy, who's unsure whether he really was responsible, must stand trial, but the plague has reappeared, and spread to the Enterprise.

HOW SHARPER THAN A SERPENT'S TOOTH?

STARDATE 6063.4

TX 5 October 1974 **WRITER** Russell Bates and David Wise

Kirk, McCoy, Scotty and Ensign Walking Bear are trapped by the ancient Mayan god Kulkukan, who wants to be worshipped and places them in a zoo. Back on the ship, Spock must try to free them.

THE COUNTER-CLOCK INCIDENT

STARDATE 6770.3

TX 12 October 1974 **WRITER** 'John Culver' [pseudonym for Fred Bronson]

The Enterprise is taking the ship's first captain, Robert April, to Babel, when an alien ship approaches at an incredible Warp 36. It's heading straight for a supernova – when the Enterprise tries to stop it, both ships fall into a dimension where time runs backwards. A rejuvenated April saves the ship just before the regular crew regress into babies.

STAR TREK II

Proposed seventies television series
No episodes made

REGULAR CAST

Captain James T Kirk: William Shatner
Will Decker: never cast
Dr Leonard 'Bones' McCoy: DeForest Kelley
Xon: David Gautreaux
'Scotty': James Doohan
Sulu: George Takei
Uhura: Nichelle Nichols
Chekov: Walter Koenig
Ilia: Persis Khambatta
Christine Chapel: Majel Barrett

BY THE MID-SEVENTIES, *STAR TREK* WAS MORE POPULAR THAN EVER.

It became clear to Paramount that it ought to be brought back in some form. The obvious outlet was cinema, and as early as 1975 the studio began making plans for a *Star Trek* film. As a couple of separate big screen projects stumbled, another Paramount scheme was taking shape: the creation of a fourth television network. It became clear that *Star Trek* would be a strong addition to the schedule. In 1977, Paramount asked Gene Roddenberry to develop a two-hour opening episode that would reintroduce the crew of the Enterprise, leading to an initial season of 13 one-hour episodes. This was to be essentially a continuation of the original series, and would be called *Star Trek II* (an alternate title, *Star Trek Phase II*, is preferred by most fans nowadays, to avoid confusion with the second movie, *Star Trek II: The Wrath of Khan*). Gene Roddenberry reassembled many of the original production team and set to work, with the hope that the first episode would debut on 1 February 1978.

Roddenberry was excited that television had moved on in the decade since the original *Star Trek* – in contemporary interviews, he cited *M*A*S*H* and *All in the Family* as exactly the sort of challenging, issue-driven shows that he felt *Star Trek* could be. He was also keen to use some of the advances in special effects technology.

In Thy Image was picked as the first episode. It was based on *Robot's Return*, an idea Roddenberry had for his rejected series *Genesis II*, about an ancient space probe that returns to Earth looking for its creator, and is unable to believe it was built by humans. The Enterprise would start the episode being refurbished for a five-year mission before a hurried launch to intercept the probe.

The first problem was that the most recognisable character, Mr Spock, wouldn't be in the show. Leonard Nimoy was worried about typecasting. His 1975 autobiography, *I Am Not Spock*, wasn't as negative about the role as the title would lead you to presume but, although he was proud of his time on the show, Nimoy wanted to move on and establish himself as a serious actor. He was also in a legal dispute with Paramount over his likeness rights, which were being used on merchandise and in advertising without his blessing.

Roddenberry's solution was simple – he introduced a new Vulcan science officer, Xon, played by David Gautreaux. Xon differed from Spock by being wholly Vulcan, not half-human, and by being young and inexperienced. He would fill the 'outsider' role that Spock had provided, without being a carbon copy, and would attempt to explore emotions 'to solve the human equation' – a form of words later used by *The Next Generation's* outsider character, Data.

Roddenberry was reportedly annoyed that the studio insisted that Leonard Nimoy was in the first episode to explain his absence from the series. Paramount were prepared to offer Nimoy $100,000 to appear in one scene, with the option of future guest appearances. This was, of course, a vast amount of money, and it seems reasonable to assume that it may have been agreed as part of a settlement of Nimoy's legal action against them. A scene was added to the first episode in which Spock told Kirk he had been offered the job of Head of the Vulcan Science Academy, and wouldn't be joining him on the second five-year mission.

William Shatner was happy to sign on as Kirk – and Paramount were keen to sign him quickly, before he learnt about Nimoy's deal. Concerned that his leading man might one day demand too much money, and aware that William Shatner was older than was conventional for a leading man (he was 46 in 1977) and that this would become more of a problem the longer the show ran, Roddenberry decided that the new first officer, Will Decker, would be a younger man in the Kirk mould. Decker idolised Kirk, and was a little blind to his faults – a dangerous characteristic in a first officer. Casting Decker proved tricky, and as the show was developed serious thought was given to dropping this 'second Kirk', who seemed to duplicate Kirk's role a little too closely.

A third new crewmember, Ilia, would be an exotic woman. A Deltan from the planet 114-Delta V, Ilia was able to read people's emotions. She and Decker had been lovers in the past, but now she had an 'intense' relationship with Kirk. Persis Khambatta, a former Miss India, was cast. Decker (played by Stephen Collins) and Ilia would eventually appear (and disappear!) in *Star Trek: The Motion Picture*, where her home planet was renamed Delta IV. *The Next Generation* featured two almost identical characters, Riker and Troi.

Harold Livingston was brought in to control scripting, and Roddenberry's assistant Jon Povill helped with matters of *Star Trek* history and continuity. Livingston approached various writers.

It's striking how much time and money was spent on *Star Trek II*. It was in pre-production for at least six months, and stories were developed from pitches into full scripts. Production paintings and models were assembled, sets were built and costume tests filmed. Casting calls were made. Some estimates have it that *Star Trek II* cost nearly $20m. If that's true, the studio spent almost as much on i t as they would ten years later on the first series of *The Next Generation* (which, of course, was actually made!).

The Enterprise was to be a refurbished ship, and the familiar look of the series was to get a makeover. The production paintings and test footage (some of which appears on *Star Trek: The Motion Picture* Special Edition DVD), suggest that *Star Trek II* would look like a seventies revamp of the original show. The Enterprise would retain the same primary colour look, the women would wear leggings under their short skirts and the men would wear short-sleeved shirts. Matt Jefferies, the designer of the original series, was working on the Paramount lot on *Little House on the Prairie*, and acted as a technical consultant.

There was tension over the scripts, with the studio worried about the dramatic potential of some of the proposed stories. Livingston and Roddenberry clashed over the scripts, leading to Livingston walking out towards the end of 1977, complaining that Roddenberry's interference made it impossible for him to do his job.

By then, the success of *Star Wars* at the cinema and – more importantly – the collapse of plans for a Paramount network had finally convinced the studio to take the first episode of the television series and prepare it for cinematic release. *In Thy Image* became *Star Trek: The Motion Picture*, and, as we'll see, it was a huge financial success. Some of the design work – notably the bridge set – survived to the movie, as did the new characters of Decker and Ilia. Some of the scripts and story ideas also survived – the first episode was the basis of the first movie, and *The Next Generation* episodes *Devil's Due* and *The Child* were dusted-off versions of *Star Trek II* scripts.

The new television series that the fans of the show campaigned for in the early seventies is now a small footnote in the history of *Star Trek*. One fascinating question about *Star Trek II*, though, is what would have happened if it had gone ahead. As the nineties – and *Voyager* – proved, the fate of the show would have been linked to the success of the new network. Without *Star Trek II*, *Star Trek* thrived – first as a series of successful movies, then returning as *The Next Generation*, a show that surpassed the original in terms of popularity and success. We'll never know, of course, if *Star Trek II* would have captured the public's imagination – it could have been a huge hit and the flagship of a network, or a massively expensive failure. All we can say with any certainty is that either way, if it had gone ahead the history of *Star Trek* would have looked radically different.

STAR TREK: STAR TREK II
EPISODE LISTING

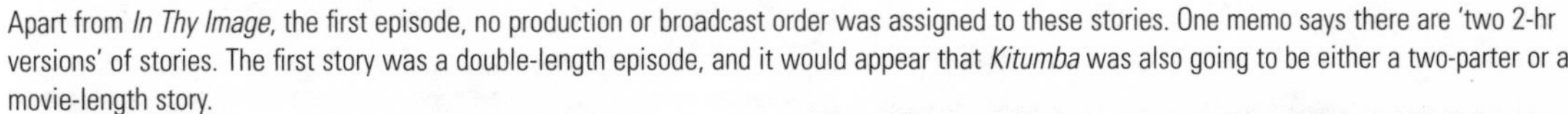

Apart from *In Thy Image*, the first episode, no production or broadcast order was assigned to these stories. One memo says there are 'two 2-hr versions' of stories. The first story was a double-length episode, and it would appear that *Kitumba* was also going to be either a two-parter or a movie-length story.

The following list would make up the pilot and 13 normal episodes ordered by Paramount. In addition, Arthur Heinemann, Ray Bradbury and Jerome Bixby were working on scripts. One of these may or may not have been *The War to End All Wars*, a script mentioned in studio documentation – equally, this might be a working title for one of the stories listed below. Alan Dean Foster also pitched a story that saw the Enterprise arrive at a planet like the US in the 1860s, where the whites were slaves and blacks their masters, although this was never developed.

IN THY IMAGE

WRITER Harold Livingston **DIRECTOR** Bob Collins

A destructive energy cloud is heading for Earth, and the Enterprise is sent to intercept it. Kirk discovers that at its heart is an ancient space probe. (Adapted to become *Star Trek: The Motion Picture*, Alan Dean Foster also worked on a version of this story, which was based on an idea by Gene Roddenberry.)

TOMORROW AND THE STARS

WRITER Larry Alexander

A transporter malfunction sends Kirk to Pearl Harbor in 1941, days before the Japanese attack. Kirk falls for a married woman and agonises about whether to warn her.

DEADLOCK

WRITER David Ambrose

The Enterprise is engaged in war games with Starbase 7 – but the commander of the base, Commodore Hunter, has been replaced by an alien and the 'games' turn real.

SAVAGE SYNDROME

WRITERS Margaret Armen and Alf Harris

A mine explodes releasing radiation that transforms the crew into primitive savages.

PRACTICE IN WAKING

WRITER Richard Bach

Scotty, Sulu and Decker fall into comas after seeing a mysterious woman in suspended animation on a drifting ship. They are in a dreamworld, and will remain there forever unless they are rescued soon.

DEVIL'S DUE

WRITER William Lansford

The planet Neuterra has been a paradise for 1,000 years, because they made a deal with a being called Komether that he could have the planet after that time. Now he wants them to make good on the deal. (Adapted for *The Next Generation.*)

THE PRISONER

WRITER James Menzies

Albert Einstein materialises on the ship, claiming to be a prisoner on an alien planet – but it's a trap to lure the Enterprise to the evil Logos.

THE CHILD

WRITERS Jon Povill and Jaron Summers

Ilia is impregnated by an energy being and her child grows unnaturally quickly (Adapted for *The Next Generation*)

KITUMBA Parts 1 and 2

WRITER John Meredyth Lucas

A Klingon defector, Ksia, has warned that the Klingons intend an invasion. The Enterprise takes on a suicidal mission to the Klingon homeworld, where Kirk meets Kitumba, boy king of the Klingons, and tries to persuade him not to listen to his hawkish advisors.

TO ATTAIN THE ALL

WRITER Norman Spinrad

An alien arrives on the Enterprise and promises every crewmember what they desire the most. (Q does this in *The Next Generation* story *Hide and Q*.)

CASSANDRA

WRITER Theodore Sturgeon

The Enterprise is inadvertently the location of the hatching of Cassandra, a creature known as the Second Monitor, that can foretell the future. The Manlikt blame their rivals, the Breet, and threaten to destroy them unless the creature is returned to them.

ARE UNHEARD MELODIES SWEET? (aka HOME)

WRITER Worley Thorne

Investigating the disappearance of the USS St Louis, the crew are held prisoner by an alien race that forces them to live out a series of sexual fantasies. The aliens need a constant supply of hormones to avoid extinction.

LORD BOBBY'S OBSESSION (aka LORD BOBBY)

WRITER
Shimon Wincelberg

As the Romulans invade the Neutral Zone, the Enterprise takes on board Lord Robert Standish, who claims he was abducted by aliens in the twentieth century... but who McCoy discovers is an alien.

STAR TREK: THE MOVIES – PART 1

The cast of Star Trek
(1979-91)

REGULAR CAST

Captain James T Kirk: William Shatner (1-7)
Mr Spock: Leonard Nimoy (1-6)
Dr Leonard 'Bones' McCoy: DeForest Kelley (1-6)
'Scotty': James Doohan (1-7)
Sulu: George Takei (1-6)
Uhura: Nichelle Nichols (1-6)
Chekov: Walter Koenig (1-7)
Christine Chapel: Majel Barrett (1, 4)
Saavik: Kirsty Alley (2), Robin Curtis (3-4)
Sarek: Mark Lenard (3-4, 5 [voiceover only], 6)
Janice Rand: Grace Lee Whitney (1, 4, 6)

Even before they'd thought of the new *Star Trek II* television series, Paramount had actively been trying to make a *Star Trek* movie. In autumn 1975, Gene Roddenberry completed a script, *The God Thing*, for a film provisionally budgeted around $3m. Paramount wasn't keen on the story, but invited Roddenberry and a number of other people, like Harlan Ellison, Robert Silverberg and Trek veterans Jon Povill and John DF Black to pitch other ideas. The brief seems to have been to make the film as big as possible, with the writers all submitting stories with epic scope – Ellison pitched an ambitious time travel story, Jon Povill wanted a story where the whole of Vulcan was possessed with a psychotic rage, Roddenberry and Silverberg had the crew meeting God (or at least awesome alien intelligences that could be God), while Black opted for a black hole story with the universe at stake.

In 1976, pre-production began on another story, *Planet of the Titans* (by Chris Bryant and Allan Scott) with Phil Kaufman (the director of *Quills* (2000) and co-creator of Indiana Jones, among other things), as director and Ken Adam (famous for the James Bond films) as production designer. *Star Wars* (1977) production illustrator Ralph McQuarrie was brought in to redesign the Enterprise and come up with other concept sketches. Paramount assigned a budget of $10m (about what *Star Wars* would cost). The story had the Enterprise fighting Klingons to salvage advanced technology from a planet that was doomed to plunge into a black hole. Gene Roddenberry reportedly had little to do with this version. There have been unconfirmed rumours that Paramount was considering completely recasting the film, with Robert Redford as Kirk and Dustin Hoffman as Spock (other reports have Paul Newman and Richard Burton) – Gene Roddenberry has since suggested this was a joke to a journalist reported as fact.

All the time the *Star Trek II* television series was in development, Paramount had one eye on making the first episode, *In Thy Image*, into a movie with a cinematic release. The thinking on whether *Star Trek* should come back as a movie or a television series seemed to change from day to day, and went through a number of permutations (not all of which were communicated to everyone involved). When the plan for a Paramount network collapsed, the studio had already done plenty of work, and spent plenty of money, on a new version of *Star Trek*. By then *Star Wars* had proved a huge hit worldwide. Every movie studio dusted off their science fiction scripts and put them into production. Paramount took *In Thy Image* and massively increased the budget.

The result was *Star Trek: The Motion Picture*. It was a huge financial success, but the studio felt it was far too expensive, and too slow. A second film quickly became inevitable, particularly as it could reuse sets and costumes made for the first movie. *Star Wars* had created a new genre of fast-paced science fantasy film, and Paramount felt *Star Trek* should fit that mould. Gene Roddenberry disagreed, but the studio had little patience for the man they thought – fairly or unfairly – was responsible for the slow pace and poor management of the first movie. Roddenberry, as he had with the TV series, found himself moved aside to the role of Executive Producer, effectively an advisor. Harve Bennett was appointed as the producer of the sequel at a meeting with Paramount mogul Charles Bluhdorn who asked him, 'Can you make it for less than forty-five fucking million dollars?' A television producer up until that point, Bennett was shocked by how much the first film had cost and suggested he could make five movies for the same amount of money. Paramount took him at his word, and set the budget at $8.5m (two weeks into the production, it was happy enough with the progress to boost the budget by another $2m). This film became *Star Trek II: The Wrath of Khan*.

Director Nicholas Meyer was not a *Star Trek* fan, and has claimed that the only thing he knew about the show when he got the job was that Spock had pointy ears (the first shot of the film is a close up of those ears). He saw the series as a futuristic updating of sea-faring stories – like Roddenberry in the sixties, one template was the *Horatio Hornblower* novels, with the script dictating a revenge story *à la Moby Dick* and a finale highly reminiscent of *Sink the Bismarck!* (1960) or any number of submarine films. The Starfleet costumes were redesigned and took their cues from early nineteenth century naval uniforms. While Roddenberry often liked to emphasise how man would have evolved by the time of *Star Trek*, Meyer was keen to bring things back down to earth – showing Kirk growing old, getting a birthday present from Spock and sharing a drink at home with McCoy. This approach extended to making the Enterprise look like it was a place people lived in – he populated the corridors with cleaning staff, the galley with cooking pots and added other details to make the Enterprise less antiseptic than in the first movie.

Everyone involved was keen to make the film faster and more action-packed than the first. It was made on a tight budget, and this prevented any thought of repeating the epic scale of the first film. The Enterprise bridge set was redressed to become the bridge of the other ship in the story, the USS Reliant, meaning that almost half of the film's scenes were shot on that one set. Perhaps the biggest contrast with the first film was that it came in on time and under budget. It broke box office records when it was released, and ended up as the fifth highest-grossing film of the year.

Star Trek II: The Wrath of Khan proved to be the template for the future *Star Trek* films – the model was, essentially, to produce mid-budget movies that pitched the crew into a quest that could be summed up in a sentence. To minimise confusion, the baddies were always the Klingons – the original plan to use the Romulans in the third film was changed, apparently at a late stage – the Klingons in it fly around in a starship called a Bird of Prey with a cloaking device. The third film saw Kirk and his surviving crew search for

Spock in... *Star Trek III: The Search for Spock*. Having found him, the fourth film saw the crew time-travelling to 1980s San Francisco in *Star Trek IV: The Voyage Home*. The fifth film, *Star Trek V: The Final Frontier*, saw the crew forced to confront God, the sixth, *Star Trek VI: The Undiscovered Country*, had them lobbying for peace with the Klingons. The studio knew that home video was becoming an increasingly important source of revenue – and that *Star Trek* fans would be avid and loyal consumers of the cassettes. They could also bank on continued goodwill for the series. It was, in other words, the closest thing that the film industry had to a sure thing.

That said, the series scored one notable success, *Star Trek IV: The Voyage Home*, which broke the $100m at the US box office (a rarity in the mid-eighties, not the necessity it's become these days). The film also did something the studio didn't think a *Star Trek* film was capable of doing: it was a mainstream success, being perhaps more popular among the general public than the fans. However, the studio didn't capitalise on this, and the fifth film, *Star Trek V: The Final Frontier*, was a critical and commercial failure.

By the early nineties, the original crew were mostly in their sixties and seventies and looking old, as shows like *The Simpsons* and *Spitting Image* were happy to remind everyone. *The Next Generation* was coming to the end of its seven year run on television and the obvious thing to do was pass the baton to the crew of The Next Generation...

STAR TREK: THE MOVIES
PART I

THE MOTION PICTURE

The refitted Enterprise is sent out to intercept a vast alien object heading for Earth

RELEASED 6 December 1979
WRITER Harold Livingston (story by Alan Dean Foster)
DIRECTOR Robert Wise
GUEST CAST Majel Barrett (Chapel), Persis Khambatta (Ilia), Stephen Collins (Decker), Grace Lee Whitney (Janice Rand), Mark Lenard (Klingon Captain), Billy Van Zandt (Alien Boy), Roger Aaron Brown (Epsilon Technician), Gary Faga (Airlock Technician), David Gautreaux (Branch), John D Gowans (Assistant to Rand), Howard Itzkowitz (Cargo Dock Ensign), Jon Rashad Kamal (Sonak), Marcy Lafferty (Chief Difalco), Michele Ameen Billy (Lieutenant), Terrence O'Connor (Chief Ross), Michael Rougas (Cleary), Susan L Sullivan (Woman), Joshua Gallegos (Security Officer), Leslie C Howard (Yeoman), Ralph Brannen, Ralph Byers, Paula Crist, Iva Lane, Franklyn Seales, Momo Yashima (Crew Members), Jimmie Booth, Joel Kramer, Bill McTosh, Dave Moordigian, Tom Morga, Tony Rocco, Joel Shultz, Craig Thomas (Klingon Crewmen), Edna Glover, Norman Stuart, Paul Webber (Vulcan Masters)

STARDATE 7412.6

Federation station Epsilon Nine monitors the destruction of three Klingon battlecruisers by a vast, mysterious object – an object that is on a direct course to Earth. On Vulcan, Spock is about to complete his Vulcan training, purging the last emotions and connections to his former life... when he, too, senses the object. On Earth, Admiral Kirk arrives at Starfleet Headquarters. He takes command of the Enterprise to investigate the object, alienating the Captain, Will Decker, who resents being usurped and is worried that the Enterprise hasn't been fully tested following its refit. Kirk suffers an early blow when Sonak, his new science officer, is killed, along with another crewman, in a transporter accident. Kirk briefs the crew – they are to intercept the object and try to prevent it reaching Earth. The crew is given 40 minutes to launch. Ilia, the navigation officer, arrives, as does a reluctant Bones. The Enterprise leaves – but there's a problem with the warp drive, which malfunctions, creating a wormhole which sucks in an asteroid that nearly destroys the ship. Spock arrives unexpectedly, and is able to fix the warp drive. The ship soon arrives at the intercept co-ordinates – the Enterprise is visited by a column of plasma energy that tries to drain the databanks, and vanishes with Ilia. Ilia quickly returns... or rather an android copy, sent by the object, V'Ger, to communicate. As Decker tries to get to know the android, Spock leaves the ship without authorisation to attempt a mindmeld. He is thrown into a coma, and rescued by Kirk. Spock explains that he wanted to make contact with a being of pure logic. V'Ger wants to talk to its creator, who it believes is on Earth. V'Ger has reached Earth, and easily deactivates the entire planetary defence system. It will destroy the Earth's 'carbon based units' (lifeforms) unless they fetch the creator. Kirk offers to explain why he can't in person, and Kirk, Spock, Bones, Decker and 'Ilia' make their way to a central structure in the heart of V'Ger. There's an ancient human space probe there, and Kirk discovers it's the Voyager VI... it is V'Ger, enhanced by an unknown machine race. It wants to complete its programming by telling its creator all it has learnt. It refuses to accept that it was created by a human. Spock suggests that it has done all it can with logic, and Decker decides to join with the Ilia android. They merge, and transcend our universe. The Earth is safe. Back in the captain's chair, Kirk orders a shakedown cruise for the new Enterprise.

QUOTES

- 'They gave her back to me, Scotty.' – *Kirk*
- 'Each of us, at some time in our lives, turns to someone: a father, a brother, a god and asks, 'why am I here? what was I meant to be?' – *Spock*

TRIVIA

- This film was based on an idea for the first episode of the proposed *Star Trek II* TV series, *In Thy Image*. The script was written by Harold Livingston, after Alan Dean Foster and Gene Roddenberry's versions were rejected.
- The original budget was $15 million. Paramount calculated that the final cost was closer to $45m, although various people involved in the production have protested that about half that figure includes development costs for aborted projects, including the *Star Trek II* series. In any event, at the time it was thought to be the biggest budget overrun in cinema history.
- It more than made its money back, though – with US box office of around $82m, and about $140 million more worldwide, and a further $140 million from total worldwide video rentals. There has also been significant income from video, LaserDisc and DVDs, particularly given that three distinct versions of the film have been released.
- The novelisation was originally credited to Gene Roddenberry, but recent editions have also credited Alan Dean Foster. In the book, Kirk has a wife (strictly speaking a partner with whom he has a fixed-term marriage contract), Lori Ciani, who is the other crewmember killed in the transporter accident with Sonak.
- Marcy Lafferty, William Shatner's wife at the time, plays DiFalco.
- Persis Khambatta was cast as Ilia during the pre-production of the *Star Trek II* television series.
- With Leonard Nimoy agreeing to play Spock, his *Star Trek II* replacement, Xon, wasn't needed. David Gautreaux preferred to play the commander of the Epsilon station than a couple of scenes as Xon, so the Vulcan character was renamed Sonak.
- The extras playing crewmen in the briefing scene were mostly played by *Star Trek* fans, contacted through the fan clubs. One was George La Forge, a fan with muscular dystrophy, after whom Roddenberry named *The Next Generation* regular Geordi.
- Jerry Goldsmith's theme music for the film would be reused as the theme music for *The Next Generation* (and for *Star Trek V: The Final Frontier*). The reverberating music that strikes up whenever we see V'Ger was created using a specially constructed instrument, the blasterbeam, which used artillery cases being hit by motorised magnets.
- Decker was also to have appeared in *Star Trek II*, but hadn't been cast for the series. Actors who read for the part include Jordan Clark, Frederick Forrest, Lance Henriksen, Art Hindle, Andrew Robinson, (later to play Garak on *Deep Space Nine*), Richard Kelton, Steven Macht (later Gene Roddenberry's first choice to play Picard) and Tim Thomersen. While no one ever says it in the film, the press kit for the film states that Decker was the son of Commodore Decker from *The Doomsday Machine*.
- There are three major versions of this film – the cinematic release (126 minutes), the TV release (138 minutes) which added or extended eleven scenes, and the director's cut (136 minutes), an extensive re-cut of the film for the 2001 DVD release, with a variety of scenes either cut, restored or re-edited, as well as substantial updating of the special effects work (the second disc includes original scenes and scenes from the TV version that didn't make it to the Director's Cut).

RATING

- A film that missed its target audience of *Star Wars* fans by opting for *2001: A Space Odyssey*-style hard science and longeurs. But *Star Trek* has never been so epic, the Enterprise has never looked so solid and impressive, and a cast long-typecast as camp sixties relics all prove they're capable of a radically different take on their familiar roles. It's almost the exact opposite of a 'romp' and it's too cold and sterile to sit easily in the *Star Trek* canon, but the Director's Cut in particular shows a sincere, intelligent, character-based movie. It's seriously under-rated.

STAR TREK II: THE WRATH OF KHAN

STARDATE 8130.3

An old enemy returns for revenge on Kirk – and ultimately he gets it

RELEASED 4 June 1982
WRITER Jack B Sowards (story by Harve Bennett and Jack B Sowards)
DIRECTOR Nicolas Meyer
GUEST CAST Bibi Besch (Carol Marcus), Merritt Butrick (David Marcus), Paul Winfield (Clark Terrell), Kirstie Alley (Saavik), Ricardo Montalban (Khan), Ike Eisenmann (Peter Preston), John Vargas (Jedda), John Winston (Kyle), Paul Kent (Beach), Nicolas Guest (Cadet), Russell Takaki (Madison), Kevin Rodney Sullivan (March), Joel Marstan (Crew Chief), Teresa E. Victor, Dianne Harper, David Ruprecht, Marcy Vosburgh (Computer and radio voices), Judson Earney Scott (Joachim – uncredited)

The Enterprise crew are training a new generation of cadets, including Spock's protégé, Saavik. Meanwhile, the crew of the USS Reliant, including Chekov, are surveying planets looking for one completely devoid of life. Chekov and Captain Terrell beam down to what they think is Ceti Alpha VI, which only has a faint trace of life. Investigating, they are captured by Khan, who was marooned here by Kirk 15 years ago. This is Ceti Alpha V – Ceti Alpha VI exploded, killing most of Khan's followers, including his wife. Khan captures the Reliant using mind control worms and swears revenge on Kirk. He discovers the Reliant was working on a secret project, Genesis, and heads to space station Regula 1, where it is based. When Carol Marcus, head of the project, thinks Starfleet has come to interfere with her project, she sends a message to Kirk, which Khan jams. Kirk takes command of the Enterprise and heads to Regula. On the way, he briefs McCoy and Spock – the Genesis Device can transform planets from lifeless rocks to inhabitable planets in minutes. Or, as McCoy points out, it can wipe clean an entire planet in the same time. As they approach Regula, the Enterprise is attacked and badly damaged by Khan, but just as Khan is about to deliver the killing blow, Kirk lowers the Reliant's shields by remote control and damages it, in turn. The Reliant is forced to retreat. The Enterprise appears crippled, and Kirk orders it to withdraw while he investigates Regula. Kirk's landing party discovers a murdered crew – and that the transporters have been used to beam something to the heart of a nearby, apparently lifeless, asteroid. They follow the trail, and meet up with Carol and David Marcus... David is Kirk's son. Chekov and Terrell attack Kirk, and Terrell kills himself trying to resist Khan. Chekov breaks the hypnotic control, and once again Khan has failed to kill Kirk.

But Khan beams up the Genesis Device, leaving them stranded. Carol shows Kirk the Genesis Cave, an Edenic environment created in the heart of a previously dead world – the proof Genesis works. Kirk reveals he has tricked Khan – the Enterprise isn't as heavily damaged as he'd claimed. They return to the ship, and lure Khan into the nearby Mutara Nebula. Kirk outsmarts Khan, and while the Enterprise loses its warp drive, the Reliant is completely crippled and everyone but Khan is killed. Rather than surrender, Khan activates the Genesis Device. Without warp drive, the Enterprise can't escape in time. Spock hurries to the engine room, and enters a high radiation area. He restores warp power and the Enterprise escapes – but Spock has received a lethal dose of radiation. Spock dies, and is given a full military funeral, his body fired into space, where it falls onto the idyllic planet the Genesis Device has created from the nebula.

QUOTES

- 'Ah Kirk, my old friend. Do you know the Klingon proverb that tells us revenge is a dish that is best served cold? It is very cold in space.' – *Khan*
- 'And I shall have him. I'll chase him 'round the moons of Nibia and 'round Antares Maelstrom and 'round perdition's flames before I give him up!' – *Khan swears revenge and misquotes* Moby Dick
- 'Of my friend, I can only say this: of all the souls I have encountered in my travels, his was the most... human.' – *Kirk's eulogy for Spock*

TRIVIA

- The budget of the film was around $10.5m. The film made $14.5m on its opening weekend in the US (a record at the time), went on to make $85m domestically and another $100m in the rest of the world. It made, ironically enough, less money than the 'flop' first film – but the smaller budget meant it was far more profitable. Total video rentals have been estimated at around $110m. These figures don't include what must be significant sales on video, LaserDisc and DVD.
- Khan and Kirk never actually meet face to face in the film, although they did in the first draft script. Nicholas Meyer – who did an extensive uncredited rewrite – has noted that Elizabeth I and Mary Queen of Scots never met, either, but that didn't stop them being arch-enemies.
- The version most often seen on television has cuts for violence – particularly the discovery of the corpses of the Regula crew – and a couple of very minor additions to the cinematic release. The 2002 Special Edition DVD is a Director's Cut that's uncut for violence but also has the additional scenes from the TV version, as well as substituting different takes and having a couple of minor re-edits in places.
- 'Revenge is a dish best served cold' has passed into common currency, seemingly as a result of this film, and has variously been cited as an old Sicilian or Russian saying. It's actually a translation of a remark ('La vengeance est un plat qui se mange froid') in *Les Liaisons Dangereuse* (1782), by Pierre de LaClos.
- ILM built a special camera for the Genesis Wave effect. An explosion that lasted less than a second was filmed by a high-speed camera (one that took 2,500 frames a second), and the sequence lasts 104 seconds on screen.
- Kim Cattrall, who went on to play Valeris in *Star Trek VI: The Undiscovered Country* (as part of a successful TV and film career), auditioned to play Saavik.
- Bibi Besch's daughter is the actress Samantha Mathis.
- In an early version of the script, the mother of Kirk's child was Janet Wallace from *The Deadly Years*, not Carol Marcus.
- This is a sequel to *Space Seed*. Fans were quick to note that, as that was a first season episode, Chekov wasn't on the Enterprise then, and so Khan shouldn't recognise him. Khan's right-hand man was Joaquin in the TV series, he's become Joachim for the film.
- This is the first *Star Trek* story to establish roughly how far in the future the series is set – the film starts with the caption 'The 23rd Century'. Meyer claims he did this to warn his dad, who'd never watched the show, that it was science fiction!
- According to the official *Star Trek Chronology*, this film takes place in 2285 and *Space Seed* in 2267 (so, 18 years earlier). However, the film explicitly states that it's 15 years since Khan was exiled to Ceti Alpha V. The script specified that Kirk was celebrating his 49th birthday, but the line was dropped – the Chronology suggests it's his 52nd.
- Judson Earney Scott played Joachim, a major supporting role as Khan's right hand man, but a mix-up with his agent meant that he wasn't credited.

RATING

- *Star Trek's* finest hour, an absolutely perfect mix of camp science-fiction action, suspense and raw emotion, with an ending that leaves a lump in the throat. Memorable, quotable, endlessly entertaining, and just as good as ever 20 years on. Not just the zenith of original *Star Trek*, it's a great film in its own right.

STAR TREK III: THE SEARCH FOR SPOCK

The Enterprise officers return to the Genesis Planet to save Spock

RELEASE DATE 1 June 1984
WRITER/PRODUCER Harve Bennett
DIRECTOR Leonard Nimoy

STARDATE 8210.3

Spock is dead. As Kirk mourns, McCoy is taken ill. Back on Earth, Kirk discovers that Spock performed a mind meld with McCoy that transferred his spirit to Bones for safe-keeping. Sarek, Spock's father, insists that they return to the Genesis Planet, which Starfleet has decreed is now off-limits, and retrieve Spock's body so that a final Vulcan ritual can be performed. Starfleet refuses to permit the journey but Kirk, Scott, Sulu, Uhura, Chekov and McCoy steal aboard the Enterprise and leave. Meanwhile, the Klingons have received reports of the Genesis Planet and, led by Captain Kruge, decide to destroy or capture this new weapon. David Marcus and

CAST Robin Curtis (Saavik); Merritt Butrick (David); Phil Morris (Trainee Foster); Scott McGinnis ('Mr. Adventure'); Robert Hooks (Admiral Morrow); Carl Steven (Spock, Age 9); Vadia Potenza (Spock, Age 13); Stephen Manley (Spock, Age 17); Joe W Davis (Spock, Age 25); Paul Sorensen (Merchantship captain); Cathe Shirriff (Valkris); Christopher Lloyd (Kruge); Stephen Liska (Torg); John Larroquette (Maltz); Dave Cadiente (Sergeant); Bob Cummings (Gunner #1); Branscombe Richmond (Gunner #2); Phillip Richard Allen (Captain Esteban); Jeanne Mori (Helm); Mario Marcelino (Communications); Allan Miller (Alien); Sharon Thomas (Waitress); Conroy Gedeon (Civilian Agent); James B Sikking (Captain Styles); Miguel Ferrer (First Officer); Mark Lenard (Sarek); Katherine Blum (Vulcan child); Dame Judith Anderson (High Priestess); Gary Faga (Prison Guard #1); Douglas Alan Shanklin (Prison Guard #2); Grace Lee Whitney (Woman in Cafeteria); Frank Welker (Spock Screams); Teresa E Victor (Enterprise Computer); Harve Bennett (Flight Recorder); Judi Durand (Space Dock Controller); Frank Force (Elevator Voice)

Lieutenant Saavik beam down from the USS Grissom to the Genesis Planet and find Spock's empty coffin and a Vulcan child, traumatised and ageing rapidly. They deduce that the Genesis Planet has brought Spock back to life. The Klingons arrive and destroy the Grissom. On the surface, a landing party takes Marcus, Saavik and Spock captive. The Enterprise arrives and is crippled by the Klingon ship. Kirk tries a bluff to rescue the prisoners, but it backfires and his son is executed. Kirk surrenders the Enterprise but activates the self-destruct sequence. The crew beam to the planet and watch as the Enterprise explodes, taking Kruge's boarding party with it. The officers rescue Spock and Saavik and discover that the Genesis Planet is dangerously unstable and will explode. Kruge, defiant to the end, beams down to the planet and battles Kirk. Kruge falls to his death. The officers take control of the Klingon Bird of Prey and escape just as the Genesis Planet explodes. The Klingon ship races to Vulcan where the fal-tor-pan ceremony is performed, reuniting Spock's spirit and body. Spock is bemused by his friends' attempt to save him. Kirk insists that the needs of the one outweigh the needs of the many.

QUOTES

- 'Klingon bastard, you killed my son. Oh... Klingon bastards, you've killed my son... You Klingon bastard!' – *There was no doubting Kirk's emotion: he was angry*
- 'How many fingers do I have up?'
  'That's not very damned funny.' – *Kirk shows the Vulcan salute to McCoy*
- 'Up your shaft!' – *Scotty to an Excelsior turbolift*
- 'My God, Bones, what have I done?'
  'What you had to do. What you always do. Turned death into a fighting chance to live.' – *Kirk and Bones watch as the Enterprise is destroyed*

TRIVIA

- Harve Bennett wrote 12 drafts of the script in six months. Despite this, he felt that the process was a lot easier than it had been on *Star Trek II: The Wrath of Khan* because the new film was a logical continuation.
- Bennett felt that Kirk had to pay a price for getting Spock back and so wrote in David's murder and the destruction of the Enterprise. Roddenberry was critical of the Enterprise's demise, as were fans at the time, but the scene itself is one of the most effective of the finished film.
- Nimoy was lured back to the franchise by the opportunity to direct. Nimoy and Bennett discussed the first script extensively with Shatner and found him to be a great support. This is the first *Star Trek* 'episode' to be directed by a member of cast, establishing a precedent for later series and movies.
- The villains were originally intended to be the Romulans but studio executives thought that the Klingons were better-known enemies. Unfortunately, a large-scale model of a Romulan ship had already been made by the time the decision was taken and so the Klingons fly a Bird of Prey, as they do in later episodes.
- Shooting began on 15 August 1983 and took 49 days. It was interrupted by a fire at Paramount Studios. William Shatner helped fight the fire and rescued a member of the film crew.
- Sulu was meant to take command of the USS Excelsior in *Star Trek II: The Wrath of Khan* but the storyline was held over to the third film. Sulu doesn't become its captain until *Star Trek VI: The Undiscovered Country*. The voice of the Excelsior's computer was provided by Leonard Nimoy.
- Several Tribbles can be seen in the background in the bar scene where McCoy tries to hire a ship. The bar is the Enterprise sickbay set redressed.
- In the best tradition of *Star Trek II: The Wrath of Khan*, the USS Grissom bridge is a redressed version of the Enterprise bridge set.
- Common cuts in TV versions of the move include the scene where Kruge kills a female mercenary and McCoy's reference to 'that green-blooded son-of-a-bitch'.
- *Star Trek III: The Search for Spock* had a budget of $17m. It made $76m at the US box office and a further $87m worldwide, smaller returns than *Star Trek II: The Wrath of Khan* on almost twice the budget. Rentals add another $90m to this, with sell-through release figures unknown.

RATING

- Ironically, given the subject matter, *The Search for Spock* is a dull and lifeless addition to *Star Trek* on the big screen. One gets the feeling that the intention was to take the original series' tack of focusing on characters and situations rather than the technology or the alien menace. Yet, there is little in terms of characterisation and even less in terms of plot. It is amazing that this hollow rendition manages to fill so much screen time.

STAR TREK IV: THE VOYAGE HOME

STARDATE 8390

The Enterprise crew rescue whales from twentieth century Earth to defeat a twenty-third century threat

RELEASE DATE 26 Nov 1986
WRITERS Steve Meerson, Peter Krikes, Harve Bennett, Nicholas Meyer (story by Leonard Nimoy and Harve Bennett)
DIRECTOR Leonard Nimoy
CAST Jane Wyatt (Amanda), Catherine Hicks (Gillian), Mark Lenard (Sarek), Robin Curtis (Lt. Saavik), Robert Ellenstein (Federation Council President), John Schuck (Klingon Ambassador), Brock Peters (Admiral Cartwright), Michael Snyder (Starfleet Communications Officer), Michael Berryman (Starfleet Display Officer), Mike Brislane (Saratoga Science Officer), Grace Lee Whitney (Commander Rand), Jane Wiedlin (Alien Communications Officer), Vijay Amritraj (Starship Captain), Majel Barrett (Commander Chapel), Nick Ramus (Saratoga Helmsman), Thaddeus Golas (Controller #1), Martin Pistone (Controller #2), Scott DeVenney (Bob Briggs), Viola Stimpson (Lady in Tour), Phil Rubenstein (1st Garbageman), John Miranda (2nd Garbageman), Joe Knowland (Antique Store Owner), Bob Sarlatte (Waiter), Everett Lee (Cafe Owner), Richard Harder (Joe), Alex Henteloff (Nichols), Tony Edwards (Pilot), Eve Smith (Elderly Patient), Tom Mustin (Intern #1), Greg Karas (Intern #2), Raymond Singer (Young Doctor), David Ellenstein (Doctor #1), Judy Levitt (Doctor #2), Theresa E Victor (Usher), James Menges (Jogger), Kirk Thatcher (Punk on Bus), Jeff Lester (FBI Agent), Joe Lando (Shore Patrolman), Newell Tarrant (CDO), Mike Timoney, Jeffrey Martin (Electronic Technicians), 1st Sgt Joseph Naradzay, USMC (Marine Sergeant), 1st Lt Donald W. Zautcke, USMC (Marine Lieutenant)

As the Enterprise officers wait on Vulcan for Spock's rehabilitation, Sarek resists Klingon attempts to extradite Kirk for his actions against them on the Genesis planet. Nevertheless, Starfleet demands that Kirk return to Earth to face nine counts of breaching regulations. Kirk decides to return and Spock accompanies him. When they arrive, Earth is threatened by a deep space probe that threatens to destroy all life on the planet. Spock realises that the probe's communication is whale-song. Kirk and crew decide to travel into Earth's past so they can rescue two whales that might be able to respond to the probe. The officers slingshot the Klingon Bird of Prey into the past and land in twentieth century San Francisco but the ship is damaged in the process. As Uhura and Chekov search for an atomic reactor, McCoy, Scotty and Sulu prepare a tank to transport the whales. Kirk and Spock head to Seaworld and meet Dr Gillian Taylor, who has been told to release two whales into the sea. Kirk tries to explain that Starfleet will take care of the whales but she understandably dismisses his claims. Meanwhile, Chekov and Uhura find an atomic reactor on a US aircraft carrier, the USS Enterprise. As guards close in, Uhura is beamed to safety but Chekov is injured and hospitalised. As Scotty fits a water tank in the Klingon ship, Kirk and Gillian join McCoy in rescuing Chekov from a hospital. McCoy quickly cures Chekov of a condition that would be fatal in the twentieth century. Gillian decides to believe Kirk and they travel out to sea where they beam the whales aboard the Bird of Prey just as a whaler comes into range. Spock makes his calculations and the Klingon ship slingshots back to the twenty-third century. Kirk releases the whales and the probe, finally getting a response to its calls, retreats into deep space. Finally, Admiral Kirk faces the Federation Council and is demoted to Captain and given a new command – the USS Enterprise, NCC-1701-A.

QUOTES

- 'Well, double dumbass on you.' – *Kirk swears*
- 'Back in the sixties he was part of the free speech movement at Berkeley. I think he did a little too much LDS.' – *Kirk explains Spock*
- 'I'm from Iowa. I only work in outer space.' – *Kirk to Gillian*
- 'Admiral! There be whales here!' – *Scotty to Kirk*

TRIVIA

- Happy with the box office returns of *Star Trek III: The Search for Spock*, Paramount executives quickly set in motion plans for a fourth film. It stalled when Shatner insisted on more money, beginning an eight-month stalemate. Pressed, Bennett developed Ralph Winter's idea of a film about the crew before they joined the Enterprise. This story, *Starfleet Academy*, was shelved when Shatner signed for $2m, but would be reconsidered for the fifth movie and has been rumoured ever since.
- Bennett and Nimoy made a conscious decision to make the fourth film lighter. In a bizarre early move, Eddie Murphy was lined up for a major part as a science teacher. Irate fans started a letter writing campaign and the idea was shelved (Murphy made *The Golden Child* instead). As a result, Steve Meerson and Peter Krikes, who developed the Eddie Murphy version, were dropped with their script. They later insisted that much of their story made it to screen and, when Bennett and Meyer were given lead writing credits, Meerson and Krikes pursued their case through the Writer's Guild.
- Rumour has it that an early pitch had Kirk on trial by the Klingons for the events of *Star Trek III: The Search for Spock*. If true, this story, entitled *The Trial of James T Kirk* would seem to have inspired the events of *Star Trek VI: The Undiscovered Country.*
- One of the women who auditioned for the role of Gillian was Kate Mulgrew, who went on to play Captain Janeway in *Voyager.*
- The punk on the bus is played by Kirk Thatcher, an associate producer of the movie, who also composed the song he's playing on his ghetto blaster, *I Hate You*. The song was performed by the band Edge of Etiquette.
- Sulu was to meet one of his ancestors in the film but the scene was never filmed as the child actor cried on set.
- One scene written but never filmed revealed that Saavik has stayed on Vulcan after becoming pregnant when 'comforting' Spock in *Star Trek III: The Search for Spock* as he underwent *Pon farr*. Their child has been alluded to in the novels, but never mentioned in the movies or on television.

- In the hospital, you can hear a call out for Dr Sandy Zober – Leonard Nimoy's wife at the time. Doctor #2 is played by Judy Levitt, Walter Koenig's wife.
- The captain of the USS Saratoga is a woman, the first female captain seen in *Star Trek.*
- Vijay Amitraj, playing another captain, was a world class tennis player who had also appeared in the James Bond film, *Octopussy.*
- The aircraft carrier USS Enterprise was actually the USS Ranger. The Enterprise was at sea when the scenes were shot.
- The film is dedicated to the memories of the crew of the Challenger, the Space Shuttle that exploded on take-off on 28 January 1986.
- *Star Trek IV: The Voyage Home* had a budget of $25m. The movie made $110 m dollars in the USA and $130m worldwide, making it, still to this day, the most financially successful film of the franchise in real terms.

RATING

- A welcome change of style and pace from the third film, *Star Trek IV: The Voyage Home* is *Star Trek*'s most overt foray into comedy. On this score, it stands up reasonably well, even though the core concept is absolutely dreadful. The cast clearly relish the freedom to mess around, with some pleasantly well-handled highpoints (Spock's colourful metaphors) and some despairingly poor low points (Kirk's reaction to Spock swimming with the whales). This is the movie that has the widest appeal, probably because it is the furthest from the show's format. Flippant and throwaway.

STAR TREK V: THE FINAL FRONTIER

STARDATE 8454.1

Spock's brother hijacks the Enterprise and sets off to meet God

RELEASED 9 June 1989
WRITER David Loughery (story by William Shatner, Harve Bennett and David Loughery)
DIRECTOR William Shatner
GUEST CAST David Warner (St. John Talbot), Laurence Luckinbill (Sybok), Charles Cooper (Korrd), Cynthia Gouw (Caithlin Dar), Todd Bryant (Klaa), Spice Williams (Vixis), Rex Holman (J'onn), George Murdock ('God'), Jonathan Simpson (Young Sarek), Beverly Hart (High Priestess), Steve Susskind (Pitchman), Harve Bennett (Starfleet Chief of Staff), Cynthia Blaise (Amanda), Bill Quinn (McCoy's Father), Melanie Shatner (Yeoman)

On the desolate 'Planet of Galactic Peace', Nimbus III, a man has all his pain somehow removed by a charismatic laughing Vulcan. Meanwhile, on Earth, Kirk is scaling a mountain in Yosemite National Park as part of a camping trip with Spock and McCoy. When he slips and falls, Spock saves him using rocket boots. Kirk, Spock and McCoy enjoy each other's company and the humans try to teach Spock campfire songs. On Nimbus III, the mysterious Vulcan, Sybok, marches into the capital, Paradise City, and takes the Federation, Klingon and Romulan ambassadors hostage. He has done it so that a starship will be sent to resolve the situation. The Enterprise, still being readied for service, is chosen, and Kirk and his friends are picked up by Uhura in a shuttle. The Enterprise is soon on its way. Negotiations don't work, and Kirk heads a rescue party that, after Uhura has lured their owners away, arrives in Paradise City on horseback. Sybok's forces prevail, and Kirk and his men are captured. Sybok travels up to the Enterprise with them in a shuttle, just as the young Klingon captain Klaa arrives, spoiling for a fight with Kirk. Kirk's shuttle crashes into the Enterprise's shuttle bay, and in the confusion, Spock gets a chance to shoot Sybok, but refuses. He reveals that he is Sybok's half-brother. As the rest of the crew falls under Sybok's influence – he has the psychic ability to rid people of the guilt of their past – Scotty breaks Kirk, Spock and McCoy from their cell. They learn that Sybok is piloting the ship to the centre of the galaxy, looking for the legendary planet Sha Ka Ree. Sybok is hoping to meet God. Klaa's ship follows. They pass through an energy barrier, and Kirk, Spock and McCoy accompany Sybok down to the planet. They meet 'God', who says he needs a starship... a bemused Kirk asks why. 'God' becomes angry, and Sybok realises he is a fraud – a powerful energy being imprisoned here because he would endanger the galaxy. Sybok is killed, Spock and McCoy get to the shuttle – but Kirk is trapped with the angry 'God' on the planet. Spock convinces the rescued Klingon ambassador to order Klaa to save Kirk, and uses the ship's weapons to destroy 'God'.

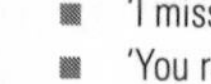

- 'I miss my old chair.' – *Kirk*
- 'You really piss me off, Jim' – *McCoy*
- 'God, I liked him better before he died!' – *McCoy on Spock*
- 'Hello, boys! I've always wanted to play to a captive audience.' – *Uhura 'entertains'*

TRIVIA

- A longstanding arrangement meant that Leonard Nimoy and William Shatner had a 'favoured nation' clause in their contracts – they were on exactly the same money and got exactly the same perks and privileges. As Nimoy had directed the last two movies, Shatner was entitled to direct and he decided to exercise that right for the fifth film.
- William Shatner's original outline, entitled *An Act of Love*, was inspired by television evangelists and saw the Enterprise travel to 'Heaven' only to discover it was really Hell.
- It is established that the Enterprise-A has 23 decks, but when Kirk and company power up a liftshaft, they fly up past Deck 78. It has also been established that the bridge deck is Deck 1, so the lowest deck should have the highest number, but here that is reversed. Less forgivable is a more basic lapse in continuity: the deck numbers appear out of sequence as they fly up past them.

- David Loughery, brought in to write the screenplay, had written the science fiction movie *Dreamscape*. The script went through a number of drafts. The studio felt Shatner's take was 'too dark', preferring the comedic appeal of *Star Trek IV: The Voyage Home*.
- A number of reports said the *Star Trek* novel *Probe* by Margaret Wander Bonanno (with 'significant creative and conceptual contributions' from Gene DeWeese) was based on the original concept for the fifth movie. It's a direct sequel to *Star Trek IV: The Voyage Home*, uncovering the origins of the probe that crippled the Earth. On her website, Bonanno explains that she's unhappy with the book, a reworked version of her *The Music of the Spheres*, but doesn't mention it ever being considered as a movie (and says she started work on it in 1990, which would seem to rule that out).
- Gene Roddenberry wasn't happy with the ambiguity in the original versions of the story and wanted it made clear that the alien wasn't a supernatural being. He later suggested that elements of the film are not 'canon' (so, officially, 'they never happened'). These included Spock having a brother, the planet of galactic peace and the journey to the centre of the galaxy... which leaves, er, the camping trip at the beginning.
- Worried that the production would exceed its $27.8m budget, the original effects-intensive ending was scaled back. In the script, 'God' unleashes an army of rock people and gargoyles that chase Kirk, Spock and McCoy back to the shuttlecraft. Budget cuts led to one 'rockman' being built, but it was decided that the special effect wasn't working, and even that was abandoned.
- It was hoped that Sean Connery would play Sybok, or failing that he'd play 'God' at the end of the film. Connery was working on *Indiana Jones and the Last Crusade* at the time (as were many of the Industrial Light and Magic people who'd normally have done the special effects), and perhaps because of this he turned down the chance. The name Sha Ka Ree is a vestige of that hope, although there are points where Lawrence Luckinbill's performance seems to be a conscious impersonation of Connery (his and Kirk's first meeting, for example).
- Kirk's fall off the mountain at the start of the movie was a stunt performed by Kenny Bates, and it holds the record as the highest fall to appear in a film.
- Todd Bryant, who played Klaa, was keen to learn Marc Okrand's Klingon language for his part, and was later credited as 'Klingon translator' on *Star Trek VI: The Undiscovered Country*.
- The first *Star Trek* film released while a TV show was in production, it came out between second season *The Next Generation* episodes *Samaritan Snare* and *Up the Long Ladder*. In cinema terms, it was released the week before *Ghostbusters II* and *Dead Poets Society*, and two weeks before *Batman*, which at least partially explains the poor box office. The opening weekend gross of $17m compared favourably with the other *Star Trek* films, but its total US box office ended up around $55m, half that of the previous film. That's not to say it was a flop: its total box office ended up at around $125m, not including video rentals and sales, so in cinemas alone the film made around $100m more than it cost to make.

RATING

- One of the worst films ever released by a major studio, the fifth *Star Trek* film has few redeeming features. Bizarrely, it's almost a remake of *The Way to Eden*, one of the poorest original episodes. The special effects work is appalling – it's difficult to believe watching it now that it was made only two years before *Terminator 2* (1991) The money runs out before the film ends, which really doesn't help. Sean Connery might just have saved it, not least because his involvement might have persuaded Paramount to increase the budget (not that it had a low budget – allowing for inflation, it cost exactly the same as the fourth and sixth films, or, to put it another way, roughly the same as the whole of season two of *The Next Generation*), but the whole film feels sloppy and inconsistent. At the very least, they could have spelt Uhura's name right in the end credits. One thing it does well is emphasise the Kirk-Spock-McCoy 'trinity', and how their friendship runs deeper even than family or religion. This gives DeForest Kelly some of his best scenes as Bones, the finest being a flashback to the death of his father. But overall, the original crew are looking old and tired – particularly as the Borg just made their debut over on *The Next Generation*.

STAR TREK VI: THE UNDISCOVERED COUNTRY

STARDATE 9521.6

Kirk is framed for the murder of a progressive Klingon leader

RELEASED 6 December 1991
WRITTEN BY Nicholas Meyer and Denny Martin Flinn (story by Leonard Nimoy, Lawrence Konner and Mark Rosenthal)
DIRECTOR Nicholas Meyer
GUEST CAST Kim Cattrall (Valeris), Brock Peters (Cartwright), Leon Russom (Chief in Command), Kurtwood Smith (Federation President), Christopher Plummer (Chang), Rosana DeSoto (Aztbur), David Warner (Chancellor Gorkon), John Schuck (Klingon Ambassador), Michael Dorn (Klingon Defense Attorney), Paul Rossilli (Kerla), Rober Easton (Klingon Judge), Clifford Shegog (Klingon Officer), W Morgan Sheppard (Klingon Commander),

USS Excelsior, now commanded by Sulu and on a mission in the Beta Quadrant, witnesses an explosion at an energy production facility on the Klingon moon of Praxis. Two months later, Spock convenes a meeting at Starfleet Command to announce that as a result of the accident, the Klingon home world will soon be uninhabitable. The Klingons' progressive leader, Gorkon, is lobbying for peace, and asking the Federation to cut down the Starfleet. Kirk agrees with Admiral Cartwright that this is their chance to defeat the Klingons once and for all, but Spock has already arranged for Kirk to bring Gorkon to Earth for a peace conference – one last mission for the crew and the ship. The Enterprise-A makes the rendezvous, and Kirk hosts an uneasy dinner with Gorkon and his General Chang. Later that night, the Enterprise appears to fire on the Klingon ship, and assassins beam over and shoot Gorkon. Kirk and McCoy beam over to help, but are too late to save Gorkon. They are arrested and sentenced to life imprisonment on Rura Penthe, a barren ice planet. Spock launches a daring mission to save them, while trying to discover the true assassins. He realises the Klingons have a ship that can fire while cloaked – they fired on Gorkon's ship. Kirk and McCoy struggle to survive, and are helped by the shapeshifter Martia. Spock rescues Kirk and McCoy just as Martia is revealed as a traitor

Brett Porter (General Stex), Jeremy Roberts (Excelsior Officer), Michael Bofshever (Excelsior Engineer), Angelo Tiffe (Excelsior Navigator), Christian Slater (Excelsior Communications Officer), Iman (Martia), Tom Morga (The Brute), Todd Bryant (Klingon Translator), John Bloom (Behemoth Alien), Jim Boeke (First Klingon General), Carlos Cestero (Munitions Man), Edward Clements (Young Crewman), Katie Jane Johnston (Martia as a child), Douglas Engalla (Prisoner at Rura Penthe), Matthias Hues (Second Klingon General), Darryl Henriques (Nanclus), David Orange (Sleepy Klingon), Judy Levitt (Military Aide), Shakti (Adc), Michael Synder (Crewman Dax)

and Kirk is about to find out who her masters are. Spock mind-melds with Valeris, discovering that she is part of a conspiracy of hawkish Starfleet officers led by Cartwright and senior Klingons who prefer the certainties of war to the uncertainties of peace. Kirk has come to realise that the peaceful Klingons need to be encouraged. The Enterprise races to Khitomer, where a peace conference is being held, they shoot down Chang's cloaked bird-of-prey with the help of the Excelsior and narrowly prevent the assassination of the Federation president. Cartwright is arrested. The Enterprise is ordered to return to Earth for decommissioning, but Kirk sends it out for one last voyage...

QUOTES

- 'I am constant as the Northern Star.'
  'I'd give real money if he'd shut up.' – *Chang and McCoy*
- 'That was not his knee. Not everybody keeps their genitals in the same place, Captain.' – *Martia, after Kirk has assaulted a fellow inmate*
- 'You've not experienced Shakespeare until you have read him in the original Klingon.' – *Gorkon*
- 'I can't believe I kissed you.'
  'Must have been your lifelong ambition.' – *Kirk objects when Martia turns into a version of him*

TRIVIA

- The studio were initially unsure about making a sixth film, after the disappointment of the fifth and awareness that a couple of the cast were in their seventies. However, the involvement of Nicholas Meyer, the 25th anniversary of the television series, a guarantee that ILM would do the effects work, and the economies of being able to reuse sets and costumes from *The Next Generation*, among other factors, persuaded studio executives to change their mind. Even so, they insisted the budget was cut from $40m to $26m.
- Early rumours were that the sixth film would be called *The Infinite Voyage*, and that the 'hook' of the plot would be Spock falling in love.
- Leonard Nimoy agreed to appear in *The Next Generation* as Spock to form a link to this story. He appeared in the anniversary story *Unification*. The film also features links to the successor series, most notably a cameo by Michael Dorn as an ancestor of Worf.
- Kirstie Alley – now famous from a role in *Cheers* – was approached to reprise Saavik, but she turned the chance down. The almost identical character of Valeris was created, and Kim Cattrall (an established movie actress who would later become famous for *Sex and the City*) was cast.
- Christopher Plummer was happy to play a Klingon on the condition that his make up wasn't as elaborate as it usually was for Klingons, a term Meyer was more than happy to agree to.
- It's more than three years since *Star Trek V: The Final Frontier*, because Sulu's been in command of Excelsior for that long (although McCoy apparently hasn't missed him – he needs telling at the briefing at the start of the film). According to the official Chronology it takes place six years after the last film.
- Sulu's command of the Excelsior followed lobbying for the actor to be given his own command. There's never been any indication that the studio shares Takei's enthusiasm for the idea, but a number of spin-off stories in the comics, books and audios have depicted missions of Sulu's USS Excelsior.
- Sulu's part in this story is revisited in the *Voyager* episode *Flashback*, which confirms that the unnamed 'Excelsior Communications Officer' played by Grace Lee Whitney is her original series character, Janice Rand.
- Christian Slater was delighted to get the chance to play a cameo role in the film as one of Sulu's ensigns (his mother, Mary Jo Slater, was in charge of casting).
- Sigourney Weaver declined the opportunity to play Martia.
- A rare critical success, with most reviewers feeling well-disposed to the original crew's last hurrah, the film did quite well at the box office, making $75M in the US, another $95M worldwide, with another $100M coming in from total video rentals (as ever, these figures don't include video and DVD sales).

RATING

- A clever deconstruction of *Star Trek*'s role in social history as well as an affirmation of its optimistic credo, *Star Trek VI: The Undiscovered Country* is the perfect send-off for the original crew and for Gene Roddenberry. Almost the first film to deal – allegorically, at least – with the collapse of the Soviet Union, Kirk's Kennedy-era hero comes to embrace and personify the new order. It feels like everything has come together – the sense of the Enterprise as a real place where epic adventures take place from the first movie, the camp action of the second, the emotional cost of the third, the humour of the fourth, the sense the crew's a family from the fifth. All the cast get something fun to do, and it's constantly exciting and intriguing. It's a real shame that Valeris was so obviously going to be Saavik; it would have been good to have that character return. This is a film that's unashamedly pitching itself as historically significant, both in *Star Trek* and real terms. Nick Meyer aims high and scores higher, and it's the perfect capstone to a legend. The only thing that could possibly spoil it is if the studio undermined another Meyer film, by deciding to commission a far inferior sequel. Surely they wouldn't?

STAR TREK: THE NEXT GENERATION

SEVEN SEASONS

175 x 44-minute and 2 x 88-minute episodes (1987-94)

REGULAR CAST

Jean-Luc Picard: Patrick Stewart
William Riker: Jonathan Frakes
Data: Brent Spiner
Troi: Marina Sirtis
Worf: Michael Dorn
Geordi La Forge: LeVar Burton
Beverly Crusher: Gates McFadden (Seasons 1, 3-7)
Wesley Crusher: Wil Wheaton (Seasons 1-4)
Natasha 'Tasha' Yar: Denise Crosby (Season 1)
Katherine Pulaski: Diana Muldaur (Season 2)

CREATED BY

Gene Roddenberry

PRODUCERS

Gene Roddenberry (Seasons 1-4)
Rick Berman (Seasons 3-7)
Michael Piller (Seasons 4-7)
Jeri Taylor (Season 7)

THE NEXT GENERATION

By the eighties, the original episodes of *Star Trek* had been running in syndication for more than ten years, and were as popular as ever. *Star Trek: The Motion Picture* had established that there was an appetite for new material, not just reruns. An obvious next step was a new television series.

The mid-seventies had seen an attempt at a *Star Trek II* television show, but as the film series prospered, it became clear that a new *Star Trek* show wouldn't feature Kirk and Spock. It must have occurred to the makers of *Star Trek II: The Wrath of Khan* that there was a potential spin-off featuring David Marcus and Saavik – as Kirk's son and Spock's spiritual daughter, they were the true 'next generation', with the twist that she was captain material, he was the scientist, and they would be lovers (or openly lovers – some fans had long speculated that Kirk and Spock's relationship went beyond friendship). The bigger and better USS Excelsior introduced in *Star Trek III: The Search for Spock* would be the perfect ship for them – particularly as the Enterprise was destroyed in that film. But Leonard Nimoy returned as Spock, the future of the film franchise was assured and David was killed off. If Paramount wanted a TV series, they'd need something completely new.

The debut of *Star Trek: The Next Generation* was announced on 10 October 1986 and publicity stressed that it wouldn't have any of the original cast – only the (all-new) Enterprise. *Star Trek* without Kirk or Spock was seen as a risk, and it was to be an expensive show, with especially high initial costs – even with some reuse of props from the movies, big investments in sets, costumes and special effects were all needed. Unable to get a TV network to commit to more than a few episodes, Paramount instead sold it straight to the syndicated market – the logic being that was where the original series had found its audience... and if the show bombed, the episodes could just be added to the end of the syndication deal for the original series. In the event, it was lapped up by the smaller stations across the country. While the original show had struggled to find an audience the first time round, *The Next Generation* would become the highest-ever rated syndicated show, a massive mainstream success that more than doubled the original series' episode tally of 79 episodes, and followed it onto the silver screen.

A hundred years on, the *Star Trek* universe had changed, as the first episode, *Encounter at Farpoint*, was at pains to make clear. The Klingons were now allies of the Federation, and there were no Vulcans to be seen. Adversaries were all new – the omnipotent Q and the rapacious, whip-wielding Ferengi. More than ever, the Enterprise was a vehicle of exploration and co-operation – the bridge was carpeted, the crew sat round a table to discuss different courses of action, the captain stayed on the ship and sent Away Teams down to planets – and at his side was the ship's counsellor, a psychologist-cum-morale officer who wore civvies. The crewmembers were allowed to have their families on board (although, oddly, only one of the officers, Beverly Crusher, was a family woman), and if it looked like the Enterprise was going to get into a fight, the officers decamped to the 'battle bridge' in the main body of the ship and left the saucer section behind, out of harm's way. The Will Decker-Ilia relationship, a young ambitious officer reunited with an exotic old flame, was recreated with the characters of Will Riker and Troi.

As the series progressed, all this touchy-feely stuff was downplayed. Patrick Stewart's brilliant, layered performance as Jean-Luc Picard came to dominate proceedings. Originally conceived as a wise old man who stayed on the bridge while his hothead of a first officer did all the action stuff, Picard was soon leaping around stories, phaser in hand – tellingly, Picard dominates the *The Next Generation* movies far more than Kirk ever did the original series. That said, all the other regulars got their moment in the sun during *The Next Generation's* run, and it's always more of an ensemble piece than the original. The Ferengi looked more ridiculous than threatening – but were quickly and successfully reinvented as miserly comic relief. The Klingons and Romulans soon re-emerged as serious recurring threats to the security of the Federation, and in the fourth season they were joined by the reptilian Cardassians. The early *The Next Generation* comics and novels, which came out soon after the series debuted, and which were clearly more influenced by the writers' guidelines than the show itself, are a fascinating glimpse at a show where Riker's the main character, the Ferengi are terrifying and formidable opponents and Picard is almost certainly Wesley Crusher's father.

After a first season that struggled to find its feet and often felt like an uneasy politically-correct attempt to recreate one of the sixties' least politically-correct shows, *The Next Generation* began to hit its stride in its second year. A key turning point was *Q Who*, which saw the introduction of the Borg, memorable and worthy foes for the new crew. The third series saw a run of good stories like *The Defector* and *Tin Man*, and spectacular ones like *Yesterday's Enterprise*. By the Borg's second appearance, in *The Best of Both Worlds* at the end of the third season, the show was a phenomenon in its own right, an international hit, and was so ambitious it was beginning to eclipse the new movies, let alone the original series. It never looked back – season four consolidated success with stories like *Future Imperfect* and *The Drumhead* and began to stretch the format with episodes like *Family* and *Data's Day*. Season five saw intelligent stories like *Darmok* and *The Inner Light* jostle with epic Klingon and Romulan space opera in *Redemption* and *Unification* (the latter saw Picard meet Spock). As with all production line television, not every episode was a classic, but the third, fourth and fifth series represent the height of the show, with episodes that were intelligent, ambitious, action-packed and funny. The sixth and seventh series saw a slight dip in quality – the debut of *Deep Space Nine* about halfway through season six must have eaten into the precious time of key people behind-the-scenes. *Chain of Command* is a highlight of season six, and there are fantastic episodes like *Face of the Enemy* and *Tapestry*, but other episodes were beginning to feel lightweight and gimmicky. Season seven has some downright peculiar episodes (*Sub Rosa*, for example), and the unmistakable feeling that the show was winding down, but it rallied for *All Good Things*, the series finale, a celebration of *The Next Generation's* own mythology and history, showing how far the show had come.

Years before most people had even heard of the internet, the new frontier had been colonised by *Star Trek* fans. It's no exaggeration to say that in the late eighties and early nineties a considerable portion of internet bandwidth was taken up with discussion of *The Next Generation.* Fans debated whether the new series was a worthy successor, traded news and trivia, nitpicked episodes, speculated on the future. It's no coincidence that the first film with a dedicated website was *Star Trek: Generations* (the site consisted of about half a dozen publicity photos and a paragraph or two of text, but seemed impossibly futuristic at the time).

Studio estimates in 1994 were that *The Next Generation* had made $511m in advertising revenue over the course of seven series, and a further $650m in merchandising. It means the show made almost $950m profit... and that figure doesn't include video rentals and sales. A 30 second advertising slot during *All Good Things* cost $700,000, easily a record for a syndicated show, and it was and is the highest-rated episode of *Star Trek* in any form. *The Next Generation* ended on a high. After filming of that episode, the cast literally had a week off before starting on *Star Trek: Generations*, the seventh *Star Trek* film, a story overtly designed to hand the movie series over to the next generation.

Ten years on, with the show still being repeated around the world and all seven series available in DVD box sets, *Star Trek: The Next Generation* remains one of Paramount's most valuable properties. It would prove an extremely tough act to follow...

STAR TREK: THE NEXT GENERATION
SEASON ONE

1.1 ENCOUNTER AT FARPOINT

The new Enterprise and its crew investigate a mysterious base on a distant planet

TX 28 September 1987 (two-hour movie)
WRITERS DC Fontana and Gene Roddenberry
DIRECTOR Corey Allen
GUEST CAST Michael Bell (Groppler Zorn), Timothy Dang (Main Bridge Security), John de Lancie (Q), David Erskine (Bandi shopkeeper), Evelyn Guerrero (Ensign), Chuck Hicks (Drugged military officer), Cary-Hiroyuki Tagawa (Mandarin Baliff), DeForest Kelley (McCoy), Colm Meaney (O'Brien), Jimmy Ortega (Torres)

STARDATE 41153.7

The vast new USS Enterprise is sent to far-distant Deneb IV to pick up the last of its bridge officers and to investigate the mysterious Farpoint Station, which seems too advanced to be the product of the native Bandi. *En route*, the ship is surrounded by a huge forcefield, and a man, Q, materialises on the bridge in a range of historical costumes. Q tells Picard that humans shouldn't come this far out into space, as they are too primitive. Picard complains that Q is being judgemental and this gives Q an idea. Picard separates the saucer section, sending it on to Deneb, and prepares to confront Q. He, Troi, Data and Tasha find themselves in a mock-up of a twenty-first century kangaroo court. Picard admits that humanity has been savage in the past – but it has outgrown that now. Q says he will test this, and releases them. Meanwhile, on Deneb, Riker meets the Farpoint administrator, Groppler Zorn, and becomes suspicious. The Enterprise arrives, and the crew begin their investigations – Troi senses great pain, but Zorn denies this. As they continue their search, another ship arrives at Deneb, and begins firing at the surface. Wary of appearing violent in front of Q, Picard instead sends a team to investigate the alien ship. They realise that the alien ship resembles Farpoint, and that it's not a ship... it's a living being capable of manipulating matter. Zorn has captured its mate, and forced it to take the form of Farpoint Station. The Enterprise transmits energy to the creature on the surface, allowing it to return to its native form. The aliens leave. Q grudgingly admits as he leaves that Picard has passed the test – but doesn't agree that the matter of humanity's nature has been settled.

QUOTES

- 'Well it's a new ship – but she's got the right name. Now you remember that, you hear?'
  'I will, sir.'
  'You treat her like a lady, and she'll always bring you home' – *McCoy advises Data*

TRIVIA

- DC Fontana was responsible for the Farpoint story, Gene Roddenberry for the scenes with Q putting humanity on trial. Originally, these were intended to be separate episodes.
- Q was named after Roddenberry's friend Janet Quarton.

- As well as its original two-hour format, this story is also available as two normal-length episodes, with a few minor cuts to scenes to help speed up the pace.
- The decision was made, relatively late in the day, to use the theme from *Star Trek: The Motion Picture* as the title music instead of a new piece. The incidental music for the episode is based on the unused main theme.
- DeForest Kelley's cameo as 'the Admiral' was kept secret, so much so that his character's name isn't referred to in the script or in dialogue.
- Colm Meaney's part is credited as 'conn ensign' and he would be seen again as a security guard in *Lonely Among Us*. He settles down to a semi-regular role as the transporter chief in the second season, and gets a surname, O'Brien, in *The Child*. Officially, although it's an odd set of duties and he has a different rank each time, all these appearances are the same character.

RATING

- An episode with a lot to introduce. The Farpoint plot is fairly light and unsatisfactory, but the Q stuff is more promising. Nowadays, the episode doesn't feel like *The Next Generation* at all and seems very slow. It's an OK start, not a brilliant one.

1.2 THE NAKED NOW

STARDATE 41209.2

The crew are infected by a virus that brings their passions to the surface

TX 5 October 1987
WRITER 'J Michael Bingham' (pseudonym for DC Fontana, story by John DF Black and 'J Michael Bingham')
DIRECTOR Paul Lynch
GUEST CAST Brooke Bundy (Sarah MacDougal), Kenny Koch (Kissing crewman), Benjamin WS Lum (Jim Shimoda), Michael Rider (Transporter Chief), Skip Stellrecht (Crewman)

The Enterprise is scheduled to rendezvous with the science vessel USS Tsiolkovsky which has been investigating the collapse of a star. As they approach, they detect a hatch being blown, killing the entire crew. The Away Team that is sent over discovers a ship-wide party had been taking place. When they return, Geordi falls ill, and infects Tasha and Wesley. Riker and Data discover that Kirk's Enterprise encountered a similar situation, as the crew succumbed to the Psi 2000 virus, and gave into their passions. Wesley takes control of the ship and Tasha seduces Data. Discipline on the ship begins to collapse – and so does the star the Tsiolkovsky was investigating. One of the engineering crew has dismantled the computer – Data uses his abilities to fix it, while Wesley buys some time by pushing the Enterprise away from the star with a repulsor beam. The Enterprise moves out of danger, and Beverly begins to administer the cure to the crew.

QUOTES

- 'Fully functional.' – *Data can deal with Tasha's attentions*

TRIVIA

- A story that's a sequel to the original series' *The Naked Time*.
- While *Encounter at Farpoint* wasn't a true 'pilot' (the series had already been commissioned), and this episode started filming only ten days after the first, a few changes were made – mostly to Troi, who was given a unique outfit and a more severe hairstyle, as well as having her 'telepathic' abilities downgraded to 'empathic' ones. The Riker-Troi romantic subplot was also downplayed. Troi was clearly a problem character for the writers early on: she didn't appear in four episodes (*Hide and Q*, *Datalore*, *11001001* and *Heart of Glory*). Marina Sirtis has since claimed that there was talk of writing her out.
- The ship's Chief Engineer is here Sarah McDougal. The first season would see a number of different engineers; the second season would see Geordi promoted to the role.

RATING

- It's perhaps not as good as the original, but it's a good chance for the cast to show a bit more range and humour than usual and to define their characters. Brent Spiner shines as Data, while Denise Crosby gets a memorable chance to be slinky.

1.3 CODE OF HONOR

STARDATE 41235.25

Proud aliens kidnap Tasha Yar and force her to fight to the death

TX 12 October 1987
WRITER Katharyn Powers and Michael Baron

The Ligonians of Ligon II possess a vaccine for the deadly Anchilles fever affecting Styris IV. The Enterprise is sent to acquire it, and the crew meet Lutan, the leader of the Ligonians. Tasha demonstrates her strength against Lutan's 'secondary' Hagon, and Lutan is impressed. Lutan kidnaps her, telling Picard he'll return her if honour is satisfied. Lutan wants Tasha as his wife, but she'll have to fight to the death with Yareena, Lutan's current 'First One', for the prize. Tasha and

DIRECTOR Russ Mayberry
GUEST CAST Jessie Lawrence Ferguson (Lutan), Michael Rider (Transporter Chief), Karole Selmon (Yareena), James Louis Walker (Hagon)

Yareena fight with poisoned spikes, and Tasha wins. Honour is satisfied. Lutan agrees to give the Enterprise the vaccine – and then Beverly revives the 'dead' Yareena. Yareena passes her favours to Hagon, who'll be the new ruler of the planet.

TRIVIA

- Tasha Yar was originally envisaged as a tough Hispanic character called Macha Hernandez, loosely based on Vasquez from the movie *Aliens*. Marina Sirtis was considered for the role, and Denise Crosby for Troi, until it was decided they should swap. The character's name was briefly Tanya Yar.
- Denise Crosby is Bing Crosby's granddaughter.
- The music for this episode was composed by *Star Trek* veteran Fred Steiner.

RATING

- An atrocious story that pleads political correctness while exemplifying racism and sexism, *Code of Honor* would have been dated if it had been part of the original sixties series, was terrible when first broadcast and has got worse with age.

1.4 THE LAST OUTPOST

STARDATE 41386.4

The Enterprise discovers more about the mysterious Ferengi

TX 19 October 1987
WRITER Herbert Wright (story by Richard Krzemien)
DIRECTOR Richard Colla
GUEST CAST Jake Dengel (Mordoc), Mike Gomez (Tarr), Darryl Henriques (Portal), Armin Shimerman (Letek), Tracey Walter (Kayron)

The Enterprise pursues a Ferengi vessel that's stolen a T9 energy converter to the Delphi Ardu system. The Enterprise becomes trapped in an energy beam, which the crew assume is a Ferengi weapon – until the Ferengi contact them, asking to be released. Research reveals that the planet below used to belong to the extinct Tkon Empire. As the power drain becomes critical, the Enterprise and Ferengi send parties down to the planet to investigate. The Ferengi attack the Away Team but a mysterious figure, Portal, appears, claiming to be the Guardian of the Tkon Empire. The Ferengi try to paint the Enterprise crew as raiders, but Riker convinces Portal that they pose no threat and the ships are released on the condition that the Ferengi return the stolen energy converter.

TRIVIA

- The name Ferengi might derive from the old Asian word 'firinghee', a disparaging term used to describe European traders.
- It's made clear here that the Federation have never seen a Ferengi – this runs counter to the impression given later that the Ferengi have been traders in and around the Federation for centuries. The earliest contact with the Ferengi has now been backdated to Archer's time (*Acquisition*).
- The first Ferengi seen is played by Armin Shimerman, who'd go on (after a number of other roles in *The Next Generation*) to play a Ferengi regular character, Quark, in *Deep Space Nine*.
- Geordi seems to fulfil the function of Chief Engineer despite not having been given the role. Sarah McDougal has vanished.

RATING

- In which the ultimate capitalists fall victim to hype and bad marketing... the Ferengi design makes them look surprisingly vicious here, but the script paints the Ferengi as little more than caricatures and makes it impossible to see them as a credible threat.

1.5 WHERE NO ONE HAS GONE BEFORE

STARDATE 41263.1

A warp drive experiment moves the Enterprise beyond space

TX 26 October 1987
WRITERS Diane Duane and Michael Reaves
DIRECTOR Rob Bowman
GUEST CAST Charles Dayton (Crewman), Victoria Dillard (Ballerina), Stanley Kamel (Kosinski), Eric Menyuk (Traveler), Herta Ware (Picard's Mother), Biff Yeager (Argyle)

Propulsion expert Kosinski arrives on the Enterprise with a mysterious alien assistant, from Tau Ceti C, to test the ship's warp engines. They run a new procedure, break the Warp Ten boundary and end up two galaxies and 300 years from home. The crew hallucinate – Picard talks to his dead mother. They are in a region of space where imagination is as real as matter. Wesley notices that the presence of the mysterious alien, the Traveler, is somehow responsible for the huge speed, and gets him to return them home. Before he fades away, the Traveler tells Picard that Wesley has great potential, but must be allowed to develop. Picard promotes Wesley to 'Acting Ensign'.

TRIVIA

- Eric Menyuk was second choice to play Data. A rumour that's persisted – despite being contradicted by some sources – is that Patrick Stewart was originally called in to audition as the android (for a long time, Gene Roddenberry had his heart set on Stephen Macht from *Cagney and Lacey* as 'Julien' Picard, the captain).
- The concept for the story closely resembles Diane Duane's *Star Trek* novel *The Wounded Sky*. Maurice Hurley extensively rewrote the script, which presented quite a special effects challenge for new director Rob Bowman.
- The Chief Engineer is Argyle in this episode.

RATING

- An odd episode that feels ambitious and intimate at the same time. It doesn't make much sense, but does have an edge and a sense of danger missing from many of this type of 'surreal' story. And Kosinski is wonderfully arrogant.

1.6 LONELY AMONG US

STARDATE 41249.3

Two opposing worlds both lobby for Federation membership

TX 2 November 1987
WRITER DC Fontana (story by Michael Halperin)
DIRECTOR Cliff Bole
GUEST CAST John Durbin (Ssestar), Kavi Raz (Singh)

The peoples of the two planets of the Beta Renna system, the Anticans and the Selay, have applied for Federation membership, but they are hostile to each other. The Enterprise is to conduct negotiations, but is hit by a mysterious energy cloud. An energy being takes control of Worf and Beverly before entering Picard. The being intends to merge Picard with the energy cloud, creating a new life-form. Picard beams into the cloud, but Riker and Data reform him using the transporters. He is unharmed, and has no memory of his possession.

RATING

- A fairly straightforward and inconsequential story, but one that takes itself far too seriously.

1.7 JUSTICE

STARDATE 41255.6

Wesley is sentenced to death by a strict alien culture

TX 7 November 1987
WRITER Worley Thorne (story by 'Ralph Willis' – pseudonym for John DF Black, and Worley Thorne)
DIRECTOR James L Conway
GUEST CAST Brenda Bakke (Rivan), Josh Clark (Conn), David Q Combs, Richard Lavin (Mediators), Judith Jones (Girl), Jay Louden (Liator), Brad Zerbst (Medical Officer), Eric Matthews, David Michael Graves (Boys)

An Away Team beams down to Rubicon III, an idyllic world of beautiful, scantily-clad people, the Edo. Meanwhile the Enterprise is hailed by an unknown ship that warns them not to 'interfere with my children below'. Wesley damages a flowerbed – and is sentenced to death. Perfection on Rubicon has been obtained by establishing random 'punishment zones' where even minor crimes carry the death penalty. Rivan, one of the Edo, is taken to the Enterprise, but the mysterious ship orders them to return her to the surface. Rivan tells them the ship is their god. Picard communicates with the ship, telling it that true justice takes circumstances into account. The 'god' is persuaded, and Wesley is released.

QUOTES

- 'Nice planet.' – *Worf, surrounded by half-naked Edo*

TRIVIA

- The original story was set in an urban dystopia, Llarof, where all crime was punishable by death. Worley Thorne's rewrite transformed the planet into a rural idyll, while Gene Roddenberry added the alien spacecraft watching over the Edo.
- This saw the first major location shoot for the series (a couple of holodeck shots in *Encounter at Farpoint* were filmed on location), at the Tillman Water Reclamation Plant in Van Nuys.

RATING

- The type of story that gave the original show a bad name, *Justice* thinks it's a profound statement about the nature of crime and punishment, but it's a silly premise with, if you'll pardon the pun, a juvenile execution.

1.8 THE BATTLE

STARDATE 41723.9

A Ferengi wants revenge on Picard for the death of his son

TX 14 November 1987
WRITER Herbert Wright (story by Larry Forrester)
DIRECTOR Rob Bowman
GUEST CAST Frank Corsentino (Bok), Robert Towers (Rata), Doug Warhit (Kazago)

DaiMon Bok of the Ferengi demands the Enterprise meets him in the Xendi Sabu system. Once there, they find an old Federation ship – Picard's last command the USS Stargazer, a 'gift' from Bok to Picard, who he calls 'the hero of the Battle of Maxia'. Nine years ago, when he commanded the Stargazer, Picard destroyed a ship that attacked him at Maxia Zeta. This was captained by Bok's son. Picard apologises to Bok, but says he was defending himself from an unprovoked attack. Picard leads an Away Team to the Stargazer and discovers a spherical device that begins to affect his mind, making him believe he is fighting the Battle of Maxia again – and he targets the Enterprise. Every Starfleet Academy cadet is taught the brilliant 'Picard Maneuvre' he used to win the original battle, so Riker is able to anticipate it. Riker contacts the Ferengi, who have mutinied against Bok's unprofitable scheme for revenge. Picard manages to destroy the sphere and escape its influence.

TRIVIA

- A number of scenes on the Ferengi ship that filled in details about their culture were dropped, as it was felt the Ferengi weren't working as the major villains they'd been designed to be.

RATING

- The first *The Next Generation* episode to really work on all levels, even managing to rehabilitate the Ferengi. It's the first of many *tour de force* performances from Patrick Stewart. A good, solid, dark episode.

1.9 HIDE AND Q

STARDATE 41590.5

Riker is granted the power of the Q

TX 23 November 1987
WRITER 'CJ Holland' (pseudonym of Maurice Hurley) and Gene Roddenberry (story by 'CJ Holland')
DIRECTOR Cliff Bole
GUEST CAST John de Lancie (Q), Elaine Nalee (Survivor), William A Wallace (Wesley Crusher at 25)

The entire crew, except Picard, are transported to a planet by Q, who wants to see if Riker can 'resist temptation'. The crew are attacked by savage aliens in Napoleonic uniforms. Q grants Riker the powers of the Q Continuum, saying that it will increase mutual understanding between the humans and the Q. Riker uses his power to transport the crew back to the ship. Picard asks Riker not to use his powers – if he does, he must leave Starfleet and join the Q. Riker regrets agreeing when there's a disaster on a mining colony – he could have prevented great suffering. Riker grows arrogant, and decides to leave – first granting his friends' greatest wishes. When Data refuses, Riker realises that he must renounce Q's gift.

QUOTES

- 'I know *Hamlet*, and what he might say with irony, I say with conviction: "What a piece of work is a man! How noble in reason! How infinite in faculty! In form, in moving, how express and admirable. In action how like an angel. In apprehension, how like a god."
'Surely you don't see your species like that, do you?'
'I see us one day becoming that, Q. Is it that which concerns you?' – *Picard spells out Gene Roddenberry's humanism to Q*

TRIVIA

- The original story was set on the Q's home planet, which was also the location of the natural disaster. Maurice Hurley used his pseudonym because he didn't like the changes.
- Riker gives Geordi his sight, makes Wesley an adult (one who looks nothing like him!) and gives Worf a mate. Data declines the chance to become human.
- A scene where Wesley gets a spear through his chest was cut by the BBC on first showing, but not from the repeats.

RATING

- A story that feels like it's from a different series when you watch it now – it's all Q, Riker and Wesley. The aliens in Napoleonic uniforms are good, the planet set is pretty bad. An effective, if obvious, morality play about getting power and your heart's desire.

1.10 HAVEN

STARDATE 41294.5

Deanna Troi prepares for her arranged marriage

TX 30 November 1987
WRITER Tracy Tormé (story by Tracy Tormé and Lan O'Kun)
DIRECTOR Richard Compton
GUEST CAST Majel Barrett (Lwaxana Troi), Raye Birk (Wrenn), Robert Ellenstein (Steven Miller), Anna Katarina (Valeda Innis), Danitza Kingsley (Ariana), Rob Knepper (Wyatt Miller), Nan Martin (Victoria Miller), Michael Rider (Transporter Chief), Armin Shimerman (Wedding Box – uncredited), Carel Struycken (Mr Homn)

The Enterprise arrives at the paradise planet Haven and Troi is sent a Betazed greeting box to announce her wedding to Wyatt Miller. It's a marriage arranged, in accordance with Betazed tradition, by her mother, Lwaxana. Deanna meets Wyatt and his family for the first time, and Wyatt tells her he's always dreamed of a certain woman – he thought it was Deanna, but it isn't. A Tarellian starship approaches Haven – the Tarellians were thought to be wiped out by biological weapons, and have a terrible disease. They beg for help as Haven is meant to have miraculous healing properties, but it becomes clear that they merely want to die in a peaceful place. The Tarellian woman making the announcement is the woman of Wyatt's dreams. He makes an unauthorised transport to the Tarellian ship, and pledges to try to cure them. Deanna admires his courage and wishes him well.

TRIVIA

- Majel Barrett, of course, had been with *Star Trek* since the beginning.
- This is the first script Tracy Tormé, son of entertainer Mel Tormé, who would go on to become a stalwart of *The Next Generation* and help to create *Sliders*.

RATING

- An odd story from a show still trying to find its feet. The resolution of the 'arranged marriage' plot is obvious the moment Wyatt mentions the woman of his dreams, but it's still breathtakingly convenient for all concerned.

1.11 THE BIG GOODBYE

STARDATE 41997.7

Picard becomes trapped in a Dixon Hill holodeck fantasy

TX 11 January 1988
WRITER Tracy Tormé
DIRECTOR Joseph L Scanlan
GUEST CAST Rhonda Aldrich (Madeline), Carolyn Allport (Jessica Bradley), Gary Armagnal (McNary), William Boyett (Dan Bell), Eric Cord (Thug), Mike Genovese (Desk Sergeant), Harvey Jason (Felix Leech), Dick Miller (Vendor), David Selburg (Whalen), Lawrence Tierney (Cyrus Redblock)

The Enterprise is on a diplomatic mission to the Jarada, who are obsessed with protocol and insist on being addressed precisely in their own complex language. Picard finds the preparations stressful, and Troi suggests he relaxes on the holodeck. Picard chooses to recreate the 1930s pulp detective Dixon Hill, and enjoys the experience so much he invites Beverly, Data and crewman Whalen along. While they are there, the Jarada contact the Enterprise and demand to speak to Picard – but there's a malfunction and Riker can't communicate with the holodeck. Oblivious, Picard and co continue to explore the world of Dixon Hill chasing mobster Felix Leech – until Whalen is shot, and seriously injured. They realise the holodeck is malfunctioning. Geordi and Wesley open the holodeck, just in time to save Picard and Beverly from Leech's boss, Cyrus Redblock. Picard hurries to the bridge and successfully addresses the Jarada.

TRIVIA

- This episode won an Emmy for Series Costuming, and Tracy Tormé won the prestigious Peabody Award for the script.
- Tormé wanted the holodeck scenes to be in black and white, and this was seriously considered at one point.
- Lawrence Tierney would later play Joe Cabot in *Reservoir Dogs*.

RATING

- The first of many, many practically identical holodeck stories in *The Next Generation, Deep Space Nine* and *Voyager*, this at least had novelty value and the fans loved it at the time. It's fun, but seems a little indulgent, both for the characters and the writers.

1.12 DATALORE

STARDATE 41242.4

Data discovers Lore, his evil brother

The Enterprise investigates Omicron Theta, the colony where Data was discovered 26 years before by the USS Tripoli, just after the human colonists had been wiped out by an unknown force. Data discovers a

TX 18 January 1988
WRITER Robert Lewin and Gene Roddenberry (story by Robert Lewin and Maurice Hurley)
DIRECTOR Rob Bowman
GUEST CAST Brent Spiner (Lore), Biff Yeager (Argyle)

laboratory containing parts for another completed android, built by the cyberneticist Noonien Soong. The android is reassembled on the Enterprise, and announces that it is Lore, an improved version of Data. He seems to have emotions, and to be rather arrogant. He soon admits he was built before Data, and was so perfect the colonists wanted him deactivated. Lore reveals that the colonists were wiped out by a Crystalline Entity, a massive space-dwelling creature. Lore incapacitates Data and takes his place, but Wesley notices, and reactivates the real Data – together, they prevent Lore from using the Crystalline Entity to destroy the Enterprise. Lore is transported into space.

TRIVIA

- The original story had Data falling for a female android. It was Spiner who suggested that Data might have an evil twin. A lot is learned about Data's origins in this story, and the revelation that he was built by a human scientist contradicts the original concept for the character: that he was built by an unknown race of aliens who wanted to use him to learn about humanity (much as V'Ger used the android version of Ilia in *Star Trek: The Motion Picture*).
- Noonien Soong, like Khan Noonian Singh, was named after an army buddy of Gene Roddenberry.
- Lore returns in *Brothers* and *Descent*, and the Crystalline Entity reappears in *Silicon Avatar*.

RATING

- Despite the hoary premise of the 'evil twin', this is a strong episode, with Brent Spiner working hard to impress in a dual role.

1.13 ANGEL ONE

STARDATE 41636.9

Federation citizens have crashed on a world run by women

TX 25 January 1988
WRITER Patrick Barry
DIRECTOR Michael Rhodes
GUEST CAST Leonard John Crowfoot (Trent), Sam Hennings (Ramsey), Patricia McPherson (Ariel), Karen Montgomery (Beata)

The Enterprise is looking for survivors from a crashed freighter, the Odin. They arrive at Angel I, a planet run by a matriarchy. Riker, particularly, is out of place as they attempt diplomacy. The survivors are found, but they want to stay, as do their wives, women from Angel I who are rebelling against the oppressive female regime. As a virus ravages the Enterprise, Riker is unable to beam the rebels to safety and they are all sentenced to death. Riker reaches a compromise – the rebels are exiled to a remote part of the planet. The Enterprise has recovered from the virus, and heads off to investigate reports of a Romulan incursion into Federation space.

TRIVIA

- Patrick Barry's original idea was to use the female-ruled planet as a metaphor for apartheid. This slowly mutated until it became a rather bizarre Prime Directive story.

RATING

- The story that does for feminism what *Code of Honor* did for race equality. That isn't a compliment. A truly lousy episode, coming at a point when the show had seemed to be finding its feet.

1.14 11001001

STARDATE 41365.9

The Enterprise is hijacked, while Riker falls in love on the holodeck

TX 1 February 1988
WRITER Maurice Hurley and Robert Lewin
DIRECTOR Paul Lynch
GUEST CAST Katy Beyer (01), Ron Brown (Drummer), Gene Dynarski (Quinteros), Alexandra Johnson (10), Iva Lane (00), Carolyn McCormick (Minuet), Kelli Ann McNally (11), Abdul Salaam el Razzac (Bass Player), Jack Sheldon (Piano Player)

The Enterprise is at Starbase 74 to upgrade its computer, a task performed by Bynars, small creatures that communicate in binary. Riker immerses himself in a holodeck simulation of a jazz bar, where he falls for Minuet, the most realistic hologram he's ever seen. Picard is also amazed by the Bynars' upgrade. The Bynars, though, fake a magnetic shield breakdown and steal the ship from its dock, with only Picard and Riker onboard. Picard threatens to self-destruct the ship, and the Bynars reveal they need the Enterprise's computer memory to save their species from an electromagnetic pulse. Picard helps them.

TRIVIA

- The title is binary notation (the base ten equivalent being 201). It's all four of the Bynars' names in a row. Indeed, if Bynars limit themselves to two digit names, it's every possible Bynar name, so it's just as well there aren't five of them!

RATING

- One of the better episodes of the season that at least has a couple of good twists, exciting sequences and is light on the moralising.

1.15 TOO SHORT A SEASON

STARDATE 41309.5

A Federation negotiator has a number of dark secrets

TX 8 February 1988
WRITER Michael Michaelian and DC Fontana (story by Michael Michaelian)
DIRECTOR Rob Bowman
GUEST CAST Marsha Hunt (Anne Jameson), Michael Pataki (Karnas), Clayton Rohner (Mark Jameson)

The Enterprise takes the frail Admiral Jameson to Mordan IV, a planet he ended a hostage situation on 40 years before, and where a similar situation has developed again. Jameson is recovering from Iverson's Disease, and also admits he's using an illegal rejuvenation technique from Cerebus II which is making him younger by the day. He also confesses that he solved the hostage problem by giving the terrorists Federation weapons – he got round the Prime Directive by giving the other side the same weapons. Karnas, the leader of the planet, has lured him to the planet for revenge. Jameson decides to go in all guns blazing, but Karnas ambushes him. Karnas watches Jameson die from his illness, then frees the hostages.

TRIVIA

- Originally a story tackling the male menopause and treating the rejuvenation as a metaphor for Alzheimer's Disease (Jameson would 'regress' to the point where he couldn't remember his wife), Fontana added the terrorism plot.

RATING

- Dodgy make-up and a talky script make for a dull episode, despite a fascinating premise.

1.16 WHEN THE BOUGH BREAKS

STARDATE 41509.1

The Aldeans kidnap a group of Enterprise children

TX 15 February 1988
WRITER Hannah Louise Shearer
DIRECTOR Kim Manners
GUEST CAST Ivy Bethune (Duana), Jessica Bova, Vanessa Bova (Alexandra), Connie Danese (Toya), Jerry Hardin (Radue), Paul Lambert (Melian), Michele Marsh (Leda), Dan Mason (Accolan), Brenda Strong (Rashella), Jandi Swanson (Katie), Dierk Torsek (Dr Bernard), Phillip N Waller (Harry Bernard)

The Enterprise stumbles across the mythical planet Aldea, which has been hidden by an enormous cloaking device. The Aldeans beam Riker, Beverly and Troi to the surface, where their leader Ranue explains his people are infertile and that he'll exchange technology for the ship's children. The Enterprise officers are horrified and refuse, so the Aldeans kidnap some children, including Wesley, and fling the Enterprise many light years away from the planet. Wesley takes charge of the children and orders them to passively resist. He discovers the utopian Aldea is controlled by the Custodian, a computer, and that the infertility is a side-effect of the cloaking device. The Aldeans return the children to the Enterprise.

TRIVIA

- Wil Wheaton's brother and sister Jeremy and Amy have non-speaking roles as two of the children taken hostage.
- Jerry Hardin is a stalwart of US television, perhaps better known as Deep Throat in *The X-Files*.

RATING

- It's another first season story that feels dull and old-fashioned. An OK episode, albeit one that feels like it was commissioned because someone was worried that the show wasn't doing enough with the 'family' concept.

1.17 HOME SOIL

STARDATE 41463.9

Federation terraformers unwittingly anger microscopic aliens

TX 22 February 1988
WRITER Robert Sabaroff (story by Karl Guers, Ralph Sanchez and Robert Sabaroff)
DIRECTOR Corey Allen
GUEST CAST Carolyne Barry (Engineer), Walter Gotell (Kurt Mandl), Elizabeth Lindsey (Luisa Kim), Gerard Prendergast (Bjorn Benson), Mario Roccuzzo (Arthur Malencon)

The Enterprise arrives at Velara III, a planet being made Earth-like by Federation terraforming engineers. Luisa Kim, the project leader, greets the Away Team shortly before a laser beam malfunction kills her colleague Malencon. Geordi and Data begin a full investigation and discover native life – tiny crystals that can combine to become sentient – which they christen 'the microbrain'. One of the scientists, Mandl, can't accept that it counts as life, but once on board the Enterprise samples of the microbrain quickly grow and take over the ship's systems, initiating contact with the crew. They tell Picard that the engineers have been draining vital salt water and that it declares war on humanity. Picard regains control by shutting down the ship's power, returns the microbrain to Velara III, then places the planet in quarantine to protect its ecosystem.

QUOTES

- 'Ugly bags of mostly water.' – *the microbrain's description of humans*

TRIVIA

- Walter Gotell played M's KGB counterpart General Gogol in all the James Bond films between *The Spy Who Loved Me* (1977) and *The Living Daylights* (1987).

RATING

- Extremely dull and cheap-looking, *The Next Generation* takes a step backwards. The weakest episode of the show's weakest season.

1.18 COMING OF AGE

STARDATE 41416.2

Wesley sits his exams while the Enterprise is investigated by Admiral Quinn

TX 14 March 1988
WRITER Sandy Fries
DIRECTOR Michael Vejar
GUEST CAST Estee Chandler (Iliana Mirren), Ward Costello (Gregory Quinn), Stephen Gregory (Jake Kurland), Robert Ito (Chang), Brendan McKane, Wyatt Knight (Technicians), John Putch (Mordock), Daniel Riordan (Rondon), Robert Schenkkan (Dexter Remmick), Tasia Valenza (T'Shanik)

Wesley beams down to Relva VII to sit his Starfleet Academy entrance exams. Admiral Quinn and his assistant Remmick beam up to inspect the ship. It becomes clear they are investigating Picard for violating the Prime Directive. When they fail to discover any evidence of this, Quinn confides in Picard that there's a conspiracy in Starfleet, and asks Picard to become Commandant of Starfleet Academy to root out the problem. Picard declines. Wesley narrowly fails his exam, losing to Mordock, the first Benzite to be accepted. Picard confides in him that he only got in on his second attempt, and Wesley vows to try again.

TRIVIA

- A show with a couple of firsts: the first time we see the new Enterprise's shuttlecraft, and the first time there's a speaking Vulcan character (previously a couple of Vulcan extras had been glimpsed).
- Quinn and Remmick return in *Conspiracy*, in which we learn more about the problems at Starfleet HQ.

RATING

- An OK episode, with the welcome introduction of some running plotlines and an attempt to make Wesley's role a bit more formal.

1.19 HEART OF GLORY

STARDATE 41503.7

Three renegade Klingons threaten the Enterprise

TX 21 March 1988

The Enterprise locates the freighter Batris in the Neutral Zone. Three Klingons are onboard, one of whom dies in sickbay. The Klingon commander, Korris, confides in Worf that he is worried that the alliance with the Federation is destroying his people's warrior spirit.

WRITER Maurice Hurley (story by Herbert Wright and DC Fontana)
DIRECTOR Rob Bowman
GUEST CAST Vaughn Armstrong (Korris), Robert Bauer (Kunivas), David Froman (K'Nera), Charles H Hyman (Konmel), Dennis Madalone (Ramos), Brad Zerbst (Nurse)

Korris wants Worf to join him. Picard learns this from K'Nera, captain of a Klingon ship that comes alongside the Enterprise. The renegades are arrested, but escape. One of the Klingons, Konmel, is killed, but Korris has a disruptor, and threatens to destroy the dilithium chamber (and the ship). Worf tries to talk Korris down, but ends the situation by shooting him. There was no honour in Korris' actions.

TRIVIA

- One of the more intriguing aspects of *The Next Generation* was the exact nature of the relationship between the Federation and the Klingons. In *Hide and Q*, Q had said the Federation had 'defeated' the Klingons, but this story started to hint that events were more subtle – although, in a move that's never repeated, the Klingon ship here has Federation emblems on it.
- Model work of the Klingon ship from the first *Star Trek* film was reused here (as it had been in *Star Trek II: The Wrath of Khan*).

RATING

- An action-packed episode, one that shakes up an often staid and dull first season. That said, it shares a number of faults that plagued the season – it's a straightforward, painfully po-faced episode.

1.20 THE ARSENAL OF FREEDOM

STARDATE 41798.2

The Enterprise becomes trapped by ancient weapons left by alien arms dealers

TX 11 April 1988
WRITER Richard Manning and Hans Beimler (story by Maurice Hurley and Robert Lewin)
DIRECTOR Les Landau
GUEST CAST George de la Pena (Orfil Solis), Julia Nickson (Lian T'Su), Marco Rodriguez (Paul Rice), Vyto Ruginis (Logan), Vincent Schiavelli (The Peddler)

The USS Drake has disappeared in the Lorenze Cluster, and the Enterprise is sent to the planet Minos to investigate. Minos is the home of arms dealers, and the ship receives an automated message inviting them to trade. Riker, Data and Tasha beam down and meet Captain Rice of the Drake... but soon realise he's a holographic replica. The Away Team is fired on by floating robots. Picard leads another Away Team to help – and the Enterprise comes under attack from orbital defences. Geordi withdraws the ship and separates the saucer section. Picard finds a computer which offers him the ultimate weapon – Echo Papa 607. Picard realises that this weapon wiped out its creators. He feigns interest in buying the weapon – and the deadly demonstration ends. The Enterprise arrives back at Minos and destroys the orbital defence mechanism.

QUOTES

- 'It's a good ship.' – *Riker tests the fake Paul by claiming he's now the Captain of the USS Lollipop*

TRIVIA

- This is the last time we see a saucer separation until *The Best of Both Worlds, Part II* – not only was the effect quite expensive, it was felt it slowed down the action. So another idea that was pushed in *Encounter at Farpoint* as a major part of the new format was quietly dropped.
- Another first season storyline was also dropped – this story was to have revealed Picard and Beverly's love for each other. The early episodes hinted that Picard and Beverly had been more than friends when she was married to Jack, with possible implications for Wesley's paternity. Later episodes would continue to suggest that they had strong feelings for each other – these are finally addressed in *Attached*.

RATING

- The message of the episode, that dealing arms is a Bad Thing which might end up doing harm, isn't exactly profound. But at least this is a fast-paced episode in an often sedentary first season.

1.21 SYMBIOSIS

STARDATE UNKNOWN

The Enterprise has to deal with two factions after the same addictive drug

The Enterprise is investigating solar magnetic field activity in the Delos system when it receives a distress signal from an Ornaran ship, the captain of which, T'Jon, seems confused and not competent to perform his duty. As their ship plummets into a planet's atmosphere, its crew prefer to beam a barrel over before saving themselves, and

TX 18 April 1988
WRITER Robert Lewin, Richard Manning and Hans Beimler (story by Robert Lewin)
DIRECTOR Win Phelps
GUEST CAST Merritt Butrick (T'Jon), Kimberly Farr (Langor), Richard Lineback (Romas), Judson Scott (Sobi), Kenneth Tigar (Margan – uncredited)

only four of the six survive – two from Ornara, two from neighbouring Brekka. The barrel contains felicium, a 'medicine' that both groups claim as their own. As the Ornarans get increasingly agitated, Beverly realises that the substance is a narcotic. The entire economy of Brekka is set up to export felicium to Ornara, a planet that's now helpless – the Sanction was the last ship capable of making the journey. Both planets are equally dependent on the trade. Picard can't intervene in this arrangement because the Prime Directive prevents it, but equally he decides it means he can't repair their ships – the two races will have to abandon their arrangement.

TRIVIA

- Merritt Butrick played David Marcus, Kirk's son, in *Star Trek II: The Wrath of Khan* and *Star Trek III: The Search for Spock.* The credits misspell his name as 'Merrit'. By coincidence, Judson Scott was also in *Star Trek II: The Wrath of Khan*, and he had also been the victim of a mix-up in the credits.
- The production order of the first season wasn't the same as the broadcast order, and this was the last story Denise Crosby filmed (and in the last scene she shot, in the cargo bay, she's waving goodbye in the background). This is presumably why *The Arsenal of Freedom* is, according to the stardate, set after *Skin of Evil*, even though Tasha is in it!

RATING

- A heavy-handed message show which, just when you think it couldn't get any heavier-handed, has Tasha Yar deliver a 'drugs are bad, mm'kay speech. Preachy and predictable.

1.22 SKIN OF EVIL

STARDATE 41601.3

Tasha Yar dies facing an entity of pure evil

TX 25 April 1988
WRITER Joseph Stefano and Hannah Louise Shearer (story by Joseph Stefano)
DIRECTOR Joseph L Scanlan
GUEST CAST Raymond Forchion (Ben Prieto), Ron Gans (Voice of Armus), Mart McChesney (Armus), Brad Zerbst (Nurse)

A shuttle containing Troi and Lt Prieto crashes on Vagra II. The Enterprise hurries to its aid, but an energy field around the shuttle blocks the transporters. An Away Team is sent down to move the passengers to safety, but they are blocked by a pool of living oil, Armus. Armus kills Tasha, who is rushed to sickbay, but too late for Beverly to do anything. Armus lets the surviving Away Team members talk to Troi – she senses great pain and loneliness from Armus. The long-departed people of this planet learned how to shed their evil like a second skin – which became Armus. Armus demands to be transported off the planet, then he'll shut down the energy field. Armus' power seems to diminish when he is angry, so Picard riles him, the field weakens and the shuttle's crew are beamed away. Picard destroys the shuttlecraft from space so that Armus can't use it. Picard leads an emotional service for Tasha, who has left a holographic message for her crewmates.

QUOTES

- 'Death is that state in which one exists only in the memories of others. Which is why it is not an end. No goodbyes, just good memories. Hailing frequencies closed, sir.' – *Tasha delivers her own eulogy*

TRIVIA

- While there's been some speculation that she was pushed – and we know that the production team had been looking to lose at least one regular character – the balance of evidence is that Denise Crosby chose to leave, reportedly because she was bored with her role and saw no prospect of it growing or developing. As the creative team began to think about the second season, they were planning to move away from the ensemble cast to concentrate more on Picard, Riker and Data. There certainly seems to have been no ill-will on either side – Crosby would return a number of times in cameo and guest appearances, starting with the third season's *Yesterday's Enterprise*, which gave Tasha a new chance for an heroic sacrifice. She also fronted the film *Trekkies*, a documentary about *Star Trek* fans and conventions.

RATING

- A story in which Tasha Yar is killed by a monster that looks like a man trying to get out of a bin bag... her death is pointless and low-key, but the funeral is effective enough. If Tasha hadn't died, people would be hard-pressed to remember anything about the episode.

1.23 WE'LL ALWAYS HAVE PARIS

STARDATE 41697.9

Picard has to deal with a scientist's time experiments – and his wife, who's an old flame

TX 2 May 1988
WRITER Deborah Dean Davis and Hannah Louise Shearer
DIRECTOR Robert Becker
GUEST CAST Kelly Ashmore (Francine), Dan Kern (Dean), Rod Loomis (Paul Manheim), Isabel Lorca (Gabrielle), Michelle Phillips (Jenice Manheim), Lance Spellerberg (Herbert), Jean-Paul Vignon (Edouard)

A temporal distortion passes over the Enterprise, and they receive a distress call from Vandor IV and the missing scientist Paul Manheim, whose specialism is non-linear time. Picard orders the Enterprise to attend, but is worried at the prospect of meeting Manheim's wife, Jenice, who he stood up 22 years before in Paris. Everyone else on Manheim's team is dead, and Paul is seriously ill. The temporal shockwaves, christened 'Manheim radiation', threaten the fabric of time and space. Data is less susceptible to the distortions, evades the elaborate security system and seals the dimensional rift. As Paul recovers, Picard and Jenice make their Paris rendezvous, courtesy of the holodeck.

TRIVIA

- The source of the title and the loose basis of the story is, of course, *Casablanca.* The original draft had Jenice named Laura and she and Picard slept together. According to Debra Dean Davis, it was Patrick Stewart who lobbied to tone down that aspect of the story. As before, scenes where Beverly confronted her feelings for Picard were also cut.
- Michelle Phillips was the wife of John Phillips of The Mamas and the Papas.

RATING

- The episode is hamstrung by the reluctance of the production team to show Picard getting too involved with a married woman. It's also a rare example of a poor performance by Patrick Stewart, who has no chemistry whatsoever with Michelle Phillips.

1.24 CONSPIRACY

STARDATE 41775.5

Picard is told there's a conspiracy that goes right to the heart of Starfleet

TX 9 May 1988
WRITER Tracy Tormé (story by Robert Sabaroff)
DIRECTOR Cliff Bole
GUEST CAST Michael Berryman (Rixx), Ursaline Bryant (Scott), Ward Costello (Quinn), Henry Darrow (Savar), Jonathan Farwell (Keel), Ray Reinhardt (Aaron), Robert Schenkkan (Remmick)

The Enterprise is heading to an easy mission on beautiful Pacifica when Picard receives a coded message from a friend, Captain Walker Keel, who asks him to divert to Dytallix B. Picard beams down alone, and Keel introduces him to a couple of allies, Captains Rixx of the USS Thomas Paine and Tryla Scott of the USS Renegade, who warn him that Starfleet has been infiltrated by aliens. Picard is sceptical, but shortly afterwards Keel's ship, the USS Horatio, is destroyed in an 'accident'. Picard sets course for Earth. At Headquarters, Admirals Quinn, Savar and Aaron invite Picard and Riker to a meal. Picard becomes suspicious of Quinn, and asks Riker to watch him – once alone, Quinn overpowers Riker and tries to infect him with a parasite. Beverly manages to stun him, and they discover a blue 'gill' sticking from his neck. At Headquarters, Picard is confronted by the other Admirals, Captain Scott and an aide, Remmick, who openly admit they are under alien control. Riker arrives, pretending Quinn succeeded in converting him – together he and Picard disable the Admirals and discover Remmick is host of the 'mother alien'. Killing him causes the other aliens to disintegrate, ending the invasion threat.

TRIVIA

- Never named in the script, fans call the aliens in this 'the blue gill aliens'. The story hints they'll return, but they haven't to date.
- Gene Roddenberry didn't like the original idea, a story called *The Assassins* where the conspiracy had no alien involvement, and concerned a group of Starfleet 'hawks' who wanted war with the Klingons.
- The scene with Remmick's death and the 'mother alien' nestling in his innards was heavily cut by the BBC for the British broadcast – although the scene appeared, uncut, in a flashback during *Shades of Gray.*

RATING

- A tense, paranoid story that deserved to be spun out over a few episodes, it's a shame the money's running out at the end of the season, so our first glimpse of Earth in *The Next Generation* is a beige corridor and the monster turns out to be a glove puppet.

1.25 THE NEUTRAL ZONE

A group revived from the twentieth century annoy the crew – but the Romulans prove a more dangerous foe

TX 16 May 1988
WRITERS Maurice Hurley (story by Deborah McIntyre and Mona Glee)
DIRECTOR James L Conway
GUEST CAST Marc Alaimo (Tebok), Gracie Harrison (Clare Raymond), Anthony James (Thei), Peter Mark Richman (Ralph Offenhouse), Leon Rippy (LQ 'Sonny' Clemonds)

STARDATE 41986.0

While waiting for Picard to return from an emergency meeting at Starbase 718, the Enterprise discovers a derelict satellite with a number of cryogenic capsules containing 'sleepers' from the twentieth century. Picard returns with bad news – two outposts near the Neutral Zone have been destroyed. After 50 years, it looks like the Romulans have re-emerged as a threat. Beverly has revived the sleepers, all of whom were frozen when they became terminally ill. They're a businessman, a housewife and a country and western singer, all of whom struggle to adjust to life in the future, and make nuisances of themselves. The Enterprise arrives near the Neutral Zone to discover two more colonies have been destroyed. A Romulan Warbird, a battleship even larger than the Enterprise, materialises – it had been using its cloaking device. Picard hails the ship and tells them they have committed an act of aggression – but it transpires that the Romulans have suffered the same sort of attacks on their outposts. The Romulans pledge to co-operate in uncovering the origin of the attacks.

QUOTES

- 'We have indeed been negligent, but no more. We are back.' – *the Romulan commander*

TRIVIA

- This story is actually the first hint of the Borg. The production team already had them in mind as a new, major threat, although a writers' strike meant that they had to scale back this story. Originally intended to be at least a two-parter concentrating on the re-emergence of the Romulans, that storyline became a subplot in a story submitted by a couple of fans about characters from our time waking up in *The Next Generation*. At this point, the aliens were imagined as a race of giant insects (and so presumably weren't called the Borg).
- Mark Alaimo later became prominent as Dukat in *Deep Space Nine*.
- A close examination of the computer screen reveals that Clare Raymond seems to be descended from the actors that played the first six Doctor Whos, as their names flash up.
- For the first time in any version of *Star Trek*, the exact year the Enterprise is from is established – Data says it is 2364 (although he had claimed to be from the 'class of '70' in *Encounter at Farpoint*).

RATING

- The season limps a little to a close – a lightweight story where three characters from our time keep getting lectured on how much better everything is by *The Next Generation*'s time doesn't mesh with the serious – and much more interesting – mystery of the destroyed outposts.

STAR TREK: THE NEXT GENERATION **SEASON TWO**

2.1 THE CHILD

Deanna Troi is impregnated by an energy being but the child threatens the lives of the crew

TX 19 November 1988

STARDATE 42073.1

While the Enterprise is *en route* to collect plague samples from Audet IX, Troi stuns the crew by announcing that she is pregnant. She says an energy sphere impregnated her. The New Chief Medical Officer, Dr Katherine Pulaski, establishes that Troi's child is growing at an unprecedented rate and will be delivered in 36 hours. Troi gives birth to a boy, who she names Ian Andrew, and he is soon the size of a

WRITER Jaron Summers, Jon Povill and Maurice Hurley
DIRECTOR Rob Bowman
GUEST CAST Dawn Amermann (Miss Gladstone), Zachary Benjamin (Young Ian), Seymour Cassel (Hester Dealt), Whoopi Goldberg (Guinan), Dore Keller (Crewman), Colm Meaney (O'Brien), RJ Williams (Ian)

four-year-old and able to talk. Meanwhile, the Enterprise crew pick up Hester Dealt and the plague samples and set course for an infected planet in the Rachelis system. However, one of the samples soon starts to grow and threatens to breach its containment module. Data discovers that Ian is emitting a form of radiation that has accelerated the growth of the deadly plague samples. Ian reverts to his natural form as a ball of energy and sacrifices himself to save the ship. He explains that he is an alien life-form, curious about the human crew, who decided to live as one of them to understand more. Deanna is saddened by the loss of her son.

TRIVIA

- Production on the second season was delayed by a writer's strike. As a result, the producers revived and extensively rewrote this script, originally penned for the seventies' *Star Trek II* series.
- At the end of the first season, the producers decided that with Wesley now part of the bridge crew, the character of Beverly was not developing as they had planned. In the fiction, Dr Crusher has been promoted to head of Starfleet Medical. Wesley is persuaded to stay with the ship by new crewmember, Guinan. Diana Muldaur took over as the ship's doctor. She preferred a 'special appearance' credit to a caption in the opening titles. She would appear in every episode of the second season, except *The Outrageous Okona* and *Q Who*).

RATING

- An uncomfortably routine episode to kickstart the much awaited second season. The plague feels like a hasty attempt to create a threat for the main story.

2.2 WHERE SILENCE HAS LEASE

STARDATE 42193.6

Nagilum, a powerful entity, toys with the crew to investigate the notion of human mortality

TX 26 November 1988
WRITER Jack B Sowards
DIRECTOR Winrich Kolbe
GUEST CAST Earl Boen (Nagilum), Charles Douglass (Haskell), Colm Meaney (O'Brien)

While exploring the Mordana Quadrant, the Enterprise encounters a strange hole in space that is without energy, matter or physical shape. The void quickly envelops the Enterprise, which is unable to escape. Suddenly, a Romulan ship decloaks and attacks. The Enterprise returns fire and the Bird of Prey is destroyed, but Picard is suspicious. Next, the Enterprise encounters its sister ship, the USS Yamato. Riker and Worf beam over but the ship is deserted. Meanwhile, the Enterprise crew find a small gap in the void. They beam back the Away Team but the hole closes and the Yamato vanishes. Suddenly, a large face appears on the viewscreen. The creature announces it is Nagilum, a powerful creature that is intrigued by the notion of human mortality. When Nagilum threatens to kill half the crew in a science experiment, Picard initiates the autodestruct sequence. Fearing another of Nagilum's tricks, Picard does not cancel the order until the Enterprise has broken free of the void. Nagilum claims to have let the crew go and expresses dismay with the humans. Picard notes that both humans and Nagilum share a sense of curiosity.

TRIVIA

- The production team approached Richard Mulligan to play the mysterious alien entity but he was unavailable. The writers paid homage to Mulligan nevertheless in the name – Nagilum is Mulligan spelt backwards. Another story has it that the spelling was Ngilam, or malign backwards.
- Writer Jack B Sowards was the credited cowriter of *Star Trek II: The Wrath of Khan.*
- The USS Yamato shares its name with a Japanese vessel of the Second World War. However, the name is more likely a nod to the animé series *Space Cruiser Yamato* (renamed *Star Blazers* in the US).

RATING

- Disappointingly standard episode that runs the old gamut of alien entity that tests humanity. It is particularly perplexing given the similarity of storylines with the previous episode, *The Child*, and the repeat appearance of Q later in the season.

2.3 ELEMENTARY, DEAR DATA

STARDATE 42286.3

A holodeck version of Professor Moriarty makes a bid for freedom

TX 3 December 1988
WRITER Brian Alan Lane
DIRECTOR Rob Bowman
GUEST CAST Daniel Davis (Professor Moriarty), Biff Manard (Ruffian), Richard Merson (Pie Man), Anne Elizabeth Ramsey (Clancy), Alan Shearman (Inspector Lestrade), Diz White (Prostitute)

Geordi, Data and Pulaski are on the holodeck, with Geordi playing Watson to Data's Sherlock Holmes. When Data solves the case immediately, Geordi reprograms the holodeck to create an adversary worthy of Data. Later, Data and Geordi hear screams and realise Pulaski has been abducted. They encounter Moriarty, who can now control the holodeck and has overridden the safety protocols. He demands to know more about the future. Geordi and Data discuss events with the senior staff who deduce that, in creating a more worthy rival, the computer has created a dangerous, sentient opponent. Suddenly, the Enterprise is rocked as control of the ship is transferred to the holodeck. Picard enters the holodeck and tells Moriarty that once the program is over, he will cease to exist. Moriarty realises his fate lies with Picard and releases control of Pulaski and the ship. Picard promises to save the holodeck program and thereby preserve Moriarty until they find a way of converting the character into matter.

TRIVIA

- Brian Lane's original ending had Picard realise that the holodeck *can* allow Moriarty to leave, but decide to leave the master criminal in the computer program just in case. Roddenberry objected on the grounds that this deceit hurt Picard's character.

RATING

- A clever little episode that explores, with some ingenuity, the more profound implications of the holodeck and the 'sentience' of its characters. Moriarty comes across as a genuinely intelligent character.

2.4 THE OUTRAGEOUS OKONA

STARDATE 42402.7

A roguish cargo ship captain brings the troubles of two worlds to the Enterprise's door

TX 10 December 1988
WRITER Burton Armus (story by Les Menchen, Lance Dickson and David Landsberg)
DIRECTOR Robert Becker
GUEST CAST William O Campbell (Thadiun Okona), Whoopi Goldberg (Guinan), Teri Hatcher (BG Robinson), Rosalind Ingledew (Yanar), Kieran Mulroney (Benzan), Joe Piscopo (Comic), Douglas Rowe (Debin), Albert Stratton (Kushell)

When the Enterprise encounters a small ship in trouble, Picard readily offers assistance and beams its captain aboard. The pilot, Thadiun Okona, is a dashing rogue who soon starts to work his charm on the female crewmembers. His joking also confuses Data, who talks to Guinan and then uses the holodeck to try to learn more about humour. Picard soon discovers that Okona is hot property when two vessels approach the Enterprise. The Straleb captain claims that Okona stole the precious Jewel of Thesia, while the Altec captain blames Okona for fathering the child of his daughter, Yanar! Picard invites both captains onto the Enterprise and discovers that Benzan, the son of the Straleb captain, is actually the father of Yanar's child – he stole the Jewel of Thesia to give to Yanar and the young couple used Okona as a courier for messages. Grudgingly, the Straleb and Altec captains reach a truce, but argue over the planet on which the child will be raised. As the crew say goodbye to Okona, Data inadvertently makes a joke – but fails to understand why the crew are laughing.

TRIVIA

- William O Campbell (Okona) was Gene Roddenberry's first choice to play Riker.
- Teri Hatcher, better known as Lois Lane in *Lois and Clark*, makes an early TV appearance as a lieutenant.

RATING

- Lightweight but fun. The mystery of Okona's crimes is a little obvious, given the almost complete lack of camouflage, but at least detracts from the appalling Data sub-plot. What is perhaps more remarkable is that it took four people to write the episode!

2.5 LOUD AS A WHISPER

STARDATE 42477.2

Peace talks are jeopardised when the assistants of a skilled negotiator are murdered

TX 7 January 1989
WRITER Jacqueline Zambrano
DIRECTOR Larry Shaw
GUEST CAST Leo Damian (Warrior/Andonis), John Garrett (Lieutenant), Richard Lavin, Chip Heller (Warriors), Colm Meaney (O'Brien), Marnie Mosiman (Woman), Thomas Oglesby (Scholar), Howie Seago (Riva)

The Enterprise arrives at Ramatis III to collect Riva, a renowned peacemaker who they hope will bring peace to the planet Solais V. Riva is deaf, and his thoughts and emotions are communicated telepathically through his chorus of three assistants, each of whom represents a different aspect of his personality. On arrival at Solais V, Riva selects a location for the negotiations and invites the leaders of the two factions to attend. As Riva speaks, one of the attendees opposed to a settlement fires at him. Riker manages to save Riva, but the blast kills the chorus. The Away Team beam back to the ship. Unable to talk, Riva attempts to communicate with the crew via sign language but it is only after Data has accessed the ship's computer that they can translate. Riva's confidence is shattered; he blames his own arrogance for the deaths. Troi manages to convince him to turn his disadvantage to an advantage and press on with the negotiations. Riva decides to return to the planet and teach both sides his sign language in the hope that through this process they will learn to respect their differences.

TRIVIA

- Howie Seago (Riva) is actually deaf and suggested a story about deafness during the writers strike at the start of the season. The shooting script had Riva learning to speak after the loss of his chorus but, a day before shooting began, Seago suggested that his character should teach the combatants sign language instead.

RATING

- The ability of the chorus to reflect different facets of Riva's personality, combined with the subservience of its members, is fascinating but doesn't move the story along. Somewhere there's a more interesting story fighting to get out.

2.6 THE SCHIZOID MAN

STARDATE 42437.5

A brilliant cyberneticist takes over Data, threatening to erase the android's personality forever

TX 21 January 1989
WRITER Tracy Tormé (story by Richard Manning and Hans Beimler)
DIRECTOR Les Landau
GUEST CAST Suzie Plakson (Selar), W Morgan Sheppard (Ira Graves), Barbara Alyn Woods (Kareen Brianon)

The Enterprise arrives at Gravesworld in response to a distress call from Kareen Brianon. Brianon is personal assistant to Ira Graves, a brilliant cyberneticist, and concerned for his failing health. A medical examination reveals Graves is in the final stages of Darnay's Disease and has less than a week to live. Graves confides in Data that he has discovered a way to transfer human consciousness into a computer. Shortly after, Data informs the Away Team that Graves has died. Back on the Enterprise, Data begins to act strangely. He delivers an emotional eulogy at Graves' memorial service and seems jealous when Kareen talks to Picard. Mechanical tests on Data show there is nothing wrong, but Troi's psychotronic test reveals two personalities vying for supremacy in Data's mind. Before Kareen departs, the android reveals that he is now Graves: the cyberneticist deactivated Data and transferred his mind into the android. Graves wants to do the same for Kareen so they can live forever. When Kareen refuses, Graves breaks her hand, unaware of his own strength. Picard confronts Graves but is knocked unconscious. When he awakens, he discovers that Data is now safe: Graves could not find it in himself to destroy Data's personality and instead transferred his knowledge into the ship's computer, losing his consciousness forever.

QUOTES

- 'I feel pity for you. Your existence must be a kind of walking purgatory: neither dead nor alive, never really feeling anything. Just existing.' – *Graves to Data*

TRIVIA

- There is an episode of *The Prisoner* with the same title. Patrick McGoohan, star of that series, was approached to play Graves.

- The love story was taken from an original pitch by Tormé in which Data meets a woman from the planet in *Datalore* who had an affair with two of the colonists. The personalities of the two colonists come alive in Data and fight for supremacy. At the same time, Beimler and Manning pitched their story about Graves implanting his consciousness in Data. Tormé combined the best from both pitches.
- Suzie Plakson makes her first appearance here as Vulcan doctor Selar. She returned later in the season as K'Ehleyr in *The Emissary*.

RATING

- A simple idea, exploited well. If there is a problem it is that the heavy-handed establishment of Graves' relationship with Data makes the problem seem a logical conclusion, when it is played as a mystery.

2.7 UNNATURAL SELECTION

Pulaski must find the source of a mysterious aging disease before she dies of the illness

TX 28 January 1989
WRITERS John Mason and Mike Gray
DIRECTOR Paul Lynch
GUEST CAST J Patrick McNamara (Taggart), Colm Meaney (O'Brien), Patricia Smith (Dr Sarah Kingsley), Scott Trost (Transporter Ensign)

STARDATE 42494.8

The Enterprise responds to a distress call from the USS Lantree but discovers that all the crew died of old age. Pulaski examines the Lantree's medical log but can only find a case of the mild Thelusian flu a few days previously. The Enterprise sets course for the Lantree's last location, Darwin Genetic Research Station on Gagarin IV, but finds that the researchers there are also aging rapidly. Only the station's genetically-engineered children appear immune to the disease. Pulaski and Data examine one child on a shuttlecraft, so as not to risk contaminating the Enterprise, but soon Pulaski begins to show symptoms of the illness. On Darwin Station she discovers the cause: when a member of the Lantree crew exposed the children to Thelusian flu, the children developed a powerful airborne antibody to kill the disease. It is this antibody that creates rapid aging in non-engineered humans. Picard and O'Brien use the Enterprise's transporter to beam Pulaski back and filter out changes to her DNA. The process works for Pulaski and later for the Darwin Station scientist, who go to work to find a cure.

TRIVIA

- Following this episode, the series writer's guide was amended to include restrictions on the use of the transporter, most importantly to prevent characters being duplicated or brought back to life each week. However, this did not stop the creation of Tom Riker in the sixth season's *Second Chances*.

RATING

- A simple story with a clearly defined threat – but one wonders why they don't solve all medical emergencies this way. Very original *Star Trek*.

2.8 A MATTER OF HONOR

Riker serves on a Klingon vessel and is thrown into conflict with the Enterprise

TX 4 February 1989
WRITER Burton Armus (story by Wanda M Haight, Gregory Amos and Burton Armus)
DIRECTOR Rob Bowman
GUEST CAST Christopher Collins (Kargan), Laura Drake (Vekma), Colm Meaney (O'Brien), Peter Parros (Tactical Officer), John Putch (Ensign Mendon), Brian Thompson (Klag)

STARDATE 42506.5

While Wesley takes care of Mendon, a Benzite ensign on an exchange programme, Riker volunteers for an exchange on the Klingon ship, the Pagh. Worf tells Riker that his duty as first officer will be to kill the captain, Kargan, should he become too cowardly, but warns him not to refuse Kargan's orders or he will be killed by the second officer, Klag. For safety, Worf gives Riker an emergency signal! On the Pagh, Riker swears allegiance to Kargan and quickly asserts his authority over Klag. Meanwhile, the Enterprise discovers bacteria eating through the hull. Discovering the same bacteria on the Pagh's hull, the Enterprise pursues to warn the Klingons. Kargan suspects Picard of planting it deliberately – and he expects Riker to battle the Enterprise. Mendon discovers a way to eliminate the bacteria, but the cloaked Pagh does not answer Picard's hail. As the tension rises on both ships, Riker uses the emergency signal. Kargan snatches it from Riker and is suddenly beamed aboard the Enterprise, and knocked unconscious by Worf. Riker takes command and orders the Enterprise's surrender. Realising Riker is trying to avoid a conflict without breaking his oath to Kargan, Picard agrees and has his officers repair the Klingon ship. Kargan is returned and strikes Riker, but admires his understanding of Klingon culture.

TRIVIA

- *A Matter of Honor* became the show's highest rated episode of season two, gaining 12.2 million viewers.
- Brian Thompson is more immediately recognisable as the recurring shape-changing alien character in *The X-Files*.

RATING

- A tightly scripted, well-structured story with tension and humour. Frakes puts in one of his best performances of the series, revelling in the wry and roguish aspects of Riker's character that are all too often forgotten.

2.9 THE MEASURE OF A MAN

STARDATE 42523.7

Picard defends Data when a Starfleet cyberneticist obtains permission to study him

TX 11 February 1989
WRITER Melinda M Snodgrass
DIRECTOR Robert Scheerer
GUEST CAST Brian Brophy (Bruce Maddox), Whoopi Goldberg (Guinan), Clyde Kusatsu (Nakamura), Amanda McBroom (Philippa Louvois), Colm Meaney (O'Brien)

At Starbase 173, the Enterprise is joined by Starfleet cyberneticist Bruce Maddox. Maddox wants to disassemble Data to study his positronic brain in the hope of creating other androids. Fearing Data's personality will be lost in the process, Picard refuses to permit the experiment. Instead, Maddox orders Data to be transferred to his team. Unable to disobey an order, Data resigns from Starfleet. Maddox claims that Data is a machine – property of Starfleet – and cannot resign. When Starfleet's legal representative, Louvois, concurs, Picard demands a hearing. Understaffed, Louvois demands that Riker act as Maddox's counsel or she will automatically rule in favour of Maddox. Riker's case is compelling, culminating with him switching Data off as final proof of his argument. Picard feels the case may be lost but Guinan convinces him that the ruling would effectively turn all artificial beings into slaves. Picard makes a fierce defence of Data's case and challenges Maddox to explain why Picard is sentient and Data is not. Maddox is unable to explain. After a tense moment, Louvois rules that Data is free to make his own choices.

QUOTES

- 'Data is a toaster.' – *Louvois to Riker*

TRIVIA

- Melinda Snodgrass worked as an attorney before writing this, her first script, which was nominated for a Writers' Guild award.
- Maddox works out of the Daystrom Technological Institute, a reference to the original series episode *The Ultimate Computer*. Poignantly, when Data packs his case to leave the Enterprise he includes a memento of Tasha Yar.

RATING

- A blunt episode lacking finesse. Drafting Riker in to prosecute adds another level, but is poorly rationalised. In the end, *The Measure of a Man* is little more than an A-level balloon debate.

2.10 THE DAUPHIN

STARDATE 42568.8

Wes Crusher falls in love with a beautiful alien queen who is not all she seems

TX 18 February 1989
WRITERS Scott Rubenstein and Leonard Mlodinow
DIRECTOR Rob Bowman
GUEST CAST Madchen Amick (Anya as Teenage Girl), J ennifer Barlow (Gibson), Paddi Edwards (Anya), Whoopi Goldberg (Guinan), Jaime Hubbard (Salia), Colm Meaney (O'Brien), Peter Neptune (Aron), Cindy Sorenson (Anya as Furry Animal)

The Enterprise arrives at Klavdia III to collect Salia and transport her to Daled IV, the planet she was born to rule. On their arrival, Wesley is struck by Salia's beauty and the two are instantly attracted to one another, to Anya's disapproval. Anya is extremely protective and demands that a patient in sickbay with an infectious disease be killed. When Pulaski refuses, Anya transforms herself into a vicious beast. Worf intercedes and Anya is confined to quarters. Meanwhile, Wes and Salia grow closer. Salia is scared by her responsibilities. When Wes suggests she stay on the Enterprise, Salia runs away. Salia visits Wes in his quarters and they kiss. Suddenly, Anya intercedes and transforms into a beast, but Salia forces Anya to back down by turning into an equally ferocious creature. Wes realises his true feelings as Salia waits to be transported down to Daled IV. They say their goodbyes. Salia transforms into her natural form, a beautiful white light, and is beamed down.

QUOTES

- 'I dream of a galaxy where your eyes are the stars and the universe worships the night... You are the heart in my day and the soul in my night.' – *Riker to Guinan, demonstrating the art of flirting to a bemused Wesley*

TRIVIA

- The episode features an early TV appearance by Madchen Amick, who would a year later find fame in David Lynch's *Twin Peaks* as Shelly Johnson.

RATING

- Wes Crusher in love. Enough said.

2.11 CONTAGION

STARDATE 42609.1

The Enterprise suffers the same technical difficulties that destroyed her sister ship

TX 18 March 1989
WRITERS Steve Gerber and Beth Woods
DIRECTOR Joseph L Scanlan
GUEST CAST Colm Meaney (O'Brien), Thalmus Rasulala (Donald Varley), Folkert Schmidt (Doctor), Carolyn Seymour (Sub-Commander Taris), Dana Sparks (Weapons Officer)

The Enterprise receives a distress call from its sister ship, the USS Yamato, in the Neutral Zone. Captain Varley explains that his crew have found the last remnants of the Iconian civilisation, also of interest to the Romulans. Suddenly, the Yamato explodes, killing all hands. A Romulan ship decloaks but Commander Taris insists they were not to blame. She tries to scare the Enterprise away but Picard is determined to investigate the loss of the Yamato and the Iconian remains. The Enterprise travels to Iconia and begins to suffer malfunctions. An automatic probe is launched from the planet but Geordi realises it is carrying a destructive computer program and it is destroyed. Nevertheless, the Enterprise has already downloaded the program from the Yamato's logs and is now on borrowed time. Worf, Data and Picard beam down to the source of the probe. Meanwhile, the Romulans threaten to destroy the crippled Enterprise, but Riker warns them of the probe. However, the Romulans also downloaded the Yamato's logs and are having problems. On the planet, Picard discovers a control centre. Data deciphers the Iconian language and opens a doorway that cycles through a number of destinations, one of which is the Enterprise bridge. Picard deduces that this is how the Iconians travelled. Data is infected by the computer program and taken back to the ship by Worf. As Picard sets the control centre to self-destruct, Data shuts down and restarts, flushing his system. Geordi realises he can do the same with the Enterprise. Picard enters the doorway but arrives on the bridge of the Romulan ship, now on self-destruct. He is saved when O'Brien transports him back. Riker tells the Romulan crew how to save their ship.

TRIVIA

- The original concept for *Contagion* was provided by Beth Woods, a *Star Trek* fan who was then working on the production office's computers.
- The episode establishes Picard's interest in archaeology and his fondness for 'Tea: Earl Grey, hot.'
- One of the alien locales seen in the Iconian Gateway (the one with two curved skyscrapers) is actually Toronto City Hall!

RATING

- Plenty of action and tension, although the story is a little overloaded with the addition of the Romulans. The destruction of the Yamato adds gravitas to the proceedings and an impressive effects sequence.

2.12 THE ROYALE

STARDATE 42625.4

The crew find the remains of a twenty-first century astronaut in the recreation of a pulp novel

While surveying the Theta 116 system, the Enterprise finds debris orbiting the eighth planet. The wreckage is that of a twenty-first century NASA spacecraft. The Enterprise picks up a structure on the planet's surface and Riker, Worf and Data are sent to investigate.

TX 25 March 1989
WRITER 'Keith Mills' (pseudonym for Tracy Tormé)
DIRECTOR Cliff Bole
GUEST CAST Sam Anderson (Manager), Gregory Beecroft (Mikey D), Leo Garcia (Bell Boy), Jill Jacobson (Vanessa), Colm Meaney (O'Brien), Noble Willingsham (Texan)

They find themselves in blackness and locate a revolving door. Beyond is a bustling twentieth century casino, but the Away Team soon find themselves unable to leave or communicate with the Enterprise. They pick up DNA traces and track them to the skeletal remains of Colonel S Richey, the Captain of the Charybdis, his diary and a novel entitled *Hotel Royale*. The diary reveals that Richey's crew was killed by an alien, but that the alien created the Royale, from the novel, as a place for Richey to live out his remaining days. Riker realises that the only way to escape is to enact the end of the book, where the casino is bought out by foreign investors. Data proceeds to win a small fortune on the craps tables and buys the Royale. The Away Team is able to leave through the revolving doors and return to the Enterprise.

TRIVIA

- *The Royale* did not have an easy transition to screen. Tracy Tormé pitched the original idea but was disappointed by Maurice Hurley's rewrites. In Tormé's original, Richey was still alive. Hurley's redraft left him dead and divided Richey's dialogue between the members of the Away Team.
- The episode also features a notorious science gaffe: the temperature of the planet is given as 291° Celsius, which is below Absolute Zero. More forgiveably, Picard wonders if someone will solve Fermat's Last Theorem – in real life it was solved in 1993!

RATING

- *The Next Generation* rarely gets more like the original series than this. Flimsy and throwaway, but a refreshingly light-hearted change of pace.

2.13 TIME SQUARED

STARDATE 42679.2

A future Picard reveals that the Enterprise will be destroyed in six hours

TX 1 April 1989
WRITER Maurice Hurley (story by Kurt Michael Bensmiller)
DIRECTOR Joseph L Scanlan
GUEST CAST Colm Meaney (O'Brien)

The Enterprise discovers a Federation shuttle pod floating in space and beams it aboard. The crew are surprised to discover it is the El-Baz, one of the Enterprise's own shuttles, and inside is an unconscious duplicate of Picard. Pulaski establishes that the duplicate's brainwaves are out of phase. Meanwhile, Data and Geordi access the shuttle's logs. The El-Baz is from six hours in the future and a log entry shows the Enterprise being destroyed by an enormous vortex. The duplicate is a future version of Picard, who escaped the disaster but is now disorientated and incoherent. Picard worries that a decision he will make will result in the death of his crew. A few hours later, the Enterprise encounters the vortex. Picard orders Warp 9 but the pull of the vortex is too strong. The Enterprise launches a probe into the vortex but the result is a strong backlash of energy that connects with both Picards. Troi reasons that the energy only wants the Captain. Picard decides to leave the Enterprise in the El-Baz to draw the vortex's attention. However, his double is so insistent on the same action that Picard deduces that he must break the cycle. He stuns the duplicate and returns to the bridge, ordering the Enterprise into the vortex. The crew are tense but Picard is proved right – the Enterprise passes through unharmed and the duplicate of Picard disappears.

TRIVIA

- *Time Squared*, provisionally titled *Time to the Second*, began life as a prelude to *Q Who?* in which the time slip was caused by Q, acting off-screen. The explanation was to come in *Q Who?* three weeks later. When the episode aired, the on-screen title was *Time*^{2}. However, when it was syndicated it was changed to the written out version used here, presumably to make it clearer to the audience.

RATING

- A neat little story with a tangible threat. The double-think problem is handled efficiently, while the notion that the future Picard may have deserted his ship makes for an interesting aside. Sadly, the ending is a confusing anti-climax.

2.14 THE ICARUS FACTOR

STARDATE 42686.4

Riker is reunited with his estranged father, while Worf marks his age of acsension

TX 22 April 1989
WRITERS David Assael and Robert L McCullough (story by David Assael)
DIRECTOR Robert Iscove
GUEST CAST Colm Meaney (O'Brien), Mitchell Ryan (Kyle Riker), Lance Spellerberg (Herbert)

En route to Starbase Montgomery, Picard informs Riker that the captain of the USS Aries is retiring and that Starfleet has offered Will the command. Riker has 12 hours to decide. On arrival at the Starbase, Riker is surprised to be briefed on the Aries' mission by his estranged father, Kyle, who he has not seen for 15 years. Riker ignores his father's attempts at reconciliation. Kyle challenges Riker to a game of anbo-jitsu, a futuristic martial art. Riker, who has never beaten his father, realises that Kyle always cheated. Kyle explains that he wanted to keep Will interested in the challenge. Their barriers start to break down and the two find some peace. Later, Riker announces that he has decided to stay on the ship – he feels he can best serve Starfleet on the bridge of the Enterprise.

Meanwhile, Wes discovers that it is the tenth anniversary of Worf's age of ascension, an important date that should be marked by a Klingon ceremony. Worf's friends arrange a version of the painful ceremony on the holodeck which Worf fiercely endures.

QUOTES

- 'You choose your enemies, you choose your friends, but family – that's in the stars.' – *O'Brien to Riker*

TRIVIA

- Director Robert Iscove wanted to play up the resentment between Riker and Kyle, but Roddenberry insisted that these base emotions had been dealt with by the twenty-fourth century.

RATING

- A flimsy filler episode that is more soap opera than *Star Trek*. Riker's relationship with his father is played out at face value rather than through a bigger story, giving it a higher status than it should have. Unfortunately, this is B-and C-plot material given top billing.

2.15 PEN PALS

STARDATE 42695.3

Data breaks the Prime Directive to aid a young girl whose planet is on the brink of destruction

TX 29 April 1989
WRITER Melinda M Snodgrass (story by Hannah Louise Shearer)
DIRECTOR Winrich Kolbe
GUEST CAST Nicholas Cascone (Davies), Nikki Cox (Sarjenka), Ann H Gillespie (Hildebrant), Colm Meaney (O'Brien), Whitney Rydbeck (Alans)

While investigating geological activity, Data answers a faint radio message from Sarjenka, a young girl on Drema IV. Some weeks later, Data informs Picard about Sarjenka: her planet is collapsing and Data requests that the Enterprise try to help. Picard is concerned that Data has broken the Prime Directive by talking to Sarjenka, whose civilisation does not have space travel. However, he is persuaded to intercede and sets course for the planet. While Wesley prepares a method of destroying the dilithium that is causing the planet's destruction, Picard reluctantly allows Data to beam down to the planet to find Sarjenka, who cannot be contacted. However, he is enraged when Data brings the girl back to the Enterprise and orders Pulaski to erase Sarjenka's memories of the encounter. Wes' planetary bombardment is a success and Sarjenka is returned home. Data apologises, but Picard knows he meant no harm. Data will remember Sarjenka, even if she will not remember him.

TRIVIA

- Snodgrass' original draft had a teaser sequence in which Data taught Wesley how to dive on the holodeck. It had to be scrapped as it would cause problems with Brent Spiner's make-up. Snodgrass also intended to have Data learn how to comfort others by being tactile through his interactions with Sarjenka, but this was lost due to the finger extensions used in Sarjenka's makeup. Snodgrass also added the holodeck scenes with Picard riding to provide something different to the usual Ready Room scenes.

RATING

- A simple idea that is undermined by Data's reasoning. It seems peculiar that Data should take such a course of action in the first place, let alone compound it with further errors.

2.16 Q WHO?

Q transports the Enterprise to an unexplored sector of space and pits the crew against the relentless Borg

TX 6 May 1989
WRITER Maurice Hurley
DIRECTOR Rob Bowman
GUEST CAST Whoopi Goldberg (Guinan), John de Lancie (Q), Colm Meaney (O'Brien), Lycia Naff (Sonya Gomez)

STARDATE

Picard is once again confronted by Q, who keeps the captain aboard an Enterprise shuttlecraft until he consents to speak to him. Picard relents and Q reveals that he wants to join the crew, claiming that the universe is more dangerous than the Federation thinks. When Picard indignantly refuses, claiming that the Federation is ready to meet any challenge, Q transports the Enterprise 7,000 light years away and vanishes. Guinan warns Picard that her people have been in this part of space and urges him to leave at once, but he is determined to explore. Soon the crew find a planet where all technology has been scooped up from the surface and they encounter a strange alien craft, a vast metal cube with no bridge that Guinan identifies as a Borg ship. Two Borg, cybernetic hybrids, part-organic and part-machine, beam into Engineering and examine the ship. Worf kills one but the other instantly develops a shield that protects against phasers and proceeds unhindered. The Borg hail the Enterprise and order the crew to surrender and be assimilated into their collective consciousness. The Borg lock a tractor beam onto the ship and dissect a section of the hull, killing 18 crewmembers. Picard fires all weapons at the source of the tractor beam and the Enterprise is freed. With the Borg ship apparently dormant, Riker leads an Away Team and finds the Borg crew in hibernation. The only active Borg merely ignore the Away Team, regarding them as no threat. Data realises that the ship is regenerating. Picard beams the Away Team back and orders warp speed, but the Borg ship soon pursues. Soon the Enterprise is straining to maintain Warp 9.65. Q warns that the Borg are relentless and will pursue the Enterprise until its engines fail. The Borg fire a weapon that disables the Enterprise and lock on another tractor beam. Desperate, Picard admits that Q was right – the Federation is not ready to face the Borg. Q is taken aback but respects Picard's honesty. With a click of his fingers, the Enterprise is thrown back to its original position.

QUOTES

- 'You can't outrun them. You can't destroy them. If you damage them, the essence of what they are remains. They regenerate and keep coming... They are relentless.' – *Q to Picard on the Borg*

TRIVIA

- *Q Who?* was a conscious and highly successful attempt to create a viable new threat for the Federation. At its core was the desire for an enemy with whom you could not reason. The original idea for an insect race was aborted due to costs but led to the idea of a hive of augmented humans.
- The episode won Dan Curry an Emmy nomination for best visual effects.
- Although the episode states that the Borg live many thousands of light years away, the suggestion is that the Borg were responsible for attacks seen in *The Neutral Zone,* which is significantly closer.

RATING

- The first appearance of the Borg remains one of the highlights of *The Next Generation's* long run. For once we see the Federation utterly at a loss, barely able to comprehend and certainly unable to defend themselves against a new enemy. It is the Borg's inhuman relentlessness that makes them so compelling. Add to this the final sense of doom and foreboding, and you have a classic episode.

2.17 SAMARITAN SNARE

Geordi is kidnapped by the Pakleds, while Picard undergoes heart surgery

STARDATE 42779.1

While Picard travels to Starbase 515 with Wesley Crusher for urgent heart surgery, the Enterprise investigates a distress signal from a Pakled ship, the Mondor. Geordi is beamed over to assist with repairs, but when the ship's power is restored the Pakleds render him unconscious and raise shields. Data discovers that the malfunctions reported by the Pakleds were simply a means to ensnare someone with engineering

TX 13 May 1989
WRITER Robert L McCullough
DIRECTOR Les Landau
GUEST CAST Daniel Benzali (Surgeon), Christopher Collins (Grebnedlog), Tzi Ma (Biomolecular Specialist), Leslie Morris (Reginod), Lycia Naff (Sonya Gomez)

skill. All the Pakled technology has been appropriated from other cultures. In retaliation, Riker claims that hydrogen emissions from the Enterprise are in fact evidence of a forcefield capable of destroying the Mondor. The Pakleds fall for the ploy and release Geordi. The Enterprise arrives at Starbase 515 to hear that the surgery to repair Picard's artificial heart is not going well. Pulaski joins the surgeons and together they are able to save the captain. A few hours later, Picard is back at his post fit and well. Wesley has passed his Starfleet exams and is permitted to stay on the Enterprise.

TRIVIA

- Dennis Putnam Bailey and David Bischoff once claimed that the first five minutes of *Samaritan Snare* were so awful that it convinced them to pitch an episode (season three's *Tin Man*).
- Grebnedlog and Reginod are the last names of the writer who pitched the story and his best friend spelled backwards. (Doniger and Goldenberg).
- In his opening monologue, Picard explains how he came by his artificial heart, a story which became the basis for season six's *Tapestry*. It's a rare case of a soliloquy where the character just gets to talk, with absolutely no attempt to liven it up in action terms. You don't get that often on TV...

RATING

- A fairly uneventful episode with little of note. Picard's brief exchange with Wesley about his past and Wes' future has potential but leads nowhere. Ultimately the potential drama to be had from Picard's heart operation is about as little as can be drained from the encounter with the Pakleds.

2.18 UP THE LONG LADDER

The Enterprise encounters the decendents of the SS Marinosa crew

TX 20 May 1989
WRITER Melinda Snodgrass
DIRECTOR Winrich Kolbe
GUEST CAST Jon de Vries (Granger), Barrie Ingham (Danilo O'Dell), Rosalyn Landor (Brenna O'Dell), Colm Meaney (O'Brien)

STARDATE 42823.2

The Enterprise investigates a distress call which they believe is from the SS Mariposa, which left Earth in the twenty-second century to explore the Ficus sector. The crew pick up life signs on the planet Bringloid V, which is threatened by solar flares. Riker begins the evacuation of the inhabitants – the descendents of the original Mariposa crew. Their leader, Danilo O'Dell, explains that a second set of colonists travelled on the Mariposa. Picard finds them on an Earth-like planet a short distance away. They are welcomed by Prime Minister Wilson Granger to his planet, Mariposa. The crew are surprised to discover that the populace are all clones. Granger explains that the Mariposans need a fresh supply of DNA, as the clones are becoming poorer copies each time. Riker and Pulaski refuse to be cloned but Granger has them incapacitated and steals some cells. Riker and Pulaski discover his actions and destroy the duplicates before they are completed. Picard persuades Granger to start a new colony with the inhabitants of Bringloid V.

QUOTES

- 'Every moment of pleasure in life has to be purchased by an equal moment of pain.' – *Danilo to Worf*

TRIVIA

- Melinda Snodgrass came up with the story as a satire on America's immigration policy, but found herself under attack from the pro-life lobby for supposedly condoning abortion.

RATING

- *Up The Long Ladder* is one of those episodes where the solution is so obvious it's barely worth going through the motions. Thankfully it skirts around the contemporary political issues without making too much of them.

2.19 MANHUNT

STARDATE 42859.2

Lwaxana Troi sets her sights on Captain Picard

TX 17 June 1989
WRITER 'Terry Devereaux' (pseudonym for Tracy Tormé)
DIRECTOR Rob Bowman
GUEST CAST Rhonda Aldrich (Madeline), Rod Arrants (Rex), Majel Barrett (Lwaxana Troi), Wren T Brown (Transport Pilot), Robert Costanzo (Slade Bender), Mick Fleetwood (Antedian Dignitary), Colm Meaney (O'Brien), Robert O'Reilly (Scarface), Carel Struycken (Mr Homn)

The Enterprise is given the task of transporting four passengers to a conference on Pacifica. The two Antedean delegates are beamed aboard in a trance-like state: it is their way of coping with space travel. The last two are Lwaxana Troi and a Betazoid ambassador, and her servant, Mr Homn. Lwaxana is undergoing the 'phase', a Betazoid mid-life cycle that greatly increases sexual drive. Her attentions are immediately focused on Picard, who makes a hasty retreat to a holodeck Dixon Hill program. Now Lwaxana makes a beeline for Riker and announces that the entire crew are invited to their Betazoid wedding. Meanwhile, the Antedean delegates waken from their coma and Riker and Data track down Picard to tell him the news. Lwaxana follows them and falls for a holographic bartender. Though relieved, Picard feels duty bound to tell Lwaxana her date is a hologram. Lwaxana gives up all hope of finding a suitable partner among the Enterprise crew. As Lwaxana prepares to leave, she is able to read the Antedeans' minds and discovers that they are assassins sent to destroy the conference. Picard is grateful for the tip off.

TRIVIA

- Tracy Tormé conceived this as a sequel to two of his earlier episodes, *Haven* and *The Big Goodbye*. He intended the Dixon Hill sequences to be more in the style of hard-boiled fiction. Patrick Stewart was to deliver scene-setting monologues in the detective movie style but this was vetoed on the grounds that voice-overs could only be used for the captain's log. Tormé was unhappy with the rewrite and had his name removed from the episode. Dixon Hill would next reappear two years later in *Clues*.
- Two cast members of note are Mick Fleetwood of Fleetwood Mac, making a guest appearance as an Antedian dignatory, and Robert O'Reilly, who would go on to play the Klingon Gowron.

RATING

- Frothy, amusing and entirely throwaway, *Manhunt* is a decent comedy episode with a few good gags. Picard's fear of Lwaxana's attentions makes it.

2.20 THE EMISSARY

STARDATE 42901.3

Worf is reunited with a former lover as the crew pursue a renegade Klingon vessel

TX 24 June 1989
WRITERS Richard Manning and Hans Beimler (story by Thomas H Calder)
DIRECTOR Cliff Bole
GUEST CAST Dietrich Bader (Tactical Officer), Georgann Johnson (Gromek), Lance Le Gault (K'Temoc), Colm Meaney (O'Brien), Suzie Plakson (K'Ehleyr), Anne Elizabeth Ramsey (Clancy)

Emissary K'Ehleyr, a half-human, half-Klingon ambassador, arrives on the Enterprise with news that Starbase 336 has heard from the Klingon ship, T'Ong. The T'Ong's crew, captained by K'Temoc, has been in hibernation and does not know the Klingon-Federation war is over. The Enterprise is sent to intercept and convince K'Temoc of the new order. Picard assigns Worf to work with the emissary, but Worf is unhappy: he and K'Ehleyr were lovers six years previously. K'Ehleyr takes out her frustrations in the holodeck by running one of Worf's training programs. Worf is impressed and soon their feelings are rekindled. The next day, Worf asks K'Ehleyr to marry him, as is tradition, but she refuses. Meanwhile, the Enterprise tracks down the T'Ong. Worf pretends to be the captain of the Enterprise, with K'Ehleyr at his right hand. After tense moments, he succeeds in persuading K'Temoc to back down. Worf takes K'Ehleyr to the transporter room, where she will beam aboard the T'Ong. K'Ehleyr admits she considered Worf's proposal and was tempted. She hopes someday their paths will cross again.

QUOTES

- 'I don't bite... Well, that's not true. I *do* bite.' – *K'Ehleyr to Worf*

TRIVIA

- *The Emissary* was based loosely on an idea from Tracy Tormé for a romance between Selar and Worf. Selar was also played by Suzie Plakson.

RATING

- A surprisingly strong character piece, largely made successful by Suzie Plakson's performance as K'Ehleyr. There is a real sense that Worf and K'Ehleyr could have been much more.

2.21 PEAK PERFORMANCE

A Starfleet tactical exercise is interrupted by an ambush by a Ferengi vessel

TX 8 July 1989
WRITER David Kemper
DIRECTOR Robert Scheerer
GUEST CAST Roy Brocksmith (Sirna Kolrami), David L Lander (Tactician), Glenn Morshower (Burke), Leslie Neale (Nagel), Armin Shimerman (Bractor)

STARDATE 42923.4

The Enterprise is joined by Kolrami, an arrogant grand strategist from Zakdorn sent to help the crew prepare for future Borg encounters. For the purpose of a war game, Riker is given command of the USS Hathaway, an 80-year-old decommissioned starship. Riker's team restore the Hathaway's engines, but Will is convinced their only hope is to outwit the Enterprise. Meanwhile, Kolrami's doubts over Riker's suitability for command are resolutely rebuffed by Picard. As the game begins, the Enterprise spots a Romulan cruiser. Although Picard quickly realises it is an illusion generated by the Hathaway, he drops his guard and Riker scores a few hits. The Enterprise makes to attack but is ambushed by a real Ferengi vessel. The Enterprise cannot take its virtual weapons offline and is damaged. Observing the war game, the Ferengi are convinced that the Enterprise is protecting valuable cargo on the decommissioned ship. Picard and Data devise a plan to fire photon torpedoes at the Hathaway that will explode just as the ship enters warp, giving the illusion of its destruction. Their plan works, but the Ferengi turn their weapons towards the defenceless Enterprise. Suddenly, the Ferengi pick up signs of another Federation ship on intercept and quickly make their escape. It is another illusion generated by the Hathaway. Kolrami is impressed by the Enterprise's captain and first officer. He is less impressed when Data forces him to a stalemate in a game of Strategema.

RATING

- Fast-paced and neatly told. There are welcome nods to the Borg encounter (*Q Who*) and Riker's decision not to take the Aries (*The Icarus Factor*), showing that *The Next Generation* is rapidly developing its own universe and history.

2.22 SHADES OF GREY

Riker is infected by alien microbes and forced to relive memories to fight the disease

TX 15 July 1989
WRITER Maurice Hurley, Richard Manning and Hans Beimler (story by Maurice Hurley)
DIRECTOR Rob Bowman
GUEST CAST Colm Meaney (O'Brien)

STARDATE 42976.1

During a geological survey of Surata IV, Riker is infected by the alien vegetation. The transporter's bio-filter is unable to remove microbes now in Riker's body. Pulaski announces that the prognosis is not good: the microbes have fused with Riker's central nervous system and cannot be removed surgically. Data and Geordi obtain a sample of the vegetation for analysis but, Pulaski discovers she can only kill the microbes by killing off the nerves they inhabit. She keeps Riker alive by sending electrical impulses into his brain – the impulses trigger positive memories such as meeting Data for the first time and former lovers. However, the memories stimulate the microbes, causing them to grow and infect more of Riker's body. Pulaski deduces that different types of endorphins may repel rather than attract. She changes the impulses and induces bad memories in Riker, including the death of Tasha Yar. The plan works, and Riker is restored to full health.

TRIVIA

- *Shades of Gray* was written to recoup the additional money spent on *Elementary, Dear Data* and *Q Who?* The linking material was shot in three days, using just the sickbay set.

RATING

- So it's come to this, a *Star Trek* clip show. Unfortunately the noble attempt to provide an overarching story simply draws a snigger after so many self-referential clip shows in different series. Do we actually think Riker might die? Abysmal.

STAR TREK: THE NEXT GENERATION
SEASON THREE

3.1 EVOLUTION

STARDATE 43125.8

Wesley infects the Enterprise with nanites

TX 25 September 1989
WRITER Michael Piller (story by Michael Piller and Michael Wagner)
DIRECTOR Winrich Kolbe
GUEST CAST Whoopi Goldberg (Guinan), Scott Grimes (Eric – scenes cut), Ken Jenkins (Paul Stubbs), Mary McCusker (Nurse), Amy O'Neill (Annette – scenes cut), Randal Patrick (Crewman)

The Enterprise prepares to launch a probe belonging to Dr Stubbs, but ends up malfunctioning and heading towards a cloud of stellar matter. The ship is brought under control just in time, but computer faults keep recurring. Wesley admits it might be his fault – his genetics project has led him to create nanites, tiny self-replicating computers. The nanites have escaped, and now they are in the computer core. Stubbs wants the core wiped clean, but Picard and Data insist they can't destroy a new life-form. Stubbs sneaks into the computer room and kills the nanites with a gamma burst. But some survive the attack, and shut down the life-support systems. The nanites enter Data and initiate negotiations with Picard – they meant no harm, they are just following their programming. Stubbs suggests the uninhabited planet of Kavis II will be a good home for them. The nanites help Stubbs launch his probe.

TRIVIA

- *Evolution* is a story written by the new producer, based on an idea by the outgoing producer. It served as a reintroduction for Beverly, who returned for the third season. Scenes with Wesley and his friends were filmed but cut.

RATING

- A story that isn't sure whether it's about scientific responsibility or mother and son relationships, so ends up being about nothing very much.

3.2 THE ENSIGNS OF COMMAND

STARDATE UNKNOWN

Data has to convince colonists to leave their home

TX 2 October 1989
WRITER Melinda Snodgrass
DIRECTOR Cliff Bole
GUEST CAST Richard Allen (Noe), Grainger Hines (Gosheven – uncredited), Mart McChesney (Sheliak), Colm Meaney (O'Brien), Eileen Seeley (Mackenzie), Mark L Taylor (Haritath)

The Sheliak Corporate, a race obsessed with legal matters, demand the evacuation of the Federation colony Tau Cygna V, granted to them in a century-old treaty. They will arrive in four days and kill any humans found there. The Enterprise is sent to arrange the evacuation, and Data is sent down. A hyperonic radiation belt surrounding the planet prevents transporters from working – the ancestors of the colonists settled here when their ship the SS Artemis crashed, and have transformed a desert world into a thriving colony. The leader of the colonists, Gosheven, insists they are staying put. Picard tries to negotiate with the Sheliak, but they are stubbornly sticking to the letter of the treaty. It becomes clear that even with the cooperation of the colonists, it will take weeks to evacuate the planet – the Sheliak insist on their deadline. Data realises that humans require action, not his well-chosen words, and destroys the colony's aqueduct with his one phaser – the Sheliak will be infinitely more destructive. The colonists are convinced. Picard uses legal trickery and a careful reading of the treaty to buy enough time to evacuate.

QUOTES

- 'This is just a thing, and things can be replaced. Lives cannot' – *Data*

TRIVIA

- This story was originally the season opener, and was made before *Evolution*, but the two were swapped before broadcast. The stardate is given as 43133.3 in the script, but not the episode.
- Granger Hines was unhappy that his dialogue was redubbed by another actor, so he had his name removed from the credits.

RATING

- A rare episode where the budget lets the story down. Yet again, Data discovers something about humans – in this case 'actions speak louder than words' – that it's difficult to believe he'd never noticed before. An episode that feels like it could have been so much better.

3.3 THE SURVIVORS

STARDATE 43152.4

Two elderly colonists have mysteriously survived a nuclear attack

TX October 9 1989
WRITER Michael Wagner
DIRECTOR Les Landau
GUEST CAST John Anderson (Kevin Uxbridge), Anne Haney (Rishon Uxbridge)

The Enterprise crew discovers that the colony on Delta Rana IV has been destroyed in a nuclear attack by an alien vessel. Eleven thousand colonists have died – but two, Kevin and Rishon Uxbridge, have survived completely unharmed. The alien vessel returns, and attacks again, apparently killing the Uxbridges. The Enterprise returns fire, destroying the craft. But there are again two life-forms on the planet – Picard beams up the Uxbridges and demands an explanation. Kevin tells them he is a member of the Douwd, an immortal race. He fell in love with Rishon 53 years before, and they retired to Delta Rana IV – which was attacked by the alien Husnock. Rishon died, and in his rage, Kevin wiped out all 50 billion of the Husnock race – since then, he has lived in guilt with a simulacrum of his wife. Stunned by the scale of the crime, and unable to judge him, Picard allows Kevin to return to the planet to recreate his former life.

QUOTES

- 'Good tea. Nice house.' *Worf fails to master the thing humans know as small talk*

TRIVIA

- Still relatively rare for *The Next Generation*, this episode saw a location shoot – a summer's day in Malibu.

RATING

- John Anderson's performance saves an old-fashioned story in a season that was starting to outgrow old-fashioned stories.

3.4 WHO WATCHES THE WATCHERS

STARDATE 43073.5

A Federation observation team is discovered by a feudal society

TX 14 October 1989
WRITERS Richard Manning and Hans Beimler
DIRECTOR Robert Wiemer
GUEST CAST James Greene (Dr Barron), Lois Hall (Dr Warren), James McIntyre (Hali), John McLiam (Fento), Kathryn Leigh Scott (Nuria), Pamela Seagall (Oji), Ray Wise (Liko)

A Federation team of anthropologists is concealed behind holographic generators, studying the culture of the planet Mintaka III, a race whose society is centuries behind humanity. The generator explodes, and attracts the attention of Liko, a local, who sees Beverly arrive with a medical team. Liko touches the damaged equipment and is given an electric shock – Beverly beams him up to sickbay to save him. She beams him back down, thinking she has erased his memory. One of the Federation team, Palmer, is missing – Troi and Riker disguise themselves and beam down to find him. They discover that Liko remembers the Enterprise, and thinks Picard is their ancient deity, the Overseer. Mintakan society is on the verge of a scientific revolution and this will set them back centuries. Picard beams the rational Nuria to the Enterprise to explain – a violation of the Prime Directive – and explains that he is from an advanced culture, but is no god. She realises the truth, but it's only when Picard is wounded with an arrow that the rest of the Mintakans accept he is flesh and blood.

QUOTES

- 'Millennia ago they abandoned their belief in the supernatural. Now you are asking me to sabotage that achievement? To send them back into the dark ages of superstition and ignorance and fear? No!' – *Picard*

TRIVIA

- For the first time, *The Next Generation* features location shooting at the Vasquez Rocks, frequently visited by the original series (most famously in *Arena*).
- The title derives from Juvenal – 'quis custodes ipso custodiet?'

RATING

- There's a clever twist – the Mintakans have already abandoned religion and seeing Picard reintroduces god into their society. The message of the episode, as proclaimed by Picard, is the bravest, most uncompromising declaration of atheist principles ever made on American TV. Although no one seems to have noticed.

3.5 THE BONDING

STARDATE 43198.7

A young boy is left orphaned by the death of a crewman... or is he?

TX 21 October 1989
WRITER Ronald D Moore
DIRECTOR Winrich Kolbe
GUEST CAST Gabriel Damon (Jeremy), Colm Meaney (O'Brien), Susan Powell (Marla Aster)

An Away Team led by Worf undertakes a survey of the home planet of the Koinonians, a race that wiped itself out in a civil war. Lt Aster triggers a booby trap and is killed. Her son, Jeremy, is on the Enterprise, and is now an orphan. Worf is troubled, and tells Troi he feels connected to the boy, who he takes time to talk to. Wesley also tries to comfort the boy, but he seems to respond better to Worf's less sentimental approach. Jeremy is visited by his dead mother, who tells him they'll live together on the planet. Picard learns that energy beings on the planet don't want Jeremy to suffer. Picard convinces them that humans can't be shielded from grief. Worf and Jeremy perform a Klingon bonding ritual, the R'uustai, a much better way of coping with loss.

QUOTES

- 'In my tradition, we do not grieve the loss of the body. We celebrate the releasing of the spirit.' – *Worf to Jeremy*

TRIVIA

- Originally, Jeremy was going to recreate his mother on the holodeck – but there were already a number of holodeck episodes in the works this season, like *Booby Trap* and *Hollow Pursuits*.

RATING

- An episode that works, and a rare one where Klingon ritual is portrayed as more like the solution than the problem. Michael Dorn gets a chance to show Worf's caring side, without diluting the character.

3.6 BOOBY TRAP

STARDATE 43205.6

Geordi falls in love with the hologram of the Enterprise's designer

TX 30 October 1989
WRITERS Ron Roman, Michael Piller and Richard Danus (story by Michael Wagner and Ron Roman)
DIRECTOR Gabrielle Beaumont
GUEST CAST Susan Gibney (Leah Brahms), Whoopi Goldberg (Guinan), Albert Hall (Galek Dar), Christy Henshaw (Julie Warner), Colm Meaney (O'Brien)

The Enterprise responds to the automatic distress call of a Promellian battlecruiser – a relic from a war fought a millennium ago. Suddenly the Enterprise loses power and is bathed in radiation, and is forced to raise shields. It's a trap, the same one that did for the Promellian ship, and designed by their enemies, the Menthar. Radiation will kill the crew in three hours. Geordi tries to work out how to get the engines working again, and goes to the holodeck to consult a hologram of the engines' original designer, Dr Leah Brahms. Data collects information about how the Promellians died, but it offers no way out. Geordi's falling for Dr Brahms, and together they work out a solution: using only thrusters, the Enterprise can use the slingshot effect to get clear. Picard destroys the asteroid field – and, to his deep regret, the battlecruiser – to prevent anyone else falling into the trap.

TRIVIA

- It seems a little odd that Geordi seems to be the only person working on the problem – back in the first season, Riker described Argyle as 'one of our chief engineers', and Geordi has a sizable staff. Later in the season, in *Hollow Pursuits*, we see a more sensible roundtable arrangement for sorting out problems that threaten the ship.
- The real Leah Brahms arrives and discover Geordi's hologram of her in *Galaxy's Child*.

RATING

- A good, sweet, story for Geordi, and one that raises lots of interesting questions about the ethics of the holodeck without beating the audience over the head with a message. Not an outstanding episode, but proof that by this stage even the average stories are well worth watching.

3.7 THE ENEMY

Geordi is stranded on a hostile planet with a Romulan

TX 6 November 1989
WRITERS David Kemper and Michael Piller
DIRECTOR David Carson
GUEST CAST Andreas Katsulas (Tomalak), Colm Meaney (O'Brien), Steve Rankin (Patahk), John Snyder (Bochra)

STARDATE 43349.2

On Galorndon Core, Riker, Worf and Geordi find a crashed Romulan scout ship. Geordi gets cut off looking for survivors, and Riker and Worf return to the Enterprise with an injured Romulan, Patahk. Patahk says he was alone, but Data discovers he's been communicating with a nearby Warbird. Only a blood transfusion from Worf will save his life... but Worf refuses, and Patahk dies. On the planet, Geordi is captured by another Romulan, Bochra. They connect Geordi's visor and a tricorder to create an emergency beacon. The commander of the Warbird, Tomalak, demands the return of Patahk, and when he learns he is dead, he powers up his weapons. Detecting the emergency signal from the planet, Tomalak is forced to concede that Patahk wasn't working alone, and as a gesture of thanks for Geordi saving Bochra's life, he withdraws across the Neutral Zone.

QUOTES

- 'We have good reason to mistrust one another. But we have even better reason to set those differences aside.' – *Picard to Tomalak*

TRIVIA

- David Carson directed *The Six Napoleons* instalment of the *Sherlock Holmes* TV series, the episode that featured Marina Sirtis.
- Andreas Katsulas puts in a memorable turn as Tomalak, and he would reappear a number of times. He would go on to play G'Kar in *Babylon 5*.

RATING

- An effective episode. Geordi gets another chance to shine, but Worf's three scenes are the most powerful and interesting.

3.8 THE PRICE

Troi falls for a negotiator who wants to secure access to a new wormhole

TX 13 November 1989
WRITER Hannah Louise Shearer
DIRECTOR Robert Scheerer
GUEST CAST Castulo Guerra (Mendoza), Kevin Peter Hall (Leyor), Elizabeth Hoffman (Bhavani), Matt McCoy (Devinoni Ral), Colm Meaney (O'Brien), Dan Shor (Arridor), Scott Thompson (Goss)

STARDATE 43385.6

The Enterprise is hosting a conference for species bidding for control of a stable wormhole discovered by the people of Barzan II, which leads straight to the Gamma Quadrant, offering a unique chance for exploration and trade. The Chrysalians are represented by Devinoni Ral, the Federation by Dr Mendoza, the Caldonians by Leyor – and the Ferengi gatecrash, led by DaiMon Goss and their scientists Kol and Dr Arridor. The Barzan premier, Bhavani, starts the negotiations for the price. Troi begins a romantic relationship with Ral, but discovers he is a part-Betazoid, and using his empathic skills to manipulate the other bidders – he convinces Leyor to drop out and gets the Ferengi and Federation fighting, so the Barzans distrust them both. Geordi and Data investigate the wormhole. The Ferengi scientists follow – and the wormhole proves unstable. The Ferengi are trapped in the Gamma Quadrant; Geordi and Data barely escape in time. Ral has taken control of the wormhole for the Chrysalians – but the wormhole is worthless.

QUOTES

- 'At the negotiating table, it can be fatal to have a heart.' – *Ral reveals his true nature to Troi*

TRIVIA

- Advance publicity for this story concentrated on the 'bed scenes' between Troi and Ral. Despite Kirk's fondness for women, this was the first time that *Star Trek* characters had been seen in bed together.
- While no one could have predicted it at the time, this story is one of the most seminal in *Star Trek* history. It established the value of a stable wormhole, a key plot point in *Deep Space Nine*. Also many years in the future, the Ferengi from this episode would reappear in *Voyager* in the episode *False Profits*.

- An entertaining episode, with some cleverly dramatised negotiations, nice reflective moments and the Ferengi now firmly established as comic relief. Troi in a nightie wielding massage oil is the icing on the cake.

3.9 THE VENGEANCE FACTOR

STARDATE 43421.9

Picard tries to negotiate with a race of space pirates

TX 20 November 1989
WRITER Sam Rolfe
DIRECTOR Timothy Bond
GUEST CAST Joey Aresco (Brull), Elikanah J Burns (Temarek), Michael Lamper (Mallon), Marc Lawrence (Volnoth), Stephen Lee (Chorgan), Nancy Parsons (Marouk), Lisa Wilcox (Yuta)

Scientific outposts have been raided by Acamarians. Picard meets with the Acamarian leader, Marouk, who explains that the raiders are called Gatherers, who broke away from the rest of society. Picard initiates peace talks between the two factions, while Riker romances the lovely Yuta, Marouk's food taster. The Enterprise goes to Gamma Hromi II and they arrange a meeting with Chorgan, the leader of the Gatherers. Yuta is the last survivor of the clan Tralesta, who were wiped out by Chorgan's people. She infects them with a microvirus. Riker discovers the truth, and is forced to kill Yuta rather than let her kill Chorgan. Chorgan is impressed, and declares a truce.

TRIVIA

- Michael Lamper is Marina Sirtis' husband – they were a couple when this episode was made, and married in June 1993.
- By now, a lively internet community was starting to grow up. One of the perennial questions they asked about *Star Trek* (along with 'who's better: Kirk or Picard?'), was 'who's stronger: Worf or Data?' This episode establishes that it's Data.

RATING

- The episode is rather dark, but the suspicion is that the gruesome moments are there to distract from a weak story. Riker's decision to gun down a woman – his lover! – is a case in point. It's great to see him make a tough choice rather than cop out... but surely with all the technology at his disposal there was another way to stop her?

3.10 THE DEFECTOR

STARDATE 43462.5

The Enterprise takes on board a high-level Romulan defector

TX 1 January 1990
WRITER Ronald D Moore
DIRECTOR Robert Scheerer
GUEST CAST John Hancock (Haden), Andreas Katsulas (Tomalak), James Sloyan (Setal/Jarok), Patrick Stewart (Michael Williams), SA Templeman (John Bates)

A Romulan scout ship heads towards the Enterprise, pursued by a Warbird. Its pilot demands asylum, which Picard grants. The Warbird returns to Romulan space. The defector claims to be a low-grade technician, Setal, and that the Romulans are planning to launch an attack from a secret base on Nelvana III to seize the Neutral Zone, and then key sectors of the Federation. He tells Picard they have time to destroy the base and prevent this. Riker and Troi interrogate Setal, but he refuses to provide any evidence for his claims. Eventually he admits he's Admiral Alidar Jarok, a very senior officer, opposed to the plans for war. Scans of Nelvana show no base – Jarok has been tricked. Two Warbirds decloak, trapping the Enterprise. Their commander, Tomalak, gloats that he's exposed a disloyal officer and captured the Federation flagship in breach of treaty, but Picard has a trick up his sleeve – cloaked Klingon ships that reveal themselves. Tomalak is outgunned and retreats. Jarok is a broken man, and commits suicide.

QUOTES

- 'Now if these men do not die well, it will be a black matter for the king that led them to it.' – *Picard quotes Shakespeare*

TRIVIA

- At one point, this was a Beverly episode in which she fell for her Romulan patient, but (thankfully?) this plotline was dropped. The episode originally opened with Data reprising his Sherlock Holmes holodeck character, but as another Paramount production was being sued over Sherlock Holmes rights, the legal people got nervous and (again thankfully?) the sequence was replaced with a scene from *Henry V*, with Patrick Stewart disguised as one of the players.
- Riker demonstrates in this episode that he's familiar with Romulan swearwords – a 'varool' is an extremely pejorative term for an unwise person. While it's handy for a production team trying to reach a family audience, it's not explained why the Enterprise's universal translator doesn't translate the Klingon or Romulan curse words.
- This is the first episode to feature the new four-foot model of the Enterprise. Smaller than the model that had been used, it was more detailed. The main difference was that it had large windows at the very front of the saucer (which are meant to be those of the Ten-Forward lounge).

RATING

- An intelligent study of the ethics of patriotism, wartime leadership, and what drives people to betray their country. Tense and twisty, this is a classic episode in a season that's building up to be something very special indeed.

3.11 THE HUNTED

STARDATE 43489.2

The Enterprise captures a criminal who is more than he seems

TX 8 January 1990
WRITER Robin Bernheim
DIRECTOR Cliff Bole
GUEST CAST Andrew Bicknell (Wagnor), James Cromwell (Nayrok), J Michael Flynn (Zaynar), Jeff McCarthy (Roga Danar), Colm Meaney (O'Brien)

Angosia III has applied to join the Federation. The Enterprise arrives in time to see a break-out from a prison colony by Roga Danar, a veteran of the Tarsian War. It becomes clear that he and his brothers in arms have been bio-chemically altered and mentally conditioned to become killing machines. Prime Minister Nayrok tells Picard that such soldiers have been unable to adapt to ordinary life, and it is an internal matter. Picard wants to help the veterans, but his hands are tied by the Prime Directive. Danar escapes and leads fellow veterans into Nayrok's chambers. Picard reminds Nayrok that he can't help him: it's an internal affair.

TRIVIA

- Budget cuts prevented a shootout at the end of the episode, an allegorical story about the government abandoning Vietnam veterans.

RATING

- An OK episode, but there's little to write home about. Ironically, the high point is Picard abandoning Nayrok for exactly the same reason he couldn't help Danar – the new, cheaper, ending.

3.12 THE HIGH GROUND

STARDATE 43510.7

Ansata terrorists threaten the Enterprise to win support for their cause

TX 29 January 1990
WRITER Melinda M Snodgrass
DIRECTOR Gabrielle Beaumont
GUEST CAST Marc Buckland (Katik Shaw), Richard Cox (Kyril Finn), Kerrie Keane (Alexana Devos), Christopher Pettiet (Boy), Fred G Smith (Policeman)

An Away Team in Rutia III's city centre witnesses an explosion – Beverly rushes to help the injured, and is captured by Ansata terrorists, who are using dimensional shifting technology. The terrorist leader, Finn, reveals that he's got some plan for the Enterprise – and that his men need treatment for side-effects of the dimensional shifting. Riker beams down to talk to the chief of police, Devos, who tells him that the Ansata have been fighting a bloody civil war for independence – and have killed innocents. Riker gets word to the Ansata movement that he is ready to negotiate, but Finn isn't – he thinks the Federation have sided with the Rutians, and intends to destroy the Enterprise. Finn shifts aboard the ship and nearly blows up the warp core, but Geordi saves the day. Finn takes Picard hostage and returns to the planet, but Wesley locates his base. An Away Team assists Devos in storming the place, and Finn is killed.

TRIVIA

- This episode wasn't shown by the BBC, presumably because of some concern about its portrayal of terrorism. It can't just be Data's line about the IRA's terrorism leading to the unification of Ireland (due in 2024, and not 2025 as the official *Chronology* states) – they could just have cut the one line.

RATING

- An action-packed episode, but one that seems to muddle its message – while there's no reason it should have been 'banned' in the UK, if the situation is meant to represent Ireland (and a character called Finn is a big hint it is), then the analogy doesn't work and it just rings hollow. Post-September 11th, its depiction of terrorism and the Rutians 'harsh' methods must take on different associations for the American audience.

3.13 DEJA Q

STARDATE 43539.1

Q has his powers stripped from him – and turns to Picard for help

TX 5 February 1990
WRITER Richard Danus
DIRECTOR Les Landau
GUEST CAST Corbin Bernsen (Q2), Richard Cansino (Garin), John de Lancie (Q), Whoopi Goldberg (Guinan), Betty Muramoto (Bre'el Scientist)

The moon of Bre'el IV has fallen from its orbit and is heading for the planet. The Enterprise has arrived to try to help. As they start work, a naked Q appears on the bridge. He's been thrown out of the Continuum, and has come here because Picard is the closest thing he has to a friend. Worf takes Q to the brig. The crew prove unable to deflect the moon. Q is preoccupied with his new mortality, baffled by sleeping and eating. He is attacked by the Calamarain, a gaseous race with a grievance against him. Data saves him, but is badly damaged. Q is impressed by the self-sacrifice, and steals a shuttle – his death will help Picard. A second Q appears in the shuttle. He is impressed by Q's selflessness, and restores his powers. Q saves Bre'el IV, and thanks the Enterprise crew by giving them all cigars, and Data an uncontrollable fit of laughter.

QUOTES

- 'There are creatures in the universe that would consider you the ultimate achievement, android. No feelings, no emotions – no pain.' – *Q to Data*
- 'You're a better human than I.' – *Q to Data*

TRIVIA

- The original story had Q faking his loss of powers and engineering a war between the Federation and Klingons.

RATING

- A great story, a comedy that's genuinely funny, but with a nice serious edge that contrasts Data and Q (Q's 'curse' of humanity is exactly what Data's been striving for all his life). It's pretty obvious Q's going to get his powers back and save the moon from the moment he appears, but it's still a satisfying moment when he does.

3.14 A MATTER OF PERSPECTIVE

STARDATE 43610.4

Riker is accused of murder – a holodeck recreation holds the truth

TX 12 February 1990
WRITER Ed Zuckerman
DIRECTOR Cliff Bole
GUEST CAST Juli Donald (Tanya), Gina Hecht (Manua Apgar), Mark Margolis (Nel Apgar), Colm Meaney (O'Brien), Craig Richard Nelson (Krag)

Riker and Geordi have been working on a space station orbiting Tanuga IV, monitoring the work of Dr Apgar into Krieger waves. Geordi reports that Apgar hasn't made a breakthrough. As Riker returns to the Enterprise, there's a power drain, and the station explodes, killing Apgar. Chief Investigator Krag beams up from the planet and arrests Riker, but Picard wants to hold a hearing. Using the holodeck, Riker reconstructs his version of events. Manua, Apgar's wife, attempted to seduce Riker, but he turned her down. Apgar catches them, and says he will lodge a formal complaint to Starfleet. Mrs Apgar then gives her version – Riker was trying to seduce her, not the other way round. Picard reluctantly agrees there's a case to answer. Data, though, has detected radiation – Krieger waves. Apgar had succeeded in his work, and was hiding it from the Federation because he could get a better price. He was trying to kill Riker as he transported, but it backfired. Krag accepts the evidence.

TRIVIA

- Not just a 'bottle' show but an episode that sees the same scenes shown three times, the story was commissioned to balance a number of expensive episodes this season, but everyone involved, particularly the director, Cliff Bole, was pleased with the result.

RATING

- An episode that doesn't really work as courtroom drama – both the Federation and Tanugans seem to make up legal procedure as they go along – but does work as television drama, and uses the holodeck cleverly. The teaser scene, with Data's harsh but fair criticism of Picard's painting ability, is very funny (and we never see Picard paint again).

3.15 YESTERDAY'S ENTERPRISE

STARDATE 43625.2

In an alternate timeline, the Federation and Klingons are at war

TX 19 February 1990
WRITER Ira Steven Behr, Richard Manning, Hans Beimler and Ronald Moore (story by Trent Christopher Ganino and Eric A Stillwell)
DIRECTOR David Carson
GUEST CAST Denise Crosby (Tasha Yar), Whoopi Goldberg (Guinan), Christopher McDonald (Richard Castillo), Tricia O'Neill (Rachel Garrett)

The Enterprise detects a starship emerging from a temporal rift... and then everything has changed. The Enterprise-D is now a warship, with Tasha Yar as security chief, and the Federation is losing a war against the Klingons. The other ship is the Enterprise-C, which has travelled 22 years forward in time. It's badly damaged, and the Enterprise-D beams survivors aboard. Only Guinan has any sense that things are wrong – and a vague feeling that Tasha shouldn't be there. The captain of the Enterprise-C, Rachel Garrett, says they were on the way to answering a distress call from the Klingon outpost on Narendra III when they were attacked by Romulan Warbirds. They escaped through the temporal rift. Data calculates that if the Enterprise-C had stayed, it would have been destroyed – but such an honourable sacrifice would have impressed the Klingons, and the war would probably have been avoided. Tasha falls for the Enterprise-C's first officer, Castillo. Picard tells Garrett she has to return to her own time – if nothing else, her crew's prospects in the present are as bleak as in the past. The Klingons attack the two ships as they prepare for the Enterprise-C's return, and Garrett is killed. Tasha Yar volunteers to go back with the Enterprise-C, to give them a fighting chance. Guinan convinces Picard that this will set things right and prevent the war. As three Klingon battlecruisers attack, Picard places his own Enterprise in danger to buy the older ship enough time to return to the rift. Riker is killed, and the Enterprise is seconds from destruction when the Enterprise-C enters the rift and the original timeline is restored. Only Guinan has any sense of what has just occurred...

QUOTES

- 'Let's make sure that history never forgets the name Enterprise.' – *Picard*

TRIVIA

- The episode was written in three days (and, judging by the credits, by just about everyone who was in the building at the time – Michael Piller also did substantial uncredited work) to fit with the availability of Denise Crosby and Whoopi Goldberg.
- This was the merging of two similar story ideas – one in which the Enterprise-C appears in the present and Picard has the dilemma of whether to tell them that soon after returning to their own time they met a terrible end, and another where Vulcan history was accidentally changed and the Enterprise found itself in a timeline where the Vulcans and Romulans were the cruel masters of the galaxy.
- The episode won an Emmy for sound editing and nominations for music and sound mixing.

RATING

- Bleak, dark, deterministic and brilliant, with great use made of Picard and Guinan. It briefly slips you into a timeline where you wish they'd kept Tasha Yar. Everything's kept at a human level and there's minimal technobabble. It's around this point that even the sceptics started realising *The Next Generation* was something special.

3.16 THE OFFSPRING

STARDATE 43657.0

Data has a daughter...

TX 12 March 1990
WRITER Rene Echevarria
DIRECTOR Jonathan Frakes
GUEST CAST Nicolas Coster (Haftel), Leonard John Crowfoot (Robot Lal) Judyanne Elder (Ballard), Hallie Todd (Lal), Diane Moser, Hayne Bayle, Maria Leone, James G Becker (Crew in Ten-Forward)

Data summons his friends to his laboratory – he has created a child for himself, a robot called Lal, by copying patterns from his positronic brain. Picard is concerned that he didn't ask permission, but Data notes that no other crewmembers have to have the decision to have children authorised. Lal chooses to resemble a young human female, and rapidly begins to develop a personality. Admiral Haftel contacts the Enterprise, and says Lal should be sent to the Daystrom Institute for study – he arrives to see Lal for himself. Lal is finding it difficult to socialise with other children. Data learns of Haftel's plans, and strongly objects. Lal kisses Riker, and is concerned about her lack of emotions. Guinan offers her a job in Ten-Forward. Haftel orders Data to surrender Lal. Picard countermands the order, convinced Lal has rights. Lal begins demonstrating emotions, but this is a sign that her positronic brain is failing. Haftel tries to help, but Lal dies. Data, absorbs Lal's memories and resumes his duties.

QUOTES

- 'It would seem you have actually improved on yourself, Data.'
  'Is that not the goal of every parent?' – *Picard and Data*

TRIVIA

- Jonathan Frakes became the first *The Next Generation* cast member to direct an episode – he would continue to direct TV episodes, before taking charge of the movies *Star Trek: First Contact* and *Star Trek: Insurrection*, and has branched out to work on *Roswell* and the live action *Thunderbirds* movie.

RATING

- Cited by Patrick Stewart as one his favourite episodes, *The Offspring* is a good example of a *Star Trek* story which discusses a moral issue, even if that issue ('would an android make a suitable parent?') is a little... artificial, and was dealt with pretty comprehensively in the previous season's *The Measure of a Man*.

3.17 SINS OF THE FATHER

STARDATE 43685.2

Worf must clear his father's name

TX 19 March 1990
WRITERS Ronald D Moore and W Reed Morgan (based on a teleplay by Drew Deighan)
DIRECTOR Les Landau
GUEST CAST Charles Cooper (K'mpec), BJ Davis (Assassin – uncredited), Teddy Davis (Technician), Chris Doyle (Assassin – uncredited), Thelma Lee (Kahlest), Patrick Massett (Duras), Tony Todd (Kurn)

As part of the Starfleet Exchange Programme, Klingon Commander Kurn has been posted to the Enterprise. Kurn soon rubs the crew up the wrong way – all except Worf, who he treats too politely. When Worf complains, Kurn explains that they are brothers, and that their father, Mogh, was accused of helping the Romulans massacre the colony at Khitomer where Worf was found, and has been judged a traitor by the High Council. When Worf tells Picard he wants to go to the Klingon homeworld to right the wrong, the captain says the Enterprise will go with him. On the homeworld, Worf challenges Duras, his father's enemy, to an honour duel. Kurn is wounded by assassins, and Picard steps in as Worf's second for the duel. It becomes clear that it was Duras' father who was the traitor – but Duras is powerful, and this news will split the Empire. Worf accepts discommendation, giving up his honour for peace.

QUOTES

- 'I am a Klingon. If you doubt it, a demonstration can be arranged.' – *Worf kicks ass*
- 'Today is a good day to die, Duras, and the day is not yet over.' – *Worf means business, and unknowingly coins himself a catchphrase*

TRIVIA

- This is the first (but by no means the last) time *Star Trek* showed the Klingon homeworld. It marked a turning point for Worf, who from now (and into *Deep Space Nine*) would have stories based around a huge family saga.

- The guttural Klingon language had first appeared in the opening scenes of *Star Trek: The Motion Picture*, but from here on it was developed into a full language by linguist Marc Okrand, and before long whole Klingon dictionaries and linguaphone-style tapes were available to fans. Based on a line in *The Undiscovered Country*, even a Klingon version of *Hamlet* has been published – although plans to translate the Bible into Klingon hit trouble when there were theological differences among the translators. No, honestly. As many hardcore fans will attest, Klingon is an easy language to learn, although it always sounds like a Welshman trying to start a fight. A bluffer's tip to get people to stop speaking Klingon is to shout '*mev yap*!' ('that's enough') at them, although purists would prefer '*bljatlh e ylmev*' (pronounced 'bee-jattle ee yee-mev', meaning 'be quiet'). The Klingon for 'I don't speak Klingon' is *tlhlngan Hol vljatlhlaHbe* (pronounced 'tuh-lingan khol vee-jattle-lack-bee').
- Meanwhile, back in the real world, this episode won Emmys for production design and set decoration.

RATING

- The Klingons get a rich and fascinating culture, and Worf and Picard are pitched into the heart of it. A great episode, tainted now only by the knowledge that it will spawn many inferior Klingon sequels. The original *Star Trek* ran out of new ideas before its third season ended, but by the same point, *The Next Generation*'s only warming up.

3.18 ALLEGIANCE

STARDATE 43714.1

Picard is abducted and replaced by an impostor

TX 26 March 1990
WRITERS Richard Manning and Hans Beimler
DIRECTOR Winrich Kolbe
GUEST CAST Stephen Markel (Kova Tholl), Jocelyn O'Brien (Haro), Jeff Rector, Jerry Rector (Aliens), Reiner Schone (Esoqq)

Picard vanishes from his quarters and materialises in a small cell, which he is sharing with three aliens: Kova Tholl of Mizar II, Mitena Haro (a Bolian Starfleet cadet), and Esoqq of Chalna. The claustrophobic surroundings add to the mutual suspicion and recrimination. Meanwhile, an impostor Picard appears on the Enterprise – he orders the ship away from its scheduled rendezvous with the USS Hood and towards the Lonka Cluster. This Picard is a lot more relaxed than the real one, joining the officers at their poker game, attempting to woo Beverly and singing drinking songs in Ten-Forward. The real Picard realises that Haro is an impostor, and she reveals herself to be one of a race of identical telepaths who have kidnapped them to discover more about individuality and leadership. Picard returns to the Enterprise just as Riker becomes suspicious of his impostor, and they confine the aliens in a forcefield. The aliens don't like the experience, and realise the error of confining others.

TRIVIA

- A story that fulfills two needs – to save money after the expensive *Yesterday's Enterprise*, and to give Patrick Stewart something to do. Earlier in the year, Stewart had told the producers he was thinking of leaving at the end of the season. They persuaded him that he would be given more, particularly comedy and action. Both this and the next episode fit that bill.

RATING

- A fun episode, with Patrick Stewart getting to do both a serious and comic plot in the same week, and clearly relishing it.

3.19 CAPTAIN'S HOLIDAY

STARDATE 43745.2

Picard goes on holiday – and becomes embroiled in the quest for the ultimate weapon

TX 2 April 1990
WRITER Ira Steven Behr
DIRECTOR Chip Chalmers
GUEST CAST Michael Champion (Boratus), Max Grodenchik (Sovak), Jennifer Hetrick (Vash), Deirdre Imershein (Joval), Karen Landry (Ajur)

Picard is persuaded to take a holiday on the pleasure planet Risa, where he decides to catch up with his reading, starting with *Ulysses*. However, he soon meets Vash, an attractive archaeologist who's looking for a mythical artefact, the Tox Uthat. To fund her trip to Risa, Vash has swindled a Ferengi, Sovak, who's come looking for her. Two Vorgons from the twenty-seventh century are also looking for the Tox Uthat. Picard locates it, and he and Vash hike to its location where they are joined by the Ferengi and Vorgons and start digging. It's a bluff, though: Vash has already retrieved it. The Vorgons are revealed as criminals. The Enterprise arrives and Picard orders it to destroy the Tox Uthat. He bids farewell to Vash.

TRIVIA

- Vash would return in *Q-Pid* and *Q-Less*.
- Gates McFadden was surprised to see Jennifer Hetrick – the year before, McFadden had sold her house to her.

RATING

- Patrick Stewart gets the 'sex and shooting' story he'd wanted for ages, and makes the most of it. A confident, funny story that's very entertaining and a nice change from a lot of the previous 'heavy' episodes.

3.20 TIN MAN

STARDATE 43779.3

A nervy Betazoid helps contact an unusual life-form

TX 23 April 1990
WRITER Dennis Putnam Bailey and David Bischoff
DIRECTOR Robert Scheerer
GUEST CAST Michael Cavanaugh (Robert DeSoto), Harry Groener (Tam Elbrun), Colm Meaney (O'Brien), Peter Vogt (Romulan Commander)

The USS Hood transfers a first contact specialist, Tam Elbrun, to the Enterprise, which heads to the Beta Stromgren system, home of a collapsing star. A mysterious life-form, dubbed 'Tinman,' has been discovered. Elbrun has made preliminary contact with it, and knows it calls itself Gomtuu. The Romulans are known to be active in the area, adding urgency to the mission. As they arrive in the system, a Romulan Warbird decloaks – they want to destroy the creature, but it destroys them. Gomtuu is the last of its kind – Data and Elbrun beam over to communicate. Gomtuu is lonely, and Elbrun decides to stay with it. A second Romulan Warbird arrives for revenge – Gomtuu creates a shockwave which pushes the Enterprise and the Romulan ship away, then sets off with Elbrun to explore the galaxy.

TRIVIA

- Based on the writers' 1975 short story *Tin Woodman*, which was nominated for a Nebula award.

RATING

- Another strong episode, although Gomtuu perhaps isn't as weird as the script seems to demand, and Elbrun becomes very annoying very quickly.

3.21 HOLLOW PURSUITS

STARDATE 43807.4

Shy Reg Barclay retreats into a fantasy holodeck world rather than deal with his problems in the real one

TX 30 April 1990
WRITER Sally Caves
DIRECTOR Cliff Bole
GUEST CAST Charley Lang (Duffy), Colm Meaney (O'Brien), Dwight Schultz (Reg Barclay)

Engineer Reg Barclay is spending a great deal of time in the holodeck, where he's created a version of the Enterprise in which he's universally feared or respected. In reality, he's recently been assigned to the flagship, and finds it difficult to cope. When he's late for yet another shift, Riker and Geordi suggest he should be transferred. Picard is more forgiving, and suggests Geordi get to know him. Geordi realises Barclay is chronically shy, and discovers another of his holodeck scenarios, with fantasy versions of the officers. Geordi orders Barclay to see the ship's counsellor – not knowing that Troi is the object of Barclay's fantasies. Meanwhile, a series of minor technical problems afflict the ship, coinciding with the arrival of some medical supplies. Reg is assigned to clear up the problem – but prefers to escape to the holodeck. Riker, Troi and Geordi enter the holodeck, and Riker is furious to discover himself represented as a squeaky midget. Troi suggests it's all healthy fantasy – until she's confronted with 'the Goddess of Empathy', a scantily clad version of herself. The technical problems have spread to the warp engines, which begin to accelerate out of control. While the other engineers are baffled, Reg deduces that the medical supplies were contaminated with invidium, which has affected the systems. He saves the ship in the nick of time, earning the respect of the crew.

TRIVIA

- Geordi confides to Barclay that he once fell in love on the holodeck, a reference to *Booby Trap*.

RATING

- It's nice to see not everyone on the Enterprise is perfect. A sensitive character piece, with a well-balanced performance by Dwight Schultz making Barclay sympathetic and pathetic by turns.

3.22 THE MOST TOYS

STARDATE 43872.2

Data is stolen by a collector

TX 7 May 1990
WRITER Shari Goodhartz
DIRECTOR Timothy Bond
GUEST CAST Jane Daly (Varria), Colm Meaney (O'Brien), Nehemiah Persoff (Palor Toff), Saul Rubinek (Kivas Fajo)

Data is transporting hazardous hytritium to the Enterprise from the Kovis, the ship of trader Kivas Fajo, when his shuttlecraft explodes. While the Enterprise crew mourns, Data wakes up to discover himself as an exhibit in Fajo's collection. Data allies himself with Varria, Fajo's bullied assistant. Riker becomes suspicious – they had taken the hytritium on board to treat water contamination on Beta Agni II... contamination which looks deliberate. Picard realises what Fajo has done, and they begin to search for the Kovis. Data and Varria stage an escape, but Fajo catches them and kills Varria. Data aims his phaser at Fajo – but is beamed over to the Enterprise. Fajo is arrested.

TRIVIA

- Fajo was originally played by David Rappaport, star of *Time Bandits* and a well-known British actor and personality. One idea (not taken up) was that Fajo's ship would have doors and furniture scaled to Rappaport's tiny size. Rappaport attempted suicide on the weekend break after two days of filming (and would succeed soon afterwards). Publicity photos of Rappaport in the role had already been issued, and most of his scenes had been completed.

RATING

- Remarkably, the episode doesn't bear any signs of the tragedy and turmoil behind the scenes. It's another strong episode where Data is treated as a thing, rather than as a person, and is driven to the brink of committing murder in anger. Michael Dorn gets a memorable scene where he laments that, once again, he has been promoted because a comrade has been killed.

3.23 SAREK

STARDATE 43917.4

Ambassador Sarek arrives for a conference – but he's terminally ill

TX 14 May 1990
WRITER Peter S Beagle (story by Marc Cushman and Jake Jacobs)
DIRECTOR Les Landau
GUEST CAST William Denis (Ki Mendrossen), John H Francis (Ensign), Mark Lenard (Sarek), Colm Meaney (O'Brien), Joanna Miles (Perrin), Rocco Sisto (Sakkath)

Ambassador Sarek arrives on the Enterprise to complete his crowning achievement – contact between the Federation and the Legarans. Picard is warned by Sarek's staff that he is an old man, and tires easily. It becomes clear Sarek is seriously ill. He has Bendii Syndrome, a Vulcan illness affecting the very old which means his emotions are 'leaking' telepathically. Sarek is in denial about his condition, and becomes angry. Picard offers to mind-meld with the ambassador and to take on his anguish to give him enough breathing space to finish the negotiations. Picard is in agony as Sarek concludes his negotiations. Sarek thanks Picard – they now share an intimate bond.

TRIVIA

- Sarek is, of course, Spock's father, but this link is never mentioned in this episode. Picard casually mentions, though, that he met Sarek at his son's wedding.
- Sarek was in one of the original drafts of *Yesterday's Enterprise*. The present story was always about an ambassador with an illness that meant he lost self-control, but it wasn't always about Sarek.
- One of the pieces played at the Mozart concert is actually by Brahms.

RATING

- An episode that could have simply pressed fanboy buttons is, instead, a moving story of a great man brought low by old age and illness. Mark Lenard is brilliant, but Patrick Stewart steals the show with an extraordinary performance.

3.24 MÉNAGE À TROI

STARDATE 43930.7

Lwaxana Troi, Deanna and Riker are kidnapped by a Ferengi

TX 28 May 1990

The Enterprise has been attending a trade conference on Betazed, which has included the Ferengi for the first time. Lwaxana Troi has caught the eye of Ferengi delegate Tog, but she rebuffs his advances. Wesley is preparing to go to Starfleet Academy. Picard orders Riker to take some shore leave on Betazed, and the first officer takes Deanna Troi on a

WRITER Fred Bronson and Susan Sackett
DIRECTOR Robert Legato
GUEST CAST Majel Barrett (Lwaxana Troi), Frank Corsentino (Daimon Tog), Ethan Phillips (Dr Farek), Peter Slutsker (Nibor), Carel Struycken (Mr Homn), Rudolph Willrich (Reittan Grax)

picnic... where they are joined by her mother, who starts dropping hints they should get married – thus killing the romantic mood. Tog beams in to interrupt, and kidnaps the three of them, taking them to his ship, the Krayton. Tog has a business proposal for Lwaxana – her telepathy could bring him great profits, and in return he'll spare Deanna's life. Lwaxana almost tricks Tog into getting him to signal the Enterprise. Riker escapes his cell and makes the call. Wesley misses his rendezvous to help track the Krayton. The Enterprise intercepts the Ferengi ship and Picard convinces Tog that he's Lwaxana's jealous lover. Tog releases his hostages.

TRIVIA

- Body doubles were used for the Trois' 'nude scene'.
- Wesley is promoted to full Ensign at the end of the episode.

RATING

- A lightweight story that is fun, even if having Lwaxana, the Ferengi *and* a 'Wesley mopes around' subplot all in one episode does stretch the viewers' goodwill a little. Picard's 'declaration of love' is surprisingly funny.

3.25 TRANSFIGURATIONS

STARDATE 43957.2

The Enterprise discovers a mysterious man with amnesia and miraculous healing abilities

TX 4 June 1990
WRITER René Echevarria
DIRECTOR Tom Benko
GUEST CAST Charles Dennis (Sunad), Mark LaMura ('John Doe'), Colm Meaney (O'Brien), Patti Tippo (Temple), Julie Warner (Christy Henshaw)

An Away Team finds an injured man on a planet in the Zeta Gelis cluster. He has complete amnesia, but is good company and heals supernaturally quickly. The officers discover a star chart in his escape pod and work out where he is from. As the man recovers, he is wracked by strange yellow energy. He kills Worf while trying to steal a shuttlecraft... but then uses his powers to bring him back to life. The Enterprise is approaching the man's home, Zalkon. The ship is paralysed by the Zalkonians, but the mystery man's memory has returned, and he releases the Enterprise. He is approaching a new stage in evolution, and his people fear him. He transforms into an energy being and vows to help his people understand the changes that are coming.

TRIVIA

- Another story that was originally a love story for Beverly (see *The Defector*).

RATING

- A straightforward and small-scale episode that's a little lost in a season with such great and memorable stories.

3.26 THE BEST OF BOTH WORLDS Part I

STARDATE 43989.1

The Borg arrives in Federation space and assimilate Picard into the Collective

TX 1 July 1990
WRITER Michael Piller
DIRECTOR Cliff Bole
GUEST CAST Elizabeth Dennehy (Shelby), George Murdock (Hanson), Colm Meaney (O'Brien), Whoopi Goldberg (Guinan)

The Federation has lost contact with Jure 4, one of its outermost colonies. Starfleet believes the Borg is responsible, and assign Lt Comm Shelby and Admiral Hanson to the Enterprise to help investigate. Shelby is keen to become the next first officer of the Enterprise, an attitude that unnerves and irritates Riker, even though he admits to Deanna he's thinking of moving on. The crew prove the Borg are behind the attack and start working on new defences, but these will take some time. The Borg Cube is located and the Enterprise is sent to intercept it. The Borg hail Picard and demand he personally surrender. Picard orders a quick getaway. The Enterprise shelters in a nebula but is forced to make a break for it. The Borg pursue, beam aboard and capture Picard. As the Borg Cube turns and heads for Earth, the Enterprise follows. Riker oversees the development of a weapon that will destroy the Borg Cube – and Picard, if he isn't rescued. Shelby leads an attempt to rescue their Captain, but when she finds Picard he has been assimilated – turned into a Borg. The Enterprise is hailed and the Borg Picard steps forward – he is now Locutus, spokesman for the Borg. Riker orders the destruction of the Borg.

QUOTES

- 'Data was available. I took him. We came.' – *Shelby proves she has what it takes to command a starship*
- 'I am Locutus of Borg. Resistance is futile. Your life as it has been is over. From now on, you will service us.' – *Locutus*
- 'Mr Worf... fire.' – *Riker's response*

TRIVIA

- This episode was nominated for the Special Visual Effects Emmy.
- It's unclear who or what the title refers to – the point of the assimilation is that Picard becomes fully Borg, not a human/Borg hybrid who'd represent 'the best of both' species. Riker gets to be Captain without leaving the Enterprise, but it's not exactly ideal circumstances. The shooting script featured a scene in which Riker sings a song about whether he should stay or go!

RATING

- Tense and foreboding, confident and seminal, ending on an extraordinary cliffhanger, this is simply the best episode of *The Next Generation* – there are other great episodes, but nothing else comes close to this one.

STAR TREK: THE NEXT GENERATION
SEASON FOUR

4.1 THE BEST OF BOTH WORLDS Part II

As the Borg destroy the Starfleet, Riker launches a desperate bid to destroy the Collective

TX 24 September 1990
WRITER Michael Piller
DIRECTOR Cliff Bole
GUEST CAST Elizabeth Dennehy (Shelby), Whoopi Goldberg (Guinan), Colm Meaney (O'Brien), Todd Merrill (Gleason), George Murdock (Hanson)

STARDATE 44001.4

The Enterprise fires its new weapon, but the Borg Cube is undamaged. Locutus explains that Picard's knowledge has been assimilated into the Borg collective – they had already adapted to the weapon. As the Borg leave for Sector 001, Earth, the Enterprise crew begin emergency repairs. Meanwhile, Admiral Hanson reports that the Federation is amassing an armada of ships at Wolf 359 to repel the Borg Cube. Hanson promotes Riker to Captain. Surprisingly, Riker decides to appoint Shelby as his First Officer. After 12 hours, the Enterprise is operational once more and follows in the wake of the Borg Cube. Meanwhile, Hanson reports that the Federation has engaged the Borg. The Enterprise arrives too late: Wolf 359 is a floating graveyard of Federation ships. As the Borg ship approaches Earth, Riker hatches a plan to use Picard's knowledge to their advantage. Riker uses a daring strategy involving separating the ship, a tactic planned with Picard, to distract the Borg long enough for Data and Worf to capture Locutus. Riker is pleased that Locutus can still function as part of the collective on board the Enterprise. He asks Data to establish a neurological link with the Borg to implant an instruction. As Data accesses the collective, the Borg bombard the Enterprise. Picard is able to break free of Borg control and urges 'Sleep'. Data correctly surmises that Picard is suggesting he implant an order that the Borg ship regenerate, or sleep. Just as Riker is about to ram the Borg ship, Data succeeds and the Borg Cube is suddenly inactive. The Enterprise makes a hasty exit as the Borg Cube explodes. Beverly is able to remove the Borg implants, restoring Picard to health, but the psychological impact of his experience haunts him.

QUOTES

- 'What do you remember?'
- 'Everything.' – *Beverly to Picard, once he is freed from the Collective*

TRIVIA

- The summer hiatus saw a spate of rumours that Shelby would join the crew as a semi-regular. Fuel was added when it was reported that Wil Wheaton was to leave, creating a space at helm. It is not certain that this was ever a serious consideration, but there were many rumours to the contrary.

RATING

- Although not as gripping as part one, this is still fantastic stuff. The final scene, where we see these events will have a lasting impact on Picard, is delightfully underplayed.

4.2 FAMILY

STARDATE 44012.3

As the Enterprise is repaired, Picard, Worf and Wesley are reunited with their families

TX 1 October 1990
WRITER Ronald D Moore
DIRECTOR Les Landau
GUEST CAST Theodore Bikel (Sergei Rozhenko), David Tristan Birkin (Rene Picard), Georgia Brown (Helena Rozhenko), Dennis Creaghan (Louis), Samantha Eggar (Marie Picard), Whoopi Goldberg (Guinan), Jeremy Kemp (Robert Picard), Colm Meaney (O'Brien), Doug Wert (Jack Crusher)

While the Enterprise is repaired at McKinley station, the crew take time to visit their families. Worf is discomforted to receive news that his human foster parents, Sergei and Helena Rozhenko, will be visiting the ship. Meanwhile, Picard returns to his family home in Labarre, France, after an absence of 20 years. He is warmly received by his sister-in-law and nephew, neither of whom he has met before. However, his older brother, Robert, is less keen on Jean-Luc's return. Back on the Enterprise, the Rozhenkos wax lyrical about their son's achievements, but receive only Worf's sullenness. Slowly, Worf comes to enjoy his parents' visit. Also on the Enterprise, Beverly finds an old holographic message recorded by her late husband, Jack, for Wesley. Wesley is moved by the recording. Meanwhile, Picard is offered a job on the Atlantis Project by Louis, an old friend. Though Jean-Luc seriously considers the offer, Robert derides his brother's fascination with technology. When Robert's son, Rene, reveals a fascination with starships, Robert rebukes Jean-Luc for stimulating Rene's interest. Later, their relationship worsens. Robert reveals his resentment that Jean-Luc broke the family rules and his jealousy of his career. He begins to probe Jean-Luc for details of what happened to him on the Borg ship. Unable to stand Robert's bullying any longer, Jean-Luc lunges and the two men fight in the vineyard. Picard's anger turns to amusement and the two men laugh. Jean-Luc, horrified by the deaths he caused as Locutus, is grateful for the release of tension. The brothers put aside their differences. Picard returns to the Enterprise.

TRIVIA

- *Family* is a break from the traditional format of *Star Trek*. At first the production crew struggled to make it fit by having a science fiction story on board the Enterprise at the same time as Picard's emotional journey on Earth. Early versions had a child stowaway on the ship and members of the crew disappearing into a wormhole. Eventually, Rick Berman decided to abandon the usual format and pursue the family theme throughout.

RATING

- Wonderful small-scale stuff dominated by superb performances by Patrick Stewart and Jeremy Kemp. There is a real sense of character and history running through the events in France. The Worf and Wesley storylines, although interesting and thematically important, take valuable screen time away from the Picard family story.

4.3 BROTHERS

STARDATE 44085.7

Data is reunited with Lore and Noonien Soong and is offered an emotion chip

TX 8 October 1990
WRITER Rick Berman
DIRECTOR Rob Bowman

While the Enterprise rushes a sick child to Starbase 416, Data covertly sets a new course, then beams down to a verdant planet and finds a small dwelling in which he is surprised to find Dr Noonien Soong, his creator, whom he believed was killed by the Crystalline Entity. On the Enterprise, sensors pick up Soong's presence on the planet below just as an unmanned ship enters orbit. The ship is piloted by Lore, Data's twin brother, who was also drawn by Soong's homing device. Lore and Data are soon at odds, but Soong interrupts to reveal he is dying. He

GUEST CAST Cory Danziger (Jake Potts), James Lashly (Kopf), Colm Meaney (O'Brien), Adam Ryen (Willie Potts), Brent Spiner (Noonien Soong/Lore)

has been plagued by his failure with Lore and has brought Data to the planet to give him an emotion chip. Soong, however, is tired and decides to sleep. The next day, he implants the chip in Data – but it is actually Lore in Data's uniform. Lore is unbalanced and throws Soong across the lab. Meanwhile, Riker and Worf arrive with an Away Team and discover Data in Lore's clothes. Soong sadly notes there was only one emotion chip. He tells Data how to remove the programming that brought him to the planet. Soong refuses the offer of medical aid and, saying goodbye to Data, decides to die alone on his planet. The Enterprise continues its course and the sick child makes a full recovery.

TRIVIA

- Rick Berman's first draft did not include Lore. The writing team made the suggestion to add an element of jeopardy.
- From the outset there was a desire to have Brent Spiner play all three roles, but technical considerations were a worry. For a time, Keye Luke, who appeared as Donald Cory in the *Star Trek* episode *Whom Gods Destroy*, was considered to play Dr Soong.

RATING

- A technical feat well achieved, but really not terribly interesting. There's very little in the Lore concept that is new, plus the story feels like an alternative draft of season two's *The Schizoid Man*.

4.4 SUDDENLY HUMAN

STARDATE 44143.7

Picard helps a human teenager, lost for years among Talarians, come to terms with his heritage

TX 15 October 1990
WRITERS John Whelpley and Jeri Taylor (story by Ralph Phillips)
DIRECTOR Gabrielle Beaumont
GUEST CAST Chad Allen (Jono), Sherman Howard (Endar), Barbara Townsend (Connaught Rossa)

The Enterprise picks up a distress call from a Talarian spacecraft. They crew find five teenagers on board, one of whom is a human called Jono. Jono insists that he and his friends be reunited with their Captain, Endar, but Beverly discovers signs of abuse. By using Jono's DNA, Beverly discovers Jono is Jeremiah Rossa, the sole survivor of a Talarian attack on Galen IV 11 years previously. Jono, however, is resolutely Talarian and refuses to accept his true past. Troi persuades Picard, the only person Jono seems to respect, to reason with the boy. Though reticent, Picard tries hard to understand Jono, who declares his allegiance to Endar. Picard is determined to convince Jono of his heritage and introduces Jono to Admiral Connaught Rossa, his only surviving relative. Later, Picard challenges Jono to racquetball, during which Jono starts to recall the events of his parents' death and come to terms with his past. After, Jono seems more comfortable in the company of Wesley and others. Picard feels he has broken down Jono's barriers. However, that night, Jono feels guilty for betraying Endar and stabs Picard. Picard recovers quickly. Three Talarian ships converge on the Enterprise to retake Jono. Riker makes a stand, but is interrupted by Picard. The Captain has realised the folly of his actions and allows Jono to return to Endar.

TRIVIA

- The production team received a number of letters from angry viewers who complained that the episode condoned child abuse by letting Jono return to his abusers.

RATING

- A simple story that narrowly avoids becoming a trite tale of teenage angst. Jono's stabbing of Picard comes as a genuine surprise. However, the episode suffers for not explaining the crew's reasoning for trying to convince Jono, when one would have expected this moral dilemma to be their first concern.

4.5 REMEMBER ME

STARDATE 44161.2

Beverly finds herself on a version of the Enterprise where the crew slowly disappear

Beverly talks to old friend Dr Dalen Quaice who is retiring from Starfleet. Prompted by Dalen's sadness over losing his wife, Beverly seeks out Wesley but finds him busily creating a warp bubble, based on the calculations of expert Kosinski. Beverly returns to Dalen's quarters

TX 22 October 1990
WRITER Lee Sheldon
DIRECTOR Cliff Bole
GUEST CAST Bill Erwin (Dalen Quaice), Colm Meaney (O'Brien), Eric Menyuk (The Traveler)

but he cannot be found and no one remembers him coming on board. Wesley suggests Dalen may have been trapped in a warp bubble and removed from space-time. Soon the rest of the crew start to vanish and Beverly, the only one to remember them, starts to doubt her own sanity. When a vortex appears on the bridge, Beverly resists its pull. In fact, Beverly is the one caught inside the warp bubble and the vortex is an attempt by Wesley to reach her. Kosinski's assistant, known as The Traveler, explains that Beverly has created her own reality in the warp bubble based around the idea of losing close friends. With the Enterprise buckling about her, Beverly runs to main engineering where she first saw the vortex. When it appears again, created by Wesley and The Traveler, she dives through just in time to the real Enterprise.

QUOTES

- 'If there's nothing wrong with me, maybe there's something wrong with the universe...' – *Beverly muses on her predicament*

TRIVIA

- Sheldon's first two drafts had Beverly in a dream. The Traveler and warp bubble were added in the third draft to bring a more satisfactory resolution to the story.

RATING

- A simple little puzzle that works well, largely due to strong direction. Unfortunately, McFadden's performance is not quite there, and her discussions with the ship's computer mark a low point.

4.6 LEGACY

STARDATE 44215.2

The crew unite with Tasha Yar's sister to find a missing Federation freighter

TX 29 October 1990
WRITER Joe Menosky
DIRECTOR Robert Scheerer
GUEST CAST Colm Meaney (O'Brien), Christopher Michael (Man), Don Mirault (Hayne), Beth Toussaint (Ishara Yar), Vladimir Velasco (Tan Tsu)

The Enterprise answers a distress call from a Federation freighter in orbit around Turkana IV, the birthplace of Tasha Yar. Picard reluctantly permits an Away Team to beam down and find the freighter crew. On the planet, Riker meets Hayne, leader of one of the planet's warring factions, the Coalition, who suspects his opponents, the Alliance, have captured the survivors. He offers the aid of Tasha's sister, Ishara, in their search. The Enterprise soon receives a signal from one survivor, who says they are being held in an Alliance prison compound. Ishara beams down to act as a decoy, but is wounded when a security implant in her body sets off Alliance sensors. She is beamed back to the ship. Geordi determines that the freighter crew are near Alliance Headquarters. Data suggests a way of removing the security implant, which Beverly does. Data is supportive when Ishara contemplates joining Starfleet, but Picard and Troi are more suspicious. Ishara and the Away Team beam into Alliance headquarters. The Enterprise team quickly find the freighter crew but Ishara steals away. Data finds her at the Alliance's defence systems – her mission is to destroy their defences and she will kill Data if he tries to stop her. However, Riker and Data are able to stun her and repair any damage. Ishara is returned to the Coalition. Riker must explain to Data about betrayal.

TRIVIA

- *Legacy* was *The Next Generation*'s eightieth show and, as such, was the point at which the show beat the original *Star Trek* episode tally. When the Enterprise is redirected to Turkana IV, it leaves behind a journey to a dig on Camus II, the planet on which the last episode of the original *Star Trek* is set.

RATING

- A fairly mundane story that starts to work as they play it through Data's eyes. Data's childlike innocence had to be shattered somehow, and the use of Tasha's sister makes it all the more effective.

4.7 REUNION

STARDATE 44246.3

K'Ehleyr returns to the Enterprise with Alexander, Worf's son

TX 5 November 1990
WRITERS Thomas Perry, Jo Perry, Ronald D Moore and Brannon Braga (story by Drew Deighan, Thomas Perry and Jo Perry)
DIRECTOR Jonathan Frakes
GUEST CAST Charles Cooper (K'Mpec), April Grace (Hubbell), Patrick Massett (Duras), Robert O'Reilly (Gowron), Suzie Plakson (K'Ehleyr), Michael Rider (Security Guard), Jon Steuer (Alexander), Basil Wallace (Klingon Guard #1), Mirron E Willis (Klingon Guard #2)

K'Ehleyr beams aboard with her son, Alexander, and Worf discovers he is the boy's father. K'Ehleyr tells Picard of her mission: the Klingon Empire is on the brink of civil war. K'Mpec, leader of the High Council, is dying, and two factions, led by Gowron and Duras, are vying for power. K'Mpec tells Picard that for months he has been poisoned with small amounts of veridium six, for which there is no cure. K'Mpec wants Picard to arbitrate in the power struggle after his death – no one else can be trusted. Picard is reluctant, but concedes. Shortly after, K'Mpec dies. Soon, Duras and Gowron arrive and Picard tells them the leadership ceremony will begin shortly. Worf knows Gowron has been a troublesome figure in the High Council, but is acutely aware that Duras framed Worf's father for the massacre at Khitomer, leading to Worf's discommendation. As the ceremony begins, an explosion kills two Klingons. K'Ehleyr buys time for Picard to investigate and discovers the truth about Duras. Riker and Geordi discover the explosive device used a substance normally used by Romulans, and suspicion grows. While Beverly deduces that the device was implanted in the arm of one of Duras' comrades, Duras attacks and mortally wounds K'Ehleyr. Worf beams aboard the Klingon vessel to challenge Duras to a fight to the death. Riker leads an Away Team to rescue Worf, but arrives just in time to see him kill Duras. Later, Picard announces that Gowron will succeed K'Mpec, but urges Worf to consider resigning. Worf declines and they settle on a formal reprimand. Worf then returns to Alexander and admits he is the boy's father.

QUOTES

- 'Worf, you killed Duras. I consider that no small favour. But what you ask is impossible.' – *Gowron*

RATING

- A busy episode with tremendous pace and tension. Worf's story is neatly plotted to intersect with the leadership struggle and K'Ehleyr's death is truly shocking. We are left with the distinct feeling that Gowron is hardly a better candidate for Klingon ruler.

4.8 FUTURE IMPERFECT

STARDATE 44286.5

Riker falls unconscious on an Away Team mission and awakens 16 years later

TX 12 November 1990
WRITERS J Larry Carroll and David Bennett Carren
DIRECTOR Les Landau
GUEST CAST Chris Demetral (Jean-Luc/Ethan), April Grace (Hubbell), Andreas Katsulas (Tomalak), Carolyn McCormick (Minuet), George O'Hanlon Jr (Transporter Officer), Dana Tjowander (Barash), Patti Yasutake (Ogawa)

The Enterprise investigates strange energy readings coming from Alpha Onias III, an uninhabited planet bordering the Neutral Zone. Riker loses consciousness during the mission and reawakens in sickbay 16 years later. Beverly explains that Riker contracted a virus on Alpha Onias III but it only became active recently and destroyed his memory of the last 16 years. She tells him that he has been Captain of the Enterprise for nine years and has a son, Jean-Luc, by a wife who died two years previously. He is soon contacted by Admiral Picard who tells Riker that he must transport Romulan Ambassador Tomalak, whom Riker remembers as a staunch enemy, to a peace negotiation on Outpost 23, the heart of Federation defences in the Neutral Zone. However, Riker becomes suspicious when the computer is slow to answer questions about his past. When he sees footage of his wife, who resembles a woman he once created on the Holodeck, Riker realises the time warp is a trick to make him reveal the location of Outpost 23. Riker confronts Tomalak and the Enterprise façade melts away, revealing a Romulan holodeck. Tomalak explains that Riker was captured during the Away Team mission and they built a new reality for him using neural scanners. Riker is put in a cell with Ethan, a young captive who was forced to play Riker's son in the charade. However, the boy is not all he seems and Riker calls his bluff. Again, the world around him melts away revealing Alpha Onias III. Ethan reveals himself to be an alien called Baresh who is desperate for companionship. Riker and Baresh beam back to the Enterprise.

TRIVIA

- The first draft did not involve the Romulan ploy, but led inexorably to the unmasking of Ethan as Baresh. The double-bluff was added to beef up the fourth act and to add another twist.

RATING

- The first of the mind-warp episodes that were ultimately to become staple fodder for later seasons. Here, however, it works well, and an interesting view of the future is proposed.

4.9 FINAL MISSION

STARDATE 44307.3

Wesley fights to keep Picard alive when they are marooned on a desert moon

TX 19 November 1990
WRITERS Kasey Arnold-Ince and Jeri Taylor (story by Kasey Arnold-Ince)
DIRECTOR Corey Allen
GUEST CAST Kim Hamilton (Songi), Mary Kohnert (Tess Allenby), Nick Tate (Dirgo)

Picard informs Wesley that he has been accepted into Starfleet Academy. His final mission on the Enterprise will be to accompany Picard to Pentarus V, where the Captain will mediate a dispute. While the Enterprise leaves to investigate a radioactive freighter, Picard and Wesley travel to the planet in the Nenebek, an ageing shuttlecraft piloted by Dirgo. The shuttle malfunctions and crashes on the desert moon of Labda Paz. They head to a rock outcrop for shelter and water. The Enterprise tows the freighter into a sun and, after only several hours, is able to head in search of their crewmates. Picard and Wesley finally reach the outcrop and discover water, but it is protected by a force field. Dirgo shoots at the forcefield and summons a robot sentry. He shoots at the sentry and causes a rockslide that seriously injures Picard. Later, Dirgo tries again to get past the sentry and dies in the process. As night falls, Picard grows weaker and Wesley can do little more than watch over him. Wesley manages to deceive the sentry and unlock the force field, gaining access to the water desperately needed by Picard. An Away Team rescues Picard and Wesley shortly after.

TRIVIA

- Pentarus V was conceived as an ice planet, but this was changed to a desert world to enable location filming.
- Nick Tate is better known as Alan Carter in *Space: 1999*.

RATING

- A suitable out-story for Wesley with a few quiet character moments. Ultimately the threat is a little weak, but the force field puzzle helps the story along.

4.10 THE LOSS

STARDATE 44356.9

When the Enterprise is trapped by two-dimensional beings, Troi loses her empathic powers

TX 21 December 1990
WRITERS Hilary J Bader and Alan J Adler and Vanessa Greene (story by Hilary J Bader)
DIRECTOR Chip Chalmers
GUEST CAST Kim Braden (Janet Brooks), Whoopi Goldberg (Guinan), Mary Kohnert (Tess Allenby)

The Enterprise detects an anomaly pulling at the ship and Troi collapses in her quarters in pain. She recovers and is called to the bridge, but finds her empathic powers have left her. Beverly discovers Troi has brain damage and tells her she may have lost her powers forever. Troi refuses to accept this and returns to work. Troi finds it difficult to counsel others and starts to become angry and desperate. Data and Geordi discover that the Enterprise is being pulled by a cluster of two-dimensional beings. Troi resigns. When Riker goes to see her, she breaks down in distress. It is only Guinan who convinces Troi that her natural instincts are still intact. The Enterprise, meanwhile, is being towed towards a cosmic string. Picard tries to break free by making a controlled jump to warp speed, but fails. The beings, however, seem to sense the presence of the ship. Picard asks Troi to find a way to communicate with the beings. She and Data realise the beings are drawn to the cosmic string. Data projects a fake string that momentarily confuses the creatures, giving the Enterprise its chance to escape. The ship resumes its course and Troi's powers return. She senses that the cosmic string is the beings' home. Their sense of longing temporarily confused her abilities, but they have now returned.

TRIVIA

- Stories about Troi losing her empathic powers had been pitched for some time, but each proved a little lightweight. Hilary Bader, then an intern on the show, pitched a B-story about two-dimensional beings and the two themes were put together.

RATING

- Troi loses her empathic powers while the Enterprise is caught in the grip of two-dimensional beings – the jokes are just too obvious. Hey, it's a Troi episode – how good did you think it was going to be?

4.11 DATA'S DAY

A day in Data's life sees the marriage of Keiko O'Brien and the murder of a Vulcan ambassador

TX 7 January 1991
WRITERS Harold Apter and Ronald D Moore (story by Harold Apter)
DIRECTOR Robert Weimer
GUEST CAST Rosalind Chao (Keiko Ishikawa), Shelly Desai (V'Sal), April Grace (Hubbell), Colm Meaney (O'Brien), Sierra Pecheur (T'Pel), Alan Scarfe (Mendak)

STARDATE 44390.1

O'Brien and Keiko are getting married and Data has been asked to give the bride away. On the day, Keiko has wedding jitters and asks Data to tells Miles she can't marry him. O'Brien is upset but Data is confused. Meanwhile, Vulcan ambassador T'Pel arrives on the Enterprise. Her curt manner puts all on edge except Data. Picard asks Data for information about the deployment of Romulan forces then sets course for the Neutral Zone. Data then tries to mediate between Keiko and O'Brien but is still unable to understand. He is then summoned to T'Pel's quarters where the Vulcan orders Data to reveal information about the ship's defences. Data refuses as T'Pel does not have authorisation. Later, Data takes dancing lessons from Beverly on the holodeck. Although he can mimic her moves, dancing with a partner is more tricky. Meanwhile, the Enterprise meets a Romulan Warbird, the Devoras. T'Pel beams aboard but the transporter beam is interrupted and the ambassador is killed. The Romulan commander, Mendak, accuses Picard of foul play and the two ships head back to their own space. However, Data discovers that T'Pel was not really killed – the Romulans faked the accident. Picard plots an intercept course for the Devoras and, during a tense stand-off, learns that T'Pel was a Romulan spy. The Enterprise returns to Federation space, where Keiko and Miles are finally married.

QUOTES

- 'There may be a correlation between humour and sex... The need for more research is clearly indicated.' – *Data muses on Riker's ability with women*

TRIVIA

- Harold Apter originally pitched the story *A Day In the Life of the Enterprise* in the third season, but the writing team struggled to make it work before they settled on Data as the viewpoint character. The decision to marry O'Brien was a reflection of the production team's appreciation of Colm Meaney. At one point, the writing team considered replacing Wesley with a female conn officer who would get together with O'Brien.

RATING

- Taking the 'day in the life' style of storytelling, *Data's Day* has a unique feel but not an entirely satisfactory one. The number of storylines Data is involved in merely detracts from the T'Pel storyline. Dancing on the holodeck has a nasty taste of one of those scenes designed to show off the real-life talents of the cast, and does little but irritate.

4.12 THE WOUNDED

A renegade Starfleet captain threatens the Cardassian-Federation peace

TX 28 January 1991

STARDATE 44429.6

The Enterprise is attacked by a Cardassian vessel, the Trager. Its commander, Gul Macet, is acting in retaliation for the destruction of a Cardassian space station. Picard consults Starfleet and is told that Captain Maxwell of the USS Phoenix carried out the assault and is now threatening the Cardassian-Federation peace. Ordered to intercept the Phoenix, Picard invites Macet and his aides to join the Enterprise crew in their search. Maxwell's former colleague, Miles O'Brien, reveals that

WRITER Jeri Taylor (story by Stuart Charno, Sara Charno and Cy Chermak)
DIRECTOR Chip Chalmers
GUEST CAST Marc Alaimo (Gul Macet), Rosalind Chao (Keiko), Bob Gunton (Benjamin Maxwell), John Hancock (Haden), Colm Meaney (O'Brien), Marco Rodriguez (Glen Telle), Tim Winters (Glinn Daro)

Maxwell's family was killed by Cardassians but cannot believe his former Captain would seek revenge. The Enterprise locates the Phoenix, which destroys two more Cardassian ships then pursues a supply ship supposedly illegally carrying weapons. When Picard's hails are unanswered, he gives the coordinates of the Phoenix to Macet. Maxwell suspects the Cardassians are rearming for a war with the Federation and attacks another Cardassian vessel which he believes carries arms. Macet denies this but refuses to let Starfleet officers board the ship. Maxwell urges Picard to board the Cardassian vessel but Picard threatens to cripple the Phoenix if it does not retreat. O'Brien beams aboard the Phoenix and convinces Maxwell to turn himself in. Picard tells Macet that he knows Maxwell was right, and warns against starting a war.

QUOTES

- 'It's not you I hate, Cardassian. It's what I became, because of you.' – *O'Brien to Daro*

TRIVIA

- Rick Berman suggested the song at the end ('The Minstrel Boy' by Thomas Moore) after hearing it used in *The Man Who Would be King*.

RATING

- *Star Trek* does *Heart of Darkness*. The Cardassians come across as an intelligent, sinister adversary. Dark, doom-laden and thought-provoking.

4.13 DEVIL'S DUE

STARDATE 44474.5

Picard tries to free a planet from the tyrannical regime of a female devil

TX 4 February 1991
WRITER Philip Lazebnik (story by Philip Lazebnik and William Douglas Lansford)
DIRECTOR Tom Benko
GUEST CAST Marta Dubois (Ardra), William Glover (Marley), Paul Lambert (Howard Clarke), Thad Lamey (Devil Monster), Tom Magee (Klingon Monster), Marcelo Tubert (Jared)

The Enterprise crew come to the rescue of Dr Howard Clark, a researcher on Ventax II whose science station was attacked by the local inhabitants, who are terrified by the reappearance of Ardra, their version of the devil, who promised them 1,000 years of prosperity in return for enslavement thereafter. Picard beams down to the planet to calm the Ventaxian leader, Acost Jared, but is surprised by the sudden appearance of Ardra, a beautiful female, come to collect on her deal with the Ventaxians. Ardra claims to have many names on different worlds and scares Worf by transforming into Fek'Ihr, a creature from Klingon mythology. Data investigates Ardra's claim and finds it to be legally binding – moreover, the Enterprise, in orbit around Ventax II, can also be claimed. Picard insists Ardra is a fraud and determines to expose her. While Geordi tries to uncover the source of Ardra's power, Data uncovers an obscure legal practice which Picard employs to delay Ardra. Data is appointed as judge and ordered to be impartial. Ardra performs illusions to convince Data that she is the claimant and gave the Ventaxians a new society. Picard claims it was Jared's ancestors who made their peace and prosperity a reality. However, Jared is terrified by Ardra and insists her claim is fair. Deflated, Picard orders a recess but Geordi arrives with news of Ardra's power source: a cloaked ship in orbit. Picard uses the Enterprise's resources to duplicate Ardra's illusions and convinces Jared he has nothing to fear from Ardra. Data dissolves the contract and Ardra is arrested.

TRIVIA

- *Devil's Due* began life as an episode for the *Star Trek II* series, uncovered when Piller trawled old scripts for season three. An early rewrite by Philip Lazebnik was deemed too funny and revised several times. As well as the loss of much of the humour, the devil became female. *Devil's Due* became the highest rated episode since *Encounter at Farpoint*.
- Marta Dubois had auditioned for Troi. Ardra transforms into the Counselor at one point.

RATING

- A neat idea to focus on a returning deity, but this time an evil one. Unfortunately, the trial format provides little excitement and tends to drag. Picard's unmasking of Ardra is one that could have been accomplished at any time.

4.14 CLUES

STARDATE 44502.7

Suspicion falls on Data when the Enterprise crew cannot remember their last 24 hours

TX 11 February 1991
WRITERS Bruce D Arthurs and Joe Menosky (story by Bruce D Arthurs)
DIRECTOR Les Landau
GUEST CAST Rhonda Aldrich (Trixie), Whoopi Goldberg (Guinan), Thomas Knickerbocker (Gunman), Colm Meaney (O'Brien), Pamela Winslow (McKnight), Patti Yasutake (Ogawa)

Passing through a wormhole, the Enterprise crew are knocked unconscious. As they revive, Data – who wasn't affected – explains that they were out for 30 seconds. Beverly discovers a full day's growth on one of her plants and realises Data is not telling the truth. Data gives an unconvincing explanation, prompting Picard to order an investigation. Troi senses she is being possessed by an alien life form but dismisses this as an hallucination. When Geordi finds that the planet is abnormal, Data reveals that his actions are not his own. Beverly discovers that Worf's wrist has been fractured and reset. Picard suspects Data is lying to protect the crew and orders a return to the planet. Data explains that the Enterprise encountered a race of isolationists who stun intruders and transport visiting ships out of their system. As Data's memory was not affected, the aliens ordered the ship destroyed. Picard agreed to have each crew member's memory erased and ordered Data to lie. Picard is able to convince the aliens to give the crew another chance and this time orders the crew not to leave any clues behind.

TRIVIA

- Long-time fan Bruce Arthurs submitted this speculative script when he was working as a postman in Phoenix, Arizona. The story passed to Joe Menosky for the rewrite.
- The episode bears a striking resemblance to the *Red Dwarf* episode *Thanks For The Memory*, first transmitted in 1988.

RATING

- A clever episode with a strong mystery at its core. Data's actions are genuinely creepy and remain so to the end. It's a strong concept episode which makes excellent use of Data, without making him the star.

4.15 FIRST CONTACT

STARDATE UNKNOWN

The Enterprise crew are charged to make first contact with an alien race

TX 18 February 1991
WRITERS Dennis Russell Bailey, David Bischoff, Joe Menosky and Ronald D Moore (story by Marc Scott Zicree)
DIRECTOR Cliff Bole
GUEST CAST Steven Anderson (Nilrem), George Coe (Durken), Michael Ensign (Krola), George Hearn (Berel), Bebe Neuwirth (Lanel), Sachi Parker (Tava), Carolyn Seymour (Mirasta)

During an Away Team mission on Malcor, Riker is injured and rushed to an alien hospital. The doctors realise he's an alien and keep his presence quiet to avoid alarm. Meanwhile, Picard and Troi visit the science minister, Mirasta, and explain that the Federation has been watching her planet for some time. Her civilisation is on the verge of major changes and news of aliens would threaten the balance. Meanwhile, one of the doctors spreads rumours of an alien invasion. The Malcorian leader, Durken, is brought to the Enterprise and is suspicious, but is soon convinced by Picard that their intentions are friendly. On the planet, Riker tries to escape but is cornered by scared locals. When Durken returns, one of his ministers, Krola, reports Riker's presence and claims that the Federation is spying. Picard assures Durken that the surveillance was innocent. Krola investigates Riker, determined to prove guilt. When he fails, Krola turns Riker's phaser on himself. However, Beverly takes Krola back to the Enterprise and revives him – the phaser was set to stun. Durken is shocked by Krola's actions and asks that the Federation cease activity on his planet until his people can be encouraged to accept outsiders.

TRIVIA

- *First Contact* was pitched by Marc Scott Zicree during season three. Michael Piller suggested that the episode take the aliens' point of view – *The Day the Earth Stood Still* with the Enterprise crew as the invaders.

RATING

- Another hallmark experimental episode, *First Contact* gives us a fascinating glimpse of *Star Trek* from the perspective of another species. The play on the motifs of alien invasion stories is cleverly handled. All in all, the episode reflects the more intelligent approach displayed generally throughout season four.

4.16 GALAXY'S CHILD

STARDATE 44614.6

Geordi meets Leah Brahms, the engineering genius he fell for in a Holodeck simulation

TX 11 March 1991
WRITER Maurice Hurley (story by Thomas Kartozian)
DIRECTOR Winrich Kolbe
GUEST CAST Lanei Chapman (Rager), Susan Gibney (Leah Brahms), Whoopi Goldberg (Guinan), April Grace (Hubbell), Jana Marie Hupp (Pavlik)

Picard informs Geordi that Dr Leah Brahms of the Theoretical Propulsion Group is coming to inspect his work. Geordi is excited – he previously fell for a holographic version of her – but the real Brahms is ascerbic and highly critical of Geordi's work. Meanwhile, the Enterprise sets course for the Alpha Omicron system to investigate strange sensor readings. The crew discover a large blue whale-like life-form made of plasma energy. The creature emits a dampening field that damages the ship. Picard is forced to return fire and accidentally kills the creature. A second sensor sweep reveals that the creature was about to give birth. The Enterprise's phasers are used to cut the child free but the infant attaches itself to the ship and suckles on its energy. Geordi tries to make peace with Brahms but their frosty relationship is exacerbated when Leah encounters Geordi's holodeck version of her. They have to put aside their differences to deal with the energy drain. Data discovers that the mother was *en route* to a large energy source in an asteroid belt. However, the infant calls for more of its kind who arrive to feast on the Enterprise. Geordi and Brahms conceive an idea to use a harmonic frequency to 'sour' the Enterprise's energy. The idea works and the baby returns to the asteroid belt. Picard congratulates the two engineers, who start a real friendship.

TRIVIA

- In *All Good Things*, Q shows a version of the future where Leah and Geordi are married with children.

RATING

- A neat exploration of fantasy and reality that works well alongside the more generic infant child plot. Susan Gibney is an excellent foil for LeVar Burton, providing him with the opportunity to put in one of his better performances.

4.17 NIGHT TERRORS

STARDATE 44631.2

Troi must find a solution when the crew become aggressive and paranoid

TX 18 March 1991
WRITERS Pamela Douglas and Jeri Taylor (story by Shari Goodhartz)
DIRECTOR Les Landau
GUEST CAST Lanei Chapman (Rager), Rosalind Chao (Keiko), Whoopi Goldberg (Guinan), Craig Hurley (Peeples), Colm Meaney (O'Brien), Duke Moosekian (Gillespie), Deborah Taylor (Chantal Zaheva), Brian Tochi (Lin), John Vickery (Andrus Hagan)

The Enterprise locates the USS Brattain, a science ship that has been missing for several days. An Away Team finds Captain Zaheva murdered in her chair: the crew are dead, save their Betazoid counsellor, Hagen, who is shocked and cannot speak. Troi tries to communicate with Hagen but the images she experiences are vague. Soon after she begins to have nightmares. Beverly confirms that the crew of 34 killed each other. Geordi is unable to restart the Brattain's engines so Picard tows the stricken vessel to Starbase 220. Soon after, members of the crew start to show signs of paranoia and aggression. Troi and Beverly warn Picard that the events of the Brattain may be about to start on the Enterprise. Picard agrees but when he orders a new course the Enterprise's engines fail. Data suggests that the ship has fallen foul of a Tyken's Rift, a rupture in space that absorbs energy, but can find no reference to it affecting behaviour. Data and Geordi try to create an explosion to free the Enterprise, but the attempt fails. An agitated Beverly discovers that the Brattain's victims all went insane from dream deprivation: Troi is the only person dreaming on the Enterprise. Troi realises that her nightmares mean something and realises Hagen is experiencing them too. She discovers that telepathic beings are trapped on the other side of the rift and inadvertently affecting the crew's behaviour. Communicating through Troi's dreams, both ships work together to create an explosion that frees them.

RATING

- Solid episode building on the age-old fascination with the crew going loopy. There's an excellent scene where Troi prevents Worf from committing suicide that is so brief it almost goes unnoticed.

4.18 IDENTITY CRISIS

STARDATE 44664.5

Geordi turns into an alien when he investigates the disappearances of his old crewmates

TX 25 March 1991
WRITER Brannon Braga (story by Timothy De Haas)
DIRECTOR Winrich Kolbe
GUEST CAST Amick Byram (Paul Hickman), Mona Grudt (Graham), Dennis Madalone (Hedrick), Maryann Plunkett (Susanna Leijten), Paul Tompkins (Breville), Patti Yasutake (Ogawa)

Geordi is reunited with Susanna Leitjen, a former crewmate on the USS Victory. She informs him that they are the sole surviving members of an Away Team to investigate mysterious disappearances on the planet Tarchannen III. Their former colleague, Hickman, recently stole a shuttlecraft to return to the planet, but the shuttle burned up on re-entry. On the planet, Geordi and Leitjen discover two Starfleet uniforms. She begins to act unusually and is beamed back to sickbay. Beverly discovers that Leitjen's blood chemistry has changed. Soon Leitjen comes out in dark blue lesions and her middle fingers fuse together. Beverly deduces that the missing officers were not abducted but transformed into an alien race. Geordi investigates an old recording of the first mission and notices an unusual shadow. He recreates the scene on the holodeck and discovers an unknown creature. He is struck down with pain when the transformation begins. Beverly isolates the alien DNA and successfully removes it from Leitjen, but Geordi does not respond to her communications and beams down to the planet. Leitjen, now recovered, joins the search for Geordi. They find Geordi communing with the other transformed Away Team members. Leitjen appeals to the last vestiges of Geordi's human side and is able to convince him to return to the Enterprise, where he is fully cured.

TRIVIA

- Fan writer De Haaf submitted *Identity Crisis*. His original story concerned two previously unknown Enterprise crewmembers. The tone was more horrific and featured many more aliens on the planet.

RATING

- A simple story, playing on well established horror themes, which has some nice touches like the use of older-style tricorders and equipment during the recording of the Victory's mission. The effects work on the transformed humans is simple but effective.

4.19 THE NTH DEGREE

STARDATE 44704.2

A mysterious alien probe turns Reg Barclay into a super-advanced human

TX 1 April 1991
WRITER Joe Menosky
DIRECTOR Robert Legato
GUEST CAST David Coburn (Brower), Kay E Kuter (Cytherian), Page Leong (April Anaya), Jim Norton (Albert Einstein), Dwight Schultz (Barclay), Saxon Trainor (Linda Larson)

The Enterprise encounters an alien probe adjacent to the malfunctioning Argus Array. Geordi and Barclay take a shuttlecraft to investigate. The probe fires an energy surge that knocks Barclay unconscious and then begins to menace the Enterprise. Barclay recovers in sickbay then amazes the crew by stepping in to destroy the probe. Geordi is surprised by Barclay's change of character and Beverly reports that Reg's brain tissue has evolved significantly – he may now be the most advanced human ever. Meanwhile, the array's reactor threatens to explode. Frustrated by the slow pace of the Enterprise computer, Barclay hooks himself directly into the system in the holodeck. Picard orders an immediate retreat from the array but discovers the bridge has lost control of the computer. Suddenly, the crisis on the array is averted and Picard is concerned when the computer responds with Barclay's voice. In the holodeck, Picard orders Barclay to disconnect himself but Barclay says this will cause his death. When the crew try to disconnect anyway, Reg sends the Enterprise 30,000 light years away. A projection of an alien being, a Cytherian, appears on the bridge and explains that the probe transformed Barclay – this is their way of researching alien races. Picard permits them to scan the crew in return for the Cytherian's database on thousands of civilisations. Barclay is restored and the ship returned to Federation space.

TRIVIA

- The return of Barclay was a priority for season four but the production team struggled to find the right vehicle. Eventually, Menosky came up with the idea of the alien probe carrying more than just sensor information.

RATING

- A welcome return for Reg Barclay, first seen in season three's *Hollow Pursuits*. The writing neatly undercuts audience expectation from the outset with the *Cyrano de Bergerac* sequence. It is sadly let down by a tried and tested *Star Trek* cop-out.

4.20 QPID

STARDATE 44741.9

Q creates a Robin Hood fantasy to prompt Picard to confess his true feelings for Vash

TX 22 April 1991
WRITER Ira Steven Behr (story by Randee Russell and Ira Steven Behr)
DIRECTOR Cliff Bole
GUEST CAST John de Lancie (Q), Jennifer Hetrick (Vash), Clive Revill (Sir Guy of Gisbourne), Joi Staton (Servant)

As Picard prepares a lecture for an archaeology conference, he is surprised to be reunited with Vash. Vash is still interested in Picard but irked that he has never mentioned her to his crewmates. Picard is uncomfortable with her presence and concerned when she announces her intentions to visit a planet that is off-limits to outsiders. To Picard's great annoyance, Q arrives determined to repay his debt to Picard by match-making. Without warning, Q transforms Picard into Robin Hood, accompanied by the officers as his Merry Men. Q, playing the Sheriff, tells Picard that Vash, now Maid Marian, will be beheaded the next day and challenges Picard to abandon her if he genuinely doesn't care for her. Vash, meanwhile, promises to marry Sir Guy of Gisbourne to save herself. When Picard arrives alone, she is critical of his efforts. When Sir Guy arrives, she turns Picard over. Q is amused, until he realises Vash is playing for time. Picard and Vash are held in the dungeon and set for execution the next day. As Picard awaits execution, the Merry Men arrive disguised as monks. Amid the confusion, Vash and Picard escape. Picard and Sir Guy fight a duel and Guy is killed. Q is impressed and returns the Enterprise crew to their ship. Vash arrives soon after and reveals that she is now to explore the universe with Q.

QUOTES

- 'What does he want?'
  'He wants to do something nice for me.'
  'I'll alert the crew.' – *Riker and Picard on Q's reappearance*
- 'Sir, I protest. I am *not* a merry man.' – *Worf*

TRIVIA

- 1991, for some reason, was a year when a number of Robin Hood projects appeared. As well as the Kevin Costner film *Robin Hood: Prince of Thieves*, there was a lesser-seen film starring Patrick Bergin.
- Marina Sirtis was keen on Vash's black outfit in this story, and suggested Troi should wear something similar.

RATING

- Errol Flynn meets *Star Trek* in an amusing if decidedly peculiar episode. The relationship between Picard and Q is perhaps the most interesting underscore, showing as it does the kind of uneasy camaraderie that makes these episode so much fun.

4.21 THE DRUMHEAD

STARDATE 44769.2

A retired admiral launches a witch-hunt that questions the loyalty of the crew

TX 29 April 1991
WRITER Jeri Taylor
DIRECTOR Jonathan Frakes

An explosion in the dilithium chamber damages the Enterprise. When an investigation reveals that information was passed to the Romulans, suspicion falls on a visiting Klingon officer, J'Ddan. Admiral Norah Satie, aided by a Betazoid, Sabin Genestra, is brought out of retirement to conduct an enquiry. Satie discovers that J'Ddan did pass information, but that he wasn't responsible for the explosion. Sabin suspects crewman Simon Tarses is lying, but Picard refuses to arrest him without proof. When it's determined that the explosion was an accident, Satie still

GUEST CAST
Earl Billings (Thomas Henry), Bruce French (Sabin Genestra), Spencer Garrett (Simon Tarses), Ann Shea (Nellen Tore), Jean Simmons (Norah Satie), Henry Woronicz (J'Ddan)

insists Tarses is hiding something. When Satie discovers that Tarses is part Romulan, she enlists Worf to uncover all he can about the crewman. Picard is disturbed by the witch-hunt and talks to Tarses, satisfying himself that he's innocent. Picard appeals to Satie for the investigation to end, but she refuses and calls in Admiral Henry. When the trial resumes, Satie calls Picard to give evidence, suspecting he too may be a traitor. Picard gives an impassioned plea for reason, quoting Satie's father, a former judge. Satie is enraged and denounces Picard, dredging up elements from his past and launching a tirade of baseless accusations. Henry is disgusted by Satie's paranoia and ends the trial.

QUOTES

- 'We think we have come so far. The torture of heretics, the burning of witches is ancient history. Then, before you can blink an eye, it suddenly threatens to start all over again.' – *Picard*

TRIVIA

- *The Drumhead* came about in response to the studio's request for an extra episode in the season. Although studio executives had another clips show in mind, the team fought to produce an episode that would cost the same but have more merit. The germ of the idea came from Ron Moore, but was heavily worked on by Jeri Taylor. According to Jonathan Frakes, who directed the episode, *The Drumhead* cost $250,000 less than a regular episode.
- The episode has a notable quest star, Jean Simmons, as Satie. Simmons has been a major film actress since the 1940s, with appearances in Lean's *Great Expectations* (1946), Powell and Pressburger's *Black Narcissus* (1947), *Guys and Dolls* (1955) and the epic eighties TV series *North and South* (also featuring Jonathan Frakes) and *The Thorn Birds*.

RATING

- Starfleet's version of the McCarthy trials of the 1950s. It's wonderfully well told – you can feel control of the story slipping further and further away from Picard. A clever study of paranoia that for once makes good use of the trial setup. Simmons' performance is phenomenal and raises the standard of the rest of the cast.

4.22 HALF A LIFE

Lwaxana Troi falls in love with an alien scientist who has only days to live

TX 6 May 1991
WRITER Peter Allan Fields (story by Ted Roberts and Peter Allan Fields)
DIRECTOR Les Landau
GUEST CAST Majel Barrett (Lwaxana Troi), Michelle Forbes (Dara), Terence McNally (B'Tardat), Colm Meaney (O'Brien), David Ogden Stiers (Timicin), Carel Struycken (Mr Homn)

STARDATE 44805.7

Lwaxana Troi is aboard the Enterprise to welcome Dr Timicin, one of Kaelon II's leading scientists, and the two are soon infatuated. Timicin needs the Enterprise's help to recharge his planet's dying sun. They perform a test in an abandoned system but the sun rises to dangerous temperatures. Picard contacts the Kaelonian minister for science, B'Tardat, and explains the setback. Meanwhile, Lwaxana discovers that Timicin will soon reach 60 years, at which point he must commit suicide, as is the Kaelonian tradition called The Resolution. Picard refuses to confine Timicin. However, Lwaxana convinces Timicin to devote more time to his experiments. Prompted, Timicin asks Picard for asylum and Picard agrees. Shortly after, Timicin's daughter, Dara, beams aboard and pleads with Timicin to obey the traditions of their world – she is ashamed that he is turning his back on his heritage. Timicin relents and tells a broken-hearted Lwaxana that he intends to go through with the ritual. She returns to Kaelon II with Timicin to show support in his final days.

TRIVIA

- Peter Allan Fields' poignant take on the plight of the elderly won him his place as a staff writer during season five. Fields later moved on to co-produce *Deep Space Nine*.

RATING

- *Half a Life* – half a plot. Dull and unimaginative, there's barely a concept on which to hang an episode. The desire to bring back Lwaxana Troi rises above reason once more.

4.23 THE HOST

STARDATE 44821.3

Beverly falls in love with a Trill but cannot adjust when the symbiont is transferred to a new host

TX 13 May 1991
WRITER Michel Horvat
DIRECTOR Marvin V Rush
GUEST CAST Robert Harper (Lathal), Franc Luz (Odan), William Newman (Kalin Trose), Nicole Orth-Pallavicini (Kareel), Barbara Tarbuck (Leka Trion), Patti Yasutake (Ogawa)

Beverly Crusher has fallen in love with Odan, a Trill ambassador, who is being escorted to Peliar Zel to resolve a dispute. The people of the Alpha and Beta moons of the planet are arming for war. Riker escorts Odan, but on their return they are fired on. Odan is critically injured and rushed back to the Enterprise. Beverly examines Odan and finds a parasite living in his body. As she prepares to remove it, Odan reveals that his body is a host that can wither and die but the parasite must be found a new body. Another Trill host will arrive too late, so Riker volunteers to be a temporary host so Odan can complete his mission. Beverly performs the transplant, but cannot get used to seeing Odan as Riker. Dismayed, Odan resigns himself to staying away from Beverly. The negotiations continue and Odan must convince the factions to accept his new body. The discussions are successful, and Beverly also comes to accept the situation. Odan returns to be removed from Riker's body but the Trill ship is delayed, endangering his life. The Enterprise sets an intercept course for the Trill vessel. When the new host arrives, Beverly is stunned to find it is a woman. Once the operation is complete, Beverly sadly announces that she cannot adjust to the constant changes they would face in their lives.

TRIVIA

- With Gates McFadden in the later stages of pregnancy during filming, director Martin Rush had to shoot Beverly in tight shots, or with objects in the way on wider angles, to avoid the sight of her bulge.

RATING

- Although continuing a recent theme of unconvincingly quick romances, *The Host* at least explores the nature of what Beverly is feeling. Her difficulties with the new host bodies are interesting, and the presence of a female host at the end creates a rich backdrop for stories about the Trills that would be picked up in *Deep Space Nine*.

4.24 THE MIND'S EYE

STARDATE 44885.5

Geordi is brainwashed by the Romulans and used to sabotage the Klingon-Federation alliance

TX 27 May 1991
WRITER René Echevarria (story by Ken Schafer and René Echevarria)
DIRECTOR David Livingston
GUEST CAST Majel Barrett (Computer Voice), Larry Dobkin (Ambassador Kell), John Fleck (Taibak), Colm Meaney (O'Brien), Edward Wiley (Vagh)

En route to Risa, Geordi is captured by Romulans. Romulan scientist Taibak brainwashes him using his VISOR. The process is observed from the shadows by a Romulan commander. Some time later, Geordi is returned to the Enterprise, unaware that he is still being controlled. Meanwhile, Governor Vagh of the Klingon planet Krios accuses the Federation of aiding a group of rebels. When Vagh produces Federation weapons issued to the activists, Special Emissary Kell asks Picard to investigate. Data and Geordi discover the weapons are Romulan. Picard tries to assure Vagh that the incident is a Romulan ploy to drive the Federation and Klingon Empire apart, but his efforts fail when the Klingons intercept a shipment of weapons sent from the Enterprise to the rebels. The Enterprise is surrounded by Klingon ships. Kell tries to appease Vagh and invites him aboard the Enterprise. However, Kell is a Romulan sympathiser who manipulated Geordi into sending the weapons to the rebels. He orders Geordi to kill Vagh before they are discovered. Data discovers e-band emissions and traces them to Geordi and Kell. Deducing the truth, he arrives just in time to prevent Geordi killing Vagh. Kell is implicated and arrested..

TRIVIA

- Denise Crosby makes her first (uncredited) appearance as Sela, who watches from the shadows as Geordi is tortured. Sela was played by a body double with Crosby's voice dubbed on.
- For his first *Star Trek* shoot, director David Livingston studied John Frankenheimer's work on *The Manchurian Candidate*, on which the episode is based.

RATING

- The episode neatly revives the notion of the Klingon civil war, first broached in *Reunion* but which was to reach its peak at the end of the season. Geordi's brainwashing is well done and Burton is good throughout.

4.25 IN THEORY

STARDATE 44932.3

Data begins a romantic relationship with crewmember Jenna D'Sora

TX 27 May 1991
WRITERS Joe Menosky and Ronald D Moore
DIRECTOR Patrick Stewart
GUEST CAST Rosalind Chao (Keiko), Whoopi Goldberg (Guinan), Colm Meaney (O'Brien), Michele Scarabelli (Jenna D'Sora), Pamela Winslow (McKnight)

Jenna D'Sora, on the rebound from boyfriend Jeff Arton, finds a shoulder to cry on with Data. Data seeks advice from a number of his colleagues and decides to pursue the relationship. Their first date is unpromising. D'Sora tries to get Data to appreciate the difference between love and logic, but Data cannot understand. Data picks a fight with Jenna, having observed that conflict can sometimes strengthen the bond between people, but Jenna finds his actions artificial. Meanwhile, the Enterprise investigates the Mar Obscura, a dark matter nebula. As the Enterprise passes through the phenomenon, parts of the ship begin to phase in and out of normal space. When the ship reaches a planet, they are surprised to find it does not exist. Suddenly it shimmers into view and Data deduces that the nebula is causing gaps in space. With the ship in danger, Picard orders a new course but Data observes that the Enterprise is too large to navigate between the gaps. Instead, Picard pilots a shuttlecraft through the nebula, guiding the Enterprise to safety. Afterwards, Jenna tells Data she cannot see him again: she fears her previous boyfriend was unemotional and she may be following a pattern. Data sees her point and discontinues the relevant program immediately, blankly wishing Jenna goodbye.

QUOTES

- 'I would be delighted to offer any advice I can on understanding women. When I have some, I'll let you know.' – *Picard to Data*

TRIVIA

- Data's cat, first seen in *Data's Day*, is given a name here – Spot, the name of the real cat who played her (a role shared by two other cats, Monster and Brandy).

RATING

- Pretty much wallpaper for Patrick Stewart's directorial debut. Data's love story had been on the cards since the first season but, sadly, the episode has little to offer that isn't obvious. The nebula is clumsily crowbarred in to add jeopardy.

4.26 REDEMPTION Part I

STARDATE 44429.6

Worf resigns his Federation commission to fight for his family's honour

TX 17 June 1991
WRITER Ronald D Moore
DIRECTOR Cliff Bole
GUEST CAST Majel Barrett (Computer Voice), Denise Crosby (Sela), JD Cullum (Toral), Whoopi Goldberg (Guinan), Clifton Jones (Helmsman), Nicholas Kepros (Movar), Barbara March (Lursa), Robert O'Reilly (Gowron), Tom Ormeny (Klingon First Officer), Ben Slack (K'Tal), Tony Todd (Kurn), Gwynyth Walsh (B'Etor)

En route to the Klingon homeworld, where Picard is to attend the accession of Gowron as Leader of the High Council, the Enterprise is intercepted by a Klingon vessel. Picard is surprised to see Gowron, who reveals that his rival, Duras, has amassed a rebel faction and is preparing to wage civil war. Reminding Picard of Duras' hand in Worf's discommendation, Gowron asks Picard to ban Duras' family from the Council. Picard insists this is beyond his powers. Worf asks Gowron to restore his family name, but Gowron claims it would cause too much dissent at this time and refuses. Instead, Worf takes leave to join his brother, Kurn, who reveals that he has his own alliance to defy both Gowron and Duras and restore their name. Worf, however, insists they remain loyal to the leadership and decides to back Gowron in return for their honour. At the accession, Duras' sisters, Lursa and B'Etor, insist that Duras' illegitimate son, Toral, be allowed to challenge Gowron for leadership. The Council leaves Picard with the casting vote, but he rightly suspects that the Duras sisters are in league with the Romulans. Picard refuses Toral's right of candidature and, in response, members of the High Council move to Toral's side, showing their support. Meanwhile, Worf meets with Gowron and offers his brother's ships in return for their family honour. Gowron asks for Federation help but Worf refuses. Soon they are under attack from Duras' allies. Gowron issues a request for Federation help but Picard refuses to get involved. Worf is able to beat off the attackers. Gowron rushes through the ceremony and immediately restores Worf's family name. On Gowron's behalf, Worf asks Picard to bring the Federation in on Gowron's side. Picard stands firm. He orders Worf to return to the ship but the Klingon officer resigns his commission. As the Enterprise leaves, the Duras sisters meet with their allies, the Romulans – led by Sela, who is the double of Tasha Yar.

TRIVIA

- In an amusing aside, Guinan beats Worf's best score in the phaser range.

RATING

- Strong stuff that brings to a head the run of Klingon stories that really got going with *Sins of the Father.* Klingon politics and power struggles always work better than episodes about Klingon ceremonies or rites of passage. And there's still the sense that Gowron is the devil we didn't know. The low-key episode ending works well, coming as it does with little foreshadowing.

STAR TREK: THE NEXT GENERATION
SEASON FIVE

5.1 REDEMPTION Part II

STARDATE 45020.4

Picard moves to prevent the Klingon civil war engulfing the whole Quadrant

TX 23 September 1991
WRITER Ronald D Moore
DIRECTOR David Carson
GUEST CAST Fran Bennett (Shanti), Timothy Carhart (Hobson), Stephen James Carver (Helsman), Denise Crosby (Sela), JD Cullum (Toral), Whoopi Goldberg (Guinan), Michael G Hagerty (Larg), Clifton Jones (Craig), Nicholas Kepros (Movar), Jordan Lund (Kulge), Barbara March (Lursa), Colm Meaney (O'Brien), Robert O'Reilly (Gowron), Tony Todd (Kurn), Gwynyth Walsh (B'Etor)

Worf fights on Gowron's side, but begins to suspect that the Duras faction is being supplied by the Romulans. Picard decides to intervene to expose Romulan involvement to prevent a victorious Duras from forming a Klingon-Romulan alliance. He wins approval from Starfleet Command for a non-aggressive blockade of the Neutral Zone, and commands a fleet of ships that sets up a tachyon web that will detect cloaked ships. Worf is kidnapped by Duras and tortured. Data takes command of one of the fleet, and faces prejudice from its crew. He wins their support by acting on his own initiative to detect a Romulan vessel that would have evaded the web. The Romulans withdraw rather than risk detection, weakening the Duras faction. Gowron assumes control of the Klingon Empire. Worf returns to the Enterprise, where the crew wonder how Sela can be related to Tasha Yar.

QUOTES

- 'Worf has been captured by Duras. I hope he dies well.' – *Gowron*

TRIVIA

- By all accounts, Denise Crosby herself came up with a way she could still make guest appearances in the show despite her character Tasha Yar being killed (twice!) The answer is a little convoluted: Sela is the daughter of the Tasha Yar from *Yesterday's Enterprise*, a Tasha from a timeline that didn't 'really' happen. Tasha survived the end of that episode, was captured by the Romulans and had Sela... who handed her in to the Romulan authorities when she was four. Tasha died trying to escape them.

RATING

- An episode with a scope, complexity and action sequences that would have been unthinkable when *The Next Generation* started, the twenty-fifth year of *Star Trek* starts with a vast threat to the Federation and, for once, it shows us rather than tells us. An extraordinary episode, one that really does look like a movie.

5.2 DARMOK

STARDATE 45047.2

The crew struggle to communicate with aliens who have abducted Picard

TX 30 September 1991
WRITER Joe Menosky (story by Philip Lazenbnik and Joe Menosky)
DIRECTOR Winrich Kolbe
GUEST CAST Richard James (Tamarian First Officer), Ashley Judd (Robin Lefler), Colm Meaney (O'Brien), Paul Winfield (Dathon)

The Enterprise is on a mission to attempt contact with The Children of Tama, an enigmatic race whose language has baffled previous explorers. Meeting in neutral territory over El-Adrel IV, the Tamarians send a message that seems nonsensical. Frustrated, the alien captain holds out two daggers and says 'Darmok and Jalad at Tanagra', then beams Picard off the Enterprise and down onto the planet. The Tamarians block attempts to rescue Picard, leading Riker and Worf to assume they are hostile. Data and Deanna's attempt to analyse the Tamarian language gets nowhere. Meanwhile, Picard finds himself by a campfire with the Tamarian captain, who continues to speak apparent nonsense at him. When the alien captain offers Picard a dagger, he refuses to fight. It becomes clear that isn't the alien's intent, either – Picard will need it to help fight off a wild creature, one too powerful for either to face alone. The Enterprise manages to beam Picard off the planet, but only for a moment, and in that moment, the creature mortally wounds the alien captain. Picard has come to realise that the Tamarians speak in metaphor – they are constantly alluding to their myths. The alien wants peace. This revelation comes as the Tamarian ship and the Enterprise finally lose patience and move to attack one another. Picard arrives back at the last moment, contacts the Tamarians and manages to communicate with them using the phrases he has learnt, averting war. Dathon, the alien captain is dead, but his sacrifice has created a connection between their people.

QUOTES

- 'Darmok and Jalad at Tanagra', 'Shaka when the walls fell', 'Temba, his arms wide' – if that's the *translation*, no wonder communication has proven difficult!

TRIVIA

- Paul Winfield is 'the black man who dies in science fiction films' – including *The Terminator* and *Star Trek II: The Wrath of Khan.* Of course his character dies in this too.
- The alien effect here was the first use in *Star Trek* of the 'morphing' software that had made such an impression in *Terminator 2* earlier in the year, and which would rapidly become ubiquitous in science fiction films.

RATING

- A story that deliberately starts out looking like a remake of *Arena*, but which quickly becomes something far more challenging and idiosyncratic, *Darmok* is one of the best *The Next Generation* episodes, and it's certainly the cleverest.

5.3 ENSIGN RO

STARDATE 45076.3

A rebellious officer is brought aboard the Enterprise to deal with a crisis on Bajor

TX 7 October 1991
WRITER Michael Piller (story by Rick Berman and Michael Piller)
DIRECTOR Les Landau
GUEST CAST Majel Barrett (Computer voice), Frank Collinson (Gul Dolak), Michelle Forbes (Ro Laren), Whoopi Goldberg (Guinan), Jeffrey Hayenga (Orta), Scott Marlowe (Keeve Falor), Cliff Potts (Kennelly), Ken Thorley (Mr Mot), Harley Venton (Transporter Officer)

Bajoran extremists attack a Federation colony. Bajoran Ensign Ro is brought aboard the Enterprise to get Orta, a militant, to agree to resettlement. Ro was court-martialed some years ago for causing the death of an Away Team, and the crew resent her presence. After his Away Team is taken hostage tracking Orta in the Valo system, Picard confines Ro to quarters. But she is on a secret mission to lure Orta out of hiding then allow the Cardassians to destroy his ship, preserving the peace. Picard and Ro conspire to make sure the Cardassians destroy an empty ship, and reveal it was the Cardassians who raided the colony to get Starfleet support to persecute the Bajorans. Impressed by Ro, Picard offers her a place on his crew.

QUOTES

- 'We live in different universes, you and I. Yours is about diplomacy, mine is about blankets.' – *Keeve*

TRIVIA

- It was felt that the regular crew had become a little too settled and friendly, and Ro was introduced to put the cat among the pigeons. The production team were also acutely conscious that once Yar left, the two women in the crew were in stereotypically feminine 'caring' roles. By accident or design, Ro Laren is the exact opposite of Troi: belligerent and feisty with a spiky relationship with Riker. Michelle Forbes had impressed the producers in *Half a Life*, and the role was reportedly written with her in mind.
- This episode introduces the Bajorans and sketches in their character and the nature of the dispute with the Cardassians. As such, this episode would prove to be seminal, as (along with *The Price*) it sets up the situation seen in *Deep Space Nine*. This certainly wasn't the intention at the time – the idea of a spin-off series was floating around by summer 1991, but wouldn't be formally proposed until early 1992.
- The real life inspiration for the Bajoran situation would be a subject of discussion over the years. Fans tended to polarise between those who saw them as thinly-veiled Palestinians and those who saw them as thinly-veiled Israelis – and further polarise between whether it was a fair or accurate representation of that side. Rick Berman has always said they were not meant to represent a particular group, but the common experience of refugees becoming freedom fighters and/or terrorists. In production at the time of the first Gulf War, the experience of the Iraqi Kurds might have been on the writers' minds.

RATING

- Rather like the *Itchy, Scratchy and Poochy* episode of *The Simpsons*, where the whole story revolves around the new character being introduced into a long-running show. Ro is a strong character, well played, but the story requires the regulars to be uncharacteristically a bit too dim, mistrusting and wrong for it to be entirely successful.

5.4 SILICON AVATAR

STARDATE 45122.3

The Crystalline Entity returns, and a scientist is determined to destroy it

TX 14 October 1991
WRITER Jeri Taylor (story by Lawrence V Conley)
DIRECTOR Cliff Bole
GUEST CAST Susan Diol (Carmen Davila), Ellen Geer (Kila Marr)

Riker leads an Away Team helping colonists settle on Melona IV when it is attacked by the Crystalline Entity that wiped out Data's home colony of Omicron Theta. Two colonists are killed, but Riker and Data save the rest by getting them into caves. The Enterprise rescues them, and is joined by Dr Kila Marr, whose son, Renny, was killed on Omicron Theta and who has vowed to kill the Entity. She hates Data because of Lore's role in that attack, but warms to him when she realises he has stored details of Renny and can even imitate his voice. Picard wants to contact the Entity, Marr wants to kill it. She pretends to change her mind, and works on a graviton pulse emitter that lures the Entity out near the Brechtian Cluster. She then uses it to destroy the Entity, saying she did it for Renny. Data tells her Renny would not have approved.

QUOTES

- 'The sperm whale on Earth devours millions of cuttlefish as it roams the oceans. It is not evil... it is feeding. The same may be true of the Entity.' – *Picard to Dr Marr. Fair comment, but a bit insensitive seeing as it did kill her son*

TRIVIA

- A story pitched by a new writer which tickled the fancy of the production team, because it brought back a silly monster (from *Datalore*) and had a title they loved, although they claimed not to understand what it meant. For the record: Data is the robot representation (or 'silicon avatar') of Marr's lost son, whose memory and voice are stored within him.

RATING

- One of the show's worst baddies returns – but the Crystalline Entity is genuinely threatening this time, and makes for a good threat in a nice Roddenberryesque morality tale. Quite why none of the crew realise that Dr Marr is a) barking mad and b) up to no good is never made clear, though, because she doesn't exactly hide it. It has some nice touches and twists, like a lovingly set up same-old-Riker-romance subplot which is abruptly ended when the monster kills the girl in the teaser. This was below average for the season, but compares well with a lot of *Star Trek* made since.

5.5 DISASTER

STARDATE 45156.1

The Enterprise is disabled, its crew placed in jeopardy – and Troi is the acting captain

TX 21 October 1991
WRITER Ronald D Moore (story by Ron Jarvis and Philip A Scorza)
DIRECTOR Gabrielle Beaumont
GUEST CAST Cameron Arnett (Mandel), Rosalind Chao (Keiko O'Brien), Erika Flores (Marissa), Michelle Forbes (Ro), John Christopher Graas (Jay Gordon), Jana Marie Hupp (Monroe), Colm Meaney (O'Brien), Max Supera (Patterson)

The Enterprise is immobilised when it hits quantum filaments, a rare space phenomenon. Areas of the ship are completely cut off by the damage. Picard is stuck in a lift with a broken ankle and three children who'd won the chance of a guided tour of the ship. Worf is stuck in Ten-Forward with the heavily-pregnant Keiko O'Brien. Geordi and Beverly are trapped with a hazardous cargo. Ro and Miles O'Brien are on the bridge with Deanna Troi – the ranking officer, and so the Acting Captain. The bridge is aware that the engines have been damaged, and could explode at any moment – Ro demands that Troi separates the saucer section, leaving the rest of the ship to its fate. Unknown to the bridge, Riker and Data make their way to Engineering in an attempt to restore power. To get past one hazard, Data disconnects his head and uses his body as a circuit breaker. Picard gets the children to safety, Worf helps deliver the O'Briens' daughter. Troi plays a hunch, and sends power from the bridge to Engineering. Riker connects Data's head to the ship's computer, where he averts disaster and repairs the engines. The ship heads for Starbase 67 for repairs.

TRIVIA

- It's odd that Troi needs to have a warp core breach explained to her – it's fairly basic *Star Trek* knowledge, and she saw one in *Contagion*. But the writers redeem themselves by getting her to ask if a quantum filament is anything like a cosmic string (*The Loss*), and earn bonus points for Ro and O'Brien's withering response to her ignorance of basic technobabble.
- The O'Briens' daughter, Molly, isn't named until the next episode. A year later, when she reappears in *Deep Space Nine*, she's already a 'three-year-old' toddler.

RATING

- Entertaining – perhaps a little *too* funny, as the jokes undermine the grave situation the ship and its crew are in. The ending's a little rushed, too. But it's a very likeable episode.

5.6 THE GAME

STARDATE 45208.2

Wesley Crusher returns to discover the Enterprise crew addicted to a new computer game

TX 28 October 1991
WRITER Brannon Braga (story by Susan Sackett, Fred Bronson and Brannon Braga)
DIRECTOR Corey Allen
GUEST CAST Diane M Hurley (Ensign), Ashley Judd (Robin Lefler), Colm Meaney (O'Brien), Katherine Moffatt (Etana Jol), Wil Wheaton (Wesley Crusher), Patti Yasutake (Ogowa)

On holiday on Risa, Riker falls under the spell of Etana Jol, who gives him a computer game headset. He returns to the Enterprise at the same time Wesley Crusher pays the ship a visit. While Wesley sparks up a friendship with Ensign Robin Lefler, Riker distributes the game to his fellow officers. The addictive game spreads through the crew. Under the influence of the game, Beverly disables Data. Wesley becomes suspicious, and discovers that the game raises serotonin to dangerous levels. Wesley and Robin make fake headsets when they realise Data – the only crewman who won't be affected by the game – was sabotaged. With even Picard under the thrall of the game, the Enterprise makes a rendezvous with Etana Jol's ship. She wants them to distribute the game throughout Starfleet. Wesley has repaired Data, though, and Data uses an optical burst pattern (a series of flashing lights) to break the game's spell. Etana Jol is arrested.

QUOTES

- 'I never met a chocolate I didn't like.' – *Troi*

TRIVIA

- This is the second appearance of Robin Lefler, who was never seen again on television, but is a regular character in Peter David's *New Frontier* series of *Star Trek* novels. Ashley Judd turned down a chance to play her again later in the season in *The First Duty*, but has gone on to enjoy a successful Hollywood career.
- Gene Roddenberry died on 26 October 1991, just before this episode was broadcast.

RATING

- A fun episode, even if it's a bit odd to imagine Wesley as having more willpower than the whole crew of the Enterprise put together.

5.7 UNIFICATION Part I

STARDATE 45233.1

Ambassador Spock is missing... has he really defected to the Romulans?

TX 4 November 1991
WRITER Jeri Taylor (story by Rick Berman and Michael Piller)
DIRECTOR Les Landau
GUEST CAST Erick Avari (B'ljik), Majel Barrett (Computer Voice), Mimi Cozzens (Soup Woman), Karen Hensel (Admiral), Graham Jarvis (Dokachim), Norman Large (Neral), Mark Lenard (Sarek), Joanna Miles (Perrin), Leonard Nimoy (Spock), Daniel Roebuck (Romulan), Stephen D Root (K'Vada), Malachi Throne (Pardek)

Starfleet has a picture of Ambassador Spock on Romulus, and they are worried he has defected. Picard is ordered to find him and return him to the Federation. On Vulcan, Sarek tells Picard that Spock has made contact with Pardek, a reformer in the Romulan senate. The Enterprise heads for Klingon space, and Picard persuades Gowron to lend him a Bird of Prey to infiltrate the Romulan sector. The Enterprise investigates the destruction of a Vulcan ship, the T'Pau. Sarek dies. The Enterprise discovers that smugglers are raiding a shipyard for decommissioned vessels. Picard and Data head to Romulus, disguised as Romulans, and are captured by Romulan soldiers, who lead them to a cave. A shadowy figure emerges: Spock.

TRIVIA

- The twenty-fifth anniversary story. Leonard Nimoy had been approached about a *The Next Generation* appearance as early as the second season, when a proposed story, *Return to Forever*, would have seen the twenty-fourth century Spock meeting himself from both the era of the TV series and the movies, but he wasn't keen. He agreed to do *Unification* because it tied in with the soon-to-be-released *Star Trek VI: The Undiscovered Country* (he was an executive producer of the film).
- Many fans were disappointed that Spock only appeared right at the end of the episode, but Nimoy's schedule only allowed five days of filming.
- Venerable actor Malachi Throne had been in *Star Trek* before, as the voice of The Keeper in the very first episode, *The Cage* and as Mendez in *The Menagerie*. Contemporary publicity drew attention to the fact he'd been in the very first *Star Trek* story.
- *Star Trek VI: The Undiscovered Country* was inspired by the end of the Cold War, and *Unification* draws some inspiration from the reunification of Germany that followed (although that aspect of the script is decidedly undeveloped).

RATING

- Keeping Spock in the shadows actually works very well, and allows the regulars to shine in a story that, like *Redemption*, shows just how large and well-populated the *Star Trek* universe had become, and which has a very funny scene where Picard is just trying to get some sleep. A fine episode that doesn't let nostalgia interfere with a show that's perfectly successful in its own right. It's clear that *The Next Generation* is the West Germany side of the two *Star Trek*s being unified here.

5.8 UNIFICATION Part !!

STARDATE 45245.8

Spock and Picard discover that the Romulans are intent on conquest

TX 11 November 1991
WRITER Michael Piller (story by Rick Berman and Michael Piller)
DIRECTOR Cliff Bole
GUEST CAST William Bastiani (Omag), Denise Crosby (Sela), Susan Falldender (Romulan), Norman Large (Neral), Harriet Leider (Amarie), Leonard Nimoy (Spock), Vidal Peterson (D'Tan), Daniel Roebuck (Romulan), Stephen D Root (K'Vada), Malachi Throne (Pardek)

Spock tells Picard that Pardek thinks Romulan society is changing, and the unification of the Romulans and Vulcans is possible. Riker learns the smugglers were taking ship components to Galorndon Core, and heads there. Picard, Spock and Data are captured by Sela, who explains they are preparing an invasion of Vulcan. They'll use Spock (or a hologram of him) to announce that the craft are a peace delegation. The Enterprise rushes to intercept the force after Spock broadcasts a warning – but the Romulan ships are destroyed by a Romulan Warbird, as the senate fear the invasion will fail. Spock chooses to stay on Romulus to seek peace. Before Picard leaves, he and Spock mind meld, so Spock can remember his father.

QUOTES

- 'I was involved with 'cowboy diplomacy', as you describe it, long before you were born.' – *Spock to Picard*

- 'Do you find you have missed your humanity?'
'I have no regrets.'
'No regrets'. That is a human expression.'
'Yes. Fascinating.' – *Data and Spock compare notes*

TRIVIA

- This episode was filmed before part one, because of Nimoy's limited availability.
- Spock's line that he could never forgive himself for what happened to Kirk was a reference to Kirk being captured by the Klingons in *Star Trek VI: The Undiscovered Country*. It led to rumours on the internet that Kirk was to die at the end of the film.
- Advertising rates for this episode were unprecedented for a syndicated show – $200,000 for a 30-second slot (and about twice the average for *The Next Generation* up to this point). Viewing figures were also unprecedented: a Nielsen rating of 14.6 against prime-time competition. That's more than that week's *Cheers*, *Roseanne*, football and baseball matches.

RATING

- A bit too much of a romp, and far too talky and studio-bound, the 'Romulan invasion of Vulcan' looks pedestrian and not a little underfunded. However, Patrick Stewart and Leonard Nimoy are great value together, and they, at least, don't disappoint. This is a very good episode, just not the barnstormer it deserves to be.

5.9 A MATTER OF TIME

STARDATE 45349.1

A time traveller arrives on the Enterprise

TX 18 November 1991
WRITER Rick Berman
DIRECTOR Paul Lynch
GUEST CAST Shelia Frankin (Felton), Matt Frewer (Berlingoff Rasmussen), Shay Garner (Female Scientist), Stefan Gierasch (Hal Mosely)

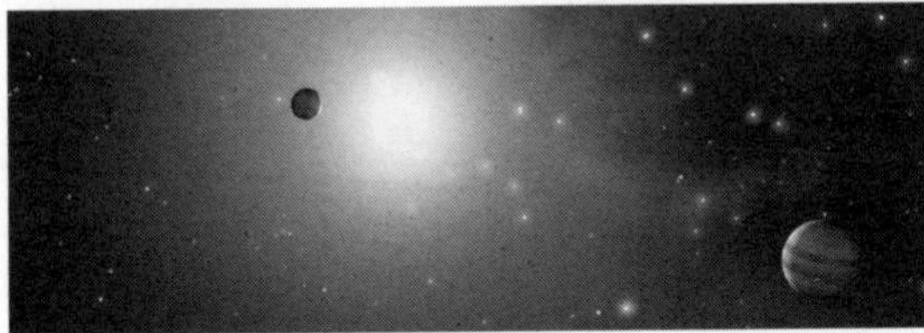

An asteroid has crashed into Penthara IV and the Enterprise is trying to prevent a nuclear winter. Rasmussen, a time traveller from the twenty-sixth century, arrives and is keen to study the Enterprise and its 'artefacts'. The crew rapidly become impatient with him as he asks them to fill in questionnaires. Troi senses deception, but on the surface he is annoyingly cheerful. Geordi comes up with a plan that will either save Penthara or destroy it – triggering an electrostatic discharge in the atmosphere. Rasmussen refuses to disclose whether history says it works, but the Pentharans consent to it, and it saves the planet. Rasmussen decides to leave, but Picard orders his time pod searched, as things have gone missing. Rasmussen says that only Data can be allowed in the pod, because he will be able to keep his secrets. Once inside, Rasmussen kidnaps Data – he's from the twenty-second century, and stole this time pod from the real owner. He's planning to go back home and 'invent' twenty-fourth century technology, including Data himself. Picard had deactivated Rasmussen's stolen phaser, though, and Data apprehends him. The time pod returns home automatically, leaving Rasmussen stranded in his future.

TRIVIA

- Robin Williams is a *Star Trek* fan and was keen to make a guest appearance. However, schedule changes on *Hook* made it impossible to play Rasmussen, a part written for him.

RATING

- ...but just imagine what it could have been. Matt Frewer puts in a good performance, but like Lawrence Luckinbill in *Star Trek V: The Final Frontier*, he's the understudy, and the original casting would have made this episode into something special.

5.10 NEW GROUND

STARDATE 45376.3

Worf's son is proving to be a problem child, as is a new spacedrive system

TX 6 January 1992
WRITER Grant Rosenberg (story by Sara Charno and Stuart Charno)
DIRECTOR Robert Scheerer

Worf's adoptive mother brings his son Alexander to the Enterprise, saying the boy needs a role model. Worf reluctantly agrees to take him under his wing. Meanwhile, the Enterprise is monitoring tests of the 'soliton wave', a way of pushing spacecraft at warp speeds without the need for warp engines. Alexander proves to be a handful – he is anti-social, and steals a toy. Worf tries to teach him Klingon codes of honour, but Alexander is unresponsive. The soliton wave project goes wrong, and the Enterprise is forced to

GUEST CAST Brian Bonsall (Alexander); Georgia Brown (Helena Rozhenko); Jennifer Edwards (Kyle); Sheila Franklin (Ensign Felton); Richard McGonagal (Ja'Dar)

put itself at danger to dissipate the wave before it hits an inhabited planet. It succeeds, but Alexander is trapped in a damaged part of the ship. Worf and Riker rescue him.

QUOTES

- 'You not only dishonour yourself, but your family. You dishonour me.' – *Worf sketches in the basics of Klingon ethics*

TRIVIA

- With the part of Alexander now a semi-regular one, it was recast. Brian Bonsall had starred in the sitcom *Family Ties*, and so was a young actor used to the rigours of production-line television.
- Worf tells Alexander about Kahless, and gives us the Klingon side of a story first heard in *The Savage Curtain*.

RATING

- An episode where neither the A nor B plots amount to much, and don't fit together at all. The Worf/Alexander story sends out all sorts of mixed messages about Worf as a father. It wouldn't be so bad if the very next episode didn't do much the same story a lot better...

5.11 HERO WORSHIP

STARDATE 45397.3

A young boy copes with the loss of his parents by emulating Data

TX 27 January 1992
WRITER Joe Menosky (story by Hilary J Bader)
DIRECTOR Patrick Stewart
GUEST CAST Steven Einspahr (Teacher), Sheila Franklin (Felton), Joshua Harris (Timothy), Harley Venton (Hutchinson)

The Enterprise discovers the heavily-damaged USS Vico on the edge of a 'black cluster', an area full of dangerous collapsed protostars. An Away Team beams over to recover the ship's records, and Data rescues a boy, Timothy. He claims the ship was attacked by aliens, but the crew can find no traces of that. Timothy is traumatised, and becomes fascinated by Data, his saviour – especially when he learns Data doesn't have feelings. Timothy begins to copy Data's mannerisms and speech patterns. Troi suggests it's his temporary way of coping with loss, and encourages Data to spend time with Timothy. As they become friends, Timothy confides that he was the one that destroyed the Vico by playing with the computer. This can't be true, though – he's blaming himself for something that wasn't his fault. As the Enterprise explores the black cluster, it's subject to incredible gravitational forces. By listening to Timothy, Data makes sure the Enterprise doesn't make the same mistake as the Vico did – raising shields just makes the situation worse, the solution is to *lower* them. The Enterprise flies to safety.

QUOTES

- 'They say imitation is the greatest form of flattery' – *Data*

TRIVIA

- Counsellor Troi manages to spend a great deal of time with Timothy, but despite that and her empathic powers, she can't tell that he's lying about the Vico being attacked, even though Picard, Geordi and Data all can.

RATING

- A twist on the 'Data wanting to be human' story, with a good performance by Joshua Harris. The limitations of the episode's length means Timothy gets over his trauma remarkably quickly (a matter of hours, it seems!), but a good episode nonetheless.

5.12 VIOLATIONS

STARDATE 45429.3

Telepathic aliens release the unpleasant memories of the crew

Three Ullians are onboard. They are historians who can recover long-forgotten memories telepathically. They are an open race, and don't understand some of the crew's reluctance to undergo the process. That night, Troi dreams of a romantic encounter with Riker... but he

TX 3 February 1992
WRITER Pamela Gray and Jeri Taylor (story by Shari Goodhartz, T Michael Gray and Pamela Gray)
DIRECTOR Robert Wiemer
GUEST CAST Majel Barrett (Computer Voice), Craig Benton (Davis), Eve Brenner (Inad), Rosalind Chao (Keiko O'Brien), Rick Fitts (Dr Martin), Ben Lemon (Jev), David Sage (Tarmin), Doug Wert (Jack Crusher)

turns into one of the Ullians. Troi falls into a coma and is diagnosed with Iresine Syndrome. Riker and Beverly are also affected before Picard suspects the Ullians. Troi wakes, and agrees to let Jev probe her memories. She sees Tarmin assault her, but realises Jev is framing him. Worf and Data save her, and research shows that Jev is responsible for many similar crimes. Jev is taken into custody and dropped off at Starbase 440.

TRIVIA

- Shari Goodhartz pitched a rape-metaphor story, one which a number of other writers worked on before it was made. Various drafts had other crewmen revealing their fears – Geordi's memories of a fire when he was a child weren't used here, but were referred to in *Hero Worship.*

RATING

- If you were visited by a group of telepaths who specialised in recovering memories, and everyone suddenly started having traumatic dreams, how long would it take you to suspect your guests could be behind it? It seems to take the Enterprise crew an age. An OK episode, but a formulaic one.

5.13 THE MASTERPIECE SOCIETY

The Enterprise discovers a colony of the genetically 'perfect'

TX 10 February 1992
WRITER Adam Belanoff and Michael Piller (story by James Kahn and Adam Belanoff)
DIRECTOR Winrich Kolbe
GUEST CAST John Snyder (Aaron Conor), Dey Young (Hannah Bates), Ron Canada (Martin Benbeck), Shelia Franklin (Felton)

STARDATE 45470.1

A stellar core fragment is endangering the hitherto unknown population of Moab IV, so the Enterprise contacts their leader, Aaron Conor. The colony has been isolated for 200 years. They live in a biosphere where everyone has a specific role, and there's a delicate genetic balance. Troi and Conor fall for each other, while Geordi and the colonist Hannah manage to deflect the fragment. Hannah tells Geordi there are cracks in the biosphere – she is lying, hoping to leave the colony with a group of 22 others who resent the eugenic society. If they leave, though, the delicate balance of the society will be destroyed. Picard agrees to take them.

QUOTES

- 'I wouldn't want to live my life knowing that my future was already written, that my boundaries had already been set.'
  – Picard to Troi

TRIVIA

- John Snyder was incorrectly credited as 'John Synder' on first broadcast of this episode.

RATING

- An OK story, but one that doesn't really get to grips with the big themes it's trying to address, like whether a utopia can ever be built around an evil idea (the treatment of the disabled – Geordi is told his blindness would have been detected during his mother's pregnancy and he would have been aborted) or the influence of genetics on individuality. Instead it's all too predictable. Picard's actions at the end – destroying an entire civilisation for the sake of less than two dozen people – are also far more serious than the script allows.

5.14 CONUNDRUM

The Enterprise crew lose their memories – but have orders to complete a military strike

TX 17 February 1992

STARDATE 45494.2

The crew are knocked out by a burst of green energy. When they awake, they've lost their memories. The executive officer, Kieran MacDuff, helps them to access the ship's computer, and they discover they work for the Federation, which is at war with the Lysian Alliance, and their mission is to destroy Lysian Central Command. Riker remembers strong feelings for both Ro and Troi – and is happy to express them. They discover their

WRITER Barry M Schkolnick (story by Paul Schiffer)
DIRECTOR Les Landau
GUEST CAST Erich Anderson (MacDuff), Michelle Forbes (Ro Laren), Liz Vassey (Kristin), Erick Weiss (Crewman)

names and ranks from the computer, and set about their task. They easily destroy some of the Lysian defences. Picard becomes suspicious – the Enterprise is leagues ahead of the Lysian technology. Why wasn't the war won long ago? Against MacDuff's advice, he contacts the Lysians, who tell him they at war with the Satarrans. MacDuff is a Satarran agent who's engineered this situation. Picard expresses his deep regret to the Lysians for the damage his ship has done.

QUOTES

- 'I feel as though I've been handed a weapon, sent into a room and told to shoot a stranger.' – *Picard to MacDuff*

TRIVIA

- Originally a story about a government using mind control to recruit troops, it metamorphosed into a 'bottle show' that emphasised the characters and personalities of the regular cast.

RATING

- A replay of *Clues* with added action, the addition of MacDuff as a crewman the audience know is an intruder but the amnesiac crew don't even question is a stroke of genius, and the first half of the episode is brilliant. It can never live up to the teaser scene, though, and while there are some nice touches (like Worf assuming he's captain and being visibly grumpy after the truth is revealed, and an amnesiac Riker seducing both Ro and Troi), the progression of the story quickly becomes predictable.

5.15 POWER PLAY

STARDATE 45571.2

The Enterprise and its crew are hijacked by evil spirits

TX 24 February 1992
WRITER Rene Balcer, Herbert J Wright and Brannon Braga (story by Paul Ruben and Maurice Hurley)
DIRECTOR David Livingston
GUEST CAST Majel Barrett (Computer voice), Rosalind Chao (Keiko O'Brien), Michelle Forbes (Ro Laren), Colm Meaney (O'Brien), Ryan Reid (Transporter Technician)

The Enterprise gets a distress call from the unexplored moon of Mab-Bu VI, which is affected by powerful electrical storms. Riker, Troi and Data take a shuttle to investigate. The shuttle crashes, injuring Riker, but O'Brien risks his life to beam down with a pattern enhancer which boosts the transporters. As they beam out, all of them except Riker are touched by a strange cloud. Troi, Data and O'Brien, possessed, seal off Ten-Forward and take hostages, demanding that the ship be moved to the moon's south pole. They say they are from the USS Essex, lost here 200 years ago, and all they want is to find peace. But Picard doesn't believe them – they have acted violently, and the truth is revealed: they are convicted criminals from Ux-Mal, exiled here 500 years ago. Picard allows himself to be taken hostage, and the rest of the aliens are beamed into the cargo bay. Picard threatens to destroy them unless they return to the planet. The aliens are forced to agree.

TRIVIA

- Herb Wright added the idea that the aliens resembled vengeful ghosts after a fair few other writers had tried to get this story to work. Like *The Next Phase*, a story designed as a 'bottle show' evolved into an effects-intensive story.

RATING

- It's nice to see Marina Sirtis and Colm Meaney play against type, and Brent Spiner deserves a mention for playing an evil Data who's nothing like Lore. It's an effective, tense episode. Nothing remarkable, but very watchable.

5.16 ETHICS

STARDATE 45587.3

Worf wants to commit suicide after being crippled in an accident

TX 2 March 1992
WRITER Ronald D Moore (story by Sara Charno and Stuart Charno)
DIRECTOR Chip Chalmers

Worf loses the use of his legs following an accident in a cargo bay. Klingon honour requires him to commit suicide, but Riker refuses to help him. Picard suggests he honours Worf's culture, but Riker discovers that technically Worf's son, Alexander, should assist his father to die. Dr Toby Russell comes on board to try to heal Worf – Worf rejects partial mobility, and Russell tells him she has a radical new technique, using genetronics, that is untried and might result in his death. When the Enterprise assists with a disaster aboard the

GUEST CAST Brian Bonsall (Alexander), Caroline Kava (Toby Russell), Patti Yusutake (Ogowa)

transport ship Denver, Beverly becomes concerned that Russell puts her research over the lives of her patients and relieves her of duty. Worf can't bring himself to get Alexander to help him to die, and agrees to try Dr Russell's treatment. It doesn't work and Worf appears to die but a number of redundant organs unique to Klingons prevent his death. Alexander helps his father with his physiotherapy.

QUOTES

- 'Suicide is not an option.' – *Riker tells Worf*

TRIVIA

- Klingons have two livers, 23 ribs, an eight-chambered heart... and a back-up synaptic system which gives them the handy ability to come back from the dead to resolve ethical issues in series drama without killing a regular character.

RATING

- As the name suggests, *Ethics* deals with big ethical issues, but the 'debate' is pitched at a pretty banal level. Besides, it's obviously much ado about nothing because we know Worf's going to get better by the end of the episode. The way he does so is a particularly weak cop-out.

5.17 THE OUTCAST

STARDATE 45614.6

Riker breaks a taboo when he falls in love

TX 16 March 1992
WRITER Jeri Taylor
DIRECTOR Robert Scheerer
GUEST CAST Megan Cole (Noor), Melinda Culea (Soren), Callan White (Krite)

The androgynous J'Naii are looking for a missing shuttle. The Enterprise locates it in 'null space', and Riker and J'Naii scientist Soren work to recover it. The two hit it off, and Soren confides that 'hir' sexual orientation is frowned upon by the J'Naii, and 'hir' kind are 'cured' with brainwashing. After s/he's injured, s/he confesses 'hir' love of Riker. The J'Naii notice the close relationship, and Soren is arrested. Riker gatecrashes Soren's hearing, but fails to convince them to be tolerant. Picard warns him against interfering, but with Worf's help Riker finds Soren – only to discover Soren's conditioning has worked and all feelings for Riker have been erased.

TRIVIA

- A number of letter-writing campaigns over the years had suggested that *Star Trek* should include a gay character or otherwise explore the theme of homosexual relationships in the tolerant, diverse Federation. Gene Roddenberry had stated that 'it wouldn't be a problem' in his future, echoing the sentiments over the 'inter-racial kiss' in *Plato's Stepchildren* – what bothered sections of a twentieth century audience wouldn't even register as an issue in a tolerant future. The episode proved to be one of the most talked-about 'issue' stories, but opinion was sharply divided about its intended message and the actual message it gave out.

RATING

- If Soren had been played by an androgynous-looking man, this would have been quite a daring episode. As it is, this is the episode in which *Star Trek* 'tackles' homophobia by having a heterosexual man fall in love with a beautiful woman. Another serious issue, another banal treatment.

5.18 CAUSE AND EFFECT

STARDATE 45652.1

The Enterprise crew start getting a sense of déjà vu

TX 23 March 1992
WRITER Brannon Braga
DIRECTOR Jonathan Frakes
GUEST CAST Michelle Forbes (Ro Laren), Kelsey Grammer (Morgan Bateson), Patti Yasutake (Ogowa)

The crew fails to save the Enterprise after the warp engine is damaged and it explodes, killing everyone on board. The officers play poker, but Beverly is called away to see to a dizzy Geordi. She has a strong sense of déjà vu. The ship hits some sort of distortion in time: a ship emerges, and they try to deflect it with the tractor beam. The crew fails to save the Enterprise after the warp engine is damaged and it explodes, killing everyone on board. The officers play poker, but Beverly is called away to see to a dizzy Geordi. She has a strong sense of déjà vu, and hears voices that night. Picard has déjà vu. The crew fails to save the Enterprise after the warp engine is damaged and it explodes, killing everyone on board. Everyone on the ship now has déjà vu. Beverly realises that Geordi's dizziness is being caused by interference with his VISOR. The crew realise they are in a time loop – they implant a subspace message in Data. The crew fails to save the Enterprise after the warp engine is damaged and it explodes, killing everyone on board. As events replay themselves, Data realises from the message that he should decompress the shuttlebay, not use the tractor beam. This time, the Enterprise dodges the emerging ship. They realise they've spent 17 days in a time loop. The other ship is the USS Bozeman, and they've been trapped, completely unaware of the fact, for 90 years.

TRIVIA

- Kelsey Grammer is famous for his parts in *Cheers* and *Frasier*. His cameo was kept a surprise. It was hoped that Kirstie Alley – another *Cheers* stalwart, of course – could reprise her role as Saavik to play his first officer, but this proved impossible to arrange.
- The original script had a Constitution class ship (like Kirk's original Enterprise) trapped, but few props from the original series had survived and it was easier to use re-dressed items and uniforms from the movies.

RATING

- Having the same few scenes replayed over and over with only minor differences ought to feel like a swizz, but this is surprisingly effective, with each replay becoming more oppressive for the crew. A good example of a 'bottle show' that feels like more than a way to save a bit of money.

5.19 THE FIRST DUTY

STARDATE 45703.9

Wesley is involved in a cover-up at the Academy

TX 30 March 1992
WRITER Ronald D Moore and Naren Shankar
DIRECTOR Paul Lynch
GUEST CAST Walker Brandt (Jean Hajar), Jacqueline Brooks (Brand), Richard Fancy (Saltelk), Shannon Fill (Sito), Ed Lauter (Albert), Robert Duncan McNeill (Locarno), Richard Rothernberg (Cadet), Ray Walston (Boothby), Wil Wheaton (Wesley Crusher)

A terrible accident has occured while Starfleet Academy cadets, including Wesley Crusher, were practicing a flying display. Joshua Albert was killed. The inquiry quickly establishes discrepancies in the surviving cadets' stories. The squadron's leader, Locarno, says Albert panicked. Wesley confronts Locarno later for sullying the name of their comrade. Locarno warns the survivors to stick to the story they prepared. Wesley testifies, but previously unseen sensor data contradicts his account. It's clear to Picard and Beverly that he is lying. Picard realises that the cadets were planning a Kolvoord Starburst, a dangerous flying stunt, and it went tragically wrong. However, he can prove nothing, and implores Wesley to tell the truth. Just as he and his friends are about to escape punishment through lack of evidence, Wesley interrupts the judgement and confesses. His squadron is formally reprimanded.

QUOTES

- 'The first duty of every Starfleet officer is to the truth, whether it's scientific truth or historical truth or personal truth.'
  – Picard spells it out to Wesley

TRIVIA

- Moore and Piller argued whether Wesley should do his duty or protect his friends. Piller won, insisting Wesley tell the truth.
- This was the first time Starfleet Academy had been seen (barring the flight simulator in *Star Trek II: The Wrath of Khan*), and was filmed in the Tillman Water Reclamation Plant in Van Nuys.
- Boothby, the Academy groundskeeper, had been mentioned a couple of times, but this was the first time he'd been seen. Ray Walston was a well-known face on American TV for playing the title role in the sitcom *My Favorite Martian*.
- Robert Duncan McNeill went on to play Tom Paris in *Voyager*. Originally, he was to play Locarno in that show but it was felt that the character's crime here was too serious a weight for a regular in the show to carry.

RATING

- Powerful courtroom drama, this is a well-constructed story which doesn't resort to cop-outs, reset buttons or any other excuses. One of the very best *Star Trek* episodes.

5.20 COST OF LIVING

STARDATE 45733.6

Lwaxana Troi is getting married to someone completely unlike herself

Parasites invade the Enterprise after it destroys their native asteroid. Lwaxana Troi turns up – she wants to get married on the Enterprise to Campio from Kostolain. He is a very staid and quiet man, quite unlike his fiancée. It's clear that Erko, Campio's protocol

TX 20 April 1992
WRITER Peter Allan Fields
DIRECTOR Winrich Kolbe
GUEST CAST Majel Barrett (Lwaxana Troi, Computer Voice), Brian Bonsall (Alexander), Patrick Cronin (Erko), Tracy D'Arcy (Young lady), George Edie (Poet), Christopher Halstad (First Learner), Tony Jay (Campio), David Oliver (Young Man), Albie Selznick (Juggler), Carel Struyken (Mr Homn)

officer, disapproves of the relationship. Lwaxana befriends Alexander, and the two sneak off to the holodeck. The ship starts suffering failures as the parasites eat the nitrium in the ship's structure. Picard orders the ship to the nitrium-rich Pelloris Field. Lwaxana shocks Campio by wanting to get married naked, in the traditional Betazed fashion, and he leaves.

TRIVIA

- Majel Barrett (Computer Voice) talks to Majel Barrett (Lwaxana Troi) as she enters the holodeck.

RATING

- A scrappy episode that's in all sorts of places, none of them very interesting or entertaining.

5.21 THE PERFECT MATE

Picard falls for a woman who can be anything he desires

TX 27 April 1992
WRITER 'Gary Perconte' and Michael Piller (story by René Echevarria and 'Gary Perconte,' pseudonym for Reuben Leders)
DIRECTOR Cliff Bole
GUEST CAST Majel Barrett (Computer Voice), Mickey Cottrell (Alrik), Famke Janssen (Kamala), April Grace (Hubbell), Max Grodenchik (Par Lenor), Charles Gunning (Miner Three), David Paul Needles (Miner One), Tim O'Connor (Briam), Roger Rignack (Miner Two), Michael Snyder (Qol)

STARDATE 45761.3

The Enterprise is taking Kriosian ambassador Briam to Valt Minor with a mysterious peace offering. Two Ferengi are rescued by the Enterprise. One sneaks into the cargo bay and reveals the peace offering to be a beautiful woman, Kamala, who offers herself to Picard, thinking he is Alrik, leader of the Valtese. Briam tells Picard she is a rare empathic metamorph, who becomes whatever her partner desires. She consents to her task, marriage to Alrik. The Ferengi try to pressure Briam into selling them Kamala, and knock him out when he refuses. They are arrested and dispatched to Starbase 117. Picard must now present Kamala to Alrik. There is strong mutual attraction between Picard and Kamala, and he's the first person to ever suggest she has value as an individual, but they know their duties. Alrik must never know Kamala loves Picard. The wedding goes ahead. Briam and the Enterprise crew are baffled as to how Picard resisted Kamala's charms.

QUOTES

- 'If you need me, I'll be on holodeck four.' – *Riker makes his excuses and leaves, after meeting Kamala and being suitably impressed*

TRIVIA

- Famke Janssen went on to play Bond bad girl Xenia Onatopp in *GoldenEye*, and Jean Grey in the X-*Men* films (which also star Patrick Stewart). She later turned down the role of Dax in *Deep Space Nine*.
- Tim O'Connor played Dr Huer in the early eighties *Buck Rogers in the 25th Century* TV show.

RATING

- An OK episode, but one that feels like its rough edges have been smoothed out – we don't really get any sense of the potential horror of Kamala's duty, we just get Beverly talking about it.

5.22 IMAGINARY FRIEND

The imaginary friend of one of the children on board the Enterprise comes to life

TX 4 May 1992
WRITER Edithe Swenson and Brannon Braga (story by Ronald Wilkerson, Jean Matthias and Richard Fliegel)

STARDATE 45832.1

Ensign Sutter visits Troi with his daughter, Clara. He's worried she spends too much time talking to her imaginary friend Isabella. Troi reassures him that this is all perfectly normal. The Enterprise heads into the FGC-47 nebula, and an energy sphere enters the ship undetected. Clara is surprised to really see Isabella. Isabella is jealous of Clara's friendship with Alexander, and tells Clara that everyone on the ship will die – which, naturally, terrifies her. Troi tries to reassure her that Isabella isn't real, but Isabella shows

DIRECTOR Gabrielle Beaumont
GUEST CAST Jeff Allin (Daniel Sutter), Shay Aster (Isabella), Brian Bonsall (Alexander), Shelia Franklin (Felton), Whoopi Goldberg (Guinan), Noley Thornton (Clara Sutter), Patti Yasutake (Ogawa)

herself and knocks Troi out. Energy beings start draining the ship's shields. Isabella appears to Picard, saying that Clara has convinced them that the Enterprise is crewed with bullies. Picard explains that Clara has a child's perspective, and adults have to impose rules on children. Isabella releases the ship and apologises to Clara for scaring her.

TRIVIA

- The alien was friendly in the early drafts of the scripts, and merely curious about the Enterprise, but this was turned on its head by Braga (and sounds remarkably like *The Child*).

RATING

- A little by-the-numbers, it's a creepy at first – the scene where Troi gets attacked by the 'imaginary' friend is both very funny and straight out of a horror film – but it's soon not too hard to see where this story is going.

5.23 I, BORG

STARDATE 45854.2

The Enterprise recovers a survivor from a crashed Borg ship

TX 11 May 1992
WRITER René Echevarria
DIRECTOR Robert Lederman
GUEST CAST Jonathan Del Arco (Hugh Borg), Whoopi Goldberg (Guinan)

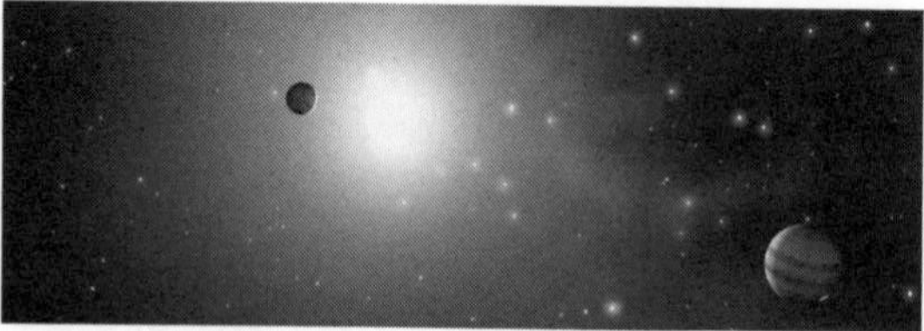

Charting the Argolis Cluster, the Enterprise detects a signal from a nearby moon and discovers a crashed Borg scout ship with one injured survivor. Beverly refuses to leave the Borg to die. The Borg is brought aboard the Enterprise, under heavy guard. As Beverly treats it, Picard reckons this is a chance to attack the collective – they could perhaps introduce a virus to this Borg and return it to the others. The Borg recovers and is baffled that humans are helping it. Geordi christens the Borg Hugh, and Hugh becomes more cooperative. Guinan lodges a complaint with the Captain – his initial instincts to leave it were right. When she meets Hugh, though, she's shocked that it confesses to feeling lonely. Geordi and Data have created the Borg-killing virus, but Geordi admits to Picard that he's got reservations about using it. Picard talks to Hugh, and tries to trick him by playing Locutus. But Hugh no longer wants to assimilate, and considers himself an individual. Picard tells him that he can return to the Collective. Hugh wants to – he knows the Borg will come after him and doesn't want to put his new friends in danger. Hugh is beamed back down to the moon, where the Borg collect him.

TRIVIA

- The production team faced a problem. There was constant pressure (and a desire) to bring back the Borg, but they were worried about how they could top *The Best of Both Worlds*, how they could afford to make such an episode, and how they could reintroduce a race so powerful they could practically wipe out Starfleet with only one ship. *I, Borg* was a conscious attempt to tell a small-scale Borg story, and the result was Michael Piller's favourite of the season. Fan reaction was more mixed.
- Jonathan Del Arco had auditioned to play Wesley Crusher.

RATING

- No, no, no! The Borg turn out to be really nice if you only take the time to get to know them – and possible to eradicate if you show them optical illusions. A fantastically tense premise and first half is squandered by a story that seems hell-bent on ruining everything that makes the Borg interesting in the first place. It's OK – great, in fact – that the Enterprise crew have reservations about killing Hugh... but it would be so much more effective if the Borg didn't reciprocate. From now on the Borg are just another alien race.

5.24 THE NEXT PHASE

STARDATE 45092.4

Geordi and Ro become intangible and ghostlike, and need to defeat the Romulans

TX 18 May 1992

The Enterprise assists a stricken Romulan ship, but Geordi and Ro are lost in a transporter accident beaming over. There's an immediate danger to address: the Romulan ship is facing a warp core breach. Data saves the Romulan ship and ejects the core. Ro and Geordi are on the Enterprise... but only they can see each other, and they pass through solid objects. Ro reckons they are ghosts, which Geordi

WRITER Ronald D Moore
DIRECTOR David Carson
GUEST CAST Brian Cousins (Parem), Michelle Forbes (Ensign Ro), Thomas Kopache (Mirok), Shelby Leverington (Brossmer), Kenneth Messerole (McDowell), Susanna Thompson (Varel)

refuses to accept. They discover Beverly filing their death certificates. Data detects chroniton particles, a sign of a cloaking device, and begins to investigate. Ro and Geordi follow Data to the Romulan ship, where they discover an experimental interphasic generator – there is a phantom Romulan on the Enterprise, plotting to rig the ship to explode when it goes to warp. After a chase through the Enterprise, the Romulan is killed, but the ship is still in danger. Ro and Geordi go to their own memorial service and attract Data's attention by generating a lot of chroniton particles. Restored to normal, much to everyone's astonishment, they can warn the crew of the Romulan booby trap.

TRIVIA

- The 'phasing' effects were simple enough to create, but proved very time-consuming.

RATING

- An episode that's exuberant and just great fun, with a lot of thought put into the little details. One highlight is Geordi pushing the Romulan through an outer bulkhead and into space.

5.25 THE INNER LIGHT

STARDATE 45944.1

Picard experiences a whole new life

TX 1 June 1992
WRITER Morgan Gendel and Peter Allan Fields (story by Morgan Gendel)
DIRECTOR Peter Lauritson
GUEST CAST Scott Jaeck (Administrator), Jennifer Nash (Meribor), Richard Riehle (Batai), Margot Rose (Eline), Daniel Stewart (Young Batai), Patti Yasutake (Ogawa)

Picard is knocked out by a blast of nucleonic particles from a mysterious probe. He wakes up to find himself tended by Eline, a woman who calls him 'Kamin' and says she's his wife. With no obvious way to escape, and no obvious threat, Picard takes time to explore: this is the town of Ressik on the planet Kataan. Five years pass, and Picard has come to accept that whoever he was, he is now Kamin the iron weaver. He is learning the flute and applying his knowledge to try to solve the planetary drought. He wants to build atmospheric condensers, but the Kataan elders laugh at his theories. Seven more years pass, and Picard names his son Batai after his deceased best friend. Twelve more years pass, and Picard's teenage daughter Meribor helps him with his science experiments. They both realise the planet is doomed. Years pass, but no one will admit that Picard's theory is right. Picard becomes a grandfather, but his beloved Eline dies of old age. When Picard is 85, his children launch a probe – soon this will be all that is left of Kataan. Picard wakes on the bridge of the Enterprise, mere minutes after he was knocked unconscious. Inside the probe, they discover Kamin's flute. Picard retires to his room and plays the flute.

QUOTES

- 'Live now. Make now always the most precious time. Now will never come again.' – *Picard to Meribor, his daughter*

TRIVIA

- Daniel Stewart is Patrick Stewart's son.

RATING

- One of the gems of *Star Trek*, with an astonishing performance by Patrick Stewart, who's given not just centre-stage, but the whole episode. Indeed, the episode's only weakness is that it cuts back to the Enterprise a couple of times. This is an extraordinary examination of Picard's character and a celebration of life, family and happiness. Great drama, not just great *Star Trek*.

5.26 TIME'S ARROW Part I

STARDATE 45959.1

After discovering Data's head buried on Earth, the trail leads to the nineteenth century

The Enterprise has been recalled to Earth, where an archaeological team has discovered Data's head while investigating nineteenth century San Francisco. The cavern where it was found has been bombarded by trilolic waves, suggesting aliens were present. A fossil

TX 15 June 1992
WRITER Joe Menosky and Michael Piller (story by Joe Menosky)
DIRECTOR Les Landau
GUEST CAST Marc Alaimo (Frederick Le Rouque), Michael Aron (Jack the Bellboy), Whoopi Goldberg (Guinan), Jerry Hardin (Samuel Clemens), Michael Hungerford (Roughneck), Barry Kivel (Doorman), John M Murdock (Beggar), Milt Tarver (Scientist), Ken Thorley (Seaman), Sheldon Peters Wolfchild (Joe Falling Hawk)

from Devidia II is also discovered, and the ship heads there to discover high levels of temporal disturbance. Data vanishes into a different time continuum. He witnesses strange beings draining the energy from humans, and recognises an Ophidian alien. He materialises in nineteenth century America. Data discovers Guinan there (at lunch with Mark Twain) – this is Guinan from the past, so she doesn't know about the Enterprise, but believes Data. Back in the twenty-fourth century, a full Away Team detects the subspace field that swallowed Data. They are hit by a beam of light that transports them into the past...

TRIVIA

- Ideas bandied around for this finale included setting the story in the 1990s, when it was shown, or in the sixties, to tie in with the original series.

RATING

- ...and this is why they shouldn't do time-travel stories. An episode that's trying so hard not to be *Star Trek IV: The Voyage Home* that it's not sure what it is trying to do, and a nineteenth century that feels like a holodeck recreation rather than the real thing. A strangely bland finale to a season that had its faults as well as its triumphs, but was never this soulless.

STAR TREK: THE NEXT GENERATION
SEASON SIX

6.1 TIME'S ARROW Part II

STARDATE 46001.3

The crew travel into Earth's past to prevent an alien crime and save Data

TX 21 September 1992
WRITER Jeri Taylor (story by Joe Menosky)
DIRECTOR Les Landau
GUEST CAST Michael Aron (Jack the Bellboy), Majel Barrett (Computer Voice), William Boyett (Policeman), Alexander Enberg (Young Reporter), Van Epperson (Morgue Attendant), James Gleason (Dr Appollinaire), Whoopi Goldberg (Guinan), Jerry Hardin (Samuel Clemens), Pamela Kosh (Mrs Carmichael), Bill Cho Lee (Male Patient), Mary Stein (Alien Nurse)

Picard's team arrive in nineteenth century San Francisco in search of Data. They discover two Devidians, disguised as a doctor and nurse, are stealing the neural energy from the diseased population and using it as sustenance. The Away Team battle the Devidians, taking their time-travel device. Data arrives in time to take them to safety. The officers deduce that Data's head was used as a focusing device to allow the aliens to time-travel and return to the cavern, unaware that Clemens is following them. The aliens arrive and retake the device, activating the time portal. A sonic boom throws Guinan against a wall and knocks Data's head off his body and into the time rift. The alien doctor jumps into the rift, pursued by Clemens and the Away Team save for Picard, who stays with the injured Guinan. The group arrive on Devidia II and beam back to the Enterprise, where Troi tries to convince Clemens that Earth's future is secure. The Enterprise crew prepare to destroy the alien cavern, but first send Clemens back in time to rescue Picard. Picard says his farewells to Guinan and returns home, shortly before the alien habitat is destroyed.

TRIVIA

- It was suggested in early discussions that the second episode should return to the officers several months after the first part. The crewmembers were to have obtained jobs in the meantime and would meet up regularly at a cafe run by Picard, where the food was terrible.
- Jerry Hardin was cast for his physical similarity to Mark Twain. He was so enamoured with the part that he went on to do a one-man show about Twain's life.

RATING

- Badly structured, self-indulgent and phenomenally boring, Time's Arrow is one of the worst *The Next Generation* stories. The constant time-hopping smacks of an ill-thought out premise – not even a characteristically strong performance from Hardin can hide the pointlessness of the addition of Clemens.

6.2 REALM OF FEAR

Barclay must face his fear to battle a creature living in the transporter beam

TX 28 September 1992
WRITER Brannon Braga
DIRECTOR Cliff Bole
GUEST CAST Majel Barrett (Computer Voice), Thomas Belgrey (Crew Member), Colm Meaney (O'Brien), Renata Scott (Hayes), Dwight Schultz (Reginald Barclay), Patti Yasutake (Ogawa)

STARDATE 46041.1

The Enterprise finds the USS Yosemite trapped in a plasma stream, but Barclay is too scared of the transporter process to beam aboard to help. After counselling, he manages to join the Away Team. Only one body can be found. As they beam back, a mysterious creature appears and touches Barclay mid-transport. Barclay is shaken and his arm begins to emit light where he was touched. Meanwhile, Beverly discovers that the Yosemite crew died when their bodies were hit with high-energy plasma. Barclay is too shaken to concentrate and is relieved of duty. Convinced that there is something trapped in the transporter beam, Barclay enlists O'Brien's help and transports back to the Yosemite. Barclay encounters the creature again and informs Picard, who orders an investigation. Beverly examines Barclay and discovers he, too, has the plasma infection. Data and Geordi discovers that the plasma particles are life forms, some of which now reside in Barclay. He is transported again, to separate the particles. Confronted by the creature, Barclay takes its hand and beams back with it. Back on the landing pad, the crew are surprised to find the creature is actually a member of the Yosemite crew. The other two crewmen are rescued and Barclay congratulated.

TRIVIA

- Piller thought that Braga's original pitch was too close to the *Twilight Zone* episode *Nightmare at 20,000 Feet* in which a character (played by William Shatner) sees a creature sitting on the wing of his airplane.

RATING

- A clever little poser that has a strong element of horror and mystery. Again, a good use of Barclay, demonstrating that you don't need to focus efforts on the main cast all the time. There should be more episodes like this.

6.3 MAN OF THE PEOPLE

Troi is used to store the evil thoughts of a Federation diplomat

TX 5 October 1992
WRITER Frank Abatemarco
DIRECTOR Winrich Kolbe
GUEST CAST Majel Barrett (Computer Voice), Lucy Boryer (Janeway), Stephanie Erb (Liva), Susan French (Sev Maylor), JP Hubbell (Ensign), Chip Lucia (Ves Alkar), Rick Scarry (Jarth), George D Wallace (Simmons), Patti Yasutake (Ogawa)

STARDATE 46071.6

The Enterprise rendezvous with the Dorian to collect a Lumerian ambassador, Ves Alkar, and his mother, Sev Maylor, and transport them to the Rekag-Seronia system, where Alkar is to mediate in a dispute. Though Alkar takes to Troi, Maylor shows an instant dislike. Later, Maylor dies and Alkar asks Troi, as an empath, to perform the funeral meditation. After, Troi starts to age rapidly. She attacks the two peace delegates, Jarth and Liva, on their arrival. The next day, Troi is a white-haired old woman. When Alkar refuses to let Troi join him at the negotiations, she rushes at him with a knife, stabbing Picard. Troi is restrained and taken to sickbay. Picard orders an autopsy of Maylor which reveals she is infact a prematurely aged 30-year-old woman. Picard beams to the negotiations. Alkar reveals that he used both Maylor and Troi, channeling his dark thoughts into them in order to keep his emotions clear for the negotations. When Alkar refuses to free Troi, Beverly puts Troi in suspended animation, an almost deathlike state that severs Alkar's link. Alkar tries to perform the funeral rite with Liva but, as the ritual is about to take place, Picard transports Liva to safety. Alkar dies and Troi is revived.

TRIVIA

- *Man of the People* was rushed through script committee when *Relics* was pushed back to accomodate James Doohan's schedule.

RATING

- A neat retelling of *The Picture of Dorian Gray*, as referenced in the name of Alkar's ship. The important difference – that Alkar is keeping himself pure for negotiations, not indulging his debauchery – shows that this is a well thought-out adaptation.

6.4 RELICS

STARDATE 46125.3

Scotty is rescued from a transporter and helps Geordi save the Enterprise

TX 12 October 1992
WRITER Ronald D Moore
DIRECTOR Alexander Singer
GUEST CAST Majel Barrett (Computer Voice), Lanei Chapman (Rager), James Doohan (Montgomery Scott), Stacie Foster (Bartel), Ernie Mirich (Waiter), Erick Weiss (Kane)

The Enterprise receives a distress call from the USS Jenolen. The ship has crash-landed on the surface of a Dyson sphere. Riker takes an Away Team and discovers that someone has been stored in the transporter's pattern buffer for 75 years. It is Montgomery Scott. Scotty is excited by the new Enterprise but begins to miss his old ship, fearing he is too old to start over. While Geordi and Scotty are on the Jenolen, retrieving records, the Enterprise activates a door on the Dyson sphere and is pulled inside by a tractor beam. Data reports that the star is unstable and the Enterprise's shields will only hold for three hours. Scotty and Geordi restore impulse power on the Jenolen. They activate the portal and prevent the doors from closing by using the Jenolen's shields. The Enterprise charges at the Jenolen and, at the last moment, beams Geordi and Scotty aboard before destroying the Jenolen and making a speedy escape. Grateful, Picard gives Scotty a shuttlecraft to allow him to continue to explore the universe.

QUOTES

- 'NCC One Seven Oh One – no bloody A, B, C or D.' – *Scotty tells the holodeck computer which bridge he wants*

TRIVIA

- One cut scene saw Troi counsel Scotty. This explains the small peck Scotty gives Troi before he leaves.
- The original Enterprise bridge, as seen on the holodeck, was a composite of original sixties footage (taken from *This Side of Paradise*) and a physical recreation of the Engineering section.

RATING

- The welcome return of James Doohan, but the story is really painting by numbers. Scotty's sense of loss is played out through a drab, uneventful problem. Meanwhile, the use of the transporter to store Scotty is too close a concept to *Realm of Fear*, two episodes previously. There should be some story editing going on here.

6.5 SCHISMS

STARDATE 46154.2

The Enterprise crew are being abducted by aliens from subspace

TX 19 October 1992
WRITER Brannon Braga (story by Jean Louise Matthias and Ron Wilkerson)
DIRECTOR Robert Wiemer
GUEST CAST Majel Barrett (Computer Voice), Lanei Chapman (Rager), Angelina Fiordellisi (Kaminer), Angelo McCabe (Crewman), John Nelson (Medical Technician), Ken Thorley (Mott), Scott T Trost (Shipley)

Riker uncharacteristically oversleeps. Meanwhile, sensors report an explosion in Cargo Bay Four, but there is no sign of damage. The next day, Geordi and Data investigate the sensors but can find no problem. Geordi's VISOR begins to malfunction and he heads to sickbay. On his return, Data can't remember their meeting. Suspicious, they run a full diagnostic of the cargo bay and discover a subspace signal. Meanwhile, Riker discovers that three other crewmembers have experienced his odd feelings. Worf reacts badly to scissors when he gets a haircut. They all have memories of a strange room that they recreate on the holodeck. Beverly discovers that someone has been experimenting on the group and Data realises he was off the ship for 90 minutes the previous day. Geordi deduces that aliens from subspace are abducting the crew. Riker takes a homing beacon with him the next time he is abducted allowing Geordi to find the source of the rift and close it. Riker rescues another crewman and jumps through the rift just before it closes.

QUOTES

- 'Felis catus is your taxonomic nomenclature/An endothermic quadruped, carnivorous by nature...' – *The opening lines of Data's* Ode to Spot

TRIVIA

- Braga's original ending had an alien claw wrap around Riker's bed in sickbay, but this proved too costly.

RATING

- An interesting take on alien abductions, though no effort is made to communicate with the aliens or work out what they are up to.

6.6 TRUE-Q

STARDATE 46192.3

A young girl discovers she shares Q's powers

TX 26 October 1992
WRITER René Echevarria
DIRECTOR Robert Scheerer
GUEST CAST Olivia d'Abo (Amanda), John P Connolly (Lote), John de Lancie (Q)

At Tagra IV, the Enterprise collects Amanda, a young student. When an explosion threatens to rip through Engineering, Amanda is forced to reveal her secret ability to make objects appear by visualising them, and saves the ship. Q arrives and tells Picard that Amanda is one of his kind: he has come to take her to the Continuum. Picard, however, thinks Amanda should make her own choice. Meanwhile, he orders an investigation into the deaths of Amanda's parents, who died in an accident. Q tries to tempt Amanda with an offer to train her to use her powers. Amanda is excited and confused. However, an attempt to transport Riker into a romantic fantasy fails. Meanwhile, Picard confronts Q, who admits the Continuum executed Amanda's parents and he has been sent to judge her. Picard informs Amanda, who furiously summons Q. Q claims to have decided to let Amanda live, but she must choose either to join him in the Continuum or stay on the Enterprise and promise not to use her powers. Amanda immediately decides to stay but feels forced to use her abilities when Tagra IV threatens to self-destruct from years of pollution. Amanda reverts the planet into a garden paradise. Amanda reluctantly accepts that she is a Q and joins the Continuum.

TRIVIA

- Echevarria's script was originally titled *Q Me?* It was one of several Q stories pitched for the season. Early pitches had Q splitting each crew member into twins that emphasised opposite parts of their personality, and a version of the Olympics.
- Echevarria originally gave the girl the name Samantha, in a sly reference to the sixties sitcom *Bewitched.*
- The episode was based on material submitted by Matthew Corey, who was 17 at the time.

RATING

- A story of adolescence played through the acquisition of Q powers. It's an attempt to make Q more malevolent, but it just doesn't work. The episode diverts attention away from the Picard-Q relationship, the only thing that makes these shows watchable.

6.7 RASCALS

STARDATE 46235.7

A transporter accidents transforms Picard, Ro, Keiko and Guinan into children

TX 2 November 1992
WRITER Allison Hock (story by Ward Botsford, Diana Dru Botsford and Michael Piller)
DIRECTOR Adam Nimoy

When a transporter beam malfunctions, Picard, Ro, Keiko and Guinan arrive on the Enterprise as 12-year-old children. Beverly establishes that their minds have not regressed. Picard tries to resume command but the crew do not take him seriously and he is reluctantly persuaded to pass authority to Riker. Geordi realises that the transporter can be used to reverse the transformation, but at that moment the Enterprise is attacked and left stranded. Two Ferengi beam aboard, declaring the ship to be salvage, and threaten the crew with execution if they resist. Guinan and Picard realise their size gives them a tactical advantage and sneak through the ship collecting weapons. They are soon faced with the problem of reaching the bridge. Picard throws a

GUEST CAST Majel Barrett (Computer Voice), David Tristan Birkin (Young Picard), Brian Bonsall (Alexander), Rosalind Chao (Keiko), Michelle Forbes (Ro Laren), Whoopi Goldberg (Guinan), Mike Gomez (DaiMon Lurin), Hana Hatae (Molly), Isis Jones (Young Guinan), Caroline Junko King (Young Keiko), Colm Meaney (O'Brien), Morgan Nagler (Kid #1), Megan Parlen (Young Ro), Michael Snyder (Morta), Tracey Walter (Berik)

tantrum and is sent to Riker, who he claims is his father. Picard manages to tell Riker to allow the ship's systems to be accessed through the schoolroom. When the Ferengi demand access to the ship's computer, the young officers overpower them. Beverly and O'Brien use the transporter to restore the officers to their true ages.

TRIVIA

- *Rascals* was originally submitted for series four but polarised the writing team. Jeri Taylor and Michael Piller pressed on with the idea but it went to several rewrites before the treatment was agreed.
- Whoopi Goldberg appeared at the request of Adam Nimoy, son of Leonard, for his first *Star Trek* directorial assignment.
- David Tristan Birkin had previously played René Picard in *Family*, and got the part in this episode at Patrick Stewart's suggestion.

RATING

- *Rascals* sounds like a terrible idea but is redeemed by four excellent child actors, particularly David Tristan Birkin as the young Picard. The highlight is an awkward scene between O'Brien and Keiko.

6.8 A FISTFUL OF DATAS

STARDATE 46271.5

Worf, Alexander and Troi battle holodeck Wild West bandits that look like Data

TX 9 November 1992
WRITER Robert Hewitt Wolfe and Brannon Braga (story by Robert Hewitt Wolfe)
DIRECTOR Patrick Stewart
GUEST CAST Majel Barrett (Computer Voice), Brian Bonsall (Alexander), Jorge Cervera Jr (Bandito), Joy Garrett (Annie), John Pyper-Ferguson (Eli Hollander)

Geordi takes the Engineering computer offline to explore ways to use Data as an emergency backup system. As they establish an interface, Data experiences strange energy fluctuations. Meanwhile, on the holodeck, Worf, Alexander and Deanna apprehend vicious killer Eli Hollander, a Wild West villain. Just as Data experiences the energy disturbance, Alexander is abducted by a new character, Eli's father Frank, who bears a startling resemblance to Data. Frank offers to swap Alexander for Eli. Worf realises there is something wrong but cannot order the program to end. Deanna suggests that if they play out the whole story, the program will end of its own accord. Geordi discovers that the ship's leisure systems have infiltrated Data's memory. Worf agrees to meet Frank for an exchange of hostages. After the handover, Frank's men fire at Worf, but the bullets have no effect: Worf has created a forcefield from items on the holodeck. Worf and Deanna run the Hollander gang out of town and Geordi returns Data and the ship's computer to normal.

TRIVIA

- Wolfe's original pitch majored on a manipulative land baron. Ira Stephen Behr, working in the adjacent office on *Deep Space Nine*, suggested they pay homage to *Rio Bravo* instead. The first draft of this version, *The Good, The Bad and the Klingon*, had Alexander take on the role of Troi's son. It was later decided that Alexander would have written himself a better part, making him a deputy.

RATING

- An episode where the title must have come before the story. Amazingly, it was this turgid script that earned Wolfe a place at the writing table for *Deep Space Nine*.

6.9 THE QUALITY OF LIFE

STARDATE 46307.2

Data insists that minute mechanisms have become sentient

TX 16 November 1992
WRITER Naren Shankar (story by LD Scott – uncredited)
DIRECTOR Jonathan Frakes

On arrival at Tyrus VIIA, the Enterprise crew are shown the abilities of exocomps by their creator Farallon. Exocomps are minute mechanisms that can create their own tools and repair faults at a microscopic level. Farallon wishes to use exocomps to complete her work on a new mining technology. However, when Data sees one exocomp stop functioning rather than enter a dangerous conduit, he suspects that the mechanisms have become sentient. Farallon is angered when her experiments are

GUEST CAST Majel Barrett (Computer Voice), Ellen Bry (Dr Farallon), David Windsor (Kelso)

temporarily halted. Geordi and Data conduct further tests which seem to contradict Data's theory, but eventually suggest that the creatures are alive. Geordi and Picard visit the research station on the planet but there is a malfunction and a threat of radiation. Farallon suggests that the exocomps could be used to save the officers. Three exocomps are transported to the station and enable Geordi and Picard to beam back. One exocomp stays behind to allow its colleagues to return. The exocomp's sacrifice force Farallon to revisit her judgment of them.

TRIVIA

- Scott's original pitch played up the notion of overlooked sentience all around us. This was unfortunately translated as Data insisting that plug sockets have feelings too. Shankar was keen for the mechanism to be alien-looking and with no real familiarity or 'cuteness'. The metacomps were changed to exocomps when the production office discovered that there was a company trading under the first name.

RATING

- An interesting premise but one that doesn't really lend itself to visuals. Overall, for all that it has some good points to make, this one just looks and feels drab.

6.10 CHAIN OF COMMAND Part I

When Picard is sent on a secret mission, the Enterprise crew suffer a new captain

TX 14 December 1992
WRITER Ronald D Moore (story by Frank Abatemarco)
DIRECTOR Robert Scheerer
GUEST CAST Majel Barrett (Computer Voice), Ronny Cox (Edward Jellico), John Durbin (Gul Lemec), Natalija Nogulich (Nechayev), Lou Wagner (Solok), David Warner (Gul Madred)

STARDATE 46357.4

When Picard, Worf and Beverly are reassigned to undertake a top-secret mission against the Cardassians, the Enterprise crew gain a new captain. Jellico quickly changes procedures, causing anxiety among the crew and Riker in particular. Troi tries to persuade Jellico to be less abrasive, but he dismisses her qualms. Later, Jellico tells Picard that he expects a war between the Federation and the Cardassians and does not expect Picard to return. Soon after, Picard, Worf and Beverly set out on their mission: Picard reveals they are to locate and destroy terrible genetic weapons that the Cardassians have created and stored on Celtris III. On the Enterprise, Jellico meets a senior Cardassian, Gul Lemec, and riles him. The approach backfires when Lemec reveals that he is aware of Picard's secret mission. On Celtris III, Picard's team locate a sealed cavern, but it is empty. Realising it is a trap, the party escape but Picard is captured. Gul Madred warns the captain that he will face interrogation and must answer all questions or die.

QUOTES

- 'Get that fish out of the ready room.' – *Jellico gets settled in*

TRIVIA

- *Chain of Command* was conceived as a crossover with new sister series *Deep Space Nine*. The scene with Solok was written for Quark. However, the production schedules slipped and it was discovered that *Chain of Command* would air before *The Emissary*.
- Picard's fish – seen since the beginning of the show – is a Lion fish (*Pterois Volitans*) called Livingston, which is presumably a reference to supervising producer David Livingston.

RATING

- A strong set-up, but a peculiar mix of characters to send on an Away Team mission. The better stuff is with Ronny Cox's Jellico, who is not played as the arch-villain but as a slightly more abrasive character. We get the sense that Jellico should be a captain, it's just that he's not the one we know and love.

6.11 CHAIN OF COMMAND Part II

Picard is tortured by a ruthless Cardassian, Gul Madred

STARDATE 46360.8

Picard is injected with a truth serum and reveals the details of his secret mission. Madred explains that it was all a trap: they want to know about Federation defences. When Picard insists he knows

TX 21 December 1992
WRITER Frank Abatemarco
DIRECTOR Les Landau
GUEST CAST Majel Barrett (Computer Voice), Ronny Cox (Jellico), John Durbin (Gul Lemec), Heather Lauren Olson (Jil Orra), David Warner (Gul Madred)

nothing, he is tortured. Later, Lemec informs Jellico that Picard is being held. When Riker demands they mount a rescue mission, Jellico has Riker relieved of his post. Data, now First Officer, and Geordi deduce that the Cardassian weapons were a ploy. They also realise that Picard is probably being tortured for information he does not have in advance of a Cardassian attack. Against advice, Jellico takes the Enterprise to Minos Korva, where he believes the Cardassians may make their first move. Meanwhile, Picard maintains a battle of wills with Madred, although he appears to be weakening. Jellico decides to enter Cardassian space in a shuttlecraft, but is persuaded that Riker should pilot the ship. They lay mines in the path of any attacking fleet. Gul Lemec contacts the Enterprise, furious, but Jellico says he will not detonate the mines if the Cardassians withdraw and return Picard. Soon after, Picard arrives back on the ship and relieves Jellico, revealing to Troi that Madred had broken him.

QUOTES

- 'I would have told him anything... anything at all. But more than that, I *believed* that I could see five lights.' – *Picard to Troi*

TRIVIA

- *Chain of Command* was intended to be one episode but was expanded to two parts when producers decided they needed another bottle show to save money. The original ending, which had a face off between two fleets, had to be cut.
- Patrick Stewart, a supporter of Amnesty International, fought for the intensity of the original script to remain. Stewart was nude for the interrogation scene. His incredible, intense performance earned him a Screen Actors Guild Award nomination in 1993/4 (Dennis Franz won the award for *NYPD Blue*)

RATING

- Much better than part one with two hugely impressive performances by Patrick Stewart and David Warner, who revel in the battle of wills. The final moments where Picard is ready to break are agonising.

6.12 SHIP IN A BOTTLE

STARDATE 46424.1

Moriarty returns, able to leave the holodeck, and demands freedom for himself and his companion
TX 25 January 1993
WRITER René Echevarria
DIRECTOR Alexander Singer
GUEST CAST Majel Barrett (Computer Voice), Stephanie Beacham (Countess Regina Bartholemew), Daniel Davis (Professor Moriarty), Dwight Schultz (Barclay), Clement Von Franckenstein (Gentleman)

While Geordi and Data enact another Sherlock Holmes mystery on the holodeck they notice a few anomalies. Barclay investigates and is met by Moriarty, who claims to have been so perfectly created by the computer that he's become alive. Picard orders a medical examination and Beverly finds to her astonishment that Moriarty has indeed become flesh and blood. Moriarty begs Picard to bring to life his lover, Countess Regina Bartholemew, but Picard wishes to understand the mysterious events first. Moriarty takes control of the computer and refuses to give up control unless Picard grants his wish. Data discovers that Moriarty isn't real – Picard, Data and Barclay are all living out his fantasy on the holodeck. Moriarty convinces Riker to transport him to reality, then demands a shuttlecraft. As Moriarty and the Countess leave on the shuttle, he releases control of the ship's computer. Picard ends the simulation: the shuttlecraft voyage was also a holodeck fantasy, and Moriarty is now safely stored away.

QUOTES

- 'Our reality may be much like theirs. And all this might just be an elaborate simulation running inside a little device sitting on someone's table...' – *Picard*

TRIVIA

- By the sixth season, the Arthur Conan Doyle estate had dropped the apparent embargo placed on the use of Sherlock Holmes characters by Paramount in retaliation for *Young Sherlock Holmes*. Piller recalled a pitch made by Echevarria in season three about a holodeck character who thought he was on board.

RATING

- Fairly well constructed stuff, although the foreshadowing of the solution is a little heavy. Picard's final speech, quoted above, is wonderfully self-referential.

6.13 AQUIEL

STARDATE 46461.3

Geordi falls for a lieutenant who is implicated in murder

TX 1 February 1993
WRITER Brannon Braga and Ronald D Moore (story by Jeri Taylor)
DIRECTOR Cliff Bole
GUEST CAST Majel Barrett (Computer Voice), Reg E Cathey (Morag), Wayne Grace (Governor Torak), Renée Jones (Aquiel Uhnari)

At a subspace relay station on the Klingon border, the Enterprise crew find the remains of Lieutenant Aquiel Uhnari and her pet dog, who's still alive. Geordi discovers that Aquiel had a relationship with missing Lt Rocha. Aquiel was also fearful of a Klingon named Morag, and damage to a shuttlecraft suggests a Klingon attack. Klingon Governor Torak arrives accompanied by Aquiel, alive. Aquiel claims that Rocha attacked her and she escaped in the shuttle – the body was that of Rocha. While Picard talks to Morag to uncover the truth, Geordi befriends Aquiel. She is distressed to discover that she is suspected of murder. Riker and Worf interrogate Aquiel but she is adamant, and gains Geordi's sympathy. Later, Geordi discovers that Aquiel deleted messages from Rocha's log but she claims he sought to make her appear dangerous to Starfleet. They grow closer. As Beverly examines cells she's found, the residue suddenly mimics her hand, becoming a perfect replica. She believes Rocha may have been killed by the life-form, which may have taken his form and attacked Aquiel. Suddenly, Aquiel's dog transforms into the creature and attacks Geordi but he manages to defend himself. Geordi and Aquiel part, hoping to meet again.

TRIVIA

- Piller's suggestion on Taylor's pitch was to play it as the movie *Laura*, in which a man falls for a woman who appears to be dead but is later found alive. In the original story, Aquiel is the murderer, but this was dropped because of similarities to *Basic Instinct*. The desperate suggestion that the dog was the guilty party actually gave the writers something new to work with.

RATING

- Remarkably dull for a story with potential. Aquiel should be the murderer. The problem is that the storytelling is stale.

6.14 FACE OF THE ENEMY

STARDATE 46519.1

Troi goes undercover as a Romulan to aid a defector

TX 8 February 1993
WRITER Naren Shankar (story by René Echevarria)
DIRECTOR Gabrielle Beaumont
GUEST CAST Majel Barrett (Computer Voice), Dennis Cockrun (Alien Captain), Robertson Dean (Pilot), Barry Lynch (DeSeve), Scott McDonald (N'Vek), Carolyn Seymour (Toreth), Pamela Winslow (McKnight)

Troi awakens on board a Romulan vessel as a Romulan officer. N'Vek, the Romulan subcommander, tells Troi that she must pretend to be Major Rakal of the Tal Shiar, and give orders to transport cargo to a certain point, if she wishes to return to the Enterprise. Meanwhile, Stefan DeSeve, a Starfleet officer who defected to the Romulans, beams aboard the Enterprise. DeSeve tells Picard that Spock wants the Enterprise to rendezvous with a freighter and take its cargo into Federation space. On the Romulan ship, N'Vek reveals the Warbird's cargo: a high ranking member of the Romulan senate is defecting to the Federation. N'Vek works for the Romulan underground and explains that Rakal was killed so that Troi could replace her. The Romulans find the freighter but N'Vek quickly destroys it, claiming he acted on Troi's orders. Commander Toreth is furious but is ordered to cloak and later told to set course for Draken IV. Suddenly, the Romulan sensors pick up the Enterprise. Toleth tries to open fire, but Troi steps in and takes command. She hails Picard and asks to be beamed over. As soon as Picard lowers shields, Troi opens fire, simultaneously transporting the Romulan senator to the Enterprise. The weapons fire is ineffective and Toreth realises the truth, killing N'Vek. However, he is too late to prevent Troi beaming back to the Enterprise.

TRIVIA

- The first story treatment had Beverly as the main character but this was changed to Troi as it was felt her empathic abilities would make her better suited to espionage. The story was loosely based on an old pitch that had Q transport the entire crew onto a Romulan Warbird where they would wake up as Romulans.

RATING

- Far and away the best use of Troi in the series, and one where Marina Sirtis rises to the challenge magnificently. The narrative is a little skewed for dramatic effect – Troi wakes up apparently confused – but it has far more pace and tension than much of the rest of the season. Cracking stuff.

6.15 TAPESTRY

STARDATE UNKNOWN

Q gives Picard the chance to make a different choice at a key point in his life

TX 15 February 1993
WRITER Ronald D Moore
DIRECTOR Les Landau
GUEST CAST Majel Barrett (Computer Voice), JC Brandy (Marta Batanides), Clint Carmichael (Nausicaan #1), Clive Church (Maurice Picard), John deLancie (Q), Marcus Nash (Young Picard), Rae Norman (Penny Muroc), Ned Vaughn (Corey Zweller)

Picard is seriously injured when an Away Team is attacked. As his artificial heart fails, Picard finds himself in a white room. Q arrives, welcoming Picard to the afterlife. He gives Picard the opportunity to explore any regrets he may have and Picard notes the time he lost his real heart in a fight with three Nausicaans. Q transports Picard back into his past, where he has the opportunity to relive the event. Picard joins his friends Marta and Corey for a game of dom-jot with the Nausicaans. The Nausicaan cheats and Corey asks Picard to rig the table, but in this version Picard refuses. Corey rigs it, but Picard intervenes. Corey is furious but Marta is impressed with Picard's maturity and they sleep together. The next morning, Marta feels they have ruined their friendship. Q congratulates Picard on losing both his closest friends. That night, when a Nausicaan riles Corey, Picard prevents his friend from attacking, disgusting Corey and Marta. Picard suddenly finds himself back on the Enterprise, now as a lieutenant. He is a reliable science officer who has never taken any risks. Picard tells Q he would rather die than live that life. Q transports Picard back to the incident and this time Picard is stabbed through the heart. The next moment, he awakens in sickbay – Beverly assures him he will be all right.

QUOTES

- 'Welcome to the afterlife, Jean-Luc. You're dead.' – *Q welcomes Picard*
- 'I would rather die as the man I was than live the life I just saw.' – *Picard to Q*

TRIVIA

- *Tapestry* was based on an earlier pitch, *A Q Carol*, in which Q's Ghost of Christmas Past made Picard relive the failures in his life: his family, the Stargazer, Jack Crusher and the Nausicaan incident. Ronald Moore pared this down to the episode with the Nausicaans, interested as he was in the denouement of Picard's early life as a rebel.
- It is ironic that early versions of *Face of the Enemy* were rejected for being too similar to *Quantum Leap* when *Tapestry* could be a direct lift. There is a rather cute moment when Picard looks in a mirror and sees himself – cocking a snook to the other show.

RATING

- A wonderfully clever, well-crafted episode with more that its fair share of incident, pathos and wit. Patrick Stewart turns in a fantastic performance, driven on by a script that has an intelligence and substance quite uncommon to the series. Each of John De Lancie's comic cameos is a gem. Definitely one of the show's finest hours.

6.16 BIRTHRIGHT Part I

STARDATE 46578.4

Worf investigates claims that his father did not die at Khitomer

When the Enterprise visits Deep Space Nine, Worf is contacted by a Yridian named Jaglom Shrek who claims that Worf's father, Mogh, did not die at the Khitomer Massacre. Shrek offers to take Worf to a remote Romulan prison camp where his father is a prisoner. Meanwhile, Bashir, Data and Geordi examine a cylinder found in

TX 22 February 1993
WRITER Brannon Braga
DIRECTOR Winrich Kolbe
GUEST CAST James Cromwell (Jaglom Shrek), Siddig El Fadil (Dr Julian Bashir), Jennifer Gatti (Ba'el), Richard Herd (L'kor), Cristine Rose (Gi'ral)

space. Suddenly, an energy bolt hits Data. He finds himself in an eerie dream version of the Enterprise, and face to face with Dr Soong. Later, Picard encourages Data to explore the meanings of his dream, which he does in a series of paintings. Worf lands at a planet in the Carraya sector. He finds a female Klingon bathing, but she is bemused by his attempts to rescue her: this is her home. She is escorted away by a Romulan. Data recreates his accident and again sees Soong. This time Soong explains that he is proud of his creation and that Data is becoming more than a machine. Meanwhile, Worf talks to an elderly Klingon, L'Kor. Worf prepares to help the 73 Klingon captives escape but is suddenly held by two of them. L'Kor will not let Worf go – the Klingons have no intention of leaving...

QUOTES

- 'Would you like to talk about what's bothering you or do you want to break some more furniture?' – *Troi to Worf*

TRIVIA

- *Birthright* had its origins in two story pitches. The first, by George Brozak, concerned a colony of Klingon prisoners too proud to return home. Brozak's story had a lot of similarities to a story in development for *Deep Space Nine* and was rejected. The second, by Daryl Mallett, Arthur Holcomb and Barbara Wallace, had Worf hear that his father may be alive. The strands were combined by Braga. Piller liked the writing of the conflict between Worf and a Romulan guard, Tokath (who appears in part two), with its similarities to the Nicholson/Saito relationship in *The Bridge On The River Kwai*, and suggested it become a two-parter.
- The episode features the first crossover of a character from *Deep Space Nine*, although the original intention was to use Dax and not Bashir.

RATING

- A brain-numbingly slow story that should never have been given a second episode. Data's dream sequences are an interesting concept but no more and feel like a hastily added filler to pad out the two-parter.

6.17 BIRTHRIGHT Part II

STARDATE 46579.2

Worf finds Klingon survivors living in peace with Romulans

TX 1 March 1993
WRITER René Echevarria
DIRECTOR Dan Curry
GUEST CAST James Cromwell (Jaglom Shrek), Jennifer Gatti (Ba'el), Richard Herd (L'kor), Sterling Macer Jr (Toq), Christine Rose (Gi'ral), Alan Scarfe (Tokath)

The Klingons tell Worf that, after Khitomer, the Romulan leader Tokath ordered that they be kept alive. Shamed, they do not wish to return home in disgrace. Tokath insists that the Romulans and Klingons have learned to live together: he has married Gi'Ral and they have had a daughter, Ba'el. Tokath implants Worf with a tracking device. Worf, however, begins to revive in the Klingons a sense of their cultural heritage, much to Tokath's horror. Tokath orders Worf's execution. When Worf stands, determined to die with honour, he is joined by Toq, and other young Klingons. Toq explains that a Romulan supply ship will allow the Klingons to leave but they must never reveal the location of the camp. Worf sends a message to the Enterprise to collect him and the young Klingons. He claims he did not find any prison camp. Picard accepts his explanation.

TRIVIA

- Despite needing to pad out the first episode, the first cut of *Birthright Part II* overran by nine minutes. Scenes showing the growing relationship between Worf and Ba'el were cut as was a tense scene when Gi'ral defends her interspecies marriage.

RATING

- A distinctly peculiar episode in which the Klingons and Romulans appear so happy that Worf's actions are simply destructive and unnecessary. The notion of Worf's racism is something that never really gets tackled head-on, when it's the most interesting aspect of the script.

6.18 STARSHIP MINE

STARDATE 46682.4

Picard battles alien thieves who board the Enterprise while it gets a spring clean

TX 29 March 1993
WRITER Morgan Gendel
DIRECTOR Cliff Bole
GUEST CAST Alan Altshuld (Pomet), Majel Barrett (Computer Voice), Tim De Zarn (Satler), Marie Marshall (Kelsey), Glenn Morshower (Orton), Tom Nibley (Neil), Arlee Reed (Waiter), Tim Russ (Devor), David Spielberg (Hutchinson), Patricia Tallman (Kiros)

The crew arrive at Arkaria Base where the Enterprise is to be exposed to a routine baryon sweep. Bored by the conversation of their host, Calvin Hutchinson, Picard returns to the ship to collect his saddle to go horse riding. On board, Picard is confronted by Devor, one of a number of criminals who have taken control of the Enterprise. Picard overpowers Devor but discovers the Enterprise is now being shut down and he cannot beam back to the base. He is captured and brought before Kelsey, the leader of the criminals, who are busy setting up a forcefield to protect them from the baryon sweep while stealing trilithium resin, an explosive waste material from the Enterprise's warp engines. Meanwhile, the base administrator, Orton, is in league with Kelsey. He kills Hutchinson and injures Geordi. Picard destroyes the forcefield and escapes but is caught again by Kelsey, *en route* to Ten-Forward, the last place that the baryon sweep will touch. Picard fights Kelsey as the baryon sweep approaches. At the last minute, Kelsey beams off the ship and Picard orders Data to stop the sweep. Picard is saved and watches as the trilithium explodes on Kelsey's shuttlecraft.

QUOTES

- 'I only wish I had the opportunity to use it – on a horse.' – *Picard escapes with his saddle*

TRIVIA

- *Starship Mine* emerged as a conscious attempt to do *Die Hard* in space. Stewart leapt at the opportunity, doing several of his own stunts.

RATING

- Wonderfully light stuff that is notably violent for *Star Trek*. The set-up with Hutchinson's boring host is brilliant, providing an amusing and realistic reason for Picard to return to the ship. Great fun.

6.19 LESSONS

STARDATE 46693.1

Picard falls in love with a new crewmember but is torn between heart and duty

TX 5 April 1993
WRITERS Ronald Wilkerson and Jean Louise Matthias
DIRECTOR Robert Wiemer
GUEST CAST Wendy Hughes (Neela Daren)

Picard meets the new Head of Stellar Cartography, Neela Daren, and is fascinated by her. After a musical recital, the two recognise their mutual love of music and grow closer. Picard soon falls for Neela but is concerned that a relationship with a member of the crew will threaten his objectivity. The Enterprise is called to Bersallis III where firestorms threaten the inhabitants. Riker assembles six Away Teams and Picard reluctantly lets Neela lead one of them. The evacuation is slow and, once over, Riker announces that two of the teams did not make it back – including that led by Neela. Picard is dismayed. Later, Worf informs Picard that survivors have been found. Neela is safe but Picard realises he cannot put her in a position of danger again. Neela agrees to leave the Enterprise but makes Picard promise not to give up his music.

TRIVIA

- Story writers Ronald Wilkerson and Jean Louise Matthias, who had pitched *Imaginary Friend* and *Schisms*, were given the opportunity to turn their ideas into a teleplay for this one. René Echevarria made a few uncredited tweaks to the script at the end.

RATING

- *Star Trek* meets *Brief Encounter*. It is odd that the Head of Stellar Cartography would lead an emergency evacuation Away Team – does the Enterprise really not have six people better able to lead such a mission?

6.20 THE CHASE

STARDATE 46731.5

The Enterprise competes against other races for the DNA fragments of an ancient civilisation

TX 26 April 1993
WRITER Joe Menosky (story by Ronald D Moore and Joe Menosky)
DIRECTOR Jonathan Frakes
GUEST CAST Majel Barrett (Computer Voice), John Cotran Jr (Nu'Daq), Salome Jens (Humanoid), Norman Lloyd (Professor Richard Galen), Maurice Röeves (Romulan Captain), Linda Thorson (Gul Ocett)

Galen, an eminent archaeologist, tries to convince Picard to join him on a year-long expedition. When Picard refuses, Galen leaves angry. Moments later, the Enterprise hears that Galen's ship is being attacked by Yridians. The Yridians are destroyed by Galen, who also dies. The crew discover strange blocks of numbers in Galen's computer and set course for Ruah IV, a planet that Galen just visited, and then Indri VII in search of answers. Beverly discovers that the numbers relate to DNA fragments. Picard sets course for Loren III, the only nearby planet where life could be sustained. They soon find Cardassian and Klingon vessels on the same trail. Both have DNA fragments and eventually agree to join theirs with those of Galen – they are still missing one fragment. When Picard deduces where it is, Gul Ocett, the Cardassian, attacks the other ships and leaves at speed. Picard pursues to the Vilmoran system where they are joined by a Romulan vessel that has been following them cloaked. While the parties argue, Picard and Beverly find the last fragment and activate a mysterious program. A hologram explains that the genetic puzzle was put together in the hope that cultures would co-operate to find the answer. The figure urges the travellers to remember their similarities not differences. The alien races leave, disappointed.

TRIVIA

- *The Chase* was pitched during season five but had a more comic feel, a kind of *It's a Mad, Mad, Mad, Mad World* in space. The heavy comic overtones stalled the script for over a year. Looking again at the pitch, Menosky was inspired by Carl Sagan's novel *Contact* in which the *pi* calculation holds the secrets of the universe. Menosky suggested the same could be done with DNA.
- Linda Thorson is better known as Tara King, Steed's final companion in *The Avengers*. Salome Jens would later have a returning role in *Deep Space Nine* as the female shapeshifter.

RATING

- A pretty silly episode where the ending is a distinct anti-climax, little more than the payoff to a rather lame joke. Despite this, rumour has it that Piller was so enamoured with the final script that he suggested it as the season cliffhanger!

6.21 FRAME OF MIND

STARDATE 46778.1

Riker finds himself in an alien asylum where he is told the Enterprise is a delusion

TX 3 May 1993
WRITER Brannon Braga
DIRECTOR James L Conway
GUEST CAST Alan Dean Moore (Wounded Crewmember), Andrew Prine (Administrator), David Selsburg (Doctor Syrus), Susanna Thompson (Jaya), Gary Werntz (Mavek)

En route to Tilonus IV, Riker starts to feel paranoid. Troi feels that he is merely getting into character for a role as a mental patient in a ship's play. However, on the opening night, the set becomes an actual cell in a Tilonus asylum. Riker finds himself trapped in the ward with an alien therapist, Syrus, who explains the play is a delusion. An attendant, Mavek, tells Riker he was brought to the hospital for killing a man. Riker becomes agitated and wakes on the Enterprise. Beverly believes Riker had an anxiety dream about the play. At the performance, Riker angrily confronts an alien crewmember who appeared in his dream. He is taken to sickbay and soon finds himself back in the asylum. Convinced he is going insane, Riker asks Syrus for help. Picard, Troi and Worf appear to him and try to convince him to return to the Enterprise, but Riker dismisses them as a delusion. That night, Worf and Data break into Riker's cell and transport him back to the Enterprise. Picard tells Riker he was abducted during an undercover mission to Tilonus IV but Riker is unsure. He eventually awakens in an alien lab and, seeing his undercover clothing, realises the Enterprise is his reality. He escapes and returns to the ship.

TRIVIA

- Braga pitched a hastily put-together idea when another story fell through late in the season and it was written in three days.

RATING

- A stream of consciousness story that is, at first, quite interesting but actually presents no real mystery. Of course, the Enterprise is Riker's reality! The ultimate mind f#?k episode.

6.22 SUSPICIONS

STARDATE 46830.1

Beverly investigates the death of a scientist when an experimental shield fails

TX 10 May 1993
WRITER Joe Menosky and Naren Shankar
DIRECTOR Cliff Bole
GUEST CAST Majel Barrett (Computer Voice), Whoopi Goldberg (Guinan), James Horan (Jo'Bril), Joan Stuart Morris (T'Pan), Tricia O'Neil (Kurak), John S Ragin (Dr Christopher), Peter Slutsker (Dr Reyga), Patti Yasutake (Ogawa)

Beverly faces a formal enquiry for misconduct. She recently invited experts onto the Enterprise to hear Ferengi scientist Reyga, who had developed a new shield for shuttlecraft to protect it from a star's corona. When Kurak, a Klingon, insists the experimental shuttle should not be piloted by Reyga, Takaran scientist Jo'Bril offers and is supported by Vulcan T'Pan and her husband Dr Christopher. Jo'Bril pilots the shuttle but dies after a build-up of baryon particles. Beverly is concerned as the precise cause of death cannot be found. Later, Reyga is found having committed suicide. Beverly, suspicious, orders an autopsy, against Ferengi tradition. Picard has her relieved of duty. Beverly pilots the experimental shuttle into the star's corona. The shield holds. Suddenly, Beverly is confronted by Jo'Bril – he put himself into a psychic trance, a Takaran talent. Jo'Bril sought only to discredit Reyga but now has his invention too. Beverly manages to reach Jo'Bril's phaser and kills him. She is reinstated.

TRIVIA

- *Suspicions* did not have an easy transition to screen. The story was taken to writers' conference five times in two years and the final script had three rewrites. The original story was a noir thriller with Worf that used flashbacks to recount the mystery. Another key element early on was the discovery that warp travel pollutes the universe (a storyline later used in *Force of Nature*).

RATING

- A standard mystery with a pretty obvious twist. McFadden puts in a lacklustre performance, engendering little interest for the character or the viewer.

6.23 RIGHTFUL HEIR

STARDATE 46852.2

Worf witnesses the return of legendary Klingon warrior god, Kahless

TX 17 May 1993
WRITER Ronald D Moore (story by James E Brooks)
DIRECTOR Winrich Kolbe
GUEST CAST Majel Barrett (Computer Voice), Kevin Conway (Kahless), Charles Esten (Divok), Alan Oppenheimer (Koroth), Robert O'Reilly (Gowron), Norman Snow (Torin)

Worf has been trying to summon a vision of Kahless, the greatest Klingon warrior who is prophesied to return. Picard grants him leave to try the ceremony on Boreth, home to the followers of Kahless, led by Koroth. Worf is stunned when Kahless appears, but doubts it is the real Kahless. Nevertheless, Worf intercedes when Gowron claims Kahless is just a trick to let Gowron's enemies to take power. Bloodshed is averted but the Klingons are wracked with doubt. Worf confronts Koroth, who reveals that Kahless is a clone implanted with memories to make him believe he has returned. Koroth insists the Klingons need a Kahless to counter Gowron's corruption. Despite this, Worf tells Gowron the truth but insists the Klingons need a moral leader. He persuades Gowron to appoint Kahless as Emperor – Gowron will still rule, but Kahless will guide and help restore the Empire's honour. Worf still feels spiritually unfulfilled until the clone reminds him to follow the teachings of the real Kahless.

QUOTES

- 'Have you ever fought an idea, Picard? It has no weapon to fight, no body to kill.' – *Gowron to Picard*

TRIVIA

- Rumour has it that Brooks' original pitch, which focused on the political machinations of Klingon clerics, was named *Jurassic Worf*. Moore added ingredients from other stories, bringing back Kahless, who first appeared in the original series' *The Savage Curtain*. Another resurrection was the legend of Kahless' death at the hands of Molor, which had been in *Birthright, Part II*.

RATING

- A key story that sets up a number of aspects of Klingon life, notably its religion, afterlife and the passage of the Empire to a medieval constitutional system. Sadly, it looks and feels like a late season-filler.

6.24 SECOND CHANCES

Riker discovers he has a double, created eight years earlier in a transporter accident

TX 24 May 1993
WRITER René Echevarria (story by Mike Medlock)
DIRECTOR LeVar Burton
GUEST CAST Mae Jemison (Palmer)

STARDATE 46915.2

The Enterprise is at Nervala IV where, eight years previously, Riker led the evacuation of Starfleet researchers while a Lieutenant on the USS Potemkin. Beaming down, Riker finds his exact double, Lieutenant Riker, who claims the transport was a failure, leaving him stranded on the planet. Geordi discovers that a freak transporter incident created identical Rikers who have since led separate lives. Lieutenant Riker is disappointed when he finds Commander Riker's actions in the intervening years appear to have wrecked his chance of romance with Troi. Nevertheless, Lieutenant Riker and Troi grow closer. Meanwhile, Commander Riker is irked when Picard chooses Lieutenant Riker's data retrieval plan over his. He is understanding when Troi reveals her relationship with his double but warns her to be careful – the Lieutenant is the same Riker that caused them to break up. When Lieutenant Riker is posted to the USS Ghandi, Troi is unsure she can join him. Later, the two Rikers beam to Nervala IV to retrieve the researchers' data. Commander Riker saves his double when the building collapses. Lieutenant Riker has adopted his middle name, Thomas, and joins the Ghandi, but Troi decides not to join Tom – Will Riker promises to watch over Troi.

TRIVIA

- Medlock's pitch was designed to meet fan demands for a Troi-Riker romance without jeopardising either character in the long run.
- Dr Mae Jemison, who has a cameo here, is an astronaut and the first black woman in space.

RATING

- A clever way of getting Troi and Riker together. Frakes is given another decent script and once again rises to the occasion.

6.25 TIMESCAPE

Picard, Geordi, Data and Troi find the Enterprise frozen in time on the brink of destruction

TX 14 June 1993
WRITER Brannon Braga
DIRECTOR Adam Nimoy
GUEST CAST Michael Bofshever (Romulan/Alien)

STARDATE 46944.2

Returning to the Enterprise in a shuttle, Picard, Troi, Geordi and Data find themselves frozen in time. When they wake, they discover the shuttle has been in constant operation for 47 days. Data deduces that they are in a temporal disturbance where time moves 50 times faster than normal. They arrive back at the Enterprise to find the ship under attack from a Romulan Warbird, firing at point blank range. The scene is frozen, as though a photograph. The officers beam to the Enterprise wearing protective forcefields and find the crew motionless. The warp core is breached and the explosion is expanding – the scene is not frozen but moving forward at an infinitesimally small speed. Picard suffers a bout of temporal narcosis and has to be taken back to the shuttle. While the others beam to the Warbird, Picard watches as the Enterprise explodes – then comes back together again. On the Warbird, Geordi is attacked by a Romulan who is not frozen in time – when Troi removes his armband, he becomes motionless. The moving Romulans are actually aliens who are trying to retrieve their young from inside the warp core. Data controls the time distortion and buys Picard time to interrupt a power beam between the Enterprise and the Warbird. The Warbird and aliens are destroyed.

TRIVIA

- With the sixth season rapidly approaching its conclusion, another story idea fell through. Braga picked up on an idea pitched by Mark Gerhed O'Connell about the Enterprise caught in time like amber. Braga's unofficial working title was *Deep Time*.

RATING

- An episode with an eerie feel but a rather technical and laboured dénouement. Adam Nimoy adds some nice touches – the first 'Romulan' to move is a great moment.

6.26 DESCENT Part I

STARDATE 46982.1

The crew encounter a vicious breed of Borg that offers Data a chance to experience emotions

TX 21 April 1993
WRITER Ronald D Moore (story by Jeri Taylor)
DIRECTOR Alexander Singer
GUEST CAST Stephen James Carver (Tayar/Borg #2), Brian Cousins (Crosis), Richard Gilbert-Hill (Bosus/Borg #1), Stephen Hawking (Himself), John Neville (Isaac Newton), Natalija Nogulich (Admiral Nechayev), Jim Norton (Albert Einstein)

Data's holodeck poker game with Newton, Einstein and Hawking is interrupted when the Enterprise receives a distress call from Ohniaka III. A large alien vessel of unknown origin in orbit. Riker, Worf and Data beam to the surface and find a new breed of Borg: vicious, fast and intent on killing rather than assimilating. Data becomes enraged and violently kills a Borg – he experienced anger. Later, Data tries to recreate the Borg attack in the holodeck but cannot repeat the emotion. Another Borg attack leads the Enterprise to the MS 1 colony. Picard is suspicious that the Enterprise was the nearest ship in both cases. The strange vessel is there again but disappears into a distortion in space. This time the Enterprise pursues. When Borg beam aboard, one is captured and refers to himself as Crosis – the Borg have individuality. Later, Crosis offers Data the chance to feel emotion again. Data and Crosis take a shuttlecraft and leave the Enterprise. The crew follow through a subspace distortion and find themselves at a planet, 65 light years away. A heavily armed Away Team beam down and Picard, Geordi and Troi rush into a building. They are surrounded by Borg – led by Data's brother, Lore.

QUOTES

- 'I got angry.' – *Data's matter- of-fact analysis*

TRIVIA

- Taylor and Moore's original ideas were based around Conrad's *Heart of Darkness*, with Data's descent. The cliffhanger ending was a matter of some discussion, with the hot favourite for a while being Data's dreams (see in *Birthright, Part I*) turning into nightmares. Lore was introduced to knit together the themes of descent into darkness and the Borg return. Also, the title is a bad pun – Descent/Dissent – that pulls the two plot strands together thematically.

RATING

- Pap. *The Next Generation* ruined the Borg with *I, Borg* and try to make a virtue of their actions here. *Descent* is simply compounding one error with another.

STAR TREK: THE NEXT GENERATION
SEASON SEVEN

7.1 DECENT Part II

STARDATE 47025.4

Lore's plan to use Data and the Borg to conquer the Federation unravels

TX 20 September 1993
WRITER René Echevarria
DIRECTOR Alexander Singer

Lore explains that Hugh's emotions left a faction of the Borg isolated and aimless. He and Data can become their leaders. Troi notices that Data is only demonstrating negative emotions. Geordi tries to rig a kedion pulse that might trigger Data's more benevolent side. Before he can, Data leads Geordi away to conduct an experiment to turn him into an android. Data pulls back at the last moment. The Enterprise, commanded by Beverly, comes under attack from a Borg ship, and they have to leave orbit, marooning the crew on the

GUEST CAST Michael Reilly Burke (Goval), Brian Cousins (Crosis), Alex Datcher (Taitt), Jonathan del Arco (Hugh), James Horan (Barnaby), Benito Martinez (Salazar)

planet. Riker and Worf find Hugh cowering in a cave. Beverly destroys the Borg ship by luring it into the sun and manipulating a metaphasic shield. Hugh resents the Enterprise crew for abandoning him, but leads them to Lore's base. After a confrontation, Data prevents Lore from killing Picard and deactivates his brother. He keeps Lore's emotion chip.

TRIVIA

- Once again, the resolution of the story was left until after the summer break. Beverly's battle against the Borg ship grew as the story evolved, while the return of Hugh (from *I, Borg*) didn't seem to grow in the telling.

RATING

- An OK episode, but as a season-opener with Lore and the Borg, it ought to be better than that. In retrospect, it feels a lot like early *Voyager* – very slickly made, but no one's heart seems to be in it. The only real highlight is Data's torture of Geordi, which is quite creepy.

7.2 LIAISONS

STARDATE UNKNOWN

Picard is marooned with a woman who loves him

TX 27 September 1993
WRITER Jeanne Carrigan Fauci and Lisa Rich (story by Roger Eschbacher and Jaq Greenspon
DIRECTOR Cliff Bole
GUEST CAST Rickey D'Shon Collins (Eric Burton), Paul Eiding (Loquel), Michael Harris (Byleth), Eric Pierpoint (Voval), Barbara Williams (Anna)

The Enterprise is hosting a cultural exchange with the Iyaarans. Picard greets their ambassadors, then leaves in a shuttle with an Iyaaran pilot, Voval, to meet their leader. The crew have mixed fortunes with their guests – Troi finds Loquel likeable if obsessed with food, Worf and Byleth end up fighting. Picard's shuttle crashes, and Voval is knocked unconscious. Picard wakes to being tended by a human woman, Anna. She smashes the shuttle's communications system and tells Picard she loves him. Picard realises he is not as ill as Anna claims. He soon realises 'Anna' is really Voval, who's changed form to explore love, a concept unknown to the Iyaarans. Loquel and Byleth were studying pleasure and anger, explaining their odd behaviour.

TRIVIA

- A story whose A-plot owes a lot to *Misery*, the Stephen King story that had recently been filmed. A number of rewrites, including extensive uncredited work at the last minute by Brannon Braga, made the aliens ever more quirky.

RATING

- A monumentally average story, which aims for a type of quirky humour but misses. It's pretty clear Patrick Stewart's heart isn't in it, and the episode never sparks into life.

7.3 INTERFACE

STARDATE 47215.5

Geordi defies Picard to try to rescue his mother

TX 4 October 1993
WRITER Joe Menosky
DIRECTOR Robert Wiemer
GUEST CAST Warren Munson (Marcus Holt), Madge Sinclair (Silva LaForge), Ben Vereen (Edward LaForge)

The USS Raman is trapped in the atmosphere of Marijne VII. Geordi perfects a remote probe he can control using his VISOR, effectively 'being' in a place in which no human can survive. As he prepares his mission, he gets news that his mother's ship, the USS Hera, has been lost. While the USS Excelsior and USS Noble look for the ship, Geordi presses on, and discovers the Raman's crew are dead. He then gets burned hands when the probe gets hot, something that should be impossible. The next time he uses the probe, Geordi is astonished to find his mother alive on the Raman. She asks him to send the Raman to a lower orbit. Geordi realises there are energy beings on the Raman who can only exist at fierce temperatures. They will die unless the ship is lowered. He defies Picard and lowers the ship. Picard understands why.

TRIVIA

- The episode under-ran, which was extremely unusual for a series that usually had to trim episodes. A scene with Riker and Geordi was filmed during *Phantasms* to make up the time.

RATING

- An episode that spends a long time setting up a gimmick, the probe, then doesn't do very much with it. It's a good episode for Geordi, though, and entertaining enough.

7.4 GAMBIT Part I

STARDATE 47135.2

Picard is undercover posing as a smuggler

TX 11 October 1993
WRITER Naren Shankar (story by Christopher Hatton and Naren Shankar)
DIRECTOR Peter Lauritson
GUEST CAST Alan Altshud (Yranac), Caitlin Brown (Vekor), Robin Curtis (Tallera), Bruce Gray (Chekote), Sabrina LeBeauf (Glusti), Stephen Lee (Bartender), Richard Lynch (Arctus Baran), Cameron Thor (Narik), Derek Webster (Sanders)

Troi and Riker are investigating Picard's death – he's been vaporised in a bar on Dessica II. The Enterprise trails his murderers to Baradas III, a planet once used by the Vulcanoid Debrune. An Away Team is attacked by mercenaries on the surface, and Riker is captured by their leader, Arctus Baran, and sent to his ship. Riker discovers Picard there, posing as a crewman, Galen. Picard explains that the mercenaries' phasers can be set to 'transport' – they use them to steal items and beam them straight back to their ship. For some reason, they are concentrating on stealing Romulan artefacts across the Taugan Sector. On the Enterprise, Acting Captain Data heads for Calder II, the next logical target for the mercenaries. Picard tries to convince Baran not to use violence, but he is ordered to open fire on the Enterprise...

TRIVIA

- Robin Curtis played Saavik in *Star Trek III: The Search for Spock* and (briefly) in *Star Trek IV: The Voyage Home.*
- There were 70 phaser effects in this one episode, easily the most of any *The Next Generation* story.
- Christopher Hatton was at college when he pitched this story, and also managed to get *Thine Own Self* accepted.

RATING

- It's blindingly obvious that Picard isn't dead, so the story starts off on a moment of false jeopardy. It's a romp, with a lot of fun to be had as Picard and Riker hurl insults at each other, and about as much action in this episode as there was in the whole of the first season. But it doesn't really add up to much, and doesn't deserve to be a two-parter (it would have been nice to see *Lower Decks*, say, expanded instead).

7.5 GAMBIT Part II

STARDATE 47160.1

Picard discovers the truth behind the smugglers' schemes

TX 18 October 1993
WRITER Ronald D Moore (story by Naren Shankar)
DIRECTOR Alexander Singer
GUEST CAST Caitlin Brown (Vekor), Robin Curtis (Tallera), Martin Goslins (Setok), Sabrina LaBeauf (Glusti), Richard Lynch (Arctus Baran), Cameron Thor (Narik), James Worthy (Koral)

The Enterprise receives only minor damage, but Data lets Baran's ship escape, following it to the Hiralyn system, where it rendezvous with a Klingon ship. Picard learns that the artefacts are early Vulcan, not Romulan. One of the crew, Tallera, tells Picard she's an undercover agent for the Vulcans. Baran is working for Vulcan isolationists who are assembling a powerful ancient weapon, the Stone of Gol – a telepathic weapon. The Enterprise accosts the Klingon ship. Riker and Picard beam to the Enterprise to get the artefact back, and Picard pretends to kill Riker. Returning to the smugglers' ship, Picard engineers a mutiny, kills Baran and takes command. He sends the ship to Vulcan, where Tallera reveals she is actually working for the isolationists. She tries to use the Stone of Gol, but Picard thinks peaceful thoughts, and the weapon is useless. Tallera is taken into custody.

TRIVIA

- Stretching the story to two parts, the whole Stone of Gol plot hadn't featured in Christopher Hatton's original pitch.
- Goral was played by an NBA basketball player and a fan of the show, who was keen for a cameo role. He features as the extremely tall captain of the Klingon trading ship.

RATING

- An oddly rushed ending, given the length of the story. As with *Unification*, *The Next Generation*'s version of Vulcan isn't visually very interesting, and a story only hints at what sounds like a, if you'll pardon the word, fascinating political situation on the planet.

7.6 PHANTASMS

STARDATE 47225.7

Data's dreams are troubling

TX 25 October 1993
WRITER Brannon Braga
DIRECTOR Patrick Stewart
GUEST CAST David L Crowley (Workman), Bernard Kates (Sigmund Freud), Clyde Kusatsu (Nakamura), Gina Ravarra (Tyler)

Data's dreaming program is generating nightmares, such as eating Deanna, who's turned into a cake, and meeting workmen who are digging up the ship's plasma conduits. Data consults a holodeck Sigmund Freud and the real Troi. Both Troi and Geordi agree it's a healthy part of Data's development – until he stabs Troi in a waking nightmare, despite deactivating his dreaming program. Beverly discovers interphasic creatures around the ship extracting cellular peptides from the crew's bodies – Data has somehow unconsciously registered their presence. Picard and Geordi enter a holodeck simulation of Data's dreams. Using the information they find, Data generates an interphasic pulse that drives out the creatures.

TRIVIA

- A miscommunication meant that the first 'Deanna cake' to arrive wasn't suitable.

RATING

- An interesting episode, one with some memorable visuals. Data's stabbing of Deanna is surprisingly graphic, and the interphasic aliens are quite nasty, too. A striking and idiosyncratic episode.

7.7 DARK PAGE

STARDATE 48254.1

Lwaxana Troi harbours a dark secret

TX 1 November 1993
WRITER Hilary J Bader
DIRECTOR Les Landau
GUEST CAST Majel Barrett (Lwaxana Troi), Amick Byram (Ian Andrew Troi), Kirsten Dunst (Hedril), Normal Large (Maques), Andreana Weiner (Kestra Troi)

Lwaxana Troi is teaching the telepathic Cairn people about spoken language, and it has left her tired. Troi is worried about her mother, and medical tests suggest she should avoid using telepathy until she is rested. When she defies this, she collapses. A traumatic event in her past has caused the coma. One of the Cairn, Maques, lets Troi enter her mother's mind, but there are troubling images in there, no solution. Troi discovers that seven years of her mother's diary have been deleted. Entering her mind again, Troi learns she had an elder sister, who died in a drowning accident. Lwaxana has felt guilty about this ever since, but confronting the memories brings closure.

TRIVIA

- Child actor Kirsten Dunst appeared before her startling role opposite Tom Cruise and Brad Pitt in *Interview With the Vampire*. She has, of course, gone on to a successful Hollywood career, most notably as Mary-Jane in the *Spider-Man* movies.
- Teddy and Buck, the wolves who play the wolf that chased Deanna, were already Hollywood stars, having appeared in the Kevin Costner movie *Dances with Wolves*.
- The story was always about the telepathic revelation and curing of a trauma, but at various stages it was Geordi, Beverly, and then Deanna's trauma.

RATING

- A story that's trying to give Lwaxana Troi a darker side that doesn't suit the character, but which works well in its own terms. It's not as fresh as it might be, resembling a lot of previous Troi stories revolving around telepathy, like *Night Terrors* and *Violations*. It also resembles *Phantasms*... the previous episode.

7.8 ATTACHED

STARDATE 47304.2

Picard and Beverly discover their true feelings for each other

TX 8 November 1993
WRITER Nicholas Sagan
DIRECTOR Jonathan Frakes

The Kes hope to join the Federation, even though they share the planet Kesprytt III with the isolationist Prytt. Picard and Beverly travel to the planet, but are taken prisoner by the Prytt, who suspect the Federation and the Kes of ganging up on them. Riker discovers that the Kes are equally paranoid. Meanwhile, Picard and Beverly escape, but discover that they are attached by a telepathic device that means they can read each other's thoughts. They realise how strongly they

GUEST CAST Robin Gammell (Mauric), Lenore Kasdorf (Lorin), JC Stevens (Kes aide)

are attracted. Picard was in love with Beverly, but kept his feelings in check. As the Kes ambassador, Mauric, begins to suspect that the Federation is in league with the Prytt, Riker threatens the Prytt with invasion. The isolationists quickly locate Picard and Beverly, who return to the ship. Beverly and Picard agree to remain just friends.

TRIVIA

- Nicholas Sagan is the son of physicist Carl Sagan, and tried pitching a number of *Deep Space Nine* stories before *The Next Generation* staff picked this idea.
- It continued the seventh season's theme of returning to old plot lines to tie them up as the series drew to a close. The first season had hinted at Beverly and Picard's mutual attraction, and while that had subsequently been downplayed, every so often the two characters seemed on the verge of declaring their love for each other (most recently in *QPid*). The original script had the two kissing, then a scene break which left it open just how far the two went, but this was toned down in the final version. The production team were reluctant to make the relationship more permanent with the end of the series (and the films) looming.

RATING

- A rather contrived way of getting two characters to talk to each other, and it all feels a bit neat, but this does at least pay off one of the most long-running and undeveloped of the show's storylines in a way that's entertaining, logical and doesn't quite flick the reset switch at the end.

7.9 FORCE OF NATURE

STARDATE 47310.2

A brother and sister go to terrible lengths to make their case

TX 15 November 1993
WRITER Naren Shankar
DIRECTOR Robert Lederman
GUEST CAST Lee Arenberg (Prak), Majel Barrett (Computer Voice), Michael Corbett (Rabal), Margaret Reed (Serova)

The USS Fleming is missing in the Hekaras Corridor, a narrow channel through an area of space flooded with tetryon particles. The Enterprise investigates, and is fired on by a Ferengi ship that was attacked by a Federation buoy that fired a verteron pulse. The Enterprise helps the Ferengi repair the damage – and shortly afterwards is itself attacked by a verteron pulse. Rabal and Serova, siblings from Hekaras II, beam aboard. They believe warp drive is destroying the fabric of space. Data discovers they might be right. Geordi is devastated when an impatient Serova sacrifices herself and puts the Enterprise and the Fleming in danger. Geordi saves the ship. Starfleet imposes a new limit – starships are not to travel above Warp 5 without permission.

TRIVIA

- Originally a story about Geordi's reaction to the death of his mother which would feature his sister and a crisis of faith as he came to worry that he was doing more harm than good with his warp engines. This family element was dropped when it was felt that too many crewmembers' families were showing up during the season.
- Data's cat, Spot, was male in *Phantasms*, but is female here (and is from now on). Data's quest for the perfect cat food recipe has reached 'feline supplement 221', suggesting that he's come up with a new formula, on average, every five days.

RATING

- A rather obvious environmental allegory which doesn't work, but which does manage to introduce a ridiculously arbitrary 'speed limit' across the *Star Trek* universe for no readily-apparent story reason. A weak episode.

7.10 INHERITANCE

STARDATE 47410.2

Data's long-lost mother arrives on the Enterprise

TX 22 November 1993
WRITER Dan Koepel and René Echevarria (story by Dan Koepel)
DIRECTOR Robert Scheerer
GUEST CAST Fionnula Flanagan (Juliana O'Donnell Soong Tainer), William Lithgow (Pran Tainer)

The Enterprise helps to warm the cooling magma of the Atrea IV colony. One of the scientists, Juliana, tells Data she was once married to Dr Soong. She's Data's mother. Data is suspicious, as there's been no hint of her existence before, but she amuses the crew with stories of a young Data. Eventually she admits to him that she didn't want Soong to create Data, after Lore proved such a failure. Data begins to accept her, but has some reservations. When she is injured in a cave, it becomes clear she is an android. Juliana is a replica of Soong's wife, who died. She has no idea that she's an android. Data doesn't reveal that to her, but tells her he knows Soong loved her.

TRIVIA

- A story designed to sort out Data's rather convoluted history, which had been established in *Datalore, Brothers, Silicon Avatar* and *Descent.*
- A subplot involving Data discovering a hiccupping subroutine was dropped. Thank heavens.

RATING

- A story with a good twist – good because it's so obvious, in retrospect. It's a simple story, and Fionnula Flanagan puts in a fine performance, all the more amazing when it seems pretty clear the writers aren't sure about the back story, so she must have been rather confused by it all. This isn't the first time a close relative of a crewmember turns out to have a dark secret this season, and it won't be the last. It would have been the best episode ever if Juliana had been Brent Spiner in drag.

7.11 PARALLELS

STARDATE 47391.2

Worf is trapped travelling through alternative realities

TX 29 November 1993
WRITER Brannon Braga
DIRECTOR Robert Wiemer
GUEST CAST Majel Barrett (Computer Voice), Mark Bramhall (Gul Nador), Wil Wheaton (Wesley Crusher), Patti Yasutake (Ogawa)

Worf begins to doubt his sanity when he returns from a bat'telh competition on Forcas III to find tiny details changing all the time. An error he makes results in Geordi's death. Then he is on an the Enterprise where he is married to Troi. Data notices that in Worf's account of what happens, Geordi always plays a prominent role – whenever he uses his VISOR, there's a shift. They test the theory... and Riker's in command of the Enterprise. Data realises Worf is trapped in a quantum fissure where 285,000 parallel universes intersect and the VISOR affects this. Worf begins to search for his Enterprise more methodically, but a group of warlike Bajorans from one universe attack the fissure and various Enterprises start popping into existence. They can synchronise and stabilise the fissure, but one crew, from a universe where Riker is one of the few to survive the Borg, doesn't want to go back, but is destroyed. Worf is back home, and intrigues Troi with the idea they were married.

TRIVIA

- The original idea was to use Picard, who had already featured heavily in the season (and who, perhaps more importantly, would do his own phasing through the timeline in *All Good Things*).
- There are seven alternate realities seen in the story – one much like the original, one where Ogawa is the doctor, one where Worf and Troi are married with two children, one where Riker's in command, one where the Bajorans are the aggressors and the Cardassians are allies of the Federation (one is a bridge officer on the Enterprise), one where Wesley serves as a lieutenant (the script suggested Tasha, but Denise Crosby wasn't available), and one where the Borg won in *The Best of Both Worlds.*

RATING

- A fun episode, one that gives Worf a story that isn't about honour and fighting (cheekily, it starts with him coming back from an adventure that sounds just like every other Klingon story). The show is playing around with its own mythos and format, and this is another one of those episodes where the cast gets to enjoy playing slight variations on their usual themes.

7.12 PEGASUS

STARDATE 47457.1

Riker's old ship holds secrets best left buried

TX 10 January 1994
WRITER Ronald D Moore
DIRECTOR LeVar Burton
GUEST CAST Michael Mack (Sirol), Terry O'Quinn (Pressman), Joyce Robinson (Ensign Gates – uncredited), Nancy Vawler (Blackwell)

Picard gets a Priority One command to rendezvous with the USS Crazy Horse in the Devolin system. Admiral Pressman beams aboard – 12 years ago, he and Riker had served on the USS Pegasus, and Riker is worried to learn that the current mission concerns its last mission. The ship was lost with all but nine crew. Now the wreck has been located in the Devolin system, and Picard is ordered to recover it before the Romulans can. A Warbird is already in the system. Meanwhile, Pressman reveals to Riker that he has sealed orders that Picard is not aware of – certain technology is to be recovered from the Pegasus. They locate the vessel – impossibly deep within an asteroid. Picard learns that there was a mutiny against Pressman on the Pegasus that was covered up, and Riker was less than forthcoming at the enquiry. Riker refuses to talk about it, angering

Picard. It's revealed that the Pegasus had an experimental cloaking device that could also phase through matter. This violates the Treaty of Algeron, which maintains peace between the Federation and Romulans. The Enterprise escapes the Romulans by installing the device, but Picard places Pressman under arrest and assures the Romulans that he will fully inform them of what has happened.

QUOTES

- 'I have a lot of friends at Starfleet Command, Captain.'
  'You're going to need them.' – *Pressman and Picard*

TRIVIA

- An episode that seems almost deliberately designed to do a few things Gene Roddenberry would have vetoed – an explanation why Starfleet doesn't use cloaking devices, mentions of 'Starfleet Intelligence', the depiction of a Starfleet 'black ops' military project and warmongering Starfleet officers.
- Joyce Robinson was an extra who appeared as the helm officer in many episodes – this was the only time she got a line of dialogue. She was named in *Phantasms.*

RATING

- Riker's dilemma (loyalty versus duty) is the same, and resolved in exactly the same way, as Wesley's in *The First Duty* (also by Moore), and the ending's reminiscent of *The Enterprise Incident.* Those were good episodes, and so's this one.

7.13 HOMEWARD

STARDATE 47423.9

Worf's brother breaks the Prime Directive to save a primitive tribe

TX 17 January 1994
WRITER Naren Shankar (story by Spike Steingasser and William N Stape)
DIRECTOR Alexander Singer
GUEST CAST Susan Christie (Tarrana), Penny Johnson (Dobara), Brian Markinson (Vorin), Edward Penn (Kateras), Paul Sorvino (Nikolai Rozhenko)

Boraal II's atmosphere will not be able to sustain life within 38 hours. Worf's adoptive human brother, Nikolai Rozhenko, has been observing the small population there, and wants them rescued, but that would break the Prime Directive. A disguised Worf goes down to retrieve his brother, and discovers him sheltering villagers under a deflector shield. Picard is adamant – they can not interfere – and Nikolai beams up. Shortly afterwards, Worf discovers that his brother has beamed the villagers up into a holodeck recreation of their caves. Nikolai confesses to Picard that he plans to resettle them on another planet, using the holodeck to smooth the transition. Picard has to acquiesce and the crew locate Vacca VI in the Cabral sector as a suitable replacement. They will be none the wiser. However, the holodeck starts to malfunction and one of the villagers, Vorin, manages to escape the holodeck and wander the ship. His memory can't be erased, and he commits suicide rather than live a lie. Another villager, Dobara, reveals she is pregnant with Nikolai's child. The villagers are resettled and Nikolai opts to stay with them to help them adjust.

TRIVIA

- This is the first episode where Michael Dorn is seen out of his Klingon make-up, although he does have a small prosthesis on his nose.

RATING

- A story that does something clever with the holodeck, but when all's said and done, it's not an epic quest, it's a group of people being tricked into wandering around a room on the Enterprise.

7.14 SUB ROSA

STARDATE 47423.9

Beverly falls for an old family friend – a ghost

TX 31 January 1994
WRITER Brannon Braga (story by Jeri Taylor, based on material by Jeanna F Gallo)

Beverly attends her grandmother Felisa Howard's funeral on Caldos IV, a colony based on Scottish culture. That night, Beverly is woken by a caress – but there's no one in her room. A local, Ned Quint, tells her that there's a ghost, and blows out a candle in Felisa's house. An electrical storm starts to affect the weather control on the planet. Beverly becomes aware of Ronin, a handsome young man who says he loved her grandmother as well as her ancestors. The environment problems spread to the

DIRECTOR Jonathan Frakes
GUEST CAST Ellen Albertini Dow (Felisa Howard), Shay Duffin (Ned Quint), Michael Keenan (Maturin), Duncan Regehr (Ronin)

Enterprise. Ronin wants Beverly to take the candle to the Enterprise. Felisa's body is the source of strange energy readings – they exhume the body, and discover that Ronin is an immortal anaphasic life form with a parasitic relationship with generations of Howard women. Beverly manages to kill him by destroying the candle, a little to her regret.

TRIVIA

- 'Sub rosa' is Latin for 'under cover'.
- Even though it looks as if the churchyard was filmed on location, this was an all-studio episode. It was also the first to use new CGI software, the Video Toaster, that was used to animate the green mist.

RATING

- Without a doubt, the oddest episode of *The Next Generation*, featuring a planet of Scots who seem to be descended from Scotty, not from anyone who can do the accent, and an Anne Rice-style dark fantasy ghost story. It might be trying to tell a tale in the style of *The X-Files* (halfway through its first series when *Sub Rosa* was shown), but it's way off that mark.

7.15 LOWER DECKS

STARDATE 47566.7

Four junior officers deal with life and death serving on the Enterprise

TX 7 February 1994
WRITER René Echevarria (story by Ronald Wilkerson and Jean Louise Mattias)
DIRECTOR Gabrielle Beaumont
GUEST CAST Bruce Beatty (Ben), Alexander Enberg (Taurik), Shannon Fill (Sito Jaxa), Dan Gauthier (Sam Lavelle), Don Reilly (Joret Dal) Patti Yasutake (Ogawa)

Four young officers – Ogawa, Lavelle, Taurik and Sito – await their evaluation reports. Lavelle doesn't think Riker likes him, and he's right... but Riker can't see how alike the two men are. Sito, a Bajoran, knows there is a black mark against her for what happened at the Academy (see *The First Duty*), but Worf is highly impressed by her. The Enterprise diverts from a rendezvous with USS Clement and heads to the Argaya system. Geordi and Taurik beam a Cardassian aboard, under conditions of strictest secrecy, and Ogawa is brought in to help treat him. After Worf teaches Sito to be bold and direct, she confronts Picard – she wants to be judged on her merits, not her past. Picard reveals that he is considering her for a dangerous mission. She is introduced to Joret Dal, the Cardassian. He is a Federation spy who needs to get back to Cardassian space. Sito is to accompany him as a 'hostage', in case he is stopped by a patrol. Sito accepts the assignment and leaves. Shortly afterwards, the wreckage of her escape pod is discovered. Sito is dead. Her friends are devastated, and it sours the news that Lavelle has been promoted.

QUOTES

- 'Perhaps next time you are judged unfairly, it will not take so many bruises for you to protest.' – *Worf teaches Sito a hard lesson*

TRIVIA

- Fans assumed that at least some of the characters from this show would appear in *Voyager*, which had been announced by this point and would debut the following January. There were good grounds for thinking this (Season five had introduced Ensign Ro and had further increased O'Brien's role in the show, with an eye to moving both of them over to *Deep Space Nine*), but this show was never considered as anything other than a one-off.

RATING

- A show that quickly sketches in some young, likeable characters who we come to care about. If only some of them had made it to *Voyager*. It's a good episode, one that (like *Tapestry*) shows us the familiar crew through the eyes of the junior officers. Because the new characters aren't regulars, there's a real sense of jeopardy, and as it turns out it's an entirely justified one.

7.16 THINE OWN SELF

STARDATE 47611.2

Data loses his memory on a pre-industrial planet

A probe has crashed on Barkon IV, scattering radioactive debris. Data is sent to retrieve it, but suffers amnesia when the radiation affects his positronic brain. He wanders into a village, spreading radiation sickness. The townsfolk have no idea what is afflicting them, and

TX 14 February 1994
WRITER Ronald D Moore (story by Christopher Hutton)
DIRECTOR Winrich Kolbe
GUEST CAST Majel Barrett (Computer Voice), Kimberly Cullum (Hia), Ronnie Claire Edwards (Talur), Michael G Hagerty (Skoran), Andy Kossin (Apprentice), Richard Ortega-Miro (Rainer), Michael Rothhaar (Garvin)

suspicion quickly falls on Data. Back on the Enterprise, Deanna is taking the tests that see her promoted to Commander. An angry mob attacks Data, exposing his circuitry. Data is killed by the mob (or so they think) and buried. He is recovered by Riker and Beverly. He cures the villagers of radiation sickness.

TRIVIA

- Deliberately written as a homage to *Frankenstein*, with an angry mob of villagers pursuing Data with a pitchfork.
- Patrick Stewart has his smallest part as Picard – one line.

RATING

- An episode that's a rare thing as *The Next Generation* draws to a close – a Data episode that's not effects-intensive and which allows Brent Spiner to play Data well, rather than revel in multiple roles. A simple story, but one that's solid and works.

7.17 MASKS

STARDATE 47615.2

Data becomes the repository for the knowledge of a dead civilisation

TX 21 February 1994
WRITER Joe Menosky
DIRECTOR Robert Wiemer
GUEST CAST Rickey D'Shon Collins (Eric Burton)

The Enterprise is investigating a comet when they discover it's the archive of a dead civilisation from the D'Arsay system that has been dead for 87 million years. A sensor scan activates a replication program that begins restructuring areas of the ship to resemble the dead planet. It also affects Data, who begins speaking in the voices of various characters from the extinct culture. Picard orders the destruction of the archive when sections of the Enterprise transform into jungle – but Engineering falls victim before the order can be carried out. Data has taken to wearing the mask Masaka, one of the legendary characters who represents the sun. Picard puts on the mask of Korgano, the moon, and chases the sun away. The ship and Data return to normal.

TRIVIA

- The comet was created using CGI by the same studio that created the comet in the *Deep Space Nine* opening credits.

RATING

- Brent Spiner seems to have had a clause in his contract that he got to play a certain number of stories out of character, to prove he didn't just do androids. He gets to work through his repertoire here, but one suspects that the finale, where he and Patrick Stewart face each other in ridiculous-looking masks (Stewart's is real handcrafted silver, but looks like tinfoil), doesn't appear on either of the actors' showreels. This story isn't half as meaningful as the people making it seem to think.

7.18 EYE OF THE BEHOLDER

STARDATE 476221.1

Troi investigates the suicide of a young officer

TX 28 February 1994
WRITER René Echevarria (story by Brannon Braga)
DIRECTOR Cliff Bole
GUEST CAST Nancy Harewood (Nara), Nora Leonhardt (Marla E Finn), Tim Lounibos (Dan Kwan), Johanna McCloy (Mattie Calloway), Mark Rolston (Walter Pierce), Dugan Savoye (William Hodges)

Lt Kwan has committed suicide by throwing himself into the plasma stream of the ship's engines. Troi investigates, getting an overwhelming sense of fear and panic when she looks into the plasma screen, which she deduces is an empathic echo. She and Worf investigate further. Troi feels herself briefly transported back eight years to the initial construction of the ship. Kwan was working there at the time, as was one other crewman: Walter Pierce. Troi and Worf become close, but Troi is jealous to see Worf with Kwan's girlfriend. Pierce stirs up further trouble between them. Troi kills Worf in her anger, then finds herself facing the plasma stream. Worf stops her – it's only been moments since she first looked at the plasma stream. Pierce committed murder eight years before, after catching his lover with another man. Kwan, an empath, picked up on that, and re-enacted it. Troi would have, too, if Worf hadn't restrained her.

TRIVIA

- There was some debate about whether Gene Roddenberry would have let one of his characters commit suicide (except in the name of the greater good, of course). The rule seemed to be that humans didn't, but aliens could – Worf wanted to in *Ethics*. Kwan's death isn't actually suicide, though.
- Nora Leonhardt had been Marina Sirtis' stand-in for many years. Here she plays the murdered woman in the flashbacks, and gets a couple of lines.
- Worf and Troi sleep together in this episode, after a relationship that's been hinted at since *Parallels*. However, this big step is part of the hallucination, something that some of the actors and writers seemingly forget about later in the season.

RATING

- Quite a creepy episode, albeit another one that has Troi investigating something and becoming the terrified victim by the end. There's a little confusion as to where Troi's hallucination begins, and the ending feels like a cop-out. But the episode works, and at least none of the crew's families show up.

7.19 GENESIS

STARDATE 47653.2

The crew revert to animalistic lower life-forms

TX 21 March 1994
WRITER Brannon Braga
DIRECTOR Gates McFadden
GUEST CAST Majel Barrett (Computer Voice), Carlo Ferro (Dern), Dwight Schultz (Reg Barclay), Patti Yasutake (Ogawa)

Picard and Data take a shuttle to retrieve a test torpedo. Beverly treats two expectant mothers – newly-wed Ogawa and Data's cat, Spot, as well as treating Barclay for Urodelan Flu. The crew begin to act oddly, with Troi feeling cold and Riker unable to think straight. Worf has a growth on his neck – a venom sac. The entire crew is affected. Picard and Data return to find the Enterprise drifting. Data discovers that a vaccine Beverly created for Barclay has activated introns, regressive parts of their cells, and they are regressing at different rates down the evolutionary ladder. Barclay has become a spider-like creature, Troi an amphibian and Riker an apeman. Spot's kittens are normal, although Spot's reverted to an iguana. Picard fights off a bestial Worf while Data follows up that clue and finds a cure. The crew quickly revert to normal, and the condition is named Barclay's Protomorphosis Syndrome.

TRIVIA

- This episode saw a huge effort on the part of the make-up team, and extra hours for the regular cast who underwent extensive makeup jobs. Michael Dorn was, for once, one of the least made-up characters, but scheduling meant that his stunt double Rusty McLennon played what the script called 'the Worf-beast'.
- Gates McFadden directed the episode which, by accident or design, fitted her previous experience as choreographer of the Jim Henson movie *Labyrinth*. She understood the technology (and just importantly the limitations) of the puppetry involved.

RATING

- Gates McFadden proves herself to be adept at directing horror – it's very rare that *Star Trek* makes you jump. The make up is imaginative and well-realised. The problem, though, is the story, which manages to be predictable while making no sense at all.

7.20 JOURNEY'S END

STARDATE 47751.2

Wesley rebels against Picard to save a colony of Indians

TX 28 March 1994
WRITER Ronald D Moore (story by Shawn Piller and Antonio Napoli)
DIRECTOR Corey Allan
GUEST CAST George Aguilar (Wakasa), Tom Jackson (Lakanta), Erik Menyuk (Traveler), Natalija Nogulich (Alynna Nechayev), Richard Poe (Gul Evek), Ned Romero (Anthwarta), Jack Wert (Jack Crusher), Wil Wheaton (Wesley Crusher)

The Enterprise is ordered to evacuate the colony of Dorvan V, which has been ceded to the Cardassians in the recent peace treaty. The planet is occupied by American Indians, who'd opted to maintain their own culture rather than submit to the homogeneity of the Federation. Picard pleads their case, but the Cardassians arrive and aren't interested in compromise. Wesley is with the Enterprise on leave from Starfleet Academy. He meets the colonist Lakanta, has a vision of his father, telling him to 'find his own way', and warns the Indians of a plan to abduct them from the planet using the transporters. Picard is furious, and Wesley resigns his commission. Lakanta is The Traveler, and together he and Wesley stay on the planet to help Wesley take his first steps to a new plane of existence. The Indians agree to live under the Cardassians, renouncing Federation citizenship.

TRIVIA

- Another attempt to tie up loose ends before the series ends – this time, reconciling The Traveler's prediction for Wesley in *Where No One Has Gone Before* with the headstrong cadet seen in *The First Duty*.
- The show took advice from Native Americans, who were happy for characters to refer to the colonists as 'Indians', but who didn't want them identified as Hopi tribe, as the original script specified.
- The next time we see Wesley is in *Star Trek: Nemesis*, as a (non-speaking, in the theatrical release) guest at Riker and Troi's wedding. There is no sign there that he's transcended our plane of reality; indeed, he's wearing Starfleet dress uniform.

RATING

- There's the usual clichéd modern Hollywood version of Indians – all traditions, stubborn refusal to leave land and dreamquests, vying with Wesley whinging. It's not exactly an appealing prospect. The episode only seems to exist to pay off the Traveller's first season prediction for Wesley.

7.21 FIRSTBORN

STARDATE 47779.4

Alexander and Worf become embroiled in Klingon politics

TX 25 April 1994
WRITER René Echevarria (story by Mark Kalbfeld)
DIRECTOR Jonathan West
GUEST CAST Majel Barrett (Computer Voice), Brian Bonsall (Alexander), Rickey D'Shon Collins (Eric Burton), Michael Danek ('Kahless'), Barbara March (Lursa), Colin Mitchell (Gorta), Armin Shimerman (Quark), John Kenton Shull ('Molor'), James Sloyan (K'Mtar/Alexander), Joel Swetow (Yog), Gwynyth Walsh (B'Etor)

Worf tries to pique Alexander's interest in Klingon culture by taking him to a celebration of the festival of Kot'baval on Maranga IV. Assassins from the Duras faction try to kill them, but they are saved by a Klingon called K'Mtar. Alexander wants to learn more from K'Mtar, but K'Mtar is frustrated that Worf's son lacks the killer instinct natural to Klingons. Worf becomes angry at K'Mtar's attitude. The Enterprise tracks down the Duras sisters, discovering that the knife used in the assassination attempt belonged to B'Etor's son. But she is pregnant with her first child. K'Mtar reveals the truth – he is Alexander from 40 years in the future. In his future, Alexander was a pacifist, and unable to prevent his father's dishonourable death. Worf realises that Alexander must find his own future, not have anyone's version of Klingon culture imposed on him.

TRIVIA

- An episode beset with availability issues: Patrick Stewart was filming a stint of *Saturday Night Live*, Suzi Plakson wasn't available to return as K'Ehleyr, child actor Brian Bonsall could only work limited hours, and the holodeck fight sequence ate up most of those.
- Alexander is now 'ten', despite being only three when K'Ehleyr died in *Reunion*, less than three years ago. Presumably, B'etor's son is born before *Star Trek: Generations*, but we don't know if he dies with his mother.
- The original episode had a Klingon/Federation ship from the future with a future Riker, but this was changed, presumably to avoid a clash with the future seen in *All Good Things*.

RATING

- A story with elements of the *Back to the Future* films and the animated episode *Yesteryear*. Again, it's abruptly tying up old story elements involving families, and it's not entirely satisfying, but the identity of K'Mtar is a good surprise.

7.22 BLOODLINES

STARDATE 47829.1

A Ferengi threatens to kill Picard's long lost son

TX 2 May 1994
WRITER Nicholas Sagan
DIRECTOR Les Landau
GUEST CAST Lee Arenberg (Bok), Majel Barrett (Computer Voice), Ken Olandt (Jason Vigo), Amy Pietz (Sandra Rhodes), Michelan Sisti (Tol), Peter Slutsker (Birta)

DaiMon Bok sends a holographic message to Picard – he is going to avenge his son's death by killing Picard's son, Jason Vigo. About 24 years before, Picard had a relationship with Miranda Vigo, so it's possible that the Jason Vigo on Camor V is his son. In any case, the young man is in great danger, so the Enterprise heads there. Genetic testing proves that Picard is the father, and the Enterprise heads after Bok. Beverly discovers that Jason has Forrester Trent Syndrome. Picard and Jason struggle to get on, and it's clear Jason has drifted in life without a father figure. Bok kidnaps Jason, and Picard transports after them. He knows that Jason isn't really his son – Bok has resequenced Jason's DNA, giving him the disorder that Beverly detected. Picard convinces Bok's crewmates that there is no profit in Bok's quest and Jason is freed. Jason says he will try to sort out his life.

TRIVIA

- Evidence, if it was needed, that Patrick Stewart had a degree of creative input to the show by now – this was a story suggested by him. He felt that the events of *The Battle* hadn't been fully resolved.
- A rare example of a continuity mistake – this story calls the system in *The Battle* Xendi Kabu, not Xendi Sabu.
- The role of Bok was recast, although Lee Arenberg was already a Ferengi veteran, having appeared in *Force of Nature*, and the *Deep Space Nine* story *The Nagus* in different Ferengi roles.

RATING

- The Picard-Jason relationship is a little too reminiscent of the Kirk-David relationship one in *Star Trek II: The Wrath of Khan*, although it's interesting to see an 'ordinary person' suddenly thrust into the life-and-death Starfleet situations. A story that's OK but not brilliant.

7.23 EMERGENCE

STARDATE 47869.2

The Enterprise seems to have developed sentience

TX 9 May 1994
WRITER Joe Menosky (story by Brannon Braga)
DIRECTOR Cliff Bole
GUEST CAST Vinny Argiro (Hitman), David Huddlestone (Conductor), Thomas Kopache (Engineer), Arlee Reed (Hayseed)

Picard and Data are discussing *The Tempest* on the holodeck when the Orient Express nearly runs them over. It's the first of a series of computer faults, which Data puts down to interference from a magnascopic storm. Riker, Worf and Data return to the holodeck, where seven programs are overlapping. Data surmises that the Enterprise has become sentient, and is working through its thoughts on the holodeck. The Enterprise flies itself to a white dwarf star and collects vertiform particles. It is trying to create a new life-form, but runs out of vertiforms. The crew uses the holodeck to persuade the ship to go to the MacPherson Nebula with more of the particles. A new life-form is created and leaves the ship, which returns to normal.

TRIVIA

- Keen to visit the holodeck one last time, the writers originally planned a final Dixon Hill story, but failed to find a new angle.

RATING

- An episode that's seemingly there to show how far effects had come on in seven years, and to show some more surreal holodeck images before the series ends. The story is the usual holodeck-affecting-reality one, but the visuals are very impressive.

7.24 PRE-EMPTIVE STRIKE

STARDATE 47941.7

Ro infiltrates the Maquis, and finds much to admire there

TX 16 May 1994
WRITER René Echevarria (story by Naren Shankar)
DIRECTOR Patrick Stewart
GUEST CAST Shannon Cochran (Kalita), Michelle Forbes (Ro Laren), John Franklin-Robbins (Macias), Natalija Nogulich (Alynna Nechayev), Richard Poe (Gul Evek), William Thomas Jr (Santos)

Ro returns after a year, promoted to Lieutenant. The Maquis crisis is growing, and she's been ordered to infiltrate the rebel group in the Demilitarised Zone. She soon discovers a Cardassian plot to bring in biogenic weapons for use against the Maquis. Ro stages a raid on the Enterprise to steal medical supplies, gaining the trust of her Maquis colleagues. Picard can see she's beginning to sympathise with the Maquis cause, and Riker is ordered to help her round up the cell she's made contact with. Ro's mentor, Macias, is killed in an ambush and Ro decides to join the Maquis. She holds Riker hostage until she and the Maquis can get away. She tells Riker to pass a message to Picard: she's sorry she betrayed his trust in her.

TRIVIA

- Another loose end is tied up. Michelle Forbes' agent had made it clear that she wouldn't return, but Jeri Taylor phoned the actress herself and she agreed to do one episode. The story originally had less involvement from the series regulars, and made more of the biogenic weapon story.

RATING

- An episode where *The Next Generation* slips into *Deep Space Nine* territory. Michelle Forbes is excellent, far better than the material, and it's not hard to see why she hadn't been keen to spend seven years as second in command to Avery Brooks. The story presents the character with the only logical, send-off, but it feels a little too tired to be fully successful.

7.25 ALL GOOD THINGS

As Picard moves through past, present and future, Q returns to pass judgement on humanity

DOUBLE-LENGTH EPISODE
TX 23 May 1994
WRITER Brannon Braga and Ronald D Moore
DIRECTOR Winrich Kolbe
GUEST CAST Majel Barrett (Computer Voice), Alison Brooks (Chilton), Denise Crosby (Tasha Yar), Stephen Matthew Garvey (Ensign), Andreas Katsulas (Tomalak), Tim Kellehar (Gaines), Pamela Kosh (Jessel), Clyde Kusatsu (Nakamura), John de Lancie (Q), Colm Meaney (O'Brien), Patti Yasutake (Ogawa)

STARDATE 47988.1

Picard tells Worf and Troi he is slipping through time. In the future, Picard is suffering from Irumodic Syndrome, senility. In the past, he approaches the Enterprise-D for the first time with Tasha Yar. In the present, Starfleet informs him of a vast spatial anomaly. This anomaly has appeared in all three time zones. The future Picard seeks advice from Data, a professor at Cambridge. They head into the Klingon Neutral Zone in the USS Pasteur, commanded by Beverly Picard, to investigate the anomaly. Suddenly, Picard is in Q's courtroom. Q tells him it is time for the verdict in his trial of humanity – they are guilty, and are to be destroyed. Picard gets a ship to the anomaly in all three time zones. The anomaly erupts with 'anti-time'. Admiral Riker arrives with the future Enterprise-D to save the Pasteur from the Klingons. Across three time zones, Picard and Data realise that the anomaly has formed in the future and is working backwards through time – Q informs Picard it will eventually reach back billions of years and prevent life on Earth from ever forming. Picard sacrifices himself and the Enterprise across all three timezones – and the anomaly collapses. Q congratulates him on his insight – this is just a glimpse of humanity's potential. Picard joins the officers' poker game for the first time, telling them 'the sky's the limit'.

QUOTES

- 'You had such potential. But then again, all good things must come to an end' – *Q to Picard*

TRIVIA

- This was the highest-rated episode of *The Next Generation*, indeed of any episode of *Star Trek* (it got a Nielsen rating of 15.4, and was the most-watched television programme of the week in 13 of 19 areas of the United States) and won the Hugo Award for Best Dramatic Presentation.
- The script was produced at the same time as the one for *Generations*. Patrick Stewart went on record that he far preferred *All Good Things*. It may also have given him déjà vu: the story is a nod to Charles Dickens' *A Christmas Carol*, the subject of an acclaimed one-man stage show that Patrick Stewart has taken around the world and would later adapt for television.
- An early draft of the script had the future crew stealing the Enterprise-D from a museum, sneaking past holographic versions of their younger selves. The cast was unhappy that the sequence was dropped. The 'past' sequence was to have the Enterprise conn officer (played by Christian Slater) falling out with Picard and demanding a transfer, thus just missing out on the chance to appear in *The Next Generation* – the character's name was Lt Sutcliffe, after the 'fifth Beatle'.
- Picard calls O'Brien 'Chief' in the 'Farpoint' scenes, and shouldn't, as he didn't get that title until later – in *Encounter at Farpoint* he was a conn officer.
- The future Data has ten pet cats.

RATING

- After a shaky last season, *All Good Things* is a real return to form. Indeed, it's one of the best episodes of the most successful incarnation of *Star Trek*, a true celebration of the characters and situations that made the show so great. A real rollercoaster ride, it demonstrates how far the show has come – and makes good on the long forgotten plot of Q judging humanity from *Encounter at Farpoint* – as well as how much mileage there was left. Everyone gets a chance to shine, little character moments, cute stuff and their moment of glory, and fittingly it's another tour-de-force for Patrick Stewart. Fantastic stuff.

STAR TREK: THE MOVIES – PART II

The cast of The Next Generation
(1994-2002)

REGULAR CAST

Captain Jean-Luc Picard: Patrick Stewart (7-10)
William Riker: Jonathan Frakes (7-10)
Data: Brent Spiner (7-10, also plays B-4 in 10)
Deanna Troi: Marina Sirtis (7-10)
Worf: Michael Dorn (7-10, and as Worf's grandfather, also called Worf, in 6)
Geordi La Forge: LeVar Burton (7-10)
Dr Beverly Crusher: Gates McFadden (7-10)
Wesley Crusher: Wil Wheaton (cameo in 10)
Guinan: Whoopi Goldberg (7, cameo in 10)

Star Trek: Generations saw Kirk and Picard meet up thanks to the magic of time travel, and ended with Kirk's death. The baton had been passed from the original series to _The Next Generation_, and it was hoped that a younger crew would boost the Star Trek movies. The slow pace and generally unspectacular set pieces of the seventh film, (the only notable action sequence, the destruction of the Enterprise, had already been done in _Star Trek III: The Search for Spock_ and was an old-fashioned and rather primitive piece of model work, when most films had switched to computer-generated effects) led to a wild over-reaction for the second _The Next Generation_ feature, _Star Trek: First Contact_, a time-travelling epic battle against the Borg, set against the backdrop of humanity's crucial discovery of warp drive leading to first contact with the Vulcans – perhaps the key event in _Star Trek_'s future history.

This pendulum swing continued – the ninth film in the series, *Star Trek: Insurrection*, was a pastoral character piece which the cast were happy to declare was the first *Star Trek* 'date movie'. Meanwhile, the production values of the *Star Trek* television series were higher than ever. A common complaint about *Star Trek: Insurrection* was that it looked and felt more like a television episode than a movie. The movie industry had moved away from mid-budget films with mid-budget returns – *Star Trek: Insurrection* was a surprisingly expensive film that didn't live up to expectations.

It was four years (the longest gap between the release of the films) before the tenth movie, *Star Trek: Nemesis*. The latest, and reportedly last *Next Generation* film, *Star Trek: Nemesis* was an attempt to re-tell *Star Trek II: The Wrath of Khan* with a script by the writer of *Gladiator*, added action set-pieces and a huge FX budget. The intention seemed to have been to recast *Star Trek* movies in the image of current action blockbusters, but it didn't capture the imagination of movie-goers. *Star Trek: Nemesis* was a disappointment at the box office. It had a strong opening weekend, only very narrowly beaten to the Number One slot by Jennifer Lopez vehicle *Maid in Manhattan*, but plummeted out of the chart within a couple of weeks. Costing almost twice as much as *Star Trek: First Contact*, it made about half as much at the box office.

After four films, it's fair to say that *The Next Generation* has not matched its huge television success in the movies. The ensemble, character-driven, nature of the show doesn't suit the medium. *Star Trek: First Contact* works, but the other three are seriously flawed. Perhaps the main problem is that while the movies with the original cast were clearly more lavish than the series they were spun off from, the *The Next Generation* movies were often less impressive than some of the television episodes. If you can watch *The Best of Both Worlds* and *All Good Things* on television, why would you want to pay money to see *Star Trek: Insurrection*?

None of these films lost money, even just in terms of US domestic box office. When the video rentals and sales are taken into account, a film like *Star Trek II: The Wrath of Khan* must be one of Paramount's most profitable features ever. DVD has provided a new excuse for reissuing the films, then reissuing them again as Special Editions, then again in boxsets. *Star Trek: Nemesis* has already paid for itself, and will be a steady seller on DVD and the formats that succeed it long after people have forgotten who Jennifer Lopez is.

As such, it's very unlikely that *Star Trek: Nemesis* is really the last *Star Trek* film. Patrick Stewart has been careful not to rule out a return to *Star Trek* films, while also saying he's not interested in doing another *The Next Generation* movie. Rumours abound that the next film will cherry-pick the best characters from the various series and have them serve under Picard as part of some sort of Federation 'special forces' group. A cunning plan, if true, it would give the most popular and enduring characters more mileage, as well as freeing the producers from having to hire complete casts (including a few actors who were lucky to be on television, let alone deserving a movie career) and allowing a more fluid, innovative approach to storytelling in a *Star Trek* film. If nothing else, it lets fans speculate just who would make the team... assuming there are seven regulars, then... Picard, Worf, T'Pol (Vulcans are very long-lived), Seven of Nine, Odo, the Doctor and O'Brien?

The ten *Star Trek* movies are unique – a spin-off from a television series that makes for a steady movie 'franchise' that's been around for nearly a quarter of a century in its own right and has survived a complete change of cast. Their contribution to *Star Trek* as a whole includes stories that are the most epic in scope, the funniest comedy, the most spectacular action, the most emotional moments, the most quotable quotes. At the same time, the people making them are the first to admit they've got it wrong at least as often as they've got it right. There's always been an uneasy relationship between the demands of the loyal *Star Trek* audience and the mainstream one. In 1975, Paramount was convinced that *Star Trek* was the ideal format for an epic film that would storm the box office, blending high concept science fiction with characters the audience cared about and spectacular special effects. They were almost certainly right... but we've still not had that *Star Trek* film.

STAR TREK: THE MOVIES
PART II

STAR TREK: GENERATIONS

Picard enlists the help of Kirk to prevent a murderous scientist destroying all life on a planetary system

RELEASED 18 November 1994
WRITERS Ronald D Moore and Brannon Braga
(story by Rick Berman, Ronald D Moore and Brannon Braga)
DIRECTOR David Carson
CAST Malcolm McDowell (Soran), James Doohan (Scotty), Walter Koenig (Chekov), William Shatner (Kirk), Alan Ruck (Captain Harriman), Jacqueline Kim (Demora), Jenette Goldstein (Science Officer), Thomas Kopache (Comm Officer), Glenn Morshower (Navigator), Tim Russ (Lieutenant), Tommy Hinkley, John Putch, Christine Jansen (Journalists), Michael Mack (Ensign Hayes), Dendrie Taylor (Lieutenant Farrell), Patti Yasutake (Ogawa), Granville Ames (Transporter Chief), Henry Marshall (Security Officer), Brittany Parkyn (Girl with Teddy Bear), Majel Barrett (Computer Voice), Barbara March (Lursa), Gwynyth Walsh (B'Etor), Rif Hutton (Klingon Guard), Brian Thompson (Klingon Helm), Marcy Goldman, Jim Krestalude, Judy Levitt, Kristopher Logan, Gwen Van Dam (El Aurian Survivors), Kim Braden (Picard's Wife), Christopher James Miller (Picard's Nephew), Matthew Collins, Mimi Collins, Thomas Alexander Dekker, Madison Eginton, Olivia Hack (Picard's children)

STARDATE UNKNOWN

Kirk launches the USS Enterprise, NCC-1701-B. During the voyage, the ship comes across two El-Aurian ships trapped in a vast energy ribbon. Kirk takes command but the Enterprise is caught in the energy. Kirk repairs the deflector relays and saves the Enterprise, but when Scotty and Chekov go to find him, part of the hull and Kirk are missing. 48650.1: 78 years later. Picard is saddened when he receives a personal message. Meanwhile, Data successfully installs an emotion chip, a product of his creator Dr Noonien Soong, and begins experiencing the new sensations. The Enterprise is lured by a distress call. An El-Aurian, Dr Tolian Soran, kidnaps Geordi and doctors his VISOR to transmit images back to a Klingon ship commanded by Lursa and B'Etor. Geordi is returned to the Enterprise. The Klingons agree to transport Soran to Veridian III in return for his trilithium explosive. Picard discovers that Soran is 300 years old and a survivor of the El-Aurian transport ships, like Guinan. Guinan explains that the energy ribbon is the Nexus, a temporal anomaly inside which a person can experience all he desires: Soran wishes to enter the Nexus to recreate the family he has lost. Meanwhile, Picard reveals to Troi that his brother and nephew have died in a fire on Earth – Jean-Luc is now the last Picard. Data and Picard deduce that Soran plans to destroy the Veridian sun and enter the Nexus at the expense of millions of lives.

While Picard beams down to Veridian III to find Soran, the Duras sisters spy information about the Enterprise's shields. They decloak and fire through the shields, damaging the Enterprise. The Enterprise is able to fight back and destroys the Klingon ship, but Soran escapes to the planet below. The Enterprise saucer section crash-lands on the planet. Soran and Picard fight as the Nexus approaches. Soran destroys the Veridian sun, destroying the planet and the Enterprise crew and transporting himself and Picard into the Nexus. For a moment, Picard is reunited with his family at Christmas. An echo of Guinan tells Picard that he can leave the Nexus before he entered it and prevent Soran from destroying the Veridian sun. Picard decides he needs help and locates Kirk, an inhabitant of the Nexus living out his years on a farm in Iowa. Picard convinces Kirk to save the Universe one last time and together they leave the Nexus before the detonation. As Kirk battles with Soran, Picard tries to sabotage the explosive. Kirk throws Soran off the bridge but they find that the bomb's controls have been cloaked. In a final desperate moment, Kirk obtains a remote control that decloaks the bomb, but falls into the chasm. Picard is able to stop the missile launch, creating an explosion that kills Soran, and runs to Kirk, just in time to see him die. Picard buries Kirk and the crew are rescued by the USS Farragut.

QUOTES

- 'There was a time when I wouldn't hurt a fly. Then the Borg came. And they showed me that if there is one constant in this whole universe, it's death.' – *Soran*
- 'He must be the only engineer in Starfleet who doesn't go to Engineering.' – *B'Etor is frustrated by Geordi*
- 'I don't need to be lectured by you. I was out saving the universe when your grandfather was in diapers.' – *Kirk to Picard*
- 'Don't let them promote you. Don't let them transfer you. Don't let them do anything that takes you off the bridge of that ship because while you're there... you can make a difference.' – *Kirk to Picard*
- 'It was... fun... Oh my.' – *Kirk's last words*

TRIVIA

- Brannon Braga and Ronald Moore wrote *Star Trek: Generations* while completing work on the last season of *The Next Generation.* A key scene included in their first draft was the destruction of the Enterprise, based on a drawing in Sternbach and Okuda's *Star Trek: The Next Generation Technical Manual* (looking at the book, a number of drawings seems to have made their way onto screen, including a communications array and details of the warp core breach).

- When Braga and Moore mooted the idea of Kirk's death, the studio insisted that they consult Shatner. They were surprised that he accepted the idea from the outset. Originally, Kirk was shot in the back by Soran but this did not play well with audiences and a new, more heroic ending for Kirk had to be filmed.
- The horse, home and farm where Kirk lives in the Nexus are all owned by William Shatner.
- There is a cryptic line in the film where Soran says of Geordi's interrogation that the engineer's 'heart wasn't in it'. This is a reference to a probe used by Soran to start and stop Geordi's heart, which was filmed but cut. Crusher also later refers to the probe and the full torture scene makes it into the novelisation.
- Dom Perignon created three bottles of their '2265' vintage specially for the film, reportedly the first time they'd ever done such a thing. The first bottle was filmed smashing against the side of the Enterprise-B at its launch, the second was sold for £1,200 in a wine auction at the Royal Albert Hall in 1995. The third had been an auction item at a Star Trek convention the previous year... until Marina Sirtis dropped and broke it while showing it off.
- The destruction of Lursa and B'Etor's ship is reused footage from *Star Trek VI: The Undiscovered Country*.
- The model of the Enterprise B is a modified version of that of the Excelsior, first seen in *Star Trek IV: The Voyage Home* and several episodes of *The Next Generation* subsequently.
- Kirk's final words, 'Oh my,' were apparently ad-libbed on location.
- Tim Russ, later Tuvok in *Voyager*, has a small role as an officer on the Enterprise-B.
- Most of the Enterprise-D sets were destroyed during filming. The exceptions – crew quarters, transporter room and engineering, were redressed and reused as parts of the USS Voyager.
- The second transport ship trapped in the energy ribbon at the beginning of the film is the SS Robert Fox, a reference to the Federation Ambassador in *A Taste of Armageddon*.
- A last-minute panic came 50 hours before filming was to begin in the studio when the crew discovered that the captain's chair had been stolen from the bridge set! A new one had to be constructed in the time.
- *Star Trek: Generations* had a budget of $35m and made $23m back in its opening weekend. It went on to make $75m in the USA and $120m worldwide, with rentals in excess of $110m.

RATING

- A fairly lacklustre beginning to *The Next Generation* in the cinemas. There's nothing inherently wrong with the core idea, but the scripting doesn't get the concepts across either quickly or simply. Because the Nexus is such an intangible notion, the threat is diluted. The scenes with Kirk at the end seem horribly out of place and there's an unhealthy clash of styles. The final battle on the bridge – a fist-fight between three actors with a collective age of 168 – is drab and anti-climactic. What's really missing is *The Next Generation*'s sense of family and community. Their first movie should involve everyone in the fray, not give it all to Picard.

STAR TREK: FIRST CONTACT

STARDATE 50893.5

The Enterprise crew battle to prevent the Borg from changing Earth's history

RELEASED 22 November 1996
WRITERS Brannon Braga and Ronald D Moore (story by Rick Berman, Brannon Braga and Ronald D Moore)
DIRECTOR Jonathan Frakes
CAST Alfre Woodard (Lily), James Cromwell (Zefram Cochrane), Alice Krige (Borg Queen), Michael Horton (Security Officer), Neal McDonough (Lt. Hawk), Marnie McPhail (Eiger), Robert Picardo (Holographic Doctor), Dwight Schultz (Lt. Barclay), Adam Scott (Defiant Conn Officer), Jack Shearer (Admiral Hayes), Eric Steinberg (Porter), Scott Strozier (Security Officer), Patti Yasutake (Ogawa), Victor Bevine, David Cowgill, Scott Haven, Annette Helde (Guards), Majel Barrett (Computer Voice), C J Bau (Bartender), Hillary Hayes (Ruby), Julie Morgan (Singer in Nightclub), Ronald R Rondell (Henchman), Don Stark (Nicky the Nose), Cully Fredricksen (Vulcan), Tamara Lee Krinsky (Townsperson), Don Fishcer, J R Horsting, Heinrich James, Andrew Palmer, John David Weigand, Dan Woren, Robert L Zachar (Borg)

Picard is haunted by nightmares of his assimilation into the Borg. He awakens to hear that the Borg have destroyed a colony and are heading to Earth, but is told to patrol the Neutral Zone. Picard fears that Starfleet feels he may compromise the mission. He breaks orders and joins the fleet, saving Worf and the crew of the Defiant before taking control of the starships. The combined attack destroys the Borg Cube but an escape pod creates a temporal vortex and lands on Earth in the past. Twenty-first century Earth is assimilated. Picard decides to follow the pod into the past and prevent the Borg changing history. They arrive on the day before unconventional rocket scientist Zefram Cochrane is due to make the first warp journey and make first contact. The Enterprise destroys the Borg ship, but is too late to prevent it damaging Cochrane's complex. The officers rescue Lily, one of Cochrane's workers, and take her back to the Enterprise for medical treatment. Geordi, Riker and Troi help put Cochrane's program back on schedule. Meanwhile on the Enterprise, two crewmembers are attacked. Picard realises that Borg survivors have transported onto the ship and are assimilating it. As Picard hunts down the Borg, the medical officers scramble into an air vent, losing Lily in the process.

Data is captured by the Borg and introduced to the Borg Queen, who gives him human sensations of touch. On Earth, Geordi persuades Cochrane of their mission by showing him the Enterprise in orbit. Cochrane is uncomfortable with the heroic image Geordi holds of him and resorts to drink. On the Enterprise, Lily obtains a weapon and demands answers from Picard. They hide in the Dixon Hill holodeck program. Picard disables the safety measures and kills the Borg, but Lily is disturbed by the ferocity of his attack, and his casual disregard for the Borg foot-soldiers, once his crewmen. As the Borg Queen seduces Data, Picard, Worf and Hawk discover the Borg are trying to contact their twenty-first century counterparts using the Enterprise's main deflector. They are able to stop the attempt, but lose Hawk in the process. The senior officers suggest that they destroy the Enterprise but Picard refuses to sacrifice the ship. It is only when Lily reminds Picard of the story of Ahab and his downfall that Picard realises his error. He orders the ship's evacuation and initiates the self-destruct. On Earth, Cochrane, Geordi and Riker board the Phoenix for the first warp voyage and launch into orbit. Picard tries to rescue Data but finds him a willing slave to the Borg. Data disables the Enterprise's self-destruct and gives control of the ship to the Borg. The Borg target the Phoenix but at the last moment Data betrays them, releasing a gas into Engineering that destroys all organic material. As Picard scrambles to safety, Data drags the Borg Queen into the gas, killing her. Cochrane is able to complete his flight and returns to Earth to receive its first alien visitors – the Vulcans. The Enterprise crew witness the event and return to the twenty-fourth century.

QUOTES

- 'I'm a doctor, not a doorstop.' – *the emergency medical hologram protests when he is used to hold back the Borg*
- 'Timeline! This is no time to argue about time! We don't have the time... What was I saying?' – *A drunk Deanna Troi*
- 'I will not sacrifice the Enterprise – we've made too many compromises already, too many retreats. They invade our space and we fall back. Decimate entire worlds and we fall back. Not again. The line must be drawn here. This far, no further. And I will make them pay for what they've done.' – *Picard's Ahab moment*
- 'Borg? Sounds Swedish.' – *Lily*

TRIVIA

- Braga and Moore reputedly thought that *Deep Space Nine* was to be cancelled when they were called to Rick Berman's office – only to be asked to write the second *The Next Generation* movie. The Borg were a feature from the outset with the Borg Queen, added to personalise the enemy. Braga suggested a time-travel element, but there was debate over the time period, with Renaissance Italy apparently a contender. Once they settled on the near future, Braga and Moore latched onto using Zefram Cochrane, the creator of warp drive, who appeared in the original series episode *Metamorphosis.*
- The part of Zefram Cochrane was reportedly offered to Tom Hanks, but filming coincided with his movie *That Thing You Do* (1996). James Cromwell, alias Farmer Hoggett in the *Babe* movies and Captain Smith in *LA Confidential* (1997), got the part – and became the first actor in the show to utter the words 'star trek'.
- The footage of the Phoenix's launch from Montana is reused in the *Enterprise* title sequence. James Cromwell reprised the role of Cochrane for the pilot episode, *Broken Bow,* in which he is seen dedicating the Warp 5 Complex.
- Perennial *Star Trek* favourite *Moby Dick* is a large part of the theme of the movie. Patrick Stewart would go on from *Star Trek: First Contact* to film a TV version of the Melville novel in which he played Ahab.
- The bartender in the Dixon Hill sequence is played by Ethan Phillips, alias Neelix in *Voyager.* In the background of the same scene, Jonathan Frakes can be spotted playing the trombone in the band.
- The character of Ensign Lynch is reportedly a reference to a *Star Trek* fan of the same name who established a website and reviewed every episode of *The Next Generation* and *Deep Space Nine.*
- Jonathan Frakes reportedly gained the nickname 'Two-Takes Frakes' for his fast shooting style on the movie.
- The location for first contact, a missile silo in Montana, is a reference to a site that has been a popular haunt for UFO sightings for more than 20 years.
- The Enterprise-E is a Sovereign Class ship (Enterprise-D was Galaxy Class). Animators at Industrial Light and Magic also created new classes of ship for the battle against the Borg at the beginning of the film, including Akira, Sabre and Steamrunner class.
- *Star Trek: First Contact* was the first Star Trek movie to receive a rating higher than PG. It was rated PG-13 in the US and 12 in the UK. It had a total budget of $45m and made $30m on its opening weekend. It made $90m on the domestic market and an estimated $150m worldwide. Rentals have been in excess of $200m.

RATING

- Leagues ahead of *Star Trek: Generations, Star Trek: First Contact* has the tempo and tone of a hit from the first scene. Patrick Stewart revels in the Ahab plot, with some fantastically tense scenes between Picard and Lily. Picard's confrontation with Worf is particularly noteworthy. If there's a problem it's that the Zefram Cochrane plot gets a bit more time than its worth, but this is a small price to pay for the action on the Enterprise. This isn't difficult stuff, but it's directed with vigour by Frakes and has something that the other *The Next Generation* movies lack – tone. All in all, one of the better movies, with any cast.

STAR TREK: INSURRECTION

Picard refuses to let an idyllic civilisation be destroyed

RELEASED 11 December 1998
WRITER Michael Piller (story by Rick Berman and Michael Piller)
DIRECTOR Jonathan Frakes

STARDATE UNKNOWN

The Federation is undergoing a joint scientific mission with the Son'a in a planet in the 'Briar Patch', an area of space cut off from the rest of the galaxy. Data is on the mission, which is concealed from the 600 peaceful natives who live in a rural idyll. Suddenly, Data goes berserk, and reveals himself to the natives. Admiral Dougherty contacts Picard to ask for Data's schematics – they need to shut him down. The Enterprise heads for the planet, and Picard and Worf recover Data. Dougherty is keen for Picard to leave – the villagers have taken their survey team hostage. But when Picard beams down, he discovers that the team are fine... indeed, their health has improved. The crew of the Enterprise are feeling better than they have for years. Geordi has his sight for the first time in his life. Worf is the only one to suffer, as he seems to be reliving puberty. Picard meets the beautiful Anij, and realises she's centuries old. Data is repaired, although he has amnesia, and together he and Picard discover a Federation

GUEST CAST F Murray Abraham (Ru'afo), Donna Murphy (Anij), Anthony Zerbe (Dougherty), Gregg Henry (Gallatin), Daniel Hugh Kelly (Sojef), Michael Welch (Artim), Mark Deakins (Tournel), Stephanie Niznik (Kell Perim), Michael Horton (Daniels), Bruce French (Son'a Officer #1), Breon Gorman (Curtis), John Hostetter (Bolian Officer), Rick Worthy (Elloran Officer #1), Larry Anderson (Tarlac Officer), D Elliot Woods (Starfleet Officer), Jennifer Tung (Ensign), Raye Birk (Son'a Doctor), Peggy Miley (Cuzar), Lee Arnone-Briggs (Starfleet Librarian – scenes deleted), Claudette Nevins (Son'a Officer #2), Max Grodenchik (Alien Ensign – scenes deleted), Greg Poland (Elloran Officer #2), Kenneth Lane Edwards (Ensign), Joseph Ruskin (Son'a Officer #3), Zachary Williams (Ba'ku Child), McKenzie Westmore (Ba'ku Woman), Phillip Glasser (Young Ru'afo – scenes deleted), Amy Miller (Dabo girl – uncredited), Brian Scheu (Artim's Friend – uncredited)

holoship in a nearby lake – Dougherty and Ru'afo, the leader of the Son'a, are planning to relocate the population. The Son'a are ancient and dying, only kept alive by constant surgery. Dougherty tells Picard he is acting with the authority of the Federation Council, which wants to harness the healing powers of the metaphasic radiation that bathes the planet. Picard decides to disobey the direct orders of the Council and save the villagers. His bridge officers won't let him go alone. Riker and Geordi stay behind to take the Enterprise out of the Briar Patch and contact the Federation to show how unpleasant the Son'a plans are. Meanwhile, Picard and the others lead the villagers to safety. Ru'afo has had enough – he launches an attack on the village and sends ships to destroy the Enterprise. When Dougherty objects, Ru'afo kills him. Picard leads the villagers to caves, but many are abducted by the Son'a transporters. Eventually, Picard is caught. It becomes clear that the Son'a and Ba'ku are genetically identical. The Son'a are young rebels, who left the planet to go into the wider galaxy. Ru'afo is consumed with desire to destroy the Ba'ku, and he activates the Collector, a device that will collect the metaphasic radiation, killing anyone on the surface. Picard beams across and sets the Collector to self-destruct before Ru'afo can stop him. The Enterprise beams Picard to safety, Ru'Afo is killed. As the villagers return home, Picard vows to return to Anij as soon as he can.

QUOTES

- 'Smooth as an android's bottom, Data.' – *Riker shows off his new unshaved face*
- 'Have you noticed how your boobs have started to firm up?'
  'Not that we care about things like that in this day and age.' – *Troi and Beverly compare notes*

TRIVIA

- Patrick Stewart (an Associate Producer of the movie) turned down the first script he read, describing it as 'dark and dreary'. In that draft, Picard killed Data, and the Starfleet Admiral was Duffy, an old friend of Picard's, making the dispute more heated and personal. Stewart also said publically that he was concerned that any *Star Trek* film would compare unfavourably to the new *Star Wars* movie in production at the time. He pushed for the film to be lighter, and liked the idea of a film about the 'fountain of youth'.
- The film had the working titles of *Nemesis* (eventually used for the tenth movie), *Rebellion, Millennium, Defiant, Betrayal, Sacred Honor* and *Stardust*. For a long time, it looked like it was going to be called *Prime Directive*, but this was apparently changed because Patrick Stewart hated the title.
- Originally Ru'Afo was to die falling through the rings of the planet, getting younger and younger as he fell. One rumour claimed Max Grodenchik played the young Ru'Afo, but Phillip Glasser is credited, despite the fact the scene didn't make the final cut. Grodenchik played an alien Ensign in another cut scene.
- The budget was around $58m ($12m of which reportedly went to Patrick Stewart, with $5m to Brent Spiner), and had been increased by the studio, who were happy with the film, but wanted a more spectacular effects-driven ending. Reports had it that the film tested well, particularly among women, which gave Paramount high hopes that it would reach a mainstream audience and become a surprise hit – initial marketing even described the film as 'a romantic comedy'. In the event, it performed much the same as *Star Trek: Generations*, and substantially below *Star Trek: First Contact*, making $22m on its opening weekend, going on to make about $70m in the US, and $120m more worldwide. Video rentals made up about another $110m worldwide.
- Pre-publicity seemed designed to tease fans with hints about the 'Troi and Riker bubble bath scene' and Picard falling in love, leading to rumours of nudity and a possible R-rating. As ever, the truth was far less raunchy. It has a PG rating in the UK, but only for two examples of bad language. British science fiction magazine *Dreamwatch* broke the news that Arnold Schwarzenegger was to have a cameo role (he didn't).
- This is the only *Star Trek* film with no scenes set on Earth.
- In the scene where the bridge officers catch Picard about to leave for the planet, Picard orders Riker and Geordi to stay on the ship. Oddly, the others are already in civilian clothes, Riker and Geordi aren't.
- Part of Michael Dorn's deal when he signed on as a regular on *Deep Space Nine* was that he wouldn't lose his place in *The Next Generation* movies. *Star Trek: First Contact* established a sensible reason why he was on the Enterprise (he's leading the attack against the Borg in the Defiant, and is taken on board when the ship was damaged). One of the funnier jokes in *Star Trek: Insurrection* is that when Picard asks Worf what he's doing on board, they're interrupted before he can explain.

RATING

- A film that feels like a reaction against *Star Trek: First Contact*, and which is deliberately smaller-scale and more character-driven. It takes care to portray the crew, particularly Picard, as rounded, decent people. However, it's just not very exciting. The central problem is that it's difficult to care about the Ba'ku, who come across as rather twee and unmemorable. It's certainly a school of thought that the fate of billions in the Federation *is* more important than preserving the good life for this handful of people who've deliberately downshifted. Apart from Anij, none are really drawn in as characters. Actresses often claim that there are few parts for older women – Anij ought to be a great role: a smart, funny, strong person who inspires Picard to disobey the Federation he holds so dear. As it is, though, Donna Murphy just can't hold her own against Patrick Stewart, and we have to rely on Picard telling us what he admires about her, we never get round to seeing it. While there are more action set pieces than you remember, and it's far more ambitious than the 'television episode on the big screen' fans said it was at the time, it's really hard to believe that the budget is more than double that of *Star Trek VI: The Undiscovered Country*, made only seven years before. Characters mention several times how the Federation is in real trouble, what with the Dominion War, the Cardassians and the Borg... and every time they do, it strikes you that it would have been much more interesting to watch the Enterprise tackle those than taking a few hundred villagers for a walk through the hills.

STAR TREK: NEMESIS

Picard battles his younger clone, who takes control of the Romulan Empire

RELEASED 13 December 2002
WRITER John Logan (story by John Logan, Rick Berman and Brent Spiner)
DIRECTOR Stuart Baird
CAST Brent Spiner (B-4), Tom Hardy (Shinzon), Ron Perlman (Viceroy), Shannon Cochran (Senator Tal'aura), Dina Meyer (Commander Donatra), Jude Ciccolella (Commander Suran), Alan Dale (Praetor Hiren), John Berg (Senator), Michael Owen (Helm Officer Branson), Kate Mulgrew (Admiral Janeway), Robertson Dean (Reman Officer), David Ralphe, J Patrick Mccormack (Commanders), Wil Wheaton (Wesley Crusher), Majel Barrett (Computer Voice)

STARDATE 56844.9

The Romulan leadership is assassinated when they reject calls to unite with the Remans, led by Shinzon. Meanwhile, Picard raises a toast to Riker and Troi, newly-weds about to join the USS Titan. *En route* to Betazed, Worf picks up a positronic signal, similar to Data's brain, coming from Kolarus III. Picard, Data and Worf discover an android, identical to Data, which identifies itself as B-4. Data downloads his memory into B-4, hoping to accelerate its learning process, but to no avail. As they puzzle over B-4, Admiral Janeway orders the Enterprise to Romulus where Shinzon has been made the new Praetor, the leader. After hours of waiting in orbit around Romulus, the Enterprise is suddenly dwarfed by a massive battleship, the Scimitar, that decloaks next to them. The Praetor's Viceroy leads the officers to Shinzon. They are stunned to discover that Shinzon looks like a younger Picard. Shinzon claims to have Shalaft's Syndrome, a rare disease that Picard shares, suggesting a blood link. Beverly establishes that Shinzon is actually a clone of Picard. They crew are mystified, as are Shinzon's supporters in the Romulan military who cannot fathom his obsession with Picard. Later, Shinzon tells Picard that he is the product of a Romulan plot to replace the captain with a clone. When the plan lost favour, he was sent to the dilithium mines of Remus, where he was cared for by one Reman, now his Viceroy. Shinzon wants freedom for his Reman brothers but Picard is suspicious.

Back on the Enterprise, Picard discovers that the ship's computer has been infiltrated and that the Scimitar is carrying thalaron radiation, a banned substance, suggesting it has a deadly weapon. That night, Troi's mind is infiltrated by Shinzon and the Viceroy. She is able to beat back their attempts to bond with her. Suddenly, Picard and B-4 are transported to the Scimitar: Shinzon planted B-4 and has used the android to access the Enterprise computer. Shinzon takes a blood sample from Picard before leaving. However, B-4 is actually Data, who realised Shinzon was using B-4 and has been feeding the Remans false information. Data and Picard steal a small craft and escape. Beverly discovers that Shinzon needs a blood transfusion to survive. Picard realises that Shinzon will come after him and plans to use the thalaron radiation weapon against Earth.

The Enterprise joins the Starfleet to intercept the Scimitar but the cloaked vessel quickly disables the ship's warp drive. Picard tries unsuccessfully to reason with Shinzon. The Enterprise receives welcome support from the Romulan collaborators, now disenchanted with Shinzon. Troi realises that she can use her mental link with the Viceroy to locate the cloaked Scimitar. The Enterprise fires on the Scimitar, forcing it to decloak, but loses its shields in the process. While Worf and Riker pick off Reman footsoldiers, Picard rams the crippled Enterprise into the Scimitar. Picard kills Shinzon in hand-to-hand combat, but it is too late to escape the Scimitar alive. Suddenly, Data arrives and beams Picard to safety before destroying the thalaron device and himself in the process. As the officers mourn, Picard struggles to explain Data's uniqueness to B-4 – but catches a small glimpse of his old friend in the new android.

QUOTES

- 'You are me! The same noble Picard blood runs through our veins. Had you lived my life, you'd be doing exactly as I am... Consider that, Captain... I can think of no greater torment for you.' – *Shinzon*
- 'We will *all* honour the Betazoid traditions. Now, if you'll excuse me, I'll be in the gym.' – *Picard prepares for Troi and Riker's naked wedding*
- 'You have the bridge, Mr Troi.' – *Picard to Riker*
- 'My life is meaningless as long as you are still alive. What am I while you exist? A shadow? An echo?' – *Shinzon to Picard*

TRIVIA

- The movie had its origins in a chance meeting between Brent Spiner and John Logan in Las Vegas. Spiner suggested that Logan, who had recently shared an Oscar nomination for his script of *Gladiator* (2000) and was working on *The Time Machine* (2002), write a *Star Trek* movie. Logan's pitch to Berman was a series of scene ideas, including the Romulans and Remans, the Enterprise crashing into another ship and the marriage of Riker and Troi in the first scene. Together, Logan, Berman and Spiner came up with a story about family and the nature/nurture debate. Patrick Stewart reportedly objected to the original draft, which had Shinzon as an unknown child, leading to the introduction of the clone plotline.
- As late as November 2000, a director had not been assigned to the movie. Berman ruled out Frakes on the grounds that he was busy with a movie for Paramount and Nickelodeon, *Clockstoppers* (2002). Instead, Stuart Baird directed *Star Trek*'s tenth cinematic outing. His previous directorial assignments include *Executive Decision* and *U.S. Marshals*. He had previously served as an editor on films such as *Superman*.
- The original cut of the movie was three hours long. Fifty minutes of additional footage was cut for the cinematic release. The most significant deletions relate to Shinzon's obsession with Troi, showing him tormenting the counsellor and leading to the rape scene that appears in the movie. Other deleted scenes include an extended cut of the wedding sequence featuring Wesley, more on Worf and his diplomatic duties, and all scenes featuring Steven Culp as Commander Martin Madden (Culp is credited but does not appear). There is also an extended ending in which Riker and Troi join the USS Titan, Picard gets a new First Officer (Madden) and a new chair with seat belt, and Beverly Crusher leaves to take a post at Starfleet Medical.
- Logan reportedly took inspiration for the Remans from Max Schreck's character, Graf Orlok, in the film *Nosferatu* (1922). Shinzon is a Chinese name meaning 'heart' and a Japanese name meaning 'new existence', although Logan claimed he had no idea what the name means.
- Jude Law was originally considered for the role of Shinzon. Michael Shanks, who played Dr Daniel Jackson in the *Stargate SG-1* TV series, read for the part. Tom Hardy, who had recently appeared in *Black Hawk Down*, was discovered when a former agent of Patrick Stewart recommended the actor to him.
- Ron Perlman is perhaps better known as the Beast in the TV series of *Beauty and the Beast*. Alan Dale, who plays the leader of the Romulan Senate, played Jim Robinson in Aussie soap *Neighbours*. He appears here with his *24* co-star, Jude Ciccolella (Commander Suran).
- Wil Wheaton (Wesley Crusher) was apparently asked back after he spoke to LeVar Burton on a special celebrity *Star Trek* edition of *The Weakest Link*. Wesley's scenes were cut from the final movie and he can only be seen as a non-speaking guest in the wedding scene.
- Bryan Singer makes a brief cameo appearance in the movie. Singer had already directed Patrick Stewart in *X-Men* (2000) and they were about to start work on *X-Men 2* (2003)
- The chair thief strikes again! After losing one captain's chair shortly before the filming of *Star Trek: Generations*, another went missing during filming for this movie. Scott Bakula, recording *Enterprise* on the next-door sound stage, presented Patrick Stewart with a small wooden chair, engraved with the word 'Kaptin,' as consolation.
- The Enterprise-E bridge was fixed on a moving base to allow the whole set to rock during battles. The British press quoted Patrick Stewart as saying that the cast could have just rocked from side to side and the producers could have saved themselves $1!
- The film has a few cute references to the rest of the franchise, including a manoeuvre named after Kirk, mentions of the Dominion War and the starship USS Archer. In the first draft, Seven of Nine was to make a cameo appearance, but Jeri Ryan landed the part of Ronnie Cooke in *Boston Public*, a TV show about a Boston high school and was otherwise engaged. Instead, Kate Mulgrew makes a brief cameo as Admiral Janeway. An early draft gave Ashley Judd's character, Robin Leffler from *Darmok* and *The Game*, a cameo.
- The wine that the crew drink at the end of the movie is Chateau Picard, a reference to the Picard family vineyard seen in *Family*.
- By the time of *Star Trek: Nemesis*, Picard has been captain of the Enterprise-E longer than he was captain of the Enterprise. According to the dates given in the official *Star Trek Chronology*, Picard is 74 years old in this story.
- *Star Trek: Nemesis* is the lowest-grossing movie of the franchise. The budget for *Star Trek: Nemesis* was around $70m, with a further $40m for marketing. A large portion of the budget was reportedly given to Digital Domain, James Cameron's visual effects company. Market analysts were sceptical, with *Business Week* observing that only one *The Next Generation* movie (*Star Trek: First Contact*) had broken the $100m takings figure that marks a blockbuster. The movie was released shortly after the James Bond outing *Die Another Day* and the second Harry Potter movie and only five days before Peter Jackson's *The Lord of the Rings: The Two Towers*. The analysts weren't wrong: the opening weekend saw a disappointing $18.75m taken at the box office. By the second weekend, the movie dropped from second in the charts to ninth, with a feeble $26m to its name. In light of the box office returns, Patrick Stewart, speaking at the opening of the *Star Trek: The Adventure* exhibition in Hyde Park, stated that *Star Trek: Nemesis* would be the final journey for (most of) *The Next Generation* cast.

RATING

- An astonishingly frustrating film, largely down to a very uncomfortably constructed final cut. This is a rich film, with many elements and plenty of mood, but the cut shows there is no concept of what it is *about*. At its heart, there's a very small-scale story around nature or nurture, with two Picards who have been raised differently and made different choices in life. Then there's the silent threat of an enormous battlecruiser, capable of destroying planets without warning. It's also littered with story problems – why doesn't Shinzon destroy the Earth first and then go after Picard? Picard is sure to come looking for him. Add to this annoying little details like the docking bay of smaller ships that are never used, the Troi storyline that is cut for time, and a rushed ending with characters departing off-screen, and you have a film that sets up more than it ever pays off. Disappointing, given that there's something worth making at the core of this.

STAR TREK: DEEP SPACE NINE

SEVEN SEASONS

170 x 44-minute and 3 x 88-minute episodes (1993-99)

REGULAR CAST

Benjamin Sisko: Avery Brooks
Odo: Rene Auberjonois
Julian Bashir: Siddig El Fadil
(credited as Alexander Siddig, seasons 4-7)
Jadzia Dax: Terry Farrell (Seasons 1-6)
Jake Sisko: Cirroc Lofton
Miles O'Brien: Colm Meaney
Quark: Armin Shimerman
Kira Nerys: Nana Visitor
Worf: Michael Dorn (Seasons 4-7)
Ezri Dax: Nicole de Boer (Season 7)

CREATED BY

Rick Berman and Michael Piller
(Based on Star Trek created by
Gene Roddenberry)

EXECUTIVE PRODUCERS

Rick Berman and Michael Piller

The autumn of 1991 saw the twenty-fifth anniversary of *Star Trek*, and the fifth season of *The Next Generation* reach new ratings highs – it would have easily been a top ten show if it was networked, rather than syndicated. Studio estimates were that each episode made over a million dollars profit.

It was pretty clear that *The Next Generation* would continue for a couple more years – but equally clear that (as with any show) it was at its peak and becoming more of a stretch to keep the series fresh the longer it carried on. The cast were well aware of the success of *The Next Generation*. With most of the main players only contracted until the end of the sixth season, some, notably Patrick Stewart and Brent Spiner, started openly saying they were looking to move on and develop a film career. 1991 also saw *Star Trek VI: The Undiscovered Country*, a sixth *Star Trek* film that served as a deliberate swansong for the original cast, as well as a bridge between *Star Trek* and *The Next Generation*. All these factors made it seem self-evident that *Star Trek VII* would feature *The Next Generation* crew (in the event, the cast all signed up for a seventh and final series before that).

While the jump to movies would solve a lot of the problems facing *The Next Generation*, it would also leave a big hole on TV, and on Paramount's budget sheets. The solution was obvious – a third *Star Trek* live action series. In late 1991, the thoughts of the production team turned to this. The two shows would run in parallel for a couple of years at least, and so the first question was how to differentiate them. It was quickly decided that the show would not be set on a starship. When word of a new *Star Trek* series emerged there was a great deal of speculation about the premise, most of it easy to rule out. One suggestion was a series set in the Klingon Empire. Make-up requirements alone, though, would make this incredibly expensive and time-consuming, and would have ruled that out straight away. George Takei had long lobbied for a series where Sulu commanded a ship, but the production team had already said it would be set at the time of *The Next Generation* and that it wouldn't be set on a starship, and the idea was never seriously considered. The smart money was on a Starfleet Academy series, particularly after *The First Duty*, a *The Next Generation* episode set there, had proved successful. However, producers Michael Piller and Rick Berman seem to have decided fairly quickly to set the series on a starbase.

Gene Roddenberry died on 26 October 1991. While Berman and Piller were always keen to stress the importance of Roddenberry's vision for *Star Trek*, the new series perhaps was a reaction against some of his restrictions. Pre-publicity stressed it would be a 'darker and grittier' *Star Trek* than viewers were used to. They stuck to Roddenberry's view that humanity wasn't selfish in the twenty-fourth century and co-operated, rather than argued – a rule that often infuriated writers on *The Next Generation* faced with a bridge full of officers agreeing with each other. However, the starbase would have a diverse staff and so there would be plenty of opportunity for 'character conflict'.

The series – called *Starbase 362* (a starbase never mentioned in the series itself) and *Star Trek: The Final Frontier* at points in its genesis – started to shape up. The basic premise of the show was taken from a couple of *The Next Generation* episodes. The starbase would orbit Bajor, a planet recovering from a recently ended war, a situation established in the episode *Ensign Ro*. Indeed, the character of Ensign Ro would make the jump to the new series from *The Next Generation*, as would Colm Meaney's semi-regular character Miles O'Brien and his wife and daughter. Starfleet would have a strategic interest in Bajor because a stable wormhole had been discovered nearby – as established in *The Price*, such a wormhole opened up lucrative trade and exploration routes. The Starfleet personnel would be a long way from home, and wouldn't be able to rely on Federation technology – the station they lived in was a relic of the war, and had been stripped by its builders, the warlike Cardassians, when they abandoned the planet. The Cardassians – who'd withdrawn shortly before the wormhole was discovered, and swiftly decided to reverse that decision – would be the recurring baddies, but the format allowed any number of familiar and unfamiliar people and races to come to the station. To announce its remoteness from Earth, the station – and the series – was given the name Deep Space Nine. The idea was that the station was like a frontier town of the Wild West – all sorts of people would come through.

It was a radical shift of emphasis, and the show hit a fair few teething problems. It was a complicated set up, with a lot of back story. It's perhaps fair to say that the show's Bible, the document that drew up the house style for the series, went into far too much detail. It set very clear guidelines as to characters' backgrounds and exactly what each character thought about everyone else. That sounds useful, but it came to feel restrictive. Odo wasn't just a grumpy hardbitten sheriff, he was a shape-changer. Who slept in a bucket. Who was there during the Cardassian occupation and had worked for the enemy. Who had a mysterious origin. Who was an amnesiac. Who resents his human form. Very little of this was usable, and the writers floundered with him, and with a few of the other characters for a while, until they boiled them down to essentials (Odo is cynical, lonely, has a line in deadpan humour and is fond of Kira – and that, in a nutshell is all you need to know about him).

When the casting didn't match the characters (Odo was originally conceived as a 'Clint Eastwood type'), it led to further confusion among the writers. Rather than growing into their roles and building on what worked on screen, the actors and writers often found themselves forcing square pegs into round holes. During the first season, none of the characters blossomed in the way Picard or Data had during the first season of *The Next Generation*.

Rumour has it that Tony Todd and Michael Clarke Duncan were approached to play station commander Ben Sisko. Both are charismatic performers. Avery Brooks is a talented actor, capable of outstanding supporting work in films such as *American History X*, but seemed uncomfortable and stiff at first in the leading role. He wasn't helped by the story requirements that Sisko couldn't fully impose his authority on the situation, or by being shown in head-to-head scenes with a sparkling Patrick Stewart in the first episode, which practically invited the viewers to think he was a poor comparison.

There were other problems with the casting and set-up: the key character, Ro Laren, had to be dropped from plans for the show, when actress Michelle Forbes didn't want to commit to the series. Two of the more skillful actors, Armin Shimerman and Rene Auberjonois, were buried under make-up that meant their faces didn't move. After Famke Janssen turned down the chance to play Dax, Terry Farrell was brought in at the last minute (actually, on the eleventh day of filming). The parent-son relationship between Ben and Jake Sisko featured heavily in the first episode, but was quickly relegated to subplots. Siddig El Fadil was far more cultured than his 'hothead' character. Which left Colm Meaney's O'Brien as the only character who wasn't lost in make-up or a convoluted back story. Gradually, it was the supporting characters, not weighed down by expectation or pages of background notes, that started to steal the show: the Ferengi, Quark, Rom and Nog; the Klingons; and above all, the Cardassians, Garak and Dukat. It's ironic that one of the most popular characters was Morn, a fat alien that sat at the bar and said nothing.

After the then-most expensive first episode in TV history ($12m), the show struggled for the first year, mainly because the writers seemed to obsess about what the show was not. Starfleet saw Deep Space Nine as a second-rate posting, and for a while, the writers seemed to want to give the new show slow versions of traditional *Star Trek* stories – a common complaint from viewers was that the format made the crew reactive, rather than active: adventure came to them, they didn't seek out adventure. The second season saw an effort to recover, with more attention paid to the Gamma Quadrant (a remarkably colourless place until the end of the second season), and the writers becoming more comfortable that they knew the strengths and weaknesses of the regular cast and their characters.

Although no one on the *Deep Space Nine* staff would ever admit it, the series gained a shot in the arm when rival series *Babylon 5* started. It, too, was set on a vast space station run by humans and overrun by various scheming alien factions. *Babylon 5* was itself a conscious attempt to react against (and cash in on) the success of *The Next Generation.* The pilot episode of *Babylon 5* was broadcast 22 February 1993, weeks after the first episode of *Deep Space Nine.* The series proper started on 26 January 1994, exactly halfway through the second season of *Deep Space Nine.* Notably less lavish than its rival and watched by far fewer people, *Babylon 5* nevertheless felt more progressive because it used then-extraordinary computer graphics to create armadas of spacecraft and stage space battles, while *Deep Space Nine* often had characters looking at displays and reporting on what they were seeing, rather than letting us see them. *Babylon 5*'s greatest innovation, though, was that it was a running series, not a set of self-contained episodes. The first season built up a complex ongoing story that got the internet bulletin boards buzzing in a way that *Deep Space Nine* singularly failed to. It had its faults, but *Babylon 5* also had a sense of direction that generated a real sense of anticipation. After a revamp for its second season, *Babylon 5* started snatching some of the prestigious awards that had long gone, seemingly automatically, to *The Next Generation.*

The other factor was that *The Next Generation* ended in May 1994, a couple of weeks before the end of season two of *Deep Space Nine.* A fourth *Star Trek* series, *Voyager*, was due to start in January 1995, but was going to the UPN, a smaller network. *Deep Space Nine* was now the highest-rated syndicated show. But by now, other shows were following the lead of *The Next Generation* and debuting in syndication – for the first time *Star Trek* had rivals for the title of 'most-watched syndicated show'. *Hercules, Xena: Warrior Princess* and *Baywatch* took turns with *Deep Space Nine* at the top of the charts. *Deep Space Nine* had the highest ever ratings for the premier of a syndicated show, and was always in the top ten, but failed to match the spectacular success of its predecessor. As such, the studio executives started to pay more attention to a show that seemed to be underperforming. The third season saw moves to make it more dynamic. The crew gained a small, heavily-armed starship, the USS Defiant, so they could take the action to their opponents – the Dominion, a vicious power from the Gamma Quadrant that was ruled by the Founders... who Odo discovered were his own people, leading to a new dynamic for one of the show's most popular characters.

Deep Space Nine got, effectively, a second pilot episode in the form of its season four opener, the double-length *The Way of the Warrior*, which saw Worf join the regular cast, the threat of an invasion from the Dominion, an evil empire on the other side of the wormhole, the Klingons end their alliance with the Federation, a new shaven-headed look for Sisko and the largest and most sophisticated space battle yet seen in *Star Trek* in any form, including the movies. The studio had asked for a spectacular opening episode, and it worked, pulling in record ratings. This kicked off four years of intricate plotting as the Quadrant became embroiled in the Dominion War. Over the years, as the stories progressed, the balance of power would shift, alliances would forge and collapse, and the series began to explore every aspect of warfare and war stories. At the same time, *Deep Space Nine* was developing into a show that could do genuinely funny comedy episodes when so minded.

Deep Space Nine was the most ambitious *Star Trek* series, but it was weighed down by an over-complicated set-up. The Bajoran situation did little to add to the drama, with some of the weakest episodes being those that dwell on some local ritual or petty political power struggle. A series about a starbase by a wormhole would have been a perfectly good setting, and far easier for new viewers to get into. Alternatively, it could have been a political thriller that concentrated on Starfleet assisting the Bajorans, rather than slotting that stuff round the normal *Star Trek* fare of peculiar visitors and ships in distress. Trying to do both, it often fell between two stools. A series created as a reaction against, and to stand in contrast to, *The Next Generation* and the movies, it really does a good job of deconstructing a lot of *Star Trek's* clichés and assumptions. But that's a game for the fans, not something that's going to endear it to a mass audience. *In the Pale Moonlight*, where Sisko lies to get the Romulans to join forces with the Federation, is a wonderfully subversive episode of *Star Trek*, but it's pretty tame as drama. *Duet* is powerful television when compared *with Move Along Home*, but not when compared with any episode of *Twin Peaks*, *The X-Files* or *ER*.

Then again, *Deep Space Nine* is funnier than people give it credit for. There's real character development over the seven years for all the regulars. It's sexier, more violent, more problematic and less sanitised than you'd expect from *Star Trek.* Ironically, it's the standalone episodes, and usually ones not set on the station, that really work. *Trials and Tribble-ations*, *The Visitor*, *Children of Time* and *Far Beyond the Stars* are as good as *Star Trek* gets, and it's easy to forget that that's very good indeed.

STAR TREK: DEEP SPACE NINE
SEASON ONE

1.1 EMISSARY

STARDATE 43997

Sisko joins Deep Space Nine and discovers his spiritual destiny

DOUBLE-LENGTH EPISODE
TX 3 January 1993
WRITER Michael Piller (story by Michael Piller and Rick Berman)
DIRECTOR David Carson
GUEST CAST Marc Alaimo (Gul Dukat), Gene Armor (Bajoran Bureaucrat), Majel Barrett (Computer Voice), Felicia M Bell (Jennifer Sisko), Megan Butler (Lieutenant), Cassandra Byram (Conn Officer), Diana Cignoni (Dabo Girl), Stephen Davies (Tactical Officer), Judi Durand (Computer Voice), Aron Eisenberg (Nog), Lynnda Ferguson (Doran), April Grace (Transporter Chief), Max Grodenchik (Ferengi Pit Boss/Rom), John Noah Hertzler (Vulcan Captain), Thomas Hobson (Young Jake), Donald Hotton (Monk #1), Lily Mariya (Ops Officer), Kevin McDermott (Alien Batter), Frank Owen Smith (Curzon Dax), William Powell-Blair (Cardassian Officer), Steven Rankin (Cardassian Officer), Stephen Rowe (Chanting Monk), Camille Saviola (Kai Opaka), Patrick Stewart (Picard/Locutus), Joel Swetow (Gul Jasad), Parker Whitman (Cardassian Officer)

The Battle of Wolf 359. Lieutenant Commander Benjamin Sisko escapes the destruction of the USS Saratoga with his son Jake, but his wife is killed. Stardate 46379.1 – three years later. Commander Sisko is assigned to Deep Space Nine, a station in Bajoran space, and charged to oversee its repair after years of Cardassian occupation. Sisko receives a cool reception from Major Kira Nerys, a Bajoran who led the resistance against the Cardassians but who views the Federation equally suspiciously. The Enterprise docks at DS9 and Picard and Sisko have a frosty meeting. Picard orders Sisko to see that the Bajorans enter the Federation. Kira suggests that the Bajorans need to unite behind their spiritual leader, Kai Opaka. Opaka has prophesied Sisko's arrival and gives him a powerful, mystical orb – his destiny is to obtain eight other orbs stolen by the Cardassians. Sisko meets the rest of his crew, including Jadzia Dax, a Trill and old friend of his.

Shortly after the Enterprise departs, a Cardassian warship arrives. Gul Dukat demands the orb, but Sisko claims to have no knowledge of it. Dax discovers that the orbs may originate from the Denorios Belt. Sisko and Dax take a runabout to the belt and suddenly find themselves transported to a distant part of the Universe through a wormhole, a rift in space. The orb transports Dax back to DS9 but Sisko is left stranded on a distant planet. Kira immediately seeks to move DS9 to the mouth of the wormhole, to claim it for Bajor, while Odo, a shape-shifting security officer found in the Denorios Belt, is disquietened that the wormhole may hold the secret to his origins.

On the planet, Sisko communicates with the force that created the orbs by conversing with images of his wife and child, created by the force. They start to understand each other and Sisko accepts that emotionally he is trapped at the moment of his wife's death. It is time to move on. Meanwhile, O'Brien moves DS9 to the wormhole, but they are intercepted by the Cardassian ship. The wormhole closes around the ship, transporting it to Sisko's destination. Kira is contacted by Gul Jasad, who accuses DS9 of destroying the ship and declares war. A battle ensues but suddenly the wormhole opens and Sisko's runabout appears – towing the damaged Cardassian ship. Later, Sisko tells Picard he intends to keep his post on the station. He also talks to Kai Opaka, who reveals that Sisko will call on the Bajoran prophets again to protect Deep Space Nine.

QUOTES

- 'The game wouldn't be worth playing if we knew what was going to happen...' *Sisko to a Wormhole alien*

TRIVIA

- The opening scene as scripted featured more of the Borg battle, but much was cut for cost. Despite this, the episode went on to win the Emmy for Outstanding Special Visual Effects in 1993.
- There were a few last-minute casting problems. The original actor to play Gul Dukat was replaced with Marc Alaimo, who had played Gul Macet, the first Cardassian to appear in the series in *The Next Generation*'s *The Wounded.* Terry Farrell was the last of the principals to be cast, and joined the established team eleven days into filming.
- John Noah Hertzler (Vulcan captain) is the actor later known as JG Hertzler, who would later play Klingon General Martok.

RATING

- A solid start to the series – better than *Encounter at Farpoint*. Sisko's emotional storyline, building on *Best of Both Worlds*, is powerfully done. Looking back, it's amazing how much is set up and how many tantalising hints are left in the air. From the outset, *Deep Space Nine* is thinking long-term, heralding a distinctly new approach to *Star Trek*.

1.2 PAST PROLOGUE

STARDATE UNKNOWN

Major Kira is torn between the Bajoran resistance and her duty to the Federation

TX 10 January 1993
WRITER Katharyn Powers
DIRECTOR Winrich Kolbe
GUEST CAST Vaughn Armstrong (Gul Dunar), Susan Bay (Admiral Rollman), Barbara March (Lursa), Jeffrey Nordling (Tahna Los), Andrew Robinson (Garak), Richard Ryder (Bajoran Deputy), Gwynyth Walsh (B'Etor)

Bashir meets Garak, an enigmatic Cardassian believed to be a spy. Meanwhile, the station crew rescue a Bajoran whose ship is under attack from the Cardassians. The pilot, Tahna Los, once served with Kira as a resistance fighter of the Khon-Ma. The Cardassians demand Tahna, but Kira succeeds in obtaining asylum for the Bajoran. Odo is suspicious when Klingon sisters Lursa and B'Etor arrive and follows them to a secret meeting with Tahna. The Klingons demand payment in return for an item. Odo informs Sisko, who becomes suspicious of Kira. Meanwhile, Lursa and B'Etor make a deal with Garak to sell Tahna to the Cardassians. Kira is shocked to discover that Tahna is still a member of the Khon-Ma and came to recruit her. Garak conceals Bashir during another meeting with Lursa and B'Etor, and the Klingons reveal that they are selling Tahna a powerful explosive. The Cardassians swoop against Tahna but he has the explosive and threatens to use it. Tahna hopes to destroy the wormhole – without it, the Cardassians and the Federation will lose interest in Bajor. Kira battles with Tahna and the bomb explodes harmlessly on the other side of the wormhole, but she is left to wonder if she has helped or hindered her people.

TRIVIA

- Garak's use of a tailor's shop as a front is a reference to *The Man from UNCLE*, in which the spies use Del Floria's Tailor Shop for cover. Co-producer Peter Allan Fields was formerly a writer on *UNCLE*. The directory graphic located on the Promenade set includes an entry for Del Floria's, along with other in-joke outlets.
- Susan Bay makes her first appearance as Admiral Rollman. Bay is the wife of Leonard Nimoy.

RATING

- A solid start to the regular series with more colour added to the Bajoran political situation. The trust between Odo and Kira is neatly established, plus we have the first appearance of fan favourite Garak. The major problem is Tahna's ploy – if the bomb is powerful enough to irradiate the system, won't Bajor be affected also?

1.3 A MAN ALONE

STARDATE 46421.5

Odo is implicated in the murder of a Bajoran killer

TX 17 January 1993
WRITER Michael Piller (story by Gerald Sanford and Michael Piller)
DIRECTOR Paul Lynch
GUEST CAST Edward Laurance Albert (Zayra), Stephen James Carver (Ibudan), Rosalind Chao (Keiko), Aron Eisenberg (Nog), Max Grodenchik (Rom), Yom Klunis (Old Man), Peter Vogt (Bajoran Man #1)

Odo spies Ibudan, a Bajoran murderer, gambling in Quark's bar and orders him to leave. Later, Odo asks Sisko to have the man expelled, but neither attempt works. Ibudan is found murdered in the holosuite. An investigation suggests that a shapeshifter was responsible, and so Odo falls under suspicion. Meanwhile, Keiko is given permission to set up a school. O'Brien supports his wife when the task proves problematic. The station's inhabitants eye Odo warily and Sisko has him relieved of duty. Bashir is determined to prove Odo's innocence and experiments on DNA found in the holosuite, attempting to make the fragments mutate into the form of their owner. Sisko has to order more security when Odo is attacked by an angry mob. Bashir discovers that the murdered man was a clone created and murdered to frame Odo. Odo returns to duty and finds the real Ibudan hiding on a ship and arrests him for murder.

QUOTES

- 'Everyone wants a piece of the new frontier.'
  'I'm sure you've tried to sell it to most of them.' – *Quark and Odo*

TRIVIA

- Max Grodenchik is formally credited here as Rom. Although referred to on screen as Rom in *Emissary*, he was then credited as 'Ferengi Pit Boss.'
- The name Zayra is a tribute to Zayra Cabot, an assistant to Jeri Taylor who was then serving as producer on *The Next Generation*.

RATING

- Another neat little episode, really designed to show more of the station and set up the culture. In these early days, DS9 is trying to play up the claustrophobia and the wider cultural issues. Though there is little to the story, we get more of a sense of how the station ticks, including firmer foundations for the Ferengi.

1.4 BABEL

STARDATE 46423.7

The station's inhabitants are exposed to a mysterious alien virus

TX 24 January 1993
WRITERS Michael McGreevey and Naren Shankar
(story by Sally Caves and Ira Steven Behr)
DIRECTOR Paul Lynch
GUEST CAST Lee Brooks (Aphasia Victim), Matthew Faison (Surmak Ren), Geraldine Farrell (Galis Blin), Todd Feder (Federation Male), Ann Gillespie (Nurse Jabara), Jack Kehler (Jaheel), Frank Novak (Businessman), Richard Ryder (Bajoran Deputy), Kathleen Wirt (Aphasia Victim), Bo Zenga (Asoth)

While fixing a replicator, O'Brien unwittingly activates an alien device and starts acting strangely. Bashir diagnoses an unusual case of brain dysfunction. Shortly, Dax also succumbs to the virus. Sisko orders a quarantine. Meanwhile, Odo discovers that Quark has been illegally using the replicator, inadvertantly contaminating his customers. Bashir discovers that the virus has become airborne. As more and more inhabitants succumb to the virus, Kira discovers an alien device and suspects Cardassian sabotage. Bashir believes the device was created by Bajorans. Sisko asks Kira to investigate, but time is short: O'Brien has a high fever and may die. Sisko also contracts the virus and starts speaking gibberish, making his orders impossible to understand. Kira contacts Surmak Ren, a Bajoran scientist, and forcibly transports him to her Runabout. Surmak eventually agrees to develop an antidote. The cure is developed just in time.

TRIVIA

- The file picture of Dekon Elig is Dan Curry, the Visual Effects Producer.
- Jaheel is transporting a shipment of Sahsheer, a crystal from Andromeda first referred to in the original series episode *By Any Other Name*.

RATING

- More grist to the mill for the flourishing Odo/Quark relationship and some good stuff between Sisko and Jake. Again, the series is playing on the claustrophobia of the station and blurring the morality of the Bajoran resistance.

1.5 CAPTIVE PURSUIT

STARDATE UNKNOWN

The station becomes the battleground for an alien hunt

TX 31 January 1993
WRITERS Jill Sherman Donner and Michael Piller
(story by Jill Sherman Donner)
DIRECTOR Corey Allen
GUEST CAST Kelly Curtis (Miss Sarda), Gerrit Graham (The Hunter), Scott MacDonald (Tosk)

A damaged alien vessel limps through the wormhole to the station. The passenger, a reptilian alien named Tosk, is suspicious of O'Brien's offers of help and is fascinated by the mix of races on the station. O'Brien is equally suspicious of Tosk, who requires little sustenance and sleep. Later, Odo finds Tosk investigating a junction box and arrests him. Tosk refuses to talk, frustrating Sisko and O'Brien, who feels guilty for bringing Tosk to the station. Later, three of Tosk's people arrive. There is a short phaser battle before the aliens free Tosk. The alien leader tells Sisko he is hunting Tosk. Reluctantly, Sisko releases Tosk to the aliens, under the Prime Directive. Kira suggests Tosk could seek asylum but Tosk proudly refuses. However, O'Brien stuns the hunter and helps Tosk make his escape. Sisko reprimands O'Brien but is quietly sympathetic with his actions.

TRIVIA

- This episode was originally entitled *A Matter of Breeding*.
- Scott MacDonald would later reappear in the fourth season's *Hippocratic Oath* as the Jem'Hadar, Goran'Agar.

RATING

- An interesting episode that shows some of the differences between *The Next Generation* and *Deep Space Nine*. There's a greater willingness to bend Starfleet rules. Most notably, Sisko ignores first contact procedures when meeting our first visitor from the Gamma Quadrant. There's a sense that *Star Trek* wants to do something different here.

1.6 Q-LESS

Q and Vash arrive with an alien artefact that threatens the safety of the station

TX 7 February 1993
WRITER Robert Hewitt Wolfe (story by Hannah Louise Shearer)
DIRECTOR Paul Lynch
GUEST CAST Laura Cameron (Bajoran Woman), Van Epperson (Bajoran Clerk), Jennifer Hetrick (Vash), John de Lancie (Q), Tom McCleister (Kolos)

STARDATE 46531.2

Dax returns from the Gamma Quadrant with an unseen hitch-hiker, Vash, Picard's archaelogist lover. After Vash stores her artefacts on the station, she hears the Daystrom institute is interested in her adventures and will offer her free passage home. O'Brien starts to tell Sisko all he knows about Vash but they are interrupted when the station suffers a power loss. Later, Q visits Vash in her quarters, keen to revive their partnership. She is also contacted by Quark who, having heard of her artefacts, arranges for an auction, for a percentage of the takings. Bashir asks Vash out on a date but Q makes him too tired to turn up! Vash asks Sisko to help rid her of Q. The next day, there is another power loss but this time the officers discover a series of hull fractures. Q is not responsible as previously thought, although he hints that Vash may be more dangerous to the station than they think. They deduce that the cause of the problems is the artefact being auctioned by Quark. O'Brien beams it off the station where it explodes, revealing a winged alien creature. Vash and Q exchange goodbyes – before Vash hatches another archaeological expedition with Quark.

QUOTES

- 'You hit me! Jean-Luc never hit me'
  'I'm not Jean-Luc.' – *Q and Sisko*

TRIVIA

- Robert Hewitt Wolfe's first draft featured only Vash but he was asked to include Q.
- The Daystrom Institute was first mentioned in *The Ultimate Computer*.

RATING

- Fairly low-level stuff for a Q episode, although not without its moments. Q is intrinsically a *The Next Generation* character, with relationships and motifs set up for that crew. It's when we see the differences that we have fun, not least Sisko planting a punch on Q's nose. The artefact is an obvious threat, although playing on O'Brien's expectations to muddy the waters is a neat trick.

1.7 DAX

Sisko fights to prevent Jadzia's extradition for a murder apparently committed by Curzon Dax

TX 14 February 1993
WRITERS DC Fontana and Peter Allan Fields (story by Peter Allan Fields)
DIRECTOR David Carson
GUEST CAST Fionnula Flanagan (Enina Tandro), Anne Haney (Judge Renora), Gregory Itzin (Ilan Tandro), Richard Lineback (Selin Peers)

STARDATE 46910.1

Dax is taken hostage by Ilon Tandro, an alien from Klaestron IV, and two others. Tandro accuses Dax of the murder of his father 30 years previously. Sisko realises Tandro is accusing Curzon Dax, not Jadzia, but when he talks to Jadzia she is quiet. Sisko insists on an extradition hearing. He argues that Jadzia is different to Curzon and succeeds in buying time. Meanwhile, Sisko orders Odo to investigate Tandro's claims. Odo speaks to Tandro's mother, Enina, who reveals that her husband is obsessed: Tandro suspects Dax because Dax is the only person without an alibi. The hearing resumes and Sisko defends Jadzia, but in the recess she asks him to stop his efforts. The reason becomes apparent when Odo discovers that Curzon and Enina had an affair 30 years previously – Dax has a motive. Jadzia is shamed by the revelation, but will say no more. As Tandro cross-examines Dax, he is surprised to see Enina arrive. Enina reveals that she and Curzon were together when Tandro's father was killed. Dax is freed.

TRIVIA

- *Dax* marks the return to *Star Trek* of series stalwart Dorothy Fontana. It was a problematic script and co-producer Peter Allan Fields made a second pass at it.

RATING

- A pretty standard 'trial' format episode, but one that acts as a good vehicle to explore the complexities of the Trill/symbiont relationship and the potential consequences. There is a more interesting story around guilt that doesn't quite get told, but the episode hangs together nevertheless.

1.8 THE PASSENGER

Bashir is possessed by a violent killer intent on stealing a shipment

TX 22 February 1993
WRITER Morgan Gendel, Robert Hewitt Wolfe and Michael Piller (story by Morgan Gendel)
DIRECTOR Paul Lynch
GUEST CAST Caitlin Brown (Ty Kajada), Christopher Collins (Durg), James Harper (Rao Vantika), James Lashly (Lt George Primmin)

STARDATE UNKNOWN

Kira and Bashir respond to a distress call from Ty Kajada, a security officer transporting a murderer, Rao Vantika, who has taken over their ship. Vantika tries to kill Bashir then dies. On the station, Kayada urges Bashir to run tests: Vantika has faked his death before. Sisko discovers Vantika may have been after deuridium, which would prolong his life. Vantika orders Quark to hire mercenaries to obtain the deuridium. The next day, Dax deduces that Vantika has transferred his consciousness into someone else. Suspicion falls on Kajada, but she falls from a balcony and claims she was pushed by Vantika. Dax discovers a device used by Vantika to transfer his consciousness to another. Meanwhile, the mercenaries meet Vantika – who is in Bashir's body. Vantika captures the deuridium freighter. Sisko locks onto the freighter but Vantika threatens to kill Bashir's body. Dax disrupts Vantika's brainwave patterns, allowing Bashir to lower the freighter's shields and be beamed back to the station. Bashir is purged and Kajada vaporises Vantika's remains.

TRIVIA

- An early pitch by Morgan Gendel, writer of *The Next Generation*'s Hugo Award-winning *The Inner Light*, had Kajada pursuing Vantika, unaware that the deceased criminal was waiting in her mind.
- Caitlin Brown (Ty Kajada) went on to play Na'Toth, assistant to Narn Ambassador G'Kar, in the first season of *Babylon 5*.

RATING

- Sadly not as much of a mystery as the writers think it is. However, the muddying of the waters around Quark makes him a very interesting character. This is something *Star Trek* had not done before.

1.9 MOVE ALONG HOME

The officers become pieces in an alien board game, thanks to Quark's cheating

TX 14 March 1993
WRITERS Frederick Rappaport, Lisa Rich and Jeanne Carrigan-Fauci (story by Michael Piller)
DIRECTOR David Carson
GUEST CAST Joel Brooks (Falow), Clara Bryant (Chandra), James Lashly (Lt George Primmin)

STARDATE UNKNOWN

Sisko greets a new race, the Wadi, but is disappointed when they seem interested in Quark's bar. Falow, the Wadi leader, is angered when Quark fixes the Dabo table and insists that they now play their game, Chula. Meanwhile, Sisko awakens and finds himself in an alien environment, where Falow urges him to move along. Sisko finds Dax, Kira and Bashir trapped in the same reality. In the bar, Quark rolls the die and moves his pieces. The officers meet a Wadi girl and mimic her actions to pass through a forcefield. The girl tells them they are at the Third Shap. In the bar, Quark moves to the next level of the game and wins a payoff. Falow tells Quark he can take a risky route and double his winnings. Quark realises the officers are experiencing the game for real and steers them away from the risky route. Quark wins more, but another roll results in Bashir being whisked from the board and placed in a holding area. Panicking, Quark uses the shortcut. Falow tells Quark he must sacrifice one of his pieces for the others to survive. Quark refuses and the board decides. Sisko, Dax and Kira stumble into an abyss. Suddenly, all the players are back in the bar. Falow reveals they were never in danger – but they wouldn't have been put through it if Quark's hadn't cheated.

TRIVIA

- The working title for the episode was *Sore Losers*.
- The original script called for an elaborate maze for the game but this had to be scaled back to meet the budget. Equally, the original concept had the principals in real danger.

RATING

- Throwaway and quite fun, but the 'they were never really in danger' revelation is a horrible cheat on the audience. There are a few welcome Odo-Quark moments but little else to recommend this episode.

1.10 THE NAGUS

Quark becomes Grand Nagus but finds himself a target for assassination

TX 21 March 1993
WRITER Ira Steven Behr (story by David Livingston)
DIRECTOR David Livingston
GUEST CAST Lee Arenberg (Gral), Aron Eisenberg (Nog), Barry Gordon (Nava), Max Grodenchik (Rom), Tiny Ron (Maihar'du), Wallace Shawn (Zek), Lou Wagner (Krax)

STARDATE UNKNOWN

Quark and Rom are visited by Krax and his father, Grand Nagus Zek, leader of the Ferengi business empire. Quark worries that Zek wants the bar, but the Nagus merely wants to host a conference there. More Ferengi arrive, including Gral, who dislikes Krax. To everyone's surprise, Zek announces that he is stepping down – and Quark will succeed him! Gral offers to 'protect' the new Grand Nagus in return for the pick of business in the Gamma Quadrant. Zek dies and the Ferengi hold the ceremony in the bar. It is interrupted when someone tries to assassinate Quark. Odo suspects the culprit is Maihar'du, one of Zek's party. In fact, it was Krax – and Rom, determined to take over his brother's bar! They lure Quark into an airlock when Odo and Maihar'du arrive – with Zek. The Grand Nagus faked his death to test his son's worthiness to be his successor and has been disappointed. He thanks Quark for his help and leaves. Quark is impressed by Rom's treachery and proudly congratulates his brother!

QUOTES

- 'Once you have their money... never give it back.' – *Rom quotes the First Rule of Acquisition*

TRIVIA

- David Livingston stepped over from production management to storyline and direct.
- The original story was a *Godfather* pastiche. Ira Behr turned it into a Ferengi episode, introducing the Rules of Acquisition.

RATING

- An amusing episode that completes the regeneration of the Ferengi from rather wet capitalist baddies to comedy characters. Wallace Shawn is wonderful in his first appearance as the gnarled Grand Nagus.

1.11 VORTEX

Odo investigates claims that other shapeshifters live in the Gamma Quadrant

TX 18 April 1993
WRITER Sam Rolfe
DIRECTOR Winrich Kolbe
GUEST CAST Majel Barrett (Computer Voice), Gordon Clapp (Hadron), Cliff DeYoung (Croden), Leslie Engelberg (Yareth), Kathleen Garrett (Vulcan Captain), Randy Oglesby (Ah-Kel/Ro-Kel)

STARDATE UNKNOWN

An alien from the Gamma Quadrant, Croden, kills one of two Miradorns in an armed robbery in Quark's bar. The surviving Miradorn, Ah-Kel, is determined to get revenge. Odo arrests Croden, who claims to have encountered 'Changelings' before. Croden offers to take Odo to other Changelings, showing him a stone that can morph. They take a runabout and pass through the wormhole. While Dax and Sisko contact Croden's people, the Rakhari, and discover that he is a wanted criminal, Croden tries to gain Odo's trust. Ah-Kel discovers Croden has left the station and pursues. In a cavern, Croden reveals the morphing stone is the key to a stasis chamber that houses his daughter, Yareth, sole survivor of his family. He charges Odo to take care of Yareth while he faces the Rakhari authorities. Suddenly, an explosion knocks Odo unconscious. Croden saves Odo and they escape, tricking Ah-Kel into destroying his own ship. Odo surprises Croden by giving him and Yareth to the Vulcans for protection from retribution. Grateful, Croden gives Odo the stone.

QUOTES

- 'I'm a security chief, not a combat pilot.' – *Odo*

TRIVIA

- Morn, a regular at Quark's bar, is accused of talking too much. Morn (an homage to Norm from *Cheers*) never talks on camera!

RATING

- One of those episodes that's perhaps more useful than good. We get to known more about Odo and there are tantalising hints that the show returns to later. We're left with more questions unanswered at the end than we had at the beginning.

1.12 BATTLE LINES

STARDATE UNKNOWN

Sisko, Kira, Bashir and Kai Opaka are stranded on a moon where the deceased come back to life

TX 25 April 1993
WRITER Richard Danus and Evan Carlos Somers (story by Hilary Bader)
DIRECTOR Paul Lynch
GUEST CAST Jonathan Banks (Shel-la), Majel Barrett (Computer Voice), Paul Collins (Zlangco), Camille Saviola (Kai Opaka)

While visiting the Gamma Quadrant, Sisko, Kira, Bashir and Kai Opaka are fired on by artificial satellites and crash on a moon. Opaka is killed and the crew are captured by battle-scarred inhabitants. Golin Shel-la, the alien leader, reveals that his people, the Ennis, are at war with the Nol-Ennis. Both sides are trapped on the moon by the satellites. Suddenly, they are ambushed by the Nol-Ennis, led by Zlangco, and Shel-la is killed. Kira scares them off – and is stunned when she is greeted by Kai Opaka. The other casualties also come back to life. As punishment for their war-mongering, the inhabitants must fight and die for eternity. Sisko decides to take the inhabitants off the moon and convinces Shel-la to arrange a peace with Zlangco, but the negotiations descend into violence. Meanwhile, Bashir discovers that dying on the moon makes the body dependent on microbes only available on the planetoid. Opaka is told she cannot leave, but she has already decided to stay – the moon is the answer to her personal prophecy. The officers find a way to divert one of the artificial satellites and are able to escape, leaving Kai Opaka behind.

TRIVIA

- Sisko defines the Federation as a coalition of more than 100 planets who have joined together for scientific development, cultural growth and military defense. It is one of the few definitions of the Federation given on screen.

RATING

- Fairly tame stuff, treading a familiar path about the pointlessness of war. Ultimately, the high concept gets in the way of any emotion. While it might have got away with it elsewhere, this episode falls within a run of decent ones and feels a little weak by comparison. Nevertheless, it does write out Opaka, setting up the battle for power on Bajor that would run into the second season.

1.13 THE STORYTELLER

STARDATE 46729.1

O'Brien is made the spiritual defender of a Bajoran village

TX 2 May 1993
WRITER Kurt Michael Bensmiller and Ira Steven Behr (story by Kurt Michael Bensmiller)
DIRECTOR David Livingston
GUEST CAST Amy Benedict (Woman), Aron Eisenberg (Nog), Jim Jansen (Faren Kag), Kay E Kuter (The Sirah), Jordan Lund (Woban), Lawrence Monoson (Hovath), Gina Philips (Varis Sul)

Sisko and Kira mediate a land dispute between the Paqu and the Navot, two peoples of Bajor. They are surprised to find Varis Sul, the Tetrarch of the Paqu, is a 15-year-old girl. Nog takes an interest in Varis. Meanwhile, Bashir and O'Brien beam down to help the Sirah, an elderly Navot, protect the village from the Dal'Rok, a fierce entity. The village magistrate, Faren Kag, insists that if the Sirah dies, the entire village will die. That night, the Sirah tells a story, that keeps the Dal'Rok, an energy cloud, at bay. Suddenly, the Sirah collapses and the Dal'Rok attacks. It is driven back, but the Sirah dies. O'Brien becomes the new Sirah, angering Hovath, who claims he is the rightful heir. That night, O'Brien tries to keep the Dal'Rok at bay but fails. Hovath steps in and the Dal'Rok is defeated. O'Brien and Bashir make a quiet exit. On the station, Nog suggests that Varis can find piece with the Novat by trading her Paqu land for something her people want. Varis is struck and devises a solution to keep both sides happy. She thanks the smitten Nog with a kiss.

QUOTES

- 'Opportunity plus instinct equals profit.' – *Nog quotes the Ninth Rule of Acquisition to Varis Sul*

TRIVIA

- *The Storyteller* began life as a script for the first season of *The Next Generation*. Piller remembered seeing the pitch and resurrected it.

RATING

- Pretty bland stuff as a story, but it gives some welcome breathing-room for the relationship between Bashir and O'Brien to develop. Ultimately, it is difficult to see how any suggestion Nog might make could avert a civil war!

1.14 PROGRESS

STARDATE 46844.3

Kira faces up to her change of principles since her move to the Federation

TX 9 May 1993
WRITER Peter Allan Fields
DIRECTOR Les Landau
GUEST CAST Michael Bofshever (Toran), Aron Eisenberg (Nog), Terrence Evans (Baltrim), Brian Keith (Mullibok), Annie O'Donnell (Keena), Daniel Riordan (First Guard), Nicholas Worth (Lissepian Captain)

The Bajoran government is to tap the molten core of the fifth moon, Jeraddo, and has ordered an evacuation. A Bajoran farmer, Mullibok, and his friends, Baltrim and Keena, have refused to leave. When Minister Toran insists that Kira evict the farmers, there is a struggle with Baltrim, and Mullibok is shot. Distressed, Kira has Mullibok stabilised and vows to stay with him. Sisko tells Kira she has left her Bajoran life and must move Mullibok. The next day, Kira tries again, but Mullibok will not leave while his farm stands. Kira damages the farm but Mullibok still refuses to leave, insisting that if he leaves he will die. Kira cannot convince him and leaves. On the station, Jake and Nog sell Quark's Cardassian yamok sauce to a trader in return for self-sealing stem bolts. They then find the trader's original customer for the stem-bolts – and trade them for seven tessipates of land. When they hear the Bajoran government wants to buy land, Jake and Nog try to sell theirs to Quark, but he has already caught on to their game.

TRIVIA

- Terrence Evans (Baltrim) appears in season two's *Cardassians* as the adopted father of an orphan.

RATING

- An uncomfortable episode where the Kira story is not balanced by that of Jake and Nog. Brian Keith puts in an enigmatic performance as Mullibok, who cleverly probes and tries to use Kira's emotions. The ending is left deliberately ambiguous, but it is hard to see how Mullibok would ever forgive Kira.

1.15 IF WISHES WERE HORSES

STARDATE 46853.2

The officers are visited by their fantasies but the station is soon in danger

TX 16 May 1993
WRITERS Nell McCue Crawford and William L Crawford and Michael Piller (story by Nell McCue Crawford and William L Crawford)
DIRECTOR Robert Legato
GUEST CAST Michael John Anderson (Rumpelstiltskin), Rosalind Chao (Keiko), Hana Hatae (Molly), Keone Young (Buck Bokai)

As the officers investigate strange thoron emissions from a space rupture, O'Brien reads Molly the story of Rumplestiltskin and is amazed to see the character appear in the room. Soon Sisko is talking to Buck Bokai, a long-dead baseball hero, and Bashir is relishing his time with a flirtatious duplicate of Dax! The emissions are making their fantasies real. The real Dax and Bashir discover that when this phenomenon last appeared it destroyed the Hanoli system. The three fantasy creatures plot to stay by cultivating Bokai's relationship with Sisko. The rupture expands, causing panic on the station. O'Brien launches an altered photon torpedo, to no effect. Sisko realises the rift is also a figment of their imagination and the rift and illusions vanish. Later, Bokai reappears and reveals that he and his fellow creatures are exploring the galaxy – only the imaginations of the station inhabitants' placed them in danger. He disappears.

TRIVIA

- The original pitch made heavy use of the holosuite, but this was dropped when producers heard that *The Next Generation* had a big holodeck story in production, *Ship in a Bottle.*

RATING

- A conscious attempt to look at the preferred method of first contact by other creatures. Simple, harmless fun that is worth a glance. It's a pity that the aliens have such a weak rationale for their behaviour.

1.16 THE FORSAKEN

STARDATE 46925.1

As Odo resists the advances of Lwaxana Troi, the station computer is taken over

TX 23 May 1993
WRITERS Don Carlos Dunaway and Michael Piller (story by Jim Trombetta)
DIRECTOR Les Landau
GUEST CAST Benita Andre (Anara), Majel Barrett (Lwaxana Troi), Michael Ensign (Ambassador Lojal), Jack Shearer (Ambassador Vadosia), Constance Towers (Ambassador Taxco)

A delegation of Federation ambassadors arrives at the station, including Lwaxana Troi, who takes a shine to Odo. Meanwhile, as O'Brien struggles with the station computer, an uninhabited ship arrives through the wormhole. Suddenly the computer co-operates and communicates with the ship. Odo tries to evade Lwaxana's advances but gets stuck in a lift with her when the power fails. As they remain trapped, Odo fast approaches the time when he must revert to his liquid state. O'Brien is bemused by the computer's behaviour and suspects its personality has changed – it now demands constant attention, like a child. The officers suspect that the computer downloaded a non-biological life-form from the ship. O'Brien tries to purge the computer but it is resistant and sets fire to a corridor, endangering the diplomats. In the lift, Lwaxana improvises a basin with her dress and Odo reverts to his liquid form. O'Brien constructs a sub-program the entity can play with and traps it, regaining control of the station computer. Odo returns to human form and says goodbye to Lwaxana, who leaves a hint of romance in the air.

QUOTES

- 'This is no computer – this is my arch-enemy.' – *O'Brien to Sisko*

TRIVIA

- This episode, originally titled *Only the Lonely*, was written to bring Lwaxana Troi to DS9. Barrett would later reprise the role in *Fascination* and *The Muse.*
- The episode reveals that Odo must revert to his liquid form every 16 hours.

RATING

- Amusing and simple, although it trades heavily on the Odo story to the detriment of the rest. Despite Lwaxana's brashness, this is a potent vehicle for exploring Odo, revealing as much about his psychological make-up as his physical abilities. He is fast becoming a very interesting character.

1.17 DRAMATIS PERSONAE

STARDATE UNKNOWN

The officers undergo personality changes from a Klingon scientific discovery

TX 30 May 1993
WRITER Joe Menosky
DIRECTOR Cliff Bole
GUEST CAST Stephen Parr (Valerian), Randy Pflug (Guard), Jeff Pruitt (Ensign), Tom Towles (Hon'Tihl)

Kira is enraged when Sisko allows Valerians to dock at the station, believing that they are arming the Cardassians. Just then, a Klingon science vessel comes through the wormhole and explodes. A Klingon is beamed aboard, shrouded in a strange violet light. Odo discovers that the Klingons were sent to obtain something that would make the enemies of the Empire tremble. Suddenly, Odo is paralysed with pain. When he awakens he discovers the officers acting out of character. As Kira plans a mutiny, Odo guesses that the last events of the Klingon ship are being replayed on the station. The Klingon ship's log reveals that alien energy spheres on board are responsible. As tensions escalate between the officers, Odo lures all the infected officers into one space then activates a signal designed by Bashir to counter the effects of the energy spheres. The violet light is purged and released into space.

TRIVIA

- Menosky's original concept concerned an eternal power stuggle between modes of behaviour transmitted through a telepathic virus. The power struggle originated with the fall of an alien civilisation.

RATING

- An episode that, by letting actors go beyond their characters, shows the confidence that the *Deep Space Nine* team had after only one season. Brooks in particular manages to break the emotionally controlled Sisko to show his range.

1.18 DUET

Kira investigates a Cardassian patient who she believes is a war criminal

TX 13 June 1993
WRITER Peter Allan Fields
(story by Lisa Rich and Jeanne Carrigan-Fauci)
DIRECTOR James L Conway
GUEST CAST Marc Alaimo (Gul Dukat), Robin Christopher (Neela), Norman Large (Lissepian Captain), Tony Rizzoli (Kainon), Ted Sorel (Kaval), Harris Yulin (Aamin Marritza)

STARDATE UNKNOWN

A Cardassian, Marritza, arrives at the station suffering from Kalla-Nohra, a condition he could only have contracted as an officer at a Bajoran forced labour mine. As Bajor demands extradition, Sisko allows Kira to question Marritza. He blames the atrocities on his leader, Gul Darhe'el. Meanwhile, Gul Dukat also demands Marritza. Sisko stalls for time. Marritza reveals that he is really Gul Darhe'el and now boasts about his crimes, but Odo is suspicious. Odo discovers that Marritza asked for information about Kira earlier and Dukat confirms that Darhe'el is dead. Marritza relents and reveals that he sought to take on Darhe'el's identity to draw attention to Cardassia's war crimes and force Cardassians to accept their guilt. Kira refuses to let Marritza die for this reason, but he is killed by a Bajoran, waging war against all Cardassians. Kira is dismayed.

QUOTES

- 'What you call genocide, I call a day's work.' – *Marritza*

TRIVIA

- This episode's working title was *The Higher Law*.
- The writing team were influenced by Robert Shaw's play *The Man in the Glass Booth*, about a Jewish businessman who is kidnapped by Israeli intelligence and put on trial for war crimes.
- *Duet* is another late-season 'bottle show' to recoup budget.

RATING

- A strong story with plenty of depth and tone. By playing on Kira's emotions, the writers ensure plenty of twists and turns. The ending is notably strong, suggesting a change in one of the main characters. One of the best episodes of the first season.

1.19 IN THE HANDS OF THE PROPHETS

A Bajoran cleric creates a crisis on the station

TX 20 June 1993
WRITER Robert Hewitt Wolfe
DIRECTOR David Livingston
GUEST CAST Philip Anglim (Vedek Bareil), Rosalind Chao (Keiko), Robin Christopher (Neela), Michael Eugene Fairman (Vendor), Louise Fletcher (Vedek Winn)

STARDATE UNKNOWN

A visiting Bajoran, Vedek Winn, objects to Keiko teaching a non-religious scientific explanation of the wormhole. Winn is supported by Kira and warns of the consequences if Keiko's lessons continue. Meanwhile, O'Brien, working with Neela, his Bajoran apprentice, discovers the remains of Ensign Aquino in a power conduit. As Odo investigates the death, Keiko finds many Bajorans turning against her. Winn leads a silent walkout of the Bajoran families. Sisko tries to enlist the help of Vedek Bareil, a candidate for the new Kai, but he fears losing popularity. Odo reports that Aquino was killed by a phaser when he tried to stop someone stealing a runabout. Suddenly, the school is set on fire. Sisko confronts Winn, who quietly nods her thanks to Neela. Later, Neela tells Winn that the officers know about the runabout, but Winn insists their secret plan must succeed. Bareil arrives on the station and joins Winn. O'Brien discovers that Neela disabled the weapons detectors. Sisko prevents Neela from killing her target, Bareil, which was Winn's plan all along.

TRIVIA

- Louise Fletcher (Vedek Winn) won an Oscar for Best Actress for her portayal of Nurse Mildred Ratched in *One Flew Over the Cuckoo's Nest* (1975) with Jack Nicholson.
- Bareil's garden sanctuary, one of the few locations permitted in the first season, is close to the Paramount backlot and was used for the holodeck scenes in *The Next Generation*'s *Encounter at Farpoint*.

RATING

- Bajoran religion neatly bookends the first season with a story that draws heavily on present day arguments about teaching approaches in schools. The socio-political power games promise more than we get, largely because Bajor is just too generic, and sadly the series never really capitalises on the backdrop it sets up.

STAR TREK: DEEP SPACE NINE
SEASON TWO

2.1 THE HOMECOMING

A legendary Bajoran is alive but a Cardassian prisoner, and Kira attempts to rescue him

TX 27 September 1993
WRITER Ira Steven Behr (story by Jeri Taylor and Ira Steven Behr)
DIRECTOR Winrich Kolbe
GUEST CAST Marc Alaimo (Gul Dukat), Michael Bell (Borum), Leslie Bevis (Freighter captain), Richard Beymer (Li Nalas), Max Grodenchik (Rom), Frank Langella (Jaro – uncredited), Paul Nakauchi (Romah Doe)

STARDATE UNKNOWN

Quark is given a Bajoran earring by a Boslic trader. Kira recognises it as belonging to the great resistance leader Li Nalas, believed to be dead, but actually a prisoner on Cardassia IV. Kira convinces Sisko that Li Nalas would stabilise the situation on Bajor, and he considers her rescue plan. The Alliance For Global Unity, a Bajoran isolationist group also known as 'the Circle', are becoming more active and their influence has spread to the station – they vandalise some areas, and brand Quark with their symbol. Sisko agrees to Kira's plan, as long as she takes O'Brien along. Their runabout heads for Cardassia IV, and they soon discover 12 Bajoran life-signs in a labour camp. They breach the camp's security and escape with Li Nalas. Gul Dukat quickly releases the other prisoners. Kira is reprimanded by Minister Jaro for not following orders, but privately he congratulates her. Li Nalas is overwhelmed by his hero's welcome – he was, in reality, only a minor resistance figure. Sisko convinces him he could be a symbol of hope for the new Bajor. Jaro agrees Li Nalas should have an important role... and gives him Kira's job on the station. Kira is to return to Bajor.

TRIVIA

- The location used for Cardassia IV was the Soledad Canyon in California, which proved to be freezing at night and extremely hot during the day. The cast and crew hated every minute of location filming here... but the show would revisit it in a couple of future episodes.

RATING

- Bajor had always been a bit too generic to be interesting. This is an honest attempt to make the planet a bit richer. It's solid, rather than spectacular, but it does suggest that the production team are learning from the strengths and weaknesses of the first season.

2.2 THE CIRCLE

Kira meets the leader behind civil unrest on Bajor

STARDATE UNKNOWN

Kira is replaced by Li Nalas, without Sisko's consent, and goes to Vedek Bareil's monastery to clear her head. There, she encounters the Third Orb, of prophecy and change. The Circle is getting bolder – the group's emblem is even scrawled on the door to Sisko's office.

TX 4 October 1993
WRITER Peter Allan Fields
DIRECTOR Corey Allen
GUEST CAST Peter Anglim (Vedek Bareil), Richard Beymer (Li Nalas), Louise Fletcher (Vedek Winn), Mike Genovese (Zef'No), Bruce Gray (Chekote), Anthony Guidera (Cardassian), Frank Langella (Jaro – uncredited), Stephen Macht (Krim), Eric Server (Peace officer)

Odo learns that the Kressari have sold weapons to the Circle, and smuggles himself aboard a Kressari ship to investigate. Kira is abducted by hooded Circle agents. She discovers their leader is Minister Jaro. He needs her to tell him how Sisko and Starfleet would react to a Circle coup, but Kira refuses. Sisko leads a team that beams in to rescue her. Odo reveals that the Kressari were a front for a Cardassian gun-running operation. Jaro and Winn plot, unaware that it's the Cardassians supplying them. Starfleet tells Sisko that it would break the Prime Directive to interfere in Bajoran local affairs, and he is ordered to evacuate. The Bajoran government move to occupy Deep Space Nine, and order all non-Bajorans to leave...

TRIVIA

- Bareil was originally written as an older man.
- The location filming for the monastery took place at Griffith Park in LA.

RATING

- A stronger episode than the season opener, and perhaps the first episode *of Deep Space Nine* that couldn't possibly be rewritten as an episode of *The Next Generation*. It hits a lot of the right notes, and makes the politics interesting and character-driven.

2.3 THE SIEGE

STARDATE UNKNOWN

Bajoran forces arrive to retake the station

TX 11 October 1993
WRITER Michael Piller
DIRECTOR Winrich Kolbe
GUEST CAST Philip Anglim (Vedek Bareil), Richard Beymer (Li Nalas), Katarina Carlson (Bajoran officer), Rosalind Chao (Keiko O'Brien), Aron Eisenberg (Nog), Louise Fletcher (Vedek Winn), Max Grodenchik (Rom), Hana Hatae (Molly O'Brien), Frank Langella (Jaro – uncredited), Stephen Macht (Krim), Steven Weber (Colonel Day)

Sisko briefs his officers as the Bajoran ships approach. Meanwhile, Dax and Kira take a subimpulse Raider that Kira hid on Lunar V during the occupation to Bajor, to give the authorities proof that The Circle is being supplied by the Cardassians. The Bajoran ships dock at the station, but it's deserted – Sisko's men are hidden in the ducts. Kira and Dax are shot down and captured by security forces on Bajor. Sisko confronts the Bajoran Colonel Day and tells him that they are using Cardassian weapons, but he doesn't believe the 'Federation lie'. The security patrol works for Vedek Bareil, and they get Dax and Kira to the authorities. Jaro denies the accusations, but it becomes clear they are true. Colonel Day refuses to believe this, and tries to kill Sisko – Li Nalas sacrifices his life to save Sisko. The command of Deep Space Nine is returned to Starfleet.

TRIVIA

- Frank Langella was keen to work on the show, and appeared in all of the first three episodes of the second season, but didn't want to be credited.

RATING

- It's odd that they kill Li Nalas after so much build-up. But this is another strong episode.

2.4 INVASIVE PROCEDURES

STARDATE 47182.1

Another Trill wants to be Dax's host – but that will kill Jadzia

TX 18 October 1993
WRITERS John Whelpley and Robert Hewitt Wolfe (story by John Whelpley)
DIRECTOR Les Landau
GUEST CAST Megan Gallagher (Mareel), John Glover (Verad), Steve Rankin (Yeto), Tim Russ (T'Kar)

A plasma disruption in the Denorios Belt leads to the evacuation of the station, except for key personnel. When a ship is damaged in the storm, Dax brings it in to dock. The crew, including Klingon mercenaries and a Trill, Verad, accost their rescuers at gunpoint. Odo escapes. The group takes control of the station, and it becomes clear that Verad wants the Dax symbiont implanted in him – a procedure that will kill Jadzia. He has been rejected as a host, and wants to prove he is suitable. Sisko tries to convince Verad Dax to save Jadzia, but he refuses. Sisko manages to drive a wedge between Verad and his lover, Mareel. Sisko shoots Verad, and the symbiont is returned to Jadzia in time. Verad is inconsolable, and Jadzia shares in that grief.

TRIVIA

- Tim Russ had already made appearances in *The Next Generation* and *Star Trek: Generations*, and would go on to play Tuvok in Voyager. Here he plays a Klingon.

RATING

- The problem with this sort of story is that you know the ending. They aren't going to kill Dax, so you know the end of the episode almost as soon as the premise is established. This episode exposes just how vague the whole host/symbiont concept is.

2.5 CARDASSIANS

STARDATE 47177.2

Garak helps settle the matter of a Cardassian boy adopted by a Bajoran

TX 25 October 1993
WRITER James Crocker (story by Gene Wolande and John Wright)
DIRECTOR Cliff Bole
GUEST CAST Marc Alaimo (Dukat), Dion Anderson (Zolan), Rosalind Chao (Keiko O'Brien), Sharon Conley (Luson Jomat), Terrence Evans (Proka Migdal), Karen Hensel (Deela), Robert Mandan (Kotran Pa'Dar), Vidal Peterson (Rugal), Andrew Robinson (Garak), Jillian Ziesmer (Asha)

Bashir tries to find out more about Garak over tea, but Garak is silent as ever on the subject. They see a Bajoran man and a savage young Cardassian boy together. Dukat contacts Sisko about the pair. The father, Proka, adopted the boy, Rugal, during the war and says he cares for him. An alien called Zoran tells Sisko that Proka abuses the boy as revenge for the occupation. Dukat wants the boy repatriated. Bashir wonders why Dukat is suddenly so interested in war orphans, but Dukat can't answer, making Sisko suspicious. Dukat claims Rugal is the son of an important politician, Kotran Pa'Dar. Garak and Bashir realise a senior Cardassian has arranged for Rugal to be left on Bajor, to humiliate Pa'Dar. Despite the social stigma, Pa'Dar wants Rugal to return. Sisko decides that Rugal must go to his father.

TRIVIA

- The episode reintroduced Garak, who'd become a fan favourite after his appearance in *Past Prologue*. This episode was, in part, designed to allow him to become a semi-regular character.
- The Cardassians' name for the station, Terok Nor, is mentioned here for the first time, along with other hints about the occupation that would bear fruit in future episodes.

RATING

- There's a fantastic scene where O'Brien and Rugal have – or rather don't have – a meal together. This is an important episode for the ongoing story. We find out a lot about the Cardassians, and it makes good use of Garak – who's far more interesting than half the regulars.

2.6 MELORA

STARDATE 47229.1

Bashir could cure an alien Ensign confined to a wheelchair

TX 1 November 1993
WRITERS Evan Carlos Somers, Steven Baum, Michael Piller and James Crocker (story by Evan Carlos Somers)
DIRECTOR Winrich Kolbe
GUEST CAST Daphne Ashbrook (Melora Pazlar), Peter Crombie (Fallit Kot), Don Stark (Ashrok), Ron Taylor (Klingon chef)

Melora Pazlar is confined to a wheelchair in normal gravity – her race, the Elaysians, are from a low gravity planet. She insists she doesn't need special treatment, but Sisko insists that Dax accompanies her on a trip to the Gamma Quadrant. Quark is dealing with an old business associate, Fallit Kot, who has just been released from prison. He's convinced Quark informed on him. Bashir develops a 'cure' for Melora, and she walks in normal gravity – but if she continues the treatment, it will become irreversible. Kot attacks Quark and steals 199 bars of latinum. Kot hijacks the Orinoco with Melora, Dax and Quark onboard and escapes, with Sisko, Bashir and O'Brien in hot pursuit. Melora overpowers Kot by switching off the gravity. On her return to the station, she tells Bashir she wants to remain a true Elaysian.

TRIVIA

- Melora had originally been thought of as a regular character, but the logistical difficulties of getting a wheelchair through the Deep Space Nine set ruled this out.
- Daphne Ashbrook would go on to play Grace Holloway, would-be companion to Paul McGann's Doctor in the 1996 *Doctor Who* TV movie.

RATING

- A fairly straightforward episode that demonstrates why Melora shouldn't have been a regular character – despite the intentions of the script, she's little more than a gimmick, and saves the day because of that gimmick.

2.7 RULES OF ACQUISITION

STARDATE UNKNOWN

Quark discovers secrets while conducting sensitive negotiations

TX 8 November 1993
WRITER Ira Steven Behr (story by Hilary J Bader)
DIRECTOR David Livingston
GUEST CAST Emilia Crow (Zyree), Max Grodenchik (Rom), Tiny Ron (Malhar'du), Wallace Shawn (Zek), Brian Thompson (Inglatu), Helene Udy (Pel)

The Grand Nagus Zek wants Quark to negotiate with the Dosi from the Gamma Quadrant, to buy 10,000 vats of tulaberry wine. Pel, a wine waiter, acts as Quark's assistant. The Dosi want to negotiate direct with the Nagus, who asks Quark to increase the order to 100,000 vats. Dax discovers Pel is a disguised woman – females are second-class citizens among the Ferengi. Quark and Pel become close. The Dosi storm out because the Nagus won't deal with them. When Quark and Pel follow them to their homeworld, the Dosi say the Karemma are more powerful and might be able to help. Quark realises that the Nagus is using the negotiations to find out more about The Dominion, a mysterious political organisation the Nagus considers the key to the Gamma Quadrant. The Nagus rewards Quark for uncovering information about the Karemma. He is shocked to discover Pel is a woman, but doesn't punish her – he strips Quark of his reward.

TRIVIA

- This started out as a Riker story for *The Next Generation*, called *Profit Margin*.
- The episode title was misspelled *Rules of Aquisition* on first transmission.

RATING

- *Yentl* with Ferengi. The Dosi are very silly, the Ferengi are still very silly. It's played too broadly, and the more serious elements of the story, like the discrimination against Pel and Zek's subtle espionage, get lost.

2.8 NECESSARY EVIL

STARDATE 47262.5

An old murder case returns to haunt Odo, Quark and Kira

TX 15 November 1993
WRITER Peter Allan Fields
DIRECTOR James L Conway
GUEST CAST Marc Alaimo (Dukat), Max Grodenchik (Rom), Robert MacKenzie (Trazko), Katherine Moffat (Pallra)

Quark is paid by the beautiful Pallra to retrieve a strongbox that's been in one of the station's shops since the occupation. He and Rom recover the box, and open it to discover a list of Bajoran names. Quark is attacked with a phaser by a Bajoran. Odo threatens to charge Rom with the attack, and Rom confesses all. Odo remembers back five years, when Gul Dukat asked him to solve the murder of Vaatrick, the owner of the shop and Pallra's husband. Pallra had accused her husband of having an affair with Kira. That was when Odo discovered Kira was a member of the resistance – she'd been the prime suspect for the murder, but had actually been sabotaging the station at the time. Pallra was the new prime suspect, but there was no evidence. Back in the present, by getting one name from the list, Odo is able to piece together what Pallra is doing: it's a list of Bajorans who collaborated with the Cardassians, and she's blackmailing them. Odo tells Kira that to know about the collaborators, Vaatrick must have been one himself. Pallra didn't kill her husband, Kira did, looking for the list. He's not sure he'll be able to trust her again.

TRIVIA

- Writer Peter Allan Fields included a few references to another show he had written for, *Columbo*. At one point, Odo even says 'One more thing... ' when questioning his prime suspect.

RATING

- A clever, well-made episode that deals with the compromises and dodgy deals in Odo, Quark and Kira's past. It has some nice twists – unlike too many *Star Trek* episodes – doesn't go for an easy resolution. One of the best *Deep Space Nine* episodes.

2.9 SECOND SIGHT

STARDATE 47329.4

Sisko falls for a mysterious woman... and then meets her double

TX 22 November 1993
WRITERS Mark Gehred-O'Connell, Ira Steven Behr and Robert Hewitt Wolfe (story by Mark Gehred-O'Connell)
DIRECTOR Alexander Singer
GUEST CAST Mark Erickson (Piersall), Richard Kiley (Seyetik), Salli Elise Richardson (Fenna/Nidell)

Sisko is in a good mood after striking up a relationship with a woman called Fenna. Also on the station is Gideon Seyetik of New Halana, a terraformer who's hoping to revive the dead star Epsilon 119 using a new protomatter technique developed by his Blue Horizon project. When Sisko meets Seyetik's wife, Nidell, she resembles Fenna, but denies ever meeting Sisko. He later meets Fenna, who denies being Nidell, but leaves before Sisko can press her. As Sisko accompanies Seyetik to Epsilon 119, Fenna appears in Sisko's quarters. She's an energy being, and her appearance has made Nidell collapse. Seyetik confesses: Nidell hates her husband, but their people mate for life. His wife is a psychoprojective telepath, and Fenna is a projection of her unconscious frustration. Seyetik commits suicide by flying a shuttle into Epsilon 119, restarting it, and freeing Nidell.

TRIVIA

- Originally a Bashir story, it was felt that not enough attention was being paid to Sisko and the focus shifted to him. Rewrites also toned down the hints that Seyetik is an abusive husband.

RATING

- An episode that falls several types of flat, with Kiley and Avery Brooks not at their best and working with weak material. It also suffers from being set up as a mystery but having a twist that's impossible to guess – 'of course... she's psychoprojective... should have seen that coming'. Ultimately, this is a character piece that fails to explore any of the three protagonists.

2.10 SANCTUARY

STARDATE 47391.2

Millions of asylum-seekers seek refuge on Bajor

TX 29 November 1993
WRITER Frederick Rappaport (story by Gabe Essoe and Kelley Miles)
DIRECTOR Les Landau
GUEST CAST Robert Curtis-Brown (Vedek Sorad), Michael Durrell (Hazar), Aron Eisenberg (Nog), Andrew Koenig (Tumak), Deborah May (Haneek), Betty McGuire (Vayna), Leland Orser (Gai), William Schallert (Varani), Nicholas Shaffer (Cowl), Kitty Swink (Rozahn)

Four crewmembers are retrieved from a damaged ship that's emerged from the wormhole. They are Skrreea, from a matriarchy that believes that the wormhole is the 'eye of the universe' that will lead them to Kentanna, which they will make into paradise. They were the victims of the T-Rogarans for centuries, but that race was wiped out by The Dominion, which then conquered their planet in turn. Sisko agrees to organise a mass resettlement of many millions of Skrreea. Sisko selects Draylon II for the asylum-seekers. Haneek, the Skrreean leader, befriends Kira, and believes that Bajor is Kentanna, but the Bajorans refuse to take them. Haneek's son is killed trying to land on Bajor. This shocks the Skrreeans, who realise that Bajor is no paradise.

TRIVIA

- Andrew Koenig is the son of Walter Koenig, who played Chekov. Kitty Swink is Armin Shimerman's wife.

RATING

- A couple of nice ideas – the Skrreea are rather unpleasant to look at, there are millions of them after refuge – helps make this a cut above the usual type of *Star Trek* we could label as 'crude analogies'. There's no easy answer to the problem, and the story's grown up enough to admit it.

2.11 RIVALS

STARDATE UNKNOWN

A charming conman takes Quark's business away from him

TX 3 January 1994
WRITER Joe Menosky (story by Jim Trombetta and Michael Piller)

A charming conman, the El-Aurian Martus Marza, is working on the station, swindling old ladies out of their savings. Odo arrests him, and he's given a mysterious 'gambling device' by his cellmate, who blames it for bad luck then dies. Martus is released without charge, the first event in a run of good luck he has. He opens a rival to Quark's bar, and even lures Rom to work for him. His customers have great luck,

DIRECTOR David Livingston
GUEST CAST Barbara Bosson (Roana), K Callan (Alsia), Rosalind Chao (Keiko O'Brien), Max Grodenchik (Rom), Albert Henderson (Cos), Chris Sarandon (Martus Mazur)

encouraging trade, and there are strange coincidences and quirks of fate throughout the station. Dax investigates, and discovers the gambling devices really do work. Sisko has them destroyed and Martus arrested. Quark bails him out – he wants his rival off the station.

TRIVIA

- Martus Marza is from the same people as Guinan, the El-Aurians, and was intended as a recurring character. However this episode went down poorly with viewers and the staff, so this was his only appearance.
- The episode had the working title *The Butterfly Effect*.

RATING

- A dreadful attempt at a comedy story, the sparring between Quark and his rival just doesn't work. Since that's the key to the episode, what's left is poor plotting disguised as the effects of the gambling device and a few set-pieces that couldn't even have looked that good on paper.

2.12 THE ALTERNATE

STARDATE 47391.7

The scientist who first examined Odo has new clues to his past

TX 10 January 1994
WRITER Bill Dial (story by Jim Trombetta and Bill Dial)
DIRECTOR David Carson
GUEST CAST Matt MacKenzie (Weld Ram), James Sloyan (Mora Pol)

Mora Pol, the scientist who investigated Odo when he was first found, comes to the station. Odo is uncomfortable – he treated him as an experimental subject, not a person. Mora has found DNA like Odo's on L-S VI, a planet in the Gamma Quadrant. They travel there with Dax, finding ruins, and get caught in blasts of volcanic gas. They retrieve a life-form that may be related to Odo's species, but it defies analysis then gets loose on the station. A monstrous creature menaces the station. The crew assume it's the life-form, but Mora realises it's Odo, who's been affected by the gas. Bashir and Mora remove the traces of gas, curing Odo, who has a new respect for his former tormentor.

TRIVIA

- Mora Pol was written as a dual role for Rene Auberjonois, with the fascinating implication that Odo had modelled his 'human' form on his tormentor. However, the show was already effects-laden, so the idea was dropped.
- A homage to *Forbidden Planet*, perhaps the key inspiration for *Star Trek* in the first place, Odo's bestial form strongly resembles the Id monster at the end of that movie.

RATING

- It seems you can't be a *Star Trek* character without an uneasy relationship with your father or surrogate father, and Odo proves no exception. This episode isn't sure whether the Freudian stuff is more important than the Jungian stuff, and ends up as a lukewarm mix of the usual stuff about coming to a new respect for daddy and a monster movie plot that just isn't scary enough.

2.13 ARMAGEDDON GAME

STARDATE UNKNOWN

O'Brien and Bashir help disarm two warring races – but they are betrayed

TX 31 January 1994
WRITER Morgan Gendel
DIRECTOR Winrich Kolbe
GUEST CAST Darleen Carr (E'Tyshra), Larry Cedar (Nydom), Rosalind Chao (Keiko O'Brien), Bill Mondy (Jakin), Peter White (Sharat)

Bashir and O'Brien have discovered a way to destroy Harvesters, biomechanical gene disruptors used by both sides of the T'Lani/Kellerun war. They are disarming the stockpiles on a munitions ship over T'Lani III. Just as they are about to destroy the last one, Kellerun soldiers launch a raid. O'Brien and Bashir escape to the surface of the planet, although O'Brien has been infected. Sisko is told they have died in an accident. Keiko isn't convinced – her husband doesn't drink coffee in the afternoon, like the surveillance tape shows. Sisko and Dax head to T'Lani III to investigate. The Kellerun and T'Lani ambassadors admit to O'Brien and Bashir that to ensure peace, they want to wipe out everyone with knowledge of the Harvesters – including the Starfleet officers. Sisko and Dax rescue them, barely escaping as a T'Lani cruiser fires on them, destroying the USS Ganges. Back on the station, Bashir cures O'Brien, who tells his wife he's had a long afternoon, and needs a coffee.

TRIVIA

- Originally, the weapon bonded with O'Brien, meaning that he had to die to achieve disarmament. This was deemed too similar to *Dramatis Personae*. Sequences of Bashir and O'Brien on the run were scaled back for budgetary reasons.
- The episode was nominated for the Hairstyling Emmy award, but didn't win.

RATING

- A nice character piece, and the first time we really see Bashir and O'Brien's relationship. The twist right at the end is another nice character moment, as well as a genuinely funny joke. And never mind Patrick Stewart not winning an acting Emmy – it's a travesty the hairdos in this episode didn't win their award.

2.14 WHISPERS

O'Brien suspects that everyone on the station is conspiring against him

TX 7 February 1994
WRITER Paul Robert Coyle
DIRECTOR Les Landau
GUEST CAST Majel Barrett (Computer Voice), Susan Bay (Rollman), Rosalind Chao (Keiko O'Brien), Hana Hatae (Molly O'Brien), Philip LeStrange (Coutu), Todd Waring (DeCurtis)

STARDATE 47582.1

O'Brien has been away preparing for the Paradan peace talks, but when he gets back to the station everyone is acting strangely. He suspects Keiko is trying to poison him, and Sisko seems to be assigning him duties to keep him out of the way. His access to the station logs has been downgraded, and he discovers Sisko has been communicating with Paradan rebels. He confronts people with his fears, but they tell him he doesn't understand. O'Brien takes a runabout to Parada II but is mortally wounded by guards. O'Brien learns that he is a replicant killer, designed to activate during the talks – the real O'Brien has been abducted. The replicant dies, with Sisko commending it for its heroic behaviour.

TRIVIA

- Colm Meaney is in every scene of this story, something of a rarity even for episodes that concentrate on a particular character.
- The runabout USS Mekong debuts, to replace the USS Ganges.

RATING

- A twist that owes a great deal to the works of Philip K Dick, but is nevertheless a surprise. We see that even a duplicate O'Brien is a man of integrity and determination. The episode ends too quickly, but that's preferable to dragging it out.

2.15 PARADISE

Sisko and O'Brien are trapped on a planet where technology doesn't work

TX 14 February 1994
WRITERS Jeff King, Richard Manning and Hans Beimler (story by Jim Trombetta and James Crocker)
DIRECTOR Corey Allen
GUEST CAST Majel Barrett (Computer Voice), Michael Buchman Silver (Vinod), Julia Nickson (Cassandra), Gail Strickland (Alixus), Steve Vinovich (Joseph), Erick Weiss (Stephan)

STARDATE 47573.1

Sisko and O'Brien search for M-class planets in the Gamma Quadrant, and discover one in the Orellius system. It's populated, and is bathed in a duonetic field that stops all technology from working. They are captured, and the people explain that they were heading for Gemulon IV but made an emergency landing on Orellius. They were stranded here. The colonists don't want to be rescued, though, as this is an idyllic planet in many ways. A Romulan ship reports it has spotted Sisko's ship and it is traced back to Orellius. It becomes clear that life on Orellius is harsh – a woman dies from a simple insect bite, and Sisko is locked in a boiling hot prison cell. O'Brien discovers that the colony's leader, Alixus, deliberately landed the ship here and set up the duonetic generator. O'Brien switches off the generator, allowing them to be rescued. However, none of the colonists want to leave, and they may even repair the generator.

TRIVIA

- Aware that a lot of the stories revolved around technical solutions, there was a desire to do an episode where the characters couldn't use the tricorders, phasers and so on that they would normally use. As the story got passed around its various writers, the irony was that the 'duonetic field generator' was added, and proved to be yet another technological solution to the plot.

RATING

- Mixed messages abound in this story, which can never quite work out whether Alixus is a good or bad person. It's probably because asking whether technology is 'good' or 'bad' is a fairly banal thing to do in the first place. Nevertheless, it's a good episode for Sisko, who gets to be determined in adversity.

2.16 SHADOWPLAY

STARDATE 47603.3

Odo and Dax discover a village plagued by mysterious disappearances

TX 21 February 1994
WRITER Robert Hewitt Wolfe
DIRECTOR Robert Scheerer
GUEST CAST Philip Anglim (Vedek Bareil), Martin Cassidy (Male villager), Trula M Marcus (Female villager), Kenneth Mars (Colyus), Noley Thornton (Taya), Kenneth Tobey (Rurigan)

Dax and Odo are investigating Omicron particles on a planet in the Gamma Quadrant. They find a generator in a village, but are captured by townsfolk who think they are responsible for recent mysterious disappearances. They persuade them otherwise, and begin an investigation. They meet Rurigan, the elder, and his granddaughter Taya. The little girl says that no one ever leaves the valley. Dax discovers that the village and villagers are all holograms, and switches off the generator. Rurigan survives – he is real. His home planet of Yadera Prime was destroyed by the Dominion, and he recreated it here, with the population growing and developing as they would have otherwise. He believes his life is now over, but Dax persuades him to reactivate the holograms and live out his life there.

TRIVIA

- The original story featured a holodeck prison which O'Brien and Dax kept escaping, only to find they were still on the holodeck.
- O'Brien's rank is given, for the first and only time, as Senior Chief Specialist.

RATING

- An OK story that benefits from great acting, with Ken Tobey and Rene Auberjonois on superb form. This isn't the most original story (there were plenty of stories where androids didn't realise they were androids), but it's a nice, watchable episode.

2.17 PLAYING GOD

STARDATE UNKNOWN

Dax discovers a tiny universe and trains a potential Trill host

TX 28 February 1994
WRITERS Jim Trombetta and Michael Piller (story by Jim Trombetta)
DIRECTOR David Livingston
GUEST CAST Majel Barrett (Computer voice), Geoffrey Blake (Arjin), Chris Nelson Norris (Alien Man), Richard Poe (Cardassian), Ron Taylor (Klingon Host)

Arjin, a young Trill, is on the station while Dax assesses his suitability as a host. After helping Arjin stun some Cardassian voles that are over-running the station, she takes him to the Gamma Quadrant, where she becomes concerned he's too arrogant. The runabout snags on something in space. Dax likens it to 'space seaweed', but when she analyses it, she realises it's a proto-universe, one that will grow and displace our universe. Sisko realises that to destroy it would be to kill untold trillions of life-forms. Dax continues to test Arjin, suggesting he doesn't seem to have clear reasons for becoming a host. It is only by his expert piloting that they manage to replace the proto-universe where they found it. Arjin has come to realise he must have a sense of purpose to become a host, not vice-versa.

TRIVIA

- An episode with three separate Dax plotlines, all quite lightweight. Later revisions played down the micro universe in favour of the trainee Trill story.
- The Cardassian voles have little Cardassian-like ridges on their foreheads and noses!

RATING

- Another episode about symbionts and hosts that seems a bit too vague on the details. The proto-universe story is also a little undefined. The Cardassian voles – and the Cardassian gloating on the subject – are much more fun.

2.18 PROFIT AND LOSS

STARDATE UNKNOWN

Quark meets an old flame – who's now a Cardassian dissident

TX 21 March 1994
WRITERS Flip Kolber and Cindy Marcus
DIRECTOR Robert Wiemer
GUEST CAST Mary Crosby (Natima Lang), Michael Reilly Burke (Hogue), Andrew Robinson (Garak), Heidi Swedberg (Rekelen), Edward Wiley (Gul Toran)

Odo accuses Quark of stealing a small cloaking device. Meanwhile, the crew of a disabled Cardassian ship are beamed to the station, Professor Natima Lang and her students. Quark recognises Natima – they had a short relationship, and Quark is still besotted. O'Brien discovers their ship was fired on by the Cardassians – Natima admits she is a dissident. The Cardassians arrive in force to arrest Natima, who Gul Dukat accuses of being a terrorist. Quark offers Natima the cloaking device, if she agrees to stay with him. She stuns him, but immediately regrets it. She is arrested – the Bajorans have agreed to swap her for Bajoran prisoners. Gul Toran tells Garak he will be welcomed back to Cardassia if he kills Natima before she's handed over. Odo and Quark conspire to smuggle Natima off the station, but Garak blocks them... before deciding to let them leave. He is told he will never be allowed back to Cardassia, then kills Gul Toran. Quark and Garak have both lost what they want most.

TRIVIA

- The working title was *Here's Looking at You*, and was going to be a pastiche of *Casablanca*, but the production team became worried about infringing copyright. This hadn't stopped *The Next Generation* when they made *We'll Always Have Paris* – or numerous other movie-makers.
- The production of this episode was affected by the earthquake in Los Angeles.
- Mary Crosby is, like Denise and Bing, part of the Crosby showbiz dynasty (she's Bing's daughter, Denise's aunt).

RATING

- Quark seems out of character as a romantic lead, and the episode never quite decides whether it's comedy or tragedy. Another episode with a premise that the script can't bring to life and sees the actors try to hold things together.

2.19 BLOOD OATH

STARDATE UNKNOWN

Three old Klingons seek out Dax to help settle an old score

TX 28 March 1994
WRITER Peter Allan Fields
DIRECTOR Winrich Kolbe
GUEST CAST Michael Ansara (Kang), Bill Bolender (the Albino), William Campbell (Koloth), John Colicos (Kor), Christopher Collins (Head guard)

Three old Klingons show up on the station – Kang, Kor and Koloth, comrades of Curzon Dax. Jadzia Dax warmly welcomes them, and they tell her they have tracked down the Albino. Eighty years before, Dax and the Klingons drove away the marauding Klingon Albino, but he returned to kill the Klingons' firstborn with a genetic virus. They swore to kill him. The female Dax eventually persuades them that she should join their quest. When Kang proposes a frontal assault on the Albino's stronghold, Dax suspects he wants an heroic death, and he confesses that he has arranged this last battle with the Albino. Dax bombards the planet with tetryon particles, disabling the Albino's weapons. The four of them launch their attack. Koloth is killed, Kor is wounded, Kang almost defeats the Albino but his bat'leth breaks at a crucial moment, and he is fatally wounded. Dax fights the Albino, but can't bring herself to kill him. Kang does the honours, then dies, honour satisfied.

TRIVIA

- The Klingons Kang, Kor and Koloth were all from the original series – *Day of the Dove*, *Errand of Mercy* and *The Trouble with Tribbles* respectively. It was quickly decided that they would resemble the 'knobbly' Klingons introduced in the first movie, rather than the more swarthy ones of the original series. No explanation was given for their transformation.
- John Colicos reprised his role 27 years after he'd last performed it, probably a record at the time for a television actor returning to the same role.
- The working title was *The Beast*.

RATING

- What's clearly meant to be a tough *The Magnificent Seven*-style story of revenge comes across more like *The Wizard of Oz*, with cute Dax following some cuddly old Klingons off to see the Albino. The music's very stirring, though, and the episode really works.

2.20 THE MAQUIS Part I

STARDATE UNKNOWN

Colonists in the Demilitarised Zone fight the Cardassians

TX 25 April 1994
WRITER James Crocker (story by Rick Berman, Michael Piller, Jeri Taylor and James Crocker)
DIRECTOR David Livingston
GUEST CAST Marc Alaimo (Gul Dukat), Amanda Carlin (Kobb), Bernie Casey (Cal Hudson), Bertila Damas (Sakonna), Steven John Evans (Guard), Michael A Krawic (Samuels), Tony Plana (Amaros), Richard Poe (Gul Evek), Michael Rose (Niles)

A Cardassian freighter explodes as it leaves the station. Meanwhile, Hudson, a friend of Sisko's from Starfleet, tells him that he fears the peace treaty favours the Cardassians over the colonists in the Demilitarised Zone. Gul Dukat shows Sisko proof that colonists were behind the destruction. Taking a runabout into the Demilitarised Zone, Sisko realises the colonists have started an armed uprising. Hudson and Gul Evek argue about the colonists' right to defend themselves. Both sides are clearly arming their own colonists. Sakonna, a Vulcan woman, approaches Quark looking to buy weapons. She abducts Dukat and takes him to an asteroid in the Badlands. Kira gets a message claiming credit for the destruction of the freighter from a group called 'the Maquis'. Tracking down Dukat to the asteroid, Sisko discovers the leader of the Maquis: Hudson.

TRIVIA

- This story, along with *The Next Generation* episodes *Journey's End* and *Pre-Emptive Strike*, laid a lot of groundwork for *Voyager*. This episode introduced the Maquis, a group of human outlaws who'd make up a proportion of the USS Voyager's crew.

RATING

- An episode that introduces a lot. The identity of the secret boss of the Maquis comes from a suspect list with only one name on it, but it's a good episode.

2.21 THE MAQUIS Part II

STARDATE UNKNOWN

The Maquis go to war

TX 2 May 1994
WRITER Ira Steven Behr (story by Rick Berman, Michael Piller, Jeri Taylor and Ira Steven Behr)
DIRECTOR Corey Allen
GUEST CAST Marc Alaimo (Gul Dukat), Michael Bell (Drofo Awa), Amanda Carlin (Kobb), Bernie Casey (Cal Hudson), Bertila Damas (Sakonna), Natalia Nogulich (Nechayev), Tony Plana (Amaros), Michael Rose (Niles), John Schuck (Legate Parn)

Hudson tries to persuade Sisko to side with the Maquis, but he refuses. Odo arrests Quark for selling arms to Sakonna. Legate Parn of the Cardassians tells Sisko that Dukat will be punished for arming the Cardassian colonists in the Demilitarised Zone. Sakonna fails to mind meld with Dukat, but Dukat turns informer, and tips them off that the Cardassians are using Xepolites as gun-runners. They intercept a Xepolite ship. Quark convinces Sakonna that her actions are illogical as it's making peace less likely. She reveals that the Maquis will attack a secret Cardassian weapons dump. The Federation stops the Maquis attack, with both sides suffering heavy losses. Sisko lets Hudson escape. The Maquis survive as a political and military force.

QUOTES

- 'It's easy to be a saint in paradise.' – *Sisko*

TRIVIA

- One of the ironies of the Maquis is that while they were only brought in to *Deep Space Nine* to set up a group to use in *Voyager*, far better use of them was made in *Deep Space Nine*, where their political beliefs and hatred of the Cardassians were more applicable.

RATING

- Action sequences! Finally! *Deep Space Nine* kicks up a gear and starts questioning some of the basics of *Star Trek* – has human nature really changed, or are the Federation's values simply one more luxury in a wealthy society?

2.22 THE WIRE

STARDATE UNKNOWN

Garak has a pleasure-inducing wire in his brain, and it's killing him

Bashir realises that Garak is in pain, but Garak denies it. When Garak collapses, Bashir discovers an implant in his brain. When pressed, Garak says it was given to him by Enabran Tain, head of the Obsidian Order, the Cardassian Secret Police. It releases endorphins, easing

TX 9 May 1994
WRITER Robert Hewitt Wolfe
DIRECTOR Kim Friedman
GUEST CAST Paul Dooley (Enabran Tain), Ann Gillespie (Jabara), Andrew Robinson (Garak), Jimmie F Skaggs (Glinn Boheeka)

pain – it's designed to allow the user to resist torture, but Garak has become addicted to it because he resents his exile, which was imposed when he murdered a man. Bashir deactivates the device, which has become deadly. When Garak awakes, he confesses he was exiled for saving Bajoran lives. The device is still killing Garak and Bashir goes to Tain, who gives him the information that he needs to save Garak. He also tells the doctor that Garak has lied to him. Garak cheerfully admits it when he recovers.

TRIVIA

- Originally Kira was the user, but it was felt this impacted too much on the series, so a supporting character was made the addict.
- The Obsidian Order was originally the Gray Order, but *Babylon 5*'s Minbari were ruled by the Gray Council, so this was changed.

RATING

- A Garak episode, and a welcome one. We're starting to see what makes the Cardassians tick (and, just as importantly, different from the Klingons and Romulans). As he's a supporting character there's a chance Garak might die, too, so there's some suspense when compared with stories like *Invasive Procedures* and *Necessary Evil* where a major character is 'dying'.

2.23 CROSSOVER

STARDATE UNKNOWN

Kira and Bashir end up in the Mirror Universe

TX 16 May 1994
WRITERS Peter Allan Fields and Michael Piller (story by Peter Allan Fields)
DIRECTOR David Livingston
GUEST CAST John Cothran Jr (Telok), Stephen Gevedon (Klingon), Dennis Madalone (Marauder), Jack R Orend (Human), Andrew Robinson (Garak)

Returning through the wormhole, Kira and Bashir's runabout is escorted back to the station by a Klingon ship. Kira meets a version of herself, the Intendant of the station, who explains that this is a parallel universe where the Bajorans are an important part of the Klingon-Cardassian axis. This formed a century ago, when the human Empire collapsed. Kirk's intervention (in *Mirror, Mirror*) weakened the human Empire, leaving the Klingons and Cardassians to move in and enslave humanity. Bashir is sent to process ore, while Kira is given the run of the station because she intrigues the Mirror Kira so much. There are twisted versions of Sisko, Garak and Odo – Quark is much the same, but is arrested and executed for helping humans escape. Garak wants to kill the Mirror Kira and replace her with the good one. He threatens to kill Bashir unless Kira goes along with the plan. Kira tries to get Sisko on side, but he's reluctant. Bashir has met the Mirror O'Brien, but both are captured during an escape attempt in which they kill the Mirror Odo. When Kira threatens them, Sisko starts a mutiny, getting Kira and Bashir back to their runabout. The two of them escape back to their own universe.

TRIVIA

- This is a sequel to the *Star Trek* episode *Mirror, Mirror*. The *Deep Space Nine* crew would return to the Mirror Universe in *Through the Looking Glass, Shattered Mirror* and *The Emperor's New Cloak*, while the Mirror Universe would come to them in *Resurrection*.
- The working title of the episode was *Detour*.

RATING

- An episode that packs a lot in, so ends up feeling a bit rushed. Nana Visitor camps and vamps it up as the Mirror Kira, and if she doesn't quite convince, she at least entertains. It's difficult to determine a point or a moral – unlike the *Star Trek* story, the Mirror versions of the *Deep Space Nine* crew don't tell us much about the originals. But it's a fun change of pace.

2.24 THE COLLABORATOR

STARDATE UNKNOWN

As elections loom – one candidate's shady past surfaces

TX 23 May 1994
WRITERS Gary Holland, Ira Steven Behr and Robert Hewitt Wolfe (story by Gary Holland)

Bajor is electing a new Kai, or religious leader, choosing between Vedek Bareil (Kira's lover) and Vedek Winn. Meanwhile, a former collaborator has come to the station, to much hostility. He passes information to Winn that a monk, Prylar Bek, was a collaborator whose actions led to the deaths of 43 Bajorans at the Kendra Valley Massacre. He also tells him that Prylar Bek was working for Bareil at the time. Kira investigates, and discovers evidence that implicates Bareil, who insists

DIRECTOR Cliff Bole
GUEST CAST Philip Anglim (Vedek Bareil), Louise Fletcher (Vedek Winn), Charles Parks (Eblan), Bert Remsen (Kubus Oak), Camille Saviola (Kai Opaka), Tom Villard (Prylar Bek)

it was for the greater good – many more Bajorans would have died otherwise. Bareil withdraws from the election and Winn is duly elected. Kira realises that it was Kai Opaka who was the real collaborator – for the good of Bajor, Bareil has protected her reputation.

TRIVIA

- This episode was transmitted in the same week as *All Good Things*, the last episode of *The Next Generation.*

RATING

- A dark episode that overturns a few apple carts, and actually makes Bajor seem like an interesting place, which is pretty impressive. It's another story about the murky motivations during the Cardassian occupation of Bajor, when *everyone* seems to have committed at least one secret murder and slept with someone on the other side. But it's entertaining stuff.

2.25 TRIBUNAL

O'Brien is arrested and tried by the Cardassians

TX 6 June 1994
WRITER Bill Dial
DIRECTOR Avery Brooks
GUEST CAST Majel Barrett (Computer Voice), John Beck (Raymond Boone), Rosalind Chao (Keiko O'Brien), Julian Christopher (Cardassian Voice), Caroline Lagerfelt (Makbar), Richard Poe (Gul Evek), Fritz Weaver (Kovat)

STARDATE 47944.2

O'Brien meets an old friend from the USS Rutledge, Raymond Boone. Shortly afterwards, he, Keiko and Molly set off on holiday in a runabout when they are stopped by a Cardassian patrol, and the Chief is taken to Cardassia Prime. Odo is allowed to serve as his nestor, or legal advisor. O'Brien's voiceprint authorised the transfer of photon warheads to his runabout – the Cardassians suspect he's a Maquis sympathiser. Kira realises the voiceprint has been altered somehow. She suspects Boone, whom Bashir discovers is a surgically-altered Cardassian. O'Brien has been tortured, and his trial goes badly. Sisko arrives in the nick of time with Boone, and O'Brien is released to return to his holiday.

TRIVIA

- This was Avery Brooks' first time as director, and the first time *Star Trek* had shown the Cardassian home planet, Cardassia Prime, which was seen to be a stark, harsh place.

RATING

- Avery Brooks gets a great performance out of Colm Meaney, one that makes you realise just how wasted his talents had been on *The Next Generation* – it really does stand up well with Patrick Stewart's performance in *Chain of Command Pt II.* A great episode, where the fact a character is clearly innocent of the trumped-up charge is the point of the story, not the great 'revelation' at the end.

2.26 THE JEM'HADAR

Sisko discovers more about the Dominion – and stirs a hornet's nest

TX 13 June 1994
WRITER Ira Steven Behr
DIRECTOR Kim Friedman
GUEST CAST Majel Barrett (Computer Voice), Aron Eisenberg (Nog), Sandra Grando (Second Officer), Molly Hagan (Eris), Michael Jace (First Officer), Alan Oppenheimer (Keogh), Cress Williams (Talak'talan)

STARDATE UNKNOWN

Sisko heads into the Gamma Quadrant with Jake, Nog and Quark. On a wooded planet, they are attacked by Eris, a telekinetic woman who is being pursued by fierce warriors, the Jem'Hadar. Eris tells them they work for the Dominion. Captured by the warriors, they learn that The Dominion is run by the mysterious 'Founders'. They want Sisko's knowledge of the Alpha Quadrant. A Jem'Hadar ship heads for the station, and issues a declaration – they have destroyed the main Bajoran colony in the Gamma Quadant, New Bajor, and will not tolerate further incursions from the Alpha Quadrant. The Galaxy-class USS Odyssey arrives as the station crew fit extra weapons to the station and runabouts. The Odyssey and a pair of runabouts head to the Gamma Quadrant to rescue Sisko and his party. The Jem'Hadar attack, and Sisko escapes home... but a Jem'Hadar suicide attack destroys the Odyssey. Odo realises Eris could have escaped at any time – she's a spy. She beams away, but not before warning that Sisko doesn't realise what he's begun... Sisko vows to be ready for the Dominion attack.

TRIVIA

- The working title of the episode was *The Dominion.*
- Eris is a Vorta, one of the bureaucrats of The Dominion, but she's the only one to demonstrate telekinesis. One idea hinted at but never really developed is that The Dominion can offer genetic enhancements as an incentive to work for them. This is exactly what the Suliban do in *Enterprise.*

RATING

- Not before time, we get a sense of threat from the Gamma Quadrant. The USS Odyssey is clearly modelled on the Enterprise-D – it's not only the same type of ship, it's got a bald captain. The Jem'Hadar destroy it, basically so the viewers get to see how hard they are. The rest of the episode is about as subtle, but it does what a season finale needs to do – set up a threat for the future.

STAR TREK: DEEP SPACE NINE **SEASON THREE**

3.1 THE SEARCH Part I

STARDATE 48212.4

Sisko acquires the Defiant but the warship is overpowered by the Jem'Hadar

TX 26 September 1994
WRITER Ronald D Moore (story by Ira Steven Behr and Robert Hewitt Wolfe).
DIRECTOR Kim Friedman
GUEST CAST John Fleck (Ornithar), Martha Hackett (T'Rul), Salome Jens (Female Alien), Kenneth Marshall (Michael Eddington)

As Kira prepares for a possible Jem'Hadar invasion, Sisko returns to the station with an experimental warship, the Defiant, equipped with a cloaking device provided by the Romulan T'Rul. Sisko plans to reason with the Founders, the leaders of The Dominion, or else demonstrate Federation firepower. Odo is replaced by Lieutenant Commander Eddington and resigns. Nevertheless, he joins the Defiant at the request of the Bajorans. In the Gamma Quadrant, T'Rul operates the cloaking device and they escape the Jem'Hadar. Quark contacts the Karemma, with whom he has traded, who inform him of a Dominion communications base on Callinon VII. Dax and O'Brien survey the base, but Jem'Hadar ships approach and Sisko has to leave them behind. Meanwhile, Odo tells Kira that he is drawn to the Omarion Nebula. Suddenly, the Defiant is attacked by three Jem'Hadar ships. They are boarded and Kira is knocked unconscious. She awakens in a shuttlecraft with Odo, who has set course for the Omarion Nebula.

QUOTES

- 'A little surprise for The Dominion...' – *Sisko unveils the Defiant*

TRIVIA

- Ira Behr and Robert Wolfe conceived the Defiant as an antidote to the squeaky-clean technology of *The Next Generation.* Though the writers fought hard to have a cloaking device on the ship, giving rise to the idea of a Romulan presence, it had apparently disappeared after the second episode of *The Search.* Only later would it become a firm fixture.
- Martha Hackett would go on to play Seska on *Star Trek: Voyager.*
- The episode sees the introduction of Michael Eddington, the engimatic officer who would become Sisko's nemesis in later episodes.

RATING

- High octane stuff to kick-start the third season, although the Defiant is a distinct change of concept. Still, the sheer insanity of the Defiant – a craft so well armed that it almost self-destructs when used – makes for fun viewing!

3.2 THE SEARCH Part II

STARDATE UNKNOWN

Odo discovers he is one of the Founders

TX 3 October 1994
WRITER Ira Steven Behr (story by Ira Steven Behr and Robert Hewitt Wolfe)
DIRECTOR Jonathan Frakes
GUEST CAST Dennis Christopher (Borath), Diaunté (Jem'Hadar Guard), Christopher Doyle (Jem'Hadar Officer), William Frankfather (Male Shapeshifter), Martha Hackett (T'Rul), Salome Jens (Female Shapeshifter), Kenneth Marshall (Michael Eddington), Tom Morga (Jem'Hadar Soldier), Natalija Nogulich (Admiral Nechayev), Andrew Robinson (Garak)

Odo and Kira arrive at the homeworld of Odo's people in the Omarion Nebula. A female shapeshifter welcomes Odo but is hostile towards Kira. Meanwhile, Sisko and Bashir abandon the Defiant and meet up with O'Brien and Dax. The Federation is negotiating with a Founder, Borath, but the Romulans have been excluded from the talks. Odo learns that he was sent out as a child to explore the universe then return to his homeworld, where the Changelings have sheltered from persecution by the 'solids'. Kira is suspicious after she detects a power source behind a locked door. On the station, Sisko learns that the Federation has signed the Bajoran sector, the wormhole and DS9 over to The Dominion. The Jem'Hadar get out of hand and kill T'Rul. Incensed, Sisko, Garak, Dax, Bashir and O'Brien steal a runabout and set out to close the wormhole forever. Garak is killed, but the others succeed. Odo opens the locked door and finds Jem'Hadar soldiers. He and Kira are taken to a room where Sisko and the Defiant crew are hooked into an alien device that is making them experience the events on DS9. The Jem'Hadar are researching Federation reponses to an invasion. The female shapeshifter reveals that they are the Founders. The officers take the Defiant and return through the wormhole.

TRIVIA

- Natalia Nogulich reprises her role as Admiral Nechayev, first seen in *The Next Generation*'s *Chain of Command*. Nogulich was to play X in *The X-Files*, and recorded a few scenes, but was replaced by Steven Williams.
- Jonathan Frakes makes his *Deep Space Nine* directorial debut.

RATING

- An episode that fools you the first time, but wins no awards for cheating the audience. It's all smoke and mirrors, while your attention should be on Odo. Sadly, the fantasy events set up a season three that is more interesting than the one we actually get.

3.3 THE HOUSE OF QUARK

STARDATE UNKNOWN

Quark becomes the reluctant leader of a Klingon House

TX 10 October 1994
WRITER Ronald D Moore (story by Tom Benko)
DIRECTOR Les Landau
GUEST STARS Mary Kay Adams (Grilka), John Lendale Bennett (Kozak), Carlos Carrasco (D'Ghor), Rosalind Chao (Keiko), Max Grodenchik (Rom), Robert O'Reilly (Gowron), Joseph Ruskin (Tumek)

A drunken Klingon, Kozak, falls on his knife and dies. Quark takes credit for killing Kozak in self-defence, but is soon confronted by Kozak's brother, D'Ghor, who will only spare Quark if Kozak died honourably in battle. Kozak's widow, Grilka, learns the truth and takes Quark to the Klingon homeworld where she marries him to take control of her husband's House. Gowron agrees to consider Grilka's demand that Quark succeed Kozak as ruler of the House. Quark discovers D'Ghor has been weakening Kozak's assets, priming it for takeover. Quark and Grilka tell Gowron, but are out-manoeuvred – D'Ghor has been told the truth about Kozak's death by Rom and now demands a fight to the death. Quark faces D'Ghor, but throws his sword down. As D'Ghor makes to strike, Gowron intercedes, disgusted that D'Ghor would kill an unarmed Ferengi. He grants control of the House to Grilka. Quark is grateful for a divorce.

QUOTES

- 'A brave Ferengi... Who would have thought it possible?' – *Gowron's final comment on Quark*

TRIVIA

- Joseph Ruskin made his first appearance as Tumek, a role he would reprise in season five's *Looking for par-Mach in All the Wrong Places*.
- The episode marks the temporary departure of Keiko from the station. The writers needed to free up Colm Meaney for movie work and to explore the Bashir-O'Brien sparring in more depth.

- Mary Kay Adams played Na'Toth in the second season of *Babylon 5*. The original actress to play Na'Toth, Caitlin Brown, appeared in the first season *Deep Space Nine* episode *The Passenger*.

RATING

- Ludicrous on paper, but actually quite fun to watch. Gowron makes a surprisingly neat transition to DS9, which stands the series in good stead for later seasons. Quark's amusing relationship with Grilka is too good to let pass and is later revived in season five's *Looking For par-Mach in All The Wrong Places.*

3.4 EQUILIBRIUM

STARDATE UNKNOWN

Jadzia is endangered when Dax recalls a previous host

TX 17 October 1994
WRITER René Echevarria (story by Christopher Teague)
DIRECTOR Cliff Bole
GUEST CAST Lisa Banes (Dr Renhol), Nicholas Cascone (Timor), Jeff Magnus McBride (Joran Belar), Harvey Vernon (Yolad)

Dax is haunted by strangely familiar sounds and hallucinations. Bashir discovers that she has dangerously low levels of the drug that allows the Trill to bond with the host. Sisko and Bashir take Dax to the Trill homeworld where she is treated by Dr Renhol. Dax experiences a second hallucination, set 100 years earlier, in which she is being pursued by Trill officials. Timor, an un-joined Trill, explains Dax is experiencing a memory from one of Dax's previous hosts. Suddenly, Dax hallucinates the murder of a Trill doctor by a masked figure, Joran Belar. Dax goes into neural shock and may have to be transplanted, killing Jadzia. Sisko suspects Timor is hiding something and contacts Joran's brother, Yolad, who reveals Joran was not deemed suitable as a host but was probably joined anyway. Sisko realises the symbiont was Dax, proving that half the Trill population can be hosts, not one in 1,000 as previously thought. Aware that the revelation would cause chaos, Dr Renhol fights to save Jadzia. Timor helps Dax come to terms with her new memories.

TRIVIA

- The episode marks the first appearance of Joran, a murderer and one of Dax's previous hosts. The actor, Jeff Magnus McBride, is a performance magician and the use of masks came from his stage show. Joran would later be played by Avery Brooks in *Facets* and Leigh J McCloskey in *Field of Fire.*

RATING

- A clever little story that has consequences that resonate through later seasons. The notion of past lives is haunting and handled well, while the overly operatic Joran makes for an interesting villain. There's much more to go at here.

3.5 SECOND SKIN

STARDATE UNKNOWN

Kira awakens as a Cardassian and ordered to report back on her secret mission

TX 24 October 1994
WRITER Robert Hewitt Wolfe
DIRECTOR Les Landau
GUEST CAST Billy Burke (Ari), Christopher Carroll (Gul Benil), Cindy Katz (Yteppa), Tony Papenfuss (Yeln), Lawrence Pressman (Ghemor), Andrew Robinson (Garak), Gregory Sierra (Entek), Freyda Thomas (Alenis Grem)

Kira is bemused to discover she was supposedly incarcerated in a Cardassian prison ten years previously. When she investigates, she is kidnapped and awakens on Cardassia – as a Cardassian. Entek tells her she is Iliana Ghemor, an agent of the Obsidian Order, who was given the memories of the real Kira. Kira is met by her supposed father, Ghemor, but refuses to accept this reality. On the station, Garak informs Sisko that Kira has been kidnapped and they set course for Cardassia with Odo. Meanwhile, Kira begins to doubt herself when Entek enunciates thoughts Kira has had, but never told anyone else. Nevertheless, she tries to escape but is captured. Ghemor is heartbroken but decides to get Kira away from Cardassia. Kira realises Ghemor is a dissident – Entek is using Kira's similarity to Iliana to make Ghemor reveal himself. Entek and two agents arrest Kira and Ghemor but Sisko, Garak and Odo intercede. Garak kills Entek. Back on the station, tests reveal that Kira is Bajoran. Ghemor vows to find his real daughter but feels close to Kira.

TRIVIA

- Wolfe originally pitched this idea to *The Next Generation* but it was not used. For *Deep Space Nine*, he proposed the radical suggestion that O'Brien was a deep cover Cardassian officer, who replaced the real O'Brien during the Cardassian war. The flaw was Molly O'Brien, leading Wolfe to use Kira instead. During writing, Wolfe realised that the key was that someone is who they believe themselves to be, and as a result Kira's 'real' identity as a Cardassian was lost.

RATING

- Good high-concept stuff, from the same roots as the Next Generation's *Face of the Enemy* and *Frame of Mind.* This time, however, there's a compelling reason for the prosthetics and a potent story to figure out. Again, there's more to go at here, hence the storyline is revived in season five's *Ties of Blood and Water.*

3.6 THE ABANDONED

STARDATE 48214.5

Odo tries to change the instincts of a Jem'Hadar child

TX 31 October 1994
WRITERS D Thomas Maio and Steve Warnek
DIRECTOR Avery Brooks
GUEST CAST Leslie Bevis (Boslic Captain), Matthew Kimborough (Alien High Roller), Hassan Nicholas (Jem'Hadar Boy), Bumper Robinson (Teenage Jem'Hadar), Jill Sayre (Mardah)

Quark buys a wrecked ship and finds a newborn child inside. The child has an accelerated metabolic rate and grows into an eight-year-old in a few hours. A few hours later, it turns into a mature Jem'Hadar warrior. Sisko decides to send the Jem'Hadar to Starfleet for study but Odo objects, having once been a subject of study himself, and tries to reason with the boy. Meanwhile, Sisko is concerned for Jake, who is dating Mardah, a Dabo girl. His disquiet seems to ease when the three have dinner together. The Jem'Hadar boy shows deference to Odo, a Founder, but still hungers for violence despite Odo's efforts. When a Starfleet vessel arrives, the Jem'Hadar refuses to leave and pulls a phaser on Sisko. Odo reluctantly concedes that he cannot change the boy. The Jem'Hadar is returned to the Gamma Quadrant.

TRIVIA

- We learn here that the Jem'Hadar have little need for food and are addicted to ketracel white, although the drug is not named.

RATING

- More insights into the Jem'Hadar, played out through a fairly standard 'teenage angst' story for both the warrior and Jake. We get the first glimmers of Jake's literary career in his conversations with Mardah, although their relationship would soon be over.

3.7 CIVIL DEFENCE

STARDATE UNKNOWN

The officers accidentally activate Cardassian civil defence systems on the station

TX 7 November 1994
WRITER Mike Krohn
DIRECTOR Reza Badiyi
GUEST CAST Marc Alaimo (Gul Dukat), Danny Goldring (Legate Kell), Andrew Robinson (Garak)

O'Brien, Sisko and Jake accidentally activate an automated Cardassian security program. A pre-recorded message from Gul Dukat warns of a workers' revolt. They are able to escape through a ventilation duct before lethal gas is released to kill the workers. Dukat warns that the workers have escaped and Ops and the Security office are locked down. Dax, trapped in Ops, inadvertantly activates another program to release the deadly gas in five minutes. Garak breaks into Ops and convinces Kira to destroy the life support system, stopping the gas. Another message from Dukat warns that the station will self-destruct in two hours! To their surprise, Dukat beams into Ops to gloat at the predicament. However, when he tries to beam out, his old leader appears on screen, informing Dukat that his codes have been revoked to prevent Dukat deserting his post! Dax succeeds in shorting out the station's force fields, allowing Sisko, Jake and O'Brien to redirect the fusion bomb blast harmlessly.

TRIVIA

- Although the episode originated with Mike Krohn, it went through numerous rewrites which involved most of the writing team. The final version sets up Dukat's predatory interest in Kira, which is picked up in *Return to Grace* and *By Inferno's Light.*

RATING

- Amusing stuff, especially Dukat's discovery that his leader didn't trust him. It's an action-packed episode filled with classic comedy capers. Sadly, Dukat's nasty interest in Kira is tainted with the light-hearted feel of the episode and is only later resolved satisfactorily.

3.8 MERIDIAN

STARDATE 48423.2

Dax falls in love with a man who must return to another dimension

TX 14 November 1994
WRITER Mark Gehred-O'Connell (story by Hilary Bader and Evan Carlos Somers)
DIRECTOR Jonathan Frakes
GUEST CAST Jeffrey Combs (Tiron), Brett Cullen (Deral), Christine Healy (Seltin), Mark Humphrey (Lito)

Sisko, Dax, Bashir and O'Brien find a planet that has just appeared in the Gamma Quadrant. A female inhabitant, Seltin, reveals that her planet, Meridian, shifts between dimensions. Dax is drawn to another Meridian, Deral, who explains that Meridian will appear for 12 days and then disappear for another 60 years. Each reappearance gets shorter and Meridian becomes less stable. Dax, in love with Deral, discovers that the cause is an imbalance in a nearby sun. The officers can stabilise Meridian, allowing it to stay for 30 years, but not before the planet disappears again for another 60 years. Deral decides to join Dax in the Alpha Quadrant. Seltin is dismayed by Deral's decision – the small society cannot afford to lose him. Instead, Dax decides to stay on Meridian. However, Dax's presence interferes with the dimensional shift. Sisko beams her to the Defiant, allowing Meridian to shift dimensions, but leaving her without Deral for another 60 years.

TRIVIA

- Jeffrey Combs (Tiron) makes the first of many appearances in *Deep Space Nine.* He later appears as Brunt and the Vorta Weyoun.

RATING

- *Star Trek* meets *Brigadoon* in an appallingly schmaltzy episode. Unsurprisingly, Dax forgets the wet Deral and we hear no more about him. There's more success with a second storyline involving Quark's sleazy holosuite program, and a fantasy about Kira, but its all throwaway stuff.

3.9 DEFIANT

STARDATE 48467.3

The Defiant is stolen by Tom Riker

TX 21 November 1994
WRITER Ronald D Moore
DIRECTOR Cliff Bole
GUEST CAST Marc Alaimo (Gul Dukat), Majel Barrett (Computer Voice), Michael Canavan (Tamal), Shannon Cochran (Kalita), Jonathan Frakes (Riker), Robert Kerbeck (Cardassian Soldier), Tricia O'Neil (Korinas)

Commander William Riker visits the station and tours the Defiant. Suddenly, he stuns Kira and steals the ship, warping out of the sector. The commander is really Thomas Riker, Riker's double, created by a transporter accident, who now works for the Maquis. Sisko and Gul Dukat join forces to hunt down Riker. On the Defiant, Riker sets course for the Orias system, where renegade Cardassians are amassing an invasion force. Sisko pursues but Korinas, an agent of the Obsidian Order, insists the system is under the Order's control and threatens to destroy trespassers. Dukat sends ten ships after the Defiant, but is surprised when three ships belonging to the Order arrive. Riker attacks but is outgunned. Dukat lets the Defiant return to Federation space in return for its sensor logs on the Order's activities in the Orias system. Riker surrenders to save his Maquis colleagues.

QUOTES

- 'Terrorists don't get to be heroes.' – *Kira to Tom Riker*

TRIVIA

- One idea pitched was that the Maquis would gain strength throughout the third season. Sisko would discover that the reason was a new leader, Tom Riker. Sadly, the whole thread was completed in the first few minutes. The rest of the episode was based on *Fail Safe*, a Cold War thriller, and placed Sisko in the enemy war-room, forced to shoot down one of his own ships.

RATING

- A fun episode seeing the welcome return of Frakes in front of the camera. More importantly, it's an interesting vehicle to set up the power struggle within the Cardassian empire. As ever, Marc Alaimo is a delight as Dukat.

3.10 FASCINATION

STARDATE UNKNOWN

When Lwaxana Troi visits the station, the inhabitants get amorous!

TX 28 November 1994
WRITER Philip Lazebnik (story by Ira Steven Behr and James Crocker)
DIRECTOR Avery Brooks
GUEST CAST Philip Anglim (Vedek Bareil), Majel Barrett (Lwaxana Troi), Rosalind Chao (Keiko), Hana Hatae (Molly)

It is the Bajoran Gratitude Festival, and the officers are to be reunited with their loved ones. However, Kira is too busy to spend time with Bareil, O'Brien is cool with Keiko and Odo hides from Lwaxana Troi. When Lwaxana experiences a headache, Jake suddenly confesses his love for Kira while Bareil makes a play for Dax. A second headache and Dax makes for Sisko! Meanwhile, Keiko announces that she must stay on Bajor for her work, annoying O'Brien. Lwaxana has another headache – and Kira and Bashir race to the infirmary for a passionate clinch. At the festival, Sisko evades Dax, Dax punches Bareil and Jake pursues Kira, but she is preoccupied with Bashir. Keiko arrives to make amends with O'Brien, but is interrupted by Quark – who declares his love for her! Sisko and Odo realise Lwaxana's last headache was near Quark – Bashir discovers that Lwaxana has Zanthi Fever, a Betazoid illness that projects amorous feelings onto others nearby. Sisko is bemused to find it only works on people who already have a latent attraction. Bashir cures everyone – and O'Brien and Keiko are reunited.

QUOTES

- 'You humans never learn. You let your women go out in public, hold jobs, wear clothing and you wonder why your marriages fall apart.' – *Quark offers some advice to O'Brien*

TRIVIA

- *Fascination* was conceived as a light episode to raise spirits in advance of the gloom and doom of *Past Tense*. The crew were also given the freedom to innovate, putting more colour into the scenes and bathing some sets in pink light.
- In the episode, Lwaxana Troi has information about the Changelings, but does not reveal her source. In the shooting script, Lwaxana explains she heard it from Admiral Nechayev, who she describes as a sister she never had.

RATING

- A silly episode, but amusing nevertheless. The latent attraction between some of the characters is a useful revelation to leave in the air. Yet, amid the *Midsummer Night's Dream* levity, there is the pressure on Keiko and Miles, adding a bit more weight to the show.

3.11 PAST TENSE Part I

STARDATE 48481.2

Sisko is transported into Earth's past at a crucial time of social change

TX 2 January 1995
WRITER Robert Hewitt Wolfe (story by Ira Steven Behr and Robert Hewitt Wolfe)
DIRECTOR Reza Badiyi
GUEST CAST John Lendale Bennett (Gabriel Bell), Henry Hayashi (Male Guest), Patty Holley (Female Guest), Richard Lee Jackson (Danny Webb), Tina Lifford (Lee), Jim Metzler (Chris Brynner), Frank Military (BC), Dick Miller (Vin), Al Rodrigo (Bernardo), Bill Smitrovich (Michael Webb), Eric Stuart (Stairway Guard)

Sisko, Dax and Bashir beam down from the Defiant to San Francisco but find themselves in the year 2024. Sisko and Bashir are arrested and taken to Sanctuary District, a ghetto for the homeless, unemployed and mentally ill. Meanwhile, Dax is found by a businessman, Chris Brynner, who gives her an ID card so she can set out to find the others. Sisko realises that a crucial event in Earth's history, the Bell Riots, is about to unfold. The inhabitants will take hostages and their leader, Gabriel Bell, will sacrifice himself to save them. The event led to major social change. Meanwhile, Kira, Odo and O'Brien deduce that the officers have travelled in time. On Earth, Sisko and Bashir get involved in a scuffle for Bashir's food card and a bystander is killed – Gabriel Bell. When Kira tries to contact Earth, she discovers that Starfleet has vanished – history has changed. In Sanctuary District, the inhabitants take hostages. As the riot begins, Sisko identifies himself as Gabriel Bell.

TRIVIA

- Concerned by the increasing numbers of homeless people on the streets of Santa Monica, Wolfe submitted a screenplay, *Cold and Distant Stars*, in which Sisko suffers amnesia and lives a life on the streets in 1990s Earth. Ira Behr suggested as inspiration the Attica Prison riot of 1972, where prisoners rioted against inhumane conditions. Amazingly, as the episode was in pre-production, Los Angeles council proposed shutting the city's homeless people into a fenced industrial area.
- The episode alludes to a Starfleet policy on Temporal Displacement which is picked up in season five's *Trials and Tribble-ations.*

RATING

- *Past Tense* begins as a standard time-travel episode but quickly develops into a potent social commentary. There's a richness and awful reality to the darker side of twenty-first century Earth, as well as a real sense of sacrifice that ultimately resulted in the Starfleet we know. Finally, we're seeing *Star Trek*'s soft underbelly.

3.12 PAST TENSE Part II

STARDATE UNKNOWN

Sisko impersonates Gabriel Bell to ensure that history takes its course

TX 9 January 1995
WRITERS Ira Steven Behr and René Echevarria (story by Ira Steven Behr & Robert Hewitt Wolfe)
DIRECTOR Jonathan Frakes
GUEST CAST Mitch David Carter (Swat Leader), Clint Howard (Grady), Richard Lee Jackson (Danny Webb), Tina Lifford (Lee), Jim Metzler (Chris Brynner), Frank Military (BC), Dick Miller (Vin), Al Rodrigo (Bernardo), Bill Smitrovich (Michael Webb), Deborah Van Valkenburgh (Detective Preston), Daniel Zacapa (Henry Garcia)

As Sisko takes charge of the riot, Dax realises he and Bashir are in danger. Meanwhile, Kira and O'Brien beam into different time periods, but cannot find the officers. Sisko, aided by family man Webb, negotiates with Police Detective Preston, who promises to take their concerns to the governor. Preston later meets Dax, but she cannot convince him to help her find her crewmates. Sisko and Webb refuse to give up the hostages. Dax is captured trying to enter Sanctuary District, but enables Sisko and Webb to use the computer. Soon the events in Sanctuary District are common knowledge. The Governor orders in the troops. As Kira and O'Brien locate Dax, troops burst into Sanctuary District, killing Webb and many others. Sisko takes a bullet for a hostage. As the National Guard take over, Sisko and Bashir are allowed to leave and swap their ID cards with two dead men, restoring the timeline. The remaining hostages promise to tell the truth about the plight of Sanctuary District.

TRIVIA

- *Past Tense* was originally a single-parter but gained a second episode when Michael Piller observed that the hostage scene could be extended for almost a full episode. This bottle show helped to recoup the expense of part one.
- The part of Grady was originally written for Iggy Pop, but the singer was touring Europe and unable to do it. Instead, Frakes cast Clint Howard, brother of film director Ron Howard and better known to fans as Balok in the original series episode *The Corbomite Maneuver*. Iggy Pop later appeared as the Vorta Yelgrun in season six's *The Magnificent Ferengi*.

RATING

- A slightly disappointing second part that lacks the frantic activity of the first. This time, the writers just about manage to stay the right side of preachy. Interestingly, the two-parter goes some way to redrawing Bashir as a more mature character.

3.13 LIFE SUPPORT

STARDATE 48498.4

Bareil is seriously injured on the eve of a Bajoran-Cardassian peace treaty

TX 30 January 1995
WRITER Ronald D Moore (story by Christian Ford and Roger Soffer)
DIRECTOR Reza Badiyi
GUEST CAST Philip Anglim (Vedek Bareil), Kevin Carr (Bajoran), Aron Eisenberg (Nog), Louise Fletcher (Kai Winn), Ann Gillespie (Nurse), Eva Loseth (Riska), Andrew Prine (Legate Turrel), Lark Voorhies (Leanne)

Vedek Bareil is seriously injured when a Bajoran transport is damaged at the station. Kai Winn tells Sisko that she and Bareil are on a secret peace mission to Cardassia – Bareil is the driving force. Bareil is stabilised but in a critical condition. Winn asks Bashir to find a way to let Bareil continue his work. Bashir has a drug that would do so, but it could reduce Bareil's chance of recovery. Winn begins the talks but needs Bareil, whose organs are failing. Bashir wants to put Bareil in stasis, but the Vedek wants to help. When Winn consults Bareil the next time, his brain begins to fail. On Kira and Winn's insistance, Bashir uses artificial brain implants to revive Bareil again. Bareil is horrified that he can no longer experience emotions. However, he is able to complete the negotiations and the treaty is signed. Bashir leaves Kira alone with Bareil, who dies.

QUOTES

- 'I don't care about your negotiations and I don't care about your treaty. All I care about is my patient and right now he needs more treatment and less politics.' – *Bashir to Winn*

TRIVIA

- The original pitch for *Life Support* saw Bashir bring a deceased Federation ambassador back to life to complete negotiations with the Romulans. A kind of Dr Frankenstein, Bashir has to let his monster die. The writers decided on Vedek Bareil to add weight and converted the Romulans to Cardassians. Bareil's death did not go unnoticed: the production team was inundated with angry letters from a fan group called The Friends of Vedek Bareil.

RATING

- *Life Support* is a powerful, emotional episode that is entirely undercut by a ludicrous Jake-Nog comedy sub-plot. If only the writers had held their nerve, this could be one of the show's better moments. Instead it treads an uncomfortable line and becomes a dull 'weepy' towards the end.

3.14 HEART OF STONE

Odo reveals his feelings to Kira when she is trapped by a crystalline organism

TX 6 February 1995
WRITERS Ira Steven Behr and Robert Hewitt Wolfe
DIRECTOR Alexander Singer
GUEST CAST Majel Barrett (Computer Voice), Aron Eisenberg (Nog), Max Grodenchik (Rom), Salome Jens (Female Shapeshifter)

STARDATE 48521.5

Kira and Odo pursue a Maquis ship to a deserted moon. In the caverns, Kira is trapped by a crystalline structure that grows over her foot. Odo tries unsuccessfully to call for help. When he returns, both of Kira's legs are trapped. Odo and Kira decide to find a frequency that will shatter the crystal, but time is against them and Kira could be encased. They try all frequencies but the crystal does not shatter. With the moon unstable, Kira orders Odo to leave but he refuses and confesses that he is in love with her. Kira says she is in love with him too but Odo becomes suspicious and demands to know what happened to the real Kira. Kira and the crystal structure morph into the female shapeshifter Odo encountered before. She hoped to trick Odo into thinking Kira had died to persuade him to return home. Odo rescues Kira and they return to Deep Space Nine, but he does not reveal his true feelings to her. Meanwhile, Sisko is persuaded to write Nog a reference to enter Starfleet Academy.

QUOTES

- 'Of course everything that goes wrong is your fault – it says so in your contract.' – *Quark to Rom*

TRIVIA

- Alhough the episode was expected to major on the Odo-Kira story, it was the Nog storyline that drew fan acclaim.
- The episode 'introduces' the never-seen character of Ensign Vilix'pran, an alien male who gives birth by sprouting offspring like buds. In later episodes, we hear that Vilix'pran is pregnant again and that Jake babysits for him.
- The episode also makes reference to the Bajoran-Cardassian peace treaty, negotiated in *Life Support*.

RATING

- The moment we have been waiting for, only for it to be a cheat on the audience. Like *The Search*, to which this is a sequel, the mind games are a disappointing dénouement. The final scene is a poignant coda. Meanwhile, the Nog sub-plot, much acclaimed by fans, feels like a whimsical distraction.

3.15 DESTINY

Sisko must fulfil his destiny when a Bajoran prophecy seems set to come true

TX 13 February 1995
WRITERS David S Cohen and Martin A Winer
DIRECTOR Les Landau
GUEST CAST Erick Avari (Vedek Yarka), Jessica Hendra (Dejar), Wendy Robie (Ulani Belor), Tracy Scoggins (Gilora Rejal)

STARDATE 48543.2

Two Cardassian scientists arrive to help the crew establish a subspace relay in the Gamma Quadrant, allowing communications through the wormhole. Vedek Yarka warns of a prophecy that the wormhole will be destroyed. Sisko points out holes in the prophecy, but they suddenly come true. Kira is convinced of the prophecy when the Defiant encounters a rogue comet *en route* for the wormhole. She tells Sisko that he, the Emissary, must make a decision as is foretold. Sisko is dismissive and sends a test signal that collapses the wormhole and draws the comet closer. O'Brien modifies the Defiant's phasers to vaporise the comet, but this merely splits the comet into three sections. The officers discover that Dejar, one of the Cardassian scientists, is a member of the Obsidian Order and sabotaged the efforts to close the wormhole to The Dominion. Kira and Sisko take a shuttlecraft and surround the three comet fragments in a field that allows them to pass through the wormhole safely. The comet slivers act as filaments that boost communications through the wormhole. Kira realises that the prophecy was misinterpreted. The revelation makes Sisko reconsider his own prophesied role.

TRIVIA

- *Destiny* began life as a second-season script, but early drafts floundered around the promise of a prophecy of joy and miracles.
- Tracy Scoggins appeared in the last season of *Babylon 5* as Captain Elizabeth Lochley and *Lois and Clark* as Cat Grant.

RATING

- Tried and tested stuff made interesting by Sisko and Kira's conflict of interest. Sadly it descends into some awful exposition towards the end, where the self-evident prophecy is painstakingly explained.

3.16 PROPHET MOTIVE

Ferengi culture is threatened when the Grand Nagus abandons his materialism

TX 20 February 1995
WRITERS Ira Steven Behr and Robert Hewitt Wolfe
DIRECTOR Rene Auberjonois
GUEST CAST Juliana Donald (Emi), Max Grodenchik (Rom), Bennet Guillory (Medical Big Shot), Tiny Ron (Maihar'du), Wallace Shawn (Zek)

STARDATE UNKNOWN

The Grand Nagus announces that he has rewritten the Rules of Acquisition. Quark and Rom eagerly read the volume, but are disturbed to find the first rule tells them to return money if it is requested! Quark is horrified by Zek's determination to change Ferengi culture – and his hope to mould Rom into a new type of Ferengi. Zek also plans to return an orb to the Bajoran people as a gift. The orb shows Quark a vision that reveals the Nagus was given the new Rules by the aliens in the wormhole. Realising that something has happened to Zek, Quark takes him into the wormhole. The wormhole aliens explain that they reverted Zek to his younger, less materialistic self. Quark asks them to restore Zek and promises that the Ferengi will never bother them again in return. The aliens agree and Ferengi tradition is secured.

QUOTES

- 'Greed is eternal' – *Quark quotes the Tenth Rule of Acquisition*

TRIVIA

- Rene Auberjonois had previously directed theatre and sitcoms, but *Prophet Motive* marks his graduation to TV drama.
- A sub-plot, in which Bashir is nominated for the Carrington Award but knows he won't get it, is a sly reference to *The Next Generation*'s nomination for best series in its seventh year. The award went to *Picket Fences*.
- The story idea originated in a speculative script written by Ira Behr for the sit-com *Taxi*. The episode, entitled *Uncle Sylvester*, featured a con man who appears to have turned over a new leaf. It was never produced.

RATING

- Fun stuff, with Wallace Shawn putting in another stellar performance as Grand Nagus Zek. Interestingly, some of the changes that the possessed Zek proposes are pushed forward by Quark's mother Ishka in later seasons. The Quark-Zek relationship remains one of the show's highlights.

3.17 VISIONARY

O'Brien uncovers a Romulan plot to destroy the station, at the cost of his own life

TX 27 February 1995
WRITER John Shirley (story by Ethan H Calk)
DIRECTOR Reza Badiyi
GUEST CAST Annette Helde (Karina), Dennis Madalone (Atul), Bob Minor (Bo'rak), Jack Shearer (Ruwon), Ray Young (Morka)

STARDATE UNKNOWN

After Romulans arrive on the station, O'Brien suffers a bout of radiation poisoning and observes himself talking to Quark. Although Bashir blames the sickness, O'Brien finds himself observing different parts of his day and eventually see a brawl between Romulans, Klingons and Quark. O'Brien waits in Quark's for the brawl to erupt and sees himself appear, open a wall panel and die when shot by a phaser hidden within. O'Brien looks at the panel, but can find nothing. Later, the Romulans occupy a room opposite the wall panel. Odo suspects the Klingons. Meanwhile, O'Brien jumps into the future and the future Bashir tells him how he died. Dax discovers that the time jumps are caused by a quantum singularity reacting to the radiation poisoning.

Another time shift, and O'Brien watches as the wormhole collapses. O'Brien exposes himself to radiation and, with his future self, discovers the singularity is inside a cloaked Romulan ship. The real O'Brien becomes dangerously ill and lets his future self take over and warn Sisko: the Romulans plan to end the Dominion threat by destroying the station and the wormhole. Sisko expels the Romulans.

TRIVIA

- The episode was based on a story by Ethan Calk, a Texas schoolteacher, who recounted the concept to René Echevarria. The team brought in John Shirley, a science fiction author with a reputation for handling high concepts, who wanted to write for screen.

RATING

- A peculiar episode, if we are being charitable. The fact that O'Brien from now on is not *technically* the same as the one before is at first an astonishing revelation but in practice means nothing. Unfortunately, the same can be said for the rest of the episode, which descends to *The Next Generation*-levels of technobabble at the expense of an emotional story.

3.18 DISTANT VOICES

Bashir fights to save himself while trapped in a telepathically-induced coma

TX 10 April 1995
WRITERS Ira Steven Behr and Robert Hewitt Wolfe (story by Joe Menosky)
DIRECTOR Alexander Singer
GUEST CAST Nicole Forester (Dabo Girl), Ann Gillespie (Nurse), Victor Rivers (Altovar), Andrew Robinson (Garak)

STARDATE UNKNOWN

Bashir tries to prevent an alien named Altovar from stealing a substance from the infirmary, but is knocked unconscious. When he awakens, he finds he is 25 years older and the station is deserted and malfunctioning. Bashir narrowly escapes Altovar and stumbles upon Kira, O'Brien, Odo and Dax who seem oblivious to him. Bashir hears whispering and deduces that it is the distant crew, stating that he is in a telepathically induced coma. He has three hours to live. Bashir realises that the station represents his state of health – fix the station and he will survive. The officers are parts of his personality, but are captured by Altovar. Rapidly ageing, Bashir finds Kira dead and Odo dying. Altovar kills Quark and pursues Bashir who, now 100, has a broken hip. In Ops, Garak urges Bashir to give up and the doctor realises that Garak represents Altovar. Bashir returns to the infirmary and manages to destroy Altovar in a forcefield. He regains consciousness in the real sickbay.

QUOTES

- 'Chief, you must be my doubt – my indecision.'
  'No I'm not.' – *Bashir and O'Brien*

TRIVIA

- The original pitch, was a deep, symbolic episode where the aspects of Bashir's personality were represented by new characters.
- The episode won Michael G Westmore (Makeup Artist Supervisor) and his team of ten make-up artists the Emmy for Individual Achievement in Makeup for a series in 1995.

RATING

- A potentially menacing episode that never cranks up the mood high enough. There's a real horror in Bashir's experience that is lost amid the more esoteric material.

3.19 THROUGH THE LOOKING GLASS

Sisko is taken to the mirror universe where he must rescue his wife, Jennifer

TX 17 April 1995
WRITERS Ira Steven Behr and Robert Hewitt Wolfe
DIRECTOR Winrich Kolbe
GUEST CAST Felicia M Bell (Jennifer Sisko), Max Grodenchik (Rom), John Patrick Hayden (Cardassian Overseer), Dennis Madalone (Marauder), Andrew Robinson (Garak), Tim Russ (Tuvok)

STARDATE UNKNOWN

Sisko is abducted by the Mirror O'Brien and taken to the parallel universe. The Mirror Sisko, leader of the Terran forces against the Klingon-Cardassian alliance, has been killed. O'Brien wants Sisko to pretend to be his double and convince scientist Jennifer Sisko, the double of Sisko's late wife, to join the Terrans, or die. Sisko is captured by Kira and meets Jennifer. Jennifer despises Sisko, but is surprised when he apologises and reveals he has come to save her. O'Brien causes a diversion, allowing Sisko and Jennifer to escape. When Kira traps Sisko, he reveals that he has started the station's self-destruct sequence and is the only person who can stop it. Kira is forced to release the Terrans. Sisko and Jennifer escape. Sisko kisses Jennifer goodbye.

TRIVIA

- Tim Russ makes his second appearance in *Deep Space Nine*, this time as the mirror Tuvok on Terok Nor. As with Spock's alter ego in *Mirror, Mirror*, Tuvok seems closer to his 'real' universe version than any of the other characters.

RATING

- More mirror universe fun for Sisko, who appears to bed Jadzia and Kira! Nana Visitor puts in another sterling performance as the over-the-top Intendant, while doubling for the alternative Sisko frees Avery Brooks to put more into his performance. Fun stuff, but there's only so many times you can do this.

3.20 IMPROBABLE CAUSE

STARDATE UNKNOWN

Garak and Odo uncover an alliance between the Obsidian Order and the Romulans

TX 24 April 1995
WRITER René Echevarria (story by Robert Lederman and David R Long)
DIRECTOR Avery Brooks
GUEST CAST Darwyn Carson (Romulan), Paul Dooley (Enabran Tain), Carlos LaCamara (Retaya), Julianna McCarthy (Mila), Andrew Robinson (Garak), Joseph Ruskin (Informant)

Garak's shop is destroyed in an explosion but he is coy about the reason. Odo recognises the *modus operandi* and tracks down a Flaxian named Retaya. Retaya reveals nothing and when Garak and Odo pursue his ship it explodes before it enters warp. Odo discovers the Romulans hired Retaya, and five Obsidian Order agents were killed on the same day as the explosion. Odo deduces that Garak faked his own death. Garak explains that he and the others worked for Enabran Tain, the former head of the Obsidian Order. They look for Tain but are intercepted by a Romulan warbird. Tain is on board and reveals that he ordered the attempt on Garak's life: the Romulan Tal Shiar and the Cardassian Obsidian Order have joined forces to destroy the Founders. Tain wanted to kill anyone with information on him, but offers Garak a place at his side. Despite Odo's warning, Garak accepts.

QUOTES

- 'Who would want to kill me, a simple tailor?' – *Garak*

TRIVIA

- Lederman and Long's original pitch did not include Enabran Tain, first featured in season two's *The Wire*.

RATING

- Strong stuff for Garak. Paul Dooley makes a welcome reappearance as Tain, the enigmatic former leader of the Obsidian Order. On first viewing, you keep expecting a writer's trick to get out of a tight corner, but the ending comes as a genuine surprise.

3.21 THE DIE IS CAST

STARDATE UNKNOWN

A combined Romulan-Cardassian fleet launches an attack on the Founders

TX 1 May 1995
WRITER Ronald D Moore
DIRECTOR David Livingston
GUEST CAST Paul Dooley (Enabran Tain), Kenneth Marshall (Michael Eddington), Leland Orser (Lovok), Andrew Robinson (Garak), Leon Russom (Vice Admiral Toddman), Wendy Schenker (Romulan Pilot)

Colonel Lovok of the Tal Shiar and Enabran Tain lead a fleet of ships into the Gamma Quadrant to wipe out the Founders. Garak is ordered to interrogate Odo. Meanwhile, Sisko discovers what is happening and defies Admiral Toddman by taking the Defiant in search of Odo. When the Defiant's cloak fails, Eddington reveals that he sabotaged it on Toddman's orders. Garak interrogates Odo with a device that prevents him changing form. Breaking apart, Odo finally reveals a secret: he wants to rejoin the Founders. Odo's life is spared when Lovok and Garak suggest they can study him. The fleet arrives at the Founders' planet and opens fire, but it is deserted. Suddenly, they are attacked by 150 Jem'Hadar ships. Garak rescues Odo with help from Lovok, who is actually a Founder. It was a ruse to destroy the Romulans and Cardassians. Odo refuses to join the Founders. Garak and Odo are rescued and returned to the Alpha Quadrant.

QUOTES

- 'I tried to deny it... I tried to forget, but I can't. They are my people... and I want to be with them... in the Great Link.'
  – *Odo reveals his secret to Garak*

TRIVIA

- Ronald Moore decided to use the Garak-Odo relationship as the core of the episode and push it to its limits. The episode required significant make-up and costume work to achieve Odo's torture and painfully slow dessication.

RATING

- Momentous stuff that really shows the Federation is in trouble. Still, it is the smaller moments between Garak and Odo, reminiscent of *Chain of Command part II*, that make this episode work. There's some extraordinarily intense acting between Auberjonois and Robinson that the director rightly lets play out in full with no fancy camera moves. Odo's revelation – he wants to return home – seems momentarily small fry, but has massive implications. Overall, powerful stuff.

3.22 EXPLORERS

STARDATE UNKNOWN

Sisko and Jake recreate an ancient Bajoran space flight

TX 8 May 1995
WRITER René Echevarria (story by Hilary J Bader)
DIRECTOR Cliff Bole
GUEST CAST Marc Alaimo (Gul Dukat), Bari Hochwald (Dr Elizabeth Lense), Chase Masterson (Leeta)

Sisko decides to build an ancient spacecraft that allowed the Bajorans to explore their star system. Jake eventually decides to join Sisko on the maiden voyage. Gul Dukat is dismissive of the endeavour. On the voyage, Jake reveals that he has been offered a writing fellowship in New Zealand. Sisko is pleased, but sad that Jake may be leaving. However, Jake intends to delay by a year to keep his father company. Suddenly, one of the solar sails gives way. Sisko manages to regain control. Then, the Bajoran craft is surrounded by light and leaps to warp speed. The craft leaves warp, but Sisko has no idea where they are. Gul Dukat sends a message that they are in Cardassian space. Sisko and Jake have proven that the Bajoran spacecraft worked as legend suggested. Dukat reluctantly congratulates them for proving that the Bajorans beat the Cardassians into space.

TRIVIA

- Bader's pitch was heavily influenced by Thor Heyerdahl's epic voyage from Peru to Tahiti, as described in *The Kon-Tiki Expedition*. The first draft featured Sisko and O'Brien, but the producers decided to pursue the father-son story instead.

RATING

- A disappointingly aimless episode that seems to drift. The sub-plot, in which O'Brien and Bashir get drunk and recognise their friendship, although trite, at least gives rise to humour. A much decried episode and sadly rightly so.

3.23 FAMILY BUSINESS

STARDATE UNKNOWN

Quark's mother must return illegally-held profits to the Ferengi tax man

TX 15 May 1995
WRITERS Ira Steven Behr and Robert Hewitt Wolfe
DIRECTOR Rene Auberjonois
GUEST CAST Jeffrey Combs (Brunt), Mel Green (Secretary), Max Grodenchik (Rom), Penny Johnson (Kasidy Yates), Andrea Martin (Ishka)

Brunt, an agent of the Ferengi tax service, hands Quark a Writ of Accountability for mismanaging a family member. Quark's mother, Ishka, has been making profit against Ferengi law. Quark and Rom return to Ferenginar to convince Ishka to confess, but she insists she only earned three bars of latinum for investing part of her monthly donation from Quark and refuses to confess her wrongs. Quark is angry, even more so when he discovers Ishka has been trading under numerous aliases. Ishka insists Quark is just jealous of her business sense and dares Quark to report her to the revenue service. Quark heads to Brunt, but Rom arrives insisting Ishka wishes to split her profits with Quark. Quark is pleased, but Rom has lied to protect their mother. Ishka signs the confession and hands back the money, but later tells Rom that she only declared a third of her profits!

TRIVIA

- This episode sees the first visit to the Ferengi homeworld, named here for the first time as Ferenginar. We are also introduced to Kasidy Yates, Sisko's girlfriend, previously known only to be a freighter captain.
- Kasidy reveals that her brother is from Cestus III, a planet mentioned in the original series episode *Arena*.

RATING

- A surprising episode in which the humour of the situation does not fully displace the poignant family moments between Quark and Ishka. There's a sense of loss and regret that is surprisingly well conveyed from beneath the layers of latex and make-up each Ferengi actor had to suffer.

3.24 SHAKAAR

STARDATE UNKNOWN

Kira reunites with her former resistance cell leader to oppose Kai Winn

TX 22 May 1995
WRITER Gordon Dawson
DIRECTOR Jonathan West
GUEST CAST John Doman (Lenaris Holem), Louise Fletcher (Kai Winn), Sherman Howard (Syvar), Harry Hutchinson (Trooper), William Lucking (Furel), Duncan Regehr (Shakaar), Diane Salinger (Lupaza), John Kenton Shull (Security Officer)

On the eve of becoming First Minister, Kai Winn asks Kira to obtain reclamators held by a group of farmers, led by Kira's former resistance cell leader, Shakaar. Shakaar who explains that he, Furel and Lupaza had been promised the reclamators for one year to boost exports. Winn sends troops to arrest Shakaar, enraging Kira, who escapes with Shakaar to the mountains. Shakaar is weary and can no longer run, so sets an ambush. As they wait, Kira and Shakaar realise they will be injuring comrades and call a cease-fire. They are taken to Winn's office, where Shakaar tells her he intends to run for election. Winn, realising the contest will reveal the folly of her actions, decides not to stand.

TRIVIA

- Gordon Dawson, a friend of Sam Peckinpah, pitched this story to *The Next Generation,* but the idea was never developed. An early version developed for *Deep Space Nine* focused on the opening of a costly Bajoran museum at the expense of local farmers. The writers latched on to pursuing Winn's rise to power, a rich vein that would be exploited to the end of season seven.
- Duncan Regehr (Shakaar) previously appeared in the *The Next Generation* episode *Sub Rosa.*

RATING

- Another journey into recent Bajoran history, made all the more palatable by strong performances by Visitor and Regehr. There are a few quiet scenes that set up their relationship neatly. Of greater significance is Winn's dogmatic leadership, which provides plenty of grist for the mill in future.

3.25 FACETS

STARDATE 48959.1

Jadzia faces Dax's previous hosts during a Trill rite of passage

TX 12 June 1995
WRITER René Echevarria
DIRECTOR Cliff Bole
GUEST CAST Majel Barrett (Computer Voice), Jefrey Alan Chandler (Guardian), Aron Eisenberg (Nog), Max Grodenchik (Rom), Chase Masterson (Leeta)

Jadzia undertakes the Trill Rite of Closure, in which the memories of previous hosts are transferred into other bodies. Kira becomes Lela, Dax's first host, O'Brien becomes Tobin, Leeta becomes Emony, Quark becomes Audrid, and Bashir becomes Torias. Jadzia is disturbed to come face-to-face with Sisko as Joran, the murderer who briefly hosted Dax. Joran tries to kill her, but Jadzia resists. Later, Jadzia admits she has put off the ritual as she feels unworthy compared to Dax's previous hosts, notably Curzon, whose memories are transferred into Odo. Odo/Curzon morphs to take on the appearance of both people. Curzon is delighted to see Sisko again. Jadzia talks about her insecurities but Curzon is little comfort. Moreoever, Curzon reveals that he and Odo have decided to stay as they are – his memories will not be returned to her. Sisko offers to reason with Curzon, but Jadzia decides she must face him herself. She convinces him to rejoin with her. Jadzia finally gains her self-confidence.

TRIVIA

- Based on the book *Sybil* by Flora Rhea Schreiber, about the true story of the first woman diagnosed with multiple-personality disorder. Behr struggled to find the dark secret that would necessitate the personalities, as in *Sybil*, but settled on the Trill ritual.

RATING

- Another Dax episode, after *Equilibrium* and *Meridian*, that doesn't quite hit the mark. The highlight this time is the performances from the regulars – particularly Avery Brooks, who puts in a sinister performance as Joran.

3.26 THE ADVERSARY

STARDATE 48962.5

A Changeling seeks to use the Defiant to start a war

TX 19 June 1995
WRITERS Ira Steven Behr and Robert Hewitt Wolfe
DIRECTOR Alexander Singer
GUEST CAST Jeff Austin (Bolian), Majel Barrett (Computer Voice), Kenneth Marshall (Michael Eddington), Lawrence Pressman (Krajensky)

Admiral Krajensky orders newly promoted Captain Sisko to take him to the Tzenkethi homeworld, where a coup threatens Federation citizens. *En route*, they receive a distress call from Barisa Prime, which is under attack by the Tzenkethi. Sisko tries to communicate with Starfleet command, but the ship has been sabotaged. He discovers that Krajensky is a Changeling. The Founder escapes and takes control of the Defiant, intending to start a war between the Federation and the Tzenkethi. As they hunt the Changeling, Dax is found unconscious. The officers pair up but become suspicious of each other. Bashir takes blood samples from each, and Eddington is suspected, but a duplicate Bashir is found. The Changeling escapes again as the Defiant closes on the Tzenkethi. As Sisko initiates the self-destruct sequence, Odo battles his Changeling duplicate. Before the Changeling falls into the warp core, it tells Odo: 'You're too late. We're everywhere.'

TRIVIA

- The original script featured Sisko visiting his father and discovering that the Changelings had infiltrated Earth. However, the network did not want a cliffhanger and instead the episode was scaled back to focus on a Changeling threat close to home and concentrate on building paranoia. The episode borrowed inspiration from *The Thing* (1951 and 1982).

RATING

- Paranoia, pure and simple, although the game is never raised as high as it could go. We finally get to see Michael Eddington make his move, an action that foreshadows his move to the Maquis in season four's *For the Cause*. It's pensive, low-key stuff with a sting in the tail that sets up the next season well.

STAR TREK: DEEP SPACE NINE
SEASON FOUR

4.1 THE WAY OF THE WARRIOR

STARDATE 49011.4

The Klingons act unilaterally to fight the Dominion

DOUBLE-LENGTH EPISODE
TX 2 October 1995
WRITERS Ira Steven Behr and Robert Hewitt Wolfe
DIRECTOR James L Conway
GUEST CAST Marc Alaimo (Dukat), Christopher Darga (Kaybok), Judi Durand (Station Computer Voice), JG Hertzler (Martok), William Dennis Hurt (Huraga), Penny Johnson (Kasidy Yates), Obi Ndefo (Drex), Robert O'Reilly (Gowron), Andrew Robinson (Garak), Patricia Tallman (Weapons Officer)

The crew prepare to fight the Changelings but find themselves inadequate. A Klingon ship arrives, and its captain, Martok, asks for shore leave. Sisko agrees... and an entire fleet decloaks. Martok gives Kira and Sisko a blood test to prove they aren't Changelings. The Klingons quickly cause problems – everything from bar brawls to intercepting ships on lawful business (like Kasidy Yates' ship, the Xhosa). Sisko forces them to withdraw and requests help from Starfleet in dealing with the Klingons. They assign Worf, who quickly discovers that the Klingons are planning an invasion of Cardassia, which they believe has been infiltrated by the Changelings. Martok's fleet sets course. Gowron arrives at the station, and strips Worf of his lands and title for not joining the attack on Cardassia. Sisko warns Dukat about the attack, and offers to take the Detappa council, the civilian leaders, to safety in the Defiant. They rescue them in a space battle, then return home, being pursued. The Klingon fleet attacks the station, which has new defences. It's a fierce battle, and the Klingons board the station. Sisko tells Gowron a Starfleet task force is on the way – and they should be fighting The Dominon, not each other. Gowron agrees, and withdraws, but warns Sisko he won't forget what he has done. Worf becomes the station's Strategic Operations Officer.

QUOTES

- 'We were like warriors from the ancient sagas. There was nothing we could not do.'
  'Except keep the holodecks working right.' – *Worf and O'Brien remember their days on the Enterprise*

TRIVIA

- Michael Dorn was happy to do a guest appearance, but it took a little while to finalise the deal that saw him become a regular. The writers were keen to move Worf's character along – a necessity, anyway, because Kira and Odo fulfilled the 'security chief' role.
- The budget was more than seven times the normal budget for a couple of episodes.
- While *Babylon 5* was pioneering CGI animation for its space fleets, this episode used traditional models for the Klingon armada, including commercially available toys – even small Klingon Christmas ornaments for ships seen in the distance.
- Talking of *Babylon 5*, Patricia Tallman is a stuntwoman who played Lyta Alexander in that series. She doubled for Michelle Forbes in the movie *Kalifornia* (miscredited as 'Tillman'), and was also Laura Dern's student double in *Jurassic Park*, where she was mis-credited as 'Patrick' Tallman.

RATING

- Wow. It's almost a different show, one that revels in action and old *Star Trek* icons, and which isn't scared by comparisons with *The Next Generation*. The influence of *Babylon 5* seems clear, as Sisko bellows at people to get off his station while vast fleets of ships fly by outside. This is a great episode.

4.2 THE VISITOR

Jake Sisko is an old man who remembers his father's death, long ago

TX 9 October 1995
WRITER Michael Taylor
DIRECTOR David Livingston
GUEST CAST Majel Barrett (Computer Voice), Aron Eisenberg (Nog), Galyn Gorg (Korena), Rachel Robinson (Melanie), Tony Todd (Jake Sisko)

STARDATE UNKNOWN

A young writer, Melanie, comes to Jake Sisko's house in the Bayou. Jake is an old man who stopped writing when he was 40, and she wants to know why. He tells how his father was killed investigating a subspace inversion in the wormhole. Young Jake kept seeing his father's ghost. Without Sisko, the Bajorans ceded to Cardassian protection and the two went to war with the Klingons. Jake remained as most personnel evacuated Deep Space Nine. Ben Sisko reappeared, but his temporal signature was unstable and he soon vanished again. Dax and O'Brien kept trying to recover him, but the Federation turned the station over to the Klingons. Jake settled on Earth, wrote a novel, got married... and briefly saw his father again. He gave up writing to study subspace mechanics. He teamed up with old friends, including Nog, now a Starfleet captain, and they went to the wormhole with the subspace flux isolator he designed. He met his father in the wormhole, who told him to live his own life... he has done so, and written some more, but now his life is nearly over. Melanie leaves, and Ben appears. Jake tells him to dodge the energy discharge that killed him. Sisko does so, and this time, he survives.

QUOTES

- 'There's only one first time for everything, isn't there, and only one last time, too.' – *Jake*

TRIVIA

- Rachel Robinson is the daughter of Andrew Robinson, who plays Garak.
- The episode was nominated for a Hugo Award. It was a tough field, though – it was up against *Apollo 13, Toy Story, Twelve Monkeys* and the deserved winner, *Babylon 5*'s finest episode, – *The Coming of Shadows*.
- The future sequences use the same Starfleet uniform design as *All Good Things*.

RATING

- A clever episode, one that doesn't pretend Sisko has been written out of the series, but concentrates on the cost of bringing him back. Tony Todd puts in an exceptional performance – if he really did audition for Sisko, you can only be baffled why he wasn't cast. Once again, there are real shades of *Babylon 5*, with old men, destinies and dire hints of future wars and chaos. This is one of the best episodes of any incarnation of *Star Trek*.

4.3 HIPPOCRATIC OATH

STARDATE 49263.5

O'Brien and Bashir clash when they are captured by the Jem'Hadar

TX 16 October 1995
WRITER Lisa Klink (story by Nicholas Corea and Lisa Klink)
DIRECTOR Rene Auberjonois
GUEST CAST Michael H Bailous (Jem'Hadar #1), Steven Davies (Arak'Taral), Roderick Garr (Regana Tosh), Scott MacDonald (Goran'Agar), Jerry Roberts (Meso'Clan), Marshall Teague (Temo'Zuma)

Bashir and O'Brien detect a subspace magnaton pulse on Bopak III in the Gamma Quadrant, the sign of a warp core explosion. They land and are captured by the Jem'Hadar. Their leader, Goran'Agar, tells Bashir about ketracel white, a drug all Jem'Hadar take. They are dependent on this isogenic enzyme, so that the Founders can ensure their loyalty. Goran'Agar has weaned himself off the drug, but none of his men can. O'Brien doesn't think they should help, and tries to escape. Bashir disagrees and pulls rank. O'Brien destroys Bashir's research. The Jem'Hadar start recriminations, but Goran'Agar lets the humans escape. Meanwhile, on Deep Space Nine, Worf tries to catch Quark smuggling illegal Tallonian crystals – but only interferes with Odo's plan to bring down the whole smuggling ring.

TRIVIA

- The Worf subplot was added to keep the popular character a presence in the show – and had him confront Quark and Odo, two more fan favourites.
- Rene Auberjonois was originally to direct The Visitor, but Colm Meaney was making a film, *The Van* (a Roddy Doyle adaptation, like *The Commitments* and *The Snapper*), so the schedule was shifted around.

RATING

- Another strong episode – one that's essentially just a Prime Directive story, but which pitches it at a personal level between Bashir and O'Brien and puts a strain on their friendship in a very un-*Star Trek* way.

4.4 INDISCRETION

STARDATE UNKNOWN

Kira and Dukat investigate the wreckage of a lost Cardassian ship

TX 23 October 1995
WRITER Nicholas Corea (story by Toni Marberry and Jack Trevino)
DIRECTOR LeVar Burton
GUEST CAST Marc Alaimo (Dukat), Cyia Batten (Ziyal), Roy Brocksmith (Razka), Penny Johnson (Kasidy Yates), Thomas Prisco (Heler)

Razka Karn, a smuggler, gives Kira a piece of metal from the lost Cardassian ship the Ravinok. Six years ago, it vanished with its cargo of Bajoran prisoners, among them Kira's friend, Lorit Akrem. Sisko – who's offended Kasidy by not being enthusiastic at the news she's moving to the station – hears that the Cardassians are sending Dukat to accompany Kira on her search mission to Dozaria, where the metal was found. They find the wreckage, including the body of Tora Naprem, a Bajoran who Dukat had an affair with – and evidence that at least some survived. Dukat confesses that they had a daughter, Tora Ziyal. If she survived, Dukat will have to kill her to avoid disgrace. They discover the Breen using the survivors to mine dilithium ore. Kira and Dukat infiltrate the mine and they discover that Lorit died two years ago, but that Ziyal survives. Dukat breaks down in tears – he will be proud to take his daughter home.

QUOTES

- 'If my daughter is still alive, I'll have no choice but to kill her' – *Dukat*

TRIVIA

- Taking its cue from the series' roots in Western movies, this is clearly influenced by *The Searchers* (1956).
- Once again, as with *The Homecoming*, Nana Visitor found herself on location in the extreme conditions of Soledad Canyon. This time, landslides meant that some scenes had to be completed in the studio.
- LeVar Burton had directed episodes of *The Next Generation*, but this was his *Deep Space Nine* debut.

RATING

- Back to the usual fare of *Deep Space Nine* – Bajorans and Cardassians coming to terms with their dodgy pasts. But this is a sharp, focused episode that doesn't let back story swamp the story in hand.

4.5 REJOINED

STARDATE 49195.5

Dax breaks a Trill taboo by falling for a former host's wife

TX 30 October 1995
WRITERS Ronald D Moore and René Echevarria (story by Rene Echevarria)
DIRECTOR Avery Brooks
GUEST CAST Kenneth Marshall (Michael Eddington), James Noah (Hanor Pren), Tim Ryan (Bejal Otner), Susanna Thompson (Lenara Khan)

A Trill team interested in wormholes arrives at the station. The leader is Dr Lenara Khan, whose symbiont was married to Torias Dax when it was hosted by Nilani. Trill are not meant to recommence relationships from a past life, 'reassociation', and face exile for doing so... this in turn means the symbiont dies with the host. They grow close, though, and it becomes clear that they have more in common than Torias Dax and Nilani Khan did. They end up kissing. Dax saves Khan from a plasma leak, but Khan has decided to return to Trill, rather than face social ostracism. Dax is heartbroken.

TRIVIA

- The episode bears some resemblance to the first Trill story, *The Next Generation* episode *The Host*.
- The episode courted, and generated, controversy by featuring two women kissing, but by 1995 it wasn't exactly shocking for most TV viewers. In the UK, the 'taboo' had long been broken (*Rejoined* has never been cut in the UK, even for afternoon timeslots).
- Avery Brooks banned any publicity photographs of the kiss from being taken, to the annoyance of the studio publicity department.

RATING

- A straightforward episode, bogged down a little by having to explain the ever-complicated Trill to the casual audience. The fact that it's a 'lesbian' relationship does make the taboo a little more easy to identify with, but it's fairly run-of-the-mill stuff.

4.6 STARSHIP DOWN

STARDATE 49263.5

The Defiant is trapped by two Jem'Hadar ships

TX 6 November 1995
WRITER David Mack and John J Ordover
DIRECTOR Alexander Singer
GUEST CAST Jay Baker (Stevens), James Cromwell (Hanok), Sara Mornell (Carson) FJ Rio (Muniz)

The Defiant meets a Karemma vessel deep in the Gamma Quadrant. Minister Hanok complains about a trade agreement with the Federation: they used the Ferengi as middlemen and Quark has fiddled the figures to his advantage. While Sisko sorts out the mess, Worf captains the Defiant but the crew find him hard to adjust to. Jem'Hadar warships approach, and attempt to attack the Karemma ship. The Defiant defends, and the two ships hide in the atmosphere of a gas giant. But the Jem'Hadar can detect them, and seriously damage the Defiant. The crew destroy one warship with a modified probe. Quark and Hanok are forced to work together to defuse an unexploded torpedo. They become fast friends, and Hanok learns the excitement of taking risks. O'Brien converts the deflector dish into a phaser, and Worf destroys the remaining Jem'Hadar ship.

TRIVIA

- The production team did their research, modelling the gas giant on Neptune and trying to keep as scientifically accurate as possible.
- James Cromwell had appeared a couple of times in *The Next Generation*, and would go on to play Zefram Cochrane in *Star Trek: First Contact*. He's best known for pig flick *Babe*, which earned him an Oscar nomination for Best Supporting Actor.

RATING

- Like *Balance of Terror*, this is basically a submarine movie, but sometimes the analogies don't quite work – it's hard to get too worked up about a compartment flooding with nitrogen. This is basically pure action, though, and works well on those terms.

4.7 LITTLE GREEN MEN

STARDATE UNKNOWN

Quark and his colleagues crash in Roswell in 1947

TX 13 November 1995

As Nog prepares to join Starfleet Academy, Quark auctions off his possessions! Quark gets a new shuttle he's owed by his cousin Gaila and he, Rom and Nog set off to Earth... with a little kemacite smuggling planned on the way. However, the ship has been sabotaged, and they are caught in a time vortex. They land on Earth,

WRITERS Ira Steven Behr and Robert Hewitt Wolfe (story by Tom Marberry and Jack Trevino)
DIRECTOR James L Conway
GUEST CAST Aron Eisenberg (Nog), Megan Gallagher (Nurse Garland), Max Grodenchik (Rom), Charles Napier (Denning), Conor O'Farrell (Carlson), James G MacDonald (Wainwright)

but it's 1947, their ship has crashed in Roswell, and they are captured by the military. Their universal translators don't work at first, but Quark is soon offering to trade technology for gold. They are surprised when Odo arrives – he hid on the ship, convinced Quark was up to no good. Quark plots to contact the Ferengi of this time and give them the warp coil... then to rule a Ferengi empire more advanced than any other. The military become convinced that the Ferengi are an invasion force, and they and Odo have to make a quick getaway. They find their ship in Hangar 18, and a nuclear test nearby provides the radiation that fires up the warp engines to get them home.

QUOTES

- 'All I ask for is a tall ship, and some contraband to fill it with.' – *Quark*

TRIVIA

- A homage to Fifties B-movies, the names of the human characters are those of B-movie actors Richard Denning, Richard Carlson and Beverly Garland.
- The episode features the second ever mention of a toilet in *Star Trek*... although by the twenty-fourth century, they are known as 'waste extractors'. The first toilet is in the cell Kirk, Spock and McCoy occupy in *Star Trek V: The Final Frontier*, which bears the rather wonderful (and wise) warning sign 'Do Not Use Toilet in Zero Gravity'.

RATING

- A deliberately silly episode. *Deep Space Nine* has a reputation for being a bit po-faced, but it has some of the funniest scenes in *Star Trek*. This episode is as funny as the time-travel episodes of the original *Star Trek* just thought they were.

4.8 THE SWORD OF KAHLESS

STARDATE UNKNOWN

Worf and Dax join a quest to discover an ancient Klingon artefact

TX 20 November 1995
WRITER Hans Beimler (story by Richard Danus)
DIRECTOR LeVar Burton
GUEST CAST John Colicos (Kor), Tom Morga (Soto), Rick Pasqualone (Toral)

Dax's blood brother Kor arrives on the station. He has evidence that the Sword of Kahless, stolen from the homeworld by the Hurq 1,000 years ago, has turned up in the Gamma Quadrant. Kor is attacked by a telepathic Lethean who steals the knowledge of the Sword's location. Dax, Worf and Kor take the Rio Grande through the wormhole to the Hurq homeworld, and discover the Sword in a museum. A rival group of Klingons – led by Toral – arrives to steal the Sword, the bearer of which will be the rightful ruler of the Empire. Kor and Worf trap Toral, but fight for the Sword. Dax is disgusted, and takes the Sword for herself. As the three of them make their escape, they realise the Sword will divide Klingon society, not unite it. They beam the Sword into space.

TRIVIA

- As soon as the deal to make Michael Dorn a regular was sealed, a Klingon episode was commissioned from Richard Danus, executive story editor on the third season of *The Next Generation*, the year that saw *Sins of the Father* introduce the whole Klingon political plotline.

RATING

- A fairly typical Klingon episode, with lots of talk of honour, Kahless, bat'leths and civil war in the Empire. It's at least focused, and rises above the run-of-the-mill for that.

4.9 OUR MAN BASHIR

STARDATE UNKNOWN

Dr Bashir becomes a dashing spy in a holo-fantasy

TX 27 November 1995
WRITER Ronald D Moore (story by Robert Gillan)

Bashir plays a spy on 1960s Earth in a holosuite scenario, and finds himself joined by Garak. Meanwhile, Sisko, Kira, Worf, Dax and O'Brien return to the station in the Orinoco runabout – but the ship has been sabotaged by the True Way Cardassian terrorist organisation, and Eddington only just beams them out before it explodes. The transporter patterns accidentally end up in the holosuite memory. The lost crew

DIRECTOR Winrich Kolbe
GUEST CAST Marci Brickhouse (Mona Luvsitt), Max Grodenchik (Rom), Kenneth Marshall (Michael Eddington), Andrew Robinson (Garak), Melissa Young (Caprice)

begin appearing as characters in the holosuite – Kira is Russian temptress Anastasia Komananov, Sisko is Dr Hippocrates Noah, who plans to flood the world by forcing seismologist Honey Bare (Dax) to help him. O'Brien and Worf appear as two of his henchmen, Falcon and Duschamps. Unable to turn off the simulation, Bashir has to complete the adventure and defeat the evil Dr Noah at his Mount Everest secret base. Eddington recruits Quark and Rom to use the Defiant's transporters to free the trapped crew.

TRIVIA

- Bashir's holo-fantasy owes something to James Bond and *The Man from UNCLE*. We see it again briefly in *A Simple Investigation*.
- MGM/UA, makers of the James Bond films, weren't happy with the references to 'Dr Noah'.

RATING

- It's that story again... like most of the variations on the trapped-in-the-holodeck story it seems like an excuse for the regulars to dress up, rather than an insightful pastiche. It's an episode that's not half as much fun as it thinks it is.

4.10 HOMEFRONT

STARDATE UNKNOWN

Sisko is ordered to tighten Earth security in the face of a Changeling threat

TX 1 January 1996
WRITERS Ira Steven Behr and Robert Hewitt Wolfe
DIRECTOR David Livingston
GUEST CAST Dylan Chalfy (Head Officer), Aron Eisenberg (Nog), Robert Foxworth (Leyton), Susan Gibney (Erika Benteen), Brock Peters (Joseph Sisko), Herschel Sparber (Jaresh-Inyo)

The wormhole is opening and closing seemingly at random. This is overshadowed when 27 people are killed in an explosion at a Federation-Romulan conference on Earth, and there is evidence of Changeling involvement. Sisko and Odo are summoned to Starfleet Command, and Sisko is put in charge of Starfleet security on Earth. Sisko visits his father, Joseph, and becomes worried about his health. Sisko and Leyton see the Federation President, who thinks they are being paranoid – until Odo reveals he was disguised as Sisko's briefcase, and that Changelings could be anywhere. Nog complains to Jake that the Academy's Red Squad are unfriendly. The President authorises blood testing of key staff. Odo discovers that Admiral Leyton is a Changeling. Joseph Sisko is arrested for failing to allow a blood test. Ben Sisko realises he's becoming paranoid when he suspects his father is a Changeling. Earth's entire power relay grid goes offline, rendering Earth defenceless. Sisko guesses that the wormhole's 'random' opening was actually evidence of a cloaked Dominion invasion fleet. Jake and Joseph watch in alarm as Starfleet security officers start beaming in, ready for war.

TRIVIA

- Susan Gibney had played Leah Brahms in *The Next Generation*, Brock Peters had played Admiral Cartwright in *Star Trek IV: The Voyage Home* and *Star Trek VI: The Undiscovered Country*.
- This was originally intended as the third-season cliffhanger, with *Paradise Lost* as the season-opener. This was changed at the studio's insistence, and bumping it further up the season meant this story didn't have the huge budget originally imagined. Instead of having a full-scale Dominion invasion, the production team decided to play on the paranoia surrounding such an attack.

RATING

- An effective episode, even if the glimpses of Earth in the future are, once again, fairly cheap and dull-looking. Avery Brooks seems to revel in his new role, and the episode actually starts showing the problem rather than just telling us about it.

4.11 PARADISE LOST

STARDATE UNKNOWN

The true nature to the threat on Earth is revealed

TX 8 January 1996
WRITERS Ira Steven Behr and Robert Hewitt Wolfe (story by Ronald D Moore)

Sisko and Odo wonder how The Dominion sabotaged Earth's power grid, and notice that Red Squad was stood down when all other Starfleet units were on high alert. They talk to Nog, and trick a member of Red Squad into revealing that they shut down the power grid. Leyton plans a military coup, believing that martial law is the only way to fight The Dominion. Sisko discovers a Changeling disguised as O'Brien. It says that only four Changelings were needed

DIRECTOR Rez Badiyi
GUEST CAST Mina Badie (Security Officer), Aron Eisenberg (Nog), Robert Foxworth (Leyton), David Drew Gallagher (Riley Shepard), Susan Gibney (Erika Benteen), Brock Peters (Joseph Sisko), Herschel Sparber (Jaresh-Inyo), Rudolph Willrich (Academy Commandant)

to destabilise Earth. He is confident Earth will fall easily when its time comes. Leyton frames Sisko by faking a blood test and making the President think Sisko is a Changeling. The Defiant is sent to prove that Leyton is the guilty party, but is attacked by the USS Lakota, which has been told the Defiant is part of a Changeling invasion fleet. The Lakota's captain, Benteen, a Leyton loyalist, refuses to fight fellow Starfleet officers. Without support, Leyton resigns. Sisko hopes that fear won't conquer the Federation.

QUOTES

- 'Paradise has never been so well-armed' – *Sisko*

TRIVIA

- A victim of budget cuts, the final space battle included the use of some old footage.

RATING

- An effective episode, one that makes good use of the question of whether Starfleet is the military organisation it looks like, or the bunch of peaceful explorers they always say they are. Leyton is clearly a better leader than President Jaresh-Inyo – a comedy antelope-type thing – too. In the end, the revelation that there isn't an invasion is far more shocking than scenes of pitched battle would have been, and that's a neat trick to pull off.

4.12 CROSSFIRE

STARDATE UNKNOWN

Odo must cope as Shakaar becomes closer to Kira

TX 29 January 1996
WRITER René Echevarria
DIRECTOR Les Landau
GUEST CAST Duncan Regehr (Shakaar), Charles Tentindo (Jimenez), Bruce Wright (Sarish)

Shakaar, the First Minister of Bajor, arrives on the station to lobby for the planet to join the Federation. Odo finds out that The True Way, the Cardassian extremists, are planning to assassinate him. Odo acts as Shakaar's bodyguard, finding it awkward that the Bajoran starts to get involved with Kira. Shakaar admits to Odo he has strong feelings for Kira. Distracted, Odo allows a turbolift they are in to go into freefall – the assassination attempt. Odo uses his abilities to slow the lift car. He is heartbroken when Shakaar spends the night with Kira, smashing up his office. Quark comes to complain, and when Odo confesses, the Ferengi suggests that he needs to tell Kira how he feels.

TRIVIA

- Originally, Odo was to face a choice of protecting Shakaar or Kira when the assassination attempt came. He was to choose Shakaar.

RATING

- Shakaar's not a very interesting character this time out, and the focus of the episode is on Odo, which really stacks the deck of the story. Rene Auberjonois is on fine form, and there's a lovely scene with Quark at the end.

4.13 RETURN TO GRACE

STARDATE UNKNOWN

A disgraced Dukat gains inspiration from Kira

TX 5 February 1996
WRITER Hans Beimler (story by Tom Benko)
DIRECTOR Jonathan West
GUEST CAST Marc Alaimo (Dukat), Cyia Batten (Ziyal), Casey Biggs (Damar), John K Shull (K'Temang)

Shakaar asks Kira to share intelligence on the Klingons with the Cardassians. She meets Gul Dukat, who's been demoted since returning with his illegitimate daughter. They are exiles on their battered freighter. Dukat and Kira discover that the Korma outpost has been wiped out by the Klingons, with many Bajoran and Cardassian diplomats killed, but they are unable to harm the bird of prey. Kira uses an old resistance trick of welding a ground-based disruptor from the colony onto the freighter. They ambush the Klingons, *en route* to the Cardassian planet Loval, capture the ship, and Dukat sends them to his freighter, which he blows up. Dukat is conviced this will rehabilitate him, but the civilian government want to pursue a diplomatic solution. Dukat is inspired by Kira to form a resistance against the Klingons. Kira persuades him that Ziyal should come with her, rather than fight in his one-man war.

TRIVIA

- This marks the second and final appearance of Cyia Batten as Ziyal (the first being *Indiscretion*). The character reappears in *For the Cause*, recast as Tracy Middendorf.
- This is the first appearance of Glinn Damar, seen here as Dukat's first officer.

RATING

- Marc Alaimo is always good value, and this swift reunion for the cast of *Indiscretion* is another superior exploration of the murky, interconnected relationship between Kira and Dukat.

4.14 THE SONS OF MOGH

STARDATE 49556.2

Kurn asks his brother Worf to kill him

TX 12 February 1996
WRITER Ronald D Moore
DIRECTOR David Livingston
GUEST CAST Robert DoQui (Noggra), Tony Todd (Kurn), Elliot Woods (Klingon Officer), Dell Yount (Tilikia)

Kurn arrives at the station, and demands that Worf kill him – under the terms of the Klingon ritual of mauk-to'Vor, this will restore his honour. Worf's opposition to the war with Cardassia has ruined Kurn. Dax arrives just as Worf stabs his brother, and has him beamed to the Infirmary. Bashir saves his life. Sisko has detected Klingons on 'military exercises' nearby, and he sends the Defiant to investigate. Kurn asks to help Odo with station security – but he soon allows himself to be shot, and Odo realises he has a death wish. The Defiant discovers that the Klingons were laying a cloaked minefield to cut off the station and Bajor from the Federation. Kurn and Worf are sent to discover the exact co-ordinates from the Klingons, and they infiltrate a ship. When Kurn kills a soldier, he becomes suicidal. On their return to the station, Worf asks Bashir to wipe Kurn's memory, then sends him to Noggra, a friend of his father. Kurn is now Rodek, son of Noggra, unaware of his past life.

TRIVIA

- Originally, Worf spent the story (which had the working title *Brother's Keeper*) unwilling to kill his brother, before deciding on his radical amnesia solution. This also marked the start of the Worf/Dax romance, with a scene at the beginning designed to see if Terry Farrell and Michael Dorn had chemistry together.
- This was the first appearance of Worf's mek'leth.
- Around this time, Michael Dorn suggested that Worf's Klingon exercises would make an excellent *Star Trek*-themed workout video, but Paramount vetoed the plans to release it.

RATING

- As often happens with Klingon stories, we learn about a new Klingon ritual that leads Worf to an ethical dilemma and it ends with a convenient cop-out. This gains points for having Worf agreeing to stab Kurn so readily, but the rest of the episode is by-the-numbers.

4.15 BAR ASSOCIATION

STARDATE UNKNOWN

Quark's employees form a trade union

TX 19 February 1996
WRITERS Robert Hewitt Wolfe and Ira Steven Behr (Barbara J Lee and Jenifer A Lee)
DIRECTOR LeVar Burton
GUEST CAST Jeffrey Combs (Brunt), Emilio Borelli (Frool), Max Grodenchik (Rom), Jason Marsden (Grimp), Chase Masterson (Leeta)

When Rom collapses with an ear infection, Bashir discovers the illness has progressed because Ferengi employers don't offer sick pay. Bashir suggests they should form a trade union, a prospect that offends and terrifies Rom. But when Quark cuts all his staff's wages, Rom rallies his reluctant co-workers. O'Brien, the descendant of a union activist, fuels Rom's fire and the Guild of Restaurant and Casino Employees goes on strike. Quark tries to replace them with holographic duplicates of himself. Sisko orders Odo to go easy on the strikers, and pressures Quark by asking for back rent. Brunt arrives and threatens to resolve the problem with force. Quark is worried that Brunt will injure Rom. In fact, Brunt decides that as Rom cares for Quark, hurting *him* would be more effective. Quark is badly beaten by Nausicaan thugs. He and Rom settle their dispute – they'll pretend Quark won, but Quark will give into all his brother's demands. One final bombshell is that Rom leaves his job – he'll work on the station maintenance staff from now on, making his own way in life.

TRIVIA

- An episode reminiscent of *Babylon 5*'s *By Any Means Necessary*, which featured a dock workers' dispute that was often cited as 'the sort of story *Star Trek* wouldn't ever do'. It was originally thought of as a B-plot, possibly for *Crossfire*, but it was felt it had enough material for a whole episode. The writers were looking to introduce the romance between Rom and Leeta.

RATING

- A comic story about a serious subject – one that's rarely addressed on American TV – this suffers in places from an uncertain tone. But it's a good story for Quark, showing his nasty side, and his somewhat twisted loyalties that means he can love his brother while cutting his wages.

4.16 ACCESSION

An ancient Bajoran emerges from the wormhole and declares himself Emissary

TX 26 February 1996
WRITER Jane Espenson
DIRECTOR Les Landau
GUEST CAST David Carpenter (Onara), Rosalind Chao (Keiko O'Brien), Holly Hatae (Molly O'Brien), Richard Libertini (Akorem Laan), Laura Jane Salvato (Gia), Camille Saviola (Kai Opaka), Robert Symonds (Vedek Porta), Grace Zandarski (Latana)

STARDATE UNKNOWN

Keiko announces she is pregnant again. Meanwhile, Sisko reluctantly performs a Bajoran wedding as the Emissary. Then Akorem Lam arrives in a Bajoran lightship. He's a poet who's been missing for 200 years, and claims he was saved by the beings in the wormhole. He's the true Emissary. Sisko is happy to step aside. Akorem quickly starts preaching what Sisko sees as dangerous ideas, like the return of the caste system, which will disqualify Bajor from Federation membership. Sisko has a vision of Kai Opaka, which Bashir dismisses. Kira, who has tendered her resignation, finds herself in the artists' caste and is no use at her new role. Sisko begins to see things on Bajor fall apart. A Vedek has murdered an 'unclean' monk. Sisko asks Akorem to follow him into the wormhole to ask the beings who is the true Emissary. Akorem is shocked to learn from them that Sisko is, and his appearance has been used to prove to Sisko how important the role of Emissary is. The aliens return Akorem to his own time.

QUOTES

- 'We are of Bajor. You are of Bajor.' – *the wormhole beings to Sisko*

TRIVIA

- There's a cute joke when Keiko announces she is pregnant. Worf's horrified, because he was the one who had to deliver Molly (in *The Next Generation*'s *Disaster*).
- Once again, *Babylon 5* seems to be an influence – the wormhole beings seem to have turned into Vorlons, making pithy, enigmatic statements about destiny.

RATING

- The studio is generally right about Bajoran stories, and particularly Bajoran religious stories. But this one isn't the usual nonsense, it's a clever character piece for Sisko and Kira. The central irony, that Sisko fights against Akorem's idea that everyone has a predestined role while coming to an understanding of his own part in the scheme of things, is never laboured.

4.17 RULES OF ENGAGEMENT

Worf has killed Klingon civilians and faces extradition

TX 8 April 1996
WRITER Ronald D Moore (story by Bradley Thompson and David Weddle)
DIRECTOR LeVar Burton
GUEST CAST Ron Canada (Ch'Pok), Christopher Michael (Helm Officer), Deborah Strang (T'Lara)

STARDATE 49665.3

Worf faces an extradition hearing – he's accused by the Klingon lawyer Ch'Pok of killing 141 Klingons on a passenger ship while in command of Defiant. Sisko claims it was a tragic mistake, but the Klingons think it was bloodlust. Even colleagues concede that Worf is capable of violence. Sisko orders Odo to check the background of the Klingon ship's crew. Things go from bad to worse when Worf attacks Ch'Pok after being provoked. Odo discovers that all the Klingon ship's 'passengers' had died in a vessel that crashed months earlier. Sisko turns the tables on Ch'Pok. This was a plot to make the Federation reluctant to defend convoys to Cardassia, allowing the Klingons a free hand in Cardassian space. Worf is exonerated, but admits that he would relish revenge on the Klingons.

TRIVIA

- The story was inspired by news of the US shooting down an Iranian passenger jet when it was misidentified as a missile.

RATING

- An odd misfire, because it seems like a foolproof story. In the event, it's got a strange narrative technique that doesn't work, and a cop-out ending. The interesting thing about the news story that inspired it was how the Americans responsible were never identified or (as far as we know) punished, and it would a much stronger story to see the Federation move to protect a guilty Worf.

4.18 HARD TIME

STARDATE UNKNOWN

O'Brien suffers 20 years in prison

TX 15 April 1996
WRITER Robert Hewitt Wolfe (story by Daniel Keys Moran and Lynn Barker)
DIRECTOR Alexander Singer
GUEST CAST Rosalind Chao (Keiko O'Brien), Hana Hatae (Molly O'Brien), FJ Rio (Muniz), Margot Rose (Rinn), Craig Wasson (Ee'Char)

O'Brien returns to the station traumatised. He was imprisoned on Argratha after his curiosity led to an espionage charge. He's had memories of 20 years' imprisonment implanted as punishment. He knows these memories to be false, but can't put them behind him. Bashir can't remove the memories, and O'Brien is given counselling. He remembers his kindly cellmate Ee'Char, but never tells anyone, insisting it was solitary confinement. He begins to see Ee'Char around the station, and after becoming increasingly erratic, Sisko relieves him of duty. When he gets violently angry with Molly, O'Brien becomes suicidal. Bashir talks him down, and O'Brien admits that he killed Ee'Char after snapping one day. It doesn't matter that Ee'Char isn't real, his reaction was. Bashir tells him that he mustn't allow the incident to overshadow his life, and O'Brien starts on the road to recovery.

TRIVIA

- This story contains elements salvaged from an abandoned one in which Sito, the young officer sent to her death in *Lower Decks*, returned with psychological problems due to her imprisonment.

RATING

- The same sort of thing as the previous year's *Voyager* episode *Ex Post Facto*, but done properly. The exact nature of Ee'Char is a nice little twist, one that makes you realise O'Brien is right to feel guilty and worry about what sort of man he is. Colm Meaney puts in a great performance, as ever.

4.19 SHATTERED MIRROR

STARDATE UNKNOWN

Sisko travels to the Mirror Universe to help lead a defence of the station

TX 22 April 1996
WRITERS Ira Steven Behr and Hans Beimler
DIRECTOR James L Conway
GUEST CAST Felicia M Bell (Jennifer Sisko), James Black (Helmsman), Carlos Carrasco (Klingon officer), Aron Eisenberg (Nog), Dennis Madalone (Guard), Andrew Robinson (Garak)

Jake finds Sisko talking to his dead mother Jennifer... or rather, her Mirror Universe counterpart. She tells them that the human rebels have control of the Mirror Terok Nor, and takes them there. They meet 'Smiley' O'Brien, who tells them that they stole the plans for the Defiant last time but need Sisko to fine-tune the ship. An Alliance fleet led by Regent Worf is coming to retake the station. Sisko goes to the imprisoned Kira, who realises that the Alliance will blame her for the loss of the station. She tells Sisko that the Alliance ships have a glitch in their targeting system that is vulnerable to warp shadows. Nog frees Kira, who kills Jennifer but spares Jake, so that Sisko owes him. Sisko leads the Defiant to war, sending the Klingon ships scattering.

TRIVIA

- This episode had five times the normal special effects budget.

RATING

- Everyone's having fun, but again an excursion to the Mirror Universe leads to a pretty shallow episode. Early hints that this is going to be an interesting story about Jake and his 'mother' give way to the usual comedy death scenes and the regulars acting butch. The space battle at the end is impressive, though.

4.20 THE MUSE

STARDATE UNKNOWN

Jake is inspired by an alien vampire

TX 29 April 1996
WRITER René Echevarria (story by Rene Echevarria and Majel Barrett)
DIRECTOR David Livingston
GUEST CAST Michael Ansara (Jeyal), Majel Barrett (Lwaxana Troi), Meg Foster (Onaya)

Jake is looking for writing inspiration when he sees a beautiful alien woman arrive at the station. Meanwhile, Odo is sought out by another new arrival – Lwaxana Troi, who reveals she's pregnant by her new husband, the Tavnian Jeyal. She's fled him, because she doesn't want the child raised the traditional way of his kind, exclusively by men. Jake meets his mystery woman, Onaya, who takes an interest in his writing, and gives him an antique pen. He draws inspiration from her, but as she massages his neck, she's draining his life energy. Jeyal arrives, and Odo pretends that he's to marry Lwaxana as soon as she annuls her marriage to Jeyal. Odo finds himself announcing that he genuinely does like Lwaxana, who celebrates his difference rather than fearing it. So much so, that he's disappointed when Jeyal leaves and Lwaxana says she's heading back to Betazed. Jake collapses. Sisko confronts Onaya, who says she's inspired great poets – it's cost them their life, but they created great art. Jake recovers, and has completed his first novel, *Anslem*. He hopes he can be so inspired again.

TRIVIA

- Tarbolde, one of the poets Onaya inspired was cited by Gary Mitchell in *Where No Man Has Gone Before*.
- The Lwaxana plot was Majel Barrett's idea: a story which started with her announcing she was carrying Odo's baby.
- While it's been mentioned a few times, it's never been established in even the broadest terms what Jake's novel *Anslem* is about.

RATING

- Oh deary me. Neither story in this episode is up to much – the Jake story is a writer's fantasy that should never be entertained – that sexy women love watching men type. The B-plot is an actor's idea that was never going to be entertaining.

4.21 FOR THE CAUSE

STARDATE UNKNOWN

Eddington reports that the Maquis are planning a daring theft

TX 6 May 1996
WRITER Ronald D Moore (story by Mark Gehred-O'Connell)
DIRECTOR James L Conway
GUEST CAST Penny Johnson (Kasidy Yates), Steven Vincent Leigh (Reese), Kenneth Marshall (Michael Eddington), Tracy Middendorf (Ziyal), John Prosky (Brathlaw), Andrew Robinson (Garak)

Starfleet Security representative Eddington tells the station officers that the Klingons have inflicted serious losses on the Cardassians. Starfleet is going to send Cardassia some industrial replicators to aid their recovery, and they'll be passing through the station. They'll be a prime target for the Maquis. He also suspects Kasidy Yates is smuggling for the Maquis. Meanwhile, Garak has become fascinated by Ziyal, Dukat's daughter, but is worried she has a hidden agenda. A cloaked Defiant follows Yates' ship, and sees it head for the Badlands, where it meets a Maquis ship. Sisko leads the next mission to arrest Yates himself – as he's doing so, he realises that he and the Defiant have been lured away from the station. Eddington is a Maquis, and takes control of the replicators. Sisko vows revenge, and goes easy on Yates. Garak and Ziyal become friends.

TRIVIA

- Originally about a Maquis bombing of the station, this story was to see Sisko pursue Kasidy Yates as the prime suspect. It was also to reveal that the Klingons and Maquis were working together, but this idea was dropped.

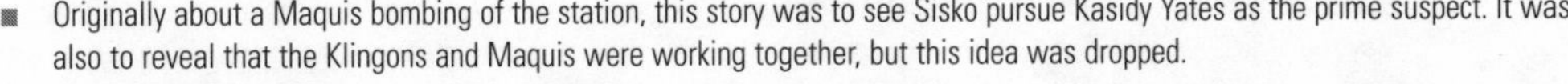

RATING

- A straightforward episode, and quite an effective one, but the twist that Eddington is up to no good is pretty obvious, and so it becomes obvious what his plan is.

4.22 TO THE DEATH

STARDATE 49904.2

The Defiant crew team up with the Jem'Hadar

TX 13 May 1996
WRITERS Ira Steven Behr and Robert Hewitt Wolfe
DIRECTOR LeVar Burton
GUEST CAST Jeffrey Combs (Weyoun), Scott Haven (Virak'kara), Brian Thompson (Toman'torax), Clarence Williams III (Omet'iklan)

Returning from defeating a Breen attack on a Bajoran colony, Sisko finds the station's been devastated by a Jem'Hadar attack. He takes the Defiant after them, and finds a damaged Jem'Hadar ship. He beams aboard the survivors – half a dozen Jem'Hadar and their leader, the Vorta Weyoun. Weyoun tells Sisko the Jem'Hadar were renegades, and he wants to destroy them, too. The renegades are looking for an Iconian gateway on Vandros IV that will allow them to travel across the galaxy instantly – Weyoun doesn't trust his Jem'Hadar commander Omet'iklan, fearing they might join the renegades. Weyoun approaches Odo and tells him the Founders still want him to join the Great Link. Odo refuses. Beaming down, they discover their phasers and communicators don't work near the gateway. They have to rely on bladed weapons and explosives. After a bloody battle, O'Brien blows up the gateway. Now energy weapons work again, Omet'iklan kills Weyoun for doubting his loyalty. Omet'iklan warns Sisko that next time they meet, he'll do the same to him.

TRIVIA

- The blade fights were cut down in post-production as it was felt they were too violent.
- The Iconians were first mentioned in *Contagion.*
- Jeffrey Combs was cast as Weyoun, having already been cast by LeVar Burton earlier in the season as Brunt in *Bar Association.* Previous Vorta had failed to make the impact the writers had hoped for, but Weyoun worked. Unfortunately, his character died at the end of the episode, but this proved less of an obstacle than it might...

RATING

- A sort of inverse of *I, Borg.* The more you get to know the Jem'Hadar, the less pleasant they are. It's not the deepest of episodes, but it finally gives The Dominion a face.

4.23 THE QUICKENING

STARDATE UNKNOWN

Bashir faces a planet ravaged by incurable plague

TX 20 May 1996
WRITER Naren Shankar
DIRECTOR Rene Auberjonois
GUEST CAST Alan Echevarria (Tamar), Dylan Haggerty (Epran), Loren Lester (Attendant), Heidi Margolis (Norva), Lisa Moncure (Latia), Michael Sarrazan (Trevean), Ellen Wheeler (Ekoria)

In the Gamma Quadrant, Kira, Dax and Bashir pick up a distress call from the Teplan system. There's a pandemic on the planet, and they soon discover that rather than cure them, the healer Trevean accelerates the effects of the plague so they die more quickly and painlessly. Bashir is told there's no cure – 200 years ago, the Jem'Hadar introduced it as punishment. The crew are unable to help, and are about to leave when they are met by the pregnant Ekoria, who wants to live long enough to deliver her baby. Bashir tries to help, but his test subjects die painfully. Bashir works on alone, and keeps Ekoria alive – not just that, her baby is free from the disease. Bashir has succeeded in innoculating the baby, and future generations will be free from the plague.

QUOTES

- 'There is no cure for the Blight. The Dominion made sure of that, and I was so arrogant I thought I could cure it in a week.' 'Maybe that was arrogant. But it's even more arrogant to say that there is no cure, just because you couldn't find it.' – *Bashir and Dax*

TRIVIA

- The working title was *The Healing Touch.*
- Torrential rain meant three filming days were lost on location.

RATING

- An episode that feels like it's about to lurch into a heavy-handed AIDS or euthanasia allegory at any moment actually works really well, and there's some very nice directorial touches. The disease, complete with CG boils, is really unpleasant.

4.24 BODY PARTS

STARDATE UNKNOWN

Quark is told he's dying, and puts his dead body up for sale

TX 10 June 1996
WRITER Hans Beimler (story by Louis P Desantis and Robert J Bolivar)
DIRECTOR Avery Brooks
GUEST CAST Rosalind Chao (Keiko O'Brien), Jeffrey Combs (Brunt), Max Grodenchik (Rom), Hana Hatae (Molly O'Brien), Andrew J Robinson (Garak)

Quark returns from Ferenginar with news he's suffering from Dorek Syndrome and has only a week to live, and so has to pay off his debts. He lists his desiccated body parts for sale, as is the Ferengi way, and soon gets an anonymous bid for 500 bars of latinum. Meanwhile Keiko is caught in a shuttle accident with Bashir and Kira, and suffers internal injuries. Her baby has been transferred to Kira's womb. Now he's back, Bashir gives Quark a second opinion and declares he isn't dying after all. Brunt arrives, and reveals that he bought Quark's body. Quark explains, but Brunt tells Quark he's either going to have to die or become a pariah for breaking a contract. Quark asks Garak to arrange to have him assassinated painlessly, and Garak is happy to help. Quark has a dream that persuades him to break the contract instead. He returns Brunt's money. Brunt strips the bar, but Quark's friends help out with restocking it.

TRIVIA

- Nana Visitor was pregnant in real life (with Siddig El Fadil's child), and received Keiko's baby as a way of explaining away Kira's appearance.
- Andrew Robinson decided to change his acting credit to Andrew J Robinson. The new name appears from this episode onwards.

RATING

- A surprisingly good Quark episode, one that presents a number of sides to the character. The Kira B-plot is extremely silly, though. Not a brilliant episode, but it works.

4.25 BROKEN LINK

STARDATE 49962.4

Odo is dying and must return home to survive

TX 17 June 1996
WRITERS Robert Hewitt Wolfe and Ira Steven Behr (story by George A Brozak)
DIRECTOR Les Landau
GUEST CAST Leslie Bevis (Freighter Captain), Andrew Hawkes (Amat'igan), Jill Jacobson (Areya), Salome Jens (Founder Leader), Robert O'Reilly (Gowron), Andrew J Robinson (Garak)

Odo collapses. Bashir discovers that Odo's mass is fluctuating, but has no idea why. Odo leaves the Infirmary to accost a Boslic freighter captain, but collapses again and the captain escapes. Odo is deteriorating. Sisko offers to go to the Gamma Quadrant and send out a distress call, to see if the Founders respond. Garak asks to go, to see if there are any Cardassian survivors of their attack against The Dominion the previous year. The Defiant is soon surrounded by Dominion warships. The female shapeshifter tells Sisko that Odo's only hope is to return to the Great Link. Odo realises they've given him the illness to force him to come home. Odo melts into the great sea of Changelings on their home planet. Garak learns there were no survivors, and tries to destroy the Changeling planet, but Worf stops him. Odo emerges, and Bashir tells him he's now biologically human. The Changelings have punished him for allying with the 'solids'. Odo is returned to the station... where he reveals that he's learned something while part of the Great Link. Gowron, head of the Klingon Empire, is a Changeling...

TRIVIA

- Nana Visitor had to practice sneezing on cue.
- Shortly after filming this episode Visitor gave birth to her son, Django.

RATING

- An episode that gives a real sense that things are moving along and changing. It's a shame though that the series never really explores the impact on Odo.

STAR TREK: DEEP SPACE NINE
SEASON FIVE

5.1 APOCALYPSE RISING

STARDATE UNKNOWN

Sisko and the officers unmask a Changeling in the Klingon High Command

TX 30 September 1996
WRITERS Ira Steven Behr and Robert Hewitt Wolfe
DIRECTOR James L Conway
GUEST CAST Marc Alaimo (Gul Dukat), Ivor Bartels (Young Klingon), John L Bennett (Towering Klingon), Casey Biggs (Damar), Robert Budaska (Burly Klingon), Tony Epper (Drunk Klingon), JG Hertzler (Martok), Robert O'Reilly (Gowron), Robert Zachar (Head Guard)

Sisko, Odo and O'Brien are altered to look like Klingons, in order to infiltrate and expose the Gowron Changeling at the Ceremony of Commendation. Gul Dukat transports the officers, and a slightly altered Worf, into Klingon territory in his bird of prey. As the Ceremony is about to begin, O'Brien and Odo narrowly escape being recognised. They set up four emitters that will force the Changeling to reveal itself. At the last minute, General Martok, Gowron's right-hand man, recognises Sisko. The emitters are destroyed and the officers are arrested and thrown into a cell. The situation looks bleak, but Martok reveals that he too believes Gowron has been replaced. They decide to go back to the hall and kill the Changeling. When Worf attacks, Gowron insists on fighting one-on-one. When Martok wonders why Sisko does not shoot Gowron, Odo realises that this Martok has no honour and must be the Changeling. Martok is exposed and Gowron, fearful that the war will not end easily, agrees to a cease-fire and has the officers safely returned to Deep Space Nine.

TRIVIA

- At the end of season four, the production team had decided that Gowron was the Changeling. Ronald Moore suggested that Martok be revealed as the shapeshifter to maintain suspense. The crew were so impressed by Hertzler's performance that they had the real Martok found and join the cast of semi-regulars from *In Purgatory's Shadow*.

RATING

- Fast-paced, heady stuff to start the fifth season. This is the episode that really marks the show getting behind the Klingons as a key feature for the next few years. Hertzler is wonderful as the imposter Martok.

5.2 THE SHIP

STARDATE 50049.3

Sisko finds a Jem'Hadar ship and enters a stalemate with a Vorta

TX 7 October 1996
WRITER Hans Beimler (story by Pam Wigginton and Rick Cason)
DIRECTOR Kim Friedman
GUEST CAST Kaitlin Hopkins (Kilana), FJ Rio (Muniz), Hilary Shepard (Hoya)

From their runabout, Sisko, Dax, Worf, O'Brien and Muniz watch as a Jem'Hadar ship crashes into a planet. They investigate and find all the crew dead. As the officers wait for the Defiant, a second Jem'Hadar craft destroys the runabout. A Vorta, Kilana, requests that Sisko return the ship. Sisko refuses. The officers realise there must be something aboard that The Dominion wants, but Muniz is seriously wounded and they have little time. Kilana tells Sisko he can keep the ship if she can have an item hidden inside, but will not say what it is. Sisko refuses, but this time explosions outside the craft rock the ship. O'Brien restores power and they try to escape, but they fear a core breach and have to cut power. In the panic, Muniz dies. As the officers take stock, Dax spots a strange liquid. It is an injured Changeling that cannot hold its form – this is what the Kilana wants. The Changeling dies. Sisko and Kilana realise that their mutual mistrust cost each of them a life. The Vorta leaves and the Defiant arrives to tow the Jem'Hadar ship back to the station.

TRIVIA

- DS9's one-hundredth episode began life as a pitch by Wigginton and Cason. The story was a version of the Alamo with the DS9 crew holed up in the ship, facing constant bombardment and slowly taking their frustration out on each other.

RATING

- A decent enough story, but one that never quite brings out the paranoia and claustrophobia of the situation. Although we have seen Muniz before (in *Hard Time*), we don't really have a sense of loss. Sadly, the stakes just aren't high enough for this one to work.

5.3 LOOKING FOR PAR'MACH IN ALL THE WRONG PLACES

Worf falls for Quark's Klingon ex-wife when she returns to the station

TX 14 October 1996
WRITER Ronald D Moore
DIRECTOR Andrew J Robinson
GUEST CAST Mary Kay Adams (Grilka), Rosalind Chao (Keiko), Phil Morris (Thopok), Joseph Ruskin (Tumek)

STARDATE UNKNOWN

Worf instantly falls for Grilka, a Klingon female who arrives at the station with Tumek and a guard, Thopok. He is horrified to discover Grilka and Quark were once married for her convenience. Worf makes his advances, but Tumek derides Worf for his discommendation – and that, having been reared by humans, he has little idea of how to woo a Klingon woman! Quark is invited to dinner with Grilka, providing Worf with an opportunity to prove his courtship skills by proxy. In the holosuite, Worf and Dax show Quark a battle that ends in the male and female warriors mating. The tuition is successful, but Thopok, observing Grilka and Quark's post-coital bliss with anger, challenges Quark to a fight to the death. Dax rigs Quark with a remote control device that allows Worf to control Quark's moves, fighting for him. Dax hints that Worf should pursue someone else, but he is oblivious to her advances. Quark fights impressively until the device fails. Stalling for time, Quark claims the Ferengi right to woo Grilka with words – while Dax and Worf fix the device. Once fixed, Quark quickly defeats Thopok and hands his sword to Grilka, allowing him to retain his honour while not killing his opponent. As Quark and Grilka fall together again, Worf succumbs to Dax.

QUOTES

- 'For a Klingon who was raised by humans, wears a Starfleet uniform and drinks prune juice, you're pretty attached to [Klingon] tradition. But that's OK – I like a man riddled with contradictions.' – *Dax to Worf*

TRIVIA

- Ronald Moore's sequel to season three's *House of Quark* draws heavily on *Cyrano de Bergerac*. The original concept focused on Worf as the title character, but early developments gave way to Quark. Instead, the writers introduced the Dax-Worf relationship, an idea that had been slowly developing, and a reflection on the on-screen chemistry of Farrell and Dorn.

RATING

- Good light-hearted stuff. The Quark-Grillka, Dax-Worf and ultimately Kira-O'Brien subplot all contribute to the episode's theme. The characters are pushed just so far to have fun without compromising them. A difficult balance but struck well here.

5.4 ...NOR THE BATTLE TO THE STRONG

Jake Sisko experiences the horrors of war first-hand

TX 21 October 1996
DIRECTOR Kim Friedman
WRITER René Echevarria (story by Brice R Parker)
GUEST CAST Elle Alexander (Female Guard), Karen Austin (Kalandra), Jeb Brown (Ensign), Danny Goldring (Burke), Mark Holton (Bolian), Andrew Kavovit (Kirby), Lisa Lord (Nurse), Greg 'Christopher' Smith (Male Guard)

STARDATE UNKNOWN

Jake and Bashir pick up a distress call from a Federation colony under attack from the Klingons. Jake persuades Bashir, despite misgivings, to take him to the battle. They are quickly asked to help the medical team treat casualties. Jake hears that the Klingons are regrouping to attack again. Suddenly, the Klingons disable the reactor and power fails. Bashir and Jake head for the power pack on their runabout, but come under fire. Jake panics and runs. He finds an injured soldier, but the man is too far gone to be helped. Jake makes it back to the cavern where he pretends he was knocked out. Bashir is annoyed with himself for putting Jake in danger, but Jake only feels worse about deserting. As Jake sleeps, the Klingons attack. The medical team evacuate, but Jake engages in a fire fight and is trapped in a rock fall. Jake awakens on the Defiant with Sisko and Bashir. Sisko is proud that his son aided the escape, but Jake writes an article to reflect the horrors of war and his personal feelings.

TRIVIA

- Brice Parker's original pitch had Jake working as a journalist in a Cardassian hospital when the Klingons attacked. For cost reasons (imagine the make-up budget!), the location and protagonists were changed. Echevarria's working title for the script was *Portrait of a Life*, but this gave way late in the day to...*Nor the Battle to the Strong*, a quotation from Ecclesiastes.

RATING

- Fairly traditional 'horror of war' stuff, but unusual for *Star Trek*. The tension builds well and we get some good performances out of Bashir and Jake, but the show never capitalises on the potential relationship that could result from these events.

5.5 THE ASSIGNMENT

STARDATE UNKNOWN

Keiko O'Brien is possessed and held hostage by a Pah-wraith

TX 28 October 1996
WRITERS David Weddle and Bradley Thompson (story by David R Long and Robert Lederman)
DIRECTOR Allan Kroeker
GUEST CAST Majel Barrett (Computer Voice), Rosalind Chao (Keiko), Judi Durand (Station Computer Voice), Patrick B Egan (Jiyar), Max Grodenchik (Rom), Hana Hatae (Molly), Rosie Malek-Yonan (Tekos)

Keiko returns to the station, possessed by an alien holding her hostage. The entity threatens to kill Keiko unless O'Brien alters the station's communications system. O'Brien complies, but soon there are more demands. O'Brien tries to tell Sisko, but the entity throws Keiko from high above the Promenade. Keiko survives but was lucky. The entity gives O'Brien 13 hours to comply. O'Brien enlists Rom's help and swears him to secrecy. Dax discovers sabotage, but O'Brien has to pretend to know nothing. Rom discovers that the sabotage will kill the aliens in the wormhole. O'Brien and Rom discover that, before her return, Keiko visited the home of the enemies of the Prophets, the Pah-wraiths. O'Brien completes the alterations and meets Keiko in a runabout. He operates a beam which frees Keiko from the Pah-wraith. O'Brien returns to the station to explain all.

TRIVIA

- Lederman and Long's original pitch was a traditional hostage story. As the writers pushed it forward, the team came up with the idea of possession and eventually the notion of 'evil' as the controlling force. The concept of evil Bajoran gods, hinted at in the first season, provided the threat.

RATING

- Rosalind Chao's performance turns a rather hokey idea into a creepy flesh-crawling episode. The moment when the Keiko entity invites O'Brien to bed is just plain nasty. Small-scale stuff that works well, especially after the big episodes of the season so far.

5.6 TRIALS AND TRIBBLE-ATIONS

STARDATE UNKNOWN/4523.7

The officers travel back in time to prevent an assassination attempt against Kirk

TX 4 November 1996
WRITERS Ronald D Moore and René Echevarria (story by Ira Steven Behr, Hans Beimler and Robert Hewitt Wolfe, based on the original Star Trek episode *The Trouble with Tribbles* by David Gerrold)
DIRECTOR Jonathan West
GUEST CAST Leslie Ackerman (Waitress), Jack Blessing (Dulmur), Charlie Brill (Arne Darvin), Charles S Chun (Engineer), James W Jansen (Lucsly), Deirdre L Imershein (Lieut Watley) – and the cast of the original *Star Trek* episode *The Trouble With Tribbles*

Sisko is visited by Lucsly and Dulmer from the Federation Department of Temporal Investigations and is ordered to reveal details of his recent travel through time. Sisko recounts that the Defiant was returning from Cardassian space with a Bajoran Orb of Time and Arne Darvin, a Klingon altered to look human. Darvin used the Orb to send the Defiant 100 years into the past, to Deep Space Station K-7 at the time of Kirk's visit. At that time, Darvin poisoned grain supplies but was unmasked by Kirk. Darvin is out to change history. As Sisko, Dax, Bashir and Worf search the Enterprise for Darvin, Odo and Worf trawl Station K-7. Bashir, O'Brien, Worf and Odo spot Darvin in the station bar, but get involved in a fight between the Enterprise crew and the Klingons. Bashir and O'Brien are arrested for fighting and questioned by Kirk – and notice Tribbles appearing on the ship. Meanwhile, Worf and Odo find Darvin on the Defiant – he has planted a bomb in a Tribble! The officers discover the bomb is in the storage compartments, where the Tribbles have eaten the grain and are dying. As Kirk opens the compartment and is covered by the creatures, Sisko finds and beams outside the exploding Tribble. The timeline is left undamaged. The agents close their investigation, leaving the officers to contend with the offspring of a Tribble Odo obtained.

QUOTES

- 'We do not discuss it with outsiders.' – *Worf to Bashir on the original series Klingons*

TRIVIA

- In 1996, the *Star Trek* franchise celebrated its thirtieth birthday in style. *The Next Generation* was putting together *First Contact* and *Voyager* had a special two-parter planned, yet *Deep Space Nine* seemed to be missing out. Ronald Moore was hesitant to bring back more of the original series cast, having resurrected Scotty for *The Next Generation*'s *Relics* and hearing of Sulu's imminent return in *Voyager*. One initial concept had the DS9 crew return to Sigma Iotia II, the gangster planet in *A Piece of the Action*. Eventually, Ronald Moore suggested that putting the DS9 characters into the past, rather than bringing past characters to *Deep Space Nine*, and latched onto a fan favourite, David Gerrold's *The Trouble with Tribbles*.
- Lucsly and Dulmer are, of course, anagrams of Scully and Mulder, the lead characters in *The X-Files*.

RATING

- *Deep Space Nine*'s finest hour: well thought-through, cleverly crafted and above all funny as hell. Few moments can top Worf's embarrassment at the original series Klingons. Technically and creatively flawless – a *Star Trek* masterpiece.

5.7 LET HE WHO IS WITHOUT SIN...

Worf's relationship with Dax hits a problem on the pleasure planet Risa

TX 11 November 1996
WRITERS Robert Hewitt Wolfe and Ira Steven Behr
DIRECTOR Rene Auberjonois
GUEST CAST Zora Dehorter (Risan woman), Frank Kopyc (Bolian Aide), Monte Markham (Pascal Fullerton), Chase Masterson (Leeta), Blair Valk (Risan woman), Vanessa Williams (Arandis)

STARDATE UNKNOWN

His relationship with Dax struggling, Worf intends to talk to her during their vacation on Risa. However, on arrival, Worf discovers that the social director, Arandis, is the former lover of Curzon Dax. Meanwhile, Worf is approached by the New Essentialists led by Pascal Fullerton, a group that wishes to restore the culture and morals of the Federation by closing Risa. That night, a group of New Essentialists storm the Solarium. Worf realises this is a stunt to make the holiday-makers feel vulnerable. He argues with Dax that she is not taking their relationship seriously. The next day, he sees Dax with Arandis and, jealous, tells Fullerton he knows how to scare the guests from the resort. Soon, a storm hits Risa. Arandis realises that the weather control has been sabotaged. Dax accuses Worf of sabotaging Risa to get back at her. Worf begins to explain his feelings and the rift begins to heal, but suddenly a powerful earthquake shakes Risa. Worf takes his tricorder back from Fullerton and the weather is restored. Worf and Dax can enjoy their holiday.

TRIVIA

- The idea for *Let He Who is Without Sin...* evolved from discussions around Eugene O'Neill's play *A Moon for the Misbegotten*, in which indulgences and excesses result in tragedy.

RATING

- *Star Trek* just isn't about romance, so it's not a good idea to put it centre-stage. *Let He Who is Without Sin...* is one of those bizarre episodes where the characters act oddly just to fulfil their story function. Ill thought-through, unimaginative nonsense.

5.8 THINGS PAST

Odo relives his guilty past on Terok Nor

TX 18 November 1996
WRITER Michael Taylor
DIRECTOR LeVar Burton
GUEST CAST Marc Alaimo (Dukat), Brenan Baird (Soldier) Victor Bevine (Belar), Louahn Lowe (Okala), Andrew J Robinson (Garak), Kurtwood Smith (Thrax)

STARDATE UNKNOWN

Sisko, Odo, Garak and Dax are found unconscious in their runabout. They awaken in the past, on the station when it was under Cardassian occupation. The rest of the inhabitants see them as Bajorans. Dax is taken to be Dukat's 'friend'. Garak scans the others and discovers they are seen as Timor Landi, Ishan Chaye and Jillur Gueta. Odo explains that these three Bajorans were wrongly executed for an assassination attempt on Dukat's life – he was Security Chief on Terok Nor at the time. Odo is put in a cell and meets Thrax, supposedly his predecessor as Chief of Security but still holding that position, and urges him to investigate further. Dax escapes Dukat and frees the others, but they are blocked by Thrax, who is revealed to be a Changeling. They are told they will be executed in two hours. Sisko is sure it all leads back to Odo. Odo tells Thrax they are from the future, but Thrax already knows. On the Promenade, Odo and Thrax watch as Sisko, Dax and Garak wait for execution. Odo insists he won't let this happen again. The scene changes and the officers watch as the three innocent Bajorans are executed, with Odo looking on wearing Thrax's uniform. Odo awakens. Bashir explains that a plasma storm caused Odo to forge a version of the Great Link with his friends. Odo's guilt forced him to relive the incident and face the truth.

TRIVIA

- LeVar Burton consciously reused horror movie techniques to create Odo's Terok Nor nightmare.

RATING

- A dream episode with a difference. Odo's guilty past is a fascinating theme that was crying out for exploration, as was Terok Nor. Auberjonois is surprisingly over-the-top at times, but on the whole puts in a decent performance.

5.9 THE ASCENT

STARDATE UNKNOWN

Quark and Odo must co-operate in order to escape death on an ice planet

TX 25 November 1996
WRITERS Ira Steven Behr and Robert Hewitt Wolfe
DIRECTOR Allan Kroeker
GUEST CAST Aron Eisenberg (Nog), Max Grodenchik (Rom)

Odo is ordered to escort Quark to a hearing eight days away. *En route*, they find a bomb on the runabout. Although they manage to limit the damage, the runabout crashes on an ice planet. Their communications system damaged, Quark suggests they take a piece of equipment to the top of a moutain, where the atmosphere may be thin enough to send a distress call. After a long trek, Quark is ready to give up. Odo encourages him to continue, but they discover there is a valley between them and the mountain – they must go down before they can climb up again. Their bickering turns into pushing and shoving, and Odo breaks his leg. Quark tries to take Odo and the equipment up the mountain but loses heart. He is shamed into trying again when Odo attempts the climb with his broken leg. Later, as Odo ponders Quark's fate, he is beamed to the Defiant. Quark succeeded in the attempt. He and Odo return to the station and comfort themselves that they still share a mutual hatred.

QUOTES

- 'I'm not trying to rescue you – I'm taking you along as emergency rations.' – *Quark to Odo*

TRIVIA

- When the production team decided to run an Odo-Quark story as the main plot, Ira Behr suggested a *Trek* version of Beckett's *Waiting for Godot.*
- There is a sly reference to Fizzbin, a fictitious game created by Kirk to get out of a tricky spot in *A Piece of the Action.* According the Quark, Fizzbin is a real game that he has mastered.

RATING

- An episode that reaches the pinnacle of the Odo-Quark relationship, no pun intended. Odo's new human frailty is brought out further to add yet more to this already burgeoning character, while Quark's sincerity and concern is nicely achieved. Sadly, in the end there's just too much of it.

5.10 RAPTURE

STARDATE UNKNOWN

Sisko experiences visions that warn Bajor not to join the Federation for now

TX 30 December 1996
WRITER Hans Beimler (story by LJ Strom)
DIRECTOR Jonathan West
GUEST CAST Louise Fletcher (Kai Winn), Penny Johnson (Kasidy Yates), Ernest Perry Jr (Admiral Whatley)

Sisko is inspired by a painting of B'hala, Bajor's lost city, to try to uncover its location, hidden in a depiction of an obelisk. Sisko recreates the obelisk on the holosuite, but is injured when the holosuite shorts out. When Sisko awakens, Bashir tells him he will have enhanced senses for the next few days. Sure enough, Sisko realises what the obelisk means and makes for the holosuite. He is interrupted by a message from Admiral Whatley – Bajor has been accepted to join the Federation and the ceremony will take place on the station. Sisko has a vision of B'hala and glimpses Bajor's future. He sets out with Kasidy Yates, his old girlfriend, who has been released from prison, and finds the lost city. The Bajorans proclaim a miracle from the Emissary. However, Sisko is weakening. Bashir insists that Sisko is in danger, but he refuses an operation in order to glean more from the visions at the expense of his own life. Aided by Kai Winn, Sisko uses an Orb of Prophecy. He warns that if Bajor joins the Federation now it will be destroyed. Sisko collapses and Jake permits Bashir to operate. Sisko is saved and, though saddened by the loss of the visions, is urged by Kasidy to appreciate what he still has.

TRIVIA

- Strom's pitch mutated beyond recognition to become a story that explored the themes of the pilot episode. The story was originally written with Kira as Sisko's compatriot, but Kasidy Yates was promoted to the main plot when Nana Visitor briefly left to have her child.
- The episode sees the first use of the new Starfleet uniforms seen in *First Contact*. Although *Deep Space Nine* had these ready for use, the cast were unable to use them until they had premiered in the eighth *Star Trek* film. The old *Deep Space Nine* uniforms were reused in *Voyager*.

RATING

- An episode that is more momentous when you think about it than when you see it. Sisko finally accepts his destiny, but a question mark remains over his powers. It's a cornerstone for seasons to come.

5.11 THE DARKNESS AND THE LIGHT

Kira is terrorised when members of the Shakaar resistance cell are killed

TX 6 January 1997
WRITER Ronald D Moore (story by Bryan Fuller)
DIRECTOR Michael Vejar
GUEST CAST Christian Conrad (Brilgar), Judi Durand (Station Computer Voice), Aron Eisenberg (Nog), William Lucking (Furel), Scott McElroy (Guard), Randy Oglesby (Silaran Prin), Matt Roe (Latha Mabrin), Diane Salinger (Lupaza), Jennifer Savidge (Trentin Fala)

STARDATE 50416.2

Kira is shocked when Vedek Latha Mabrin, a former Shakaar resistance fighter, is murdered. She then receives a sinister anonymous recording with a picture of Mabrin and a voice saying: 'That's one.' The officers suspect that the former resistance cell is now under threat. Kira makes contact with Trentin Fala, an old informer, who fears that she may be next. Fala is killed in the transporter beam – and Kira receives a second message featuring Fala's image and the words 'That's two.' Later, Kira receives a third message feauturing the face of Mobara. Later, Kira returns to her room in the O'Briens' quarters but is awoken by the sudden reappearance of Furel and Lupaza, two other resistance fighters, who have come to protect her. Furel and Lupaza offer to hunt down the killer, but Kira wants to use the law and asks them to protect her and the O'Briens' unborn child. Later, an explosion rips through the O'Briens' quarters, killing Furel and Lupaza. Kira steals Odo's list of suspects and tracks down a Cardassian, Silaran Prin. Silaran, who was disfigured by a bomb, intends to kill Kira, but will not act indiscriminately as she did. He prepares to remove the child, but Kira outwits and kills him. Sisko, Bashir and Odo arrive to bring Kira safely home.

TRIVIA

- Bryan Fuller's first pitch for *Deep Space Nine*, *The Darkness and the Light*, is a rendition of Agatha Christie's *Ten Little Indians*.

RATING

- A clever dark piece of television with tension and gravitas. Prin is a complicated character surrounded by moral ambiguities. Kira's morality is no less ambiguous, which makes for some exceptional one-on-one scenes. Visitor puts in one of her best performances, with a series of powerful monologues.

5.12 THE BEGOTTEN

Odo obtains a Changeling child and tries to raise it as he was not

TX 27 January 1997
WRITER René Echevarria
DIRECTOR Jesus Salvador Trevino

STARDATE UNKNOWN

As Kira goes into labour, Odo takes care of his own baby, a Changeling child he has purchased from Quark. Odo is displeased when Dr Mora, the Bajoran scientist who raised Odo, arrives to help. They clash: Odo wants to try encouragement, Mora is interested in using scientific measurements. Although Odo refuses to recognise Mora's expertise, he is backed into a corner when Sisko orders him to communicate with the child or give it to Starfleet. Odo and Mora use the same electric shocks once used on Odo to make the child hold a new form. They are

GUEST CAST Rosalind Chao (Keiko), Duncan Regehr (Shakaar Edon), Peggy Roeder (Y'Pora), James Sloyan (Dr Mora Pol)

amazed when the creature creates a face and looks at Odo. Odo and Mora both feel pride in the child and accept that both approaches have helped. Odo is pleased and claims his life has changed, but his happiness is cut short by news that the child is dying. Odo begs Bashir to help, but there is nothing he can do. The creature dies but merges into Odo, restoring his shapeshifting powers. Odo meets Kira, who has given birth to the O'Briens' child and handed it over. They share their life-changing senses of loss.

QUOTES

- 'Constable – why are you talking to your beverage?' *Worf to Odo – the beverage is a Changeling*

TRIVIA

- James Sloyan reprised his role as Dr Mora Pol, previously seen in *The Alternate.*

RATING

- The O'Brien baby and Odo story arcs neatly mesh together in *The Begotten.* It's testament to Auberjonois' talent that we get a real sense of Odo's feelings, despite him spending most of the time acting to a jelly. Mora Pol becomes a more rounded character in a way that helps us understand Odo a little better.

5.13 FOR THE UNIFORM

STARDATE 50485.2

Sisko takes drastic action to capture Eddington, his former security chief

TX 3 February 1997
WRITER Peter Allan Fields
DIRECTOR Victor Lobl
GUEST CAST Aron Eisenberg (Nog), Kenneth Marshall (Eddington), Eric Pierpoint (Sanders)

Sisko pursues Michael Eddington, his former Security Chief who joined the Maquis, in the Defiant. He gives the order to fire but the ship's computer fails, thanks to Eddington. As O'Brien fixes the Defiant, Sisko hears that Captain Sanders of the Malinche has replaced him in the search for Eddington. However, when Sisko hears that Eddington has attacked Cardassian colonies with a biogenic weapon, he takes the unrepaired Defiant. Sisko realises too late he has been duped; the Maquis have ambushed and disabled the Malinche. Sisko tracks Eddington down, but the Maquis disable a Cardassian civilian vessel, forcing Sisko to break off and help the innocents. Sisko realises Eddington sees himself as the hero and decides to engineer conditions under which he would give himself up. Sisko prepares to poison the atmosphere of a Maquis colony and, to everyone's astonishment, launches the missiles. Sisko tells the evacuating Maquis he is prepared to destroy every Maquis colony in the Demilitarised Zone. Eddington offers himself in return.

TRIVIA

- Writer-producer Peter Allan Fields came out of *Star Trek* retirement to pen this story about Sisko's obsession. Fields drew on Victor Hugo's *Les Miserables* to explore Eddington's psychological make-up.
- Eric Pierpoint (Sanders) is better known as Detective George Francisco, the newcomer from the television version of *Alien Nation.*

RATING

- Solid character stuff for Sisko, once again giving Avery Brooks the opportunity to show what he can do. Sisko's approach is about as subtle as smashing a door with a sledgehammer, but it works well in context. The episode is weakened only by its repeat performance later in the season as *Blaze of Glory.*

5.14 IN PURGATORY'S SHADOW

STARDATE UNKNOWN

The Jem'Hadar capture Worf and Garak as they prepare to invade the Alpha Quadrant

When the station picks up a coded Cardassian message from the Gamma Quadrant, Garak claims it is of no significance, but is later caught trying to sneak off the station. He reveals the signal is from Enabran Tain, former head of the Obsidian Order. Sisko lets Garak investigate, but insists Worf go with him. They find nothing but come

TX 10 February 1997
WRITERS Robert Hewitt Wolfe and Ira Steven Behr
DIRECTOR Gabrielle Beaumont
GUEST CAST Marc Alaimo (Gul Dukat), Paul Dooley (Enabran Tain), JG Hertzler (General Martok), James Horan (Ikat'ika), Jim Palladino (Jem'Hadar guard), Andrew J Robinson (Garak), Melanie Smith (Tora Ziyal), Carrie Stauber (Romulan)

across a Jem'Hadar invasion fleet hiding in a nebula. Worf sends a garbled message to the station. Kira is sent to investigate but Garak and Worf have been imprisoned in a detention camp where they are told they will eventually die. In the camp, Worf meets Martok, the Klingon general who was impersonated. Garak finds Tain, who is dying. Kira returns to the station with news that 50 Dominion ships are *en route*. With only Dukat to protect them, Sisko suspects he must seal the wormhole, with Worf and Garak lost. Meanwhile, Worf and Garak find Bashir in the camp – the Bashir on the station is a Changeling. As Dax and the fake Bashir work on a device to close the wormhole, Garak makes peace with his mentor before he dies. On the station, Sisko operates a particle beam to close the wormhole but it fails – and the Jem'Hadar fleet comes through.

QUOTES

- 'A man shouldn't allow his enemies to outlive him.' – *Enebran Tain to Garak*

TRIVIA

- *In Purgatory's Shadow* began life as a homage to *The Great Escape*, in which Allied Prisoners of War escape a Nazi prison camp. The Bashir Changeling was introduced when the writers decided they needed a twist to sustain the story. Reports have it that Bashir was supposedly a Changeling from three or four episodes previously, but because the revelation came to the writers so late in the day, it was too late for Alexander Siddig to make changes to his performance.
- The episode opens with a dedication to Derek Garth, a crewmember who died in a car accident during filming of the episode.

RATING

- Another key episode where things really move on. The prison camp story serves as a useful hook on which to hang a few loose ends, notably the Garak-Worf relationship, while jumping headlong into the war. The Bashir Changeling story works as a shock but there's sadly no foreshadowing to give the idea credence.

5.15 BY INFERNO'S LIGHT

STARDATE 50564.2

The Dominions join forces with the Cardassians to conquer the Alpha Quadrant

TX 17 February 1997
WRITERS Ira Steven Behr and Robert Hewitt Wolfe
DIRECTOR Les Landau
GUEST CAST Marc Alaimo (Gul Dukat), Ray Buktenica (Deyos), Judi Durand (Station Computer Voice), Don Fischer (Jem'Hadar Guard), JG Hertzler (General Martok), James Horan (Ikat'ika), Robert O'Reilly (Gowron), Andrew J Robinson (Garak), Melanie Smith (Tora Ziyal), Carrie Stauber (Romulan), Barry Wiggins (Jem'Hadar officer)

The station crew watch astonished as the Dominion fleet come through the wormhole – and turn for Cardassia. Dukat has arranged for Cardassia to join The Dominion – and he will become Cardassia's leader. In the internment centre, the prisoners plan to beam themselves back to the runabout. As the Jem'Hadar practice fighting Klingons by battling Worf, Garak tries to manufacture a transmitter. Meanwhile, Sisko persuades Gowron to restore his treaty with the Federation, in order to fight the Dominion and Cardassians together. The Bashir Changeling slips into a runabout. Later, Dukat warns that the station will be a target unless the Federation joins The Dominion. Sisko refuses. After a bout of claustrophobia, Garak finishes the transmitter. On the station, the Federation and Klingons are joined by the Romulans just as the Dominion fleet prepares to attack Bajor. In the camp, Garak is discovered, but the prisoners kill the Jem'Hadar guards. Worf continues to fight, though weakened, and his execution is ordered. Suddenly, Worf is beamed to the runabout – Garak succeeded. The real Bashir sends a message to the station but the Bashir Changeling is already piloting a trilithium explosive into the Bajoran sun which will destroy the entire combined fleet. They intercept the rogue runabout just in time. Later, the prisoners return and Martok is put in charge of the Klingon forces on Deep Space Nine but there is no time for rest. Gul Dukat sends a message to Sisko: the battle for the Alpha Quadrant has begun.

TRIVIA

- The runabout being left in orbit seems like a story oversight, and may well have been, but is referred to later by Sloan from Section 31 in season six's *Inquisition*.

RATING

- High-octane stuff but just a bit too frantic. *In Purgatory's Shadow* doesn't build all that comfortably to *By Inferno's Light* – there's almost a third episode lurking here. Still, you can't accuse it of being boring!

5.16 DOCTOR BASHIR, I PRESUME?

STARDATE UNKNOWN

Bashir's career is threatened when his parents reveal he was genetically engineered

TX 24 February 1997
WRITER Ronald D Moore (story by Jimmy Diggs)
DIRECTOR David Livingston
GUEST CAST Brian George (Richard Bashir), Max Grodenchik (Rom), Fadwa El Guindi (Amsha Bashir), Chase Masterson (Leeta), J Patrick McCormack (Rear Admiral Bennett), Robert Picardo (Dr Lewis Zimmerman)

Doctor Lewis Zimmerman informs Bashir that he has been chosen as the model for Starfleet's new medical hologram program. To be accurate, Zimmerman must perform a detailed history of Bashir, including interviewing his friends, relatives and colleagues. Bashir asks Zimmerman not to speak to his parents – and is irked when they arrive at the station. Though uncomfortable around his parents, Bashir coaches them for their interview and asks them to keep his secret for fear it would ruin his career. Later, Bashir's parents assure their son that they will not reveal that he was genetically enhanced as a child – not realising they are talking to the hologram. O'Brien and Zimmerman are stunned: genetic engineering is illegal. Fearing Zimmerman's report will result in his expulsion from Starfleet, Bashir decides to take pre-emptive action and resign. However, he later descovers that his father has decided to spend two years in a minimum security prison in return for Bashir's continued service in Starfleet. Bashir reluctantly accepts the solution, but knows that his relationship with his father has strengthened through the events.

QUOTES

- 'Think of it, Julian. If this works, you'll be able to irritate hundreds of people you've never even met.' – *O'Brien to Bashir*

TRIVIA

- The main story began life as the sub-plot in a story pitch by freelance writer Jimmy Diggs submitted during season three. When *Voyager*'s Robert Picardo, who had already appeared in *First Contact*, expressed a desire to make a guest appearance in DS9, the story was revived and elevated to the main plot.

RATING

- A peculiar episode that sets up Bashir's background almost four years too late. The revelation is ultimately not that big a deal, but does serve to explain something of Bashir's personality. Brian George puts in a wonderful performance as Richard Bashir.

5.17 A SIMPLE INVESTIGATION

STARDATE UNKNOWN

Odo falls in love with a woman on the run from a criminal organisation

TX 31 March 1997
WRITER René Echevarria
DIRECTOR John T Kretchmer
GUEST CAST Brant Cotton (Tauvid Rem), John Durbin (Traidy), Randy Mulkey (Idanian #2), Nicholas Worth (Sorm), Dey Young (Arissa)

Odo meets a beautiful woman, Arissa, who is waiting for an Idanian called Tauvid Rem. Later, he catches her breaking into the station's computer. Arissa explains that Tauvid has information about a daughter she gave up 15 years previously. Odo takes her to Tauvid's quarters, but he has been murdered. Odo then catches Arissa taking a datacrystal from Tauvid. Arissa has been working for a notorious criminal, Draim of the Orion Syndicate, and wants to leave. The datacrystal holds the information she needs to do so. As Dax and O'Brien try to decode the datacrystal, Odo tries to convince Arissa to testify against Draim. They spend the night together. The next day, Arissa offers to trade the crystal for her life. Draim agrees but instructs his assassins, Traidy and Sorm, to kill her once they have the crystal. Meanwhile, an Idanian agent informs Odo that Arissa is a sleeper agent who was given a new identity to infiltrate Draim's organisation – the datacrystal contains her real memories. Odo takes the agent to Arissa but both she and the crystal have gone. At the rendezvous, Arissa is ambushed but Odo and the Idanian agent intercede. Later, Arissa's true identity and memories are restored. She returns to her married life, leaving Odo heartbroken.

TRIVIA

- Odo's sexual coupling had been first mooted at the end of season four, when he lost his ability to shapeshift. Writers had hoped to do this story while Odo had been fixed in solid humanoid form, but the opportunity did not come along until this episode. The idea that Odo would shapeshift around his lover was saved for Kira.

RATING

- As far as *Star Trek* romances go, *A Simple Investigation* isn't that bad. It also neatly serves to distract you from the Odo-Kira relationship that is finally voiced a few episodes later in *Children of Time.*

5.18 BUSINESS AS USUAL

Quark's life is threatened when he goes into the arms business

TX 7 April 1997
WRITERS Bradley Thompson and David Weddle
DIRECTOR Siddig El Fadil
GUEST CAST Steven Berkoff (Hagath), Eric Cadora (Customer), Charlie Curtis (Talura), Tim Halligan (Farrakk), Josh Pais (Gaila), Lawrence Tierney (Regent)

STARDATE UNKNOWN

Quark is offered a cut of his cousin Gaila's weapons business – Quark will provide hospitality and virtual tests of the weapons on the holosuite while Gaila makes the sales. Quark agrees and is introduced to Gaila's associate, Hagath, who warns him not to cross him. Soon, all three are making a good deal of latinum. Odo uncovers Quark's new business and intercedes, but the Bajorans have him released as Gaila and Hagath used to provide them with munitions. Nevertheless, Quark soon loses the respect of the station's officers. Later, Quark sees Hagath fire Farrakk, another associate, and learns that Hagath had the man killed. Next, the Regent of Palamar arrives to buy weapons to kill millions of people. Quark's scruples show, but Gaila warns him that Hagath will kill them if he stops the deal. Unable to call on the officers for support, Quark decides he must stop the arms deal, even at the cost of his own life. Quark brings the Regent's enemy, General Nassuc, to the station to buy arms and engineers an encounter. Gaila and Hagath flee, pursued by Nassuc, but the Regent is killed. Quark escapes and is freed of his ties to Gaila and Hagath.

TRIVIA

- Thompson and Weddle were reportedly inspired by contemporary news reports of the trade in plutonium for warheads following the collapse of the Soviet Union. The context for the episode was the parallel disintegration of the Cardassian Empire.
- A short scene between Worf and baby Kirayoshi became the inspiration for a secondary plot in season six's *Time's Orphan.*

RATING

- A neat little story that explores the extent of Quark's greed. There's a wonderful exuberance about the story, notably Stephen Berkoff's typically heavyweight performance, while still getting under Quark's skin a bit more.

5.19 TIES OF BLOOD AND WATER

Kira helps a Cardassian dissident die in peace

TX 14 April 1997
WRITER Robert Hewitt Wolfe (story by Edmund Newton and Robbin L Slocum)
DIRECTOR Avery Brooks
GUEST CAST Marc Alaimo (Gul Dukat), Jeffrey Combs (Weyoun), Thomas Kopache (Kira Taban), William Lucking (Furel), Lawrence Pressman (Tekeny Ghemor), Rick Schatz (Gantt)

STARDATE 50712.5

Kira meets Tekeny Ghemor, a Cardassian dissident, whom she hopes will lead the opposition to the Cardassian/Dominion alliance. Ghemor, however, is dying, but may be able to help through a Cardassian ritual where he can pass his secrets to his family on his deathbed. With no living relatives, Ghemor asks Kira to be his daughter – she was once genetically altered to look like her. Kira reluctantly agrees. Ghemor struggles to share his secrets, while Kira recalls her father's death at Cardassian hands. Meanwhile, Gul Dukat arrives on a Jem'Hadar ship and beams aboard to take Ghemor. When Ghemor refuses to leave, Dukat gives Kira a file that reveals Ghemor participated in a massacre at a Bajoran monastery. Kira angrily confronts Ghemor and leaves him to die alone. Odo discovers that Kira is more angered by recalling how she fought the Cardassians instead of staying with her father as he died. Eventually, Kira relents and returns to Ghemor, allowing him to die in peace. Later she buries Ghemor next to her father.

TRIVIA

- The original pitch from husband-and-wife team Newton and Slocum was that Ghemor came to the station to die and wanted Kira to care for him. Robert Wolfe expanded on the core concept, adding Dukat for pace.

RATING

- An intelligent episode that delves into Kira's weaknesses and failings. The story isn't about Ghemor, it's about Kira and her failure to be with her father at the end. Kira comes out of the episode a more rounded, mature character.

5.20 FERENGI LOVE SONGS

STARDATE UNKNOWN

When Quark prevents his mother seeing the Grand Nagus, the Ferengi economy slides

TX 21 April 1997
WRITERS Ira Steven Behr and Hans Beimler
DIRECTOR Rene Auberjonois
GUEST CAST Cecily Adams (Ishka), Hamilton Camp (Leck), Jeffrey Combs (Brunt), Max Grodenchik (Rom), Chase Masterson (Leeta), Tiny Ron (Maihar'du), Wallace Shawn (Grand Nagus Zek)

Disappointed that he has been blacklisted by the Ferengi Commerce Authority, Quark returns home to his mother, Ishka, for comfort, but finds Grand Nagus Zek hiding in the closet! Zek and Ishka are in love and ask Quark to keep their affair secret. Quark is delighted by his family's new alliance but is disappointed when Zek refuses to restore his business license. Liquidator Brunt offers to restore Quark's license if he breaks up Ishka and Zek. Quark agrees and begins to poison Zek against his mother. The plan works: Ishka is heartbroken but Quark gets his business license. Zek makes Quark his First Clerk. Quark accepts, but discovers that Zek is not the talent he once was and the Ferengi stock market begins to slide. Quark realises that Ishka was the power behind the throne – by breaking them up, he may have destroyed the Ferengi economy! Brunt reveals it was all a set-up to enable Brunt to become Grand Nagus once Zek is thrown out of office by the Liquidators. Quark gives Zek some advice that helps him turn around the economic collapse – then reveals it came from Ishka. Quark admits his actions and Zek and Ishka are reunited.

QUOTES

- 'My *Maurauder Mo* action figures!...Have you any idea how much these are now worth?'
'Not as much as if you'd kept them in the original packaging. As I told you at the time.' – *Quark and Ishka, on some of Quark's childhood possessions*

RATING

- Flippant and lightweight, *Ferengi Love Songs* takes the comic elements of *Deep Space Nine* that little bit too far. It's not just Quark with his comic double-takes – Zek seems a throwaway character, with no semblance of reality. A good idea that needs toning down. This one goes to eleven.

5.21 SOLDIERS OF THE EMPIRE

STARDATE UNKNOWN

Worf revives the spirits of General Martok and his defeated Klingon crew

TX 28 April 1997
WRITER Ronald D Moore
DIRECTOR LeVar Burton
GUEST CAST David Graf (Leskit), Aron Eisenberg (Nog), JG Hertzler (General Martok), Scott Leva (Ortakin), Sandra Nelson (Tavana), Rick Worthy (Kornan)

General Martok is ordered to search for a Klingon ship, the B'Moth, missing on the Cardassian border. Martok takes command of the Rotarran, with Worf as temporary First Officer, and Dax as Science Officer. The rest of the crew, however, are dispirited Klingons who have suffered defeats at the hands of the Jem'Hadar. Worf insists they need a victory and Martok agrees, but wishes to act cautiously. Martok passes over the opportunity to ambush a Jem'Hadar ship and morale worsens. They find the B'Moth in Cardassian space but Martok fears it is a trap. Realising Martok is terrified of the Jem'Hadar, Worf realises he must challenge Martok for command, even if he must kill him. Worf gives the order to rescue the survivors of the B'Moth and challenges Martok. Seeing the crew and Martok's blood-lust revived, Worf allows himself to receive a wound and backs off, just as the Jem'Hadar advance. Martok's crew launch into action and defeat the Jem'Hadar before rescuing the Klingon survivors. Martok is grateful to Worf for reminding him of his duty.

TRIVIA

- Ronald Moore's original story had Worf and Martok investigate a Klingon outpost with which the Empire had lost contact. The outpost was next to a foggy river which Worf and Martok crossed to find old friends and Worf's father. The River Styx elements were removed to focus on the hard realities of life on a Klingon bird of prey.
- The Klingon war song is taken from the interactive CD-ROM *Star Trek: Klingon*, directed by Jonathan Frakes.

RATING

- With its wall-to-wall Klingons, *Soldiers of the Empire* feels like a glimpse of a *Star Trek* series that never was. It's an interesting idea, one that borrows from the genre of WWII submarine movie, much like *Wrath of Khan*, and brings Martok into the fold. Farrell has great fun as Dax in this episode – this is the side we should see more of.

5.22 CHILDREN OF TIME

STARDATE 50814.2

The Defiant crew discover a colony of their descendants

TX 5 May 1997
WRITER René Echevarria (story by Gary Holland and Ethan H Calk)
DIRECTOR Allan Kroeker
GUEST CAST Brian Evaret Chandler (Brota), Doren Fein (Molly), Gary Frank (Yedrin Dax), Jesse Littlejohn (Gabriel), Marybeth Massett (Parell), Jennifer S Parsons (Miranda O'Brien), Davida Williams (Lisa)

The Defiant crew investigates a planet surrounded by an energy barrier. Suddenly the ship is crippled. Kira is momentarily duplicated and needs help. The crew find a colony on the planet led by Miranda O'Brien. Miranda explains that, when the Defiant leaves, the barrier will cause the ship to crash-land on the planet 200 years in the past. The planet, Gaia, is populated by the descendents of the crew. Sisko realises they can change events but the colony will cease to exist. Dax's descendent, Yedrin, suggests they duplicate the Defiant, allowing one to escape and the other to crash. Later, Dax discovers that this is a cover: Yedrin intends to let the Defiant crash to save the colony. Sisko is reluctant to let history take its course, but the crew are increasingly moved by the plight of their descendants. An elderly Odo, who survived the crash and is now 200 years old, admits his love for Kira and tries to dissuade her from sacrificing herself. The Defiant prepares to leave but at the last moment veers off-course. Odo reveals that his older self reprogrammed the ship and sacrificed the colony to give their younger selves a chance.

TRIVIA

- Storywriter Gary Holland, who pitched season two's *The Collaborator* and *Voyager*'s *Dreadnought*, was Vice President of Advertising and Promotion for Domestic Television at Paramount. Holland first pitched the idea during season three, but it was not until Ethan Calk (*Visionary*) pitched an almost identical idea that the writers dusted off Holland's original idea.

RATING

- Although *Children of Time* suffers from a little too much soul-searching, it's basically solid and is elevated by the Odo-Kira moment. There's a hint at the tragedy Odo could face as he watches his friends grow old and die, but it remains bubbling under.

5.23 BLAZE OF GLORY

STARDATE UNKNOWN

Sisko must work with Eddington to prevent a full-scale war with The Dominion

TX 12 May 1997
WRITERS Robert Hewitt Wolfe and Ira Steven Behr
DIRECTOR Kim Friedman
GUEST CAST Aron Eisenberg (Nog), Gretchen German (Rebecca Sullivan), JG Hertzler (General Martok), Kenneth Marshall (Michael Eddington)

Sisko receives a message stating that the Maquis have launched undetectable missiles against Cardassia, now under Dominion control. A major war will erupt if they are not intercepted. Sisko speaks to Michael Eddington, but the former Security Chief refuses to tell Sisko how to stop the missiles. Sisko takes Eddington into custody and forces him to take him to the launch site from which the missiles can be deactivated. Eddington warns Sisko that once they arrive he will kill him. They are pursued by two Jem'Hadar ships and Eddington has to take a different plan, injuring Sisko. They arrive at the launch site on Athos IV and find two Jem'Hadar waiting. They kill the soldiers but know more will arrive. Inside the command centre, Sisko is surprised to meet Maquis prisoners and the woman who sent the message. Eddington reveals that she is his wife: there are no missiles, Eddington needed Sisko to evacuate his people. Sisko and Eddington battle the Jem'Hadar, during the escape. Eddington tells Sisko to go without him and dies helping the prisoners.

TRIVIA

- With the big plot threads being laid for seasons six and seven, the production team felt the need to resolve some loose ends. Eddington's death was to bring closure to this storyline and lay the foundations for the *Deep Space Nine* dénouement. A few Maquis were allowed to survive in case the producers of *Voyager* were to bring the ship back to the Alpha Quadrant.

RATING

- Eddington's demise marks the end of *Deep Space Nine*'s interest in the Maquis and the preparations for full-scale war against The Dominion. There are more twists this time as Eddington comes across as a more rounded person, with a life and spouse.

5.24 EMPOK NOR

STARDATE UNKNOWN

O'Brien's team come under attack when they visit a deserted Cardassian space station

TX 19 May 1997
WRITER Hans Beimler (story by Bryan Fuller)
DIRECTOR Michael Vejar
GUEST CAST Aron Eisenberg (Nog), Tom Hodges (Pechetti), Marjean Holden (Stolzoff), Jeffrey King (Amaro), Andy Milder (Boq'ta), Andrew J Robinson (Garak)

O'Brien takes a team of engineers to an abandoned Cardassian space station, Empok Nor, to salvage parts. Garak discovers two stasis tubes, perhaps containing Cardassians that have recently been activated. Meanwhile, Nog watches as the runabout drifts away from the station and explodes. O'Brien takes a group of engineers to set up a distress call, but the Cardassians find two of the remaining engineers and kill them. Garak hunts the Cardassians down and kills one. He discovers they are acting under the influence of a drug that makes them more aggressive. O'Brien suggests that this is why they were put in stasis. Two more engineers are attacked and one is killed. Garak kills the Cardassian – then stabs the second engineer, Amaro. Amaro is able to tell O'Brien about Garak before dying. Meanwhile, Garak captures Nog and dares O'Brien to try to take him. Garak and O'Brien fight hand-to-hand, but O'Brien has rigged a phaser to explode which knocks Garak unconscioius. The influence of the drug is removed and the team obtain the parts.

TRIVIA

- Bryan Fuller's original idea saw Worf and Garak investigate a deserted Cardassian ship, littered with the bodies of Obsidian Order agents who had succumbed to a drug.
- Andrew Robinson was reportedly uncomfortable with the episode, which saw Garak turn into a serial killer. Robinson had previously starred as the killer in the first *Dirty Harry* movie (1971).

RATING

- An attempt to do a claustrophobic horror story fails simply because it makes a mockery of Garak. There's a more interesting story to be told that blurs Garak's motives. Instead, the story is tried and tested stuff, with only a few enhancements to O'Brien's character worth a credit.

5.25 IN THE CARDS

STARDATE 50929.4

Jake and Nog try to buy a baseball card and end up in trouble with The Dominion

TX 9 June 1997
WRITER Ronald D Moore (story by Truly Clark and Scott Neal)
DIRECTOR Michael Dorn
GUEST CAST Jeffrey Combs (Weyoun), Aron Eisenberg (Nog), Louise Fletcher (Kai Winn), Brian Markinson (Dr Elias Giger), Chase Masterson (Leeta)

Jake tries to cheer his father up by buying a baseball card at Quark's auction. Though Jake convinces Nog to use his life's savings, they are outbid by a man named Dr Giger. They try to buy the card from Giger but he refuses. However, he later offers to trade the card for medical supplies he needs to create a machine that will give eternal life – by 'entertaining' living cells so they do not die of boredom. Meanwhile, Kai Winn tries to negotiate a non-aggression pact between Bajor and The Dominion, represented by Weyoun. Jake and Nog take the last supplies to Giger but he and his machine are gone. They tell Odo, who has no record of a visitor called Giger. However, they see Winn talking to 'Giger' and confront her. Sisko has his son arrested but Jake can't come clean, not wanting to talk about the card. Jake and Nog are transported to a Jem'Hadar ship where they ask for the baseball card from Giger, who is being held captive. Weyoun suspects they are plotting something more serious but when Jake makes up a story about Starfleet Intelligence, he decides to believe them. Jake and Nog are given the card which, as hoped, raises Sisko's mood.

TRIVIA

- *In The Cards* marks Michael Dorn's directorial debut.

RATING

- Throwaway comic stuff with some great one-liners. The preposterous concepts work simply because they stick with it so persistently. The concept of cellular ennui – where you are literally bored to death – is so ludicrous it's worth an award.

5.26 CALL TO ARMS

Starfleet abandons Deep Space Nine to The Dominion

TX 16 June 1997
WRITERS Ira Steven Behr and Robert Hewitt Wolfe
DIRECTOR Allan Kroeker
GUEST CAST Marc Alaimo (Gul Dukat), Casey Biggs (Damar), Jeffrey Combs (Weyoun), Aron Eisenberg (Nog), Max Grodenchik (Rom), JG Hertzler (General Martok), Andrew Robinson (Garak), Chase Masterson (Leeta), Melanie Smith (Tora Ziyal)

STARDATE 50975.2

When another fleet of Jem'Hadar ships comes through the wormhole and heads towards Cardassia, Sisko is ordered to stop Dominion reinforcements. He decides to mine the entrance to the wormhole, though it will precipitate war. Dax, O'Brien and Rom aim to lay a self-replicating minefield, but it cannot be activated until all have been laid, undoubtedly leaving the Defiant open to attack. With no Starfleet reinforcements, the station will be lost. As the mines are laid, Weyoun insists they will take over the station unless Sisko stops. Sisko refuses to back down and puts Martok on a war footing while endorsing Bajor's non-aggression pact. Amid the tension, Sisko marries Rom and Leeta – but the Dominion fleet is only one hour away. The station is evacuated, leaving Sisko and a skeleton crew. Martok defends the Defiant from attack and the minefield is finished. As The Dominion bears down, Sisko orders Starfleet personnel to evacuate. He tells Kira, Odo, Quark, Rom and those others who have decided to remain that the Federation fleet has destroyed Dominion shipyards in Cardassian space. Sisko joins the Defiant for a final battle while Kira, Odo and the others surrender Deep Space Nine to Gul Dukat and the Cardassian/Dominion forces.

QUOTES

- 'He's letting me know... he'll be back.' – *Dukat to Weyoun, on discovering Sisko's baseball left on the station*

TRIVIA

- For his last episode on the show, writer Robert Wolfe makes a brief cameo appearance as a wounded crewmember.
- For the final sequence, the producers decided to use computer generated imagery (CGI) in a break from the model work that had been used on previous episodes.

RATING

- Heady stuff to end the fifth season. It's a carefully crafted piece that sets up the characters for the events of season six and seven while keeping up the tension and pace. The ending is superb and is up there with *Best of Both Worlds Part 1* for sheer impact.

STAR TREK: DEEP SPACE NINE
SEASON SIX

6.1 A TIME TO STAND

STARDATE UNKNOWN

Sisko is given a mission that could change the course of the war

TX 29 September 1997
WRITERS Ira Steven Behr and Hans Beimler
DIRECTOR Allan Kroeker
GUEST CAST Marc Alaimo (Dukat), Casey Biggs (Damar), Jeffrey Combs (Weyoun), Aron Eisenberg (Nog), JG Hertzler (Martok), Barry Jenner (Ross), Brock Peters (Joseph Sisko), Andrew J Robinson (Garak)

Three months into the Dominion War, the Federation is losing. Sisko and his crew man the Defiant, watching their reinforcements being wiped out. Admiral Ross gives them a new mission – to take the Jem'Hadar ship they captured and infiltrate Cardassian territory, destroying the ketracel white storage facility. They struggle with the headsets The Dominion use to pilot the ships, and Garak volunteers. They are attacked by the USS Centaur, but it pulls away. They arrive at the asteroid storage facility, but just as O'Brien plants the explosives, they are detected and trapped in a 'net'. Sisko gambles that destroying the base will disable the net, and they outrun the explosion, but their warp drive is damaged. Without it, it will take 17 years to get back to Federation territory...

TRIVIA

- An episode influenced by World War II movie *The Guns of Navarone* (1961), starring Gregory Peck and David Niven, in which a team of Allied and Greek soldiers disable two German gun emplacements that guard a vital sea channel.

RATING

- An interesting way to pick up the sixth season, creating a real sense that the series has been going on while we were away. Unfortunately, the cliffhanger is an obviously false set-up.

6.2 ROCKS AND SHOALS

STARDATE 51107.2

Sisko and his crew are captured by the Jem'Hadar

TX 6 October 1997
WRITER Ronald D Moore
DIRECTOR Michael Vejar
GUEST CAST Lilyan Chauvin (Vedek Yassim), Paul S Eckstein (Limara'Son), Aron Eisenberg (Nog), Joseph Fuqua (Gordon), Sarah MacDonnell (Neeley), Phil Morris (Remata'Klan), Andrew J Robinson (Garak), Christopher Shea (Keevan)

Sisko's damaged Jem'Hadar ship takes refuge in a nebula, but crashes into an ocean planet. Dax is wounded, Garak and Nog are captured by Jem'Hadar soldiers who have also crashed here. Keevan, a Vorta, has been wounded, and when he learns of Bashir, he sends the soldiers to capture the Starfleet personnel. After a firefight, Sisko agrees to exchange himself and Bashir for the two hostages. Keevan wants Bashir to heal him, but reveals he only has one dose of ketracel white left. When it runs out, the soldiers will go berserk. He proposes to surrender and sacrifice his men before that happens. Sisko tries to reason with the Jem'Hadar, but is given no choice but to massacre them. Repairing Keevan's communications system, they signal for help.

TRIVIA

- The episode is influenced by the Frank Sinatra movie *None But the Brave* (1965) in which Japanese and American soldiers, stranded on a Pacific island, are forced to co-operate to survive.

RATING

- Nice small-scale stuff from Ron Moore. Sisko's dilemma doesn't have quite the weight it should, but it works nonetheless.

6.3 SONS AND DAUGHTERS

STARDATE UNKNOWN

Worf discovers that his son is no warrior

TX 13 October 1997
WRITERS Bradley Thompson and David Weddle
DIRECTOR Jesus Salvador Trevino
GUEST CAST Marc Alaimo (Dukat), Casey Biggs (Damar), JG Hertzler (Martok), Melanie Smith (Ziyal), Gabrielle Union (N'Garen), Marc Worden (Alexander), Sam Zeller (Ch'Targh)

Martok's ship, the IKS Rotarran docks at Starbase 375 to pick up reinforcements – Worf is surprised that one of the new recruits is his son, Alexander, whom he hasn't spoken to since he passed him over to his human adoptive parents. When Worf sees his son lose a barfight to an old Klingon, he worries about his chances against the Jem'Hadar. Worf tries to train Alexander with various Klingon weapons, but ends up arguing with him. Martok agrees to transfer Alexander off the ship, but it comes under attack. Alexander and the elderly Klingon volunteer to fix a plasma leak, a near-suicidal task. Luckily, they fix the leak. Worf promises to teach Alexander how to be a warrior if it means that Alexander will accept him as a father. Martok welcomes him to the House of Martok.

TRIVIA

- Another episode inspired by a classic war movie. This time the inspiration is the John Ford post-Civil War classic *Rio Grande* (1950) in which Union officer Yorke (John Wayne) trains the son he has not seen in 15 years to battle the Apaches. *Rio Grande* was also the inspiration for *A Fistful of Datas*.

RATING

- So formulaic you can sing it! Any viewer who's ever seen a Worf and Alexander episode before is about three scenes ahead of the action. It's not a bad episode, but in the middle of an arc that's doing all sorts of things that are new to *Star Trek* storytelling, its 'father and son have a problem/they argue while playing some sport/by coincidence they are placed in a life-threatening situation that makes them realise the path they are on' structure just seems old hat.

6.4 BEHIND THE LINES

STARDATE 51149.5

Sisko is promoted, and there are mixed fortunes in the war

TX 20 October 1997
WRITER René Echevarria
DIRECTOR LeVar Burton
GUEST CAST Marc Alaimo (Dukat), Casey Biggs (Damar), Jeffrey Combs (Weyoun), Aron Eisenberg (Nog), Max Grodenchik (Rom), Barry Jenner (Ross), Salome Jens (Female Shapeshifter)

On Starbase 375, Admiral Ross discovers that a vast Dominion sensor array is monitoring activity across five sectors, and Sisko comes up with a plan to destroy it. On Deep Space Nine – or Terok Nor, as the Cardassians call it – Kira starts to question Odo's loyalty to her resistance movement. The female shapeshifter tells Odo he is forgiven for his murder of another Changeling and tempts him to rejoin The Link. Odo is torn between his desire to rejoin his people and the promise he made to Kira that he would not enter The Link. Quark tells Kira that Dukat has worked out a way to disable the minefield blocking the wormhole. Kira puts in operation a plan to stop Dukat, but it fails and Rom is arrested, when Odo, bonding with the female shapeshifter, fails to play his part. Kira is furious and realises she can no longer trust him. Dax, the new commander of the Defiant scores a victory, destroying the sensor array.

TRIVIA

- The precise nature of The Link and the emotions felt have drawn different interpretations from cast and crew. Both Salome Jens and Rene Auberjonois did not feel that The Link was inherently sexual, arguing instead that it was a movement to oneness and calm or achieving a state of Nirvana. Burton, by contrast, believed it was seduction, pure and simple, and filmed it as such.
- The working title was *Life During Wartime*.

RATING

- Heady stuff for the Odo-Kira story, filled with desire and betrayal. The success of the episode is Odo's quiet transformation into something truly alien (there is a notably eerie moment when he looks down on the 'solids' from the promenade and feels pity). Finally, we get an understanding of the Founders and why they regard themselves differently to the rest of us.

6.5 FAVOR THE BOLD

STARDATE UNKNOWN

The Federation needs a major victory

TX 27 October 1997
WRITERS Ira Steven Behr and Hans Beimler
DIRECTOR Winrich Kolbe
GUEST CAST Marc Alaimo (Dukat), Casey Biggs (Damar), Jeffrey Combs (Weyoun), Aron Eisenberg (Nog), Max Grodenchik (Rom), JG Hertzler (Martok), Barry Jenner (Ross), Salome Jens (Female Shapeshifter), Chase Masterson (Leeta), Andrew J Robinson (Garak), Melanie Smith (Ziyal)

Federation morale is low, and Sisko draws up a plan to retake Deep Space Nine. Odo struggles with his loyalties – he doesn't want to betray Kira, nor can he resist The Link. Rom is sentenced to death, and Dukat refuses to be lenient. Quark's discovered that the minefield will be destroyed within a week, and The Dominion forces massing on the other side will swarm through. Jake smuggles out a message to his father to warn him. Dukat and Weyoun realise the Federation is planning an offensive. The Cardassians are distracted at a crucial moment when Damar is rough with Ziyal, angering Dukat. Sisko launches his attack, but Dukat isn't worried: he has assembled a defence fleet. Sisko's on a suicide mission.

TRIVIA

- The title comes from the saying 'fortune favours the bold'.

RATING

- Another episode that's a powerful character piece as we see how the occupation is affecting those left on the station.

6.6 SACRIFICE OF ANGELS

STARDATE UNKNOWN

Sisko takes back Deep Space Nine – and Dukat loses Ziyal

TX 3 November 1997
WRITER Ira Steven Behr and Hans Beimler
DIRECTOR Allan Kroeker
GUEST CAST Marc Alaimo (Dukat), Casey Biggs (Damar), Jeffrey Combs (Weyoun), Aron Eisenberg (Nog), Max Grodenchik (Rom), JG Hertzler (Martok), Salome Jens (Female Shapeshifter), Chase Masterson (Leeta), Andrew J Robinson (Garak), Melanie Smith (Ziyal)

The Federation fleet engages the Dominion fleet. Sisko orders them to concentrate on the Cardassian ships. Dukat prepares to destroy the minefield, knowing that if the reinforcements arrive, it will mean defeat for the Federation. He orders Kira arrested. The space battle rages, but the Dominion line holds. Quark and Ziyal break Kira, Rom and their allies out of prison, but they are too late to prevent the destruction of the minefield. Sisko heads for the wormhole, and the entire Dominion fleet. The wormhole aliens contact Sisko, and he pleads for them to save the Bajorans. He returns to the Defiant, fearing the worst, but the Dominion fleet abruptly disappears. Dukat is without his reinforcements, and 200 Federation ships are on the way. The Dominion withdraw from the station, heading for Cardassia. Ziyal refuses to go with Dukat, and Damar kills her when she admits she freed Kira. Dukat is a broken man. Sisko returns to command of Deep Space Nine – and he may just have turned the tide of the war.

RATING

- The ending is a literal deus ex machina, but it's played well. The battle scenes are fantastic eye candy, but the heart of the episode is the death of Ziyal and Dukat's reaction.

6.7 YOU ARE CORDIALLY INVITED

STARDATE 51247.5

Worf and Dax get married

TX 10 November 1997
WRITER Ronald D Moore
DIRECTOR David Livingston
GUEST CAST Shannon Cochran (Sirella), Aron Eisenberg (Nog), Max Grodenchik (Rom), JG Hertzler (Martok), Chase Masterson (Leeta), Marc Worden (Alexander)

Worf and Dax resume their wedding plans, but hit a snag when Sirella, Martok's wife, refuses to give her blessing, as is traditional. Worf, Martok and the male crewmembers hold a traditional Klingon bachelor party, but it's not the fun the humans were expecting: it involves fasting and bloodletting. Dax tries to win Sirella's favour, but when asked if she knows Klingon history, she reveals that her research shows Sirella is the daughter of a concubine – she's not of noble blood. This does not go down well, and Sirella declares her an enemy. Worf begs Dax to apologise, but she refuses, and the wedding is off. Sisko reminds Dax that she knew what she was getting into when she married a Klingon, and must follow tradition. Dax's apology wins Sirella round, and Worf and Dax are married.

TRIVIA

- The working title was *Once Upon a Wedding*.

RATING

- The Klingon wife plot is terrible, but the stag do is very funny, and it's a nice change of pace from the grim war stuff.

6.8 RESURRECTION

STARDATE UNKNOWN

The Mirror Universe Bareil takes Kira hostage

TX 17 November 1997
WRITER Michael Taylor
DIRECTOR LeVar Burton
GUEST CAST Philip Anglim (Antos Bareil), John Towey (Vedek Ossan)

Kira is taken hostage by Bareil... who is dead. This is the Mirror Universe version, on the run from the Alliance. Kira doesn't press charges, and Sisko warns her not to let his resemblance to her Bareil fool her. This Bareil's life was far from spiritual, but he's keen to hear about the Bajoran faith from Kira, and the two end up spending the night together. Bareil is exposed to the Bajoran Orb of Prophecy and Change. When Kira leaves him to recuperate, the Intendant (the Mirror Kira) appears, and it transpires Bariel is here to steal the Orb. When Quark hears about Bareil's activities in the temple, he remarks that it sounds like he's casing the joint. Kira catches Bareil stealing the Orb, and persuades him that the Orb is sacred. He agrees, and stuns the Intendant. He tells Kira he saw the two of them together on Bajor, with a family, but knows he's not worthy. He returns with the Intendant to his own universe.

TRIVIA

- LeVar Burton's directorial debut had been *Second Chances* over on *The Next Generation* – the episode with the two Rikers – so he was prepared for the challenges of bringing two Kiras to the screen. This time, he was able to use computer-controlled cameras which allowed much more dynamic shots.

RATING

- It can't help but feel like a backward step after the wars and weddings of the first few episodes – and it's clearly a lot less lavish than the season to date – but this is a perfectly fine romance story and a nice change of pace from the usual Mirror Universe stories, where the object seems to be to pile as many evil versions of the characters on screen as possible.

6.9 STATISTICAL PROBABILITIES

STARDATE UNKNOWN

Bashir is asked to work with other genetically-engineered humans

TX 24 November 1997
WRITER René Echevarria (story by Michael Taylor)
DIRECTOR Anson Williams
GUEST CAST Jeannetta Arnette (Loews), Casey Biggs (Damar), Jeffrey Combs (Weyoun), Michael Keenan (Patrick), Tim Ransom (Jack), Faith C Salie (Sarina) Hilary Shepard Turner (Lauren)

It's hoped that Bashir can help four genetically-engineered humans – Jack, Patrick, Lauren and Sarina – integrate into normal society. When they see a newscast of Damar announcing he wants to open peace talks, they read his body language and come up with new insights into his character. Sisko invites them to watch Damar more closely. The Dominion seems willing to concede territory, but Bashir's group spot that they aren't mentioning a system with the raw materials for ketracel white. This analysis impresses Starfleet, which passes on top-secret data for their analysis. The group predict total defeat for the Federation with over a hundred billion dead and recommend surrender. Sisko refuses. The group decides to pass on information to The Dominion that will lead to a swift end to the war – the Federation will lose, but with less casualties. Bashir refuses to go along with this, and he and Odo foil their plan when Sarina defects – something the rest of the group didn't foresee. They are returned to their instituition.

TRIVIA

- The working title was *Think Tank*.

RATING

- The warning they give is chilling – even though we know they're bound to be wrong – but Bashir's team are all rather irritating, and overall it's not a good episode.

6.10 THE MAGNIFICENT FERENGI

STARDATE UNKNOWN

Quark assembles a team of Ferengi to recover his kidnapped mother

TX 1 January 1998
WRITERS Ira Steven Behr and Hans Beimler
DIRECTOR Chip Chalmers
GUEST CAST Cecily Adams (Ishka), Hamilton Camp (Leck), Jeffrey Combs (Brunt), Aron Eisenberg (Nog), Max Grodenchik (Rom), Chase Masterson (Leeta), Josh Pais (Gaila), Iggy Pop (Yelgrun), Christopher Shea (Keevan)

Quark's mother, Ishka, has been taken hostage by The Dominion, and the Grand Nagus has posted a large reward. Quark assembles a team of Ferengi – Rom, Nog, Leck, Gaila and Brunt – to recapture her. Training in the holosuite reveals them to be a hapless bunch, and Rom suggests they cut a deal with The Dominion instead. Quark will exchange the Vorta, Keevan, for his mother. Arriving at The Dominion's base camp, they negotiate with Yelgrun. Things are going well, until Rom accidentally lets slip to the other Ferengi that Quark is swindling them out of most of the reward money. There's a fight... and Keevan is accidentally killed. This rather weakens their bargaining position, but Nog hits on the idea of wiring up Keevan with neural stimulators to make it look like he's alive. Yelgrun isn't fooled, but the Ferengi manage to ambush him, and they head back to the station with Ishka and a new Vorta prisoner.

TRIVIA

- Iggy Pop had injured his shoulder, meaning he couldn't do any music gigs, but he was available for acting roles. Wallace Shawn wasn't available to play the Grand Nagus – in the original story, it was the Nagus himself that was kidnapped.
- This story isn't really based on *The Magnificent Seven*, as the title suggests, but the twist is somewhat reminiscent of a film rarely regarded as a classic – *Weekend At Bernie's*.

RATING

- Harmless fun. Iggy Pop is fantastic as a muted, rather cynical Vorta. The last shot, with the reanimated corpse walking into a wall presumably until its batteries run down, is really quite distasteful.

6.11 WALTZ

STARDATE 51413.6

Dukat has been driven mad with grief

TX 8 January 1998
WRITER Ronald D Moore
DIRECTOR Rene Auberjonois
GUEST CAST Marc Alaimo (Dukat), Casey Biggs (Damar), Jeffrey Combs (Weyoun)

Sisko meets Dukat, who is being investigated for war crimes and has had a nervous breakdown since the death of Ziyal. The ship they are on is destroyed by Cardassians, and Sisko and Dukat find themselves on a nearby planet. Dukat is delusional, and imagines Weyoun and Damar telling him to kill Sisko. Dukat refuses until Sisko shows him respect. Sisko realises Dukat is deranged when he starts arguing with 'Kira'. Dukat destroys the communications system, and the two men fight. Worf is searching for them in the Defiant, but doesn't have long before he must escort a convoy. Dukat and Sisko continue to fight, and Dukat gets to the shuttle. He says he will destroy Bajor. The Defiant rescues Sisko, but Dukat has got away.

QUOTES

- 'We didn't choose to be the superior race. Fate handed us that role.' – *Dukat*

TRIVIA

- A story, with the working title *Dukat's Head*, that was designed to show just how insane and evil Dukat was. The writers were becoming worried that viewers were starting to sympathise with the character.

RATING

- A strong episode, if not a revolutionary one. Dukat is clearly as nutty as squirrel pooh.

6.12 WHO MOURNS FOR MORN?

Morn has died... so Quark looks to profit

TX 4 February 1998
WRITER Mark Gehred-O'Connell
DIRECTOR Victor Lobl
GUEST CAST Brad Greenquist (Krit), Gregory Itzin (Hain), Cyril O'Reilly (Nahsk), Mark Allen Shepherd (Morn), Bridget Ann White (Larell)

STARDATE UNKNOWN

Morn has died in an ion storm, and Quark decides to throw a memorial party, where Sisko tells him that Morn has left him everything in his will. Morn was meant to be broke, but his ex-wife, Larell, tells Quark he had a retirement fund. She wants ten per cent, and two more aliens, Krit and Nahsk, want it all. Quark haggles them down to fifty per cent, and finds a locker key. There's one bar of latinum in there, with a note that the rest is in a bank. Another alien, Hain, shows up, telling Quark that as Morn was a Lurian prince, all his assets are actually the state's. He also offers a reward for Larell. Quark learns that they were all bank robbers, and now that the statute of limitations has run out, they've come for the money. The 'partners' all try to double-cross each other and Quark, and Odo arrives to arrest them all. Quark finds the latinum... except it's just worthless gold. Sadly, Quark returns to work, and finds Morn there. Morn wanted the others out of the way. So where's the latinum? Morn vomits up 100 bars' worth of liquid latinum he'd stored in his second stomach – Quark's reward for sorting out Morn's problem.

TRIVIA

- René Echevarria did an uncredited rewrite to tone down the humour, and to make Quark less comically greedy. Originally, it was the regular cast who were after Morn's money, but this was felt to be out of character.
- It's finally revealed what 'gold-pressed latinum' is – latinum is a valuable liquid, that for ease of transport is placed in golden capsules. There are four denominations, in ascending order: slips, strips, bars and bricks.
- It took six hours to create the sound effect of Morn regurgitating the latinum.

RATING

- There are a few episodes this season that could be set in previous seasons, and they tend to stick out a bit. This is one of them, a fun little romp that feels strange among all the madness, war and death of the rest of the season.

6.13 FAR BEYOND THE STARS

Sisko dreams of being a 1950s SF writer

TX 11 February 1998
WRITERS Ira Steven Behr and Hans Beimler (story by Marc Scott Zicree)
DIRECTOR Avery Brooks
GUEST CAST Marc Alaimo (Dukat/Ryan), Jeffrey Combs (Weyoun/Mulkahey), Aron Eisenberg (Nog/Vendor), JG Hertzler (Martok/Roy), Penny Johnson (Kasidy Yates/Cassie), Brock Peters (Joseph Sisko/Preacher)

STARDATE UNKNOWN

A friend of Sisko has been killed and he's seriously considering leaving Starfleet. He starts to see members of the crew as characters from 1950s America, and Bashir diagnoses unusual synaptic patterns. Sisko finds himself in New York, 1953. He's Benny Russell, an SF writer who's writing about a space station for the magazine *Incredible Tales of Scientific Wonder*. His editor, Pabst, likes the story, but won't publish it, because he doesn't think people will believe that a Negro could command a spaceship. Benny continues to write the stories, ignoring Cassie, his girlfriend. He starts hallucinating that he is Sisko, and worries he's going mad. This provides an acceptable way to get his story published, though – it's all a dream. Reality is more harsh. A Negro teenager resembling Jake is murdered by thugs who beat up Benny. The publisher has pulped the issue with Benny's story, and demanded that he's fired. Benny has a nervous breakdown, insisting that Deep Space Nine is real. Sisko wakes up, and realises he must stay in Starfleet.

QUOTES

- 'You can pulp a story but you cannot destroy an idea... The future, I created it, and it's real!' – *Benny Russell (Sisko)*

TRIVIA

- One of the copies of *Incredible Tales* on display boasts a story called 'The Cage' by EW Roddenberry, and a cover that's the familar 'refinery' backdrop seen in stories like *The Devil in the Dark*.

- This was a rare opportunity to see the what members of the *Deep Space Nine* cast look like without any prosthetic make up.
- Herb has a Hugo Award on his desk and a memo from Pabst warning 'No one would believe that a cheerleader could kill vampires' – an in-joke, as Armin Shimerman, who played Herb, was also a regular *on Buffy the Vampire Slayer*.
- Nana Visitor's character, Kay Eaton, uses a male pseudonym, because traditionally it's thought science fiction readers don't like stories by women. The character is probably based on the late science fiction author CL Moore, who was married to author Henry Kutter. Another inspiration may have been Dorothy Fontana who, for the same reason as Kay, wrote as DC Fontana.

RATING

- Avery Brooks is sometimes criticised for being flat and inexpressive as Sisko, and sometimes that's fair comment. Here, though – as an actor and director – he puts in one of the great *tour de force* performances of *Star Trek*. It's a clever, layered script, with little touches that only hit you afterwards (like spotting that Herb is a Communist, so the polar opposite of Quark). Most importantly, it never lectures, it never even uses the word 'racism'. It simply shows us. Along with *Trials and Tribble-ations*, this is one of the two best *Deep Space Nine* episodes.

6.14 ONE LITTLE SHIP

STARDATE 51474.2

Dax, O'Brien, Bashir and their ship are all shrunk

TX 18 February 1998
WRITERS David Weddle and Bradley Thompson
DIRECTOR Allan Kroeker
GUEST CAST Aron Eisenberg (Nog), Kevin Quigley (Gelnon), Fritz Sperberg (Second Ixtana'Rax), Scott Thompson Baker (First Kudak'Etan), Christian Zimmerman (Third Lamat'Ukanship)

Dax, O'Brien and Bashir are shrunk to about an inch in height and sent in the minaturised USS Rubicon to investigate a subspace phenomenon. The Defiant monitors the experiment, but is attacked by the Jem'Hadar. The Rubicon leaves the anomaly without returning to normal size, and flies into the Defiant to discover it's been boarded by the Jem'Hadar. The minaturised crew fly to the bridge to help Sisko's efforts to retake the ship. Sisko, meanwhile, gives the warp drive a computer virus. As the Jem'Hadar are distracted by the minaturised ship, Sisko floods the Defiant with gas. The Rubicon returns to the anomaly and normal size.

TRIVIA

- Informally, the writers referred to this as *Honey, I Shrunk the Runabout*.

RATING

- On *Star Trek*, like every other show, if one episode goes over the average budget, another has to come in under the average. This, oddly, also seems to affect the quality of episodes, not just the spending. The last episode, *Far Beyond the Stars*, has a good claim to be the best *Deep Space Nine* episode, one of the classics of *Star Trek* and just great television. *Far Beyond the Stars* is perfectly judged, beautifully acted, clever and funny. *One Little Ship* redresses the balance.

6.15 HONOR AMONG THIEVES

STARDATE UNKNOWN

O'Brien goes undercover in the Orion Syndicate

TX 25 February 1998
WRITER René Echevarria (story by Philip Kim)
DIRECTOR Allan Eastman
GUEST CAST Carlos Carrasco (Krole), John Chandler (Flith), Leland Crooke (Vorta), Joseph Culp (Raimus), Michael Harney (Chadwick), Nick Tate (Bilby)

O'Brien infiltrates the Orion Syndicate, the largest criminal organisation in the Federation, to find an informant. He befriends Bilby and proves his worth as a handyman when he fixes some faulty Klingon rifles Bilby has procured. When Bilby takes O'Brien to meet his boss, Raimus, O'Brien learns that Raimus has a Vorta associate. Starfleet orders O'Brien to establish what The Dominion and the Orion Syndicate are planning. O'Brien helps rob a bank, and starts to bond with Bilby, a family man. He worries what will happen when the Federation arrest him. Bilby is ordered to assassinate the Klingon ambassador to Farius. The Dominion wants to end the Federation's alliance with the Klingons. O'Brien tips off the Federation, and realises that the Klingons will kill Bilby. He warns Bilby... who chooses to carry out the mission. He knows he will die, but this is preferable to failing the syndicate. Bilby asks O'Brien to look after his cat, and goes off to his death.

TRIVIA

- Charles Hallahan was cast as Bilby, but died before filming started. The part went to *Space:1999* veteran Nick Tate, who had previously appeared as Dirgo in *Final Mission*.

RATING

- An episode that makes you wonder about Starfleet Intelligence's recruitment and training policies. Colm Meaney can make any scene work – usually the writers seem to take that as licence to give O'Brien some terrible plots or subplots. Here, he gets a standalone, solid story that shows his integrity, and that nice blend of being brave while knowing he's not a hero. It's a nice episode with good stuff from Nick Tate, too.

6.16 CHANGE OF HEART

STARDATE 51597.2

Worf must decide whether to save Dax or complete his mission

TX 4 March 1998
WRITER Ronald D Moore
DIRECTOR David Livingston
GUEST CAST Todd Waring (Lasaran)

Worf and Dax are in a mission in the Badlands to meet a Cardassian double agent, Lasaran, who knows the location of the Founders' planet. He wants to defect, and they are to meet him on the planet Soukara. For Worf and Dax, this means a two-day jungle trek. It's tough going, but Worf and Dax enjoy each other's company – it's practically a honeymoon. They fight off a Jem'Hadar patrol, but Dax is critically injured. Worf realises he has to leave Dax to die. They kiss and he leaves, but turns back and gets her back to their runabout in time to save her life. Lasaran is killed. Sisko tells Worf he made the wrong decision – but did exactly what Sisko would have done.

TRIVIA

- A large stage usually reserved for movie sets was used to stage the jungle, but it had such much vegetation planted in it that it became difficult to move the cameras.

RATING

- The title rather gives away the ending. This is probably Terry Farrell's best performance in the series, and while you don't expect Dax to die, you are expecting some sort of cop-out that allows a win-win scenario, so the ending is a nice – or nasty – twist.

6.17 WRONGS DARKER THAN DEATH OR NIGHT

STARDATE UNKNOWN

Kira learns a dark secret about her mother

TX 1 April 1998
WRITERS Ira Steven Behr and Hans Beimler
DIRECTOR Jonathan West
GUEST CAST Marc Alaimo (Dukat), David Bowe (Basso), Tim de Zarn (Halb Wayne), Grace (Legate), Leslie Hope (Meru), Thomas Kopache (Taban)

Dukat contacts Kira on her late mother's birthday to tell her that she didn't die – she left Bajor to live with him. Kira can't disprove the allegation, so consults the Orb of Time. She travels to the past, and ends up in a refugee centre with her family, who don't know who she is. Kira and her mother Meru are taken to be 'comfort women' for the Cardassians. Meru is overwhelmed by the luxury of her new surroundings and soon becomes the mistress of Dukat. Kira is thrown out into the station's Bajoran ghettos. Angry with her mother, Kira agrees to help plant a bomb to assassinate Dukat. As she plants the bomb, she sees a message from her father – Dukat has made sure his mistress's family haven't suffered. Kira warns Meru about the bomb, and Dukat is spared. Kira returns to the station with new awareness of her family history.

TRIVIA

- The title is a quote from Shelley's *Prometheus Unbound* (1818-19): 'To suffer woes which Hope thinks infinite; to forgive wrongs darker than Death or Night.'

RATING

- Kira's back story gets another twist and more layers of compromise, secrets and sacrifice in a story that can't really get to the meat of the story and still make it to television – there aren't many shows which are aired at teatime about forced prostitution. So it's an odd story that goes far enough to leave a nasty taste, without really being nasty enough to avoid trivialising the subject matter.

6.18 INQUISITION

STARDATE UNKNOWN

Bashir is interrogated by Starfleet Intelligence

TX 8 April 1998
WRITERS Bradley Thompson and David Weddle
DIRECTOR Michael Dorn
GUEST CAST Benjamin Brown (Kagan), Jeffrey Combs (Weyoun), Samantha Mudd (Chandler), William Sadler (Sloan)

Sloan from Internal Affairs arrives to investigate a security breach: an officer is passing information to The Dominion. The senior staff are confined to quarters and it becomes clear to Bashir that the investigation is focusing on him. Sloan tells him that when he was a Dominion prisoner, the enemy may have been able to brainwash him. When Sisko asks if this is possible, Bashir realises his commander suspects him. Sloan arrives to take him to a starbase, but actually transports him to a Cardassian ship. Weyoun tells Bashir that he was indeed brainwashed, but he refuses to believe it. The Defiant attacks, and Kira and Worf rescue Bashir, who notices that something is wrong. He's in a holodeck. The program ends, and Bashir meets the real Sloan. He works for Section 31, a division of Starfleet Intelligence that eliminates threats to the Federation without having to answer to anyone. Bashir has passed their tests, and is invited to join the group. He refuses and tells Sisko – who asks him to join... Sisko would like a spy in Section 31.

TRIVIA

- There's some speculation among *Alias* fans that series baddy Arvin Sloane, a shady, unaccountable intelligence officer, is named after this Sloan. He's named after a character in the movie *Shock Corridor* (1963).

RATING

- Bashir finds himself in another holodeck espionage scenario, but this time it's deadly serious. It's a nice, strong episode, although it does commit a cardinal sin of television – it tells you about a bunch of people who sound far more interesting and dramatic than the regular set-up. Wouldn't you rather watch a show about Section 31 than another one about Bajoran ritual?

6.19 IN THE PALE MOONLIGHT

STARDATE 51721.3

Sisko will do anything to get the Romulans on his side in the war

TX 15 April 1998
WRITER Michael Taylor (story by Peter Allen Fields)
DIRECTOR Victor Lobl
GUEST CAST Casey Biggs (Damar), Jeffrey Combs (Weyoun), Stephen McHattie (Vreenak), Andrew J Robinson (Garak), Howard Shangraw (Tolar)

As The Dominion conquers Betazed, Sisko realises that unless the Romulans join forces with the Federation, the war will soon be lost. The Romulans are neutral, so Sisko has Garak find evidence that the Cardassians are planning to attack Romulus. Garak's contacts are killed, and he suggests that Sisko just fake the evidence, and recruits Tolar, a condemned prisoner, to back up the story. The Romulan Senator Vreenak sees the hologram they have faked showing a meeting between Weyoun and Damar where they discuss attacking the Romulans, but he's not convinced. Vreenak returns home to denounce the Federation as liars, but his shuttle is destroyed in an explosion. Garak planted the bomb, and his plan works – the Romulans declare war on The Dominion. Sisko has lied... but he can live with that, because he has what he wants.

QUOTES

- '...You may have just saved the entire Alpha Quadrant and all it cost was the life of one Romulan senator, one criminal, and the self-respect of a Starfleet officer. I don't know about you, but I'd call that a bargain.' – *Garak*

TRIVIA

- The episode had the working title *Patriot* and was about Jake discovering a story that painted his father in a bad light. The flashback structure of the episode (and Sisko's last line, quoted above) were taken from *The Man Who Shot Liberty Valance.*
- The title comes from the line Jack Napier says in the Tim Burton *Batman* film before killing Bruce Wayne's parents: 'Ever dance with the devil in the pale moonlight?'

RATING

- An episode that's extraordinarily dark for *Star Trek*, but there's the problem. That *Star Trek*'s darkest moment comes when one character tells a lie speaks volumes about what a bubble it exists in. Pretty much every cop show has characters lying or tricking to get a result. This is actually what they did for a living on *Mission: Impossible* – tricking someone into believing a lie to further the aims of the good guys. It's a good episode, but not half as shocking and dangerous as some fans would have you believe.

6.20 HIS WAY

Vic Fontaine, a new holographic character, offers the crew love advice

TX 22 April 1998
WRITERS Ira Steven Behr and Hans Beimler
DIRECTOR Allan Kroeker
GUEST CAST James Darren (Vic Fontaine), Debi A Monahan (Melissa), Cyndi Pass (Ginger)

STARDATE UNKNOWN

Bashir has a new holosuite program, a 1960s Vegas singer called Vic Fontaine. Vic quickly identifies that Odo has feelings for Kira, and when Kira heads to Bajor to look up her ex-lover Shakaar, Odo seeks romantic advice from the program. Vic gradually introduces him to Lola, a singer who looks like Kira. Odo prefers Kira to Lola. Vic invites Kira into the holosuite and tricks Odo into attending by saying he's perfected a Kira program. Odo and Kira have a wonderful time, a 'first date', but when Odo discovers it's the real Kira he runs away. Kira finds him and insists they have dinner. They argue, then Odo grabs Kira and kisses her. Now a couple, they thank Vic for bringing them together.

TRIVIA

- James Darren began his acting career at Columbia studios in the late 1950s. His talent as a singer was quickly picked up and he recorded a string of hits in the 1960s. In 1966, he starred in his first TV series, Irwin Allen's *The Time Tunnel*, as Dr Tony Newman before returning to recording. He continued to act, and played Officer James Corrigan opposite William Shatner in *TJ Hooker* (1983-86). Darren was focusing on his singing career when Ira Behr singled him out for the role of Vic Fontaine.

RATING

- The episode Shakespeare would have written, in the admittedly unlikely event he'd been commissioned to write a comedy episode of *Deep Space Nine*, this works at pretty much every level. It is, of course, not about starships going to battle or big fist-fights. But it is a science fiction story, using the holosuite to tell a story about a man who's too shy to talk to the girl he likes, and it does it with two regular characters and doesn't throw the reset switch at the end.

6.21 THE RECKONING

Sisko is called on to fulfil ancient prophecy

TX 29 April 1998
WRITERS David Weddle and Bradley Thompson (story by Harry Werksman and Gabrielle Stanton)
DIRECTOR Jesus Salvador Trevino
GUEST CAST Louise Fletcher (Kai Winn), James Greene (Koral)

STARDATE UNKNOWN

Sisko is shown a Bajoran tablet about the Emissary that has been rediscovered. He sends it to Dax for translation. The wormhole begins opening and closing, and Bajor suffers a series of natural disasters. Sisko agrees to return the tablet then, acting on instinct, smashes it, releasing mysterious energy. Sisko thinks he has done the will of the Prophets. Kira is enveloped in the energy, and says she is a Prophet and it is time for Sisko to face the Reckoning, when he will fight a Pah-wraith banished from the Temple. Kai Winn tells him that his defeat of the Evil One will usher in a golden age for Bajor. Dax rigs a radiation weapon to force the Prophet to leave Kira, but it takes over Jake instead. Winn uses the radiation to stop the fight, saying she has saved the station. Kira wonders what the Prophets will make of her actions.

TRIVIA

- The story team felt that *The Assignment* had done a disservice to the Pah-wraiths and struck on the idea of an epic battle between a Pah-wraith and a Prophet. Weddle and Thompson's first draft reputedly took the short-hand billing – Godzilla versus Mothra with a Mummy movie beginning – a little too far, with the possessed Kira and Winn firing lightning bolts at each other across the promenade!

RATING

- A stiff and formulaic episode, in the least formulaic season in the whole of *Star Trek*, this episode sticks out like a sore thumb.

6.22 VALIANT

STARDATE UNKNOWN

Jake and Nog join a crew of elite cadets

TX 6 May 1998
WRITER Ronald D Moore
DIRECTOR Michael Vejar
GUEST CAST Aron Eisenberg (Nog), David Drew Gallagher (Shepard), Ashley Brianne McDonogh (Collins), Courtney Peldon (Farris), Paul Popowich (Watters)

The Defiant-class USS Valiant rescues Jake and Nog. It's crewed by Red Squad, elite cadets – the Captain, Tim Watters, is 22. They were on a training mission when they were caught in Dominion space. He's vowed to complete their mission, to get the schematics of a new Dominion battlecruiser. Nog fits in perfectly as engineer, but Jake feels out of place. The crew carry out their mission, but Watters decides to destroy the battlecruiser. Jake warns that it is suicide, but Watters throws him in the brig. The attack goes badly wrong, and the Valiant is lost with all hands except Watters, Jake and Nog.

TRIVIA

- Originally a Kira and Jake story, it became clear that one adult on a crew of young cadets would look odd.
- The Defiant was originally going to be called the Valiant, and Ronald Moore had always preferred the name.

RATING

- Starfleet's elite cadets are all a bit dumb in this episode – the fact that Jake can see that and they can't just makes it more hard to believe these are the Picards and Rikers of the future. It's interesting to see this in parallel with *Voyager* – in that show, half the crew die and you wouldn't even know it. Here, the ship turns into *Lord of the Flies* very quickly. But it's all terribly predictable, and would have been even if Jake wasn't two scenes ahead of the other characters and telling them the plot.

6.23 PROFIT AND LACE

STARDATE UNKNOWN

The Ferengi discover women's rights – so Quark becomes a woman

TX 13 May 1998
WRITERS Ira Steven Behr and Hans Beimler
DIRECTOR Alexander Siddig
GUEST CAST Sylvain Cecil (Uri'Lash), Jeffrey Combs (Brunt), Aron Eisenberg (Nog), Henry Gibson (Nilva), Max Grodenchik (Rom), Andrea Martin (Ishka), Chase Masterson (Leeta), Tiny Ron (Maihar'du), Wallace Shawn (Zek)

Grand Nagus Zek announces that females will have equal rights in Ferengi law, and their civilisation collapses into chaos. Brunt is now acting Grand Nagus, and the Ferengi Commerce Authority are about to make it a permanent position. Brunt threatens Quark and Zek, and Ishka, Quark's mother, suffers a mild heart attack,and can't attend a crucial meeting. Without female representation, Zek's case will collapse. Quark asks Bashir to perform a sex change on him. Quark, or Lumba as he's now known, reacts badly to the hormones, and becomes an emotional wreck. Nilva, Brunt's associate, falls for Lumba, and she has to fight off his advances. Brunt angrily declares that Lumba is a man – but she strips, and proves otherwise. Zek is reaffirmed as Grand Nagus, and Bashir reverses Quark's operation.

TRIVIA

- A story designed to address the issue that Ferengi women are meant to be subservient, and Moogie, Quark's mother, most definitely isn't.

RATING

- Fans are divided on this episode between those who think it's the worst episode of *Deep Space Nine* and those who think it's the worst episode in the whole *Star Trek* canon. A story that could have been merely an unfunny Ferengi comedy episode decides that doesn't set the bar quite low enough, and tries to say worthy things about feminism... in an episode with Quark in a dress. If you ever decide you want to stop being a *Star Trek* fan, watch this and *Threshold* back-to-back – that should do the trick.

6.24 TIME'S ORPHAN

STARDATE UNKNOWN

An accident turns Molly O'Brien into a feral teenager

TX 20 May 1998

The O'Briens are reunited and celebrate with a family picnic, but Molly falls into an energy vortex which throws her into the distant past. The station crew bring her back, but miscalculate. When Molly returns, she's been living wild for ten years, and is feral. The O'Briens start to regain her trust, but it's a slow process. However, she becomes scared at Quark's bar, and attacks a customer with a bottle.

WRITERS Bradley Thompson and David Weddle (story by Joe Menosky)
DIRECTOR Allan Kroeker
GUEST CAST Rosalind Chao (Keiko), Hana Hatae (Molly), Michelle Krusiec (Molly at 18)

The Federation wants her put into care, but O'Brien is convinced that institutionalising Molly will kill her. He decides to send her back through the vortex. They do this – and the feral Molly sees the child, and sends her back through the portal to her family.

QUOTES

- 'I'm disappointed in you, Chief. If anyone could break a prisoner out of a holding cell and get them off the station, I'd have thought it would have been you.' – *Odo*

TRIVIA

- Originally a rejected *The Next Generation* story about Alexander – and one that bears a resemblance to the seventh season's *Firstborn*, which features an older Alexander showing up from the future.
- The episode ran extremely short, so a subplot was added in which Worf and Dax looked after the O'Brien's baby Yoshi and discussed having children of their own.

RATING

- An odd little episode, another one of those that takes 'ordinary' O'Brien and does something that would put an ordinary man into therapy for the rest of his life (as indeed happened in *Hard Time*, but we never heard about it after that episode). There's stuff in there about families and lost childhood, but it's not exactly a typical situation faced by an eight-year-old, so whatever lessons are learned are a little abstract.

6.25 THE SOUND OF HER VOICE

STARDATE UNKNOWN

The Defiant races to save a woman who's crashed on a remote planet

TX 10 June 1998
WRITER Ronald D Moore (story by Pam Pietroforte)
DIRECTOR Winrich Kolbe
GUEST CAST Penny Johnson (Kasidy Yates), Debra Wilson (Lisa Cusak – voice only)

Defiant picks up a distress call from Lisa Cusak, whose escape pod has crashed on a remote planet. They can't talk to her yet, but Cusak keeps talking. The crew are amused by this – and delighted to finally make contact. The atmosphere of the planet is low in oxygen, and she's running out of triox supplies. The Defiant might not make it in time, but the crew keep her alert by talking to her, and she's a good listener. The Defiant diverts power from the phasers to boost its speed, but arrives to discover an energy barrier around the planet. They crash through... and discover Cusak's skeleton. She's been dead for three years and the communications have been timeshifted by the metreon radiation. The crew hold a wake for her.

TRIVIA

- The episode had the working title *Voice in the Darkness*.

RATING

- O'Brien's remark that one day they might lose one of their own wins the Least Subtle Hint award. This is an episode with a twist that would have been a lot more powerful if it hadn't already been used in the *Voyager* episode *Eye of the Needle*. If you're well-versed in *Star Trek* plotting, you can see it coming about five minutes into the episode.

6.26 TEARS OF THE PROPHETS

STARDATE UNKNOWN

Sisko defies the Prophets and Jadzia Dax is killed

TX 17 June 1998
WRITERS Ira Steven Behr and Hans Beimler
DIRECTOR Allan Kroeker

Starfleet Command orders the invasion of Cardassia, and Sisko is to lead the assault. They are to start with an attack on the Chin'toka System, but are unaware that it's recently been reinforced. The Klingons and Romulans join the Federation. The Prophets warn Sisko not to go to Cardassia, but Ross tells him to choose whether he wants to be an Emissary or a Starfleet captain. Sisko takes command of the attack fleet, leaving Dax in charge of the station. Dukat is possessed by a Pah-wraith, and vows to destroy the Prophets. The attack fleet

GUEST CAST Marc Alaimo (Dukat), Casey Biggs (Damar), David Birney (Letant), Jeffrey Combs (Weyoun), James Darren (Vic Fontaine), Aron Eisenberg (Nog), JG Hertzler (Martok), Barry Jenner (Ross), Andrew Robinson (Garak)

tries to locate the power source for the defences at Chin'toka. Dukat arrives at the station, mortally wounding Dax and destroying the Orb. The wormhole implodes. The attack fleet disables the defences and Federation forces are on Cardassian soil at last. They receive an urgent message from Bashir – he's saved the symbiont, but Jadzia is dead. The Orbs have all gone dark – the Prophets have abandoned Bajor. Sisko takes a leave of absence. He has failed.

QUOTES

- 'Klingons can be quite entertaining, can't they? Every Romulan zoo should have a pair.' – *Romulan Senator*

TRIVIA

- Terry Farrell chose to leave, feeling she'd done all she could with Dax. She asked not be killed off, but it was felt that as the season had been dark, and was set during a war, this was an ideal time to kill a regular.

RATING

- An episode that feels like it's going to have a happy ending, then wrenches it away. Dax's death is pretty low-key, but all the more shocking for that.

STAR TREK: DEEP SPACE NINE
SEASON SEVEN

7.1 IMAGE IN THE SAND

STARDATE UNKNOWN

Sisko tries to rebuild his life by contacting the Prophets

TX 30 September 1998
WRITERS Ira Steven Behr and Hans Beimler
DIRECTOR Les Landau
GUEST CAST Casey Biggs (Damar), Megan Cole (Cretak), Jeffrey Combs (Weyoun), James Darren (Vic Fontaine), Aron Eisenberg (Nog), JG Hertzler (General Martok), Barry Jenner (Admiral Ross), Johnny Moran (Bajoran Man), Brock Peters (Joseph Sisko)

It has been three months since Jadzia Dax was killed. On Earth, Sisko tries to rebuild his life, focusing on contacting the Prophets. On the station, Kira is ordered to let the Romulans set up a station office. She meets Romulan Senator Cretak and arranges for him to set up a military hospital for Romulan wounded on a deserted moon of Bajor. Odo later informs Kira that the Romulans are arming the moon. Kira tells Cretak to remove the plasma torpedoes. Meanwhile, Sisko experiences a vision of a woman who turns out to be his real mother, Sarah: he was raised by his stepmother, and his father, Joseph, never told him the truth. Joseph gives Sisko a locket that belonged to Sarah that has a Bajoran inscription that says 'The Orb of the Emissary'. Sisko decides to go to the planet Tyree, where he experienced his first vision, in the hope of finding another Orb with which to contact the Prophets. He is stabbed by a Bajoran follower of the Pah-wraiths – the enemy of the Prophets – which gives credence to his suspicions. Just as he, Jake and Joseph are about to leave, they are met by a young Trill female named Ezri, Dax's new host.

QUOTES

- 'Why does everything with Klingons have to involve bloodshed?' – *Quark to Bashir*

TRIVIA

- This episode marks the first, albeit very brief, appearance of Nicole De Boer as Ezri. She has one line and was only in the studio for half a day.
- The image in the sand was recorded during *Shadows and Symbols*.

RATING

- A strangely low-key first episode, although there's a lot of activity. The attack on Sisko in New Orleans is horrible, intruding as it does on his place of refuge. Though it doesn't provide the barn-storming stuff we have come to expect from *Deep Space Nine*'s season-openers, *Image in the Sand* is well-crafted stuff, balancing a number of difficult plots well.

7.2 SHADOWS AND SYMBOLS

Sisko searches for the Orb of the Emissary

TX 7 October 1998
WRITERS Ira Steven Behr and Hans Beimler
DIRECTOR Allan Kroeker
GUEST CAST Casey Biggs (Damar), Megan Cole (Cretak), Jeffrey Combs (Weyoun), JG Hertzler (General Martok), Barry Jenner (Admiral Ross), Deborah Lacey (Sarah Alien), Lori Lively (Siana), Brock Peters (Joseph Sisko), Cuauhtemoc Sanchez (Bajoran Crewman)

STARDATE 52152.6

As Kira prepares to blockade the Romulans on the Bajoran moon, Worf, O'Brien, Bashir and Quark set out to destroy a Dominion shipyard and elevate Jadzia's spirit to the afterlife. Ezri joins Sisko, Joseph and Jake in their search for the Orb of the Emissary. On Tyree, Sisko is guided by his visions and, after a long trek, begins digging at a site. He finds an Orb case, but he hesitates to open it after receiving dangerous visions. He hastily buries the case without opening it. On the Klingon ship, Worf devises a plan to use a nearby sun to destroy the shipyard and illuminate the gates of the afterlife for Jadzia. They are successful and Jadzia's spirit can ascend. Kira's blockade prompts four Romulan warbirds to stand down. On Tyree, Ezri makes Sisko open the Orb case. A vortex erupts that forces open the wormhole and expels the Pah-wraiths who sealed it. Sisko is met by Sarah, who explains she is one of the aliens in the wormhole, who took over Sarah's body to ensure his birth and destiny.

QUOTES

- 'We shed our blood to prove we are not frightened of death.'
  'Can't you just take my word for it?' – *Martok and Quark*

TRIVIA

- Fans have been quick to point out that Ezri tells Sisko that he promised Jadzia he would make things right, a promise he made when Jadzia was dead and the symbiont was already *en route* to Trill.

RATING

- An opportunity for Nicole De Boer to show her stuff as Ezri Dax. Sisko's religious destiny is uncomfortable, given that he reverts to a regular officer the next week. Kira's Cuban Missile Crisis plot and Worf's assault on the shipyard are far easier to get a grip on.

7.3 AFTERIMAGE

Ezri Dax gets a mixed reception on her arrival at the station

TX 14 October 1998
WRITER René Echevarria
DIRECTOR Les Landau
GUEST CAST Andrew J Robinson (Garak)

STARDATE UNKNOWN

Ezri gets a mixed reception at the station: Sisko is pleased to have Dax back, Kira is awkward and Worf wants nothing to do with her. Meanwhile, Garak collapses and is rushed to the Infirmary. Ezri intends to leave and resume her role as an assistant ship's counsellor but Sisko asks her to counsel Garak, who is having claustrophobia, attacks. Worf is irked when he sees Bashir fraternising with Ezri. Ezri's concern over complications is proved when Worf warns Bashir and Quark to stay away. Meanwhile, Garak angrily claims that she is too confused about her own state to help him. Shaken, Ezri decides to resign, but comes to realise Garak's work to decode Cardassian military signals has made him feel like a traitor – his attacks are self-induced to prevent him doing these tasks. After O'Brien intercedes, Worf realises his behaviour towards Ezri is not what Jadzia would have wanted. He hopes she will not leave on his account. Ezri decides to stay and is promoted to Lieutenant.

QUOTES

- 'You have no idea who I am, do you?... Well thanks for listening.' – *Ezri tries to get a response out of Morn*

TRIVIA

- In the original story, Garak had been on a mission for Starfleet and uncovered some information but had suppressed this as a result of an attack of claustrophobia during his escape. This required Ezri's scenes with Garak to be very psychoanalytical and took the story away from Ezri the character. The answer was to scale back Garak's problem and let Ezri's vulnerability bring about the solution.

RATING

- A solid performance by De Boer, who stands up well to Andrew Robinson's terrific performance as Garak. The episode manages to drill deeper into both of the main protagonists.

7.4 TAKE ME OUT TO THE HOLOSUITE

STARDATE UNKNOWN

Sisko challenges an old Vulcan rival to a baseball competition

TX 21 October 1998
WRITER Ronald D Moore
DIRECTOR Chip Chalmers
GUEST CAST Aron Eisenberg (Nog), Max Grodenchik (Rom), Penny Johnson (Kasidy Yates), Chase Masterson (Leeta), Lou Wagner (Captain Solok)

Sisko's former classmate and rival, Vulcan Captain Solok, brings his ship to the station – and challenges Sisko to a baseball game on the Holosuite. Sisko accepts the challenge, but has only two weeks to educate his team in the game. Sisko is a hard taskmaster, but the team is not promising. When O'Brien is injured and made coach, Sisko gets Kasidy Yates, who knows the game, onto the team. Sisko throws Rom off the team for being inept and almost causes a squad walk-out. Kasidy is bemused by Sisko's competitiveness. Sisko reveals that Solok once humiliated him at the Academy and has gloated about Vulcan superiority ever since. The game begins and the Vulcans get off to a flying start. By the fifth inning, Sisko's team is losing 7-0. Then Sisko is thrown out by Odo, the umpire. Finally, they are in with a chance to score with Nog on third base. Sisko puts Rom back into the game – and the Ferengi helps Nog make it home. The relief of the team disturbs Solok. At the team celebration after, Sisko toasts the victory of his team's spirit.

QUOTES

- 'Death to the opposition!' – *Worf gets into the swing of things*

TRIVIA

- The episode was loosely based on an episode of *Fame* called *The Old Ballgame*, penned by Ira Behr.
- The Vulcan team were genuine baseball players.
- Rene Auberjonois split time between filming this episode and the part of Professor Artemus Bradford in the Matthew Broderick film version of *Inspector Gadget* (1999)

RATING

- Fun stuff, although not enough is made of the Vulcans and especially their captain, played by Lou Wagner. Worth watching for the sheer cheek of even thinking of doing this kind of story, but it's nothing you could call quality!

7.5 CHRYSALIS

STARDATE UNKNOWN

Bashir falls for a genetically-engineered woman he helps to heal

TX 28 October 1998
WRITER René Echevarria
DIRECTOR Jonathan West
GUEST CAST Aron Eisenberg (Nog), Randy James (Officer), Michael Keenan (Patrick), Tim Ransom (Jack), Faith C Salie (Sarina Douglas), Hilary Shepard Turner (Lauren)

Jack, Lauren and Patrick, the genetically-engineered people Bashir once helped, escape from the Institute to bring Sarina to him for treatment. She is in a catatonic state. While Sisko smooths Starfleet's ruffled feathers, Bashir performs an experimental procedure to re-sync her senses and her enhanced brain. There is no change and, five days later, Bashir is ready to give up hope. Suddenly, he sees Sarina on the Promenade – she is cured. Sarina is overwhelmed by her senses and fears falling asleep in case she returns to a catatonic state. Bashir takes Sarina to Quark's, hoping to widen her circle of friends. Bashir realises that Sarina should not return to the Institute and kisses her, overjoyed that he has finally met a genetically engineered person who can live an ordinary life like himself. O'Brien urges caution, but Bashir is smitten. Later, Sarina stands Bashir up and he finds her in her quarters, back in a catatonic state. Sarina's friends reveal she can talk but is afraid to. She eventually confesses that she cannot be the woman Bashir wants. Bashir realises he has pushed her when she was not ready and leaves her to discover her own life.

TRIVIA

- Echevarria's original idea saw Bashir and the genetically engineered humans complete a mission that related to Section 31. A revision saw one of the humans become 'unengineered'. Eventually, the story was scaled back to focus on the characters, resulting in the love story with Sarina that we saw on screen.

RATING

- Strong performances from Alexander Siddig and Faith Salie turn a pretty unpromising story into something with a little more depth. Though a *Star Trek* romance, it's up there with the better episodes of this genre.

7.6 TREACHERY, FAITH AND THE GREAT RIVER

STARDATE UNKNOWN

Odo learns valuable information from a defecting clone of Weyoun

TX 4 November 1998
WRITERS David Weddle and Bradley Thompson (story by Philip Kim)
DIRECTOR Steve Posey
GUEST CAST Casey Biggs (Damar), Jeffrey Combs (Weyoun), Aron Eisenberg (Nog), Max Grodenchik (Rom), JG Hertzler (General Martok), Salome Jens (Female Shapeshifter)

Odo takes a runabout to a rendezvous with a Cardassian informer and is surprised to meet Weyoun, who wants to defect and offers valuable information in return for asylum. Suddenly, they are hailed by Damar and Weyoun – the Weyoun with Odo is actually a clone, WV-Six, while the real Weyoun, WV-Seven, still works for The Dominion. When Six refuses to terminate himself, Damar and Seven besiege the craft with a Jem'Hadar ship. Six tells Odo how to destroy the ship and they escape. Six also reveals that the Founders changed the Vorta from apes into powerful beings, hence their devotion, and that the Founders are dying of an illness that is rapidly consuming them. Six suspects that Odo left too long ago to be affected and hopes he will rebuild a better Dominion. They hide in a frozen comet, but four Jem'Hadar ships intercept and they are forced to run under heavy fire. Six contacts Weyoun and Demar and offers to terminate himself to save Odo. Odo gives Six his reluctant blessing. Back on the station, Odo realises that whoever wins the war, he will lose.

QUOTES

- 'A sickness has spread through The Great Link. The Founders are dying.' – *Weyoun*

TRIVIA

- With Ira Behr on the search for an Odo-Weyoun story, Production Assistant Philip Kim pitched an idea where Sisko joined forces with Weyoun to destroy a Jem'Hadar factory in which the Founders are breeding a more deadly race of warriors named the Modain. Sisko discovers that Weyoun has tricked him and that the Modain are actually replacements for the Vorta. Behr liked the idea, added Odo and changed the Modain plot to a scheme to replace Weyoun Six with Weyoun Seven. The background story of the Vorta and the Founders sealed the deal.

RATING

- Some interesting themes are set up and others explored, not least Odo's god-like status among the Vorta. Meanwhile, there is an amusing subplot with Nog playing Milo Minderbinder from Heller's *Catch-22*, in which Eisenberg and Meaney spar wonderfully.

7.7 ONCE MORE UNTO THE BREACH

STARDATE UNKNOWN

Worf is enlisted to help an aged Klingon warrior achieve a noble death

TX 11 November 1998
WRITER Ronald D Moore
DIRECTOR Allan Kroeker

Worf is visited by Kor, a legendary Klingon warrior, who has been sidelined in his old age and wants Worf's help to let him fight and die as a Klingon. Worf approaches Martok and requests a command for Kor, but Martok was once passed over for officer status by Kor and refuses. Worf makes Kor Third Officer on Martok's flagship, Ch'Tang, where he is treated as a legend by all but the General. During a battle, Worf and Martok are incapacitated and Kor takes command, but becomes delusional. Martok recovers in time to save the ship and

GUEST CAST John Colicos (Kor), J G Hertzler (General Martok), Blake Lindsley (Synon), Neil Vipond (Darok), Nancy Youngblut (Kolana)

orders Kor off the bridge. Worf concedes that Kor is not up to the challenge and removes him from duty. However, the ship is suddenly attacked by Jem'Hadar vessels. Worf decides to draw their fire using a Klingon ship as a decoy, meaning certain death, but Martok's aide, Darok, overhears and tells Kor. Kor knocks Worf unconscious and takes command of the decoy ship. Kor has a warrior's death.

QUOTES

- 'He will succeed. He is Kor, the Damar Master.' – *Worf*

TRIVIA

- In crafting Kor's final moments, Ronald Moore was inspired by academic arguments surrounding the death of Davy Crockett at The Alamo.
- The title is taken from Henry V's entreaties to the combatants at the siege of Harfleur in the play by Shakespeare.

RATING

- Another loose thread is brought to an end, this time the legendary warrior Kor. Hertzler's venomous invective is almost shocking and adds more colour to the Klingon General, Martok. If there's a problem it's that Worf is a little thin on the ground and so the episode doesn't hold together well.

7.8 THE SIEGE OF AR-558

STARDATE UNKNOWN

Sisko helps Starfleet officers under siege from the Dominion

TX 18 November 1998
WRITERS Ira Steven Behr and Hans Beimler
DIRECTOR Winrich Kolbe
GUEST CAST Raymond Cruz (Vargas), James Darren (Vic Fontaine), Aron Eisenberg (Nog), Max Grodenchik (Rom), Annette Helde (Larkin), Patrick Kilpatrick (Reese), Bill Mumy (Kellin)

While providing supplies to AR-558, Sisko finds Starfleet troops held up in a Dominion communications array. The officers, led by Nadia Larkin, have been trying to tap into Dominion transmissions for five months and have come under sustained attack from Jem'Hadar forces and mines. Sisko decides to stay with them until the situation is resolved. The Jem'Hadar use holographic soldiers to gauge the strength of Starfleet troops. Sisko orders Ezri and Larkin's Chief Engineer, Kellin, to unmask the hidden mines and send Nog, Larkin and Reese out to find the Jem'Hadar base. They find the base, but Larkin is killed and Nog injured. While Nog recuperates, Ezri unmasks the mines and Sisko relocates them in the path of the Jem'Hadar. The first Jem'Hadar are killed, but others charge the camp. Kellin dies saving Ezri, while Quark defends Nog, and Sisko saves Bashir. Eventually, the battle is over and reinforcements arrive, allowing the survivors to leave.

QUOTES

- 'I'm sorry, Captain, but I'm an engineer not a magician.' – *Kellin*

TRIVIA

- Bill Mumy only appeared in *Star Trek* on the condition that he wasn't under heavy make-up. Mumy is more famous for the roles of Will Robinson in *Lost in Space* and Lennier in *Babylon 5*.

RATING

- An episode that is lacking a major death from a regular character to make its point. Fortunately, there are some insightful moments from Quark that help, showing the humanity of the character.

7.9 COVENANT

STARDATE UNKNOWN

Dukat returns at the head of the Bajoran followers of the Pah-wraiths

Kira's former teacher, Vedek Fala, gives Kira a crystal that transports her to Empok Nor. She is met by Dukat, now leader of the Bajoran worshippers of the Pah-wraiths. Dukat wants Kira to join them and Fala, also a convert, insists that the Cardassians have changed. She is shown Mika and Benyan, who will be the first Bajoran followers to

TX 25 November 1998
WRITER René Echevarria
DIRECTOR John Kretchmer
GUEST CAST Jason Leland Adams (Benyan), Marc Alaimo (Gul Dukat), Maureen Flannigan (Mika), Miriam Flynn (Midwife), Norman Parker (Vedek Fala), Mark Piatelli (Brin)

have a child on the station. Kira steals a phaser and aims at Dukat but the Bajoran community stand in front of the Cardassian to protect him, then overpower her. Kira berates Dukat for his affair with her mother and is surprised when he shows regret. Later, Mika's baby is born – it is half-Cardassian. Dukat claims it is a miracle, a symbol of his covenant with the Bajorans, but Kira is sure he fathered the child. Dukat tries to cover this secret by killing Mika, but Kira saves her and exposes Dukat. Dukat responds by telling the followers the Pah-wraiths want them to commit suicide and join them. Kira is locked up while the followers prepare to take poison capsules. She escapes and exposes Dukat as never intending to kill himself. Fala commits suicide; the Defiant rescues Kira and the other Bajorans.

TRIVIA

- With Dukat dropping out of the frame for much of the sixth season, the production team consciously sought a way to bring him back to the fore. At the same time, news broke of the mass suicide of the Heaven's Gate cultists based in San Diego. The event added fuel to a story conceived for Dukat and the Pah-wraiths.

RATING

- The welcome return of Dukat, accompanied by the usual verbal sparring with Kira. There's a real sense of danger opening up with Dukat that hasn't been there before as his mannered villainy gives way to power-hungry sadism. Dukat is effectively restored here to prepare for the final battle later in the season.

7.9 IT'S ONLY A PAPER MOON

STARDATE UNKNOWN

Vic Fontaine helps Nog rehabilitate after the young Ferengi loses a leg in combat

TX 30 December 1998
WRITER Ronald D Moore (story by David Mack and John J Ordover)
DIRECTOR Anson Williams
GUEST CAST James Darren (Vic Fontaine), Aron Eisenberg (Nog), Tami-Adrian George (Kesha), Max Grodenchik (Rom), Chase Masterson (Leeta)

Nog is depressed: he needs an artifical leg after the siege at AR-558. The crew try to cheer him up but Nog retreats into the Holosuite world of Vic Fontaine. Ezri briefs Vic on Nog's condition and insists his problems are psychological. That night, Nog is annoyed to see Jake and his date in the holosuite, and lashes out. Vic throws him out. Nog apologises and offers to help with Vic's finances. When Ezri tries to coax Nog out of the Holosuite, he threatens to resign his commission – he has plans to make Vic's business into a casino. Nevertheless, Nog is not limping or using his cane. Ezri insists that Nog must return to the real world. When Nog refuses, Vic ends the program. Nog is unable to restart the it: O'Brien reveals that Vic controls it. Vic reappears and persuades Nog that he must return home. Nog is grateful and later tells Vic that Quark has agreed to run the program around the clock. In essence, Vic will have a real life.

TRIVIA

- The original concept for *Paper Moon* saw three plots take place simultaneously in Vic's Lounge, with Vic as the linking character. In development, the other plots fell by the wayside and the writers reluctantly played it as a Nog-Vic story.

RATING

- Television is not about supporting characters and *It's Only a Paper Moon* is a case in point. As much as Nog and Vic may be well-liked, there isn't enough between them to sustain a subplot, let alone a main story. A misconceived episode that harms two supporting characters instead of elevating them.

7.11 PRODIGAL DAUGHTER

STARDATE UNKNOWN

Ezri discovers that her family has links to the Orion Syndicate

TX 6 January 1999
WRITERS Bradley Thompson and David Weddle

When O'Brien goes missing on a secret mission to New Sydney, Sisko enlists Ezri, whose family are from the area, to find him. Ezri returns home to her domineering mother, Yanas Tigan, and brothers Norvo and Janel, who run the family mining business. Norvo is a sensitive young man, unsuited to the family business, who is dominated by his mother. They are interrupted by O'Brien: he found Morical Bilby, the

DIRECTOR Victor Lobl
GUEST CAST Clayton Landey (Fuchida), John Paragon (Bokar), Kevin Rahm (Norvo), Mikael Salazar (Janel), Leigh Taylor-Young (Yanas)

widow of an Orion Syndicate agent, but she had been murdered. O'Brien believes she was killed by the Syndicate, but the police are dismissive. Later, a man named Bokar warns that O'Brien's life will be in danger unless he leaves. O'Brien checks out Bokar in the company's records and discovers that Morica Bilby was on the payroll when she died – linking Ezri's family to the Syndicate. Ezri asks O'Brien to keep it quiet until she talks to her family. Janel admits Morica was employed as a favour to Bokar – the Syndicate helped the business out of a crisis. Yanas is angered that Janel arranged the deal, but the culprit was Norvo, who took action when Morica tried to extort money from him. Norvo is sentenced to 30 years in prison.

TRIVIA

- This slot in the season was originally reserved for a time-travel story featuring Sisko battling his future self, who has come to warn him about things to come. Thompson and Weddle worked on the story but it didn't go anywhere. With two weeks to go before pre-production, they developed an idea from Ira Behr to explore Ezri's back story. With only two days to go, the script was rewritten again and O'Brien included, building on his relationship with Bilby established in *Honor Among Thieves*.

RATING

- Rushed and sadly misconceived, *Prodigal Daughter* feels more like a soap opera than an episode of *Deep Space Nine*. The O'Brien subplot is dashed in for some interest but barely plays out, while Ezri's back story only damages the fledgling character.

7.12 THE EMPERORS'S NEW CLOAK

STARDATE UNKNOWN

Quark and Rom enter the Mirror universe to rescue Grand Nagus Zek

TX 3 February 1999
WRITERS Ira Steven Behr and Hans Beimler
DIRECTOR LeVar Burton
GUEST CAST Peter C Antoniou (Helmsman), Jeffrey Combs (Brunt), Max Grodenchik (Rom), JG Hertzler (General Martok), Chase Masterson (Leeta), Andrew J Robinson (Garak), Tiny Ron (Maihar'du), Wallace Shawn (Zek)

Grand Nagus Zek vanishes while on a business trip to the Mirror universe. Quark receives a message from Ezri's counterpart that Zek is a prisoner of the Alliance and will be killed unless Quark gives them a cloaking device. Quark and Rom take one from a Klingon ship and travel to the Mirror universe with Ezri. They are captured by Mirror resistance leaders Bashir and O'Brien. Later, a Ferengi named Brunt retakes the cloaking device and frees Quark and the others. They take the device to the Alliance leader, Worf's counterpart the Regent, on his Klingon flagship. The Regent takes the cloaking device and throws Quark and Rom in prison. Brunt tries to persuade Ezri to secure the Ferengi's release from Kira's double, the Intendant. However, the Intendant brands Brunt a traitor and kills him. Rom reluctantly operates the cloaking device for the Regent and suddenly they are no longer required. The Regent orders an attack on the resistance, but the Klingon ship loses power – Rom sabotaged the systems. The Mirror Ezri prevents Garak from killing Quark and Rom, while O'Brien and Bashir secure the Regent's surrender, but the Intendant escapes. Quark, Rom and Zek are assured a safe trip back.

TRIVIA

- With the series fast approaching its blockbuster finale, the production team decided to combine a final visit to the Mirror universe with a Quark-Rom story.
- James Darren makes an uncredited appearance as a crazy mirror version of Vic Fontaine who tries to kill Bashir, his creator in the 'real' universe.

RATING

- A final visit to the mirror universe in which we see a far more appealing Ezri! There are some good gags, notably Brunt's chilled out Mirror counterpart and the wonderfully crazy idea of stealing a cloaked cloaking device, but the Mirror universe is just beyond appeal by now.

7.13 FIELD OF FIRE

STARDATE UNKNOWN

Ezri summons Joran, a former host, to help her solve a series of murders

TX 10 February 1999
WRITER Robert Hewitt Wolfe
DIRECTOR Tony Dow
GUEST CAST Art Chudabala (Ilario), Leigh J McCloskey (Joran), Marty Rackham (Chu'lak)

Lieutenant Ilario is found dead, killed by a rare Starfleet rifle. Meanwhile, Ezri dreams of Joran, a murderer and Dax's former host, who urges Ezri to channel his thoughts so he can help her solve the murder. When she awakens, a science officer has been killed by the same rifle. Ezri summons Joran, trying to understand the mind of a murderer, but it is a disturbing partnership. Joran urges Ezri to tap into her darker feelings. When Ezri sees an officer being pursued by Security, she assumes he is the murderer and raises a knife to kill him but is disarmed by Odo. Shaken by the incident, Ezri hears of a third murder. She discovers that all three officers are pictured laughing in photos in their quarters. She deduces that the killer is a traumatized Vulcan who cannot cope with shows of extreme emotion. Joran spots a Vulcan science officer, Chu'lak, and claims he is the murderer. Ezri discovers Chu'lak recently survived a Jem'Hadar massacre. When Chu'lak raises the experimental rifle, Ezri fires. Joran urges Ezri to kill the Vulcan but she resists and calls aid. Chu'lak confesses to the murders. Ezri buries Joran's thoughts once more.

QUOTES

- 'If you want to catch a killer, Ezri, you have to learn to think like one.' – *Joran*

TRIVIA

- With the production team writing three scripts at once, Ira Behr called in Robert Wolfe to flesh out a story idea where Odo investigates a sniper loose on the station. Wolfe quickly latched onto using Ezri, for whom he had not written, and turned the story into a case of psychological profiling. In early drafts, Ezri recreated Joran on the holosuite, but Behr suggested that Ezri internalise her relationship with the former host.

RATING

- A clever use of Trill abilities to tell a fairly routine story. There's more to this than simply talking about the battle between good and evil within us all. Ezri's decision to use Joran's dark side to help her find the killer is compelling. A clever little piece.

7.14 CHIMERA

STARDATE UNKNOWN

Odo encounters one of 'the Hundred' and is tempted to leave Kira and the station

TX 17 February 1999
WRITER René Echevarria
DIRECTOR Steve Posey
GUEST CAST John Eric Bentley (Klingon), Joel Goodness (Deputy), Garman Hertzler (Laas)

Returning to the station in a runabout, Odo and O'Brien encounter a strange protoplasm in space. Odo recognises it as one of 'the Hundred' – Changelings, like himself, sent out by the Founders to explore the galaxy. On the station, Sisko reluctantly releases the Changeling, Laas, into Odo's custody. Laas has made no contact with their species since entering space, and is curious about The Link. Kira suspects Laas hopes to lure Odo back to The Dominion and is hostile. Laas, who has experienced the prejudice of humanoids, regards Kira, Bashir, Ezri and O'Brien with hostility. Later, he urges Odo to help him find the remaining Hundred and create a new Link. Two Klingons confront Laas for shapeshifting in public and attack him. Defensive, he stabs one. The Klingons press charges and Odo insists the case is founded on prejudice. Laas claims Odo is only accepted because he has assumed human form. Kira, wanting Odo to be happy, allows Laas to escape from custody. Odo tells Laas that he loves Kira and has decided to stay. Laas leaves to continue his search.

TRIVIA

- Garman Hertzler is better known as JG Hertzler, alias General Martok. Hertzler's peculiar speech pattern was reputedly based on a bad impression of William Shatner!

RATING

- A useful set-up for the rest of the season made special by the magical moment of Kira and Odo bonding. Somehow their relationship doesn't seem hokey – although, equally, we can't see how it will last.

7.15 BADDA-BING BADDA-BANG

When Vic's casino is taken over, the officers plan a heist to get it back

TX 24 February 1999
WRITERS Ira Steven Behr and Hans Beimler
DIRECTOR Mike Vejar
GUEST CAST Jacqueline Case, Kelly Cooper, Michelle Johnston, Michelle Rudy, Kelly Sheerin (Dancers), James Darren (Vic Fontaine), Aron Eisenberg (Nog), Penny Johnson (Kasidy Yates), Marc Lawrence (Mr Zeemo), Chip Mayer (Guard), Sammy Micco (Croupier), Robert Miano (Frankie Eyes), Bobby Reilly (Countman), Andrea Robinson (Blonde), Mike Starr (Tony Cicci), James Wellington (Al)

STARDATE UNKNOWN

When Vic's lounge is bought by mobster Frankie Eyes and Vic is fired then beaten up, the officers decide to rid the program of Frankie. Unfortunately, they must do this in a way consistent with the era of the program, 1962. Odo and Kira go undercover. While Frankie flirts with Kira, Odo discovers that Frankie works for Carl Zeemo, who demands a cut of Frankie's profits. The crew plan to rob the casino, hoping that Zeemo will get rid of Frankie in retaliation. Vic convinces Frankie to let him bring in some high-gambling customers – all Starfleet officers. Kasidy realises Sisko is not visiting the lounge because of how Blacks were treated in the 1960s. She convinces him to play a key role as a major gambler. Vic co-ordinates the heist, which must be completed in six minutes the following night, when Zeemo is in town. The heist does not go smoothly, especially when Nog can't find the safe and Zeemo arrives early. Vic stalls Zeemo while the officers cover until Nog and Odo escape with the cash. Zeemo has Frankie thrown out, leaving Vic back in charge.

QUOTES

- 'To the best friends a hologram ever had. I owe you, big time.' – *Vic toasts the officers*

TRIVIA

- The episode borrows a few elements from the classic Rat Pack flick *Ocean's 11* (1960).
- Bobby Reilly (Countman) is actually Robert O'Reilly, alias Klingon Chancellor Gowron, who appears here for the only time in *Star Trek* without alien make-up.

RATING

- The last stand-alone episode of DS9 and the cast and crew sure enjoy it! It's a fun ensemble piece with no strings or hidden depths, just a few laughs along the way. Throw-away stuff, but much needed in light of what is to come.

7.16 INTER ARMA ENIM SILENT LEGES

Section 31 approaches Bashir with an assignment against the Romulans

TX 3 March 1999
WRITER Ronald D Moore
DIRECTOR David Livingston
GUEST CAST Adrienne Barbeau (Cretak), John Fleck (Koval), Cynthia Graham (Wheeler), Barry Jenner (Admiral Ross), Hal Landon Jr (Neral), Joe Reynolds (Hickam), Andrew J Robinson (Garak), William Sadler (Sloan)

STARDATE UNKNOWN

While preparing for a conference on Dominion biogenics on Romulus, Bashir is approached by Sloan, a Starfleet secret agent who previously tried to recruit him for Section 31. Sloan asks Bashir to gather information on the Romulans. Suspecting some in Starfleet still support the banned Section, Sisko urges Bashir to play along to uncover Sloan's motives. *En route*, Sloan asks Bashir to find out if a beligerent Romulan, Koval, is suffering from a degenerative disease – Sloan wants to prevent him joining the powerful Romulan Continuing Committee. Bashir deduces that Sloan wishes to accelerate Koval's illness. Admiral Ross tries to have Sloan arrested, but suffers an aneurysm. Bashir informs Senator Cretak and hopes she can use information in Koval's medical records to prevent Sloan's attempt. Bashir is captured by Koval and interrogated before being brought before the Continuing Committee: Cretak was arrested for accessing Koval's file. Bashir suspects Sloan of pursuing a personal crusade but, when Sloan is vaporized by Koval, he confronts Admiral Ross. Ross admits that Koval is a Federation mole and Sloan is still alive.

QUOTES

- 'My people have a reputation for arrogance. I'm afraid it's well earned.' – *Cretak*

TRIVIA

- Ever since *Inquisition*, the writing team had sought the right slot to bring back Sloan and Section 31. The Latin title roughly translates as 'In times of war, the laws fall silent.'

RATING

- Some clever writing lets you think Bashir is in control when Section 31 is already one step ahead of the game. Sadly, there's no exploration of Bashir's guilt, which is eloquently swept under the carpet in a fierce retort with Ross towards the end. *Inter Arma...* has all the makings of a great show, with Bashir subsumed with guilt, but doesn't have the courage of its convictions.

7.17 PENUMBRA

As Worf goes missing, Sisko is told by the Prophets to expect his greatest trial

TX 7 April 1999
WRITER René Echevarria
DIRECTOR Steve Posey
GUEST CAST Marc Alaimo (Gul Dukat), Majel Barrett (Federation Computer Voice), Casey Biggs (Damar), Jeffrey Combs (Weyoun), Judi Durand (Cardassian Computer Voice), Michelle Horn (Saghi), Salome Jens (Female Shapeshifter), Penny Johnson (Kasidy Yates), Deborah Lacey (Sarah Prophet)

STARDATE 52576.2

As Sisko completes a purchase of Bajoran land, the station hears Worf is missing in action. Sisko reluctantly calls off the search, prompting Ezri to take a runabout and search for Worf alone. While Ezri tracks down Worf's escape pod, Sisko shows Kasidy his plans for a dream home on Bajor and proposes. Kasidy accepts and Sisko asks Jake to be his best man. Meanwhile, the female shapeshifter, rapidly deteriorating, charges Weyoun with finding a cure. Ezri and Worf are ambushed by the Jem'Hadar and beam down to a planet, but have no equipment to signal for help. On Cardassia, Dukat asks Damar for a favour. He is later seen altered to look like a Bajoran. Worf and Ezri are stranded for days and fall into a passionate clinch. Later, they are found and knocked unconscious by Breen soldiers. They wake in a cell on a Breen ship. On the station, Sisko is summoned by the Prophet in his mother's body and told he must not marry Kasidy – he is about to face his greatest trial.

QUOTES

- 'There is no honour in self-pity.'
- 'You know, Worf, I've just about had enough of your Klingon aphorisms.' – *Worf and Ezri*

TRIVIA

- René Echevarria kicks off the final ten-episode arc with *Penumbra*. Subsequent episodes were provisionally titled *Umbra* and *Eclipse* to continue the metaphor, but soon became confusing in script conferences.
- Ezri's search for Worf was conceived from a need to resolve the Dax-Worf storyline of previous seasons and to place the two characters behind enemy lines, from where they would bring back news of the Breen.

RATING

- Ominous stuff to kick off the mammoth final arc, with plotlines firing off in all directions. Perhaps creepiest of all is Dukat's surgical alteration to become a Bajoran, fitting as it does the logical development of his ambitions.

7.18 'TIL DEATH US DO PART

As Dukat poisons Kai Winn against Sisko, the Captain marries Kasidy

TX 14 April 1999
WRITERS David Weddle and Bradley Thompson
DIRECTOR Winrich Kolbe

STARDATE UNKNOWN

Kai Winn arrives to assist Sisko's wedding and receives a vision that a Guide will visit her, and together they will lead Bajor's restoration. As Dukat, disguised as a Bajoran farmer named Anjohl, appears on the Promenade, Sisko tells Kasidy that they must not marry. Devastated, Kasidy prepares to leave. Dukat calls on Winn and tells her that he is the Guide. Meanwhile, the ailing female shapeshifter and Weyoun head to a rendezvous point and Worf is tortured by the Breen. Dukat suggests to Winn that Sisko is not the Emissary. She comes to believe

GUEST CAST Marc Alaimo (Gul Dukat), Casey Biggs (Damar), Jeffrey Combs (Weyoun), Aron Eisenberg (Nog), Louise Fletcher (Kai Winn), Barry Jenner (Admiral Ross), Salome Jens (Female Shapeshifter), Penny Johnson (Kasidy Yates), Deborah Lacey (Sarah Prophet), James Otis (Solbor)

that together they are part of the Prophet's plan. They kiss. Sisko decides to defy the Prophets and proposes once more to Kasidy, who accepts and makes him promise that he will not change his mind. Despite the Sarah Prophet's warning that Sisko will know only sorrow, he and Kasidy marry in a hasty ceremony. The Jem'Hadar ship reaches its destination point and Worf and Ezri are beamed aboard. They are stunned when Weyoun announces an alliance between The Dominion and the Breen.

TRIVIA

- Provisionally titled *Umbra, 'Til Death Us Do Part* was originally intended to set up Sisko's indecision around the wedding and leave the event to the next episode.
- The wedding ceremony was based on Picard's speech at Keiko and O'Brien's marriage in *Data's Day,* which was in turn based on Kirk's speech at a marriage in *Balance of Terror.*

RATING

- Winn and Dukat – Ugh! Quite possibly the most repellent concept in all of *Deep Space Nine,* but what a joy to watch! *'Til Death Us Do Part* is as much about Kasidy and Sisko as it is the fate of Dukat and Winn. Twisted, but great fun.

7.19 STRANGE BEDFELLOWS

STARDATE UNKNOWN

Winn turns to the Pah-wraiths and Damar turns against the Dominion

TX 21 April 1999
WRITER Ronald D Moore
DIRECTOR Rene Auberjonois
GUEST CAST Marc Alaimo (Gul Dukat), Casey Biggs (Damar), Jeffrey Combs (Weyoun), Louise Fletcher (Kai Winn), J G Hertzler (General Martok), Salome Jens (Female Shapeshifter), Penny Johnson (Kasidy Yates), James Otis (Solbor)

Worf and Ezri are imprisoned while the female shapeshifter and Thot Gor prepare to sign a treaty to destroy the Federation. Damar refuses to sign because concessions to the Breen would threaten Cardassia. As Kasidy struggles to come to terms with being the Emissary's wife, Dukat and Winn promise to fulfil their destiny, even if the Emissary stands in their way. On Cardassia, Worf and Ezri hear that Weyoun and Damar want them killed. Worf kills Weyoun when he claims that Ezri has feelings for Bashir. The new Weyoun clone annoys Damar by allowing Thot Gor access to classified information. He feels further isolated when there is a battle for Cardassian troops. On the station, Winn has a disturbing vision of the Pah-wraiths. When Dukat urges her to worship the Pah-wraiths, she tells him to leave. Winn talks to Kira, who urges the Kai to step down. As Worf and Ezri await execution, Ezri asks Worf if he loves her. He admits he does not love her as he did Jadzia, and Ezri realises she has feelings for Bashir. As they are led to be executed, Damar helps them escape and urges them to tell the Federation that he will help them. Meanwhile, Winn suspects that the Prophets have deserted her – and agrees to worship the Pah-wraiths.

TRIVIA

- The episode originally featured two additional scenes that were cut for length. First, Kira tells Kasidy that her father was not religious but attended services for his wife's sake. Second, Kasidy interrupts the Bajoran ceremony mid-flow and takes charge.

RATING

- With Damar coming to the fore and Weyoun's demise, there's strong material here. Sadly, the Sisko-Kasidy subplot is astonishingly lame and holds back the pace. Still, there's some resolution in this early part of the arc, providing a brief respite.

7.20 THE CHANGING FACE OF EVIL

STARDATE UNKNOWN

The Dominion-Breen attack Earth but Damar launches a counter-offensive

TX 28 April 1999
WRITERS Ira Steven Behr and Hans Beimler

As Worf and Ezri return to the station, much to Bashir's relief, news reaches the station that a Dominion-Breen fleet has attacked Earth. Though beaten off, the enemy succeeded in hitting the San Francisco heaquarters of Starfleet. On Bajor, Dukat urges Kai Winn to read the text of Kosst Amojan and release the Pah-wraiths from the fire caves. Winn opens the sacred text, but the words are hidden and must be deciphered. Ezri tries to confess her feelings for Bashir, but he is

DIRECTOR Mike Vejar
GUEST CAST Marc Alaimo (Gul Dukat), Casey Biggs (Damar), Jeffrey Combs (Weyoun), Aron Eisenberg (Nog), Louise Fletcher (Kai Winn), JG Hertzler (General Martok), Barry Jenner (Admiral Ross), Salome Jens (Female Shapeshifter), Penny Johnson (Kasidy Yates), James Otis (Solbor), John Vickery (Gul Rusot)

called away. Sisko hears that the Breen have attacked the Chin'toka system, the Federation's foothold in Dominion space. While the Defiant and the female shapeshifter head to the Chin'toka system, Damar makes preparations for Cardassia's secession. A fierce battle erupts and the crew are forced to abandon the Defiant. The Federation loses its base and the Defiant is destroyed. On Bajor, Winn kills Solbor after he discovers her true intent. Solbor's blood reveals the secret words and Dukat urges Winn to seize the power of the Pah-wraiths. Meanwhile, the station officers hear that Damar is launching a Cardassian attack against The Dominion. Sisko realises they must help Damar if they are to save the Alpha Quadrant.

QUOTES

- 'I call upon Cardassians everywhere. Resist! Resist today. Resist tomorrow. Resist 'til the last Dominion soldier has been driven from our soil.' – *Damar*

TRIVIA

- Casey Biggs (Damar) was married to Roxann Dawson, alias B'Elanna Torres.

RATING

- Winn's final descent is played out in style with Louise Fletcher putting in a masterfully arrogant and selfish performance as the Kai. The murder of Solbor is particularly shocking, with Dukat the malevolent devil on her shoulder. This is a great pairing.

7.21 WHEN IT RAINS...

STARDATE UNKNOWN

Bashir discovers the origin of the Founders' disease as Gowron takes control of Martok's forces

TX 5 May 1999
WRITER René Echevarria (story by René Echevarria and Spike Steingasser)
DIRECTOR Michael Dorn
GUEST CAST Marc Alaimo (Gul Dukat), Vaughn Armstrong (Seskal), Casey Biggs (Damar), Scott Burkholder (Hilliard), Louise Fletcher (Kai Winn), Colby French (Ensign Weldon), JG Hertzler (General Martok), Barry Jenner (Admiral Ross), Robert O'Reilly (Gowron), Andrew J Robinson (Garak), John Vickery (Gul Rusot), Stephen Yoakam (Velal)

As Winn studies the ancient Bajoran text, Sisko orders Kira to train the Cardassians in resistance tactics and gives her a Starfleet commission to ease tensions. Still not coming clean about his feelings to Ezri, Bashir studies Odo's cell samples and discovers that the Changeling is infected with the deadly Founders' disease. Odo is stunned, but insists he and Kira continue on their mission to Cardassia. On Bajor, Dukat looks on the sacred text and is blinded. Winn throws him on to the streets for his blasphemy. Meanwhile, General Martok is inducted into the Order of Kahless, but Gowron betrays him by taking command of Martok's Klingon forces. Martok is stunned when Gowron, intent on restoring the glory of the empire, sends hopelessly outnumbered Klingons into battle. Odo and Kira advise the Cardassians, but the air is tense. Odo notices the onset of the disease. O'Brien helps Bashir obtain Odo's medical records but finds that Section 31 has altered the files to prevent a cure being produced. Bashir suspects Section 31 created the disease and used Odo as a carrier – he and O'Brien vow to find the cure.

TRIVIA

- The inspiration for Damar's story was the history of Spartacus and the slave revolt.

RATING

- There's something deeply unsatisfactory in Winn's rapid disappearance, but we're given plenty to look at instead. The onset of the Founders disease is pretty horrible, while Kira teaching the Cardassians the tools of terrorism has a wonderful irony.

7.22 TACKING INTO THE WIND

STARDATE UNKNOWN

Worf challenges Gowron and Kira steals a Breen weapon

Kira is critical of a Cardassian raid, but Damar refuses to chastise Gul Rusot. Odo is weakening. As Bashir strives for a cure, Sisko berates Gowron for a reckless battleplan that injured Martok. At Cardassian headquarters, Kira and Garak plan to capture a Breen ship and create

TX 12 May 1999
WRITER Ronald D Moore
DIRECTOR Mike Vejar
GUEST CAST Casey Biggs (Damar), J Paul Boehmer (Vornar), Jeffrey Combs (Weyoun), JG Hertzler (General Martok), Salome Jens (Female Shapeshifter), Robert O'Reilly (Gowron), Andrew J Robinson (Garak), Kitty Swink (Luaran), John Vickery (Gul Rusot)

a defence. Rusot baits Kira but Damar intercedes, Garak warns Kira that she must kill Rusot before he kills her. Later, Damar hears that The Dominion has killed his family. Bashir and O'Brien plot to lure a Section 31 operative who may hold a cure for Odo's illness. Worf urges Martok to challenge Gowron before the Chancellor destroys the Empire, but Martok is hesitant. Worf begins to question himself but Ezri urges him on. Damar, Rusot, Garak and Kira bluff their way on to a Jem'Hadar ship. Odo, disguised as the female shapeshifter, helps them take control of the ship, but they hear the Breen weapon is still being installed. When Kira refuses to leave without it, Rusot panics and is killed by Damar. They take the Breen weapon and escape. Meanwhile, Worf derides Gowron's leadership and kills him in battle. Worf proclaims Martok as the Empire's rightful leader.

QUOTES

- 'Worf... if you are willing to tolerate men like Gowron, then what hope is there for the Empire?' – *Ezri urges on Worf*

TRIVIA

- In the original story, Bashir and O'Brien were to leave the station in pursuit of Section 31. However, with the budget stretched to the limit, Ronald Moore was asked to leave Bashir and O'Brien to bring Sloan to the station.

RATING

- A final stab at the Klingons from Ronald Moore. Worf revolts against the corruption within the Empire and restores honour and control, as we always hoped he would. Meanwhile, there's an almost complete contrast with Kira returning to her terrorist ways. The strong character stories just keep coming.

7.23 EXTREME MEASURES

STARDATE 52645.7

Bashir and O'Brien enter Sloan's mind to retrieve the antidote to the Founders' disease

TX 19 May 1999
WRITERS Bradley Thompson and David Weddle
DIRECTOR Steve Posey
GUEST CAST Kate Asner (Nurse Bandee), Tom Holleron (Operative), Andrew J. Robinson (Garak), William Sadler (Sloan), Jacqueline Schultz (Jessice)

Odo is dying but insists Kira leave him and return to the Cardassian resistance. O'Brien and Bashir lure Sloan to the station. When Bashir tries to use a Romulan mind probe, Sloan attempts suicide. He is stabilised but suffered brain damage and is given one hour to live. Bashir and O'Brien decide to link their minds to Sloan's to access the information. Inside Sloan's consciousness, they are offered a file by Sloan, but he is shot by a second Sloan. O'Brien and Bashir are shot at by another agent and manage to escape Sloan's brain, regaining consciousness in the infirmary. Before they can re-enter Sloan's brain, the operative dies. Soon, Bashir and O'Brien realise that they are not in sickbay but still in Sloan's brain – he is playing tricks on them. They search Sloan's mind and eventually find the information they need. Bashir and O'Brien escape Sloan's mind just before the agent dies. Bashir administers a hypospray to Odo that saves his life.

TRIVIA

- Early in the discussions around the Founders' disease, the writers had latched onto Dr Mora Pol as the unwitting accomplice in Section 31's plan to destroy The Dominion. The episode then played out much the same, with Bashir and O'Brien on one final adventure, this time into the mind of their enemy.
- First scripts were dominated by Sloan and Bashir scenes, but the writers were urged to redraft to give O'Brien more to do.

RATING

- Bashir and O'Brien get one final outing while Sloan comes to a sticky end. William Sadler's final speech as Sloan is cringeworthy, but almost works if you assume a complete lack of sincerity.

7.24 THE DOGS OF WAR

STARDATE 52861.3

Damar rallies the Cardassians as The Dominion withdraws to Cardassian space

TX 26 May 1999
WRITERS René Echevarria and Ronald D Moore (tory by Peter Allen Fields)
DIRECTOR Avery Brooks
GUEST CAST Cecily Adams (Ishka), Vaughn Armstrong (Seskal), Majel Barrett (Federation Computer Voice), Casey Biggs (Damar), Leroy D Brazile (Lonar), Jeffrey Combs (Weyoun/Brunt), Cathy Debuono (M'Pella), Paul S Eckstein (Jem'Hadar), Aron Eisenberg (Nog), Max Grodenchik (Rom), JG Hertzler (Chancellor Martok), Barry Jenner (Admiral Ross), Salome Jens (Female Shapeshifter), Penny Johnson (Kasidy Yates), Mel Johnson Jr (Broca), David B Levinson (Broik), Chase Masterson (Leeta), Julianna McCarthy (Mila), Andrew J Robinson (Garak), Tiny Ron (Maihar'du), Wallace Shawn (Zek), Stephen Yoakam (Velal)

Sisko takes command of a new ship named Defiant. Odo learns that Section 31 created the founders' disease but assures Sisko that he will not act on his own will. Kira, Garak and Damar escape a Dominion ambush on Cardassia and go into hiding. Weyoun makes a broadcast claiming that Damar has been killed and all 18 rebel bases have been destroyed. However, Kira realises Damar now has legendary status and urges him to rally the Cardassians against the Dominion. The female shapeshifter begins a strategic withdrawal to Cardassian space. Meanwhile, Quark hears that Zek has named him as his successor, but is horrified to discover that Ferenginar has adopted democracy! He decides to reject the position unless he is allowed to rule according to Ferengi tradition. News reaches Zek who approaches Rom as his successor. On Cardassia, Garak plants a bomb in a Jem'Hadar base but is stopped by guards. Kira and Damar rescue him before the bomb goes off. Damar rallies a crowd. Sisko, Ross and Martok discuss the Dominion withdrawal and agree to attack their defensive perimeter. Later, Kasidy tells Sisko she is pregnant. Sisko fears the Prophets may react negatively to this development.

QUOTES

- 'I won't preside over the demise of Ferengi civilisation! Not me! The line has to be drawn *here*! This far and no further!'
  – *Quark's strangely familiar retort*

TRIVIA

- After the shock of the Defiant's destruction in *The Changing Face of Evil*, here we see its rapid reintroduction. The hope was for an entirely new ship, but budget prevented this.
- One deleted scene featured Garak, Kira and Damar drinking in Tain's basement.

RATING

- Another sad ending, this time a last Ferengi episode and an end to the entire Ferengi culture! This could so easily have become an episode about Rom, but the story is very much played on Quark, the last of the old guard, while his brother rules a Ferenginar Quark cares little for. It's right that Quark is back there in the bar at the end of the episode – neatly playing against our expectations these seven years.

7.25 WHAT YOU LEAVE BEHIND

STARDATE UNKNOWN

Cardassian resistance grows as The Dominion is pushed back to Cardassia

DOUBLE-LENGTH EPISODE
TX 2 June 1999
WRITERS Ira Steven Behr and Hans Beimler
DIRECTOR Allan Kroeker

Power failures hit Cardassia. The female shapeshifter realises that the Cardassians are rising against The Dominion and promises retribution. Kira, Damar and Garak are astonished when Weyoun states that one Cardassian city will be levelled for each terrorist act. Kira decides they must attack The Dominion headquarters. Meanwhile, Sisko takes the Defiant into battle, but the fleet suffers heavy casualties and they are forced to reconsider their strategy. Damar's hideout is attacked and the rebels are captured. Before Kira, Garak and Damar can be executed, Cardassian soldiers revolt and free the prisoners. In Cardassian space, the Defiant crew are relieved when a Cardassian ship switches sides and attacks the Dominion fleet. The female shapeshifter orders a retreat to Cardassia and the genocide of the Cardassian race. Sisko, Ross and Martok sense victory and press on to try for a fatal blow. Meanwhile, in the fire caves on Bajor, Winn chants from the Kosst Amojan, hoping to release the Pah-wraiths. Kira, Damar and Garak lead an assault on the Dominion headquarters. Damar is killed but the resistance draws strength and continues the attack.

GUEST CAST Marc Alaimo (Gul Dukat), Kevin Scott Allen (Jem'Hadar), Casey Biggs (Damar), Rosalind Chao (Keiko), Jeffrey Combs (Weyoun), James Darren (Vic Fontaine), Judi Durand (Cardassian Computer Voice), Aron Eisenberg (Nog), Greg Ellis (Ekoor), Louise Fletcher (Kai Winn), Christopher Halsted (Jem'Hadar First), Hana Hatae (Molly O'Brien), JG Hertzler (Chancellor Martok), Barry Jenner (Admiral Ross), Salome Jens (Female Shapeshifter), Penny Johnson (Kasidy Yates), Mel Johnson Jr (Broca), Deborah Lacey (Sarah Prophet), Julianna McCarthy (Mila), Cyndi Pass (Ginger), Andrew J Robinson (Garak)

As Starfleet plans a final assault, Kira and Garak lead the ground troops. The female shapeshifter refuses to surrender. Garak kills Weyoun. Sisko requests a meeting with the female shapeshifter. Meanwhile, Winn poisons Dukat and presents him as a sacrifice to the Pah-wraiths. Odo merges with the female shapeshifter and heals her; she orders a cease fire. Odo tells Kira he is returning to his people. Meanwhile, Worf prepares to become Federation Ambassador to Kronos and O'Brien decides to teach on Earth. In the fire caves, the Pah-wraiths bring Dukat back to life as a Cardassian. Sisko experiences a vision and heads for the site. Winn is sacrificed to the Pah-wraiths and Sisko battles with Dukat. Together they fall into an abyss. Sisko awakens in a vision. The Sarah Prophet tells him he has succeded in his destiny by condemning the Pah-wraiths to the fire caves, and will soon join the Prophets. Sisko appears to Kasidy in a vision in which he explains his fate and promises to return one day. Kira leaves Odo on the Changeling homeworld, where he merges with his people to cure them. As Bashir and Ezri plan their future, Kira returns to the station as its commander and consoles Jake.

QUOTES

- 'When will you be back?'
  'It's hard to say. Maybe a year, maybe yesterday. But I will be back.' – *Kasidy and Sisko part company*

TRIVIA

- The last months in the production office were characterised by detailed discussions the prophecied sorrow that Sisko would feel and his ultimate fate. While the sorrow was neatly dealt with by Kasidy's pregnancy, this only left the writers with the understanding that Sisko would leave in some way. Early ideas had Sisko dying then being made a Prophet and fighting the Pah-wraiths on their plane of existence. Instead, the writers realised Sisko had been made their Emissary in the material world and that was where his battle must be fought and won, even at the cost of his own life.
- Sisko's demise was originally more enigmatic than the version we finally saw, with no promise of a return. In the original scene, which was filmed, Sisko says he will be close by.
- In the final battle between Sisko and Dukat, Brooks accidentally hit Alaimo for real. The actor was sent home for a few days and the Dukat and Sisko sections of the scene had to be shot separately and cut together later.

RATING

- So this is it – *Deep Space Nine* reaches the end. Even now, it's a sad episode to watch, with Jake and Kasidy left alone and the cast sent in different directions. It's not the celebration of all that is good about the series, as *All Good Things* was – and there are a number of odd plot contingencies to make the story hang together – but it has a poignancy and respectability that says *Deep Space Nine* was a different kind of *Star Trek*.

STAR TREK: VOYAGER

SEVEN SEASONS

164 x 44-minute and four x 88-minute episodes (1995-2001)

REGULAR CAST

Kathryn Janeway: Kate Mulgrew
Chakotay: Robert Beltran
B'Elanna Torres: Roxann Biggs-Dawson (credited as Roxann Dawson from Season 3)
Tom Paris: Robert Duncan McNeill
Kes: Jennifer Lien (Seasons 1-4)
Neelix: Ethan Phillips
The Doctor: Robert Picardo
Tuvok: Tim Russ
Seven of Nine: Jeri Ryan (Seasons 4-7)
Harry Kim: Garrett Wang

CREATED BY

Rick Berman, Michael Piller and Jeri Taylor (Based on Star Trek created by Gene Roddenberry)

EXECUTIVE PRODUCERS

Rick Berman, Jeri Taylor (Seasons 1-4), Michael Piller (Seasons 1-2), Brannon Braga (Seasons 5-6), Kenneth Biller (Season 7)

Voyager looked great on paper – on videotape, though, the best word to describe it is 'troubled'. Despite a charmed start, it quickly established itself as the least-watched and least-loved incarnation of _Star Trek_. It has its fans, of course, but even their discussion of the show often feels more like a post-mortem than a celebration, and has concentrated on what (and who) is to blame for its failure.

The premise of the series (which went under a number of working titles, including *The Journey Home, Outer Bounds, Galaxy's End, Galaxy's Rim, The Return, Return of the Voyager, Flight of the Voyager, Voyager's Mission, Lost Voyager, Distant Voyager* and *Far Voyager*) was that, in contrast to later episodes of *The Next Generation* and the whole of *Deep Space Nine, it* would truly 'go where no man had gone before', to the far ends of the galaxy, a lifetime's journey away from the Federation. Not only that, many of the crew would be killed, and the Starfleet personnel would need the help of the criminals they had been pursuing if they ever wanted to get home. The idea of being 'lost in space' was, of course, hardly a new one – *Lost in Space* itself, the early seasons of *Doctor Who, Space: 1999* and *Red Dwarf*, to name just a handful of shows, had been based on the same premise.

Voyager was designed as a flagship programme on the new United Paramount Network and – along with WWF wrestling – was always the star performer for the channel, consistently its highest rating show. Uniquely among *Star Trek* series, it was guaranteed a seven-year run from the outset. The budgets reflected that – whereas *The Next Generation's* seventh season (1994) had an average episode budget of $1.3m (including cast salaries that had shot up over the years), *Voyager's* was $1.8m and the sets and special effects always looked lavish (the ship crashing into a planet in *Timeless* outdoes the movie *Star Trek: Generations'* attempt). But UPN only reaches 60-80% of US households. So, whereas *The Next Generation* (first-run syndicated across America) was watched, at its height, by more than 11 million viewers a week, and *Deep Space Nine* succeeded it as the most-watched syndicated show, *Voyager* struggled to attract four million. The mainstream audience stayed away most weeks – although tellingly, the two-hour 'event' movies scored notably better. The audience was there, they just weren't biting.

It's tempting to suggest that all *Voyager's* problems can be traced to the channel it was shown on, but it also failed to capture the imagination of viewers in other countries where it was shown on the same channels (often in the same timeslots) as the other *Star* series.

Voyager had creative problems. If it really was '*Star Trek's* answer to *The X-Files*' as the pre-publicity claimed, it demonstrated that *Star Trek* didn't really understand the question – the promised mystery, paranoia, character conflict and running intrigue never showed up. The series saw a back-to-basics approach – a smaller ship than the Enterprise, in uncharted territory, full of new and unfamiliar races, the crew had to rely on their wits, not their technology or the support of the Federation.

Except... they didn't.

Although half the bridge officers – and many other crew – were killed in the first episode (and many others would die over the course of the series), this didn't noticeably affect the running of the ship, which even maintained a working holodeck. As more crewmen died or departed, the crew got larger – Stadi says the ship has a crew of 141 in *Caretaker*, it's reached 152 in both *The 37s* and *Persistence of Vision*). The first episode sets up conflict between the Starfleet and Maquis crew... but by the end of that episode, with everyone in Starfleet uniform, it's become difficult to remember who belongs to which faction. In practical terms, Janeway's tactics are little different to Picard's, and there was even more reliance on technobabble and build-a-gadget endings than the worst of *The Next Generation*. A show that should have been *Star Trek: Unplugged*, with the characters forced to use their wits, often solves its problems by invoking some strange piece of pseudoscience. Characters would exclaim things like: 'It could have something to do with anaedion emissions being produced by the Bussard collectors', (*The Haunting of Deck 12*) or 'A tachyon beam, directed at a class B itinerant pulsar, could produce enough varimetric energy to create an artificial singularity' (*Pathfinder*). The audience was expected to know – without ever being told – what a Jeffries Tube, warp core breach, plasma coil and holomatrix all were – and, preferably how they worked.

And as for no old monsters... the crew included a Klingon and Vulcan, and the Romulans show up in the sixth episode. By the end, almost all the old favourites, from the Cardassians to the Borg and Q had shown up in the Delta Quadrant. Critically, as the series progressed there was little or no sense of attrition – fans quickly started to notice that Voyager seemed to lose a shuttlecraft or fire a photon torpedo every other week, but never ran out. Except in episodes where they faced a specific problem that was resolved that week, the uniforms stayed clean and the crew became ever more comfortable with each other. Seemingly big changes to the status quo were always reset by the end of the episode. *Voyager* was, above all else, franchise television – the channels showing it want to be able to show episodes in odd blocks, or in any order. An early indicator that *Voyager* would take the safe option wherever it could was Robert Duncan McNeill's character – in *The Next Generation* episode *The First Duty*, McNeill had played an arrogant cadet, Nick Locarno, who'd helped to cover up a fatal accident he'd been involved with at the Academy. Locarno was pencilled in on the Voyager crew (as was Ishara Yar from *Legacy*, presumably in the Torres role), but the production team decided that while they wanted someone who'd been in Starfleet before becoming a criminal, Locarno's involvement in the death of a colleague made him too morally dubious. So McNeill became another, practically identical character, Tom Paris. Even before the first script was written, the writers were pulling their punches.

While the show never lived up to its own premise, that was far from being the only problem. *Star Trek* has often returned to a small number of themes or presented slight variations on certain stories.

It's got away with it through a sheer verve that *Voyager* lacked, and as a result, this series often felt like it was flogging a dead horse. Or, as the show's idiom would have it, bombarding an inert equine bioform with a phased floggion particle sweep.

The regular characters were allocated one personality trait (Janeway: mother hen, Neelix: jealousy, Harry: the need to prove himself, Tuvok: analytical sage, Chakotay: the spiritual quest, Paris: the need for redemption, Torres: the need for self-acceptance) and were rarely allowed to play anything but that trait. It made the show predictable and oddly lifeless. Only the Doctor had room to grow, and Robert Picardo's performance quickly made him a fan favourite (and earned him a cameo in *Star Trek: First Contact*). One thing that linked the crew was that there was little sense of wonder, no excitement at the prospect of exploration. Every week, the Voyager crew saw marvels and did deeds we can barely dream of... but all the time they wished they were back on Earth taking the dog for a walk. It's almost exactly the wrong way round. The great desire of every member of the crew was to not be in *Voyager* any more.

Behind the scenes, many people seemed to be having similar thoughts. Michael Piller, the co-creator, left halfway through season one, returning for the end of season two, before leaving again, unhappy with the way the show was going.

Casting Janeway, the Captain, was a tough slog. Linda Hamilton, Lindsey Wagner and Kirstie Alley are all reported to have passed on the chance to play the female captain, then called Elizabeth Janeway. Many other actresses are said to have been approached or put themselves forward: Nicola Bryant, Erin Gray, Patty Duke, Carolyn McCommick and Joanna Cassidy. Susan Gibney and Carolyn Seymour are known to have read for the role. The producers even started considering making the new captain another man, and Nigel Havers and Gary Graham read for the part.

The actress who won the part, Genevieve Bujold, the original Captain *Nicole* Janeway, walked off the set after a day. The people making *Voyager* have claimed that she was uncomfortable with episodic television, but press reports had her specifically concerned about *Voyager* itself, worrying she was playing a 'cartoon character'. Bujold reportedly played the character – or wanted to – as quiet and thoughtful, picking up on the idea in the character notes that Janeway was a scientist first, a captain second. That could well have been more interesting than Kate Mulgrew's Kathryn Janeway, who often comes across as a competent middle manager.

The writers, and even some of the producers, would, by the end of the series, be openly saying that they couldn't wait for it to be over. The production team started to have a little more fun from about halfway through the third season. The arrival of Jeri Ryan at the start of season four as Seven of Nine, a Borg crewmember who quickly established herself as Spock to Janeway's Kirk – and who was given to wearing tight outfits and a corset – certainly increased interest in the show, and seemed to enthuse the creative team. It's a stretch to say Seven had *that* much of an impact, though: the ratings were only slightly higher after she arrived, and episodes built around her did no better than the average. What did draw the viewers in were the 'movie' episodes, double-length special episodes that were heavily trailed and usually visually spectacular.

The end of season four saw the end of *Deep Space Nine*, and a series of rumours that Voyager was to return to Earth in the fifth season and start more traditional adventures – perhaps with a few cast members leaving and being replaced by popular characters from *Deep Space Nine*. Officially, this idea was never seriously considered, but even if it's merely internet rumour or convention room gossip, it demonstrates that the fan consensus was that the show wasn't working in its existing format.

So, *Voyager* is in the odd – possibly unique – position of being a failure, despite lasting for seven full seasons as the top-rating show on its network. It was conceived as a fresh, new take on *Star Trek*, but quickly lapsed to a franchise which relied on repetitive stories and things that were put in to appeal to fanboys, but which didn't actually appeal to them. Like the other *Star Trek* series, syndication means that it will be showing somewhere every day for years to come. But it doesn't seem to have any lasting legacy, beyond a brief cameo from Janeway in *Star Trek: Nemesis*. Whereas *Deep Space Nine* and *Voyager* had built on the success of an earlier show, the next series, *Enterprise*, seemed to be specifically devised to distance itself from its immediate predecessor.

STAR TREK: VOYAGER
SEASON ONE

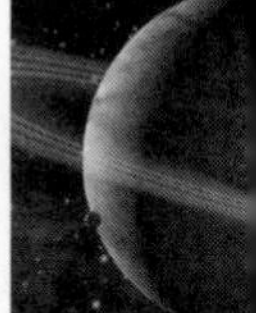

1.1 CARETAKER

STARDATE 48307.5

USS Voyager is propelled into the Delta Quadrant
TX 16 January 1995
WRITERS Michael Piller and Jeri Taylor (story by Rick Berman, Michael Piller and Jeri Taylor)
DIRECTOR Winrich Kolbe

A Maquis vessel commanded by Chakotay disappears in an area of space known as the Badlands. The state-of-the-art USS Voyager is assigned to recover it, as their security chief Tuvok is undercover on the missing ship. Janeway press-gangs Paris from a Federation prison – he knows Chakotay – and the ship heads to the Badlands, after a short stopover on Deep Space Nine. Voyager is hit by an unusual displacement wave. The ship is damaged, half the bridge crew are killed... and the ship is now 70,000 light years from Federation space; it will take more than 70 years to get back. The ship is close to the Array, a space station that's firing bursts of energy at a nearby planet. The crew suddenly find themselves on the Array. They discover the Maquis

GUEST CAST Josh Clark (Carey), Alicia Coppola (Stadi), Bruce French (Ocampa Doctor), Gavan O'Herlihy (Jabin), Stan Ivar (Mark), Scott Jaeck (Cavit), Eric David Johnson (Daggin), Basil Langton (Banjo Man), Scott MacDonald (Rollins), Jeff McCarthy (Human Doctor), Jennifer Parsons (Ocampa Nurse), Angela Paton (Aunt Adah), Richard Poe (Gul Evek), David Selsburg (Toscat), Armin Shimerman (Quark), Keely Sims (Farmer's Daughter)

crew, unconscious and suspended in a weird chamber. Three days later, they awake on their own ships – except Harry and Torres are missing. Chakotay agrees with Janeway's idea that they team up. *En route* to the nearby planet, they encounter Neelix, a local trader who says he can help them. Meanwhile, Harry and Torres wake up in the underground city of the elven Ocampa, who tell them that the Caretaker (a sporocystian being on the Array) looks after their every need. Harry and Torres have a mystery illness. Neelix has taken Janeway's Away Team to a Kazon settlement on the planet – the Kazon want the Ocampa water reserves. The Away Team escape, along with Kes, an Ocampa who's managed to leave the city. The energy bursts from the Array increase in intensity, but the Voyager crew rescue Harry and Torres. Kazon ships start to attack Voyager. Janeway returns to the Array to ask the Caretaker to send them home. But the Caretaker is dying – he wants to protect the Ocampa, as he devastated their planet, and was experimenting on Harry and Torres to try to reproduce. He is concerned that the Kazon will use his technology to destroy the Ocampa when he's dead. Janeway destroys the Array, trapping Voyager in the Delta Quadrant, but saving the Ocampa. She sets a course for home...

TRIVIA

- Filming started on Tuesday 6 September, with the first scenes shot on the existing *Deep Space Nine* sets, featuring Tom and Harry. Most of the new sets were still being finished right up to the last moment, with many of the other cast in make-up tests to finalise their look, but there were also debates about Janeway's hairstyle and Chakotay's tattoo.
- Genevieve Bujold walked out after a day-and-a-half of filming. Her first day, 7 September, had been the first scene in the script set on the bridge, and she and Winrich Kolbe had clashed about her performance, with Kolbe wanting her to be more energetic and Bujold repeatedly playing the scene in a more restrained way. The long scene, which required a lot of setting up, took 15 takes, when typically it would take two or three. The second day, scenes in the ready room with Tim Russ took even longer. Just before lunch, Bujold said, on set, 'I don't think I'm right for this.' Later, after a discussion between Kolbe and Bujold, Rick Berman, Jeri Taylor and Michael Piller went down to Bujold's trailer, and a few minutes later, production was shut down and Bujold had left.
- This was a nervous time for the other actors, who were painfully aware of the tension on set. Some got the impression the entire series would be shut down, or at least the break in production might lead the producers to rethink all the casting. In the event, shooting started again the following Monday, 12 September, with scenes that didn't feature Janeway. Within a couple of days, all such scenes had been filmed, and production was again halted before the end of the week. In the meantime, news of the problems had made the newspapers. The producers had a shortlist of four actresses based on their previous auditions, who were all called in to read for the part again. These included Kate Mulgrew and Susan Gibney. Kate Mulgrew started filming on Monday 19 September.
- Genevieve Bujold's departure was too late in the day to lose an elaborate in-joke – the harnesses in which the kidnapped crewmen hang look remarkably like those from her film *Coma*.
- Janeway's order to destroy the Array interferes with the natural development of the races involved. Ironically, given her later insistence that they follow the Prime Directive, they are only trapped in the Delta Quadrant because she breaks the code.
- *Gene Roddenberry's Andromeda* also has a pilot episode in which most of the bridge officers are killed and replaced by a bunch of criminals and misfits. There's even a character who's a hologram. The ship emerges from a spatial anomaly into a strange landscape – a dystopian far future, rather than uncharted space.
- Tim Russ had played minor roles in *The Next Generation, Star Trek: Generations* and *Deep Space Nine*. He auditioned to play Geordi LaForge in *The Next Generation*. The producers originally imagined Tuvok to be a grandfather figure for the crew.
- Chakotay's tattoo is of a slightly different design in this first episode compared with all the others. Scenes set in the Ocampa city were re-shot when it was decided to put Janeway's hair in a bun, rather than leave it loose.
- The scripts and early press releases all called the holographic Doctor 'Zimmerman', but he never gets the name in the series itself.
- *Non Sequitur* gives the stardate of Voyager's disappearance as 48307.5, but the first stardate given in the actual episode is 48315.6, when the ship is already in the Delta Quadrant.

RATING

- There's a view that the 'even' *Star Trek* films are good, the 'odd' ones are bad. This isn't necessarily supported by the films themselves, but one pattern that is true is that *Star Trek*'s first episodes keep getting better. *Caretaker* is a good episode, one that covers a lot of ground and sets up the premise of the series well. It's painfully obvious which of the Voyager officers are destined to die, and it would have been more effective to 'follow' a few of the doomed ones. The only oddity is Harry and B'Elanna's contracting, and quickly being cured of, the alien disease – it doesn't seem to serve any purpose, and is never fully explained. But this is a genuinely interesting episode. However, things have already gone wrong by the end – Paris' character arc is already over, he's redeemed; and why on earth do the Maquis put on Starfleet uniforms?

1.2 PARALLAX

STARDATE 48439.7

Voyager encounters a trapped vessel

TX 23 January 1995
WRITER Brannon Braga (story by Jim Trombetta)
DIRECTOR Kim Friedman
GUEST CAST Josh Clark (Carey), Martha Hackett (Seska), Justin Williams (Jarvin)

The Federation and Maquis crews aren't mixing – Chakotay wants Torres appointed Chief Engineer, but Janeway and her staff are horrified by the idea. Janeway is worried by Torres' temper. The ship picks up a distress signal from a quantum singularity, the result of a collapsed star. Voyager finds itself trapped in the same phenomenon. Torres suggests a way to communicate with the other ship... which turns out to be Voyager itself, stuck in a time warp. Torres and Janeway take a shuttle and use tachyons to open up a hole in the side of the singularity – Voyager escapes, and an impressed Janeway appoints Torres Chief Engineer.

TRIVIA

- When it was proving difficult to cast an actress to play Janeway, the production team briefly considered a male captain. If that was the case, various other roles were to be shuffled around. Roxann Dawson recalls being asked, having read for Torres, if she had any American Indian blood, as they were thinking of making her Chakotay. Robert Beltran's casting also seems to have been late in the day – he was formally cast on 1 September, with shooting starting on the 6th. As always with a television show, casting was a long and involved process, but Tim Russ, Robert Duncan McNeill, Roxann Biggs-Dawson and Jennifer Lien had all been selected by the end of June. Garrett Wang, Ethan Phillips and Robert Picardo had been picked out by mid-July. Robert Picardo had originally read for the part of Neelix, and was initially unhappy with his 'consolation prize' of playing the Doctor.
- Seska appears for the first time wearing a blue uniform before switching to the yellow of the engineering staff.

RATING

- A small, effective episode. It's difficult not to see the ghost of – and mourn the loss of – Genevieve Bujold's Janeway, the quiet, thoughtful scientist, as Torres and Janeway trade technobabble. The science is nonsense – you can't have a 'crack' in an event horizon, that's sort of the point. The conclusion's an awfully convenient way of solving the character conflict at the beginning.

1.3 TIME AND AGAIN

STARDATE UNKNOWN

Janeway's loyalty to the Prime Directive is put to the test

TX 30 January 1995
WRITERS David Kemper and Michael Piller (story by David Kemper)
DIRECTOR Les Landau
GUEST CAST Brady Bluhm (Latika), Ryan McDonald (Shopkeeper), Bob Rudd (Brell), Jerry Spicer (Guard), Nicholas Surovy (Makull), Steve Vaught (Officer)

Voyager is hit by a shockwave and discovers a nearby planet's population has been wiped out by a polaric energy burst. Paris and Janeway beam down, but then find themselves a day earlier – shortly before the explosion. Paris wants to warn the people there, but Janeway says it would break the Prime Directive. They discover a polaric powerplant, and some of the population are protesting about the power source, but are arrested as spies. Paris is wounded, as Janeway forces them at gunpoint to the power supply. It's now only minutes before the explosion. The crew of Voyager manage to open a portal to the past – but Janeway realises it's the portal that causes the explosion. She fires her phaser at the portal... and suddenly everyone is back on the ship unaware of what happened, as the polaric explosion never occurred.

QUOTES

- 'It seems I've found myself on a voyage of the damned.' – *The Doctor*

TRIVIA

- The first mention of the Delaney sisters, who work in Stellar Cartography and who Harry and Paris fancy. They would be frequently mentioned by the two characters (so often that some fans speculated that 'the Delaney sisters' was some kind of euphemistic code for a relationship between Harry and Paris). They get first names, Jenny and Megan, in *Prime Factors* and *The Chute* respectively. We see them once, in *Thirty Days*.

RATING

- Another anomaly marooning crewmembers, more scenes of the crew frantically assembling technobabble devices to communicate with each other and, worst of all, yet another situation created unwittingly by the crew themselves. It's an OK episode, but it's only the third one – they really shouldn't be this repetitive this quickly.

1.4 PHAGE

STARDATE 48532.4

The crew are attacked by a race that steals body parts

TX 6 February 1995
WRITERS Skye Dent and Brannon Braga (story by Timothy DeHaas)
DIRECTOR Winrich Kolbe
GUEST CAST Martha Hackett (Seska), Cully Fredericksen (Alien One), Stephen Rappaport (Alien Two)

Neelix is attacked on an away mission seeking trilithium crystals, and his lungs are removed. The Doctor designs holographic lungs for Neelix – but he can't move until his real ones are recovered. Janeway leads a team back to the planet, and they discover an organ bank. They are attacked by an alien, and recover his weapon – a combined stungun, tricorder and organ transporter. Voyager gives chase to a ship it detects, and apprehends the Vidiian crew – they suffer from the Phage, a disease which means they need constant transplants to survive. To restore Neelix's lungs would be to kill a Vidiian, but the Vidiians offer to use their advanced technology to make someone else's compatible with Neelix. Kes volunteers one of her lungs, and Neelix swiftly recovers.

QUOTES

- 'Well, if I'm going to be in here for a while, now's as good a time as any to tell you: your ceiling is hideous.'
  – *Neelix is stuck in sickbay*

TRIVIA

- The Vidiians were the Vaphorans in the shooting script, but this was changed when it was realised that no two actors pronounced the word the same way.

RATING

- An episode that starts out seeming like a bizarre remake of *Spock's Brain* which might be called *Neelix's Lungs* becomes really quite creepy about halfway through. Neelix is already far too irritating to get that concerned about whether he lives or dies, but Robert Picardo steals the show, and everything else about the episode works well.

1.5 THE CLOUD

STARDATE 48546.2

Voyager tries to retrieve rare fuel from a nebula

TX 13 February 1995
WRITERS Tom Szollosi and Michael Piller (story by Brannon Braga)
DIRECTOR David Livingston
GUEST CAST Larry Hankin (Gaunt Gary), Angela Dohrmann (Ricky), Judy Geeson (Sandrine), Luigi Amodeo (The Gigolo)

Janeway tries Neelix's attempt at making coffee and is more convinced than ever that they need new energy supplies. The ship encounters a nebula full of omicron particles, just the fuel they need. But they are attacked as they enter, and use a precious photon torpedo to escape. The nebula is a life-form they have injured. The Doctor works out a way to heal the injury and they return to the nebula to do it. Harry invites Janeway to the holodeck – some of the officers have a tavern program. Janeway hustles them at pool.

QUOTES

- 'There's coffee in that nebula.' – *Janeway*

TRIVIA

- This is the first appearance of Chez Sandrine, or Sandrine's, the holographic bar Paris creates. It was originally used as a place for the crew to relax, but would gradually be phased out.

RATING

- An almost ridiculously straightforward and predictable episode, with little in the way of drama or sense of jeopardy. And, yet again, everything that happens is entirely the crew's fault.

1.6 EYE OF THE NEEDLE

STARDATE 48579.4

Voyager finds a wormhole back home... but it's microscopic

TX 20 February 1995
WRITER Bill Dial and Jeri Taylor (story by Hilary J Bader)
DIRECTOR Winrich Kolbe
GUEST CAST Vaughn Armstrong (Telek), Tom Virtue (Baxter)

Voyager investigates a microscopic wormhole by sending a microprobe, which is quickly scanned by something on the other side. It's a Romulan ship, and the captain refuses to accept Voyager's story, believing them to be spies. Torres realises that they could beam through – if they had somewhere to materialise. The Romulan commander refuses them permission, but agrees to beam over to them. He is convinced by their story and finally offers them the chance to transport home... but Tuvok has realised the wormhole travels through time as well as space – the Romulan is from 2351, 20 years in their past. They can't go back without seriously damaging established history. The Romulan agrees to pass on the crew's personal messages to Starfleet after Voyager is lost... but Tuvok later discovers that records show he died four years ago. There is no way of knowing if the messages were ever sent.

TRIVIA

- The opening scene was originally Janeway in her holonovel. This was filmed, and ended up at the start of *Cathexis* instead.
- In the *Space: 1999* episode *Journey to Where*, the crew of the Moonbase get back to Earth, only to discover it's the past (the fourteenth century in their case).

RATING

- We know that the Voyager people won't all get home, but there's still a good amount of suspense and for the first time we get a good sense of the crew's sense of frustration and anticipation. A good episode, with a couple of really nice twists.

1.7 EX POST FACTO

STARDATE UNKNOWN

Paris is forced to relive committing a murder he says he never committed

TX 27 February 1995
WRITERS Evan Carlos Somers and Michael Piller (story by Evan Carlos Somers)
DIRECTOR LeVar Burton
GUEST CAST Robin McKee (Lidell), Francis Guinan (Minister Kray), Aaron Lustig (Doctor), Ray Reinhardt (Tolen Ren), Henry Brown (Numiri Captain)

Harry returns to Voyager from a mission on Benea, a planet at war with the Numiri, and tells the crew that Paris has been convicted of murder. Paris had been attracted to the wife of Professor Ren, who was helping them repair a columnator. Janeway and Tuvok meet Paris on the planet, and he insists he is innocent. In front of their eyes, he has some sort of fit: as part of his punishment, he's being forced to relive the murder through the victim's eyes. Tuvok establishes that it is causing permanent brain damage. He mind-melds with Paris, and understands what happened – Paris is the victim of a Numiri plot. A Benean doctor is a Numiri agent who's planted false memories.

TRIVIA

- This story is the first to explicitly state that humans no longer smoke – it's said they stopped 'centuries' ago. Gene Roddenberry was insistent on the point, and had a 'No Smoking' sign removed from the set of *The Wrath of Khan*.

RATING

- *A Matter of Perspective* with a dash of the movie *Strange Days*. The problem with this sort of story is that you know Paris isn't guilty and that he'll escape his fate. It's watchable enough.

1.8 EMANATIONS

STARDATE 48623.5

The discovery of a new element leads Harry to another dimension

TX 13 March 1995

A new element, the 247th known to Federation science, is discovered by Voyager in the rings of a Class-D planet. It could be an energy source, so an Away Team is sent to investigate. A subspace distortion forms, and Harry fails to return when the team beams back. His place is taken by a recently-deceased woman, Ptera, who is revived by the Doctor. Harry wakes up in a cenotaph on an alien world; they believe

WRITER Brannon Braga
DIRECTOR David Livingston
GUEST CAST Cecile Callan (Ptera), Jeffrey Alan Chandler (Hatil), John Cirigliano (Alien #1), Robin Groves (Hatil's Wife), Martha Hackett (Seska), Jerry Hardin (Neria)

he's returned from the next Emanation – the afterlife. The people here allow themselves to die to reach the afterlife, a belief system based around the subspace distortions. Torres fails to return Ptera home – she dies in the process. Harry is forbidden from examining the cenotaph, but he sneaks in, reasoning that he will die, return to the asteroid, and be found and saved by Voyager. The plan works. Janeway's impressed – it's not every day someone comes back from the dead.

TRIVIA

- There are 113 elements currently known to science. The 111th was discovered shortly before this episode was broadcast (8 December 1994), and has yet to be officially named (until that's assigned, it's known as 'Unununium'). Two more have been discovered since (112, 'Ununbium', in February 1996 and 114, 'Ununquadium', in January 1999). A team from Berkley claimed to have made elements 116, 'ununhexium', and 118, 'Ununoctium', but has been unable to reproduce the results.

RATING

- A strange little episode that is about terribly profound things, but isn't terribly profound. It is quite creepy, though, especially at the beginning.

1.9 PRIME FACTORS

STARDATE 48642.5

A pleasure-seeking race can get Voyager home – but refuse to intervene

TX 20 March 1995
WRITERS Michael Perricone and Greg Elliot (story by David R George III and Eric A Stillwell)
DIRECTOR Les Landau
GUEST CAST Josh Clark (Carey), Ronald Guttman (Gath), Martha Hackett (Seska), Andrew Hill Newman (Jaret), Yvonne Suhor (Eudana)

The Sikarians, renowned for their incredible hospitality, offer Voyager shore leave on their planet. As the crew enjoys themselves, and the Sikarian leader Gath woos Janeway, Harry is taken 40,000 light years on a date by a young woman, Eudana. The Sikarians have the ability to fold space... and to get Voyager at least halfway home, with Torres thinking they could modify the technology to travel the other half. Gath tells Janeway that their culture has a version of the Prime Directive – they can't give advanced technology to lesser races. Janeway reluctantly accepts this decision, but factions within the crew find this ridiculous. Harry suggests, as they love new stories, to trade the space warp for the Federation literature database. Gath grows angry, and asks Voyager to leave. Janeway realises he is shallow and only interested in gratification. Seska, Carey and Torres plan to make the exchange anyway, with another Sikarian, Jaret. They are caught by Tuvok... whose logic has led him to the same plan. He makes the exchange and gives the device to Torres, who realises when it malfunctions that it only works due to the unique geology of Sikaria. She has to destroy the device to avoid a warp core breach. Tuvok reports himself to a disappointed Janeway.

TRIVIA

- The first of the Delaney twins, Jenny (the one Harry fancies), is named in this episode.

RATING

- A nice twist on the Prime Directive story, with the boot on the other foot. The European accents and weird 'high concept' culture makes the Sikarians feel like refugees from *Barbarella* – again, you can't help but think they had Genevieve Bujold in mind. While it takes a long while to get to the meat of the story, there are some nice moral dilemmas, and (finally!) some cleverly played internal politics on Voyager.

1.10 STATE OF FLUX

STARDATE 48658.2

A traitor on board has been passing technology to the Kazon

TX 10 April 1995
WRITER Chris Abbott (story by Paul Robert Coyle)

An Away Team is scouting for food when a Kazon ship attacks – Seska goes missing in the attack, but Chakotay soon finds her. Seska tries to seduce Chakotay with soup made from stolen mushrooms, but he turns her down. Voyager gets a distress call from one of the Kazon ships – an accident has flooded it with nucleonic radiation. It appears the faulty equipment is of Federation origin. Someone on the ship has been passing

DIRECTOR Robert Scheerer
GUEST CAST Josh Clark (Carey), Anthony De Longis (Culluh), Martha Hackett (Seska)

secrets to the Kazon, violating the Prime Directive. Suspicion falls on Seska. Another Kazon ship arrives to collect the survivor of the accident. Once aboard Voyager, though, they kill him. The Doctor discovers that Seska isn't Bajoran, she's a disguised Cardassian. Chakotay confronts her, and Seska tells him she's trying to get them home. She escapes to the Kazon ship with an emergency transport before she can face justice.

TRIVIA

- Janeway speculates that the Kazon might have got their technology from another ship from the Alpha Quadrant. On its journey, Voyager will discover five such vessels: Chakotay's ship (*The Caretaker*), the Dreadnought (*Dreadnought*), the Ferengi ship (*False Profits*), the USS Raven (*The Raven*) and the USS Equinox (*Equinox*).
- A couple of reference sources state that the sour-tasting Leola root Neelix discovers here is a barb aimed at Genevieve Bujold, who played a character called Leola in the live-action *Pinocchio*. There are a couple of flaws with this theory: she doesn't play a character called Leola (she played Leona) and the film came out over a year after this episode was shown.

RATING

- An effective episode, but – as Chakotay points out – further indication that most of the Maquis are actually just agents spying on them. While Seska had been built up over a few previous episodes, the story would have packed far more of a punch if it had been one of the regulars exposed here. Or, indeed, if she or Chakotay had mentioned before that they had been lovers.

1.11 HEROES AND DEMONS

STARDATE 48693.2

The Doctor has to fight Grendel in a holodeck version of Beowulf

TX 24 April 1995
WRITER Naren Shankar
DIRECTOR Les Landau
GUEST CAST Michael Keenan (Hrothgar), Marjorie Monaghan (Freya), Christopher Neame (Unfirth)

Janeway and Torres bring photonic energy aboard the ship, and need Harry's help, but he has vanished on the holodeck. Tuvok and Chakotay go to fetch him, and discover a program running based on Beowulf. They learn that Beowulf has been killed by Grendel – and that Harry was playing Beowulf. Tuvok ascertains that Harry may have been converted into photonic energy. When they confront Grendel, they also vanish. The Doctor is sent in, as a being already made of energy. He meets Freya, a shield-maiden, and adopts the name Schweitzer. When the warrior Unfirth attacks him, the sword passes straight through him. Freya is impressed, and offers to stay with the Doctor that night 'to keep warm'. Grendel arrives, and tears off the Doctor's arm. Back in Sickbay, Paris can repair the damage. Torres has worked out that the photonic energy they bought onboard was sentient, and 'Grendel' has come to rescue it. Back on the holodeck, the Doctor tries to exchange the sample for the missing crew. Unfirth steals the sample, killing Freya, but the Doctor recovers it and makes the exchange. Harry, Tuvok and Chakotay are restored to their normal forms.

QUOTES

- 'But I've never even seen a sky or a forest... ' – *The Doctor anticipates his 'Away Mission'*

TRIVIA

- The episode had the working title *Heroes and Villains*.

RATING

- It's the same old trapped-on-the-holodeck-and-it's-affecting-the-real-world episode, but the first time the Doctor is centre stage. Robert Picardo makes the most of the chance, bringing layers of characterisation and sympathy to a script that doesn't really deserve it – the (faux) *Beowulf* setting doesn't do anything but disguise the fact this is a very straightforward story. A star is born.

1.12 CATHEXIS

STARDATE 48734.2

The crew begin to act strangely – can anyone be trusted?

Tuvok and Chakotay return in a shuttle – Tuvok is injured, Chakotay has had all his bioneural energy drained: he is brain dead. Tuvok says a ship attacked them near a dark matter nebula. As Janeway sets

TX 1 May 1995
WRITER Brannon Braga (story by Brannon Braga and Joe Menosky)
DIRECTOR Kim Friedman
GUEST CAST Michael Cumpsty (Lord Burleigh), Brian Markinson (Durst), Carolyn Seymour (Mrs Templeton)

course for the nebula, Paris and Torres both commit minor acts of sabotage which they can't remember doing. The Doctor discovers that they were possessed for a short time. Janeway's worried that she will be possessed, and transfers her command codes to the Doctor. Kes senses a presence. Tuvok attempts a mind-meld to find out more. Janeway is possessed, and fights Tuvok. Torres designs a magneton flash scan. Tuvok stuns the crew. Chakotay has been possessing them, trying to save them from Tuvok, who's been possessed by an alien in the nebula who wants to drain the crew's neural energy. The trianic-based energy being, the Komar, is flushed out by the scan, and Chakotay's mind and body are reunited.

QUOTES

- 'Just because a man changes his drink order doesn't mean he's possessed by an alien'
'Nevertheless, don't you think you should scan him or dissect him or something, just to make sure?' – *The Doctor and Neelix*

TRIVIA

- Until this episode, Tuvok had been a Lieutenant Commander. From here until his promotion in *Revulsion*, he's dropped a rank to Lieutenant. No explanation for this is given in the series – some fans speculated that he was demoted after *Prime Factors*, but there's no evidence of that in the episode, and two episodes pass before the change in rank. Presumably, it was spotted that as a Lieutenant Commander with seniority, he'd outrank Chakotay, the First Officer.
- Janeway's holonovel, which we first see here, seems to be loosely based on *The Turn of the Screw*.

RATING

- The premise of the show is that there are two factions aboard the ship who don't trust each other – they shouldn't need external help! This is a pretty standard alien possession story, the twist being there are two aliens with different agendas.

1.13 FACES

STARDATE 48784.2

The Vidiians split Torres into a Klingon and a human

TX 8 May 1995
WRITER Kenneth Biller (story by Jonathan Glassner and Adam Grossman)
DIRECTOR Winrich Kolbe
GUEST CAST Rob LaBelle (Talaxian Prisoner), Brian Markinson (Durst/Sulan), Barton Tinapp (Guard)

Sulan, a Vidiian, wakes up a Torres who is completely Klingon. He believes the Klingons are immune to the Phage, and has separated her human and Klingon sides. Sulan is becoming attracted to Torres. He's infected her with the Phage, but she hasn't contracted it. Paris and Durst are in a Vidiian prison/organ bank when they find the all-human Torres. Klingon Torres tries to escape, human Torres is scared. Sulan grafts Durst's face onto his to make himself more attractive to Torres, but she escapes. The two versions of Torres meet up, and realise they have to work together. The Klingon is killed, the human Torres escapes. The Doctor reveals that he needs to graft Klingon DNA back into her, or she will die. Torres realises that she is incomplete without her Klingon side.

TRIVIA

- The first draft of the story was set on a planet obsessed with genetic purity, the aliens' motivation for splitting Torres into a human and Klingon.
- Durst was introduced in the previous episode so that a familiar face would be killed by the Vidiians. Markinson had already been cast as Sulan so, for the first half of this episode, he's playing a double role.

RATING

- An interesting and at times horrific episode, and Rob Labelle deserves a mention for a memorable scene as a malevolent Neelix-type character. The episode takes the perennial – and deeply problematic – *Star Trek* obsession with the idea that anyone who's 'half' one culture, 'half' another must be constantly torn between the two identities and runs with it. Dawson plays the Klingon half a little too broadly, and that Torres comes across more like a cartoon than a character, but the human side is nicely played – the same as the regular Torres, and yet completely different. A good episode.

1.14 JETREL

STARDATE 48832.1

Neelix is confronted with a war criminal from his planet

TX 15 May 1995
WRITERS Jack Klein and Karen Klein and Kenneth Biller (story by James Thornton and Scott Nimerfro)
DIRECTOR Kim Friedman
GUEST CAST Larry Hankin (Gaunt Gary), James Sloyan (Ma'bor Jetrel)

Neelix is contacted by the Haakonian scientist Jetrel, the man who invented the metreon cascade which destroyed Neelix's homeworld, Rinax. Neelix refuses to meet him, but Jetrel warns he may have metremia, a blood disease, from being part of the rescue effort on Rinax. Neelix agrees to be tested, and Jetrel confirms the diagnosis. Jetrel says that using Voyager's transporters, he could retrieve a sample of metreon isotope from the ruins of Rinax, and develop a cure. Jetrel also has metremia, and asks forgiveness from Neelix, who refuses. At Rinax, Torres beams a sample onboard. Jetrel makes a move, deactivating the Doctor and doing something to the sample that turns it into organic matter. Neelix finds him, and Jetrel knocks him out. Janeway confronts him. Jetrel thinks he can use the transporter to restore the victims of Rinax to life. He nearly succeeds, with a humanoid form appearing in the transporter beam, but the transporters don't have enough power. Jetrel collapses. Neelix forgives Jetrel as he dies.

QUOTES

- 'Yes, I developed the weapon, but it was the government and the military leaders who decided to use it, not I.'
  'That must be a convenient distinction for you. Does it help you sleep at night?' – *Jetrel and Neelix*

TRIVIA

- Neelix's family referred to here consists of his father, mother and little brothers. When we see his family in *Mortal Coil*, there are no brothers but many sisters, including his favourite, Alixia.

RATING

- Another *Star Trek* tale of war crimes and an obsessive scientist gone bad. Despite being a Neelix episode, the story works, and there's something quite haunting about the idea of a scientist seeking redemption by resurrecting the dead. As ever in episodic television, there's something too hasty and easy about Neelix's offer of forgiveness.

1.15 LEARNING CURVE

STARDATE 48846.5

Tuvok gives special training to some unruly Maquis officers

TX 22 May 1995
WRITERS Ronald Wilkerson and Jean Louise Matthias
DIRECTOR David Livingston
GUEST CAST Thomas Alexander Dekker (Henry), Lindsey Haun (Beatrice), Derek McGrath (Chell), Catherine MacNeal (Henley), Scott Miles (Terek), Armand Shultz (Dalby)

Maquis crewman Dalby replaces a gel pack without permission. This is just the latest incident of Maquis crew ignoring protocol, so Janeway has Tuvok set up a crash course in Starfleet procedure. Chakotay selects four crewmembers, and Tuvok places them on a strict regime of marches and mundane tasks. The gel packs continue to malfunction. The Maquis quickly decide enough is enough, but Chakotay forces them back. Neelix suggests Tuvok tries to be more flexible, but Tuvok is more interested in the brill cheese Neelix has made – that's what's infecting the gel packs. Torres realises that heat will sterilise the packs. Tuvok and his class become trapped in the cargo bay after another malfunction, with the temperature rising rapidly. They escape into a Jeffries Tube, but one of them is trapped. Tuvok goes back for him, against Starfleet protocol, risking his life. As the emergency ends, the Maquis crew have a new respect for him – and Tuvok admits that sometimes, rules must be bent.

QUOTES

- 'Get the cheese to Sickbay.' – *Torres gives the fans a line that summed up exactly what they thought of the new show*

TRIVIA

- Four more episodes of *Voyager* were made this year, but held back to the second season – in production order, these were: *Projections*, *Elogium*, *Twisted* and *The 37s*. This was evidently a last-minute decision, as the stardates given in those episodes aren't changed, so they don't run in broadcast order.

RATING

- Again, conflict between the two factions is seen as an anomaly, not the norm, but this story at least shows the problem, rather than paying it lip service. It's another episode with a conveniently neat resolution, but the Tuvok story works. But... well, the first season of *The Next Generation* ended with them facing the Romulans – the enemy in this season finale is a lump of cheese.

STAR TREK: VOYAGER
SEASON TWO

2.1 THE 37s

STARDATE 48975.1

Voyager discovers humans abducted by aliens in 1937

TX 28 August 1995
WRITERS Jeri Taylor and Brannon Braga
DIRECTOR James L Conway
GUEST CAST David Graf (Noonan), Sharon Lawrence (Amelia Earhart), John Rubenstein (John Evansville), James Saito (Japanese Soldier), Mel Winkler (Jack Hayes)

Voyager finds a pickup truck floating in space and when they beam it onboard, it's picking up an SOS call. They land Voyager on the planet where the signal is coming from and find an aeroplane from the 1930s. Nearby is a room with eight cryo-stasis units containing eight humans. These include Amelia Earhart and her navigator. Janeway theorises that they were abducted by aliens, but finds it difficult to convince the abductees. They come under attack from more humans, who've confused them for Briori, aliens who enslaved their ancestors. A slave revolt saw off the Briori, and there's an established colony here. The colonists offer the Voyager crew and the '37s' a home. The 37s stay, the Voyager crew decide to stick with the ship.

TRIVIA

- This is the first of five times Voyager is seen to land on a planet (and the first time 'blue alert' is signalled). The other four are *Basics* (where we see it land once and it presumably lands a second time), *Demon*, *Dragon's Teeth* and *Nightingale*. The scale of the ship appears a little off on the surface – it looks smaller than the 116-metre wide ship we were told about in *Parallax*.

RATING

- Quite how a pickup truck could survive in space, let alone still have a full tank of petrol, is never explained. This is a good adventure story, albeit one that makes very little sense.

2.2 INITIATIONS

STARDATE 49005.3

Chakotay must fight a young Kazon boy

TX 4 September 1995
WRITER Kenneth Biller
DIRECTOR Winrich Kolbe
GUEST CAST Tim de Zarn (Haliz), Aron Eisenberg (Kar), Patrick Kilpatrick (Razik)

Chakotay takes a shuttle to conduct a solitary ritual honouring his father. He is attacked by Kar, a Kazon-Ogla boy who wants to earn his warrior name. Chakotay beams the boy aboard his ship, destroying the Kazon vessel. He returns Kar to his people, who hold them both in contempt. Razik, their leader, tells Chakotay he can leave if he fights the boy. Instead, Chakotay and Kar flee together. Kar and Chakotay work together to survive on a hostile moon, and Kar finds he can't murder Chakotay when he gets the chance. Instead, he kills Razik when the Kazon leader comes after them, earning his warrior name. Kar warns Chakotay that if they meet again, he'll kill him.

QUOTES

- 'Why are you so eager for me to kill you?'
  'Because there are worse things than being killed by an enemy.' – *Chakotay and Kar*

TRIVIA

- Chakotay's medicine bundle is in his shuttle when it's destroyed, but we see it in later episodes. Fans have suggested that he just replicates a new one, but surely a replicated blackbird feather doesn't count, and a replicated 'stone from a river' isn't a stone from a river at all?
- Another episode shot on location at the Vasquez Rocks.
- This is the first episode in which a Voyager shuttle is definitely destroyed. The ship has two shuttlecraft and four shuttlepods. Around 30 shuttles are destroyed during the run of the show (it's not always possible to say if a shuttle has been salvaged, and there's often some confusion whether a shuttle is a 'real' one, or one from a parallel timeline, simulation, hallucination or so on). Calculations therefore vary, but it's at least 23 real shuttles and the total number of times we see a shuttle destroyed is pushing 60. This became a cause for despair in sections of fandom, who saw it as symptomatic of a show that wasn't living up to its premise of a Starfleet ship suffering attrition, and latterly an in-joke among the writers. The producers explained the problem away by saying that the parts for shuttles could easily be replicated and replacement shuttles were built.

RATING

- An efficient piece of storytelling, one that's more interesting than the usual episodes about a warrior's duty (one of *Star Trek*'s stranger perennial preoccupations). It's formulaic, but it knows it, and so can get a couple of twists in when you're not expecting it.

2.3 PROJECTIONS

The Doctor starts confusing reality and illusion

TX 11 September 1995
WRITER Brannan Braga
DIRECTOR Jonathan Frakes
GUEST CAST Dwight Schultz (Barclay)

STARDATE 48892.1

The Doctor activates to discover the ship has been abandoned. Only Torres and Janeway are still on board, trying to prevent a warp core breach after a Kazon attack. The Doctor goes to the Bridge, using new holo-emitters, to help the Captain. He then saves Neelix from a Kazon – and discovers he is bleeding. The computer insists the Doctor is Lewis Zimmerman, his creator. When the holographic systems are shut down, everyone vanishes but the Doctor. Reg Barclay arrives. He is Zimmerman's assistant and they are orbiting Jupiter and there's been a kinoplasmic radiation surge. Voyager doesn't exist, it's simply a simulation. The way out of this is to let Voyager explode. The Doctor is talked round to this and is about to destroy the warp core, until Chakotay appears and warns him that there's a fault on the holodeck and the Doctor is about to kill himself. The Doctor hesitates, and passes the point where the ship would be destroyed. Chakotay is the real Chakotay. The Doctor returns to his Sickbay.

QUOTES

- 'I sometimes ask myself those kind of questions: who am I? What am I doing here? What's my purpose in life? Doesn't everybody?'
'Not me. I know exactly who I am and what my purpose is. I am the Emergency Medical Hologram aboard the Starship Voyager.'
– Kes and the Doctor

TRIVIA

- This is the first time we see Zimmerman, the Doctor's creator (also played by Robert Picardo).
- The Doctor refers to meeting 'banjo man' in *Caretaker* – this was a description in the script, not an expression used by any of the characters in the episode itself.

RATING

- An excellent episode that sets the scene for a number of future Doctor stories, and emphasises what a weird being he is.

2.4 ELOGIUM

Space creatures affect Kes and the ship

TX 18 September 1995

STARDATE 48921.3

The crew studies a swarm of space-dwelling life-forms, but their energy patterns disrupt the ships systems. Kes starts eating compulsively and then becomes delirious. Voyager can't find a way to move out of the way without hurting the aliens. The Doctor diagnoses Kes' condition as the 'elogium' – she has become fertile for the one

WRITERS Kenneth Biller and Jeri Taylor (story by Jimmy Diggs and Steve J Kay)
DIRECTOR Winrich Kolbe
GUEST CAST Terry Correll (Crew member #2), Nancy Hower (Wildman), Gary O'Brien (Crew member #1)

time in her life, and if she wants a child she has to do so now. Janeway isn't sure Voyager is a place for children. She asks Neelix to be the father, but he hesitates. He comes round to the idea, but now Kes isn't so sure. A larger version of the alien creatures arrives and tries to mate with the swarm. It sees Voyager as a rival. Chakotay suggests they act submissively. The plan works. The Doctor tells Kes that it wasn't her elogium after all, but a reaction to the swarm's electrophoretic field. Ensign Wildman discovers she is pregnant.

QUOTES

- 'Order the diapers, we're about to become parents!' – *Neelix*

TRIVIA

- Biller was responsible for the half of the script concerning the space creatures.
- The episode implies that Neelix and Kes' relationship hasn't been consummated.
- Ensign Samantha Wildman makes her first appearance. Her husband works on Deep Space Nine. We never see anyone named Wildman in that show, but it's a big station. Their baby was conceived on the stopover there in *Caretaker*. We learn he's a Ktaran (which may or may not be the same as the Ktarians, the race who tried to take over the Federation in *The Game*!) in *Dreadnought*. The stardate of the episodes suggest that was roughly three months ago. She has the baby in Deadlock, on stardate 49548.7, which seems consistent with a nine-month pregnancy, although *Cold Fire* (stardate 49164.8) is apparently 'ten months' after *Caretaker*. This is Wildman's first pregnancy (*Tattoo*).
- Jimmy Diggs named Wildman after a young organ donor whose organs were used to save the life of his wife.
- Some fans have objected that if Ocampan women only give birth once, then the Ocampan population would halve every generation. This would only be true if the Ocampan population, like the human one, was split roughly evenly between the two sexes. If there were twice as many women as men (and all the women had children), the generations would stay a stable size.

RATING

- A premise that makes you wonder if the people making it even watch the show. At what point did they think this was going to work? How soon were they disabused of the notion? Not the worst episode of *Voyager*, but a showcase for *Voyager* at its very worst.

2.5 NON SEQUITUR

Harry Kim wakes up on Earth, and discovers he's never been on Voyager

TX 25 September 1995
WRITER Brannon Braga
DIRECTOR David Livingston
GUEST CAST Jennifer Gatti (Libby), Louis Giambalvo (Cosimo), Mark Kiely (Lasca), Jack Shearer (Strickler)

STARDATE 49011

Harry wakes up on Earth, and even though yesterday he was on Voyager, neither his girlfriend nor friends like coffee shop-owner Cosimo are surprised to see him. He's out of his depth, and blows an important presentation to senior Admirals. Harry says he is ill, and does some research. He never served on Voyager, neither did Paris. He tracks him down to the real bar Sandrine's that's the model for Paris's holodeck version. Paris is a loser who doesn't know Harry, although he's interested in a version of history where he redeemed himself. Harry is arrested on suspicion of working with the Maquis and has a tracking device fitted. Cosimo tells him he's watching out for him – he's an alien, and Harry was in a shuttle that intersected one of their timestreams. He's living the life he would have done. Harry and Paris take a shuttle and recreate the accident. Harry arrives back in his original shuttlecraft.

TRIVIA

- The story uses the same New York street set that stands in for New Orleans in *Deep Space Nine*. Footage from *Star Trek IV: The Voyage Home* is used in establishing shots. The scene with the spacedock doors is footage originally used in *Relics*.
- Jennifer Gatti had auditioned to play Kes, having previously played a Klingon in *Birthright*.

RATING

- A good episode, although as with every visit *Star Trek* makes to Earth, you wish you could see a bit more. It's unclear, beyond a bit of lip service to Harry's loyalty to the crew, why he wants to leave his good job and beautiful fiancée to go back to see Tuvok and Neelix bickering, though, and they miss a trick by never really answering that question. It might have been more interesting to see Harry planning to settle back on Earth, then being wrenched back to the Delta Quadrant.

2.6 TWISTED

STARDATE UNKNOWN

Voyager's layout becomes jumbled up by an anomaly

TX 2 October 1995
WRITERS Kenneth Biller (story by Arnold Rudnick and Rich Hosek)
DIRECTOR Kim Friedman
GUEST CAST Terry Correll (Crewman), Judy Geeson (Sandrine), Larry Hankin (Gaunt Gary), Tom Virtue (Baxter)

Voyager hits a spatial distortion wave that cuts off sections of the ship and rearranges its layout. This quickly confuses the crew and interferes with its running. They organise into teams to search for key areas of the ship. The distortions start swallowing up crewmen. Janeway is knocked out when she comes into contact with a distortion. Tuvok theorises that the ship is turning in on itself and is going to be crushed in an hour. Torres attempts a warp shock pulse, but that just speeds up the process. Tuvok suggests that the anomaly might sort itself out. It does. Janeway recovers and reports that it was an attempt to communicate. The wave moves away, and they discover they now have a larger computer database.

QUOTES

- 'When every logical course of action is exhausted, the only option that remains is inaction.' – *Tuvok*

TRIVIA

- As ever with Federation starships, the Bridge is on deck 1. We learn here that the holodecks are on deck 6 and that Engineering is on deck 11.
- The anomaly somehow expands Voyager's computer memory by adding twenty billion gigaquads of new data. But this is never referred to again, so we'll never know what the new data was, or why it was put there.

RATING

- As with *Projections*, it's a bottle show, and it consists of characters wandering through doors to discover they aren't in the set they thought they would be. But it's actually quite a strong episode, with the crew getting steadily more frustrated.

2.7 PARTURITION

STARDATE 49068.5

Love rivals Neelix and Paris crash on an alien planet

TX 9 October 1995
WRITER Tom Szollosi
DIRECTOR Jonathan Frakes
GUEST CAST Majel Barrett (Computer Voice)

Paris falls for Kes after giving her flying lessons, and gets into a fight with Neelix. Janeway sends them both on a mission to find food supplies. They find a planet, but it's surrounded by trigemic vapours. They are forced to make an emergency landing. They shelter from the toxic atmosphere by sealing themselves in a cave. As Voyager moves to rescue them, it's attacked by an alien ship. Paris and Neelix find eggs, one of which hatches. The creature soon starts dying – it can only be revived by unsealing the cave. Looking after the alien, Neelix and Paris settle their differences. The aliens from the ship are the parents of the hatchlings. Neelix and Paris are beamed up to the ship and go for a drink together.

TRIVIA

- The stardate appears on the script, but not in the episode.
- The production team call the cave set – seen, shot from different angles with minor cosmetic variations, in *Star Trek* since the early days of *The Next Generation* – the 'Planet Hell' set. Paris uses the nickname here.

RATING

- A straightforward story with one of those ridiculously contrived premises that plague episodic television, and *Star Trek* in particular. Two characters suddenly have a dispute, they end up alone together, they have to rely on each other, they resolve their dispute. As it goes, it's an OK episode, but it's all very throwaway.

2.8 PERSISTENCE OF VISION

STARDATE UNKNOWN

The crew's deepest desires surface

Janeway relaxes in a holonovel before being called to the Bridge to make first contact with the Botha, who aren't sure whether to let Voyager through their territory. Janeway starts seeing characters from

TX 30 October 1995
WRITER Jeri Taylor
DIRECTOR James L Conway
GUEST CAST Michael Cumpsty (Lord Burleigh), Thomas Alexander Dekker (Henry), Lindsey Haun (Beatrice), Marva Hicks (T'Pel), Stan Ivar (Mark), Patrick Kerr (Bothan), Warren Munson (Admiral Paris), Carolyn Seymour (Mrs Templeton)

the holonovel in the corridors. Unable to trust her own eyes, Janeway puts Chakotay in charge of the Bothan situation. Aliens attack the ship. When an alien appears on the screen, each crewman sees someone from home. Torres diagnoses the problem as a psychoactive trance, a result of a bio-electric field from the alien ship. Kes can use her telepathy to resist and the Doctor is immune. Together, they block the force. The alien is telepathic, and admits responsibility, but flies off without further explanation. Voyager continues on its way.

TRIVIA

- In this episode Torres and Harry start fitting holoprojectors around the ship – the production team had got fed up of the Doctor being confined to Sickbay. Whenever his input was needed elsewhere, he'd appeared on viewscreens, not a terribly good way to get dramatic interaction with the rest of the crew. The next episode, *Tattoo*, sees the Doctor altering his programming so he no longer automatically says 'Please state the nature of the medical emergency' when he's activated. It's not the last time he says it, though – it's explained later that he's not sure how else to start a conversation!
- MTV VJ Kennedy has a cameo non-speaking part as a crewman.
- Although some reference sources state the alien is a Bothan, that's never stated on screen.

RATING

- A story that's not wildly different from *Projections*, which wasn't that long ago. The motivations of the Bothans are completely unknown, which makes for a rather unsatisfying ending.

2.9 TATTOO

STARDATE UNKNOWN

Chakotay discovers a planet with links to his ancestors

TX 6 November 1995
WRITER Michael Piller (story by Larry Brody)
DIRECTOR Alexander Singer
GUEST CAST Richard Chaves (Chief), Henry Darrow (Kolopak), Richard Fancy (Alien), Nancy Hower (Wildman), Joseph Palmas (Antonio), Douglas Spain (Young Chakotay)

Chakotay finds symbols like some he once saw in Central America on a planet that appears to be uninhabited, and his mind goes back to the original symbols that he found with his father, Kolopak. The Away Team finds an abandoned village, and seem to provoke a violent storm by laying down their weapons. They beam back, but Chakotay is left behind to meet the inhabitants, who speak the same language as his ancestors. When they recognise him as one of 'The Inheritors', Chakotay realises these are the Sky Spirits of his people's legends. They came to Earth 45,000 years ago, but when they returned, The Inheritors had all but been wiped out. They feared Voyager had come to attack them. Chakotay explains that mankind has moved on, and the aliens give him valuable minerals. Chakotay returns to the ship, with new respect for the ways of his people.

QUOTES

- 'I'm tired of the whining, cranky attitudes we see around here. I intend to serve as an example of how one's life and duties do not have to be disrupted by simple illness.' – *The Doctor lays down the law*

TRIVIA

- Chakotay says here that 'Captain Sulu', a Starfleet Captain patrolling the Cardassian border, recommended him for entry to Starfleet Academy. If this is Sulu from the original series, he'd be well over 100 years old, but it's been established that humans can live that long by the twenty-fourth century (McCoy's seen in *Encounter at Farpoint*). That Sulu's still a captain 60 years after taking command of Excelsior isn't necessarily a problem either – he could have been demoted, like Kirk, or chosen to stay a Captain, like Picard (who, as of *Star Trek: Nemesis*, has held the rank of Captain for 46 years). As there's a USS Excelsior mentioned in *Inheritance*, and we know that Excelsior-class ships are still in service in the era of *The Next Generation*. There's even a chance that Hikaru Sulu still commanded the same ship as he did in *Star Trek VI: The Undiscovered Country*. Chakotay says that the Sulu that recommended him was a 'he', ruling out Demora Sulu, Hikaru's daughter. But it's entirely possible that the Sulu in question is Hikaru's grandson or great-grandson. Janeway talks about Sulu in the past tense in *Flashback* – but then, that's over 20 years after Chakotay would have been at the Academy.
- In *Initiations*, Chakotay's tribe was from the deserts of North America; here, it's from the Central American jungle.

RATING

- A weird balancing act – *Star Trek's* long-standing atheism and need for scientific explanation balanced with a distinctly New Age/made-up-as-they-go-along-having-watched-*Dances-With-Wolves* take on the Native Americans. Yet another Starfleet officer has issues with his father and rejected the traditions of his culture. A resolutely average episode.

2.10 COLD FIRE

STARDATE 49164.8

Voyager encounters some Ocampa who may have access to another Caretaker

TX 13 November 1995
WRITERS Brannon Braga (story by Anthony Williams)
DIRECTOR Cliff Bole
GUEST CAST Majel Barrett (Voice of Suspiria – uncredited), Gary Graham (Tanis), Norman Large (Ocampa man), Lindsay Ridgeway (Girl)

Fragments from the alien Caretaker that Voyager took on board when they were first trapped in the Delta Quadrant begin reacting to a mysterious energy source. They follow the energy trail, suspecting it might lead them to the female Caretaker that was mentioned then. They are fired on by a space station manned by Ocampa. Kes acts as a go-between and tells the Ocampa leader, Tanis, that they come in peace. Tanis tells her that Suspiria, the female Caretaker, is nearby, and has looked after the Ocampa for centuries, and developed their psychic powers. He tutors Kes, whose powers become dangerous when she ends up boiling Tuvok's blood. Suspiria tells Janeway she will destroy Voyager for killing her mate. Kes fights Tanis with her new abilities, giving Voyager enough time to escape.

QUOTES

- 'Hurt people, help them, give life, kill. It's all the same.' – *Tanis*

TRIVIA

- The stardate appears in the script, not the final episode.
- It's stated in this episode that the events of *Caretaker* took place ten months ago.

RATING

- An episode that doesn't feel as significant as it ought to – it picks up on hints given in *Caretaker*, it has big revelations about Kes, but it feels oddly inconsequential.

2.11 MANEUVERS

STARDATE 49208.5

Seska has allied with the Kazon, and she knows Voyager's secrets

TX 20 November 1995
WRITER Kenneth Biller
DIRECTOR David Livingston
GUEST CAST Anthony De Longis (Culluh), John Gegenhuber (Kelat), Martha Hackett (Seska), Terry Lester (Haron)

Voyager picks up a Federation signal, and is attacked by the Kazon, who seem expert in knowing how to cause the maximum damage. A boarding party steals a transporter module and escapes with it. Their leader, Culluh, tells them he's teamed up with Seska. Cullah hopes to unite rival factions of Kazon behind him using Federation technology. Chakotay, feeling responsible for bringing Seska aboard, sneaks off to set things right. He beams aboard the Kazon ship and destroys the module, but is captured and tortured. Culluh wants Voyager's command codes, and tells the Majes of the other factions he has them. Seska prevents Janeway from beaming Chakotay off their ship – but not the other Kazon Majes. Janeway exchanges Chakotay for them. Seska tells Chakotay that while he was her prisoner she extracted his DNA and is now pregnant with his child.

TRIVIA

- It's established that transporters can't be used when a ship is at warp – Torres suggests a solution to beam Chakotay out: synchronising the annular confinement beam with the frequency of the Kazon warp core. In *The Best of Both Worlds*, when an Away Team is sent across to a Borg ship, O'Brien says that it's simply a matter of getting the two ships to match speed.

RATING

- A fast-paced and effective episode, one where we start to see the trail Voyager is leaving in its wake.

2.12 RESISTANCE

STARDATE UNKNOWN

Janeway needs the help of a man who thinks she's his daughter

TX 27 November 1995
WRITER Lisa Klink (story by Michael Jan Friedman and Kevin J Ryan)
DIRECTOR Winrich Kolbe
GUEST CAST Joel Grey (Caylem), Glenn Morshower (Guard #1), Alan Scarfe (Augris), Tom Todoroff (Darod)

Janeway, Tuvok, Neelix and Torres are looking for tellerium in an Alsaurian city under the occupation of the brutal Mokra. Mokra soldiers capture Tuvok and Torres. Janeway is saved by Caylem, who seems to have her confused with his long-lost daughter. Chakotay begins planning a rescue. Janeway and Caylem do the same, trying to get weapons from the resistance movement, but it's a trap. They make their escape and get into the prison via access tunnels. Voyager is attacked by the Mokra. Caylem helps to free Tuvok and Torres, but discovers his wife and daughter are dead. He is shot, and Janeway pretends to be his daughter to comfort him in his last moments.

TRIVIA

- Kes and the Doctor aren't in this episode.

RATING

- A strange episode for Janeway, and it's tempting to imagine it was originally written for another character. Seeing her pretending to be a prostitute just seems wrong, somehow.

2.13 PROTOTYPE

STARDATE UNKNOWN

Torres reactivates a robot, and plunges the ship into a civil war

TX 15 January 1996
WRITER Nicholas Corea
DIRECTOR Jonathan Frakes
GUEST CAST Hugh Hodgin (6263), Rick Worthy (3947)

Torres beams a deactivated robot aboard and works hard to find the right power source to reactivate it. When she does so, the robot says it is 3947, a worker robot created by the extinct Pralor. It wants Torres to duplicate it, but Janeway invokes the Prime Directive. 3947 kidnaps Torres and takes her to a ship from Pralor, where it meets others of its kind. Voyager can't get past the subspace defences around the alien ship. The robots launch a savage attack on Voyager, and to stop this, Torres agrees to build the prototype robot wanted by the other robots. Each robot has a unique energy code, and Torres tries to standardise this. Another ship arrives and starts firing on the first. This ship also has a robot crew. Torres discovers that the Pralor and the Cravics both built robots to fight their war. When the two races declared a truce, the robots wiped them both out and continued their fight. Torres destroys her prototype robot and is rescued by Voyager. The robots continue their war.

TRIVIA

- Kenneth Biller did substantial uncredited writing work on the episode.
- Torres says that Data is the only android known to the Federation. She clearly hasn't watched much *Star Trek*.

RATING

- Jonathan Frakes had already told a convention audience that he wasn't keen on this episode before it was broadcast. It's a rare episode that's let down by design work, but while the script doesn't sparkle, the stiff, inexpressive robots really don't help.

2.14 ALLIANCES

STARDATE 49337.4

Janeway reluctantly tries to form an alliance with the Kazon

TX 22 January 1996
WRITER Jeri Taylor
DIRECTOR Les Landau

Voyager has been badly damaged after Kazon attacks. Chakotay urges Janeway to side with some Kazon factions, allowing easier passage through their territory. Neelix is sent to the planet Sobras to negotiate with the Kazon-Pommar while Janeway contacts Cullah's faction, the Kazon-Nistrim. Neither goes well – Culluh won't talk to a woman, Neelix is thrown in prison, where he meets Mabus, a Trabe whose people rescue him. Mabus explains that the Trabe once enslaved the Kazon, but there was an uprising. Janeway forms an alliance with the Trabe, and calls a conference to negotiate a ceasefire between the

GUEST CAST Simon Billig (Hogan), Larry Cedar (Tersa), Anthony De Longis (Culluh), John Gegenhuber (Kelat), Martha Hackett (Seska), Charles O Lucia (Mabus), Raphael Sbarge (Michael Jonas), Mirron E Willis (Rettik)

Trabe and all the Kazon Majes. The pregnant Seska and Culluh attend, planning to wipe out the Trabe leadership and hijack Voyager. Janeway realises Culluh is likely to sabotage the conference, but she's not expecting the Trabe to attack. The Kazon factions think Janeway has betrayed them. Voyager's interference in the politics of the Quadrant has made their situation far worse.

QUOTES

- 'It's hard to imagine it getting much worse.' – *Janeway hasn't seen what the next episode is, yet*

TRIVIA

- Culluh died in the first draft of the script.

RATING

- An episode that perhaps deserved to be a running plot over a few episodes. As it is, it's a story that serves as unequivocal demonstration that the Prime Directive is a good thing, rather than what could have been a much more interesting exploration of the compromises and temptation to abandon their principles that ought to plague the crew.

2.15 THRESHOLD

STARDATE 49373.4

Paris breaks the Warp 10 barrier... then he and Janeway turn into salamanders

TX 29 January 1996
WRITERS Brannon Braga (story by Michael DeLuca)
DIRECTOR Alexander Singer
GUEST CAST Raphael Sbarge (Michael Jonas), Mirron E Willis (Rettik)

Paris pilots a specially adapted shuttle, the Cochrane, and in a historic flight, he breaks the transwarp threshold, hitting Warp 10 – infinite speed. He returns and appears fine, if a little awestruck by his experience. Crewman Jonas secretly sends details of the flight to the Kazon. Paris collapses, and the Doctor diagnoses massive changes in Paris' body. He stops breathing air, and despite the Doctor's best efforts, he dies. Hours later, he gets up... and now he has two hearts. He becomes paranoid and violent, and continues to evolve into the ultimate form of life. He kidnaps Janeway, and steals the Cochrane. They make a Warp 10 journey to a jungle planet. By the time Voyager catches up, they have mutated into amphibious creatures and mated. The offspring are left behind on the planet, while the Doctor is able to stabilise Janeway and Paris' DNA and return them to normal using antiproton radiation. Both are rather embarrassed by their adventures.

QUOTES

- 'Just asleep? Can you wake him?'
  'I believe so. (Shouts) Wake up, Lieutenant!' – *The Doctor revives Paris*
- 'I have to admit I'm not sure which one is the Captain.'
  'The female... obviously.' – *Chakotay and Tuvok*

TRIVIA

- In the script, the shuttle was called the Drake, but that name had already been used in *Non Sequitur*.

RATING

- The worst episode in the whole of the *Star Trek* canon? It almost certainly was up to this point. This was the exact point some of the most devout *Star Trek* fans gave up on *Voyager*, and it's not hard to see why – this even manages to break the 'worse than *Elogium*' barrier. An appalling idea for a story, very badly put together. To rub salt in the wound, the characters spend the first half saying they're making history, and the producers and actors said that it wasn't as bad as people made out.

2.16 MELD

STARDATE UNKNOWN

Tuvok investigates a murder onboard

Crewman Darwin has been murdered, and Tuvok starts an investigation. Suder, a Maquis Betazoid, is quickly identified via DNA and confesses that Darwin simply annoyed him. Tuvok can't accept that as motivation

TX 5 February 1996
WRITER Michael Piller (story by Michael Sussman)
DIRECTOR Cliff Bole
GUEST CAST Simon Billig (Hogan), Angela Dohrmann (Ricky), Brad Dourif (Suder)

for murder, but Suder can't come up with a better reason. Tuvok mind-melds with Suder, and realises that Suder is a psychopath. The meld seems to calm Suder a little, but later, Tuvok gets angry with Neelix and strangles him... in a holodeck simulation. Tuvok tells Janeway he's no longer fit for duty, and she has the Doctor treat him. But Tuvok escapes from Sickbay and goes to execute Suder. Tuvok gains enough self-control to stop himself. He returns to Sickbay to complete his rehabilitation.

QUOTES

- 'I didn't like the way he looked at me' – *Suder explains his motive*

TRIVIA

- Sussman's story, called *Genocide*, was about Tuvok melding with a racist alien, which gave vent to Tuvok's own repressed feelings about humans.
- This is the last time we see Ricky, a female holocharacter Paris said in *The Cloud* appears in all his holodeck simulations (but who patently doesn't).
- Brad Dourif has been a memorable presence in many films, including *Dune* (1984), *Alien Resurrection* (1997) and *The Two Towers* (2002), where he played Grima Wormtongue.

RATING

- Brad Dourif is always good value as an SF loony, and he helps make this episode really rather entertaining. Tuvok's sheer incomprehension at Suder's irrational violence is well played. The holodeck Neelix scene cheats the audience, though.

2.17 DREADNOUGHT

STARDATE 49447.0

Torres has to defuse a Cardassian missile she once reprogrammed

TX 12 February 1996
WRITERS Gary Holland and Lisa Klink (story by Gary Holland)
DIRECTOR LeVar Burton
GUEST CAST Roxann Biggs-Dawson (Voice of Dreadnought – uncredited), Nancy Hower (Wildman), Dan Kern (Kellan), Raphael Sbarge (Michael Jonas), Michael Spound (Lorum)

Voyager discovers a massive Cardassian missile, the Dreadnought, heading for a populated planet, Rakosa. Torres admits that it's one she and Chakotay captured and reprogrammed when she was in the Maquis. Jonas informs the Kazon of the latest developments as Torres beams over to try to defuse the missile. She thinks she's succeeded, but it soon resumes its course. The Dreadnought's computer thinks it is in the Alpha Quadrant, and thinks Torres has been compromised by the Cardassians. Janeway makes contact with Rakosa, learning that two million people will die. She decides that if Torres can't defuse the warhead, she'll ram the missile with Voyager. Torres manages to reactivate the Cardassian program. As her program and the Cardassian one quarrel, she detonates the warhead. She's beamed back to Voyager as the Dreadnought explodes.

QUOTES

- 'When a bomb starts talking about itself in the third person, I get worried.' – *Paris*

TRIVIA

- If you want to destroy Voyager – and, who hasn't, at least once? – the self destruct sequence is activated using the code 'Janeway Pi-1-1-0'. *Jetrel* established that Voyager (unlike the Enterprise and Enterprise-D) doesn't use voice print identification.
- The missile contains an explosive payload of a thousand kilos of antimatter and a thousand kilos of matter. This makes it, essentially, a giant photon torpedo, but one capable of destroying a moon. It's unclear how many weapons like this the Cardassians had in their arsenal – Torres says this is 'one of them', so it isn't unique, but we never see any in *Deep Space Nine*. Torres reprogrammed it on stardate 47582, the same date as the second season *Deep Space Nine* episode *Whispers*.
- Kes refers to her uncle Elrem (or Elrond, as some fans insist they hear) – which is odd, because according to *Elogium*, Ocampan women can only have one child.

RATING

- An episode where Torres has to outwit herself. For a story that basically consists of Roxann Dawson talking to a wall for an hour, this is surprisingly effective, and there are some real moments of tension.

2.18 DEATH WISH

STARDATE 49301.2

A member of the Q Continuum wants to commit suicide, and Q is sent to stop him

TX 19 February 1996
WRITER Michael Piller (story by Shawn Piller)
DIRECTOR James L Conway
GUEST CAST John de Lancie (Q), Peter Dennis (Isaac Newton), Jonathan Frakes (Riker), Maury Ginsberg (Maury Ginsberg), Gerrit Graham (Q2)

When a comet sample is beamed aboard, it contains a Q, Q2. He bids the crew farewell... but instead of vanishing, he accidentally makes the male crewmembers vanish instead. Q turns up, and tells Janeway that the other Q was imprisoned for repeatedly trying to commit suicide. The Qs chase each other across the universe, with Voyager caught in the middle, until Janeway demands that they stop. She decides to hold an asylum hearing. Tuvok represents Q2. Q argues that the Continuum will be affected if Q2 dies, and demonstrates the effect he's had on the universe by summoning a hippy, Isaac Newton and Will Riker. Q2 argues that the Continuum is a wasteland, and he can't face living there any longer. Janeway grants his request for asylum, but urges him to try to experience mortal life. Q2 names himself Quinn. In the morning, though, Quinn is dead. Q admits that he supplied Quinn with Nogatch hemlock.

QUOTES

- 'You have been many things... a rude, interfering, inconsiderate sadistic – ' 'You've made your point.' ' – pest. And, oh yes, you introduced us to the Borg. Thank you very much. But one thing you have never been is a liar.' 'I think you've uncovered my one redeeming virtue. Am I blushing?' – *Janeway and Q*

TRIVIA

- The other Q is called Q2 in the script, but on-screen he's simply another 'Q'.
- The writers liked the name of the actor playing the hippy character so much that they changed the character's name to match it. So Maury Ginsberg plays Maury Ginsberg, but doesn't play himself.
- This is the first of three appearances by Q in *Voyager*, the later episodes being *The Q and the Grey* and *Q2*.
- The female Q's remark on seeing Torres that she's 'always liked female Klingons' is an in-joke. Suzie Plakson played K'Ehleyr, the mother of Worf's child in *The Next Generation*, who believed herself to be the only Klingon/Human hybrid.
- In a similiar vein, Q's remark that if it wasn't for him, Tuvok would have ended up Chief Engineer on the Enterprise is a cute in-joke on the fact that Tim Russ was second choice to play Geordi LaForge in *The Next Generation*.
- The original intention was to use Geordi, not Riker, but LeVar Burton had shaved his head for another role. Jonathan Frakes (who had a production office not far from the *Star Trek* set) was happy to return as Riker.

RATING

- A very entertaining episode with an interesting dilemma at the heart of it and a sting in the tail. The Qs and Riker steal the show. The writers tie themselves in all sorts of knots when they realise that both Qs could just click their fingers and get Voyager home, and even if they didn't, Riker could have told Starfleet the ship survived (Q promises to wipe his memory).

2.19 LIFESIGNS

STARDATE 49504.3

The Doctor falls in love

TX 26 February 1996
WRITER Kenneth Biller
DIRECTOR Cliff Bole
GUEST CAST Susan Diol (Denara Pel), Rick Gianasi (Gigolo), Martha Hackett (Seska), Raphael Sbarge, (Michael Jonas), Michael Spound (Lorum)

Voyager beams aboard a Vidiian woman who's dying from the Phage. The Doctor puts her body into stasis and creates a holographic body for her as she would be without the disease. She is Denara Pel, a fellow doctor. Torres remembers her treatment at the hands of the Vidiians, and only grudgingly donates the tissue that will help Pel. While they see if it works, the Doctor and Pel spend a lot of time together. The Doctor falls for her, but is clumsy at expressing it. Paris advises the Doctor, who takes Pel on a date on the holodeck. But Pel is rejecting the graft. She doesn't want to go back to her diseased body, but the Doctor convinces her she will help her people if she lives. Voyager takes her home, and she and the Doctor share a last dance.

QUOTES

- 'Mr Paris, I assume you've had a great deal of experience being rejected by women?' – *The Doctor asks for advice*

TRIVIA

- The Doctor boasts in *Message in a Bottle* that he's had sexual relations. While it's never specified that his and Pel's relationship went that far, she would seem to be the only candidate (unless he's counting his holographic wife in *Real Life*). If he's not counting holograms, does that mean it's the phage-ravaged *real* Pel he has sex with?

RATING

- The inevitable 'Doctor in love' story, combined with the 'falling in love with someone who's sick or dying' love stories we get from time to time. It's a sweet episode, and Robert Picardo and Susan Diol have good chemistry.

2.20 INVESTIGATIONS

STARDATE 49485.2

Neelix uncovers a traitor

TX 13 March 1996
WRITER Jeri Taylor (story by Jeff Schnaufer and Ed Bond)
DIRECTOR Les Landau
GUEST CAST Simon Billig (Hogan), Raphael Sbarge (Michael Jonas), Jerry Sroka (Laxeth), Crown Prince Abdullah of Jordan (Crewman – uncredited)

Neelix learns that a crewman is leaving to join a Talaxian convoy – and is surprised to learn that it's Paris. Paris is soon taken hostage by the Kazon and Seska. Neelix realises someone on Voyager must have tipped off the Kazon, and investigates gaps in the communications log. Jonas spots him, but Neelix leaves before he can kill him. Tuvok and Neelix uncover evidence that Paris was the traitor. Janeway tells Neelix that Paris is working to uncover the traitor. Paris searches the Kazon ship, and finds that Jonas is the traitor, before escaping in a shuttle. Neelix unmasks Jonas, who falls to his death after a struggle. Paris returns a hero.

TRIVIA

- Some repeat runs (and episode guides) put this episode before *Lifesigns*, but it sets up the Kazon trap seen in this story, and the original broadcast order got it right.
- Seska's baby (conceived in *Maneuvers* around stardate 49208.5.) is due in a month. She's had it by *Basics*, the second episode of which takes place on stardate 50023.4 – that's a maximum term of less than 814.9 stardate units. This means her pregnancy has been a lot shorter than Wildman's, who conceived shortly before stardate 48307.5 and finally gives birth in the next episode on stardate 49548.7 (1241.2 units).
- The teaser features the then-Crown Prince, now King, Abdullah of Jordan as a non-speaking crewman.

RATING

- An episode that trades on the character conflict that we were promised would be a feature of the show. It's all a trick, but it's a good episode, that really gives the sense of Voyager being a community that's having a lasting effect on the Quadrant.

2.21 DEADLOCK

STARDATE 49548.7

Voyager is badly damaged, but all is not as it seems

TX 18 March 1996
WRITER Brannon Braga
DIRECTOR David Livingston
GUEST CAST Simon Billig (Hogan), Bob Clendenin (Vidiian Surgeon), Keythe Farley (Vidiian #2), Nancy Hower (Samantha Wildman), Chris Johnston (Vidiian #1), Ray Proscia (Vidiian Commander)

Voyager enters a plasma cloud to escape the Vidiians, but the warp engines stall and a proton burst cracks the hull. Harry is sucked out into space, Wildman's new baby dies and the ship is forced onto emergency power. But then Wildman's baby is fine and there's a second Kes onboard. A divergence field has formed a spatial scisson that has duplicated Voyager, but not its antimatter. So only one ship can survive. The two Janeways meet, and the Captain of the most damaged ship suggests they self-destruct her Voyager. The Vidiians raid one of the Voyagers, harvesting the crew's organs. The duplicate Janeway sends Harry and Wildman's baby to the other ship, and sacrifices her ship.

QUOTES

- 'It's all a little weird.'
  'Mr Kim, we're Starfleet officers. Weird is part of the job.' – *Harry and Janeway*

TRIVIA

- It's never specified on screen which Voyager is the 'original'. However, the production team have since clarified that the original survived. From now on, that means that Harry and Ensign Wildman's baby are actually exact duplicates of the originals.

RATING

- Harry dies again! The moment Harry dies, you know that the reset switch is going to be flicked at some point, and this episode is never quite sure whether to play that as a surprise or not.

2.22 INNOCENCE

STARDATE 49578.2

Tuvok must look after a group of children

TX 8 April 1996
WRITER Lisa Klink (story by Anthony Williams)
DIRECTOR James L Conway
GUEST CAST Richard Garon (Bennet), Marnie McPhail (Alcia), Tahj D Mowry (Corin), Sarah Rayne (Elani), Tiffany Taubman (Tressa)

Tuvok's shuttle hits electrodynamic turbulence and crashes on a moon, killing the other crewman onboard, Bennet. There is a group of frightened children already marooned there. On Voyager, Janeway meets the Prelate of Drayan II, who has minerals they need. Tuvok tries to repair the shuttle, and learns the children are worried about a creature on the planet, the morrok. When a Drayan search party arrives, it's clear they are even more frightened of them. Tuvok helps them hide from the Drayans. Janeway is told about the crashed shuttle by the Drayans, who tell them the moon is sacred ground. Two of the children have disappeared by the time Janeway and Paris arrive to pick up Tuvok. He is surprised to learn that the last child, Alcia, is 96 years old and has come here to die of old age. The Drayan ageing process is the reverse of the norm. Tuvok stays with Alcia during her dying moments.

TRIVIA

- It's stated here that the warp core can go three years without refuelling. Gratifyingly, the writers remember this in the fourth season, when it becomes a problem.

RATING

- Not a particularly good episode, not a particularly bad one. We don't really get much insight into Tuvok, though; we merely see him being a bit uncomfortable.

2.23 THE THAW

STARDATE UNKNOWN

A deadly clown feeds on the crew's fear

TX 29 April 1996
WRITER Joe Menosky (story by Richard Gadas)
DIRECTOR Marvin V Rush
GUEST CAST Tony Carlin (Kohl Physician), Thomas Kopache (Viorsa), Michael McKean (The Clown), Shannon O'Hurley (Kohl Programmer), Patty Maloney (Little Woman), Carel Struycken (Spectre)

Voyager discovers five hibernation pods on Kohl – two of the people inside are dead, and the Doctor says they died of fear. Harry and Torres hope to revive the others, but become connected to the pods and enter a dream state. This resembles a carnival, run by an evil clown. The clown depends on fear, and won't let Harry or Torres wake up so he can harness their terror. The Doctor is sent to negotiate, but the clown kills one of the other hibernating people. Janeway offers herself for the other captives. It's a trick – 'Janeway' is really a holographic image. With no fear to sustain him, the clown vanishes.

TRIVIA

- Harry plays his clarinet in the teaser, in a scene originally written for *Death Wish*, but cut for time.

RATING

- An episode that some of the cast, crew and fans really like, but it's hard to see why – it's not half as scary as it thinks it is, it's hugely derivative, and it's utterly predictable.

2.24 TUVIX

STARDATE 49655.2

A transporter accident merges Tuvok and Neelix

When Tuvok and Neelix beam back from a mission looking for nutritional plants, they are replaced by one being with both their memories. He christens himself Tuvix. The Doctor can't separate him out again, and Tuvix starts to settle in. Kes is unsettled by this new

TX 6 May 1996
WRITER Kenneth Biller (story by Andrew Shepard Price and Mark Gaberman)
DIRECTOR Cliff Bole
GUEST CAST Simon Billig (Hogan), Bahni Turpin (Swinn), Tom Wright (Tuvix)

being's love for her. Over the next couple of weeks, Tuvix settles into his new role, but the Doctor discovers a way to separate Neelix and Tuvok. Tuvix doesn't want to die, and the Doctor refuses to kill him without his consent. Janeway decides that the procedure must take place, and Tuvix is dragged from the Bridge to Sickbay, where Janeway does the deed. Tuvok and Neelix are restored.

QUOTES

- 'Lysosomal enzymes are often a sign of symbiogenesis.' – *The Doctor. No doubt the audience were one step ahead of him*
- 'All right, everybody out.' 'On whose authority?' 'Chief of Security or Head Chef. Take your pick.' – *Tuvix clears out the Mess Hall.*

TRIVIA

- The episode had the working title *Symbiogenesis.*
- Tuvix lives for two weeks.

RATING

- A stupid idea, but the episode hints that there is a great story to be had from the moral dilemma, and Tom Wright is instantly likeable and memorable. Merging two one-dimensional characters makes one interesting and rounded one. Unfortunately, the episode drops the ball by deciding to focus first on the technobabble that created him, and then on Tuvix's personality, revealing he's basically a more happy-go-lucky Tuvok who can cook. It would have been much better to focus on the other crewmembers, seeing them either befriending him or avoiding him. As it is, no one stands up for him at the end on the grounds they actually like him, and the ending is sadistic rather than sad. Fans debated Janeway's actions for years to come, but this is perhaps a symptom of problems with the way the ending is written and staged rather than any philosophical issues at its core.

2.25 RESOLUTIONS

STARDATE 49690.1

Janeway and Chakotay contract a deadly disease that forces them into quarantine

TX 13 May 1996
WRITER Jeri Taylor
DIRECTOR Alexander Singer
GUEST CAST Simon Billig (Hogan), Susan Diol (Denara Pel), Bahni Turpin (Powell)

On an Away Mission, Janeway and Chakotay are bitten by insects and infected with a virus. The progression of the virus is blocked by the atmosphere of the planet, but they'll die if they go back to Voyager. Janeway puts Tuvok in command and orders him to abandon them. The rest of the crew want to find the Vidiians, whose medical knowledge may include a cure, but Tuvok refuses. A plasma storm dashes any hope of Janeway finding a cure for herself, and she and Chakotay resign themselves to staying on the planet and grow closer. Tuvok has relented, and they contact the Doctor's Vidiian friend, Denara Pel, who has the cure. But the other Vidiians attack Voyager. Pel sends the serum over, and Voyager incapacitates the Vidiian ships. Janeway and Chakotay are rescued, and resume their more professional relationship.

TRIVIA

- A story designed to shut down the Unspoken Sexual Tension between Janeway and Chakotay, featuring the standard *Star Trek* way of getting two people to admit their true feelings for each other – marooning them and giving one or both of them a fatal condition.

RATING

- Like the next story, *Resolutions* is about shutting down a running story as much as anything else. Some fans liked the will-they-won't they Janeway/Chakotay relationship, but it was never really brought centre-stage, and often appeared as if the writers and actors were rather half-hearted about it. This is a 'business' episode, then, and works well enough in those terms, although it has to make Janeway rather hapless for the story to work.

2.26 BASICS Part I

STARDATE UNKNOWN

The Kazon take command of Voyager

Tuvok continues to try to rehabilitate Suder, the murderer. Chakotay gets a message from Seska, telling him their son is going to be taken away by Culluh. He fears a trap, but feels he owes the child his help. Voyager sets

TX 20 May 1996
WRITER Michael Piller
DIRECTOR Winrich Kolbe
GUEST CAST Henry Darrow (Kolopak), Anthony De Longis (Culluh), Brad Dourif (Suder), John Gegenhuber (Tierna), Martha Hackett (Seska)

out to help Seska, and intercepts a Kazon shuttle belonging to Tierna, an ally of Seska, who tells the crew Culluh has had the Cardassian killed. Voyager goes to the colony where the son is being held, and is attacked by the Kazon *en route*. They are being lead into a trap, so Janeway decides to attack the lead ship. Tierna commits suicide, setting off a massive explosion that leaves Voyager vulnerable. Paris gets away in a shuttlecraft, but Janeway is forced to surrender. Culluh and Seska take command and land the ship on a primitive planet. They abandon the crew there, and leave in Voyager. On board, there's only the Doctor and Suder...

TRIVIA

- There were rumours that the crew would spend the next season, or a good part of it, eking out a living on the planet's surface.
- Michael Piller had returned to the show after a stint on the short-lived *Legend* with a new sense of how modern television was made and paced. He pushed to make the show more like *ER*, with shorter scenes, a more frenetic pace and more running and character-driven stories. This clearly led to tensions between himself and Brannon Braga, who agreed that the show wasn't working, but felt that the solution was more standalone, high concept, challenging science fiction stories. He felt that the running stories like Tom pretending to be a traitor had detracted from otherwise fine episodes. Jeri Taylor's public comments at the time seem to suggest she sided firmly with Braga. The decision was made to lose running elements like the Kazon, Vidiians and some of the more prominent 'other crewmen', like Hogan and Suder. While Piller felt that the crew should become more desperate as time went on, many of the others on the production team felt they should be adapting to their situation. The year also saw the making of *Star Trek: First Contact*. Michael Piller had written a story for the seventh movie, but Ronald Moore and Braga's script had been chosen instead. They were also picked to write the eighth movie. Piller wasn't happy, feeling that they had concentrated on their first film to the detriment of the seventh season of *The Next Generation*. He felt the same was happening on *Voyager*. Michael Piller left the series at the end of the second season.
- As with the previous year, episodes were filmed as part of this season, but held back until the beginning of the next. These were (in production order) *Sacred Ground, False Profits, Flashback and Basics Part II.*

RATING

- An episode that actually feels like the show that was referred to in all the pre-publicity. Conflict and tension within the crew, actions with consequences, effective villains, and a crew hopelessly alone. The best episode of the series up to this point.

STAR TREK: VOYAGER
SEASON THREE

3.1 BASICS Part II

The crew must survive on a hostile planet and somehow regain control of Voyager

TX 4 September 1996
WRITER Michael Piller
DIRECTOR Winrich Kolbe
GUEST CAST Michael Bailey Smith (Alien #1), Simon Billig (Hogan), David Cowgill (Alien #2), Anthony De Longis (Culluh), Brad Dourif (Suder), Martha Hackett (Seska), Scott Haven (Kazon Engineer), Nancy Hower (Wildman)

STARDATE 50023.4

The Doctor tells Seska her child is Culluh's, not Chakotay's. He also discovers Suder on board, and they try to come up with a strategy to retake Voyager... but Tuvok's treatment of Suder's aggression has been so effective, he's unwilling to hurt any Kazon. On the primitive planet, the crew face the humanoid natives and dangerous eel-like monsters. Paris heads to Voyager with a group of Talaxians. The Doctor is deactivated by Seska before he can deactivate the phasers, but Suder manages it, before being killed by the Kazon. Paris boards Voyager after attacking the bridge. Seska is killed, Culluh and the baby – Cullah's, not Chakotay's – escape. Paris rescues the crew from the primitive planet and they resume course for home.

QUOTES

- 'I'm a doctor, not a counterinsurgent' – *The Doctor protests*

TRIVIA

- This is the last appearance of the Kazon. Like the Ferengi, they'd been the victims of high expectation and poor design – seen as the big recurring threat, the Kazon never caught on with the writers or audience. The writers' post mortem suggested they didn't have a goal or unifying principle, while the reaction on the internet seemed to concentrate more on their appearance, which was a little silly, while also being reminiscent of the Klingons.
- Jeri Taylor asked Michael Piller to remove elements of the show he championed but which she wasn't keen on. These included Seska and Suder, and Chakotay's baby with Seska, which turns out not to be Chakotay's baby after all.

RATING

- A rather predictable episode. Everything happens as you'd expect, and it is, in large part, an exercise in clearing the decks – Seska dies, but it's not clear why. But it's enjoyable, and for once it's cathartic when things are back to normal.

3.2 FLASHBACK

STARDATE 50126.4

Tuvok remembers his time serving with Captain Sulu

TX 11 September 1996
WRITER Brannon Braga
DIRECTOR David Livingston
GUEST CAST Michael Ansara (Kang), Boris Krutonog (Helmsman), Jeremy Roberts (Valtane), George Takei (Sulu), Grace Lee Whitney (Rand)

Tuvok suffers flashbacks when Voyager approaches a nebula it is searching for sirullium. Janeway agrees to mind-meld with Tuvok to try to discover the source of what seems to be a repressed childhood memory of him failing to save a girl from falling off a cliff. Instead of his memories leading there, Janeway and Tuvok find themselves in a memory of Tuvok's time on the USS Excelsior, 80 years ago. Captain Sulu is racing to the aid of Kirk and McCoy, who've been arrested by the Klingons. The ship passes a nebula like the one Voyager has encountered, and this time, Tuvok collapses. Tuvok can't think of a link between the girl and his time on Excelsior. They were ambushed by Klingons, and crewman Valtane was killed. The Doctor realises Tuvok has an alien virus that's disguised itself as a memory. He exposes Tuvok's brain to thoron radiation, and Tuvok recovers.

QUOTES

- 'There are times when I think back to those days of meeting Kirk, Spock and the others and I am pleased that I was part of it.' 'In a funny way, I feel like I was a part of it too.' – *Tuvok and Janeway*

TRIVIA

- This ties in with the events of *Star Trek VI: The Undiscovered Country*... sort of. In the movie, it's two months between the explosion on Praxis and Kirk and McCoy's imprisonment, whereas here they both seem to happen on the same day. Valtane is still alive at the end of the movie, but he dies before that here. A far more minor mistake is Janeway's assertion that there weren't plasma weapons in Sulu's time – there were in *Balance of Terror*.
- Nicholas Meyer is not credited for the footage from *Star Trek VI: The Undiscovered Country*.
- Juliann Medina had some (uncredited) input into the story.
- Nichelle Nichols turned down the chance to reprise the role of Uhura late in the day, and so the episode under-ran. Scenes with the regular cast were added to the start of the episode.

RATING

- This entirely lacks the wit and attention to detail that makes *Trials and Tribble-ations* such a great story. Reused footage from the movie is jarringly obvious – for one thing, Nicholas Meyer used a steadicam and David Livingston doesn't. The episode seems determined to demonstrate every flaw in *Voyager's* repertoire: it starts with an interminable scene in which Neelix tries to get Tuvok to drink fruit juice; it's slow – it's 20 minutes until we see Sulu (it's a great shot when we do); it's packed with technobabble and pseudo-psychology – the 'explanation' for Tuvok's flashbacks is gibberish; there's no humour – but there's a nebula and a hallucination and a repressed memory and an ill-defined threat. The prospect of a solo Sulu series has never been all that appetising, but the glimpses of him sparring with Kang here make it look like a banquet compared with the scenes on Voyager. And the irony is... this is actually one of the best episodes of the series.

3.3 THE CHUTE

STARDATE 50156.2

Paris and Harry are sent to a brutal prison

TX 18 September 1996
WRITER Kenneth Biller (story by Clayvon C Harris)
DIRECTOR Les Landau
GUEST CAST Don R McManus (Zio), Rosemary Morgan (Piri), Beans Morocco (Rib), Robert Pine (Liria), James Parks (Vel), Ed Trotta (Pit)

Paris and Harry are accused of planting a terrorist bomb on the planet Akritiri that killed 47 people and are sent down a metal chute to a brutal prison. They have a 'clamp' fitted that attaches to their nervous system. Janeway is told they had trilithium on their clothes, proof they had been in contact with the bomb. Paris is stabbed, and in return for his help, Harry promises to take another inmate, Zio, on an escape attempt. They climb to the top of the chute, and discover that they are on a space station. There's no chance of escape. Janeway unmasks the real bombers, but the authorities refuse to reverse the convictions of her officers. Janeway and Tuvok go to the prison, break out Harry and Paris and escape.

TRIVIA

- The other Delaney sister is named here: Megan.
- The episode had the working titles *Playground* and *The Pit*.

RATING

- There's a sub-genre of *Star Trek* stories where someone's framed for a crime they didn't commit and we see them struggling in a brutal prison. There's only one way for these stories to go, and *The Chute* duly goes there.

3.4 THE SWARM

STARDATE 50252.3

Aliens attack Voyager, and the Doctor loses his memory

TX 25 September 1996
WRITER Michael Sussman
DIRECTOR Alexander Singer
GUEST CAST Carole Davis (Diva), Steven Houska (Chardis), Robert Picardo (Doctor Lewis Zimmerman)

Aliens attack Paris and Torres' shuttle, injuring Paris, then vanish. Neelix knows about these aliens, who swarm over any intruder. Voyager continues into their territory, adjusting its shields to hide from the aliens' sensors. The Doctor is losing his memory, and the only way to restore it would be to reinitialise his program, which would wipe his personality. They go to the holodeck to consult a hologram of the Doctor's creator, Dr Zimmerman, who says that the program was only designed to run 1,500 hours before degrading. The aliens use a polaron burst to expose the ship, and swarm against it. The alien ships are all connected, though, and Voyager can set off a chain reaction. Kes and Torres graft Zimmerman's holomatrix onto the Doctor's – it works, but they can't be sure of the long-term effects.

QUOTES

- 'I can see where you get your charming personality.' 'Not to mention my hairline.' – *Torres and the Doctor meet Zimmerman*

TRIVIA

- The script called on the Doctor to sing an aria from *La Bohème*. Robert Picardo did his own singing for the episode.
- In this episode, the Doctor says his personality subroutine has grown to the point where it takes up 15,000 gigaquads of memory. This seems a lot smaller than *Lifesigns*, where he said he had a 50,000 gigaquad memory, but that seemed to be referring to his medical database, rather than his personality. Amusingly, the whole of Chakotay's consciousness only takes up 50 gigaquads in *Cathexis*. So, the Doctor has 300 times the personality of Chakotay. You can't really argue.

RATING

- This is an OK story, if a little obviously a bottle show to save money after an expensive start to the season.

3.5 FALSE PROFITS

STARDATE 50074.3

Two Ferengi lost in the Quadrant are posing as gods

Voyager heads for a system with evidence of an unstable wormhole, and quickly discovers signs of a replicator in use on the planet Takar. Chakotay and Paris go down to investigate, and discover two Ferengi,

TX 2 October 1996
WRITER Joe Menosky (story by George A Brozak)
DIRECTOR Cliff Bole
GUEST CAST Alan Altshuld (Sandalmaker), Michael Ensign (Bard), Leslie Jordan (Koll), Rob LaBelle (Kafar), Dan Shor (Arridor)

worshipped as gods in a religion based on greed which pays tributes to them. These are Kol and Arridor, two scientists who were trapped here seven years before (see *The Price*). Janeway beams them up to the ship, but the Ferengi convince her that if the gods of Takar just vanished, the society would collapse. Neelix is sent down to impersonate another Ferengi, but Kol and Arridor refuse to give up their profits. Voyager learns there's a prophecy that the gods will depart on wings of fire when three new stars appear in the sky (the Ferengi didn't know this, as you had to pay the Bard for every verse of the saga, and they thought that was a waste of money), and recreates the effect with a photon torpedo burst. The unstable wormhole opens, but the Ferengi steal a shuttle and fly into it, destabilising it before Voyager can follow.

TRIVIA

- As *The Price* ended with two Ferengi trapped in the Delta Quadrant, the only definite reference to the place prior to *Voyager* (that the Borg were from the Quadrant had been confirmed in the novels), it was inevitable that Voyager would bump into them.

RATING

- A fun episode, with some good jokes when we see the greed-related religion the Ferengi have created in their image, seemingly just to sell relics and icons to the faithful. While Janeway's concerned with the fate of the Takarians, we don't really get to know or care that much about them. And, to be honest, the Ferengi don't seem to be bad rulers – they aren't killing or oppressing people, only making them materially better off. As the Ferengi say, it's hard to see why it's any of Janeway's business.

3.6 REMEMBER

STARDATE 50203.1

Torres dreams that she is someone else

TX 9 October 1996
WRITER Lisa Klink (story by Brannon Braga and Joe Menosky)
DIRECTOR Winrich Kolbe
GUEST CAST Eve Brenner (Jora Mirell), Bruce Davison (Jareth), Charles Esten (Dathan), Athena Massey (Jessen), Eugene Roche (Jor Brel)

As Voyager takes some telepathic Enarans home, Torres has a series of dreams in which she is Korenna, a woman from Enara who loves Dathan, despite her father's disapproval. Chakotay wonders if this is connected to the Enarans' telepathy, and the Doctor confirms Torres is experiencing deliberately implanted memories. When Korenna is scarred in the next dream, Torres realises the old Enaran, Mirell, who bears the same scar, is Korenna. Her father hunted down the Regressives, Enarans who rejected technology, and she doesn't want that secret forgotten when she's dead. Korenna dies that night. Torres confronts the other Enarans, and one takes on the telepathic memories, so their people's past won't be lost.

TRIVIA

- From this episode, the actress playing Torres is, credited as Roxann Dawson, rather than Roxann Biggs-Dawson. Roxann Caballero married Casey Biggs (Damar in *Deep Space Nine*) in the mid-eighties, they divorced in the mid-nineties and she then married Eric Dawson, changing her stage name to Biggs-Dawson before dropping her previous married name from her stage name.

RATING

- The sort of episode Marina Sirtis always got lumbered with on *The Next Generation*. There are already plenty of *Star Trek* episodes that are almost the same. It's fine, but it's fundamentally about a bunch of characters we just don't care about.

3.7 SACRED GROUND

STARDATE 50063.2

Janeway must examine her faith to save Kes

TX 30 October 1996
WRITER Lisa Klink (story by Geo Cameron)
DIRECTOR Robert Duncan McNeill
GUEST CAST Becky Ann Baker (Guide), Parley Baer (Old Man #1), Keene Curtis (Old Man #2), Henry Groener (The Magistrate), Estelle Harris (Old Woman)

Kes is knocked out by an energy burst while visiting the shrine of the Nechisti Order on Nechani. The Doctor can't treat her, and the local Magistrate explains that only monks who have been through a purification ritual can survive the energy. Janeway asks to go through the ritual, and is impatient to start. She runs through a series of tests and rituals, including getting a bite from a poisonous creature, the nesset. Janeway comes to realise that she has to have faith – not in the rituals, but in her ability to save Kes. She takes Kes back through the energy field, even though all the sensor readings suggest that this will kill her. Kes recovers.

TRIVIA

- This story was Robert Duncan McNeill's debut a director, and one of Kate Mulgrew's favourites.

RATING

- A story that tries to keep things ambiguous, and to act as a critique of scientific certainty, but a story whose big character moment comes when Janeway decides to abandon rationality runs counter to the *Star Trek* Gene Roddenberry set up, where blind faith and obscure ritual were the problem, not the solution. Science certainly seems preferable to the sub-Castaneda New Age nonsense on offer here.

3.8 FUTURE'S END Part I

Voyager visits the twentieth century to prevent the destruction of Earth

TX 6 November 1996
WRITERS Brannon Braga and Joe Menosky
DIRECTOR David Livingston
GUEST CAST Ed Begley Jr (Henry Starling), Allan Royal (Braxton), Sarah Silverman (Rain Robinson)

STARDATE UNKNOWN

Voyager is fired on by the Aeon, a timeship from the twenty-ninth century commanded by Captain Braxton that blames Voyager for a temporal explosion that will wipe out Earth's star system in the future. Both ships are drawn into a temporal rift and arrive in Earth orbit in 1996. Voyager begins searching for the timeship, which has vanished. An astronomer, Rain, spots Voyager and sends them a greeting. Janeway and Chakotay find Braxton living rough – he crash-landed in 1967 and his technology was stolen by Henry Starling, who founded an electronics company. Starling wants to plan a time journey, and it's that which will destroy the Earth. Starling sends men to kill Rain, but Paris and Tuvok arrive and save her. Paris claims he's tracking down KGB agents, but Rain points out that the KGB no longer exists. Chakotay and Janeway find Braxton's timeship in Starling's office, but are caught. Starling isn't interested in their warnings, and they beam back to Voyager. They can't beam up the timeship, but Starling can use the timeship to access Voyager's database. He kidnaps the Doctor. The crew watch in horror as Voyager's arrival makes the evening news...

QUOTES

- 'Time travel. Since my first day on the job as a Starfleet Captain, I swore I'd never get let myself caught in one of these godforsaken paradoxes. The future is the past. The past is the future. It all gives me a headache.' – *Janeway*

TRIVIA

- Although they hadn't planned it at the time, these two-part, self-contained stories would become something of a Voyager tradition. UPN publicised them more than the standard episodes, and they always proved successful in the ratings.
- Janeway refers to a computer keyboard as being little better than 'stone knives and bearskins' – a nice reference back to Spock's assessment of twentieth century technology in *The City at the Edge of Forever*. She says she doesn't know about her ancestors in this era – she must do some research before *11.59*.
- Ed Begley Jr is as well known for his environmental campaigning as his acting – indeed, this role trades on the irony of him playing an evil industrialist.

RATING

- A witty script, clearly influenced by *Star Trek IV: The Voyage Home*. This is an entertaining and refreshingly light episode. The writers seem to be having some fun with the characters at last, and cutting loose a little.

3.9 FUTURE'S END Part II

The crew have to prevent a twentieth century industrialist causing disaster

TX 13 November 1996
WRITERS Brannon Braga and Joe Menosky

STARDATE 50312.5

Rain tries to lure Starling to a meeting, where the Voyager crew can ambush him. Starling shows up with the Doctor – who's now able to leave sickbay using a twenty-ninth century holo-emitter. The crew beam Starling to Voyager, but Chakotay and Torres crash a shuttle in the Arizona desert during the attempt and are captured by a survivalist group. Starling tells Janeway he wants to use the timeship to bring back even more advanced technology, and one of his men manages to

DIRECTOR Cliff Bole
GUEST CAST Ed Begley Jr (Henry Starling), Brent Hinkley (Butch), Clayton Murray (Porter), Allan Royal (Braxton), Sarah Silverman (Rain Robinson)

beam him back to his office. Tuvok and the Doctor rescue Torres and Chakotay, and they use the shuttle to destroy a truck they think has the timeship on it. But it's a trick – Starling has just launched the timeship. Starling refuses to stop, and Janeway fires on the timeship, destroying it. A time rift opens; Braxton tells them the future has been restored and he'll take them home. The Temporal Prime Directive prevents him from sending them back to arrive at Earth. The Doctor's pleased, though – he gets to keep his portable holo-emitter.

TRIVIA

- Tuvok, unlike Spock and T'Pol, isn't a vegetarian – he eats a burrito in this story.

RATING

- As with many two-parters, the second episode is far more mundane that the first, and basically just shuts down the story the first one set up. There's no great twist, and the ending feels like at least three cop-outs. But there are a couple of fun action scenes.

3.10 WARLORD

STARDATE 50348.1

Kes is possessed by a ruthless warlord

TX 20 November 1996
WRITER Lisa Klink (story by Andrew Shepard Price and Mark Gaberman)
DIRECTOR David Livingston
GUEST CAST Anthony Crivello (Adin), Charles Emmett (Resh), Galyn Gorg (Nori), Brad Greenquist (Demmas), Leigh J McCloskey (Tieran), Karl Wiedergott (Ameron)

Voyager rescues three Ilari, although one of them, Tieran, dies in Sickbay. Kes and Neelix soon split up, and Kes kills the Autarch of Ilari when he arrives on the ship. She steals a shuttle and takes it to a military camp. Kes has been possessed by Tiernan, a brutal former leader who has survived for centuries by possessing hosts. Tiernan declares himself Autarch. The Doctor designs a synaptic stimulator that will allow Kes' personality to resurface, but only has a short range. Tuvok attempts a mind-meld with Tiernan, and discovers Kes is already fighting for control. Tiernan becomes increasingly insecure and paranoid. The crew get Tiernan to leave Kes, then destroy him. Demmas, the rightful heir, becomes the new Autarch.

TRIVIA

- The Neelix/Kes relationship ends in this episode... but you'd be hard-pushed to notice. She's possessed by Tiernan at the time, and it's not made clear that her decision stands when she's back to normal. Over the years, the exact nature of their relationship seemed to vary from week to week – Neelix was always jealous and protective, but Kes would veer from wanting Neelix's baby in one episode to falling for Tom Paris a couple of episodes later.

RATING

- Another story that could have appeared in any era of *Star Trek*, with any characters. It's Jennifer Lien's turn to act evil, and it's enough of a contrast with Kes to make it quite interesting to watch, but it feels far more like a repeat than a new episode.

3.11 THE Q AND THE GREY

STARDATE 50384.2

Janeway is dragged into a civil war in the Q continuum

TX 27 November 1996
WRITER Kenneth Biller (story by Shawn Piller)
DIRECTOR Cliff Bole
GUEST CAST John de Lancie (Q), Suzie Plakson (female Q), Harve Presnell (Colonel Q)

Voyager witnesses a supernova, and shortly afterwards, Q arrives and declares he'd like Janeway to be the mother of his child. She refuses, even when Q gives her a puppy, and a jealous female Q turns up. Voyager sees a second and third supernova, and the crew start to suspect the Q are involved – supernovae are usually very rare. Q takes Janeway to the Q Continuum, which resembles the South in the American Civil War... the Q are at war. After Janeway allowed a Q to die the previous year (*Death Wish*), the old guard are fighting against the individualists. Spatial disruptions in the Continuum are so violent they are causing supernovae. Q wants a new generation of Q children with human qualities to end the war. Janeway suggests he mate with the female Q, and tries to negotiate a ceasefire, but she and Q end up in front of a firing squad. The cavalry arrive: the Voyager crew and the female Q. Q and the female Q mate and the Continuum becomes peaceful. Q asks Janeway to be the baby's godmother.

QUOTES

- 'What are you doing with that dog? I'm not talking about the puppy.' – *The female Q isn't too pleased to find Q giving gifts to Janeway*

TRIVIA

- Q redefines the concept of the long-term relationship: he's been 'involved' with the female Q for four billion years, and promises Janeway that foreplay with a Q can last decades. Although he also says later that the Q are 'way beyond sex'.
- We're told a supernova is an event that only happens every 100 years or so – in actuality, it seems that there will be one supernova every 200-300 years in a galaxy the size of ours. But as they are very bright, supernovae in other galaxies can be observed from Earth. Since 1980, one scientist, Robert Evans, has spotted 36 supernovae, an average of about two a year (and he once found three in 15 days).
- *Star Trek: First Contact* was released on the 22 November, just before this episode was broadcast. It was suggested at the time that Q was included here to attract members of *The Next Generation* audience whose appetite had been whetted by the film. Although, following that logic, you'd think they'd have brought back the Borg.

RATING

- When is a metaphor not a metaphor? The Q are meant to be omnipotent, but their civil war has all the awe, majesty and scale of a dull holodeck episode. John de Lancie holds the whole thing together in a performance that's good way beyond the call of duty in an episode that strains credibility to the limit with a resolution that's, essentially, just Janeway telling them to stop fighting and be nice. The first half – is great fun and the highlight is de Lancie's shameless face-pulling when the female Q turns up.

3.12 MACROCOSM

STARDATE 50425.1

The ship fights a giant virus

TX 11 December 1996
WRITER Brannon Braga
DIRECTOR Alexander Singer
GUEST CAST Michael Fiske (Garan miner), Albie Selznick (Tak Tak)

Janeway and Neelix return from a trade mission to the Tak Tak to Voyager to find it adrift. The ship has been overrun by venom-spitting monsters which get Neelix. Janeway arms herself, but is stung by the creatures. The Doctor explains that the ship has been attacked by a macrovirus they picked up from a mining colony. He has an antidote, but can't get near the crew to use it because the creatures are so vicious. Janeway tries to release the antidote into the air supply, but the ship is fired on by the Tak Tak, who don't want the virus to spread. Janeway sets off an antigen bomb, killing the macrovirus.

TRIVIA

- Somehow, the Voyager crew now have access to the phaser rifles that were just introduced in *Star Trek: First Contact*.
- Janeway refers to Neelix's 'lung' in this episode, a reminder of *Phage*.

RATING

- Janeway gets to 'do a Ripley' in a story clearly influenced by *Aliens*. It works, although it's never going to be as scary or relentless as the source material, and it's not a story that lends itself to thoughtfulness or optimistic philosophy of *Star Trek*.

3.13 FAIR TRADE

STARDATE UNKNOWN

Neelix becomes involved with a drug dealer

TX 8 January 1997
WRITER André Bormanis (story by Ronald Wilkerson and Jean Louise Matthias)
DIRECTOR Jesus Salvador Trevino
GUEST CAST Carlos Carrasco (Bahrat), Alexander Enberg (Vorik), James Horan (Tosin), Steve Kehela (Sutok), James Nardini (Wixiban)

Neelix asks an old friend, Wixiban, to get him a map of the Nekrit Expanse, the area of space Voyager is approaching, which is the absolute limit of his knowledge of the Quadrant. Wixiban went to prison for a crime he and Neelix committed, many years ago. Neelix accompanies Wix, but gets involved in a narcotics deal, and Wix murders a man with a phaser. Neelix keeps quiet, and Wix insists he steals warp plasma from Voyager. Paris and Chakotay are arrested for the murder. Neelix confesses, and he and Wix are allowed their freedom if they help entrap the main dealer, Tosin. Janeway realises that Neelix's motivation was to help the ship, but sentences him to two weeks cleaning the warp manifolds.

RATING

- A forgettable episode, one where you have to say that Neelix – a recidivist criminal who framed a friend, went drug-dealing with him and was an accessory to murder – gets off lightly at the end.

3.14 ALTER EGO

STARDATE 50460.3

Harry and Tuvok fall for a holodeck character

TX 15 January 1997
WRITER Joe Menosky
DIRECTOR Robert Picardo
GUEST CAST Alexander Enberg (the Vulcan), Sandra Nelson (Marayna), Shay Todd (the Holodeck woman)

The crew study an inversion nebula. Harry admits to Tuvok that he's fallen for a holodeck character, Marayna, and asks for help in controlling his emotions. Tuvok simply advises to avoid further contact with her. He later finds Tuvok talking to Marayna on the holodeck. Harry is annoyed with Tuvok, who decides that the best course is to delete Marayna. He does so, but when he returns to his quarters, Tuvok finds her there. There is some link between this and the nebula, and Tuvok finds a space station in the nebula with an uplink to Voyager. The real Marayna has a lonely life there, controlling the plasma activity of the nebula. She threatens to destroy Voyager unless Tuvok stays, but he points out that, logically, it could not be a loving relationship if it was based on blackmail. She lets Voyager to leave.

TRIVIA

- Originally an episode for Paris and Harry, it was switched – rather unconvincingly – to being a Tuvok and Harry story.

RATING

- When it gets off the holodeck, it starts to make a bit more sense, but both Harry and Tuvok seem out of character and foolish here, and this isn't a good episode.

3.15 CODA

STARDATE 50518.6

Janeway discovers that she's dead

TX 29 January 1997
WRITER Jeri Taylor
DIRECTOR Nancy Malone
GUEST CAST Len Cariou (Admiral Janeway)

Chakotay and Janeway are in a shuttle when they are killed by the Vidiians. Then they are killed again. Then they realise they are trapped in a time loop. They return to Voyager, but Janeway has contracted the Phage, and the Doctor lets her die. Janeway is back on the shuttle and is killed. This time, she sees Chakotay grieve for her. Janeway can't be seen, but Kes can sense her. Janeway meets her late father, who tells her she died. The crew holds a memorial service. She senses the Doctor trying to revive her. Her father tells her not to go back, something Janeway realises her real father would never do. An alien has disguised itself as her father to lure her to her death. Janeway awakes, recovering from injuries she got in a shuttle crash.

TRIVIA

- Jeri Taylor wrote two novels exploring Janeway's back story, *Mosaic* and *Pathways*. This episode draws on *Mosaic*.

RATING

- It's a shame that the alien entity is introduced – Janeway is facing her own demons, she doesn't actually need a demon to turn up. It's another episode that should be more powerful and interesting than it ends up.

3.16 BLOOD FEVER

STARDATE 50537.2

Torres accidentally undergoes Pon farr

TX 5 February 1997
WRITER Lisa Klink

Torres is approached by Vorik, a Vulcan ensign who wants to sleep with her. She's taken aback, but he insists she's the logical choice. She dislocates his jaw when he grabs her. The Doctor realises Vorik is going through Pon farr. Torres goes on an Away Mission, and becomes increasingly violent. Torres doesn't understand her feelings. After they are attacked by natives, Paris and Torres are left alone, but Paris

DIRECTOR Andrew Robinson
GUEST CAST Bruce Bohne (Ishan), Alexander Enberg (Vorik), Deborah Levin (Lang)

refuses to take advantage of her. Chakotay discovers the devastated remains of the Sakari civilisation, and its last survivors. Vorik arrives on the planet, and challenges Paris to a ritual battle, which Paris wins. Torres and Vorik's feelings subside. Chakotay has bad news: he thinks the Sakari were attacked by the Borg.

TRIVIA

- Pon farr was introduced in *Amok Time*, and fans had been expecting Tuvok's Pon farr. We see it in *Body and Soul*. Up until now, Pon farr is something that only Vulcan *males* experience – Saavik explicitly says so in *Star Trek III: The Search for Spock* before 'comforting' Spock. Vorik says it's something *all* Vulcans experience (and T'Pol goes through Pon farr in *The Bounty*). Vulcans have arranged marriages, and cross-checking their calenders would certainly make sense if both the men and the women are only in heat for a few days every seven years. However, neither T'Pring or Saavik are undergoing Pon farr when Spock does (it's not exactly something Vulcans can hide), so if females also undergo Pon farr, then Vulcan couples must get twice as much action as is popularly thought. Logically.
- We're told here that a holographic mate doesn't ease Pon farr, because there's no telepathic bond. This doesn't bother Tuvok in *Body and Soul*.
- There are 73 men on board – meaning that (taking the last figure given for the size of the crew, 151, from *Persistence of Vision*) more than half the crew is female. This doesn't seem to be the ratio of female crewmen we see around the ship (and the Doctor probably doesn't count as male).
- Vorik tries to rape Torres, then to murder her when she resists, but as far as we know, he's not punished.

RATING

- The inevitable Pon farr episode goes to Torres, which is at least not a predictable twist. It's not the first (or last) time we see Torres in a bad mood, though, and it takes the crew a ridiculous amount of time to work out what's wrong with her.

3.17 UNITY

STARDATE 50614.2

Chakotay discovers a Borg colony

TX 12 February 1997
WRITER Kenneth Biller
DIRECTOR Robert Duncan McNeill
GUEST CAST Ivar Brogger (Orum), Lori Hallier (Riley Frazier), Susan Patterson (Ensign Kaplan)

Chakotay and Kaplan are on a scouting mission when they detect a Federation distress call. Landing close to the source, they are ambushed and Kaplan is killed. Help arrives in the form of a beautiful woman, Riley. Voyager encounters a Borg Cube adrift, with over 1,000 dead Borg on board. Chakotay discovers that Riley used to be a Borg, but five years before an electrokinetic storm broke the link to the Collective. They landed here, but quickly started fighting among themselves. They heal Chakotay's injuries by linking with him. Voyager tracks Chakotay and beams him and Riley up. Riley wants to reactivate the Cube, to link the survivors on the planet and end their fighting. Janeway refuses, but Riley uses her link to Chakotay to convince him to sneak over in a shuttle. As soon as the link is re-established, Riley's collective destroys the Cube and return to their planet.

TRIVIA

- Apart from the first sequence of the very first episode, *Deep Space Nine* had avoided bringing back the Borg. There were reasons for that – the writers found it difficult to find a new story to tell about them that could top *The Best of Both Worlds* and it was obvious that if the whole Starfleet couldn't stop a Borg Cube, Deep Space Nine wouldn't last long (and couldn't run away!).
- After *First Contact*, the production team had a new stock of Borg costumes, sets and both old-fashioned and CG models. Bringing the Borg back, in force, would no longer be very expensive. This story re-uses Borg props and costumes from the movie.
- Chakotay says he's a vegetarian. As was pointed out in *The Next Generation*, technically, everyone who only eats replicated food is. It's an interesting moral point: while replicated beef stew, say, contains no 'real' meat, presumably it's a copy of an original beef stew which could only by made by killing an animal. Presumably, as contemporary vegetarians do, different people draw the line in different places.

RATING

- Robert Duncan McNeill's second episode as director, and it's excellent. We get three or four twists on who Riley is, and whether she's on the side of the angels. It's an interesting new take on the Borg, setting the scene for the arrival of Seven of Nine.

3.18 THE DARKLING

STARDATE 50693.2

The Doctor experiments with his dark side

TX 19 February 1997
WRITER Joe Menosky (story by Brannon Braga and Joe Menosky)
DIRECTOR Alexander Singer
GUEST CAST Christopher Clarke (Lord Byron), Stephen Davies (Nakahn), Noel de Souza (Ghandi), Sue Henley (Ensign), David Lee Smith (Zahir)

Kes falls for Zahir, a Mikhal pilot who's helping the crew. The Doctor has a new project: he's adding the personality routines of historical figures like Ghandi and Byron to his own program. Torres is worried, and offers to review his program. The Doctor becomes increasingly impatient with Kes, who's neglecting her job in Sickbay to be with Zahir. Zahir is injured by a mysterious attacker. Torres falls ill. The Doctor says it's food poisoning, but Tuvok realises that the Doctor is responsible. The Doctor kidnaps Kes, beams off the ship and, refusing to surrender, throws himself and Kes off a cliff. The two are beamed back to Voyager. Tuvok deletes the new programming.

TRIVIA

- T'Pau is briefly seen, looking nothing like she did in *Amok Time* (the extra playing her is Japanese, for one thing).

RATING

- *Star Trek* fans christened this and the next two stories 'the trilogy of terror' – three extraordinarily bad episodes, all in a row. Robert Picardo is usually great as the Doctor, but here his performance makes a bad script worse. How the Doctor can be so knowledgeable about human psychology and history and yet fail to spot that Lord Byron had a dark side is just one of the more peculiar plot holes.

3.19 RISE

STARDATE UNKNOWN

Tuvok and Neelix must co-operate to survive

TX 26 February 1997
WRITER Brannon Braga (story by Jimmy Diggs)
DIRECTOR Robert Scheerer
GUEST CAST Gary Bullock (Goth), Kelly Connell (Sklar), Lisa Kaminir (Lillias), Alan Oppenheimer (Nezu Ambassador), Geof Prysirr (Hanjuan), Tom Towles (Vatm)

Voyager is trying, without much success, to stop an asteroid bombardment destroying the planet Nezu. Neelix and Tuvok head to the planet, but their shuttle crashes. They need to get back to Voyager with a group of evacuees. Neelix suggests activating a tether linking the surface to a space station. The journey up the tether is dangerous, and Tuvok and Neelix argue about whether logic or passion will help them the most as they climb. Voyager has encountered a ship from the Etanian Order, who have directed the asteroids at the planet to make the population evacuate so they can claim it as their own. Tuvok can supply the ship with tactics to defeat the Etanians.

TRIVIA

- Tuvok and Neelix both say they don't understand each other – which either means they don't retain any memories of being merged together to become Tuvix, or that the writers forgot.

RATING

- A very dull episode, based on the premise that the audience want to see Tuvok and Neelix trade platitudes for an hour.

3.20 FAVORITE SON

STARDATE 50732.4

Harry discovers he's always been an alien

TX 19 March 1997
WRITER Lisa Klink
DIRECTOR Marvin V Rush
GUEST CAST Patrick Fabian (Taymon), Kelli Kirkland (Rinna), Kristanna Loken (Malia), Deborah May (Lyris), Cari Shayne (Eliann)

Harry fires on a Nasari vessel, without apparent provocation. He tells Janeway afterwards he had a hunch they were about to attack, and he is suspended from duty. He develops markings on his face and his blood chemistry has altered. He finds this area of space strangely familiar. He shows them Taresia, a matriarchal society. The Taresians welcome him home, claiming he's half-Taresian. The Nasari contact Voyager saying their quarrel is with Harry, as a Taresian. He wants to go back to Voyager, but the Taresians stop him. Harry discovers they've tricked him here to extract his genetic material. They plan to kill him. Harry is beamed up to Voyager as the Taresians and Nasari fight.

TRIVIA

- Kristanna Loken went on to play the Terminatrix in Terminator 3 (2003).

RATING

- Truly terrible at every level. An episode that doesn't quite sink as far as *Threshold* or *Elogium*, but seems to be trying its hardest to.

3.21 BEFORE AND AFTER

STARDATE 50973

Kes relives her whole life, backwards

TX 9 April 1997
WRITER Kenneth Biller
DIRECTOR Allan Kroeker
GUEST CAST Christopher Aguilar (Andrew), Jessica Collins (Linnis), Rachel Harris (Martis), Michael L Maguire (Benaren), Janna Michaels (Young Kes)

Kes is dying, and the Doctor places her in a bio-temporal chamber to save her life. She is suddenly with her grandson, at the morilogium, the end of her life. Then she meets her daughter, Linnis, who is married to Harry. Kes is married to Paris. As she travels back further, she learns she suffered from chroniton radiation poisoning during the Year of Hell. As she travels back further, the Doctor confirms the diagnosis. Kes keeps going back in time, and learns the temporal variance of the Krenim torpedo that bathed her in radiation. She keeps slipping back in time as the Doctor works to cure her – he saves her just before she's conceived, and she returns to normality.

TRIVIA

- An episode that shows that there were at least vague plans for *The Year of Hell* (in which we're told Janeway, Carey and Torres died), but suggests that they hadn't firmed up plans to lose Kes. It's interesting to speculate that this might have been an episode designed to assess the potential of the character and to give her one last chance.
- The stardate is the stardate given when things are back to normal – Kes would have reached the end of her nine-year lifespan around stardate 55950. Chakotay gives two stardates: 56947, and – later! – 55836.2.
- The episode features a rare mention of the Beta Quadrant, as the home of the precognitive Yattho.

RATING

- Another Kes episode where it's a different Kes, not the regular character – something of a sign that the regular Kes isn't working. Jennifer Lien, on the other hand, is great. There's never any doubt that Kes will make it, and the glimpses of the future we get are strangely unengaging.

3.22 REAL LIFE

STARDATE 50863.2

The Doctor gets himself a family

TX 23 April 1997
WRITER Jeri Taylor (story by Harry Doc Kloor)
DIRECTOR Anson Williams
GUEST CAST Lindsay Haun (Belle), Chad Haywood (K'Kath), Stephen Ralston (Larg), Wendy Schaal (Charlene), Glenn Walker Harris Jr (Jeffrey)

Voyager discovers the wreckage of a space station, and decides to investigate, discovering it was caught in a plasma tornado. Meanwhile, the Doctor has created a holographic family: a wife, Charlene, a teenage son and young daughter, Jeffrey and Belle. Torres thinks it's a little too perfect and offers to make it more realistic. The Doctor doesn't like his new family – his wife's always at work and his children are abusive. As arguments reach a head, Belle is mortally wounded in an accident. The Doctor ends the program rather than letting her die. Paris is investigating the 'space tornado' and ends up trapped in subspace. The crew manage to beam him back. Torres convinces the Doctor that he should return to the program and face the grief that real life sometimes offers up.

TRIVIA

- 'Vulky' is an insult among Klingons, meaning 'the sort of dull thing a Vulcan would do'.
- The best joke in the script is in the stage directions, and was picked up by other writers – when the Doctor is activated and deactivated, he 'zimmers in' and 'zimmers out'.

RATING

- An episode that anticipates computer game *The Sims*, but skirts the line between being a parody of banal soap opera and just being banal.

3.23 DISTANT ORIGIN

STARDATE UNKNOWN

A reptilian scientist discovers the origin of his species

TX 30 April 1997
WRITER Brannon Braga and Joe Menosky
DIRECTOR David Livingston
GUEST CAST Christopher Liam Moore (Veer), Marshall Teague (Hulak), Concetta Tomei (Odala), Henry Woronicz (Gegen)

The reptilian Gegen and his assistant Veer discover the remains of a human in a cave. It proves his theory that his people, the Voth, originated on the other side of the galaxy, millions of years ago, but the Elders of his race mock this attack on the orthodoxy. Gegen and Veer track Voyager, and use cloaking technology to examine the ship and its crew. They are eventually detected, and the crew assume that they are hostile. Veer goes into protective hibernation, and the Doctor discovers that the Voth are descended from Earth's dinosaurs. Voyager is beamed aboard a vast Voth ship, where Chakotay is deemed living proof that Gegen is right. The Elders want to suppress the knowledge of their distant origin, and to save his life and those of his crew, Gegan publically recants his theory.

QUOTES

- 'Deny that past and you deny the struggle and achievements of your ancestors. Deny your origins on Earth and you deny your true heritage.' – *Chakotay*

TRIVIA

- There are now 148 crew on Voyager.
- The body they find is Hogan, who died in *Basics Part II*. That was 'over a year ago'.

RATING

- A nice episode with a solid science fiction idea and an interesting structure – it's told from the point of view of the aliens, for a change. Henry Woronicz puts in a great performance, despite wearing one of the largest and most enveloping alien masks in the whole of *Star Trek*. All in all, a clever, witty episode, and one which has a spiky ending.

3.24 WORST CASE SCENARIO

STARDATE 50953.4

A holonovel depicts a Maquis mutiny on the ship

TX 7 May 1997
WRITER Kenneth Biller
DIRECTOR Alexander Singer
GUEST CAST Martha Hackett (Seska)

Chakotay leads a Maquis mutiny and takes control of Voyager... and then Paris walks into the holodeck. Torres has been watching a holonovel she's found hidden on the database. She and Paris are fascinated by the program, and speculate who wrote it. Just as the scenario reaches its conclusion, it abruptly stops. Whoever wrote it never finished it. Gradually, more and more people try the holonovel. Tuvok admits he wrote it – as the security chief, he was initially worried that the Maquis might revolt, and wanted to work out how to fight it. It quickly became obvious that the Maquis wouldn't mutiny, so he never finished the scenario. Paris decides to finish it himself, although a number of people offer suggestions. Tuvok helps out. The two of them quickly get trapped by the holographic Seska, who discovered the program and has boobytrapped it. As the holodeck threatens the real ship, Janeway writes the ending: Seska's phaser malfunctions and normal life on Voyager can resume.

QUOTES

- 'Loosen up' – *Janeway's advice to Tuvok*

TRIVIA

- In an interesting piece of continuity, Seska reprograms Tuvok's holonovel so that it favours the Maquis, rather than her.

RATING

- A pretty obvious trick opening, showing an 'alternative' Voyager that's so much more interesting than the regular one. If the show was really like this, it would be so much more interesting. As it is, halfway through, what could have been a clever character piece starts being played for laughs. It's an entertaining episode – and, boy, the third season needs those – but this could have been so much more.

3.25 DISPLACED

STARDATE 50912.4

The crew starts vanishing, being replaced by aliens

TX 14 May 1997
WRITER Lisa Klink
DIRECTOR Allan Kroeker
GUEST CAST Deborah Levin (Lang), James Noah (Rislan), Mark L Taylor (Jarlath), Kenneth Tigar (Dammar), Nancy Youngblut (Taleen)

Voyager's crew starts vanishing, and as every person disappears, a Nyrian takes their place. Half the crew is soon replaced in this way, and the Nyrians take control of the ship. The disappeared crewmen are on a beautiful planet, but they are prisoners. The Nyrians explain that they aren't a violent people, but they often pirate ships this way. Torres adjusts the Doctor's sight so he can locate access portals to the prison. They take control of the translocation system and beam the Nyrians to an arctic environment, where they are incapacitated. Voyager helps the other prisoners return home.

QUOTES

- 'You may find all this Klingon stuff fascinating – I don't.' – *Torres*

TRIVIA

- Tuvok talks about the 'taloth', a Vulcan rite of passage involving going out into the wilderness. We see Spock do this in the animated episode *Yesteryear*.

RATING

- As near as a bog-standard episode as it's possible to get, but it's harmless enough.

3.26 SCORPION Part I

STARDATE 50984.3

Voyager faces the Borg... and something even worse

TX 21 May 1997
WRITERS Brannon Braga and Joe Menosky
DIRECTOR David Livingston
GUEST CAST John Rhys-Davies (Leonardo Da Vinci)

Voyager has entered Borg space, but there's an area with no Borg ships in, which they christen the 'Northwest Passage'. Kes has troubling visions of the ship being destroyed and dead Borg. An armada of Borg Cubes fly straight past them at high warp – they're clearly retreating from something. They soon detect that the Cubes have been destroyed. Voyager investigates one of the dead Cubes, and detects a strange organic ship attached to the Cube. Inside the Cube, an Away Team discover Borg bodies, and Kes has a vision of Harry suffering. The real Harry is attacked by a weird new life-form, the Away Team are beamed back and Voyager makes its escape. Harry has been infected with alien cells, and the Doctor tries using Borg nanoprobes to destroy the cells. The Borg call the aliens Species 8472, and the reason there are no Borg in the Northwest Passage is simply because there's something worse there. Voyager now faces the choice of abandoning plans to go home or risk the journey through Borg space. Janeway comes up with another strategy – the Borg are incapable of assimilating Species 8472, and are incapable of innovation, so have no way to defeat them. She will tell them how to adapt their nanoprobes. She is beamed to a Borg Cube, and opens negotiations. Species 8472 attacks, destroying not just some Borg Cubes, but a whole planet. The Borg Cube with Janeway onboard retreats, dragging Voyager behind it in a tractor beam...

TRIVIA

- The first time it was confirmed on-screen that the Borg were from the Delta Quadrant was in *Star Trek: First Contact*.

RATING

- As with *The Way of the Warrior* (and, later, *The Expanse*), this is effectively a second pilot, one with big space battles, an epic scale, but which always keeps things at a human level. The big events unfurl, but we see things from the human perspective. This isn't the deepest episode of *Star Trek*, and there's something of a cheapening of the Borg, who are brought in to show how tough the new baddies are, but this is exciting, dramatic stuff and an episode that seriously raises the average of the season as a whole.

STAR TREK: VOYAGER
SEASON FOUR

4.1 SCORPION Part II

STARDATE 51003.7

Voyager gets a new crewmember – a Borg

TX 3 September 1997
WRITERS Brannon Braga and Joe Menosky
DIRECTOR Winrich Kolbe
GUEST CAST David Anthony Marshall (Annika's father – uncredited), Nikki Tyler (Annika's mother – uncredited), Erica Bryan (Annika – uncredited)

Janeway agrees to stay on the Borg Cube while Voyager gets safe passage through Borg space. She refuses to be linked to the Collective, so the Borg assign a female drone, Seven of Nine, to communicate with her. Species 8472 and their ships are made of the same material, so both should be vulnerable to the nanoprobes. They can fire the nanoprobes at them in the photon torpedos. The Doctor cures Harry. Species 8472 attack the Cube, all but ignoring Voyager. An injured Janeway, Tuvok and Seven are beamed back to their ship. Chakotay is in command, and doesn't trust the Borg. He proposes to make his own way through Borg space. Seven and other drones seize control of the ship and send it into fluidic space, the realm of Species 8472. Voyager launches its torpedoes, forcing Species 8472 to retreat. The Borg announce that they will now assimilate Voyager, but Janeway and Chakotay anticipate this. They create a power surge that breaks Seven's link with the Collective, and make their escape – with Seven still on board.

QUOTES

- 'You like harmony, cohesion, greatness. It will be your undoing' – *Seven's verdict on humanity*

TRIVIA

- Seven of Nine was introduced partly to be the 'unemotional observer' who offers comments on humanity and the values we take for granted and is seen as a vital part of any *Star Trek* format. Spock, Data, Odo and T'Pol serve this function in the other shows, and it was originally imagined that Neelix would in *Voyager*, but both he and the Doctor soon began to demonstrate a relish and deep insight into human nature. Borg make-up is elaborate and time-consuming, and there was no way a regular character could have full Borg costume and make up.
- While the character was originally a man, by the time it came to cast the role, Seven was female. Hudson Leick (Callisto in *Xena*) and Claudia Christian (Ivanova in *Babylon 5*) both read for the part. Jeri Ryan had recently been brought in to spice up failing *X-Files*-style show *Dark Skies*. She was initially reluctant to take the role.
- Hugh Borg was Third of Five, so perhaps Seven should really be Seventh of Nine. Even before she has her Borg implants removed, she's the only Borg we've ever heard without an electronic voice (even Locutus has one).
- The story of Seven's assimilation was expanded from the couple of scenes in the original script for this episode into *The Raven*, and there are cameo appearances here from her parents and the 'young Seven', Annika, before they are seen properly in that episode.

RATING

- Here's something you won't read very often in this book – the concluding episode of this two-parter is better than the original. Jeri Ryan makes her mark. A little over 75 episodes in, the series suddenly feels like it's found its feet.

4.2 THE GIFT

STARDATE UNKNOWN

Kes leaves the crew as Seven joins

TX 10 September 1997
WRITER Joe Menosky
DIRECTOR Anson Williams

Seven, demands to be returned to the Collective, but Janeway is far more interested in her past: she was a young girl, Annika Hansen, before she became assimilated. The Doctor is able to help Seven as her body starts to reject her Borg implants. Kes starts having telepathic visions. Seven tries to contact the Borg, but Kes prevents her. Seven is held in the brig, and Janeway insists that all her Borg implants will be removed. Tuvok detects that Kes is going into a state of cellular flux, transforming into a new life-form. Kes decides to leave Voyager before she endangers the ship, and becomes an energy being. As a parting gift, Kes moves Voyager to the other side of Borg space, ten years closer to home. The Doctor completes his operation on Seven – she now looks practically human.

QUOTES

- 'You can get some of the unity you require right here on Voyager.' – *Janeway tells Seven. Well, she quickly finds Neelix irritating*

TRIVIA

- The decision was made to drop Kes from the cast. While this came from the production team, not the actress Jennifer Lien, it seems to have been an amicable parting. The writers stated they'd taken the character as far as they could, which seems a little odd, as a two-year-old character with a nine-year lifespan would seem to have a rather obvious character arc in a series scheduled to run seven seasons. The show already had a large regular cast, though, and it must have been clear that Seven had more potential. It would quickly become obvious that the writers enjoyed writing for Seven – whereas the 'Kes episodes' in the previous series had often seen her acting out of character, a sure sign the writers weren't happy with her normal character.
- The Doctor says that Seven's catsuit, that he's designed, is medically beneficial. He doesn't specify whether he means for Seven herself, or for the male (and, who knows, perhaps some of the female) crewmembers.

RATING

- Do you think Kes will bump into Wesley Crusher? They have identical 'out stories', and the show doesn't break its stride as they leave. If the episode wasn't designed to show that Seven is great and Kes wasn't, then it sure feels like it.

4.3 DAY OF HONOR

Torres is forced to look inward

TX 17 September 1997
WRITER Jeri Taylor
DIRECTOR Jesus Salvador Trevino
GUEST CAST Alan Altshuld (Lumas), Alexander Enberg (Vorik), Michael A Krawic (Rahmin), Kevin P Stillwell (Moklor)

STARDATE UNKNOWN

Torres is in an even worse mood than usual, and refuses to go through the annual Klingon Day of Honor ceremony. She has to work with Seven on a transwarp conduit, but an accident means she has to eject the warp core. Paris tries to help, but Torres pushes him away. Voyager helps a group of Caatati refugees, who are shocked to see they have a Borg onboard, because their people have almost all been assimilated. Torres and Paris are sent out in a shuttle to retrieve it, and find the Caatati trying to salvage it. The Caatati destroy the shuttle, and Torres and Paris only barely beam off in time. They end up drifting in their spacesuits. The Caatati go on to attack Voyager, demanding that they hand over Seven. They are bought off with an energy matrix that can produce thorium. Paris and Torres have a heart-to-heart, and Torres admits she's in love with Paris. Voyager rescues them, and Torres realises she's followed the Day of Honor ceremony, and found out a truth about herself.

TRIVIA

- In a conversation with the editor of the *Star Trek* books, John Ordover, Jeri Taylor learned that he was planning a linked set of books based around the Klingons and their Day of Honor. She realised not only that this fit with a Torres episode she was planning, but that the lead times meant that the Day of Honor books would be coming out at the same time as the episode was broadcast. The Day of Honor concept was added to the television episode, and a novelisation of the episode (by Michael Jan Friedman) was released as part of the book series. This was said to have been the first time the books had directly influenced the television show in this way.

RATING

- A packed episode. The speed Paris and Torres get together now Kes is out of the way is a little breathtaking, but this episode is good evidence that Seven's going to be a strong character and that problems with the show are being addressed. It's a shame the Caatati are played a little too broadly, though – you can't help but feel they've got a point, but it's lost beneath all the make-up and shouting.

4.4 NEMESIS

Chakotay finds himself in the heat of battle

STARDATE 51082.4

Chakotay's shuttle is attacked, and he beams to a planet that's the battleground between the Vori and the Kradin. He's captured by the Vori, but finds himself fighting alongside them as the Kradin attack.

TX 24 September 1997
WRITER Kenneth Biller
DIRECTOR Alexander Singer
GUEST CAST Nathan Anderson (Namon), Booth Colman (Penno), Pancho Demmings (Kradin Soldier), Terrance Evans (Treen), Marilyn Fox (Vori Woman), Matt E Levin (Rafin), Michael Mahonen (Brone), Meghan Murphy (Karya), Pete Vogt (Commandant)

He finds himself at a Vori settlement, unable to leave as the Kradin commit atrocities. The Kradin contact Voyager and Tuvok accompanies one of their commando units that is trying to locate Chakotay. Chakotay is left to die after a Kradin attack, and is surprised when one of the Kradin calls his name. It's Tuvok – the Vori have been using mind control to get him to fight on their side. Chakotay doubts that either side is in the right.

TRIVIA

- Neelix says that he knows about the war, even though we're over 10,000 light years past the Nekrid Expanse, which he said was the limit of his knowledge in *Fair Trade*.

RATING

- A clever episode with a simple story – as Chakotay starts falling under the Vori influence, he starts talking like them, using words like 'nullify' rather than 'kill'. It's a Vietnam allegory, although the US military preferred the euphemism 'pacify'. The ultimate message – that war is bad and dehumanises people – isn't a surprise, but the episode works.

4.5 REVULSION

STARDATE 51186.2

The Doctor and Torres battle a psychopathic hologram

TX 1 October 1997
WRITER Lisa Klink
DIRECTOR Kenneth Biller
GUEST CAST Leland Orser (Dejaren)

Voyager receives a distress call from the Serosian hologram, Dejaren. The Doctor is keen to help, and goes with Torres on the rescue mission. Dejaren's crewmates have died from a virus, but Torres soon discovers he's lying about areas of the ship being flooded with antimatter radiation. The Doctor is sympathetic to Dejaren, but agrees to keep him busy while Torres searches the ship. He's shocked how prejudiced Dejaren is to 'organics'. Torres discovers the crew, all brutally murdered. Meanwhile, Harry chats to Seven, who is keen for him to seduce her. Back on the Serosian ship, Dejaren has cut off the Doctor and Torres, who narrowly manages to deactivate the hologram before he kills her by reaching into her body and pulling out her heart.

RATING

- An episode where the Doctor's optimism about holograms veers closely towards stupidity in places. It's pretty derivative of all sorts of slasher movies, but it does manage a couple of scary moments.

4.6 THE RAVEN

STARDATE UNKNOWN

Seven experiences visions, and wants to rejoin the Collective

TX 8 October 1997
WRITER Bryan Fuller (Story By Bryan Fuller and Harry Doc Kloor)
DIRECTOR LeVar Burton
GUEST CAST Erica Lynne Bryan (Little Girl), Mickey Cottrell (Dumah), David Anthony Marshall (Father), Nikki Tyler (Mother), Richard J Zobel Jr (Gauman)

Seven hallucinates about the Borg and a raven. The Doctor decides she's reacting to the trauma of leaving the Collective. Shortly afterwards, she attacks Neelix, threatening to assimilate him. Janeway is busy negotiating with the B'omar for safe passage. Seven takes a shuttlecraft into their territory, aggravating the B'omar. Tuvok and Paris sneak past their perimeter to catch her. Seven imprisons Tuvok, and says she's in contact with the Borg, even though Tuvok insists there is no Borg activity nearby. Seven's Borg side is reasserting itself, but she is concerned that Tuvok will be assimilated. Tuvok doesn't think there is any risk of that. On a moon, they discover a crashed, partly assimilated ship, the USS Raven. This is the ship that belonged to the Hansens, Seven's parents. Seven recalls her assimilation, but a B'omar attack breaks the spell. She and Tuvok get out of the Raven just before it is destroyed.

TRIVIA

- This episode had the working title *Resurrection*.
- Seven gets a new, brown outfit. She was six when she was assimilated, meaning she's 24. This would seem to contradict *Q Who* by having people from the Federation monitoring the Borg before Q introduced them to the Enterprise.

RATING

- The Seven stuff is great, but there's a lot of dull B'omar stuff here, too, and that drags the episode down.

4.7 SCIENTIFIC METHOD

STARDATE 51244.3

Aliens experiment on the crew

TX 29 October 1997
WRITER Lisa Klink (story by Sherry Klein and Harry Doc Kloor)
DIRECTOR David Livingston
GUEST CAST Rosemary Forsyth (Alzen), Annette Helde (Takar)

Janeway has a bad headache, the result of invisible aliens who are monitoring the crew's behaviour. Chakotay starts aging at an accelerated rate, and other crewmembers start exhibiting other signs of genetic damage. When Torres and the Doctor investigate, both are incapacitated. Seven adapts her implants and can now see aliens all around the ship, performing medical experiments on the crew. Tuvok stops her giving the crew a neuroleptic shock, suspicious of her motives. She shoots one with a phaser instead, and brings it to a tense Janeway. The alien is a Srivani, who says they are using the crew as guinea pigs – they'll cure many of their own race using this research. Janeway steers Voyager towards a binary pulsar to get the aliens off the ship. The plan works and the Doctor is able to repair the damage the aliens have done.

TRIVIA

- We find out that there are 257 rooms on Voyager.

RATING

- A story that starts out as a nice paranoia piece, then turns into a parable about animal experiments. The aliens are acting for the greater good, after all. Quite a nice self-contained story.

4.8 YEAR OF HELL Part I

STARDATE 51268.4

Voyager encounters a weapon capable of changing history

TX 5 November 1997
WRITERS Brannon Braga and Joe Menosky
DIRECTOR Allan Kroeker
GUEST CAST Rick Fitts (Zahl), Sue Henley (Brooks), Deborah Levin (Lang), John Loprieno (Obrist), Peter Slutsker (Krenim Commandant), Kurtwood Smith (Annorax)

The new Astrometrics Lab comes online, and the new mapping technology immediately plots a new course for the ship through Zahl territory. The ship hits a space-time shockwave, and then comes face-to-face with the Krenim, who have advanced technology based around time travel. They are hit with chroniton torpedos. Seven discovers a way to shield from them. Elsewhere, the Krenim captain Annorax checks the new timeline. He controls a ship with a temporal weapon, one that was responsible for the shockwave. He has altered the timelines and almost completely restored the Krenim Imperium. Annorax isn't happy, though – he wants complete restoration. He fires the weapon again. Voyager isn't affected, as Seven's shields hold. The Krenim ship they are facing is now small and unimpressive – Annorax has miscalculated. Annorax realises Voyager's shielding was the factor he didn't account for. He beams Chakotay and Paris to his ship. He fires a chroniton beam at Voyager, seriously damaging it. Janeway orders everyone but senior staff to abandon ship...

QUOTES

- 'Put Janeway out of her misery.' – *Annorax*

TRIVIA

- This episode was originally pencilled in as the season three cliffhanger, but it was felt that the Borg and the introduction of Seven should take priority. This explains why Kes said the Year of Hell started on stardate 50973 in *Before and After*.

RATING

- One thing *Voyager* does better than any other *Star Trek*, with the possible exception of the original series, is the one-off villain – Kurtwood Smith makes for a memorable baddy, a man with infinite power over the whole course of the universe, but utterly trapped by that power. The plot telegraphs the fact that everything's just going to be reset at the end, though, which undermines everything.

4.9 YEAR OF HELL Part II

STARDATE 51425.4

Voyager suffers as the Krenim continue their attacks

TX 12 November 1997
WRITERS Brannon Braga and Joe Menosky
DIRECTOR Mike Vejar
GUEST CAST John Loprieno (Obrist), Lise Simms (Wife), Peter Slutsker (Krenim Commandant), Kurtwood Smith (Annorax)

One hundred and thirty-three days after entering Krenim space, Voyager lurks in a nebula, badly damaged, with a crew of nine. On the Krenim ship, Annorax tells Chakotay to tell him all about Voyager so he can change history to send Voyager home. Annorax reveals that a mistake he made with his calculations once wiped out 50 million Krenim, including his wife, and he's been trying to repair the damage ever since and restore his wife. Paris finds a weak point on the ship, but Chakotay refuses to exploit it, believing he can work with Annorax. A year after they entered Krenim space, Paris contacts Voyager and tells them how to attack the Krenim ship. Janeway stays with Voyager as her officers rally other alien races. Together they attack the Krenim ship. They are almost wiped out, until Janeway flies Voyager straight at the Krenim ship's weak point, destroying both ships. Voyager is restored... and Annorax is at home with his wife.

QUOTES

- 'You're trying to rationalise genocide. One species is significant, one life is significant.' – *Chakotay to Annorax*

TRIVIA

- In *The 37s*, it's a major plot point that Voyager needs a bare minimum of 100 people to operate it, although the Kazon managed to get by with 89 in *Basics*. Here, the crew gets down to nine, and the ship still functions. Just.
- The crew don't remember Kes telling them about the Kremin, including how to defeat them, in *Before and After*. Then again, Torres and Janeway don't die in this version of events.

RATING

- This is a great episode, and demonstrates once and for all what a great series there could have been about a Starfleet ship facing dwindling supplies. This episode, though, comes from a parallel universe where *Voyager* was an exciting, tense show that lived up to its premise and saw characters living (and dying) on the edge. This is a great episode... but was anyone watching surprised or satisfied when everything's back to normal at the end?

4.10 RANDOM THOUGHTS

STARDATE 51367.2

Torres is arrested for violent thoughts

TX 19 November 1997
WRITER Kenneth Biller
DIRECTOR Alexander Singer
GUEST CAST Ted Barba (Malin), Bobby Burns (Frane), Rebecca McFarland (Talli), Jeanette Miller (Woman), Wayne Pere (Guill), Gwynyth Walsh (Nimira)

Torres is bumped into by a Mari man called Frane in their marketplace, and is arrested. She's accused of having a violent thought about him, or 'aggravated violent thought resulting in grave bodily harm'. She's told she'll have an engrammatic purge to remove violent images from her mind. Janeway objects – this will give Torres brain damage. She and Tuvok discover that Frane is a known offender, but the authorities insist he's been cured. Tuvok mind-melds with Torres, and realises that a telepath called Guill is selling illegal violent thoughts. Tuvok tricks Guill into thinking that he's willing to sell his own thoughts to him, and gets him to Voyager. Torres' purging is ended when Tuvok and Janeway get Guill to confess.

TRIVIA

- Flashes from the movie *Event Horizon* (1997) are included in the montage of nightmarish images, including a brief appearance by Sam Neill.

RATING

- A pretty silly premise which turns into an interesting insight into Tuvok, and the savage side he likes to keep hidden.

4.11 CONCERNING FLIGHT

STARDATE 51386.4

The Da Vinci hologram is stolen

TX 26 November 1997
WRITER Joe Menosky (story by Jimmy Diggs and Joe Menosky)
DIRECTOR Jesus Salvador Trevino
GUEST CAST John Rhys-Davies (Leonardo Da Vinci), Don Pugsley (Alien Visitor), Doug Spearman (Alien Buyer), John Vargas (Tau)

Unknown vessels swoop on Voyager and beam off items of high technology. The most important is a computer core, another is Janeway's Leonardo Da Vinci hologram, which Tuvok tracks to a nearby planet. He and Janeway beam down and discover that Da Vinci is happy – Tau, the raider, is no more brutal than the average Renaissance patron. Janeway poses as a buyer, looking for their stolen processor. They locate it in a secure facility. Janeway and Leonardo head there. Unable to beam up with the processor, they get into a glider built by Da Vinci and escape. Voyager beams the glider up.

QUOTES

- 'When are we not in prison? When are our lives free of the influence of those who have more power than us?' – *Leonardo*

TRIVIA

- Janeway reminds viewers that Kirk met the 'real' Leonardo – in *Requiem for Methuselah.*
- She uses the same command code (pi 1-1-0) to overload the core as she used to initiate the self-destruct in *Dreadnought.*

RATING

- A bit of fluff, but entertaining enough. Leonardo's enthusiasm and acceptance of his new home is fun. John Rhys-Davies is superb, in a very silly role.

4.12 MORTAL COIL

STARDATE 51449.2

When Neelix is resuscitated, he begins questioning his beliefs

TX 17 December 1997
WRITER Bryan Fuller
DIRECTOR Allan Kroeker
GUEST CAST Nancy Hower (Wildman), Robin Stapler (Alixia), Brooke Ashley Stephens (Naomi)

Neelix is killed collecting protomatter from a nebula. Janeway prepares a funeral, but Seven resurrects him with Borg nanoprobes. Neelix is distraught – he has no memory of the afterlife, The Great Forest, where he hoped to be reunited with his family. Now that the hope of seeing them again has gone, Neelix becomes angry and impatient. His body starts rejecting the nanoprobes, but Seven can repair the damage again. Chakotay takes Neelix on a visionquest, and he meets his sister, but she tells him that the afterlife is a lie. Neelix feels suicidal afterwards, and tries to beam into the nebula. Chakotay tells him not to take the vision so literally, and Neelix becomes convinced that his shipmates are his family now, and plenty of reason to live.

QUOTES

- 'You are a peculiar creature.' – *Seven has Neelix's number*

TRIVIA

- Ensign Wildman's baby was born in *Deadlock,* and finally gets a name: Naomi.
- Seven promises to use nanoprobes to revive any other dead crewmen from now on – but she never does.

RATING

- ...in which Neelix sits around a table discussing the merits of the made-up Talaxian, Klingon and Fictional Indian afterlives, then he talks to himself a lot. An episode that thinks it is saying important things, but is entirely wrong to think that. Not good.

4.13 WAKING MOMENTS

STARDATE 51471.3

Voyager is attacked by aliens for whom dreams are real

The crew have had nightmares involving the same alien – Tuvok dreamt he was naked. Several crewmembers haven't woken up, and Chakotay attempts Lucid Dreaming to discover what's going on. The alien they all saw tells him they live in the dream world, and are

TX 14 January 1998
WRITER André Bormanis
DIRECTOR Alexander Singer
GUEST CAST Mark Colson (Dream Alien), Jennifer Grundy (Ensign)

harmed by the 'waking species'. The aliens attack Voyager, but Chakotay realises he's still dreaming. He wakes, and discovers the rest of the crew are now comatose. He goes to the aliens and injects one with a stimulant that wakes him, ordering him to fix the device they use to maintain the dream state. When the Doctor threatens the aliens with a photon torpedo, they release the crew.

TRIVIA

- Roxann Dawson, like Gates MacFadden before her, gets a Starfleet-issue cardigan to wear to disguise the fact that she's pregnant.

RATING

- Not terribly scientifically accurate, but a spooky enough threat to the ship from this week's generic aliens. Chakotay's solution to the problem is, amusingly, a lot more direct and physical than the sort of battle of wills you'd expect to resolve this sort of plot.

4.14 MESSAGE IN A BOTTLE

STARDATE UNKNOWN

Voyager manages to contact a Starfleet ship

TX 21 January 1998
WRITER Lisa Klink (Story By Rick Williams)
DIRECTOR Nancy Malone
GUEST CAST Andy Dick (EMH-2), Tiny Ron (Idrin), Judson Scott (Rekar), Tony Sears (Starfleet Officer), Valerie Wildman (Nevala)

Seven locates an alien communications relay, and links up with a Starfleet vessel. Janeway sends a message, but it's distorted. They have the option of sending a holographic datastream. The Doctor finds himself on the USS Prometheus, the prototype of a new warship. The skeleton crew, though, is dead, and the Romulans have taken control of the vessel. The Doctor activates the ship's Emergency Medical Hologram, and they work together to defeat the Romulans. In the Delta Quadrant, Voyager is contacted by the owners of the communications relay, the Hirogen, who want them to leave. The two medical holograms take control of the Prometheus and use its special ability to split into three sections to destroy a pursuing Warbird. The Doctor returns to the Delta Quadrant with good news – Starfleet now know that Voyager survived and will do whatever it can to get the ship back to Earth.

QUOTES

- 'I was saving Voyager when you were a gleam in your programmer's eye.' – *The Doctor pulls rank*

TRIVIA

- Reference is made to the Dominion War, which hadn't started when Voyager left the Alpha Quadrant ('it's a long story', as the EMH rightly tells the Doctor). The Romulans are still a few months away from allying themselves with the Federation against The Dominion (*In the Pale Moonlight*).

RATING

- A great episode, albeit one which is essentially a solo effort for the Doctor, and not an episode of *Voyager* as such. But this is very entertaining, extremely funny in places.

4.15 HUNTERS

STARDATE 51501.4

The aliens who own the communications relay come after Voyager

TX 11 February 1998
WRITER Jeri Taylor
DIRECTOR David Livingston
GUEST CAST Roger Morrissey (Beta-Hirogen), Tiny Ron (Alpha-Hirogen)

Starfleet Command sends Voyager messages via the Hirogen communications relay. Voyager heads there to download the messages and comes across a ship where the pilot has been gutted. The crew get batches of letters and news – Tuvok is a grandfather, the Maquis learn that their comrades have been wiped out, Janeway's fiancé, Mark, has married someone else. Tuvok and Seven are captured by the Hirogen when they get too close to the relay. The Hirogen are hunters, and want to display their skeletons. Voyager prepares for battle, and uses the quantum singularity that powers the relay to trap the Hirogen ships. The Hirogen ships are destroyed, but so is the relay, breaking the link with the Alpha Quadrant.

QUOTES

- 'Unusual relics are prized. Yours will make me envied by men and pursued by women.' – *Why the Hirogen want Seven's skeleton*

TRIVIA

- Everyone is amazed that the Hirogen power their ships with quantum singularities, but it's been established before that the Romulans do the same.
- The Maquis met their fate in the *Deep Space Nine* episode *Blaze of Glory*. Thousands died, a handful survive, in custody.
- Janeway's ex-fiancé, Mark, gets a surname: Johnson. Paris' dad gets a first name: Owen.

RATING

- A good episode which shows us a great new baddy after a glimpse the week before and gets the ship back in touch with home without forgetting to tell an exciting and tense story. The Janeway-Mark subplot, hardly ever mentioned in the series, fizzles out.

4.16 PREY

A Hirogen hunts Species 8472

TX 18 February 1998
WRITER Brannon Braga
DIRECTOR Allan Eastman
GUEST CAST Clint Carmichael (Hirogen Hunter), Tony Todd (Alpha-Hirogen)

STARDATE 51652.3

Voyager discovers a wounded Hirogen and brings him aboard. He explains that he captured an alien but it broke free – he's anxious to recapture it. Harry discovers it's a member of Species 8472... and it's loose on Voyager. Tuvok, Seven and the Hirogen start hunting the creature. The alien communicates telepathically with Tuvok, telling him it is trying to get home and will open a singularity. Seven disobeys Janeway and refuses to help. Instead, she gives the alien to the Hirogen, and lets him escape. Janeway realises she can't trust Seven.

TRIVIA

- In a nice bit of continuity (even if it does rather demonstrate they're repeating an old plot), the Doctor tells Seven he'll use the exercises Kes taught him to become more human.

RATING

- Excellent stuff, with Tony Todd basically reprising his role in *Candyman* as a big, scary hardass. It's an ensemble piece, and balances the *Aliens*-style bughunt with the human side of things.

4.17 RETROSPECT

Seven accuses an arms dealer of attacking her

TX 25 February 1998
WRITERS Bryan Fuller and Lisa Klink (Story By Mark Gaberman and Andrew Shepard Price)
DIRECTOR Jesus Salvador Trevino
GUEST CAST Michelle Agnew (Scharn), Michael Horton (Kovin), Adrian Sparks (Magistrate)

STARDATE 51658.2

Enharan arms dealer Kovin installs a new weapons system on Voyager, with help from Seven. She gets agitated and hits Kovin. The Doctor thinks Seven is repressing a memory and hypnotically regresses her. She remembers that Kovin extracted some of her Borg nanoprobes. Kovin denies this, and Janeway begins an investigation. The accusation alone might ruin Kovin, and he runs away. Tuvok and Janeway realise he's innocent – Seven's memory is at fault. Janeway tries to tell Kovin this, but he thinks it's a trap. His ship destabilises and explodes. Seven is filled with remorse.

QUOTES

- 'When Kovin gets what he deserves, you're going to feel a lot better.' – *The Doctor tells Seven*

RATING

- A big, awkward subject – this is, essentially, about rape, the burden of proof and recovered memories. The story doesn't go down the easy route, and Seven's entirely in the wrong. Tuvok could just do a mind-meld, but doesn't. An interesting story.

4.18 THE KILLING GAME Part I

STARDATE 2 OCTOBER 1944

The crew fight Nazi Hirogen in 1944 France

TX 4 March 1998
WRITERS Brannon Braga and Joe Menosky
DIRECTOR David Livingston
GUEST CAST J Paul Boehmer (Kapitan), Mark Deakins (Hirogen SS Officer), Paul Eckstein (Young Hirogen), Danny Goldring (Alpha Hirogen), Peter Hendrixson (Klingon), Mark Metcalf (Hirogen Medic)

Janeway is a leader in the French Resistance; Seven is her munitions expert, Tuvok is a bartender. Allied Command tell them they'll soon be invading their village of St Clare. The Hirogen watch, getting the measure of their prey. The crew have been captured and hypnotically controlled with neural inter-facers to fight on the holodeck. The Doctor has to tend to their injuries. He manages to break Seven's conditioning, and she gets to the holodeck controls. American troops, including Chakotay and Paris, arrive just as the Resistance disrupts Hirogen operations at Nazi HQ. After a massive explosion, the fighting spills from the holodeck onto the ship...

TRIVIA

- This was made as a two-parter, then both episodes were shown on the same night. It wasn't edited together (although it has been on some repeat and syndication runs), so it's listed here as two episodes. The success of this story would inspire two-hour 'movies' in subsequent seasons.
- Janeway's first name in the simulation was originally Genevieve. If Ms Bujold wasn't the reason for calling her that, it was almost certainly the reason it was changed to Katrine.
- There are two holodecks on Voyager.
- Jeri Ryan really sang Seven/Mademoiselle de Neuf's rendition of 'That Old Black Magic'.
- Roxann Dawson's pregnancy isn't hidden in the episode – her holocharacter is pregnant. Which, if you think about it, does raise some interesting questions (with potentially rather unpleasant answers) as to how the holodeck simulates pregnancy.

RATING

- The Hirogen aren't much like the Nazis, and there's no real message or allegory at work, but this is a visually strong, striking and memorable story. There's something wonderful about the surreal *Predator v 'Allo 'Allo* imagery.

4.19 THE KILLING GAME Part II

STARDATE 51715.2

It's war on Voyager

TX 4 March 1998
WRITERS Brannon Braga and Joe Menosky
DIRECTOR Victor Lobl
GUEST CAST J Paul Boehmer (Kapitan), Mark Deakins (Hirogen SS Officer), Paul Eckstein (young Hirogen), Danny Goldring (Alpha Hirogen), Peter Hendrixson (Klingon), Mark Metcalf (Hirogen Medic)

The Voyager crew, all – apart from Janeway, Seven, the Doctor and Harry – still think they are fighting in World War II, but now the fight has spilled off the holodeck. The Hirogen leader refuses to shut down the simulation. Janeway blows up the neural inter-facers that are controlling the crew. The Hirogen leader captures Janeway: he wants holodeck technology as a way of uniting his people. They negotiate a ceasefire, but not all the Hirogen want to talk to their 'prey'. One officer shoots his leader, and starts hunting Janeway. She lures him to an area with damaged holo-emitters and kills him. The remaining Hirogen leave when Janeway gives them holotechnology.

TRIVIA

- The ending is rather problematic – but this is addressed in *Flesh and Blood.*
- The crew suffers 'heavy casualties' in the 19 days the 85 Hirogen hunt them, but we never learn how many people die. It's amazing there's anyone left...

RATING

- More of the same – an entertaining action romp with all the depth of a paddling pool, but a great deal of fun.

4.20 VIS À VIS

STARDATE 51762.4

An alien switches bodies with Paris

Voyager helps a vessel in need of repair. It is using an experimental coaxial warp drive. Paris helps its pilot, Steth. Steth, in turn, steals Paris' DNA record and switches bodies with him. He sends Paris off in

TX 8 April 1998
WRITER Robert J Doherty
DIRECTOR Jesus Salvador Trevino
GUEST CAST Dan Butler (Steth), Elizabeth McGlynn (Daelen)

the ship, and lives his life with not even Torres any the wiser. Paris is arrested by the Benthans and he's confronted by an old woman who wants her body back. Steth becomes violent and is stunned by Tuvok. But Steth has switched bodies with Janeway and escapes in a shuttle fitted with the coaxial warp drive. Paris catches up with him, and everyone is restored to their real body.

TRIVIA

- Crewman Kaplan is mentioned in this story, despite dying in *Unity*.
- The planet the Benthans is from is referred to as both Bentham and Benthos.

RATING

- Dan Butler plays about half a dozen roles, all very well, but despite a few nice Kafkaesque moments when Paris is trying to persuade people of his true identity, this is pretty standard stuff.

4.21 THE OMEGA DIRECTIVE

STARDATE 51781.2

Voyager discovers the most dangerous substance in the universe

TX 15 April 1998
WRITER Lisa Klink (story by Jimmy Diggs and Steve J Kay)
DIRECTOR Victor Lobl
GUEST CAST Jeff Austin (Allos), Kevin McCorkle (Alien Captain)

Voyager's computer screens all flash up the Omega symbol and Janeway starts giving unusual orders. She's following Starfleet protocol known as the Omega Directive, and only Seven understands what she is doing – the ship has detected the highly unstable Omega molecule. Seven believes they should harness Omega, which the Borg believe to be the embodiment of perfection, but Janeway is under strict orders to destroy it, because Omega destroys subspace, making warp travel impossible across vast areas of the galaxy. Janeway briefs the crew, then they rescue some alien researchers who have tried to harness it and been exposed to lethal radiation. Seven creates a harmonic resonance chamber to destroy the remaining molecules. Seven sets about destroying them, but at the last moment she sees them stabilise. As Omega is destroyed, Seven has her first spiritual experience.

TRIVIA

- The key plot point of *Scorpion* was that the Borg were incapable of research, they simply assimilated what they needed. Here, though, Seven explicitly says that the Borg researched Omega molecules.
- The working title was *The Omega Effect*.

RATING

- A straightforward episode that's a good showcase for the Janeway/Seven relationship, but which muddles its message a little, and places far too much value on Seven's faith in a molecule, which there's no good way to dramatise.

4.22 UNFORGETTABLE

STARDATE 51813.4

Chakotay can't remember falling for a beautiful woman

TX 22 April 1998
WRITER Greg Elliot and Michael Perricone
DIRECTOR Andrew J Robinson
GUEST CAST Michael Canavan (Curneth), Virginia Madsen (Kellin)

A ship decloaks in front of Voyager, and Kellin, the pilot, clearly knows Chakotay. She says she was on the ship for several weeks, but that her people, the Ramurans, produce a pheromone that blocks people's memories. She and Chakotay were lovers. She's a bounty hunter, and helped capture a stowaway. There are no computer records to corroborate her story. Other Ramurans are attempting to capture Kellin, but Voyager fights them off. Kellin admits that hers is a closed society which tracks down any people who leave. A Ramuran is onboard, and shoots Kellin with a device that slowly wipes her memories. She tells Chakotay not to forget her, and he notes down everything he can still recall in his logs to remember her by.

TRIVIA

- Virginia Madsen is a familiar face who's appeared in *Dune* (1984) and *Highlander II: The Quickening* (1991), among other films.

RATING

- A story that makes no sense – most weeks, the crew demonstrate ridiculous forensic skills, but here they can't tell whether a woman was on board the ship for weeks. Robert Beltran seems ill at ease, and it's difficult to work out what the point of the episode is. Would it be too glib to say this episode is completely forgettable?

4.23 LIVING WITNESS

Voyager is reproduced in an alien museum

TX 29 April 1998
WRITER Bryan Fuller (story by Brannon Braga)
DIRECTOR Tim Russ
GUEST CAST Rod Arrants (Daleth), Marie Chambers (Kyrian Arbiter), Brian Fitzpatrick (Tedran), Morgan Margolis (Vaskan visitor), Craig Richard Nelson (Vaskan Arbiter), Henry Woronicz (Quarren)

STARDATE UNKNOWN

Voyager is reproduced as a holographic exhibit in a museum. Seven-hundred years ago, they apparently started the civil war between the Kyrians and the Vaskans. The crew are portrayed as ruthless killers who killed millions as they let nothing stop them getting home. They sided with the Vaskans and started the war. The curator, the Kyrian Quarren, finds the Doctor's holo-emitter and manages to reactivate him. The Doctor is appalled by the depiction of Voyager, which is blatant propaganda. The Doctor recreates his own version of events, showing that the Kyrians invaded Voyager and started the war. This provokes new fighting. The Doctor says he would rather be deactivated than cause bloodshed. Many years in the future, visitors to the museum are told how this offer of self-sacrifice made the Doctor an inspirational figure who helped to heal the wounds of the two societies and oversaw the Dawn of Harmony. Eventually, they are told, the Doctor left in a ship, heading for the Alpha Quadrant.

QUOTES

- 'Facts be damned!' – *The Doctor isn't happy*

TRIVIA

- The Kyrians believed the Doctor was an android, and the one in the simulation has the same yellow eyes as Data. Seven is seen in full Borg costume again. Other differences include a Starfleet uniform with black leather gloves, Chakotay having an enormous tattoo, and Tuvok having more demonic ears.
- Tim Russ and Roxann Dawson both took the director's course at the same time, but Dawson's pregnancy meant she wouldn't direct until *Riddles* in the sixth season. She isn't in this episode, which was filmed the week she gave birth.

RATING

- One of the best episodes of *Voyager*, although the recreation of the nasty Voyager crew at the beginning isn't as much fun as the actors seem to think it is. The story also misses a trick – while there are hints that the Doctor's version is idealising the crew a little, it would have been nice to see his subjective version of events, rather than having his version as 'the truth'.

4.24 DEMON

Voyager needs deuterium – but the only source is a planet deadly to all life

TX 6 May 1998
WRITER Kenneth Biller (story by André Bormanis)
DIRECTOR Anson Williams
GUEST CAST Majel Barrett (Computer Voice), Alexander Enberg (Vorik), Susan Lewis (Transporter Technician)

STARDATE UNKNOWN

Voyager is running critically low fuel. Seven detects a source on a 'demon class' planet – as the name suggests, it's deadly to human life, with extreme levels of thermionic radiation. An attempt to beam deuterium aboard fails, and Harry volunteers himself and Paris to go down in a shuttle. They discover pools of silver liquid rich in deuterium, but their spacesuits begin to leak and they collapse. Concerned, Janeway orders Voyager to land on the planet. Chakotay and Seven search for Paris and Harry – and find them, unharmed and not wearing their spacesuits. They should be dead, and when they beam back to the ship, they collapse. It seems they have adapted to life on the planet. The Doctor discovers silver fluid in their blood. Torres and Janeway discover that the 'adapted' crewmen are actually duplicates – the fluid is a life-form. Voyager tries to lift off, but is held fast by the fluid. Janeway hurts the life-form with a nadion burst, and enters negotiations – the life-form has discovered consciousness, are lonely, and want to duplicate the whole crew. The fluid retreats and Voyager leaves – watched by duplicates of the crew.

QUOTES

- 'Now we're going down, we won't be going up again soon.' – *Tuvok gives a damage report*

TRIVIA

- *Innocence* had included a mention that the warp core would run out of fuel after three years, and this catches up with the crew here.
- There's a sequel to this story, *Course: Oblivion*.
- Why the ship's running out of deuterium is never explained – it's pretty much the most simple isotope, so it ought to be easy to replicate. And if what happens at the end isn't a violation of the Prime Directive, it's hard to see what would be.

RATING

- Exactly like *Power Play*, but with all the drama and threat painstakingly extracted from it, *Demon* has a couple of spooky moments in the middle when Harry and Paris are alone on the surface, and clever bits when it turns out they aren't evil doubles.

4.25 ONE

STARDATE 51929.3

The crew, apart from the Doctor and Seven, enter stasis as the ship passes through a nebula

TX 13 May 1998
WRITER Jeri Taylor
DIRECTOR Kenneth Biller
GUEST CAST Majel Barrett (Computer Voice), Ron Ostrow (Borg Drone), Wade Williams (Trajis Lotaric)

Voyager has met an obstacle – a Mutara class nebula with such intense sub-nucleonic radiation that the crew wouldn't survive the month-long journey through it. It will take years to go round it. Janeway orders the crew into shielded stasis capsules – Seven and the Doctor, immune to the radiation, will control the ship. Once underway, Seven adopts an efficient routine that irritates the Doctor, and the two bicker. Technical problems mount as the radiation proves unexpectedly harsh on the ship's bio-neural gel packs, and the Doctor is confined to Sickbay. Seven begins to feel lonely – she's used to being part of the collective, after all. An alien ship hails Voyager. It's Trajun Lotaric, a trader who's also passing through the nebula on his own. He initially appears friendly, then starts to sabotage the ship. The Doctor realises he's actually just an hallucination of Seven's. The Doctor's program fails with hours to go, and Seven is totally alone. She starts seeing Borg, who taunt her that she has failed. The ship's on the verge of total breakdown. Seven realises she will have to gamble on diverting power from life support to the engines to break free of the nebula. She collapses, waking in Sickbay to discover she's saved the ship and the entire crew.

QUOTES

- 'We've come 15,000 light years. We haven't been stopped by temporal anomalies or warp core breaches or hostile aliens, and I'm damned if I'm going to be stopped by a nebula.' – *Janeway*

TRIVIA

- Jim Swallow did uncredited work on the script, which was based on an idea by John Devins.
- We're told that Voyager has a crew of 151, exactly the same as the figure given in *Persistence of Vision*, despite a large number of deaths since. Once again, the ship is operated by less than 100 people, the bare minimum that was needed according to *The 37s*.
- The original Nebula appeared in *Star Trek II: The Wrath of Khan*, but it had none of the lethal properties of the nebula in this episode.

RATING

- It feels remarkably cynical – the two fan favourite characters alone on the ship, without Chakotay or Neelix spoiling things. And it really works, with great bickering giving way to a spooky story with a couple of genuine twists. The internet bulletin boards were right: kill everyone except the Doctor and Seven and this would be a great show.

4.26 HOPE AND FEAR

STARDATE 51978.2

A Federation ship arrives to take the crew home

Arturis, a trader, helps Voyager in return for passage to the next star system. He decodes a Starfleet signal, and tells them there's a Starfleet ship there waiting for them. This is the USS Dauntless, fitted

TX 20 May 1998
WRITERS Brannon Braga and Joe Menosky (story by Rick Berman, Brannon Braga and Joe Menosky)
DIRECTOR Winrich Kolbe
GUEST CAST Jack Shearer (Hayes), Ray Wise (Arturis)

with a quantum slipstream drive, and the Starfleet message tells them that it's pre-programmed to take them home. Janeway is suspicious, and Tuvok keeps an eye on Arturis. Decoding the message for herself, Janeway finds it's only about wormhole detection. When they confront Arturis, he activates the slipstream drive, taking Janeway and Seven hostage. He is angry for Janeway siding with the Borg against Species 8472 – his planet was assimilated once the Borg won, and now he wants the Voyager crew to suffer the same fate. Voyager rescues Janeway and Seven, but the slipstream drive is damaged in the attempt. Arturis is on a direct course into Borg space.

QUOTES

- 'You don't feel anger towards a storm, you just avoid it.' – *Arturis on the Borg*

TRIVIA

- With *Deep Space Nine* drawing to a close, the fan rumour was that *Voyager* would return home and start more conventional adventures inside Federation boundaries, possibly with cast members from either *Deep Space Nine* or even *The Next Generation* joining the crew. This episode seems designed to play on those rumours, but Rick Berman insists that actually returning home was never considered.
- The Dauntless is designated NX-01-A, almost the same as Archer's ship in *Enterprise*.

RATING

- A good season finale for perhaps Voyager's strongest season. This is a good ensemble piece, and one where – because it's the last of the season – there is a chance the crew could actually get home.

STAR TREK: VOYAGER
SEASON FIVE

5.1 NIGHT

STARDATE 52081.2

Voyager enters an empty area of space

TX 14 October 1998
WRITERS Brannon Braga and Joe Menosky
DIRECTOR David Livingston
GUEST CAST Steve Dennis (Night Alien), Ken Magee (Emck), Martin Rayner (Dr Chaotica)

Voyager has entered an empty area, facing two years in the void, and the crew is getting restless. Tom has started a new holonovel, *Captain Proton*, based on 1930s SF serials. Janeway is brooding in her quarters when the ship loses power, and it becomes clear they are caught in a dampening field. Aliens board the ship, but are driven away by a ship run by Malon Emck. He wants the alien they captured; in return, he'll lead them to a spatial vortex that will take them to the other end of the expanse. The Malon have poisoned the alien's people by dumping antimatter waste in the void. Janeway wants to put a stop to this by closing the vortex, but will have to stay behind in a shuttle to do so. Instead they close the vortex while they are in it, surfing the shockwave and emerging on the other side.

QUOTES

- 'Time to take out the garbage.' – *Janeway gets mean*

TRIVIA

- Captain Proton makes his first appearance – it's a holonovel based on *Flash Gordon* and *Buck Rogers*, with a dash of *King of the Rocket Men.*

RATING

- A simple enough environmental allegory, and the new race of baddies are watchable enough, but the most interesting stuff is the interactions among the crew, and the signs of strain they're starting to show.

5.2 DRONE

STARDATE UNKNOWN

A superadvanced Borg arrives on the ship

TX 21 October 1998
WRITERS Bryan Fuller, Brannon Braga and Joe Menosky (story by Bryan Fuller and Harry Doc Kloor)
DIRECTOR Les Landau
GUEST CAST Majel Barrett (Computer Voice), Todd Babcock (Mulchaey), J Paul Boehmer (Drone)

The Doctor's emitter picks up Borg nanoprobes during a transporter accident, and has created a life-form. A drone is created, but one upgraded by the Doctor's twenty-ninth century technology. He calls himself One, and starts asking about the Borg. The Collective detects him and sends a Sphere to extract him. Seven tells One the Collective is evil, and that if he is assimilated, it will become more dangerous. He beams over to the Sphere, but to disrupt it. He steers the Sphere into a nebula, where it's disintegrated. One survives, but refuses treatment for his injuries, because he knows the Borg will pursue Voyager until they have him. He dies.

QUOTES

- 'Voyager is my Collective.' – *Seven*

TRIVIA

- The Borg Sphere here is a long-range tactical vessel. The model was first used in *Star Trek: First Contact*.

RATING

- Basically *I, Borg* again, but this is much more satisfying. Boehmer is very good in what could be an unrewarding role.

5.3 EXTREME RISK

STARDATE UNKNOWN

Torres is feeling self-destructive

TX 28 October 1998
WRITER Kenneth Biller
DIRECTOR Cliff Bole
GUEST CAST Daniel Betances (The Pilot), Hamilton Camp (Vrelk), Alexander Enberg (Vorik)

Voyager needs to retrieve a probe from a gas giant after it is chased there by the Malon. Paris proposes they build a shuttle he's been working on, the Delta Flyer, which is tougher than their standard shuttles. Torres, meanwhile, takes part in dangerous holodeck scenarios. The Malon captain Vrelk hails them, and Seven's scans reveal they are also building a craft to retrieve the probe. Voyager's crew speeds up, but Torres is injured while simulating a flight. The Doctor realises she's been injured before in holodeck accidents. She admits that since she learned the Maquis were all dead, she's been feeling numb. The Malon are ready to go, and Janeway orders the Delta Flyer launched. The Away Mission is fraught with danger, but they retrieve the probe, and Torres saves the shuttle.

QUOTES

- 'Proposing the same flawed strategy over and over again will not make it more effective.' – *Tuvok*

TRIVIA

- One of Torres' risky programs is skydiving from orbit – originally the opening shot of *Star Trek: Generations*, with Kirk diving. This was new footage (and presumably the costume needed at least some alteration).
- The Delta Flyer becomes a regular feature of the series from now on.

RATING

- It's six months (15 episodes) since Torres heard about the fate of the Maquis and there's been no hint that it affected her as it does in this episode (or that she's been seriously injured). With a little build-up, this would be a great episode – as it is, it's just another one where a new problem is neatly resolved. It trivialises depression, rather than dramatising it.

5.4 IN THE FLESH

STARDATE 52136.4

Species 8472 is training to invade Earth

TX 4 November 1998
WRITER Nicholas Sagan
DIRECTOR David Livingston
GUEST CAST Zach Galligan (Gentry), Tucker Smallwood (Bullock), Kate Vernon (Archer), Ray Walston (Boothby)

Chakotay is at Starfleet Headquarters on Earth. He talks to Commander Valerie Archer, and it becomes clear she's an alien posing as a human. Chakotay beams one Ensign back to Voyager, but the alien kills himself... and reverts to his natural form: he's Species 8472. They have created a vast simulation of Earth, and must be planning an invasion. They have adapted to the Borg nanoprobes. Chakotay, Paris and Harry go back to the simulation, where Chakotay has a date with Archer, who discovers he is human and arrests him. Janeway negotiates with the alien leader, who looks like the Academy groundsman, Boothby. Species 8472 believed the humans to be hostile, after they allied with the Borg. Both sides were equally fearful of each other, but Janeway and 'Boothby' agree to work for peace.

TRIVIA

- A story based on the idea of 'sleeper' villages used by the Russians to infiltrate agents into the West during the Cold War.
- There are 128 crew on Voyager. There's a Ferengi cadet in the simulated Starfleet – in reality, there's only one: Nog, and this isn't him.
- This story sets up a new understanding between Species 8472 and the crew of Voyager, and the promise of peace. This is the last time we see them in *Voyager* (and, so, it's their last appearance to date).

RATING

- This doesn't fit what we know about Species 8472 – it feels like a shapeshifter story from *Deep Space Nine*. That said, it's a funny episode, and Chakotay gets to be a rounded human being rather than banging on about made-up Indian things.

5.5 ONCE UPON A TIME

STARDATE UNKNOWN

Neelix comforts a little girl

TX 11 November 1998
WRITER Michael Taylor
DIRECTOR John Kretchmer
GUEST CAST Nancy Hower (Wildman), Wallace Langham (Flotter), Justin Louis (Trevis), Scarlett Pomers (Naomi Wildman)

Paris, Tuvok and Ensign Wildman are in a shuttle which hits an ion storm, then crashes, seriously injuring Wildman. Neelix is given the job of keeping Wildman's daughter Naomi occupied, and he takes her to the holodeck to show her *The Adventures of Flotter*. Neelix remembers losing his own family, and Naomi overhears that her mother is hurt. Chakotay and Seven begin a race against time to dig out the shuttle from the crash site. They manage it minutes before the air runs out. Wildman is saved and reunited with her daughter.

QUOTES

- 'In accepting the inevitable, one finds peace.'
  'If that's another Vulcan saying, Tuvok, I'll stick with "live long and prosper".' – *Tuvok and Paris*

TRIVIA

- Neelix has 'sisters' here, not just the one sister, Alixia, he had in *Mortal Coil*.
- Polarising the hull of the shuttle will make it more obvious to sensors – does the same apply when Archer polarises the hull plating in *Enterprise*?

RATING

- The world really didn't need a sequel to *Mortal Coil*. This is better than that episode, but that's not exactly setting the bar very high, and if you honestly can't think of a better way to spend an hour than watching this, you're in trouble.

5.6 TIMELESS

STARDATE 52143.6

Fifteen years ago, Harry destroyed Voyager

Fifteen years in the future, Chakotay and Harry investigate the wreckage of Voyager, which is frozen in a glacier. They activate the Doctor, and Harry explains that they want to change history. In the

TX 18 November 1998
WRITERS Brannon Braga and Joe Menosky (story by Rick Berman, Brannon Braga and Joe Menosky)
DIRECTOR LeVar Burton
GUEST CAST LeVar Burton (Captain Geordi LaForge), Christine Harnos (Tessa Omond)

present, the crew celebrate creating a quantum slipstream drive that will send them to the Alpha Quadrant. Paris finds a phase variance that will destabilise the drive. Harry will take the Delta Flyer ahead and send back data on the phase variance. Harry sends the wrong data, and Voyager crashes into an icy moon. Starfleet refuses to go back to help them, and Chakotay and Harry are going to use Seven's Borg technology to send the correct data to Voyager. Captain LaForge of the USS Challenger arrives to stop them. They send the data, and in the present, Seven gets the data. The ship still crashes. Harry sends another stream of data that will disperse the slipstream. The future is erased, and in the present, Voyager continues on its way.

QUOTES

- 'Don't even try.' – *Janeway's advice on how to deal with time paradoxes*

TRIVIA

- The director presumably didn't find it too hard to persuade LeVar Burton to reprise his role as Geordi...
- There are now 153 people on Voyager. This is possibly an attempt to take the 151 'crew' figure that's frequently given, and add Seven and Naomi. But it's more people than *In the Flesh*.

RATING

- Garrett Wang is given a much more interesting and meaty part than usual and puts in a fine performance. This is one of the very best episodes of Voyager, even if it demonstrates the show's worse tendency – flicking the reset switch.

5.7 INFINITE REGRESS

Seven experiences multiple personalities

TX 25 November 1998
WRITER Robert J Doherty (story by Robert J Doherty and Jimmy Diggs)
DIRECTOR David Livingston
GUEST CAST Majel Barrett (Computer Voice), Neil Maffin (Ven), Erica Mer (Human Girl), Scarlett Pomers (Naomi Wildman)

STARDATE 52188.7

Voyager comes across Borg debris and a neural interlink frequency. Seven starts adopting different personalities: one minute she's a Klingon, the next a little girl. The Doctor isolates her, and discovers she's storing the patterns of races the Borg assimilated. The signal is damaged, though. Species 6339 have infected the Borg with a virus. Seven's neural patterns are erased, and Tuvok conducts a mind-meld to restore them. It's a chaotic mental landscape. Harry manages to disable the alien technology, and Tuvok and Seven are restored to normal.

QUOTES

- 'Subunit of Ensign Wildman.' – *Seven's description of Naomi*

TRIVIA

- The USS Tombaugh was assimilated 12 years ago, before *Q Who*.
- We've started to get enough of the history of the Borg to piece a few things together, and there's a big puzzle. They allocate each spacefaring species a number as they encounter them, not as they assimilate them, as is occasionally stated: while one usually leads to the other, there are species they don't bother with, like the Kazon – Species 329 – and species they can't assimilate, like Species 8472. It's interesting that the Ferengi are Species 180, as that implies the two races encountered each other centuries ago. In *Dark Frontier* we learn that the Borg Queen is a member of Species 125 – meaning that she's not one of the 'original' Borg (who are presumably Species 1). The Borg know they can contact their own kind in the past of *Star Trek: First Contact*, and we're told in *Dragon's Teeth* that 892 years ago they had only assimilated a 'handful' of systems. Seven's memory of that time is fragmentary, suggesting the Collective wasn't as all-embracing, and they were defeated by the Vaadwaur, suggesting they weren't as powerful. The puzzle is that the first humans to be assimilated would appear to be the Hansens, Seven's family. That was 18 years before Scorpion, and humans were designated Species 5618 (we'll learn that in *Dark Frontier*). Species 6339 were discovered four years ago, and we know one of the Borg's most recent discoveries is Species 8472. We'll meet Species 10026 in *Dark Frontier*. This means they've almost doubled the number of species they've encountered in less than 20 years, despite being active for centuries. It seems clear that they've made some massive technological leap in the last generation. We never find out what this is, but two candidates we see are the transwarp drive and the nanoprobes (which might allow faster assimilation, therefore more efficient expansion).

RATING

- A strong performance by Jeri Ryan proves she deserves all the screen time she gets, but this is a straightforward script.

5.8 NOTHING HUMAN

STARDATE UNKNOWN

An evil medical hologram is the only thing that can save Torres

TX 2 December 1998
WRITER Jeri Taylor
DIRECTOR David Livingston
GUEST CAST David Clennon (Crell Moset), Jad Mager (Tabor), Frank Welker (Alien Voice)

An alien attaches itself to Torres, and the Doctor lacks the knowledge to extract it. He and Harry create a hologram of the exobiologist Crell Moset, who reproduces his advanced lab on the holodeck. Torres objects to putting her life in the hands of a Cardassian. Crewman Tabor also raises objections – Crell used to experiment on live Bajorans, killing hundreds. Torres thinks that allowing Crell to operate will validate his research. Janeway over-rules her, and the Doctor and Crell extract the creature. The alien's comrades arrive, and the Doctor stuns it, rather than killing it, like Crell suggests. The Doctor deletes Crell from the database.

QUOTES

- 'Let's just deactivate the evil hologram and let B'Elanna die. At least we'll have our morals intact.' – *Tom*

TRIVIA

- The working title was *Not Human.*
- Perhaps this was originally a *Deep Space Nine* episode where the real Crell showed up to treat a regular character – this would make more of the objections make sense, and would make it less of a coincidence that there's a Bajoran onboard whose family was murdered by Crell.

RATING

- A very dumb premise – no one, surely, seriously suggests that we destroy all research done by people we object to? Where do we draw the line – do we stop using Pythagoras' theorem because he probably kept slaves? Crell did horrible things, but now something good has come from that. And, anyway, this is a hologram, not the real Crell. So, it's a thought-provoking episode, but one of the thoughts it provokes is 'jeez, these people are dumb'.

5.9 THIRTY DAYS

STARDATE 52179.4

Tom spends a month in the Brig

TX 9 December 1998
WRITER Kenneth Biller (story by Scott Miller)
DIRECTOR Winrich Kolbe
GUEST CAST Willie Garson (Riga), Alissa Kramer (Jenny Delaney), Heidi Kramer (Megan Delaney), Benjamin Livingston (Burkus), Warren Munson (Paris)

Paris is locked in the brig for 30 days, and recalls why: Voyager approached an ocean in space, a giant globe of water kept in check by failing containment fields. The inhabitants, the Moneans, ask for help, and Paris volunteers. When the Delta Flyer is damaged by a giant sea creature, the hull is breached and water starts pouring in. Paris discovers that the Moneans' mining operations are causing the problem, but can't persuade them how serious the situation is. He plans to destroy the oxygen mines, but Janeway fires on him before he can. He's demoted to Ensign and placed in the Brig for breaking the Prime Directive. He's been writing a letter to send to his father explaining this.

TRIVIA

- The working title was *Down Deep.*
- There's another Captain Proton sequence seen in this episode. While filming the sequence, which involved a rocket pack, Robert Duncan McNeill set fire to his bottom, and refused point blank to wear the rocket pack ever again.
- The Federation Navy is mentioned for the first time.
- The Delaney sisters appear for the only time, playing Malicia and Demonica in Tom's holodeck fantasy.

RATING

- A Prime Directive episode, but an exciting one, and one of Robert Duncan McNeill's best performances as Paris. Both the waterworld and the holodeck stuff are visual feasts.

5.10 COUNTERPOINT

STARDATE UNKNOWN

Janeway's new flame is only interested in her ship

TX 16 December 1998
WRITER Michael Taylor
DIRECTOR Les Landau
GUEST CAST Alexander Enberg (Vorik), Mark Harelik (Kashyk), Randy Lowell (Torat), J Patrick McCormack (Prax), Randy Oglesby (Kir), Jake Sakson (Adar)

The Devore stop Voyager to inspect them. They mistrust strangers, or 'gaharay', and particularly don't like telepaths. The Ship is harbouring Brenari refugees in the transporter buffers. Voyager is in this part of space because wormholes are known in a Mutara-class nebula here. They pass the inspection, then Janeway is contacted by the inspector, Kashyk, who warns her that the Devore know about the telepaths and are sending a squadron to intercept. He wants asylum, and helps her locate the counterpoint – the next place the wormhole will appear. Janeway and Kashyk kiss. The Devore detect the ship. Voyager fakes the arrival of the wormhole as cover for the refugees to escape in shuttles, through the real wormhole. Kashyk doesn't want this in the official report, and lets Voyager carry on its way.

QUOTES

- 'Let's just say I usually go on my instincts.' – *Janeway's justification for breaking the Prime Directive*

TRIVIA

- Kashyk (or, more precisely, Kashyyk) is the home planet of the Wookiees in *Star Wars*. Someone on the staff is a Star Wars fan – the Bothans and B'omar are also *Star Wars* creatures.
- There are two Vulcans on board, Tuvok and Vorik. Another telepath on the crew, the Betazoid Gerat, isn't mentioned.
- Janeway admits she broke the Prime Directive, the crime she demoted Paris for in the previous episode.

RATING

- It's a bit odd to see Janeway being romanced by, essentially, a Gestapo officer. This is a solid enough episode, though, and it's a nice change of pace.

5.11 LATENT IMAGE

STARDATE UNKNOWN

The Doctor's memories have been altered

TX 20 January 1999
WRITER Joe Menosky (story by Eileen Connors, Brannon Braga and Joe Menosky)
DIRECTOR Mike Vejar
GUEST CAST Nancy Bell (Jetal), Scarlett Pomers (Naomi Wildman)

The Doctor can't remember operating on Harry 18 months ago, as the records say he did. Seven helps him restore memories of an alien shooting Harry and Ensign Jetal. Janeway tells the Doctor she'll investigate, but he discovers it was her deleting his files. She tells him he was damaged in that incident, and refuses to tell him what happened. She eventually relents. The Doctor only had time to save one of the crewmen, and chose Harry. He had a breakdown at Jetal's funeral. He has to come to terms with conflicts within his program.

TRIVIA

- Although the flashback takes place at the end of the third season, there's no sign of Kes and Tom has his new hairstyle.

RATING

- You'd think that part of any doctor's training would be to prioritise and make life or death decisions, but this is played more as the Doctor's growing realisation that he's more than his programming. Like *Thirty Days*, it feels like the writers desperately trying to get back to the original character, but this episode works.

5.12 BRIDE OF CHAOTICA

STARDATE UNKNOWN

Aliens are at war in Tom's holonovel

TX 27 January 1999

Voyager crashes into a gravimetric barrier as Paris enjoys himself in his Captain Proton holonovel. But men from the Fifth Dimension arrive and enter discussions with the evil Dr Chaotica, who declares war on them. The visitors are photonic aliens, convinced the holodeck is real, and Tom can't convince them otherwise. Their attacks on Chaotica's

WRITERS Bryan Fuller and Michael Taylor (story by Bryan Fuller)
DIRECTOR Allan Kroeker
GUEST CAST Tarik Ergin (Robot), Jim Krestalude (Alien #1), Paul F O'Brien (Geral), Martin Rayner (Dr Chaotica)

fortress start to damage Voyager. The Doctor gets the aliens to cease-fire by pretending to be the President of Earth, while Janeway poses as the alluring Queen Arachnia and uses her irresistible pheromones to kill Chaotica's men. Tom, as Captain Proton, uses his destructo beam to destroy the fortress. Voyager realigns with normal space and the aliens withdraw.

QUOTES

- 'Unimpeachable.' – *The Doctor's verdict on his performance as the President of Earth*

TRIVIA

- There are 150 people on Voyager.
- This episode was hastily written when a small fire damaged the Bridge set (a spark set fire to the starfield backdrop curtain – the damage wasn't from the fire, it was from the sprinklers that were set off to douse it).
- Cutting between scenes on the holodeck takes the form of 1930s (and *Star Wars*)-style wipes. Which raises the question of how the people on the holodeck experience them...

RATING

- If there's one show that ought to be wary of mocking other people's science fiction clichés and formulaic storytelling, it's *Star Trek*. Nevertheless, this is a very entertaining episode. Kate Mulgrew even seems to be impersonating William Shatner when she plays Arachnia. This is one of the best episodes of *Voyager*.

5.13 GRAVITY

STARDATE 52438.9

Tuvok grapples with his emotions

TX 3 February 1999
WRITERS Nick Sagan and Bryan Fuller (story by Jimmy Diggs and Bryan Fuller and Nick Sagan)
DIRECTOR Terry Windell
GUEST CAST Leroy D Brazile (Young Tuvok), Paul S Eckstein (Yost), Lori Petty (Noss), Joseph Ruskin (Vulcan Master)

Tuvok and Paris are stranded on a planet after their shuttle falls into a gravity well, and soon meet the beautiful Noss. Tuvok helps her evade scavengers and the two become close. Paris encourages Tuvok to explore his feelings for her. Tuvok remembers his training on Vulcan. Voyager is told by the alien Yost that the phenomenon that caught their shuttle is dangerous, and it's to be sealed – trapping Tuvok and Paris forever. Noss tends to Tuvok's wounds and kisses him, and can't understand why he keeps her away. Torres manages to set up a transporter beam. Noss is taken to her homeworld, but before she goes, Tuvok mind-melds with her to show how much he liked her.

QUOTES

- 'Love is the most dangerous emotion of all.' – *Says Tuvok*

TRIVIA

- Lori Petty played Tank Girl in the under-rated, but still not terribly good, film of the same name.
- The episode was filmed at Vasquez Rocks.
- Voyager now has a crew of 152 and its 50,000 light years from home.

RATING

- A very old-school episode – practically a Kirk and Spock one. It's pretty good, although Noss is much more interesting before they can translate what she's saying.

5.14 BLISS

STARDATE 52542.3

All the crew's dreams come true

TX 10 February 1999
WRITERS Robert J Doherty (story by Bill Prady)

Voyager has found a wormhole to Earth, and Starfleet has sent a lot of good news from home. Seven isn't as optimistic, and doesn't understand why everyone else is. There's an alien ship in the wormhole that only Seven can see. Naomi Wildman and the Doctor are also unaffected by the optimism. Chakotay deactivates the Doctor and leads Seven to a suspended animation booth. Seven escapes and

DIRECTOR Cliff Bole
GUEST CAST Scarlett Pomers (Naomi Wildman), W Morgan Sheppard (Qatai)

tries to stop the ship entering the wormhole. The alien, Qatai, explains the ship is being eaten by a telepathic organism that keeps its prey happy as it devours them; he has been trapped for nearly 40 years. They team up and both their ships escape. Qatai remains with the creature, obsessed with destroying it.

TRIVIA

- T'Pel is seen, but isn't Marva Hicks, the actress who plays her in *Persistence of Vision* or *Body and Soul.*

RATING

- Another episode that feels like one from the original series. This is entertaining enough stuff.

5.15 DARK FRONTIER

Seven is brought back to the Collective

DOUBLE-LENGTH EPISODE
TX 17 February 1999
WRITERS Brannon Braga and Joe Menosky
DIRECTORS Cliff Bole/Terry Windell
GUEST CAST Kirk Bailey (Magnus Hansen), Eric Cadora (Alien), Katelin Petersen (Annika Hansen), Scarlett Pomers (Naomi Wildman), Laura Stepp (Erin Hansen), Susanna Thompson (Borg Queen)

STARDATE 52619.2

Janeway plans to raid a Borg scout ship for its transwarp coil. She assigns Seven to study her parents' logs to look for a way in. Seven vividly remembers her early years. The crew practice their mission on the holodeck, and become aware they'll have only two minutes to complete it. Seven becomes paranoid that the Borg knows about the plan. As the mission proceeds, the Collective contacts Seven, and she refuses to transport back to Voyager. The Borg Queen welcomes Seven back to the Collective. She wants to study Seven's memory, to assist the assimilation of humanity. Janeway takes the Delta Flyer to rescue Seven. Seven helps some individuals escape the Borg. The Queen warns Seven that she'll become a drone if she doesn't help create a biogenic bomb to explode in Earth's atmosphere. One of the drones guarding her is Seven's father. The Borg detects Janeway, who beams over to their ship. Janeway confronts the Queen, and Seven disrupts the power supply to the Queen. They escape, destroying a Borg ship that pursues them.

TRIVIA

- Voyager 'movie' episodes were designed with a strong cliffhanger halfway through, so that in syndication the story could be broken up into two episodes. They are written as one episode, but filmed as two, with different directors.
- Alice Krige wasn't available to reprise her movie role as the Borg Queen, but would return for *Endgame.*
- Seven gets a new catsuit (a burgundy one).
- We're told that money was abolished on Earth in the twenty-second century and the New World Economy superceded it. This ties in with what Kirk says in *Star Trek IV: The Voyage Home.*
- Janeway says it's two years since *Scorpion.*
- Chakotay says Janeway 'always' rubs her com-badge when she's about to make an unpopular decision. She hasn't done it once, in any of more than 100 previous episodes.

RATING

- A show that presses all the fanboy buttons, and some fans really love it, but this is a strangely clinical and passionless story.

5.16 THE DISEASE

Harry puts love over duty

TX 24 February 1999
WRITER Michael Taylor (story by Kenneth Biller)
DIRECTOR David Livingston
GUEST CAST Charles Rocket (Jippeq), Musetta Vander (Tal)

STARDATE UNKNOWN

Harry helps a Varro generational ship repair its warp drive, and becomes attracted to one of the crew, Tal. Harry picks up some bioluminescence after making love to Tal, and Janeway insists he stops seeing her. Harry disobeys, and he and Tal become closer. Tuvok discovers a stowaway, who tells him that many of the Varro are on the verge of mutiny. Harry and Tal run off together in a shuttle. Janeway wants to treat Harry, but this will break the bond with Tal and he refuses. Both Voyager and the Varro ship begin breaking up: they're infected by silicon parasites. The Varro ship separates into various sections, each of which has new leadership. Tal leaves, and Harry refuses treatment – he wants to feel the loss of the bond with her.

QUOTES

- 'You are such a lousy liar. Have you learned nothing from me in five-and-a-half years?' – *Paris is disappointed in Harry*

TRIVIA

- From here on, every episode has an additional advert break, and the average length of the episodes is two minutes less.
- We learn that Starfleet personnel need their Captain's permission before they have a sexual relationship with an alien species. This quite clearly isn't the case anywhere in *Star Trek* except this episode. Although we might infer that it would have been an incentive for Kirk to get promoted to captain as quickly as he does. It raises all sorts of questions – would Torres be allowed to sleep with humans and Klingons without permission, or just other half-human/half-Klingons? Did she and Tom ask Janeway's permission?

RATING

- Another rubbish 'Harry Kim in love' episode. Garrett Wang does his best, but he's doomed from the start.

5.17 COURSE: OBLIVION

STARDATE 52586.3

Voyager is disintegrating

TX 3 March 1999
WRITERS Bryan Fuller and Nick Sagan (story by Bryan Fuller)
DIRECTOR Anson Williams

Torres discovers that the ship is losing molecular cohesion, then falls violently ill. Other crewmen start suffering, and the Doctor realises they are breaking down at the molecular level. They realise it could be due to their visit to the 'demon planet' ten months and 11 days ago. They realise they are the duplicates of the Voyager crew, not the originals, and are losing their new forms because radiation from the warp drive, harmless to humans, is lethal to them. They head for a Class-Y planet, but they are fired upon. The crew mutiny against 'Janeway''s insistence they head for Earth. 'Chakotay' dies, as does 'Janeway'. 'Harry' is now in command. He sends a distress signal... but the ship has disintegrated before the real Voyager arrives to investigate.

TRIVIA

- A follow-up to *Demon*, it starts with Torres and Paris getting married... this will happen for real in *Drive*, but we don't see the ceremony there. The duplicate Tom has been demoted, the duplicate Tuvok promoted, just like the real ones.
- The duplicate Voyager has managed to modify its engines and would have got to Earth in two years!

RATING

- A cheat, of course, but the revelation of the crew's true identity is a nice twist, and a cunning way to solve a huge unresolved plot from *Demon*. But after that, it's not just the ship that falls apart, the story does, too – endless scenes of actors with slimy make-up. It's an OK episode.

5.18 THE FIGHT

STARDATE UNKNOWN

Chakotay hallucinates that he's a boxer

TX 24 March 1999
WRITER Joe Menosky (story by Michael Taylor)
DIRECTOR Rick Kolbe
GUEST CAST Carlos Palomino (The Boxer), Ned Romero (Great Grandfather), Ray Walston (Boothby)

Chakotay hallucinates that he's the Maquis Mauler, a boxer. He was knocked out on the holodeck during a boxing simulation. He hears voices, and accidentally swings at Tuvok. He's placed under restraint. Voyager finds a ship adrift, and it's clear its crew were affected like Chakotay. Voyager has become trapped in chaotic space. The voices Chakotay can hear are aliens telling him how to escape. As he boxes Kid Chaos, he realises how to escape. Voyager adjusts its deflectors and escapes chaotic space.

TRIVIA

- Chakotay says Boothby trained him as a boxer at the Academy – an odd job for a gardener.
- Is the presence of Boothby perhaps a sign that the writers planned a follow-up to *In the Flesh*, and booked Ray Walston for that? Could chaotic space once have been the fluidic space that Species 8472 come from?

RATING

- Chakotay's is at his best when he's a bit of a thug. This is a stupid premise for an episode, but a good performance from Robert Beltran.

5.19 THINK TANK

STARDATE UNKNOWN

An alien can help Voyager... for a price

TX 31 March 1999
WRITER Michael Taylor (story by Rick Berman and Brannon Braga)
DIRECTOR Terrence O'Hara
GUEST CAST Jason Alexander (Kurros), Christopher Darga (Y'Sek), Steve Dennis (Fennim), Christopher Shea (Saowin)

Alien bounty hunters, the Hazari, ensnare Voyager, which escapes but soon detects reinforcements throughout the sector. An alien, Kurros, arrives and tells Janeway he and his 'think tank' of advanced aliens can solve their problems. He wants Seven as payment. She declines to join the think tank, and the Hazari attack again. Kurros helps, but now feels that Janeway owes him. Seven discovers that Kurros hired the bounty hunters, and they trick him into thinking Seven will join him. Kurros realises its a trap. Seven deactivates the cloak on Kurros' ship, and the Hazari converge on him, demanding payment.

TRIVIA

- The think tank say that they've cured the Phage for the Vidiians.

RATING

- A pretty dumb episode, ironically, but the double – or is it triple? – cross at the end is quite fun.

5.20 JUGGERNAUT

STARDATE UNKNOWN

The crew struggle to stop a vast explosion

TX 26 April 1999
WRITERS Bryan Fuller, Nick Sagan and Kenneth Biller (story by Bryan Fuller)
DIRECTOR Allan Kroeker
GUEST CAST Lee Arenberg (Pelk), Ron Canada (Fesek), Alexander Enberg (Malon 3), Scott Klace (Dremk)

Voyager answers a distress call and finds radioactive escape pods. Two survivors, Pelk and Fesek, are Malon who have abandoned ship after a radiation leak. If the waste ignites it will destroy everything within three light years. Chakotay, Torres and Neelix beam across. The Voyager crew scoff at the idea that there's a creature, a Vihaar, made from radiogenic waste stalking the ship. The Doctor realises that it is real, and masked from sensors. It's a core worker, and he's sabotaged the ship to demonstrate to the Malon how dangerous their procedures are. They can't stop the explosion, but they can throw the freighter into a star to absorb most of the blast.

TRIVIA

- The Malons come from Malon Prime – a beautiful planet, according to Fesek.
- Danny Byrd bullied Torres at school, calling her 'turtlehead'. In *Non Sequitur,* the person on the ship instead of Harry in the alternative timeline was Daniel Byrd. There's no indication (how could there be, really?) if this is the same person.

RATING

- The problem with the Malon is that unlike, say, the Vidiians, they don't really have anything to redeem them, or an excuse for what they do. So all they really do is pollute. That said, this is a nice, tense, episode.

5.21 SOMEONE TO WATCH OVER ME

STARDATE 52647

The Doctor teaches Seven how to date

TX 28 April 1999
WRITERS Michael Taylor and Kenneth Biller (story by Brannon Braga)
DIRECTOR Robert Duncan McNeill
GUEST CAST Ian Ambercrombie (Abbot), David Burke (The Regular Guy), Brian McNamara (William Chapman), Scott Thompson (Tomin)

The Doctor helps Seven to date, to demonstrate those social skills. Paris makes a bet with the Doctor that she won't be able to keep a date for an ambassador's reception that night. Seven locates Lieutenant Chapman and announces that he is her date. He's startled, but agrees. Paris begins to suspect the Doctor is interested in Seven, although he denies it. Seven has an awkward date, which culminates in her accidentally almost ripping Chapman's arm off when they dance. Paris pays up... Seven is shocked by the bet. She announces the next day that she will no longer date as there are no suitable mates on board. The Doctor hides his disappointment.

QUOTES

- 'Perhaps there is something to be said for assimilation after all.' – *Seven doesn't fancy the idea of small talk*

TRIVIA

- The Doctor and Seven (and Robert Picardo and Jeri Ryan) sing a duet of 'You are My Sunshine'.
- We have it confirmed that the Doctor has designed all Seven's catsuits, as well as more casual clothing.
- This is the first appearance of holopub Sandrine's since *The Swarm*, and the last time we see it.

RATING

- Another story that feels like it's taking the characters backwards, Picardo and Ryan have good fun with the script and make a bunch of grown-ups acting like they're children's telly characters really rather entertaining.

5.22 11:59

An ancestor of Janeway gets involved in local politics

TX 5 May 1999
WRITER Joe Menosky (story by Brannon Braga and Joe Menosky)
DIRECTOR David Livingston
GUEST CAST Christopher Curry (Driver), James Greene (Passerby), Kristina Hayes (Field Reporter), John Carroll Lynch (Moss), Bradley Pierce (Jason), Kevin Tighe (Henry)

STARDATE

27 December 2000. Shannon O'Donnell's car breaks down in Portage Creek, Indiana and she meets bookstore owner Henry Janeway. He's the only person who won't sell up to allow the construction of the world's first arcology, Millennium Gate, a self-sustained biosphere. She agrees to help him fight the developers. Captain Janeway admires O'Donnell, an ancestor whose work helped build the first Mars habitats. As Janeway tells Paris this, he's confused – he knows all the people who helped with the Mars missions, and O'Donnell wasn't one of them. Janeway is surprised when the database backs this up – she was just a consulting engineer. Back in 2000, O'Donnell is approached by Gerald Moss, who knows she used to work for NASA. He's one of the developers and offers her a job – if she gets Henry to sell. She gets Henry to set up shop in Millennium Gate. Although Janeway will never know, without her ancestor, Millennium Gate would never have happened.

QUOTES

- 'My cousin was a prize-winning chess program.' – *The Doctor reveals his family history, and kills the conversation*

TRIVIA

- Janeway says that when the Ferengi made first contact with Earth, they saw Wall Street as a sacred place. This is peculiar, because formal first contact with the Federation was in *The Next Generation* episode *The Last Outpost*. Gradually, as the Ferengi mutated from fierce baddies to comical traders, it's been hinted that they've been around a lot longer, and the first contact between the Ferengi and Starfleet has now been backdated to the *Enterprise* episode *Acquisition*. Even given that, it's still a problem: money was abolished on Earth in the twenty-second century (*Dark Frontier*), before Archer's time.
- Seven points out that Janeway is a distant ancestor of O'Donnell's and shares little DNA. But they both look remarkably like her.

RATING

- A change of pace, and an odd way to celebrate the Millennium – in May, and pedantically pointing out that the real millennium is a year later than most people think. The disparity between Janeway's version of family history and what we see is great, and O'Donnell is an almost completely different character. An odd episode, but a sweet one.

5.23 RELATIVITY

Seven must prevent the destruction of Voyager

TX 12 May 1999
WRITERS Bryan Fuller, Nick Sagan and Michael Taylor (story by Nick Sagan)

STARDATE 52861.274

It's the day Janeway inspected Voyager for the first time... but Seven is there, disguised as an Ensign. Seven discovers a chroniton weapon, but is killed. Braxton (see *Future's End*) retrieves her from nearly six years later and beams her 500 years in the future. They are on the USS Relativity, a Federation timeship. Braxton sends Seven to the past to discover who changed history and destroyed Voyager... and Seven discovers a future version of Braxton there. He suffers from

DIRECTOR Allan Eastman
GUEST CAST Josh Clark (Carey), Jay Karnes (Ducane), Dakin Matthews (Patterson), Bruce McGill (Braxton)

temporal psychosis, and blames Janeway. After a chase through the ship, Seven meets her past self. Janeway goes back and stops Braxton. Seven and Janeway are reintegrated; Braxton is led away.

QUOTES

- 'I gave up trying to get my tenses straight years ago.' – *Braxton*

TRIVIA

- Braxton is played by a different actor – and at the conclusion of *Future's End*, the timelines were restored, so he didn't suffer the indignities he blames Janeway for. He also mentions the Takara Sector (*Timeless*).
- Seven doesn't recognise Carey, although we were never told he died before *Scorpion*.
- The Dali Paradox is a temporal fissure that slows time down (and therefore, on the face of it, it's not a paradox). The Pogo Paradox is when interference to prevent an event causes it.

RATING

- One of the best of the series, with nice glimpses of the past and future and a complex script that's always easy to follow.

5.24 WARHEAD

STARDATE UNKNOWN

A sentient bomb takes over the ship

TX 19 May 1999
WRITERS Michael Taylor and Kenneth Biller (story by Brannon Braga)
DIRECTOR John Kretchmer
GUEST CAST Steve Dennis (Alien), McKenzie Westmore (Jenkins)

The Doctor and Torres answer a distress call and find a machine embedded in rock. It doesn't realise it's a machine, and it's only when they get it on board they realise it's a radiogenic bomb. It takes control of the Doctor's holomatrix and demands that Janeway helps it find its intended target. The crew plan to trick it so Seven can inject it with nanoprobes, but the plan fails. Voyager is surrounded by more self-guided weapons. Harry persuades the bomb that it's not authorised to attack its target, and instead it detonates, destroying all the other bombs.

TRIVIA

- Paris and Torres celebrate their anniversary.

RATING

- Another evil Doctor, but this is leagues ahead of *Darkling*. That said, it's nothing brilliant, and the early scenes where the Doctor and Torres talk to the bomb are terribly silly.

5.25 EQUINOX Part I

STARDATE UNKNOWN

Voyager encounters another Starfleet vessel

TX 26 May 1999
WRITERS Brannon Braga and Joe Menosky (story by Rick Berman, Brannon Braga and Joe Menosky)
DIRECTOR David Livingston
GUEST CAST Olivia Birkelund (Gilmore), Steve Dennis (Crewmember), Scarlett Pomers (Naomi Wildman), John Savage (Ransom), Titus Welliver (Burke), Rick Worthy (Lessing)

Voyager gets a distress call from the USS Equinox, which is saved when they intercept it and extend their shields. The ship was being attacked by nucleogenic interspatial beings that suck the energy out of life-forms. Equinox was brought here by the Caretaker, and has lost the majority of its crew. It's a small ship, not kitted out for long-range missions. The Voyager and Equinox crews pool their resources, but it's clear that the Equinox's captain, Ransom, is hiding something. Janeway sends the Doctor to investigate a lab that's been flooded with radiation, and he discovers they've been experimenting on the aliens and draining them to power their warp drive. Janeway confines the Equinox crew to quarters. The EMH on the Equinox activates and deactivates the Doctor – the hologram conducted the experiments, and it's had its ethical subroutine disabled, making it amoral. Posing as the Doctor, he frees the crew of the Equinox. They steal Voyager's field generator, then flee in the Equinox, leaving Voyager unshielded. Hostile aliens start materialising all over Voyager...

QUOTES

- 'If we turn our backs on our principles, we stop being human.' – *Janeway*

TRIVIA

- Janeway tells Ransom she's never broken the Prime Directive. This is simply not true.
- Voyager is now halfway home – it's 35,000 light years to Earth.
- The Krowtonan Guard wiped out half Equinox's crew, 39 people, in the first week they were in the Delta Quadrant. They found a wormhole and avoided Borg Space.

RATING

- The adventures of the Equinox sound much more dramatic, exciting and skin-of-the-teeth than Voyager's, and the crew instantly make an impression. This is a powerful episode which, like *Year of Hell*, is so good you can only dream about how good *Voyager* could have been if it was like this all the time. Whatever *Voyager*'s faults, they're good at these double episodes.

STAR TREK: VOYAGER
SEASON SIX

6.1 EQUINOX Part II

STARDATE UNKNOWN

Janeway must tackle the aliens... and the Equinox

TX 22 September 1999
WRITERS Brannon Braga and Joe Menosky (story by Rick Berman, Brannon Braga and Joe Menosky)
DIRECTOR David Livingston
GUEST CAST Majel Barrett (Computer Voice), Olivia Birkelund (Gilmore), Steve Dennis (Crewmember), Scarlett Pomers (Naomi Wildman), John Savage (Ransom), Eric Steinberg (Ankari), Titus Welliver (Burke), Rick Worthy (Lessing)

Janeway reinforces the shields and fends off the nucleogenic life-forms. Meanwhile, Seven has shut down the engines of the Equinox and refuses to give Ransom the codes to restart them. Ransom deletes the Doctor's ethical subroutines and gets him to remove the information from Seven's implants, which will give her brain damage. Voyager attacks Equinox, damaging it, but Equinox gets away. Janeway beams members of the Equinox crew away first, though, and threatens to expose them to the aliens. Chakotay assumes it's a bluff, but it isn't. Shocked, Chakotay intervenes, and Janeway relieves him of duty. With the help of the Ankari who led Equinox to the aliens, Janeway contacts the aliens and tells them she'll lead them to the Equinox. Ransom's crew mutiny, and he is relieved of command. Janeway beams the crew to Voyager. Ransom sacrifices himself and the Equinox to beat back the aliens. The survivors from the Equinox are stripped of their ranks and join the Voyager crew.

TRIVIA

- There are five survivors from the Equinox – Marla Gilmore, Noah Lessing, James Morrow, Brian Sofin and Angelo Tassoni. None of them are ever seen again in the series.

RATING

- A bleak and brutal end to the story, with Janeway taking the gloves off and showing Ransom no mercy. It's a real shame that we don't follow the new crewmembers in the future, but that's not this episode's fault. This is good stuff.

6.2 SURVIVAL INSTINCT

STARDATE 53049.2

Other members of Nine arrive on the ship

Voyager is docked at a Markonian Outpost. Seven is confronted by a man with Borg technology, and experiences flashbacks. He gives her the Borg relays, and telepathically tells two colleagues that they

TX 29 September 1999
WRITER Ron Moore
DIRECTOR Terry Windell
GUEST CAST Vaughn Armstrong (Two of Nine), Jonathan Breck (The Dying Borg), Bertila Damas (Three of Nine), Tim Kelleher (Four of Nine), Scarlett Pomers (Naomi Wildman)

should prepare to bypass Voyager's security systems. Seven gives the relays to Torres for analysis. Three Borg enter Seven's alcove and try to re-assimilate her. They are stunned by Tuvok's security team. These are Two, Three and Four of Nine, members of Seven's unimatrix. They tell Janeway they want to be individuals. They have left the Collective but are linked telepathically, and Seven agrees to link with them to find out how this happened. This process damages the other Borg, who will have to rejoin the Collective or die. Seven decides that it is better for them to live a short time as individuals.

TRIVIA

- Marika Willkarah was on the USS Excalibur before being assimilated as Three of Nine. She joins the crew, for the brief time she has left (we never see her again).

RATING

- Another new Borg story, a variation on the *I, Borg* type of small-scale character pieces. It's interesting enough, if a little difficult to work out whether there's any point being made with relevance to the wider world.

6.3 BARGE OF THE DEAD

STARDATE UNKNOWN

Torres goes to Klingon hell

TX 6 October 1999
WRITER Bryan Fuller (story by Ron Moore and Bryan Fuller)
DIRECTOR Mike Vejar
GUEST CAST Sherman Augustus (Hij'Qa), Karen Austin (Miral), John Kenton Shull (Brok'Tan), Eric Pierpoint (Kortar)

Torres suffers concussion after her shuttle hits an ion storm. She starts seeing visions and hearing screams. She finds herself on the deck of a Klingon ship and she is told she's on the Barge of the Dead going to Gre'thor, where dishonoured souls go. She is to be joined by her mother, Miral. She wakes in Sickbay. Torres finds it hard to convince anyone this was anything but an hallucination. She then loses consciousness, and is back on the Barge. Torres tries using a ritual to save her mother, but finally opts to go to hell in her place, so that her mother can go to Sto-Vo-Kor, Klingon heaven. Miral is saved, and tells Torres that she too can be, if she lives with honour and discipline. Torres wakes in Sickbay.

TRIVIA

- Gre'thor was first mentioned in *Devil's Due.*

RATING

- The usual Klingon rubbish, a dark and dreary episode without a twist or a point.

6.4 TINKER, TENOR, DOCTOR, SPY

STARDATE UNKNOWN

An alien confuses the Doctor's daydreams with reality

TX 13 October 1999
WRITER Joe Menosky (story by Bill Vallely)
DIRECTOR John Bruno
GUEST CAST Majel Barrett (Computer Voice), Robert Greenberg (Devro), Googy Gress (the Overlooker), Jay M Leggett (Phlox)

Disappointed he's not on an Away Team, the Doctor asks Janeway to designate him a Command Hologram if there's a catastrophe, but Janeway turns down the request. The Doctor starts daydreaming that he's the Captain, and that Torres lusts after him. Phlox, an alien, is scanning Voyager, and accesses the Doctor to spy on the ship. They see his daydreams, not the reality. The Doctor dreams of heroically defeating the Borg with a photonic cannon, a weapon he just made up. The aliens think that Voyager was weakened in the attack and plan an attack of their own. The Doctor is malfunctioning, and the crew get to see his daydreams and are variously amused or offended. Phlox realises his mistake, but dare not tell his commanders. He asks the Doctor to pose as the Captain to trick his leaders, in return for warning of the attack. Janeway prompts the Doctor by a commlink, and the Doctor threatens the aliens with the photonic cannon. The aliens flee.

QUOTES

- 'The dream dreams the dreamer.' – *Talaxian proverb*

TRIVIA

- Phlox isn't the same Phlox as the doctor on *Enterprise*. The aliens are unnamed, referred to as the Hierarchy in the script, and the Overlookers in their subsequent appearances in *The Void* and *Renaissance Man*.

RATING

- The aliens look really funny, and this is a pleasant, whimsical episode. It wouldn't win any subtlety awards, but Robert Picardo manages to convey the emptiness and frustration of the Doctor's life among the broad gags.

6.5 ALICE

STARDATE UNKNOWN

Paris gets more than he bargained for with a new ship

TX 20 October 1999
WRITERS Bryan Fuller and Michael Taylor (story by Juliann deLayne)
DIRECTOR David Livingston
GUEST CAST John Fleck (Abaddon), Claire Rankin ('Alice')

Voyager is buying spare parts from a junkyard owned by Abaddon when Paris sees a small shuttle. He convinces Chakotay to let him buy it, and sets to work restoring it. The shuttle, which he calls 'Alice', has a neurogenic interface, meaning it responds to his thoughts. That night he hears a woman's voice. Paris becomes obsessed with the shuttle, worrying Torres. He steals power cells from Voyager to use. 'Alice' traps Torres and tries to kill her. Paris gets the shuttle off the ship, but it fires on Voyager then darts off at warp speed. Abaddon admits the shuttle is 'haunted', and tips them off that the shuttle will be heading to an anomaly called the Particle Fountain. Torres contacts Paris and, just as he is about to suffer a brain haemorrhage, he manages to fight 'Alice' off long enough for Tuvok to shut the ship down. Paris is beamed off as 'Alice' is destroyed in the Particle Fountain.

TRIVIA

- The working title of the episode was *The Genie*.
- One of Chakotay's arguments against buying a new shuttle is that they already have a full complement and the Delta Flyer. As many shuttles have been lost over the course of the show, it proves they have the facilities to build new ones (or, like Janeway telling Ransom in *Equinox* she'd never broken the Prime Directive, it might just be a bare-faced lie).
- The Ferengi have five stages of acquisition: Infatuation, Justification, Appropriation, Obsession and Resale.

RATING

- A story about consuming passions, there's at least a technobabble reason why Paris is so obsessed. The reason he likes the shuttle so much is never really demonstrated – we get a lot of talk about multiphasic this and optronic that, but we don't really see the passion, only the obsession.

6.6 RIDDLES

STARDATE 53263.2

Neelix has to help Tuvok recuperate

TX 3 November 1999
WRITERS Robert Doherty (story by André Bormanis)
DIRECTOR Roxann Dawson
GUEST CAST Mark Moses (Naroq)

Tuvok is attacked and suffers neuroleptic shock, which the Doctor can't reverse until he knows what weapon was used. Neelix tries to jog his memory with riddles. The locals, the Kesat, think Tuvok was attacked by a Ba'neth, a mythological shadow-being. Voyager is able to detect a fleet of cloaked Ba'Neth ships, but they flee. Tuvok is slowly recovering, and experiencing volatile emotions, lashing out at Neelix. Neelix encourages him to have some fun, and they cook a dessert. Voyager finds the Ba'Naeth and demands information on the weapon used. The Doctor can use the information to restore Tuvok's Vulcan personality. He recovers his stoic manner, but to Neelix's delight, he now appreciates the wordplay of Neelix's riddles.

TRIVIA

- Roxann Dawson finally gets her directorial debut, having had to delay it during her pregnancy.
- The twenty-fourth century equivalent of the game Animal, Vegetable or Mineral is called Species, Starship or Anomaly.
- Initial publicity said this episode was co-written by Brannon Braga.

RATING

- The writers seem determined to see Neelix and Tuvok together. As their personalities are polar opposites, they seem to think this will lead to *Odd Couple*-style watchability. It doesn't, it leads to episodes like *Rise* and this one, where both characters lose any subtlety and become mouthpieces for 'logic' and 'fun'. It's a well-directed episode, though.

6.7 DRAGON'S TEETH

STARDATE 53167.9

Voyager wakes up an ancient race

TX 10 November 1999
WRITER Michael Taylor
DIRECTOR Rick Kolbe
GUEST CAST Jeff Allin (Gedrin), Mimi Craven (Jisa), Ron Fassler (Morin), Robert Knepper (Gaul), Scarlett Pomers (Naomi Wildman), Bob Stillman (Turei)

Voyager enters a subspace corridor, and is attacked by Turei vessels that accuse the ship of trespassing in their underspace. Realising it's a misunderstanding, they push Voyager back into normal space. Janeway asks them if they could use underspace to get back to the Alpha Quadrant, but the Turei get angry and fire on Voyager, which is forced to land on a hostile planet for repairs. They realise there was once an advanced civilisation here that was wiped out centuries ago. Exploring a city, they discover aliens in stasis pods. Seven activates one of them. He is Gedrin of Vaadwaur, who explains his people built underspace and became the target of other civilisations. The Turei launch an attack, and Gedrin uses a satellite defence system to fight them off. Gedrin is happy to offer underspace technology in exchange for getting his people off the planet. Once this is done, the Vaadwaur decide to take over Voyager. They weren't peaceful explorers, but used the subspace corridors for conquest. Gedrin is horrifed that his people plan to betray those that set them free, and shuts down enough ships for Voyager to make its escape.

TRIVIA

- This was originally going to be the movie for the season, a two-parter that was intended to introduce a new regular threat. The idea was that the Vaadwaur had once dominated the Quadrant, but had been beaten back to their planet, – until Voyager let them out again, when they resumed their conquest. In the event, it was felt that the Vaadwaur weren't sufficiently interesting to justify more than this appearance. The original script said the Vaadwaur were defeated 500 years ago – one line to that effect accidentally remains in the story as broadcast.
- The title comes from the Greek myth (and the Ray Harryhausen film!) where a dragon's tooth falling to earth would grow into a fierce warrior.
- 'Today is a good day to die,' Worf's catchphrase, is revealed here to be the battle cry of Kahless.

RATING

- Tense and with lots of action, but it's not hard to see why we never saw the Vaadwaur again.

6.8 ONE SMALL STEP

STARDATE 53292.7

Voyager looks for a lost mission to Mars

TX 17 November 1999
WRITERS Mike Wollaeger, Jessica Scott, Bryan Fuller and Michael Taylor (story by Mike Wollaeger and Jessica Scott)
DIRECTOR Robert Picardo
GUEST CAST Phil Morris (John Kelly)

Voyager discovers a graviton ellipse, a rare anomaly which they manage to avoid. Chakotay and Paris are reminded of reports that one of the early Mars missions was hit by a ball of energy – they think debris from the first manned mission to Mars may be in there. A dark matter asteroid is heading for the anomaly, and interrupts their plans to retrieve any debris. When Chakotay ignores Janeway to drag the module he's found back out the Delta Flyer is badly damaged. Seven beams over to the module, discovering the body of John Kelly, the commander of the mission. He survived in the anomaly until life support ran out. As there were other ships wrecked here, he realised mankind was not alone. Just before the asteroid hits, they download the mission logs and later give Kelly a hero's burial in space.

TRIVIA

- Ares IV was a three-man mission. Kelly's crew were Andrei Novakovich and Rose Kumagawa, suggesting an American, Russian and Japanese joint mission (which contradicts the original *Star Trek*'s version of the twenty-first century, where space probes were launched by individual, competing nations). The last telemetry was received on 19 October 2032.

- The Doctor says one of his first Away Missions was to Arrakis Prime – Arrakis is the central planet in Frank Herbert's *Dune* series of books, but that planet is certainly not 'glacial' as the Doctor says here.

RATING

- Another flashback episode, although not as radical as *11.59*. *Star Trek* has always been, and for obvious and noble reasons, a strong advocate of the space program, and this is inspirational stuff, even transforming what ought to be a tragic ending into a moment of revelation. Good stuff, even if the made-up science in this episode is extremely dodgy (a 'dark matter asteroid' is just nonsense).

6.9 THE VOYAGER CONSPIRACY

STARDATE UNKNOWN

Seven is sure Voyager was lost deliberately

TX 24 November 1999
WRITER Joe Menosky
DIRECTOR Terry Windell
GUEST CAST Scarlett Pomers (Naomi Wildman), Albie Selznick (Tash)

Voyager meets Tash, whose 'catapult vessel' has a drive system that could help Voyager get home faster. Seven analyses it, and realises it's the same tetryon-based technology that brought Voyager to the Delta Quadrant. Linking herself to the ship's sensor logs, she reaches the conclusion that Janeway deliberately stranded Voyager so the Federation could establish a presence in the Delta Quadrant. Chakotay dismisses this at first, but Seven starts to uncover evidence of a Federation/Cardassian plot. She begins, in turn, to believe Chakotay has a hidden agenda, and warns Janeway. She's overloaded her mind with information. Janeway persuades her of the truth before Seven can escape in a shuttle.

TRIVIA

- We learn that the Ktarians are allies of the Federation, but sympathetic to the Maquis.

RATING

- An episode that seems, in part, to be inspired by the weird theories *Star Trek* (and *The X-Files* and *Babylon 5*) fans come up with on the internet. One problem is that Seven's theories aren't terribly convincing or imaginative. The other is that fans were really obsessing about killing Neelix and how many shuttles had been lost.

6.10 PATHFINDER

STARDATE UNKNOWN

Barclay is on Earth, trying to contact Voyager

TX 1 December 1999
WRITERS David Zabel and Kenneth Biller (story by David Zabel)
DIRECTOR Mike Vejar
GUEST CAST Majel Barrett (Computer Voice), Victor Bevine (Security Guard), Mark Daniel Cade (Technician), Richard Herd (Admiral Paris), Richard McGonagle (Pete Harkins), Dwight Schultz (Reginald Barclay), Marina Sirtis (Troi)

Reg Barclay is on Earth, trying to contact Voyager and getting to know holographic versions of its crew. Deanna Troi is growing worried about him. Barclay thinks that he can use a pulsar to contact Voyager, but his boss, Harkins, is more interested in Barclay's regular work, and takes him off duty when he discovers the holo simulation of Voyager. Troi worries that Barclay is paranoid. He sneaks to the lab, accesses the Midas Array and sends a message to Voyager. Harkins tries to stop him, so Barclay sets up a chase through the holo-Voyager. Just as Harkins is about to apprehend Barclay, the real Seven detects the experiment and replies. Barclay's faith has been justified, and he's put in charge of 'Project Voyager' by Admiral Paris.

TRIVIA

- The Enterprise-E is visiting Earth during this episode (we don't see it). This is the only specific reference to what the ship does between *Star Trek: Insurrection* and *Star Trek: Nemesis.*
- Voyager's position is now at Grid 10, Sector 3658. (In *Message in a Bottle* it was Grid 9, Sector 41751).
- Barclay has lived on Earth for two years. He's worked on a transwarp project, and has named his cat Neelix.
- The original Neelix lacks the vocal cords (and, according to Seven, the rhythm) to be a good singer.
- Barclay's hologram Voyager assumes that the Maquis crew wear Maquis uniforms. Janeway has her first season hairstyle.
- The working title was *Home Fire.*

RATING

- It's ingenious how the standing sets are utilised in a story almost entirely set tens of thousands of light years away from Voyager. This is another story where we see a fake Voyager for most of the episode. Barclay is always good value, and it's amazing how interesting and rounded Troi appears to be here.

6.11 FAIR HAVEN

STARDATE UNKNOWN

A new holovillage provides a diversion for the crew

TX 12 January 2000
WRITER Robin Burger
DIRECTOR Allan Kroeker
GUEST CAST Majel Barrett (Computer Voice), Jan Claire (Frannie), Henriette Ivanans (Maggie), Duffie McIntire (Grace), Fintan McKeown (Michael), Richard Riehle (Seamus)

Harry and Paris create a new holo-program, a simulation of the pleasant Irish village of Fair Haven. Meanwhile, Voyager is heading for an interstellar hurricane of neutron radiation. Janeway takes time off to be romanced by Michael Sullivan, a holographic bartender. Voyager clears the worst of the hurricane, and many of the crew start to relax in Fair Haven. An emergency means they have to lose a lot of the program. Janeway realises she's falling in love with Michael, and stops going, telling the computer to not let her meet Michael again.

TRIVIA

- Fair Haven is seen again in *Spirit Folk*. The working title of the episode, was *Safe Harbor* (not Harbour, as the Irish would spell it).

RATING

- The world really didn't need a Voyager/Ballykissangel crossover, and this adds nothing to the series. Like most holodeck episodes, it's indulgent and predictable.

6.12 BLINK OF AN EYE

STARDATE UNKNOWN

Voyager encounters a world in a different time frame

TX 19 January 2000
WRITERS Scott Miller and Joe Menosky (story by Michael Taylor)
DIRECTOR Gabrielle Beaumont
GUEST CAST Jon Cellini (Technician), Daniel Dae Kim (Pilot), Melik Malkasian (Shaman), Walter H McCready (Tribal Alien), Obi Ndefo (Protector), Olaf Pooley (Cleric), Kat Sawyer-Young (Astronaut), Daniel Zacapa (Astronomer)

Voyager encounters a planet at the centre of an anomaly which means every second on the ship is a day on the planet. On the planet, the appearance of a new star has already led to the formation of a new religion. Centuries and seconds later, a message is sent to Voyager telling them their presence causes earthquakes. The ship can't leave without destroying the surface. The Doctor is sent to investigate, and in the three years he's there, learns there's a space race to make contact with Voyager. A shuttle docks, but the time differential means the Voyager's crew are like statues. They help the Doctor and try to get Voyager to leave without destroying the surface of the planet. The civilisation is soon more advanced than Voyager, and has technology to allow the ship to break free.

TRIVIA

- Not to be confused with the original series episode *Wink of the Eye*, which also featured a race that lived in a faster time frame.
- The Doctor mentions he had a son on the planet, but doesn't elaborate.

RATING

- High-concept science fiction, but it doesn't quite have the surreal genius this sort of episode needs. It's clever stuff, but you get the sense it's not clever enough. That said, relatively speaking, at least it's light on technobabble.

6.13 VIRTUOSO

STARDATE 53556.4

The Doctor becomes famous

TX 26 January 2000
WRITERS Raf Green and Kenneth Biller (story by Raf Green)
DIRECTOR Les Landau
GUEST CAST Marie Caldare (Azen), Kamala Dawson (Tincoo), Nina Magnesson (Vinka), Paul Williams (Koru), Ray Xifo (Abarca)

Voyager helps repair a Qomari ship, but the Qomar, who lack social skills, think the crew are inferior. Their race has never encountered singing, and they are fascinated by the Doctor's voice. Janeway agrees to a concert, and the Qomar can't get enough of the Doctor. He plays to a packed house, and Voyager is so overwhelmed with fan mail that Seven thinks it's an attack. Janeway starts to worry the Doctor is neglecting his duty. The Doctor resigns, burning his bridges a little in his resignation speech. The Qomar contact him as he's leaving – they have a better hologram now, one that can hit the high notes, and he's no longer needed. The Doctor and the new holomatrix perform together, the Doctor's performance full of melancholy, the holomatrix technically better, but with no passion. The Qomar prefer the holomatrix. The Doctor returns to the ship.

TRIVIA

- Roberto Picardo did most of the singing for this episode, but some of the more complicated parts had to be dubbed. Garrett Wang is miming playing the clarinet and saxophone.

RATING

- A silly idea for an episode, but it's fun. Picardo shows off almost as much as the Doctor, and really shines.

6.14 MEMORIAL

STARDATE UNKNOWN

The crew suffer trauma after a battle... which they don't remember

TX 2 February 2000
WRITER Robin Burger (story by Brannon Braga)
DIRECTOR Allan Kroeker
GUEST CAST David Keith Anderson (Crewmember), Fleming Brooks (Soldier One), Robert Allen Colaizzi Jr (Dying Colonist), LL Ginter (Saavdra), Joe Mellis (Young Soldier), Scarlett Pomers (Naomi Wildman), Susan Savage (Alien Woman), Maria Spassoff (Female Colonist)

Chakotay, Tom, Harry and Neelix return from a survey mission suffering from hallucinations and anxiety attacks. They all suffer traumatic reactions to things that remind them of combat, like sounds that resemble gunfire. The Doctor thinks they are having flashbacks to a real incident, and they start to remember attacking the Nikon. They murdered 82 civilians. Soon Janeway is having flashbacks, too, as do other crewmen. They approach Tarakis, the planet in the hallucinations and discover the remains of the civilians – who all died 300 years ago. They find a large structure, a synaptic transmitter that's a memorial to the dead that literally does remind people of what happened. Some of the crew want it neutralised, but Janeway order they recharge it, so no one ever forgets.

TRIVIA

- Janeway says there's an Obelisk marking the massacre at Khitomer (see *Yesterday's Enterprise*).

RATING

- Is there anyone in the Delta Quadrant who isn't suppressing traumatic memories? This episode ought to be powerful, but it's pretty routine stuff.

6.15 TSUNKATSE

STARDATE 53447.2

Seven has to fight to entertain aliens

TX 2 September 2000
WRITER Robert Doherty
DIRECTOR Mike Vejar
GUEST CAST Jeffrey Combs (Penk), JG Hertzler (Hirogen Hunter), The Rock (Champion)

Seven and Tuvok are studying a micro-nebula when they are captured by Penk, who enslaves people to become fighters. Seven agrees to fight in exchange for medical care for Tuvok. When Chakotay, Harry, Paris and Neelix go to see a Tsunkatse match they are astonished to see Seven is one of the fighters. They can't get her beamed out – they are actually holograms, the real fight is elsewhere. The Champion knocks Seven over and wins. Penk next enters her in the Red Match, to the death. She is trained by a Hirogen, and this is also her opponent – he wants her to give him an honourable death. Voyager locates Seven and, after a battle, beams her and the Hirogen clear. The Hirogen is grateful to be free.

TRIVIA

- UPN required every program shown on the network to celebrate the addition of WWF wrestling (later WWE) to the schedules. This clearly represented a challenge for the *Voyager* team, but they obliged.
- The Rock went on from here to an acting career, with the films *The Mummy Returns* (2001) and *The Scorpion King* (2002).

RATING

- Technobabble reaches an all time low in this episode – presumably there were concerns about the levels of violence in this episode (ironically, given that WWF can be shown). So, rather than just punch people in the face, Seven wears polaron disruptors on the hands and feet that emit a bioplasmic charge when it contacts an opponent's sensors. The result of which is that all the fights look like play fights. Apart from that, this is actually a pretty entertaining episode, and anyone who thinks it's *Star Trek* dumbing down has forgotten *The Gamesters of Triskelion.*

6.16 COLLECTIVE

STARDATE UNKNOWN

Voyager takes on some Borg children

TX 16 February 2000
WRITER Michael Taylor (story by Andrew Shepard Price and Mark Gaberman)
DIRECTOR Allison Liddi
GUEST CAST Manu Intiraymi (Icheb), Marley S McClean (Mezoti), Ryan Spahn (Teenage Drone Leader), Cody Wetherill (Rebi), Kurt Wetherill (Azan)

The Borg take Chakotay, Harry, Paris and Neelix hostage – but these Borg are children. Seven is sent to negotiate, and discovers that all the adults of died of a virus. The Borg want Voyager's navigational deflector. Seven realises these Borg are not fully matured, and want to contact the Collective. They become hostile when Janeway and Seven stall them. Seven discovers that the Collective knows about the drones, but has abandoned them as irrelevant. The drones become angry, but when one attacks Seven, another protects her. The drones abandon ship as the engines malfunction. One is dying, though, and Seven comforts him. There are four Borg children, and the records show their original names were Icheb, Mezoti, Azan, and Rebi.

RATING

- Another variation on the *I, Borg/Survival Instinct* story, the twist being the Borg are children. We get nice contrasts between the human expectations of how to raise children and the Borg way, and it's interesting how clearly Seven now falls into the 'human' side. This is a strong episode, the main problem being we've seen this sort of thing many times before.

6.17 SPIRIT FOLK

STARDATE UNKNOWN

Complications ensue when Fair Haven is kept running

TX 23 February 2000
WRITER Bryan Fuller
DIRECTOR David Livingston
GUEST CAST Ian Abercrombie (Milo), Bairbre Dowling (Edith), Henriette Ivanans (Maggie), Duffie McIntire (Grace), Fintan McKeown (Michael), Richard Riehle (Seamus), Ian Patrick Williams (Doc Fitzgerald)

Paris has a car crash in Fair Haven, and one of the characters sees him walk away from it, then the car magically repair itself. The man tells his friends down the pub that Paris is from the spirit world. They decide to watch Paris, and see him play a trick on Harry, turning the woman he's with into a cow. The villagers begin to compare notes, and Michael tells Janeway about their theory. Paris realises the holodeck is malfunctioning. Soon, he and Harry are being chased by a mob of superstitious villagers. Seamus manages to hypnotise the Doctor, who tells him about Voyager. Michael persuades the villagers to calm down. The villagers and crew have a farewell party before Fair Haven is taken offline for repairs.

TRIVIA

- The cow was a big hit with the cast, with some suggesting it should become a regular character.
- The working titles were *Daoine Sidhe* and *Fairy Tale*.

RATING

- The sort of episode that makes you want to press Ctrl-alt-del. Fair Haven was a terrible idea the first time.

6.18 ASHES TO ASHES

STARDATE 53679.4

A dead crewman returns to Voyager

TX 1 March 2000
WRITER Robert Doherty (story by Ronald Wilkerson)
DIRECTOR Terry Windell
GUEST CAST Manu Intiraymi (Icheb), Kevin Lowe (Q'ret), Marley McClean (Mezoti), Scarlett Pomers (Naomi Wildman), Kim Rhodes (Lyndsay Ballard), Cody Wetherill (Rebi), Kurt Wetherill (Azan)

Lyndsay Ballard contacts Voyager... despite being a crewmember who died three years ago, and not being a human. She was re-animated by the Kobali, who reproduce by animating salvaged corpses. Harry was her friend, and believes the story. The Doctor can make her look more human, but it makes her feel sick. The Kobali catch up with Voyager, and ask to speak with Ballard, but she refuses to go back. She admits to Harry that she feels more at home with the aliens. She decides to go back, saddening Harry.

TRIVIA

- The Kobali look a lot like the Borg Queen, so perhaps she was originally of that species.

- Ballard died on stardate 51563, just before *Prey*. She was killed by the Hirogen. She has never been mentioned before, despite Harry saying she was his best friend.

RATING

- It's odd that they didn't pick a crewman we'd heard of who died – it's not as though there's a shortage of them. This is, once again, a fairly predictable and formulaic story.

6.19 CHILD'S PLAY

STARDATE UNKNOWN

One of the Borg children leaves Seven's care

TX 8 March 2000
WRITER Raf Green (story by Paul Brown)
DIRECTOR Mike Vejar
GUEST CAST Tracey Ellis (Icheb's Mother), Manu Intiraymi (Icheb), Marley McClean (Mezoti), Scarlett Pomers (Naomi Wildman), Eric Ritter (Yivel), Mark A Sheppard (Icheb's Father), Cody Wetherill (Rebi), Kurt Wetherill (Azan)

Voyager has managed to locate the parents of one of the Borg children, Icheb. This upsets Seven, who's been taking care of him. The planet they arrive at has been attacked by the Borg many times. The Brunali now keep their technology at a low level, so the Borg ignore them. Seven argues with Icheb's parents, but Icheb thinks his new knowledge can help his people. One of the other Borg children, Mezoti, misses Icheb. Seven realises that Icheb's parents lied about when he was abducted by the Borg – they didn't attack when his father said they did. They arrive back at the planet and the father is defensive when Janeway talks to him. They detect Icheb is on a shuttle heading for Borg Space. They beam Icheb back, and narrowly escape a Borg Sphere. Icheb had been given anti-Borg pathogens to infect the Borg when he was reassimilated. Icheb returns to Voyager.

TRIVIA

- Naomi calls her father's planet Ktaris, although it's previously been referred to as Ktaria VII.

RATING

- A fairly standard 'victims of the Borg' episode, with the nice twist that Icheb is basically wrenched away from his parents at the end. Usually in *Star Trek*, the solution is to return you to your parents, however abusive – or, indeed, actively evil – they are.

6.20 GOOD SHEPHERD

STARDATE 53735.2

Three crewmen aren't up to the job, and Janeway takes them in hand

TX 15 March 2000
WRITERS Dianna Gitto and Joe Menosky (story by Dianna Gitto)
DIRECTOR Winrich Kolbe
GUEST CAST Kimble Jemison (Engineer), Zoe McLellan (Tal Celes), Tom Morello (Junction Operator), Michael Reisz (William Telfer), Jay Underwood (Mortimer Harren)

Three of the crew's performance is below acceptable standards. Normally, they'd be transferred off the ship. Instead, Janeway takes them under her wing and on a mission in the Delta Flyer. An invisible force hits the shuttle and Telfer is attacked by an alien creature that writhes beneath his skin and leaps out of a wound on his neck. Harren vapourises it, against Janeway's orders. The shuttle now drifts towards the radiogenic rings of a nearby planet. Janeway orders the crew into the escape pods, but they refuse to abandon their Captain. Firing phasers into the ring, there's a huge explosion. Janeway wakes up in Sickbay. Voyager rescued them, but they demonstrated they were up to the job.

TRIVIA

- The way to remember the aspects of the subspace infrared algorithm is with the mnemonic 'Zero G Is Fun' – Zeta particle derivation, Gamma wave frequency, Ion distribution, Flow rate of subspace positrons. And to think *Voyager* has a reputation for technobabble!

RATING

- An episode that just stops suddenly. None of the crewmen is functional, let alone likeable, and it's a odd that it's taken six years for anyone to spot what a sorry bunch they are. We never see any of them again, either, so it's ultimately pointless. Not a good episode.

6.21 LIVE FAST AND PROSPER

STARDATE 53849.2

A rival crew impersonates Voyager

A group of con artists have been passing themselves off as Voyager, and some of their victims blame the real ship for not delivering what was promised. Neelix and Paris realise that Dala and Mobar, two people they

TX 19 April 2000
WRITER Robin Burger
DIRECTOR LeVar Burton
GUEST CAST Dennis Cockrum (Orek), Greg Daniel (Mobar), Francis Guinan (Zar), Kaitlin Hopkins (Dala), Scott Lincoln, Timothy McNeil (Miners), Ted Rooney (Varn)

met a few weeks back, downloaded the database from the Delta Flyer. Voyager finds the imposters' ship, which has been stopped by Varn, another victim. Thinking that Voyager is part of the scam, Varn fires on it. Voyager can only beam Dala onboard, and refuses to help them track down her victims. Janeway threatens to hand her over to 'barbaric' Telsian justice. Dala steals the Delta Flyer and escapes. Paris and the Doctor are waiting for her there. She leads them to her compatriots and they discover where their loot is. The con artists are arrested.

TRIVIA

- Dala and Zar were originally called Feydra and Zev in the script.
- Mobar says that Earth is 30,342.4 light years from Telsius – he may be making it up, but he does have access to Voyager's database, and it's roughly consistent with what we know.
- Bolomite, the substance mined on Telsius can be used in omega radiation therapy.

RATING

- Not as much fun as it thinks it is, but it's a novel idea told in an interesting enough way.

6.22 MUSE

Torres and Harry are trapped on a planet

TX 26 April 2000
WRITER Joe Menosky
DIRECTOR Mike Vejar
GUEST CAST Tony Amendola (Chorus #3), Jack Axelrod (Chorus #1), Kathleen Garrett (Tanis), Michael Houston King (Jero), John Schuck (Chorus #2), Kellie Waymire (Layna), Stoney Westmoreland (Warlord), Joseph Will (Kelis)

STARDATE 53896

Torres is badly wounded in a shuttle crash. Harry is nowhere to be seen. Torres is looked after by Kelis, a writer who wants her to be his muse. He thinks he can inspire peace between two clans with his play *Shining Ship Voyager*. On Voyager, Tuvok is exhausting himself searching for the missing shuttle. Kelis helps Torres in return for stories about Voyager, and she helps him write a play. Layna, the actress who's cast as Torres, grows jealous. Harry turns up with Starfleet supplies. Tuvok falls asleep on duty. Torres tells Harry there might be a war if she doesn't help stage the play, and returns to Kelis. She comes up with an ending that involves her leaving, and the Warlord loves it. Harry and Torres return to Voyager.

TRIVIA

- Tuvok says that Vulcans can stay awake for two weeks at a time.

RATING

- *Shakespeare in Love*, but without Shakespeare or Gwyneth Paltrow and written by Joe Menosky, not Tom Stoppard. Which means it only thinks it's *Shakespeare in Love*.

6.23 FURY

Kes returns to Voyager seeking vengeance

TX 3 April 2000
WRITERS Bryan Fuller and Michael Taylor (story by Rick Berman and Brannon Braga)
DIRECTOR John Bruno
GUEST CAST Vaughn Armstrong (Vidiian Captain), Josh Clark (Carey), Tarik Ergin (Security Guard), Nancy Hower (Samantha Wildman), Jennifer Lien (Kes), Scarlett Pomers (Naomi Wildman), Cody Wetherill (Rebi), Kurt Wetherill (Azan)

STARDATE UNKNOWN

Voyager gets a distress call from a ship piloted by an old Kes, who then attacks the ship by ramming it and using her psychic powers. She heads towards Engineering, grabs the warp core, kills Torres when she interferes, then vanishes. Kes materialises five years earlier, and knocks out the original Kes, replacing her. Janeway is worried about the Vidiians. Kes contacts the aliens, saying she'll give them the key to Voyager's defences in return for passage back to Ocampa. Tuvok is having premonitions – he sees Seven, Naomi and the Borg children. He collapses, and tachyons are discovered, indicating time travel. When the Vidiians launch a strong attack, the crew realise someone is signalling them with tactical information. Janeway confronts Kes, who blames the Captain, for forcing her to develop her powers before she was ready. Janeway kills her with a phaser. Five years in the future, this time Janeway is ready for Kes. A message from the old Kes is played, reminding her she made her own choices. Kes returns to her own ship.

TRIVIA

- In the past, the Doctor says that Ensign Wildman's pregnancy will be much longer than a human pregnancy, because the baby is half-Ktarian (a neat retroactive way of explaining one of the more obvious continuity problems in the first two seasons).

RATING

- A strange episode, but one that does what the best Kes episodes always did – have Kes acting out of character. While the story seems to be about how much things have changed in six years, nothing really has – Seven's been swapped for Kes, and some of the hairstyles are different. Compare and contrast with *All Good Things*, where Picard goes back just as far and into a completely different show.

6.24 LIFE LINE

STARDATE UNKNOWN

Zimmerman, the Doctor's creator, is dying

TX 10 May 2000
WRITERS Robert Doherty, Raf Green and Brannon Braga (story by John Bruno and Robert Picardo)
DIRECTOR Terry Windell
GUEST CAST Dwight Schultz (Barclay), Marina Sirtis (Deanna Troi), Jack Shearer (Hayes) Tamara Craig Thomas (Haley)

The first messages from the Pathfinder project reveal that the Doctor's creator, Zimmerman, is dying. The Doctor is transmitted back to the Alpha Quadrant. Zimmerman is unimpressed with his attempt to help – he's only a Mark One hologram, and no real doctors can help him. Barclay contacts Troi, wanting her to return from the Enterprise to help. Zimmerman and the Doctor continue to argue. Barclay discovers a problem with the Doctor's program. Zimmerman refuses to help. Zimmerman's holographic companion threatens to leave unless he fixes the Doctor. Zimmerman heals the Doctor, and agrees that he can try to treat him.

TRIVIA

- Two deep-space Federation vessels are only five or six years away from Voyager and have been sent to intercept.
- Hologram technology has become much more advanced in Voyager's absence. Zimmerman has developed a holographic fly, used for surveillance. EMH Mark Ones are obsolete; there are 675 in service and they are used to scrub plasma conduits – the current model is the Mark Four. Zimmerman has a holographic art collection.
- Zimmerman hasn't left Jupiter station in four years – about the time since the *Deep Space Nine* episode *Dr Bashir, I Presume.*
- The episode had the working title *I, Zimmerman.*

RATING

- Away from the ship, this is a fine episode – the crew of Voyager are used to treating the Doctor as a person, but here he's just software, and not even the latest version. As ever, Robert Picardo is good value – even supplying the original idea for the the Doctor having to cure Zimmerman.

6.25 THE HAUNTING OF DECK TWELVE

STARDATE UNKNOWN

Neelix tries to calm the Borg children by telling them a story

TX 17 May 2000
WRITERS Mike Sussman, Kenneth Biller and Bryan Fuller (story by Mike Sussman)
DIRECTOR David Livingston
GUEST CAST Manu Intiraymi (Icheb), Marley McClean (Mezoti), Zoe McLellan (Tal Celes), Cody Wetherill (Rebi), Kurt Wetherill (Azan)

The crew shut down power systems all over the ship, waking the regenerating Borg children. Neelix is there, and assures them it's only temporary. They guess that it's something to do with the ghost they've heard haunts deck 12. He tells them a story about a nebula. The crew is collecting deuterium when the nebula destabilises, and the ship is struck by an energy bolt that knocks out a lot of ship's systems. Seven is knocked out, and colourful gas floods the darkened ship. There's an electric lifeform on board, and it lived in the nebula before Voyager destroyed its home. It now wants the ship, and Janeway orders the crew to the escape pods. Janeway stays, and reassures the creature they can take it to a new nebula. It is given the whole of Deck 12 until they find a new home for it. Neelix finishes his story, and he and the Borg children hear the creature being released into its new nebula.

TRIVIA

- Neelix's favourite food is steamed chadre kab and terra nut souffle.

RATING

- A ghost story completely undermined by some of the most ridiculous technobabble and narrative tricks seen in the show. An attempt to do something a bit different (albeit one with nebulae and Janeway ordering the crew to abandon ship), but a failed attempt.

6.26 UNIMATRIX ZERO Part I

STARDATE UNKNOWN

Some Borg can escape the Collective

TX 24 May 2000
WRITERS Brannon Braga and Joe Menosky (story by Mike Sussman)
DIRECTOR Allan Kroeker
GUEST CAST Jerome Butler (Korok), Mark Deakins (Axum), Joanna Heimbold (Laura), Tony Sears (Borg Drone), Ryan Sparks (Alien Child), Susanna Thompson (Borg Queen)

Seven dreams of a beautiful forest, full of people who call her Annika. She wears a cortical monitor the next time, and meets a man called Axum, who calls this Unimatrix Zero – a place drones can go while regenerating and become individuals, the result of a recessive mutation that only one in a million drones have. It's only a matter of time before the Queen locates them. He asks for Seven's help in protecting it. The Doctor confirms that this was more than a dream, and Seven asks the crew to help. The Queen is seen dismantling drones in her quest to find Unimatrix Zero. Tuvok suggests that a Vulcan technique might help, and Janeway and Seven enter Unimatrix Zero together. Drones attack, but Janeway beats them off. The Voyager crew set up a nanovirus that will allow drones to remember Unimatrix Zero while awake, undermining the Collective. Janeway prepares to enter a Borg ship with Tuvok and Torres, disguised as drones, to activate the nanovirus, but they are detected. They beam onto the ship as the Delta Flyer is destroyed, but they are quickly assimilated.

TRIVIA

- Paris is reinstated as a Lieutenant in this episode. The Delta Flyer is destroyed.

RATING

- The Borg have been overused this season, so this story loses a lot of the impact it might have done. We see some of the crew assimilated, but we already know they'll be rescued, and it's ten years since that was first used as a season cliffhanger. It all feels a bit tired – despite some extraordinary special effects and an epic scale.

STAR TREK: VOYAGER SEASON SEVEN

7.1 UNIMATRIX ZERO Part II

STARDATE 54014.4

The Borg Queen moves to shut down Unimatrix Zero

TX 4 October 2000
WRITERS Brannon Braga and Joe Menosky (story by Mike Sussman and Brannon Braga and Joe Menosky)
DIRECTOR Mike Vejar
GUEST CAST Jerome Butler (Korok), Mark Deakins (Axum), Joanna Heimbold (Laura), Andrew Palmer (Errant Drone), Ryan Sparks (Alien Boy), Clay Storseth (Alien Man), Susanna Thompson (Borg Queen)

The assimilated Janeway, Tuvok and Torres have taken a neural suppressant to prevent being joined to the Collective. Seven goes to Unimatrix Zero to inform the free Borg what Janeway has planned. She starts to renew romantic feelings for Axum. Tuvok realises he's beginning to hear the Borg Queen. He stops Janeway and Torres from releasing a virus that will allow Borg to escape to Unimatrix Zero. Janeway is captured and taken to the Queen. The Queen is starting to destroy Cubes that have even one rogue drone on them. Janeway secretly orders Chakotay to destroy Unimatrix Zero – the Borg won't be able to escape there, but they will still be free. Voyager is helped by a Borg Sphere controlled by Korok, an assimilated Klingon who has broken free of his conditioning. The Away Team are beamed back and treated. Axum vows to see Seven again one day, as Unimatrix Zero fades away.

QUOTES

- 'Assimilation turns us all into friends.' – *According to the Borg Queen*

TRIVIA

- It's never made clear why the rogue Borg can dream up bat'leths and poles to fight off the Borg who come after them, but not phasers.
- Tuvok says he was born on Stardate 38774, but this would make him about 14 years old.

RATING

- Assimilation, once a terrifying violation of body and mind that leaves you scarred for life, is now just 'dressing up like the Borg'. This episode is meant to make you think the Borg are ruthless, but you end up feeling a bit sorry for them: the entire Collective is beaten by three Voyager officers and a bunch of people whose ultimate fantasy is to live in a studio set that looks a bit like a forest. An episode with odd pacing where no one's heart seems to be in it.

7.2 IMPERFECTION

STARDATE 54129.4

Seven's components break down as some of the Borg children leave

TX 11 October 2000
WRITERS Carleton Eastlake and Robert Doherty (story by André Bormanis)
DIRECTOR David Livingston
GUEST CAST Debbie Grattan (Wysanti), Manu Intiraymi (Icheb), Marley S. McClean (Mezoti), Michael McFall (Salvage Alien #1), Cody Wetherill (Rebi), Kurt Wetherill (Azan)

Two of the Borg children, Rebi and Azan, are returned to their people, who also take Mezoti. Icheb remains behind. Seven cries, claiming her ocular implant is damaged. The Doctor confirms the diagnosis. Seven can no longer regenerate due to damage to her cortical node, and Borg implants start appearing on her skin. Harry is sent out in the Delta Flyer to salvage parts from Borg space debris. The Doctor practices the operation to implant a new cortical node in the holodeck, killing Seven every time. He realises that they need a node from a live Borg. Icheb volunteers, having devised a plan to genetically alter himself. When Janeway refuses, he disengages his node – he'll die anyway. The two operations are successful. Seven helps Icheb to prepare for the Starfleet Entrance Exam.

TRIVIA

- The Delta Flyer was destroyed two episodes before, but returns here. Torres says she 'hopes' there's an afterlife, despite having visited it in the previous season's *Barge of the Dead*.
- This episode was meant to be shown after *Drive*, – Paris is wearing a wedding ring.

RATING

- An episode with a somewhat apposite title, this is full of stuff that isn't thought-through and which shows how unsure even the writers are about what a Borg implant is and does. That's fine... unless you're telling stories all about them.

7.3 DRIVE

STARDATE 54058.6

Paris and Torres take part in a space race

TX 18 October 2000
WRITER Michael Taylor
DIRECTOR Winrich Kolbe
GUEST CAST Cyia Batten (Irina), Chris Covics (Assistant), Brian George (O'Zaal), Patrick Kilpatrick (Assan), Robert Tyler (Joxom)

Paris and Harry take the new Delta Flyer for a test run and are joined by a small alien ship whose pilot, Irina, challenges them to a race. Her ship malfunctions, and the Delta Flyer rescues her. She's entering a race, and Paris and Harry convince Janeway that they should also enter. Torres is furious – Paris had promised to spend time with her. She tells Neelix that she thinks the relationship is over. Janeway learns that the race is the first peaceful enterprise of four local cultures – previously, they've fought each other. The race starts, and the Delta Flyer fights its way from fourth to first, but the race is stopped after an accident. Irina's ship has been sabotaged and her co-pilot has been killed. Torres becomes jealous of Paris' concern for Irina. Harry becomes Irina's co-pilot. Paris and Torres argue, and Paris stops the ship to settle the dispute. Harry realises Irina sabotaged her own ship – and has rigged the Delta Flyer to explode when it crosses the finish line. Paris and Torres realise, and eject the warp core just in time. Paris and Torres soon take the shuttle out on another mission – their honeymoon.

TRIVIA

- It's stated that Tom Paris was 'kicked out of the Academy'. He wasn't – Nick Locarno, the character Paris was based on, was.

RATING

- An episode where the big character moment plays against the rest of the episode and happens off-screen anyway. The Paris and Torres relationship was never terribly convincing or skilfully written, but bolting the wedding onto an episode where they spend the whole time saying they aren't right for each other, don't spend any time together and should split up is particularly inept.

7.4 REPRESSION

The crew suffer mysterious attacks

TX 25 October 2000
WRITERS Mark Haskell Smith (story by Kenneth Biller)
DIRECTOR Winrich Kolbe
GUEST CAST Carol Krnic (Jor), Jad Mager (Tabor), Derek McGrath (Chell), Ronald Robinson (Sek),Scott Alan Smith (Doyle), Keith Szarabajka (Teero) Mark Rafael Truitt (Yosa)

STARDATE 54090.4

Tabor is found slumped in the holodeck, his skull fractured. Tuvok starts an investigation. Another crewman, Yosa, is attacked in a Jefferies Tube. They were both Maquis. Tuvok considers Harry a suspect – his friend was killed by a Maquis years before. Harry protests, and Tuvok becomes agitated. He later attacks Chakotay, then forgets he did so. He meditates, and sees a vision of a Bajoran, Teero. He hears Teero's voice and attacks Janeway. Tuvok decides he is the attacker, and that he should be detained. His mind is being controlled by a Bajoran – he can hear Bajoran chanting in his head. A message from home contained a subliminal message, and now the Maquis rebel, influenced by Teero's mental powers. Tuvok mind-melds with Chakotay to end the rebellion.

TRIVIA

- Teero apparently knows that Tuvok and Chakotay are on the crew and what their roles on the ship are.
- Voyager is now 35,000 light years from home.

RATING

- The Maquis crewmembers only ever mention that they're members of the Maquis in episodes that revolve around it – roughly once or twice a year once we're past the first season. This is the only seventh season episode where it's an issue, and suddenly the crew are torn apart by factionalism. This sort of story would have been great... if they hadn't thrown away this whole plotline a hundred and twenty-something episodes ago.

7.5 CRITICAL CARE

The Doctor is kidnapped to work on a hospital ship

TX 1 November 2000
WRITER James Kahn (story by Kenneth Biller and Robert Doherty)
DIRECTOR Terry Windell
GUEST CAST Christinna Chauncey (Level Blue Nurse), Larry Drake (Chellick), John Durbin (Alien Miner), John Franklin (Kipp), Gregory Itzin (Dysek), Dublin James (Tebbis), John Kassir (Gar), Debi A Monahan (Adultress), John O'Heir (Husband), Stephen O'Mahoney (Med Tech), Paul Scherrer (Voje)

STARDATE UNKNOWN

The Doctor's mobile emitter has been stolen. He's activated on a crowded hospital ship, and demands to be returned home – but is compelled to help the victims of a generator explosion. Harry realises the Doctor's been replaced with a fake, and Neelix realises a trader, Gar, could have stolen him. They follow his trail. The Doctor is on Level Red of the ship, where a young patient, Tebbis, has been refused treatment because of a low TC rating, something the Doctor discovers means Treatment Co-efficient – healthcare here is rationed by social importance. Rich patients are routinely getting the cytoglobin treatment that will save Tebbis' life, and the Doctor procures some from them. It's too late. The Doctor injects the administrator, Chellick, with the virus that killed Tebbis, and hacks into the computer to lower his status to Level Red. Chellick is forced to give all Level Red patients the treatment. Voyager rescues the Doctor, who checks his ethical subroutines, but decides he has done nothing wrong.

RATING

- In the sixties, TV shows didn't tackle things like race relations or other controversial issues. The nineties were different, though. This is an effective allegory, but it is a pretty soft target and better shows made the point directly, first. What it does is make the differences between the way things work in *Star Trek* and real life more obvious: if you can replicate medicines – and doctors! – then you should treat everyone. If you've only got one dose of medicine and a roomful of patients, you have to make a choice.

7.6 INSIDE MAN

STARDATE 54208.3

A holographic Barclay arrives on the ship

TX 8 November 2000
WRITER Robert Doherty
DIRECTOR Allan Kroeker
GUEST CAST Sharisse Baker-Bernard (Leosa), Frank Corsentino (Gegis), Richard Herd (Admiral Paris), Richard McGonagle (Pete Harkins), Christopher Neiman (Yeggie), Michael William Rivkin (Nunk), Dwight Schultz (Barclay), Marina Sirtis (Deanna Troi)

The ship receives a hologram of Reg Barclay from the Alpha Quadrant. He has a plan to get them home, involving folding space around a red giant star. He's brought the necessary shield upgrades. Back on Earth, though, the real Barclay is convinced the hologram didn't make it. The Doctor isn't sure about Barclay's shield preparations, and the holographic Barclay appears shifty. He transmits to a Ferengi ship – they are planning to sell Seven's nanoprobes and loot the ship, after killing the crew. Troi and the real Barclay realise that a friend of Barclay's, Leosa, was in a position to sabotage the hologram. They question her, and discover she's a dabo girl from a Ferengi casino ship. The Doctor is suspicious of the holographic Barclay. The USS Carolina is sent to the Ferengi ship, but it won't arrive before the Voyager crew is killed. The real Barclay poses as the hologram, and reports that Janeway has discovered the plan. The Voyager crew realise that the hologram Barclay is a fake, and save Seven after he abducts her.

TRIVIA

- The Doctor suggests he and Barclay play a round of golf in the holodeck – saying 'the back nine on Geidi Prime' would be a good course. This is another reference to *Dune*. Golfballs in the *Star Trek* universe have a green blinking light in the middle.
- Voyager is now 30,000 light years from home, in Grid 898.

RATING

- A mix-and-match episode – the standard Barclay plot, the standard Ferengi plot, the standard quick-way-home-that's-too-good-to-be-true plot, and someone is once again after Seven's nanoprobes, but this is more than the sum of its parts. Marina Sirtis wears a nice bathing suit, and it is at least an entertaining episode.

7.7 BODY AND SOUL

STARDATE 54238.3

The Doctor gains a human body – Seven's

TX 15 November 2000
WRITERS Eric Morris, Phyllis Strong and Mike Sussman (story by Michael Taylor)
DIRECTOR Robert Duncan McNeill
GUEST CAST Megan Gallagher (Jaryn), Marva Hicks (T'Pel), Fritz Sperberg (Ranek), David Starwalt (Captain 2)

The Delta Flyer is attacked by a Lokirrim Captain, Ranek, who's hunting 'photonic insurgents' – holograms. He fires a disruption beam that begins to decompile the Doctor's program, so Seven downloads him into her implants and he takes control of her body. Seven and Harry are locked up, and the Doctor begins to experience touch and smell for the first time. On Voyager, Tuvok is undergoing his Pon farr. Paris keeps this secret, and tries to stabilise Tuvok while they wait for the Doctor to return. Eventually he suggests using the holodeck. The Doctor, posing as Seven, gorges himself on replicated cheesecake and gets drunk with Ranek. Regaining control of her body, Seven argues with the Doctor about what he did when controlling her body. The Doctor reassumes control to help Ranek's crew with a synaptic illness. He doesn't realise that Ranek is falling for him, until he kisses 'her'. Meanwhile, the Doctor is falling for another Lokirrim, Jaryn. Voyager attacks, injuring Ranek. The Doctor refuses to return home until he's treated Ranek. This doesn't alter Ranek's opinion of 'photonics' in general, but he appreciates the Doctor's help.

TRIVIA

- In *Blood Fever*, the holodeck couldn't help Vorik, because he needed to bond psychically with his mate. This doesn't bother Tuvok here. We learn that Vulcan's libidos increase with age.

RATING

- Possibly the best episode of Voyager. It's funny, it concentrates on the Doctor and Seven, and there's a serious message in among the comedy and nonsense. Ryan's impersonation of Robert Picardo's mannerisms is broad, but it's undeniably entertaining.

7.8 NIGHTINGALE

STARDATE 54074.7

Harry takes command to help a race of aliens

TX 22 November 2000
WRITER André Bormanis (story by Robert Lederman and Dave Long)
DIRECTOR LeVar Burton
GUEST CAST Alan Brooks (Annari Commander), Ron Glass (Loken), Manu Intiraymi (Icheb), Beverly Leech (Dayla), Scott Miles (Terek), Paul F O'Brien (Geral) Bob Rudd (Brell)

Voyager lands for a major overhaul, which is going to take a long time. Shuttles are sent out for supplies. Harry, Neelix and Seven look for dilithium in the Delta Flyer and are caught between two fighting ships, belonging to the Kraylor, who say they are on a humanitarian mission, and the arrogant Annari. Harry beams over to help the Kraylor, and is asked to take charge of the ship, because all the command crew are dead. Harry reluctantly agrees. Janeway is unaware of this, and has entered a trading arrangement with the Annari. Harry is not terribly good as a captain, and seems unable to delegate. It also becomes clear that they are testing a cloaking device. Seven tells him he should still get the Kraylor ship home – he is their Captain. He breaks the Annari blockade and returns to Voyager – but doesn't feel good about his achievement.

TRIVIA

- Harry says 'over a dozen' Voyager crewmen were killed when the ship was pulled into the Delta Quadrant.

RATING

- An Icheb subplot, where he falls for Torres and thinks she's fallen for him, does it's job of making the A-plot look good, but the writers had to stretch (or stoop) to lower the bar that far. This story, remarkably, isn't as bad as some previous Harry episodes, but it still falls far short of being worthwhile or watchable.

7.9 FLESH AND BLOOD

STARDATE 54337.5

The Hirogen fight holographic prey

DOUBLE-LENGH EPISODE
TX 29 November 2000
WRITER Bryan Fuller (story by Jack Monaco, Bryan Fuller and Raf Green)
DIRECTOR Mike Vejar/David Livingston
GUEST CAST Vaughn Armstrong (Alpha-Hirogen), Ryan Bollman (Donik), David Doty (Nuu'Bari Miner), Paul Eckstein (New Alpha-Hirogen), Spencer Garrett (Weiss), Chad Halyard (Hirogen Two), Todd Jeffries (Hirogen One), Cindy Katz (Kejal), Damon Kirsche (Nuu'Bari Hologram One), Don McMillan (Hirogen Three), Michael Wiseman (Beta-Hirogen), Jeff Yagher (Iden)

Voyager gets a distress call from a Hirogen ship and an Away Team beams over to discover a jungle simulation full of dead Hirogen. They have modified the technology Janeway gave them, and the holograms have taken control and removed the safety features. The holograms from the simulation have escaped in a ship with holo-emitters. Another Hirogen ship arrives and prepares to hunt them down. The holograms are cunning though, destroying the Hirogen ship, then firing on Voyager. They capture the Doctor and escape at warp speed. The Doctor is shocked to learn the holograms experience pain – another Hirogen enhancement. The Hirogen would hunt and kill them over and over. They now resent 'organics', and transfer memories of being hunted to the Doctor, so he understands. They want a planet of their own. The Doctor contacts Janeway and lobbies her to grant their wish. The Hirogen attack, and Iden, the leader of the holograms, thinks Voyager is in league with them. The Doctor sabotages a weapon designed to capture the holograms and voluntarily returns to the holograms' ship. Iden kidnaps Torres, an expert on holography, infuriating the Doctor. Iden shows Torres Ha'Dara (Bajoran for 'planet of light'), a world he wants the holograms to colonise. Its atmosphere is poisonous to humans. The Doctor is suspicious – especially when Iden declares himself 'Man of Light', the great deliverer of his kind. Iden intercepts a Nuu'bari ship, destroys it and 'liberates' their holograms – which aren't even sentient. Voyager arrives as the Hirogen attack the holograms' ship again. The Hirogen and holograms beam down to the planet and hunt one another. Voyager manages to deactivate the holograms, except Iden. The Doctor goes after him, hunts him down and destroys him. The Hirogen leave, and Voyager reactivates all the surviving holograms, who vow to try to live in peace.

TRIVIA

- A story that addresses the consequences of one of Janeway's more cavalier and ridiculous decisions: handing – indeed pressing into their hands – holotechnology to the Hirogen at the end of *The Killing Game*. It does compound her sin, though, when it's made clear that the holograms are based on the Doctor's program. She gave the Hirogen sentient beings to hunt!

RATING

- A big story that deserves two episodes, and which introduces one of the running themes of the series – the desire of holograms to be seen as life-forms. It's a sprawling allegory, one that conflates slavery, civil rights, animal rights and hunting, and it loses focus because of that. Iden is such a baddy, though, that it deflects from the more interesting issues raised.

7.10 SHATTERED

STARDATE UNKNOWN

Chakotay phases throughout Voyager's history

TX 17 January 2001
WRITERS Michael Taylor (story by Michael Sussman and Michael Taylor)
DIRECTOR Terry Windell
GUEST CAST Martha Hackett (Seska), Manu Intiraymi (Icheb), Scarlett Pomers (Naomi Wildman), Martin Rayner (Dr Chaotica)

Voyager hits a spatial rift, and Chakotay's body is affected by temporal flux – one half is young, the other is old. The Doctor restores him to normal, but Chakotay realises he's shifted in time: this Doctor can't leave the Sickbay. He's arrested by Janeway – this is a time before Voyager arrived in the Delta Quadrant. He then arrives in Engineering to discover the ship is under the control of the Kazon. The ship has been fractured in time, and as he's the only person that can perceive this, he must be the best person to put it right. He allies with the young Janeway, but accidentally reveals that the ship ends up in the Delta Quadrant. As they continue to fight their way across a number of time zones, Chakotay manages to get back to a few seconds before the spatial rift hits, and gives the order to power up the deflector dish, which prevents the rift from affecting the ship.

TRIVIA

- There are 37 Voyager timeframes imposed on the ship after the accident.
- Janeway sets off to the Delta Quadrant with a crew of 153.

RATING

- An episode that tries to demonstrate what a rich history the show has, but which only demonstrates how shallow and unimpressive a lot of it has been by resurrecting the macrovirus and the Kazon. This is an OK episode though.

7.11 LINEAGE

STARDATE 54452.6

Torres is pregnant, but doesn't want her child to be a Klingon

TX 24 January 2001
WRITER James Kahn
DIRECTOR Peter Lauritson
GUEST CAST Nicole Sarah Fellows (Elizabeth), Jessica Gaona (Young B'Elanna), Juan Garcia (John Torres), Javier Grajeda (Carl), Manu Intiraymi (Icheb), Paul Robert Langdon (Dean), Gilbert R Leal (Michael)

Torres faints, and when she gets to Sickbay, the Doctor realises she's pregnant. Torres is unhappy, and gets angry with Paris. The Doctor says it's going to be a girl, and will have Klingon features. Torres remembers back to when she was a child and was discriminated against. She realises that the Klingon genes could be erased from the foetus. Janeway and Paris are horrified, and Torres kicks Paris out of their room. Torres continues to remember how isolated she felt as a child. She and Paris quickly reconcile. The Doctor realises that the child will have health problems unless a lot of her Klingon DNA is removed. Icheb and Seven realise Torres has tampered with the database to produce such a result. Paris realises that Torres blames her Klingon nature for her father leaving her family. She agrees to have their Klingon child, and asks the Doctor to be her godfather.

QUOTES

- 'Good news has no clothes.' – *A Talaxian saying*

TRIVIA

- The Doctor casually corrects the baby's spine, so what else would he routinely 'correct' for? Disabled rights groups fear that mild genetic disorders will be screened for and eradicated in the future. Just where does the Federation draw the line?

RATING

- An episode that really works, mainly because the allegory works in a science fiction setting. We aren't quite at the stage where we can genetically engineer children in the womb, but it'll happen in our lifetimes, and SF is the perfect genre to act as a way of exploring the issue. This also acts as a race allegory, concentrating on how being singled out as different can hurt a child.

7.12 REPENTANCE

STARDATE UNKNOWN

Voyager transports condemned prisoners

TX 31 January 2001
WRITER Robert Doherty (story by Mike Sussman and Robert Doherty)
DIRECTOR Mike Vejar
GUEST CAST Tim de Zarn (Yediq), Jeff Kober (Iko), Gregg Poland (Voyager Security Officer), FJ Rio (Joleg)

Voyager answers a distress signal and beams passengers aboard. These are dangerous criminals, and their guards. One of the injured men, Iko, takes Seven hostage, but she quickly frees herself. The prisoners are convicted murderers, sentenced to be executed. Janeway is uncomfortable about this, but the Prime Directive means she can't interfere. She agrees to wait until another ship picks them up. The prisoners claim their convictions were unsafe. The Doctor cures Iko with nanoprobes, and these change his behaviour. They've fixed the brain damage that caused him to be violent. Iko is no longer the same man who committed the crimes, but his appeal is denied, and he's sent for execution. Seven notes that she also killed people, as a Borg, but now she's a different person. She regrets that Iko could not be spared.

TRIVIA

- Seven says she has catalogued about six billion stars. That's more than 9,000 a day since she was assimilated.

RATING

- A thoughtful meditation on the ethics of the death penalty and the sentencing of the mentally handicapped. There's some nice, subtle stuff – former prisoner Paris is the least sympathetic, because he's heard it all before. Seven shouldn't have mentioned her past, though – it exposes the blatant plot hole: Janeway felt able, indeed bound, to save Seven, why doesn't she feel the same about Iko?

7.13 PROPHECY

STARDATE 54518.2

Klingons believe that Torres is carrying the Klingon messiah

TX 7 February 2001
WRITERS Mike Sussman and Phyllis Strong (story by Larry Nemecek, J Kelley Burke, Raf Green and Kenneth Biller)
DIRECTOR Terry Windell
GUEST CAST Wren T Brown (Kohlar), Paul Eckstein (Morak), Sherman Howard (T'Greth), Peggy Jo Jacobs (Ch'Rega)

A cloaked ship attacks Voyager. It's an ancient Klingon ship, and they easily disable it. The ship self-destructs and 200 Klingons are evacuated onto Voyager. These are Klingons who are searching for the Kuvah'Magh, the Klingon saviour. Torres isn't interested, and the Klingon elder, T'Greth, isn't sure either. Their leader, Kohlar, says that even if Torres isn't carrying the saviour, they could end their wasteful journey if they pretended she was. Torres plays along. The Doctor discovers the Klingons have the nehret disease, and it's infected the baby. Some of the Klingons move to take over the ship, angry that the baby isn't their saviour. The Doctor synthesises a cure from the unborn baby's cells, and the Klingons realise that she has saved them after all.

RATING

- Even the Delta Quadrant isn't safe from Klingon episodes. Altogether now: honour blah ancient legend blah blah betraying Klingon tradition blah cloaked ship blah blah bat'leth, have you any wool? It's the usual stuff, working on the principle that the people who liked it the first time might still like it the twentieth.

7.14 THE VOID

STARDATE 54553.4

Voyager is pulled into a void

TX 14 February 2001
WRITERS Raf Green and James Kahn (story by Raf Green and Kenneth Biller)
DIRECTOR Mike Vejar
GUEST CAST Jonathan Del Arco (Fantome), Scott Lawrence (Garon), Robin Sachs (Valen Michael), Shamus Wiles (Bosaal), Paul Willson (Loquar)

Voyager is swept into a void, then raided by two ships. One of the captains explains there is no way to escape – ships sucked into the void have to fight for resources. Voyager tries to escape the void, but the warp core breaks down in the attempt. Janeway refuses to attack the other ships and proposes to form a co-operative. They find a mysterious alien, who the Doctor christens 'Fantome'. More and more races join the alliance. They need a polaron modulator and one of Janeway's allies finds one: by raiding a ship and killing its crew. Janeway refuses to use it, and some of the aliens drop out of the alliance. Fantome's people live in the void. In exchange for Voyager's kindness, they fight off the enemies long enough for the remaining alliance ships time to escape.

TRIVIA

- The animated episode *Time Trap* had a similar plot. Robin Sachs played a Minbari in *Babylon 5*... and they worship Valen.

RATING

- Another glimpse of what could have been – the show should be like this every week, with Janeway forging alliances and demonstrating how the Federation way works best... and what its limitations are. This is a decent episode.

7.15 WORKFORCE Part I

STARDATE 54584.3

The crew are forced to work for an alien race

TX 21 February 2001
WRITERS Kenneth Biller and Bryan Fuller
DIRECTOR Allan Kroeker
GUEST CAST John Aniston (Quarren Ambassador), Michael Behrens (Coyote), Robert Mammana (Security Officer #1), Iona Morris (Umali), Don Most (Kadan), James Read (Jaffen), Akemi Royer (Med Tech), Tom Virtue (Supervisor), Matt Williamson (Security Officer #2)

Seven, Janeway, Paris, Torres and Tuvok have no memory of life on Voyager or each other. They are working on a planet called Quarra as part of a workforce, and are generally happy. Tuvok has a strange flashback of life on Voyager, but it soon passes. Chakotay, Harry and Neelix return to the ship from a trading mission and discover Voyager disabled inside a nebula. The Doctor explains that the ship was flooded with radiation and abandoned. He's realised since that the radiation was a deliberate attack. Meanwhile, Janeway has fallen in love with a man called Jaffen. Voyager arrives at Quarra, and learns there are severe labour shortages on the planet. Tuvok is neglecting his inoculations, and the control over him is slipping. The unaffected crew beam down in disguise, but can't rouse their friends. Guards chase Chakotay and he finds himself trapped.

TRIVIA

- Chakotay notes that he is a vegetarian.

RATING

- A decent enough episode, which sees a lot of the cast being given a chance to demonstrate they can play different characters. As with *11.59*, Kate Mulgrew makes the most of the opportunity and sketches in a rounded, interesting human being.

7.16 WORKFORCE Part II

STARDATE 54622.4

Chakotay tries to rescue his crewmates

TX 28 February 2001
WRITERS Kenneth Biller and Michael Taylor (story by Kenneth Biller and Bryan Fuller)
DIRECTOR Roxann Dawson
GUEST CAST John Aniston (Quarren Ambassador), Majel Barrett (Narrator), Michael Behrens (Coyote), Jay Harrington (Ravoc), Robert Joy (Yerid), Don Most (Kadan), James Read (Jaffen), Damara Reilly (Alien Surgeon), Tom Virtue (Supervisor), Joseph Will (Security Officer #3), Matt Williamson (Security Officer #2)

Chakotay escapes, but is wounded. He meets up with Janeway, who's decided to move in with Jaffen. Chakotay corners her and tells her what's happened. Meanwhile, Torres is taken back to Voyager. Janeway is reluctant to leave her comfortable life, despite Chakotay's insistence that she is capable of much more. He is captured and conditioned, then leads Voyager into a trap. Seven is conducting her own investigations, and discovers that over a 100 humans all started work on the same day. The Voyager officers are beginning to gravitate towards each other, but no one quite believes Chakotay. Torres gets Voyager's transporters working, and beams the crew back. Janeway's memory returns and she says goodbye to Jaffen.

QUOTES

- 'Use a triaxilating frequency on a covariant subspace band.' – *The Doctor and Janeway, come up with a solution to the communications blackout*

TRIVIA

- The crew have been on the planet for three weeks.
- There is absolutely no reason why Jaffen can't come along with Janeway – he's a security man with no specific ties to the planet, so he's got no reason to stay and could do a job on the ship.

RATING

- The episode has the obvious ending, where everything's neatly back where it should be, but until then it's pretty good stuff.

7.17 HUMAN ERROR

STARDATE UNKNOWN

Seven attempts to experience emotion

TX 7 March 2001
WRITERS Brannon Braga and André Bormanis (story by André Bormanis and Kenneth Biller)
DIRECTOR Allan Kroeker
GUEST CAST Manu Intiraymi (Icheb)

Seven literally lets her hair down on the holodeck and then attends a simulated baby shower. She is relaxed here. She creates a new living space for herself, and decorates it. The Doctor is pleased that she's 'researching' her personal life. She gives Torres a gift for her baby, and then goes back onto the holodeck for a romantic date with a holographic Chakotay. All this distracts Seven from her work – the ship is buffeted by subspace shockwaves from alien warheads. Seven ends her relationship with the holographic Chakotay. She is suffering from headaches. The Doctor diagnoses that her implants will not allow her to experience too many emotional responses. He offers to deactivate them, but she says she isn't ready for that yet.

TRIVIA

- Seven serves the holographic Chakotay rack of lamb, and he doesn't object. The real Chakotay is supposed to be a vegetarian.

RATING

- A follow-up to Unimatrix Zero, Seven continues to explore her feelings. It's not wildly different from other holodeck episodes on this and other *Star Trek* series where shy or inexperienced characters test out a romantic relationship or live a fantasy life. The only thing that marks it out is the ending, where Seven rejects the idea of exploring things further for at least the time being.

7.18 Q2

STARDATE 54704.5

Q and his son arrive on the ship

TX 11 April 2001
WRITER Robert Doherty (story by Kenneth Biller)
DIRECTOR LeVar Burton
GUEST CAST Scott Davidson (Bolian), John de Lancie (Q), Keegan de Lancie (Q2), Anthony Holiday (Nausicaan), Manu Intiraymi (Icheb), Michael Kagan (Alien Commander), Lorna Raver (Q Judge)

Q's adolescent son arrives on the ship to learn about humanity. He's a bored teenager, but with godlike powers which he uses, variously, to remove Seven's clothes, turn Neelix into a mute and summon three Borg Cubes. Q arrives and returns things to normal. He asks Janeway, 'Aunt Kathy', to raise the boy, but she insists he should learn to be a better father. Q strips his son of his powers and tells him to learn to be a better person. Q2 cheats on various tests set for him by the crew, but soon starts improving himself and stops cutting corners. The Q judge that he has failed, but Q and Janeway appeal on his behalf, and they reverse their decision. Q is about to send Voyager home as thanks... then realises that would set a bad example to his son!

TRIVIA

- Q2 is played by John de Lancie's real son, Keegan.

RATING

- An episode that does the lazy, obvious thing with Q's son, and just makes him a silly teenager – it would perhaps have been funnier if, like Saffy in *Absolutely Fabulous* or Lisa in *The Simpsons*, that he was embarrassed by his parent and far more sensible. Any episode that leads you to speculate how you'd have done it better, while you watch it, can't possibly be doing its job right.

7.19 AUTHOR, AUTHOR

STARDATE 54732.3

The Doctor's holonovel outrages the crew

TX 18 April 2001
WRITERS Phyllis Strong and Mike Sussman (story by Brannon Braga)

Voyager sets up Operation Watson, a direct communications link home. The Doctor is finishing off a holonovel, and contacts a literary agent on Earth. The book, *Photons be Free,* is a parody of his adventures on Voyager, with thinly disguised characters like Captain Jenkins and Three of Eight. The story concerns a holographic Doctor who's bullied. The Doctor is at pains to say that he's not badly treated,

DIRECTOR David Livingston
GUEST CAST Brock Burnett (Male ND), Joseph Campanella (Arbitrator), Juan Garcia (John Torres), Barry Gordon (Broht), Jennifer Hammon (Female ND), Richard Herd (Admiral Paris), Robert Ito (John Kim), Dwight Schultz (Barclay), Irene Tsu (Mary), Kim Lorinne Vozoff (Irene Hansen), Heather Young (Sickbay ND)

but holograms like him are in the Alpha Quadrant, and he hopes to raise the profile of this issue. The Doctor realises he might offend people, but the agent has it published anyway: under Federation law, holograms have no rights. Janeway and a Federation Arbitrator declare that the Doctor is a 'person' under the law, and all the copies of his holonovel are recalled for revision. A few months later, some mining holograms are inspired by his book.

QUOTES

- 'As far as I know, Captain, you haven't executed any of my patients.' – *The Doctor says, explaining that Captain Jenkins is fictional. He's forgotten that Janeway did precisely that, over his objections, in* Tuvix

TRIVIA

- The crew of the USS Vortex, the Doctor's 'fictional' ship, include Captain Jenkins, Katanay, Tulak, Marseilles, Torrey and Kymble.

RATING

- An episode where the holonovel isn't half as funny as the writers seem to think it is, but which has a good performance from Robert Picardo. No one mentions, though, that *The Measure of a Man* established that Data was sentient, possibly hoping the viewers won't remember they already did this episode (and they did it again in *The Child*).

7.20 FRIENDSHIP ONE

STARDATE 54775.4

Voyager gets a mission from Starfleet

TX 25 April 2001
WRITERS Michael Taylor and Bryan Fuller
DIRECTOR Mike Vejar
GUEST CAST Josh Clark (Carey), Peter Dennis (Hendricks), Ashley Edner (Yun), David Ghilardi (Alien Lieutenant), Bari Hochwald (Brin), Ken Land (Verin), John Prosky (Otrin), John Rosenfeld (Technician #1), Wendy Speake (Technician #2)

Janeway gets a mission from Starfleet: locate the Friendship One probe, which was launched in 2067. They calculate its location... and find a planet in the depths of nuclear winter. An Away Team discovers wreckage and is attacked by aliens. The radiation was caused when the probe crashed into the planet, and the aliens think the humans did so to soften them up for invasion. Voyager attempts to help, but the aliens are hostile, and kill Carey. Voyager fires specially-adapted photon torpedoes to neutralise the atmospheric radiation, retrieves the wreckage of the probe and continues on its way.

TRIVIA

- The probe carries a Kirk-era Starfleet logo. It was launched 200 years before Kirk's time, and about 100 before Starfleet.
- Carey, first seen in *Caretaker*, is killed here.

RATING

- The alien victims in this episode are such a generic bunch that it's impossible to sympathise with them – you feel more sorry for the probe they got in the way of. Mix in peculiar ideas about DNA, radiation and atmospheres, and this is a weak episode.

7.21 NATURAL LAW

STARDATE 54827.7

Chakotay and Seven are marooned on a primitive planet

TX 2 May 2001
WRITER James Kahn (story by Kenneth Biller and James Kahn)
DIRECTOR Terry Windell
GUEST CAST Brooke Benko (Transporter ND), Ivar Brogger (Barus), Robert Curtis Brown (Ambassador), Matt McKenzie (Port Authority Officer), Autumn Reeser (Girl), Paul Sandman (Healer), Neil C Vipond (Kleg)

Seven and Chakotay's shuttle hits an energy barrier, and they only just beam to safety on a beautiful planet. Meanwhile, Paris has to take a safety course after flying recklessly through Ledosian territory. Chakotay and Seven make contact with the primitive locals, the Ventu. They have a sophisticated culture that is threatened by a Ledosian plan to dismantle the energy barrier and develop their planet. Seven and Chakotay make contact with Voyager and say that the Ventu way of life should be preserved. The Ledosians object. Paris swerves away from his safety course to rescue the expedition team a split-second before the energy barrier goes back up. Paris has failed his course, but the Ventu may be safe from the Ledosians.

QUOTES

- 'We found one of the shuttle's wings.' – *Harry says. Their shuttles don't have wings*

TRIVIA

- Rumoured, and publicised, as the episode where Chakotay and Seven become lovers. As with Deanna and Worf in the last few episodes of *The Next Generation*, some of the writers seemed very keen to push the 'relationship', others completely ignored it.

RATING

- A pretty dull episode, at the point where the series should be picking up momentum as it heads for the home straight. Nothing really happens, it's not about anything, and the characters don't learn from their experiences.

7.22 HOMESTEAD

STARDATE 54868.6

Neelix meets a colony of his own people, and makes a choice

TX 9 May 2001
WRITER Raf Green
DIRECTOR LeVar Burton
GUEST CAST Julianne Christie (Dexa), Christian R Conrad (Miner), Rob Labelle (Oxilon), Ian Meltzer (Brax), Scarlett Pomers (Naomi Wildman), John Kenton Shull (Nocona)

Voyager detects a colony of Talaxians inside an asteroid. They go to investigate, but are knocked out by a concussive blast. Neelix wakes up being tended by Talaxian widow Dexa, who says they were caught in a mining explosion – a group of miners is threatening them and their asteroid habitat. The Talaxians prove intolerant of the human crewmen, but are delighted to see Neelix. He's disappointed by their intolerance, though. The miners give the Talaxians three days to leave. Neelix asks Janeway to intervene, and it's clear he's attracted to Dexa. Neelix attempts to establish a shield grid over the asteroid, and rallies the Talaxians to defend their home. He is torn: he wants to stay here, but has duties on Voyager. Janeway appoints him Federation Ambassador to the Delta Quadrant, and Neelix remains behind.

TRIVIA

- Voyager's sensors apparently can automatically locate Talaxians deep within an asteroid, but can't detect large quantities of explosives right next to the ship. And this, surely, represents Janeway breaking the Prime Directive?

RATING

- Neelix leaves, the downside being that we first have to get a 'Neelix leaves' episode. This is pretty standard stuff, the twist being that, as the series is nearly over, the regular character can stay behind instead of make their excuses and leave. It would have been much more powerful to have, say, Janeway stay behind at the end of *Workforce*.

7.23 RENAISSANCE MAN

STARDATE 54890.7

The Doctor has to imitate his crewmates

TX 16 May 2001
WRITERS Phyllis Strong and Mike Sussman (story by Andrew Shepard Price and Mark Gaberman)
DIRECTOR Mike Vejar
GUEST CAST Alexander Enberg (Vorik), Tarik Ergin (Tactical), Andy Milder (Nar), JR Quinonez (Overlooker/Doctor), David Sparrow (Alien/Doctor), Wayne Thomas Yorke (Zet)

The R'Kaal have banned warp travel, and want to disassemble Voyager as punishment for breaching the ban. Janeway tells Chakotay she's agreed, and they'll settle on an M-Class planet. She's acting strangely, but the Doctor says she's not under any undue influence. Chakotay makes up a story about Janeway's past, and reveals she's an impostor, but she knocks him out. The impostor is the Doctor, wearing a holographic disguise. Aliens have Janeway hostage, and are forcing him to do their bidding. He disguises himself as Chakotay and Torres to further his plan of delivering gel packs for Janeway's return.The Doctor is chased off the ship by the crew when Tuvok detects his deception. The Doctor's holomatrix is decompiling. He rescues Janeway, who's furious with him, but he seems to be dying. He makes a number of deathbed confessions, including the fact he loves Seven, but Torres saves him, leaving him embarrassed.

TRIVIA

- It's established as early as *Encounter at Farpoint* that if you want to find out where an officer is, the computer tracks them (or, it's established later, their com-badge). No one thinks to do this in this episode.

RATING

- That most painful of *Star Trek* episode types: the comedy that just isn't funny. After seven years of incursions, invasions, traitors, rebellions and other various attacks, you'd think Tuvok (or, more precisely, whoever replaced him as Head of Security after his sacking) would have learned enough to be able to stop a rogue hologram.

7.24 ENDGAME

STARDATE 54973.4

Voyager returns home – but Janeway isn't satisfied

DOUBLE-LENGTH EPISODE
TX 23 May 2001
WRITERS Kenneth Biller and Robert Doherty
(story by Rick Berman, Kenneth Biller and Brannon Braga)
DIRECTOR Allan Kroeker
GUEST CAST Vaughn Armstrong (Korath), Iris Bahr (Female Cadet), Grant Garrison (Cadet), Richard Herd, (Admiral Paris), Manu Intiraymi (Icheb), Alice Krige (Borg Queen), Amy Lindsay (Lana), Lisa Locicero (Miral Paris), Miguel Perez (Physician), Joey Sakata (Engineering Officer), Richard Sarstedt (Starfleet Admiral), Dwight Schultz (Reginald Barclay), Ashley Sierra Hughes (Sabrina), Matthew James Williamson (Klingon)

It's ten years since Voyager returned, and it's now a museum. Janeway is an Admiral, Harry is a Captain, Paris is a novelist, Torres is a Federation Liaison with the Klingons, and the Doctor – who's called 'Joe' – is married to a human. Miral Paris, the daughter of Tom and Torres, contacts Janeway to arrange an exchange with a Klingon, Korath. Janeway goes to visit Tuvok, who is suffering from an Alzheimer's-like illness. She acquires some Chronexaline, a drug that helps protect against time travel. She visits Chakotay's grave, saying she's going to put things right. She steals an experimental time-travel device from Korath and heads into the past.

Twenty-six years earlier, Torres keeps undergoing false labour, and Seven and Chakotay are romantically involved. The ship detects a nebula full of wormholes and enters... to discover it is swarming with Borg. Admiral Janeway's ship appears and the Admiral gets Captain Janeway to close the rift behind her. She says she's here to take Voyager home. The Borg Queen monitors the transmission... The two Janeways meet, and the Admiral tells the Captain she should use the wormholes – they'll get home faster. She asks her younger self to trust her judgement. The crew begins upgrading the ship using Admiral Janeway's future technology, which includes upgraded shields that the Borg can't get past. They enter the nebula, using transphasic torpedoes that can each destroy a Borg Cube. There's a vast Borg structure at the heart of the nebula, one of only six transwarp hubs, leading to conduits that could take them anywhere in the galaxy. Captain Janeway wants to destroy it, but Admiral Janeway says they should use it to get home. The Admiral tells her that if she attacks it, Seven will be one of 23 crew to die, Tuvok will go mad and Chakotay will never recover from the blow. All the officers agree with the Captain – better to die fighting for what they believe in. The Admiral suggests they could both get home and destroy the Hub. She'll do a deal with the Queen – passage home in return for a defence against transphasic torpedoes.

She goes across, and the Borg Queen simply assimilates Janeway for the knowledge – but the Admiral has a neurolytic pathogen in her blood designed to destroy the Borg. The Borg Queen starts to fall apart, as does the Borg technology. Voyager flies into a transwarp hub, following a Borg Sphere heading for Earth. In the Alpha Quadrant, Starfleet assembles a fleet to intercept the Borg ship. The Sphere explodes as it emerges, and Voyager emerges from behind it. As Torres gives birth to a girl, the Starfleet ships escort Voyager back to Earth.

TRIVIA

- The rumours were that Janeway would leave earlier in the season, that there would be a ten-episode arc showing them getting home the hard way à la *Year of Hell*, that they would settle on a planet, that they'd be destroyed... in the event, they simply find a wormhole.
- The Borg have a transwarp aperture very close to Earth. That they've never used. And that Seven doesn't know about.

RATING

- So it ends, not with a bang but with a temporal anomaly. Janeway's actions seem selfish – she's willing to change an entire timeline for the sake of making history a little better: exactly the crime that Annorax was guilty of in *The Year of Hell*. This is a mish-mash of that story, *Timeless* and *All Good Things*, and seems determined to be as undramatic as possible. It would be quite clever to start with Voyager getting home... as long as the rest of the episode wasn't trying to generate tension from whether they will. It' looks lovely, but feels like a rehash of better episodes. It's full of technobabble, it throws character developments around at random... as such, it's the perfect send-off for a series that promised so much, but delivered so little. We could at least have seen them set foot on Earth...

ENTERPRISE

TO DATE: TWO SEASONS

51 episodes (including a double first episode) (2001-)

REGULAR CAST

Jonathan Archer: Scott Bakula
Phlox: John Billingsley
T'Pol: Jolene Blalock
Malcolm Reed: Dominic Keating
Travis Mayweather: Anthony Montgomery
Hoshi Sato: Linda Park
Charlie 'Trip' Tucker: Connor Trinner

CREATED BY

Rick Berman and Brannon Braga
(Based on Star Trek created
by Gene Roddenberry)

EXECUTIVE PRODUCERS

Rick Berman and Brannon Braga

While *Voyager* and *Deep Space Nine* both ran for seven years, neither caught the public imagination or entered their consciousness in the same way *Star Trek* and *The Next Generation* did. There was never any real prospect of either ever following their predecessors onto the movie screens. Inevitably, after 21 seasons, 'new' *Star Trek* had built up an enormous back story and, in places, it seemed to be sagging under the weight of it all. As *Voyager* finished, it was clear that there would be a new *Star Trek* series, and it was equally clear that it would need to have a clear hook for a mainstream audience. Another major concern was that *The Next Generation* was still a viable and popular series – the very obvious step of doing the adventures of the Enterprise-F – Star Trek: The Next-But-One Generation – would undermine that.

The way round both of these problems was to go back to basics – and back in time. Once again, there were rumours of a Sulu series, although this doesn't seem to have been considered. Once again, rumours of a *Starfleet Academy* show circulated. In the event, the production team went even further back than Kirk's time, to the very earliest days of Starfleet. *Enterprise* shows the launch of the first Enterprise, a ship whose existence had never been hinted at before.

The show seems keen to distance itself from the rest of the franchise. The opening credits aren't the traditional star field, but a potted history of human exploration. The theme tune is a Russell Watson ballad hated by fans, but which sums up the show's premise quite nicely, and is an uplifting tune in the same vein as the themes to *Smallville*, *Ally McBeal* and many other shows. The show is most definitely not called *Star Trek: Enterprise*. Not surprisingly, some fans felt the show was trying to hide its origins, to turn its back on fans.

And therein lies the problem.

Enterprise is a good series, but it's too *Star Trek*ky for the mainstream audience that gave up the franchise when *The Next Generation* ended, and a lot of *Star Trek* fans say it's a betrayal of everything they're a fan of in the first place. As Michael Piller had complained as early as the second season of *Voyager*, *Star Trek*'s problem is that television moved on to shorter scenes, larger casts, ongoing stories and sophisticated storytelling. *Enterprise* is one of the most expensive shows on TV, with some episodes of the second and third season costing more than $5m each. It's got special effects and other design work leagues ahead of any other show – better than a lot of movies. But while it claims to be a radical, back-to-basics *Star Trek* for a new millennium, its storytelling techniques have barely changed since the sixties. *Star Trek* has become its own genre, and it now looks slow, staid and simplistic. Whereas other SF shows have moved with the times, *Enterprise* makes cosmetic changes.

The relationship with the past and with the fans just shouldn't be a problem. Fans, even when they are as numerous, organised and committed as *Star Trek* fans, are a tiny proportion of the audience. Some of the things fans get worked up about are, generously, rather counter-intuitive. Jolene Blalock's T'Pol is criticised for being 'too sexy' – this despite the fact that she's a strong, rational, powerful female character, and that the actress is a keen ambassador for the show, and for *Star Trek* in general. T'Pol may epitomise the *FHM* generation of actresses, but surely that's better than any portrayal of women in either *Star Trek* or *The Next Generation*. A broader problem, for fans, is 'continuity'. Nineties *Star Trek* became almost theological in its endless iterations and reiterations of the show's history and fictional world. The latest version of the *Star Trek Encyclopedia*, a bare-bones A-Z of the names and concepts of the show, runs to over 600 pages. *Enterprise* has not contradicted what's been established, yet fans complain about the spirit – if Captain Archer's so hot, why did Kirk and Picard never mention him?

A serious problem – for both the fans and the mainstream viewers – is that it's easy to spot writers, directors and even actors who have previously worked on the franchise in the *Enterprise* credits. Many of these people are very talented, and a *Star Trek* show is always going to place unusual demands on whoever makes it. It would be foolish to throw away all the experience gained over the years. But *Enterprise* isn't made by an all-new team with fresh ideas and radical reinterpretation. It's made by much the same team that made *Voyager*, some of whose names have appeared on hundreds of previous *Star Trek* episodes.

Fans blame Rick Berman, the executive producer. This is clearly simplistic. Berman, for a start, is a very talented producer who has appointed and manages a skilled team. Most American shows have to go to repeats halfway through a season as their makers struggle to keep to schedule. For over 15 years, Berman's overseen a production line that has brought out one episode a week, every week... two episodes when two shows were running. The *Star Trek* shows are technically demanding, too. The amazing thing about *Star Trek* since 1987 is not that some of it is good, it's that something so complex can be made to a weekly schedule. If, as some fans demand, Berman stepped aside, there would be few people willing and able to do his job.

The problem, it seems, isn't with the skills but with the mindset of the writers and producers. If you've produced so much *Star Trek*, it must be difficult to see beyond that. Like a lot of American TV there's a story team in place whose job at times seems to be to make quirky pitches more bland or to add irrelevant plots to suck the momentum from the main story. There must be very little time to watch other shows if you're one of the makers of *Star Trek*. It must be tempting to think you know exactly what works and what doesn't. If you know which risks you can take, they aren't risks, and *Enterprise* has consistently failed to demonstrate ambition.

So, while the opening credits make the show look like *The Right Stuff: The Next Generation*, the worst episodes of *Enterprise* could just as easily be episodes of any *Star Trek* show of the past 15 years. *Enterprise* has lost some of the worst indulgencies of recent *Star Trek*, like the holodeck and the endless technobabble, but stories still work to the same logic. Characters are still obsessed with their fathers, have debates about moral dilemmas that wouldn't tax a smart 13-year-old, have dreams and visions with banal symbolism, don't spot that their friend is possessed by an alien until he starts shooting at them, all their opponents fly ships that are about the same size as our heroes', with weapons that have to hit the ship three times before the Chief Engineer tells the Captain the ship cannae take much more, and they can still do clever things to reconfigure the sensors or torpedoes to save the day.

For Earth's first starship, life on the Enterprise seems very leisurely, and instead of being sent on missions, the ship flies around looking for trouble. We get little sense of history, little sense of what Earth thinks of the mission. The Enterprise is meant to be flying ever outwards, but there's no sense of the increasing isolation from Earth. While it was never going to be 'realistic', it doesn't feel like space missions do in the early twenty-first century. There seems to be a mindset that the Enterprise can only face low-level challenges – Kirk, Picard or Sisko face Klingon battlefleets that will overrun the Federation, Archer faces half a dozen Klingons who are bullying a small colony.

Having the freedom from 40 years of accumulated *Star Trek* continuity was a godsend, after *Voyager* and (particularly) *Deep Space Nine* were weighed down by things the audience needed to know. Even if you watch the show every week, things like the Trill, The Dominion or the Bajorans were hard to sum up simply. The first episode of *Enterprise*, *Broken Bow*, has a few broad uses of *Star Trek* lore that everyone knows about, the Vulcans and Klingons. That's fair enough, and even a casual viewer will see that the Vulcans in *Enterprise* are subtly different to those of Spock's time – Vulcans in *Enterprise* don't mind-meld, but they do start wars. There's something very interesting being hinted at there. However, having started with a blank slate, the makers of *Enterprise* have proceeded to fill it with the same old stuff. By the end of the second season we've seen Tellarites, Tholians, Tribbles, Nausicaans, Romulans, and even Ferengi and Borg, species that were very specifically from areas of the galaxy that mankind barely knew even in Picard's time, 200 years after Archer's. The only significant addition to the mythos so far, the Suliban and the Temporal Cold War, is interesting and different (if a little underdeveloped), and demonstrates that the writers can score a big hit when they create rather than recreate. We're now at the stage where it seems every episode has to have a cute joke that follows the formula of one character saying they should introduce something we've seen is established practice in another *Star Trek* series – the holodeck, humans mating with Vulcans, families on starships – and a second character mocking the idea as far-fetched.

It's a paradox that affects many long-running series – you want it to be made by people who understand and respect the past, but also by those who are capable of innovation and killing the odd sacred cow. You want something that will appeal to the existing fanbase, but which doesn't alienate the casual or mainstream viewer. It is possible: *Smallville* has taken the Superman legend and ruthlessly recast it in the mould of teen soaps, deleting anything that doesn't work for a contemporary audience. There are viewers who don't realise it's a show about Superman, and there are certainly Superman fans who hate it, but the show demonstrates a deep love, respect for and knowledge of what has gone before, it's firmly in the spirit of the original, it's following the past to the letter more often than it appears to be, and it's a huge hit. Both the *X-Men* movies and the *New X-Men* comic written by Grant Morrison have taken a vast, sprawling, convoluted decades-long continuity and ditched it for a pared-down, character-driven drama. Back to basics there means getting to the heart of the situation and the characters and recasting them for a contemporary audience, not just doing the same stuff but being more coy about references to the past.

Enterprise isn't character-driven. More than 50 episodes in, it doesn't feel like an ensemble piece. The writers have concentrated on Archer, T'Pol and Trip to the point where Hoshi, Travis and Reed virtually disappear for episodes at a time – even the other characters remark that they don't really know Reed or Travis. We've rarely seen what motivates them, what enthuses and scares them. Archer, Trip and Reed are practically interchangeable.

For whatever reason, the actors haven't really made their mark in the way former *Star Trek* casts have. Scott Bakula often appears surprisingly stiff, given the warmth, intelligence and humour he demonstrated on *Quantum Leap* – you get the sense he's not being given the freedom and creative control he had on that show. However, even on low power, he dominates the show. John Billingsley, like Robert Picardo and Brent Spiner before him, has taken what might have been a gimmicky character, Dr Phlox, and made him very rounded and appealing. The star of the show, though, is Jolene Blalock. She has a gift of a role with T'Pol, but has made the most of it. At first glance, she's merely eye candy, and indeed during the first season, the writers found little for her to do but smoulder. But Blalock's approached the least subtle of roles with a clever understatement that makes you feel that both the character and the actress are holding back for fear of outclassing those around her. She's easily the funniest, sexiest, smartest regular actor to be cast in *Star Trek* in 15 years, and the second season saw her get some plum drama and comedy.

At its best, *Enterprise* is a great show. One strength has been 'haunted ship'-type stories. Later Starfleet generations can use their sensors to know what they're getting into, and their transporters to get out of there. Every *Star Trek* series has had a shaky start before settling down (and then going off a bit as the show draws to a close), and there are signs that *Enterprise* is moving in the right direction. The main criticism of *Enterprise* is that it doesn't feel as exciting, forward-looking and dangerous as the premise demands.

Let's get this in perspective – *Enterprise* is the most watchable *Star Trek* since the sixth season of *The Next Generation*, a decade ago. If the first episode had been a one-off TV movie, fans would be breaking down Paramount's doors for more. But it ought to be doing what *The Next Generation* did, mixing it with the big boys. Phlox's sickbay episodes should be *ER*, T'Pol should be as compelling as Sydney Bristow in *Alias*, the scientific investigations should be as beautifully articulated as *CSI*, the politics as passionate and relevant as *The West Wing*, the character interactions as beautifully managed as *Six Feet Under*, the comedy should be as sharp as *Frasier*, the ethical debates should leave *The Shield* in the shade. Fifty episodes in, with something like $150m spent on it, *Enterprise* should be far better than it is, and we should be able to sum it up with something more positive than 'well, at least it's better than *Voyager*'.

ENTERPRISE
SEASON ONE

1.1 BROKEN BOW

DATE 16 APRIL 2151

Earth's first starship is launched to take an injured alien home

DOUBLE-LENGTH EPISODE
TX September 26, 2001
WRITERS Rick Berman and Brannon Braga
DIRECTOR James L Conway
GUEST CAST Vaughn Armstrong (Maxwell Forrest), Jim Beaver (Daniel Leonard), Chelsea Bond (Lorillian Mother), Melinda Clarke (Sarin), James Cromwell (Zefram Cochrane – uncredited), Ethan Dampf (Alien Child), Marty Davis (Young Jonathan Archer), Van Epperson (Alien Man), Jim Fitzpatrick (Williams), John Fleck (Silik), Gary Graham (Ambassador Soval), Ron King (Farmer Moore), Diane Klimaszewski, Elaine Klimaszewski (Butterfly Dancers), Thomas Kopache (Tos), Tom 'Tiny' Lister Jr (Klaang), Ricky Luna (Carlos), Mark Moses (Henry Archer), Joseph Ruskin (Suliban Doctor), Peter Henry Schroeder (Klingon Chancellor), Jason Grant Smith (Fletcher), Byron Thames (Crewman), Matt Williamson (Klingon Council Member)

A Klingon ship crashes in Broken Bow, Oklahoma, and the pilot is attacked by mysterious aliens. He kills them, but is shot by a farmer. Jonathan Archer sees returning the injured Klingon as the perfect chance to finally launch the Enterprise, Earth's first starship, which the Vulcans have been blocking for years. Archer quickly assembles a crew, including Hoshi, a linguist he needs to communicate with the Klingon, and the Denobulan doctor, Phlox, who is treating him. The Vulcans insist that they send an observer, T'Pol, along. After a ceremony, the Enterprise is warping towards the Klingon homeworld. Klaang, the Klingon, regains consciousness as the ship is attacked by more of the mysterious aliens. They abduct Klaang, but one alien is captured, and Phlox identifies it as a Suliban who's been genetically engineered. Archer refuses to give up, and tracks the Klingon to the busy trading port at Rigel X. Archer meets up with a female Suliban, Sarin, who tells him about a 'Temporal Cold War' – the Suliban are being used as agents to stir up trouble in the Klingon Empire. Suliban lead by Silik attack, injuring Archer and killing Sarin. While he recovers, T'Pol sends the Enterprise after the Suliban, finding a mothership – the Helix – in the atmosphere of a gas giant. Archer and Tucker infiltrate the Helix, and free Klaang. Archer is left behind, and discovers a chamber where time is distorted, and a mysterious figure from the future communicates orders to Silik. Archer narrowly escapes when he is beamed back to the Enterprise. The ship takes Klaang to the Klingon homeworld, where Archer earns a curt 'thank you'. As the Enterprise leaves, they receive word from Starfleet: their exploration mission is officially underway.

QUOTES

- 'Imagine it. Thousands of inhabited planets at our fingertips. And we'll be able to explore those strange new worlds and seek out new life and new civilizations. This engine will let us go boldly where no man has gone before.' – *Zefram Cochrane*

TRIVIA

- The closing theme of this episode is an instrumental version of *Faith of the Heart*, the opening theme. Subsequent episodes use a piece of music by Dennis McCarthy.

RATING

- An excellent start, a clever blend of *Star Trek* traditions, like Klingons and alien dancing girls, and intriguing new elements like the time-travelling baddies and the spiky relationship with the Vulcans. An episode that introduces the new characters well, it has some nice variations in tone, from comedy to action. It's a shame the transporter is used as a deus ex machina – it's not so much that you see the solution coming, it's that after 700 previous episodes of *Star Trek* it's hard to get excited about seeing it.

1.2 FIGHT OR FLIGHT

DATE 6 MAY 2151

Archer decides that discretion is the better part of valour when they encounter a hostile alien

The Enterprise finds a ship floating in space and Archer decides to take a closer look. It's been damaged in a firefight, and they detect faint life signs. Archer, Reed and Hoshi enter a ship in spacesuits – the air temperature is below freezing. They discover an alien machine

TX 3 October 2001
WRITERS Rick Berman and Brannon Braga
DIRECTOR Allan Kroeker
GUEST CAST Brett Baker (Crewman #2 – uncredited), Jeff Ricketts (Alien Captain), Efrain Riguerda (Translator Voice), Max Williams (Crewman – uncredited)

suspending the crew and draining their blood. Archer decides to leave before whoever did this comes back and threatens the Enterprise, but feels guilty, and turns back. Phlox does an autopsy on one of the crewmen and discovers that triglobulin is being drained. A hostile vessel matching the technology of the alien machine arrives and opens fire on the Enterprise. A fourth ship also arrives, but problems with the translator make them think the Enterprise is responsible for the abductions. Hoshi manages to convince the alien captain of the truth. Teaming up, they destroy the hostile ship. The Enterprise's new allies are the Axanar.

TRIVIA

- One of Kirk's medals was the Palm Leaf of Axanar in *Court Martial*, and the planet was also the site of a battle fought by Garth (*Whom Gods Destroy*).

RATING

- An episode dealing with Hoshi's hopes and (mainly) fears, it's quite an eerie episode.

1.3 STRANGE NEW WORLD

DATE UNKNOWN

The Enterprise discovers an idyllic world with a secret

TX 10 October 2001
WRITERS Mike Sussman and Phyllis Strong (story by Rick Berman and Brannon Braga)
DIRECTOR David Livingston
GUEST CAST Rey Gallegos (Crewman), Henri Lubatti (Ethan Novakovich), Kellie Waymire (Elizabeth Cutler)

The Enterprise has discovered an unspoilt world, and Archer quickly arranges a landing party. Trip, Travis, T'Pol and crewmen Cutler and Novakovich join Archer (and Porthos!) on the surface. As night falls, Archer returns to the ship, but the others stay behind on a camping trip. After ghost stories, they retire for the night, but storms start up, and they need to shelter in nearby caves. They begin to imagine humanoid figures around them – Cutler sees T'Pol talking to the aliens, and it doesn't allay any suspicions when she denies it. A mission to rescue them in the shuttlepod fails. Novakovich has become disturbed, and they risk beaming him to the ship. He's injured in the attempt, and Phlox discovers he's got tropolisine – a hallucinogen found in pollen – in his bloodstream. Affected by the pollen, Trip is now paranoid about T'Pol. Phlox develops an antidote, inaprovaline, but Trip's paranoia means he won't let Archer bring it near. Archer tricks Trip, and T'Pol stuns him. As the winds subside, the crew begin hiking back through a beautiful morning to the shuttlepod.

TRIVIA

- Porthos, Archer's pet beagle, gets to go on his first Away Mission, much to T'Pol's disdain.

RATING

- It's very odd to switch focus to minor crewmen Cutler and Novakovich before the main ones are firmly established – if viewers were still joining the show, it would be very confusing. This is an episode that starts with a lovely sense of wonder, all the crew stopping to just look out the window at the new planet. If it ends up as a more standard story of crew seeing things and getting paranoid, it's at least a well-told one.

1.4 UNEXPECTED

DATE UNKNOWN

Trip discovers he's pregnant after visiting an alien ship

TX 17 October 2001
WRITERS Rick Berman and Brannon Braga
DIRECTOR Mike Vejar
GUEST CAST Mike Baldridge (Dillard), Julianne Christie (Ah'Len), John Cragen (Crewman), Christopher Darga (Klingon Captain), Regi Davis (Klingon First Officer), Drew Howerton (Steward), TL Kolman (Alien Man), Randy Oglesby (Trena'L)

The Enterprise is suffering a series of malfunctions. The crew discover a cloaked ship behind them, draining their plasma exhaust. This is a damaged Xyrillian vessel, which Archer offers to help repair. Trip is sent over, and has to undergo a painful acclimatisation process. The alien ship is weird and disorientating, and Trip finds it difficult to function there at first. He adapts, and flirts with Ah'Len, an alien engineer. They spend time in a holographic chamber together and engage in telepathic contact. The teraphasic coils fixed, Trip returns to the Enterprise. He soon discovers a strange growth on his body. Phlox gives him the good news: he's pregnant. They have to track the Xyrillian vessel for advice, and discover the fault has recurred, and it's trailing a Klingon battle cruiser. The Klingons are angry when they are told about the aliens, forcing Archer to negotiate on their behalf. The Klingon Captain agrees to spare the Xyrillians in return for their holographic technology, and has a good laugh at Trip's expense. Ah'len transfers the embryo to another host.

QUOTES

- 'Three days. You were only there for three days and you couldn't restrain yourself.'
  'I'm telling you Captain, I was a complete gentleman the entire time.'
  'I imagine that's a question of how you define "gentleman".' – *Archer, Tucker and T'Pol*

TRIVIA

- We learn that Trip is both the first pregnant human male, and the first human to successfully mate with an alien (he's certainly not the last in *Star Trek...*)

RATING

- A 'male pregnancy' story sounds terrible, but this pulls it off, with a blend of humour, genuine humanity and freakiness. An early sign that Connor Trinner is going to be a useful member of the cast, this is a good episode.

1.5 TERRA NOVA

DATE UNKNOWN

The Enterprise investigates the mystery of a lost Earth colony

TX 24 October 2001
WRITER Antoinette Stella (story by Rick Berman and Brannon Braga)
DIRECTOR LeVar Burton
GUEST CAST Erick Avari (Jaymin), Mary Carver (Nadet), Greville Henwood (Akary), Brian Jacobs (Athan)

Seventy-five years ago, the Earth ship Conestoga left to found a colony on Terra Nova, but transmissions soon ceased. The Enterprise is sent to find out what happened. No life is detected, but there are unusual radiation readings. Archer leads a landing party that finds the colony in ruins, but no sign of bodies. They are attacked by cave-dwellers in body armour who injure Reed and take him hostage. T'Pol realises they are human. Archer and Phlox allow themselves to be caught, and discover the cave-dwellers, who call themselves 'Novans', blame Earth for the poison rain that destroyed the colony. They don't think they are humans, even when Archer shows them pictures of the early days of the colony. T'Pol learns that an asteroid collision caused a radioactive cloud, and Phlox realises that the water is still poisoned and the Novans will have to leave. Archer tells the Novans to relocate to the southern hemisphere, which is safe.

TRIVIA

- According to *Encounter at Farpoint*, Earth in the 2070s was recovering 'from the post-atomic horror' and it didn't look like it was in a position to launch colony ships.

RATING

- The first major misfire of the show, *Terra Nova* isn't really about anything, and the big revelations are never anything but predictable. Perhaps it's because the 'first human colony' is presented so pessimistically, but the whole episode just feels wrong.

1.6 THE ANDORIAN INCIDENT

DATE UNKNOWN

The Andorians attack a Vulcan monastery, claiming the Vulcans are spies

TX 31 October 2001
WRITER Fred Dekker (story by Rick Berman, Brannon Braga and Fred Dekker)
DIRECTOR Roxann Dawson
GUEST CAST Jeffrey Combs (Shran), Steven Dennis (Tholos), Bruce French (Vulcan Elder), Jamie McShane (Tactical Crewman), Jeff Ricketts (Keval), Richard Tanner (Vulcan Initiate)

Archer decides to visit a Vulcan monastery, P'Jem. T'Pol briefs them to stay respectful, and she, Archer and Trip go down. The place is deserted, except for one elder, who insists they leave. Archer spots a blue-skinned alien, one of the Andorians who have occupied the planet. Their leader, Shran, claims that this is a Vulcan listening post, but the Vulcans insist there is no technology there. On the ship, Reed detects the Andorian ship, and begins planning a rescue. Archer is also planning an escape, and works out a route through some underground tunnels. There's a firefight as Reed arrives just as Archer escapes. They track the last of the Andorians to the reliquary, where the sacred artefacts are kept. Archer finds a huge underground base – the Vulcan sensor array Shran was talking about. Archer gets T'Pol to take readings of the place and hand them to the Andorians as proof. Shran has what he came for, and leaves.

TRIVIA

- The Andorians first appeared in *Journey to Babel*, and others have been glimpsed over the years in places like *Whom Gods Destroy*, *Star Trek IV: The Voyage Home* and *The Offspring*. The *Enterprise* versions, for the first time, have flexible antennae, which are radio controlled and each require a separate operator.

RATING

- If there was one person in the audience that didn't see the twist coming, it would be extraordinary. Despite that, it's a good episode for Archer and T'Pol, and an important one for the running plotlines. There's a fine mix of threat and intrigue, and a nice contrast between Archer's naive and direct approach and the Vulcans' shiftiness disguised as restraint.

1.7 BREAKING THE ICE

DATE UNKNOWN

Reed and Travis become trapped on a comet

TX 7 November 2001
WRITERS Maria Jacquemetton and Andre Jacquemetton
DIRECTOR Terry Windell
GUEST CAST William Utay (Vanik)

The Enterprise has discovered the largest known comet, and it contains the rare mineral eisilium. Reed and Travis are sent with a drilling rig to get samples. The Vulcan ship the Ti'Mur arrives, not to investigate the comet, but to observe the Enterprise. Archer is annoyed they won't help or even come over, and suspects they are up to something. Reed and Travis build a snowman with pointy ears. Trip discovers that T'Pol has been sent a secret message from the ship. Whatever it says, T'Pol isn't happy. Archer invites Captain Vanik over, but dinner is a frosty occasion. A test blast on the comet's surface alters its rotation, and places Reed and Travis in danger. Meanwhile, T'Pol confides in Trip that she has been ordered back to Vulcan, or her wedding will be cancelled. The shuttlepod becomes trapped as it is due to leave the comet. Archer tries to rescue the shuttlecraft, but the grappler doesn't work. He swallows his pride and asks the Vulcans to use their tractor beam. The shuttlepod is saved. T'Pol decides to stay on the Enterprise.

TRIVIA

- The striking Vulcan ship designs are partly based on Matt Jeffries' initial sketches for Kirk's Enterprise. Designer Doug Drexler took the basic idea of a long thin body projecting from a loop-shaped engine, making the shape more like some of the Vulcan architecture that's been seen in the films. It also looks unlike the Enterprise, making it clear that the Vulcans haven't co-operated with the humans. While Drexler has never mentioned it, it's also a little reminiscent of the Romulan Warbird, which has its engines mounted on a loop.

RATING

- An episode that was probably designed as a showcase for Reed and Travis is hijacked by the far more intriguing T'Pol subplot. The twist that T'Pol isn't plotting against the ship ought to be predictable, but it comes as something as a relief.

1.8 CIVILIZATION

DATE 31 JULY 2151

Archer disguises himself to explore a medieval planet and falls for a feisty scientist

TX 14 November 2001
WRITERS Phyllis Strong and Michael Sussman
DIRECTOR Mike Vejar
GUEST CAST Charlie Brewer (the Alien), Diane DiLascio (Riann), Wade Andrew Williams (Garos)

The Enterprise has discovered a new civilisation, the Akaali, a society roughly equivalent to Earth's Renaissance. T'Pol is shocked when Archer decides to go down himself, rather than send a probe. The crew soon detect an antimatter reactor on the planet – other off-worlders have beaten them here. On the surface, the landing party learn that many people living in the city with the reactor are suffering from a sickness caused by tetracyanate 622 in the water supply. Archer locates the reactor underneath a shop, and breaks in. He is attacked by an Akaali woman, Riaan, who's also deduced that the shop has something to do with the sickness, and blames Archer. Together, they see the real owner, Garos, a Malurian. Archer and Riaan have to kiss to avert suspicion. They then follow men with crates to a rendezvous with a shuttlecraft. Archer reveals his identity to Riaan. They discover the aliens are mining the planet for veridium isotope. As they attempt to sabotage the mine, a Malurian ship attacks the Enterprise. Trip beams the reactor into space, next to the Malurian ship, then destroys the reactor with a torpedo. The explosion cripples the enemy ship. Archer rounds up the Malurians on the surface, and Phlox provides Riaan with a cure for the plague.

QUOTES

- 'Starfleet could have sent a probe out here to make maps and take pictures but they didn't. They sent us, so that we could explore with our own senses.'– *Archer*

TRIVIA

- Items seen in the antiques shop include a variety of old props from the *Star Trek* storeroom.

RATING

- It feels like a Riker episode of *The Next Generation*, and the story doesn't amount to much, but there's something cathartic about seeing a Starfleet officer who isn't restrained by the Prime Directive starting a gunfight in an alien street.

1.9 FORTUNATE SON

DATE UNKNOWN

The Enterprise helps a freighter fight off pirates

TX 21 November 2001
WRITER James Duff
DIRECTOR LeVar Burton
GUEST CAST Vaughn Armstrong (Maxwell Forrest), Danny Goldring (Nausicaan Captain), Charles Lucia (Keene), Lawrence Monoson (Ryan Cross), Kieran Mulroney (Shaw), Elyssa D Vito (Girl), D Elliot Woods (Boy)

The cargo freighter Fortunate has sent a distress signal, and the Enterprise is sent to help. The Acting-Captain, Ryan, tells Archer they were attacked by Nausicaan pirates. Archer stays to help with the injuries and repairs – but the crew of the freighter are worried they'll discover their secret: they have a Nausicaan prisoner they are torturing for information. T'Pol detects the alien's lifesign. Ryan is unrepentant, and traps Archer and his team, before detaching the module they are in. The Fortunate fires on the Enterprise and leaves. The Enterprise rescues the crewmen. The Fortunate picks a fight with a Nausicaan base, but it goes badly, and Nausicaans board the freighter. Archer negotiates a cease-fire, but Ryan refuses to go along with the terms until the Nausicaans demonstrate the human ship is outgunned. The real captain, Keene, has recovered and demotes Ryan. He, at least, is grateful for Archer's help.

TRIVIA

- The Nausicaans first appeared in *The Next Generation* (they're the aliens who stabbed Picard through the heart when he was young – *Tapestry*). This is their first appearance on *Enterprise*.

RATING

- A nice episode, a rare *Star Trek* story where both sides in a dispute are equally wrong and equally hot-headed.

1.10 COLD FRONT

DATE UNKNOWN

Alien stargazers are invited aboard – but one is a Suliban agent

TX 28 November 2001
WRITERS Steve Beck and Tim Finch
DIRECTOR Robert Duncan McNeill
GUEST CAST John Fleck (Silik), Joseph Hindy (Prah Mantoos), James Horan ('Future Man'), Leonard Kelly-Young (Sonsorra), Michael O'Hagan (Fraddock), Lamont D Thompson (Alien Pilgrim), Matt Winston (Daniels)

The Great Plume of Agosoria is a protostar that erupts every 11 years – a feature of a number of local alien religions. The Enterprise is hosting a meeting of some pilgrims. On a tour of the ship, one of the pilgrims slips away from the group and disconnects a conduit. He's a Suliban agent. Soon, the Enterprise is caught in a plasma storm and hit by plasma lightning – there ought to be a chain reaction that destroys the ship, but because the conduit has been disconnected, the ship is saved. Trip's confused about how the conduit came undone, until crewman Daniels approaches Archer. He reveals he's from 900 years in the future, and has come back to find Silik, the Suliban Archer met on their first mission. He proves his case by having futuristic technology. They find Silik, who admits he saved the ship, but gets away and kills Daniels. Archer prevents Silik from stealing Daniels' technology. Silik escapes, and Archer orders Daniels' room to be sealed off.

TRIVIA

- James Horan is credited, in various places, as 'Future Man', 'Man' and 'Mysterious figure'. Fans speculate that because his identity is being kept secret, he must be a character we know. Prime suspect is that it's a future version of Archer himself, but posts to internet lists and boards have suggested just about every character, male and female, who's ever been seen across the franchise.

RATING

- A scrappy episode, but one that adds a new twist to the Temporal Cold War. There are tantalising hints, but nothing really meaty enough to get excited about.

1.11 SILENT ENEMY

The ship is attacked by an alien vessel

TX 16 January 2002
WRITER André Bormanis (story by André Jacquemetton and Maria Jacquemetton)
DIRECTOR Winrich Kolbe
GUEST CAST Jane Carr (Mary Reed), John Rosenfeld (Mark Latrelle), Paula Malcomson (Madeline Reed), Guy Siner (Stuart Reed)

DATE I SEPTEMBER 2151

The Enterprise is laying communications buoys when an unidentified ship arrives, then warps away without answering their hails. Setting that aside, Archer sets Hoshi the mission of finding out what Reed's favourite food is: it's his birthday, and Archer wants to give him a treat. The alien ship returns, fires on the Enterprise and warps out again. Archer has Reed and Tucker fit phase cannons to the ship – a job there wasn't time for before its first mission. Reed can't understand why Hoshi is so interested in him, suspecting romantic intentions. The mystery ship arrives again, this time crippling the ship's power system. Two aliens board, but are chased off the ship. Tensions rise on the crippled ship, as Reed tries to test the cannons. T'Pol discovers that the aliens have planted surveillance devices. The alien ship returns. This time, the Enterprise is armed, and the phase cannons prove unexpectedly powerful, seriously damaging the alien vessel, which retreats, never to be seen again. The officers convene to give Reed his birthday cake. He's amazed that it's pineapple – his favourite.

TRIVIA

- British actor Guy Siner played Grüber in *'Allo 'Allo.*

RATING

- When you hear Archer say he doesn't really know Reed, it's almost impossible not to hear the writers sitting around a table saying the same thing. We find out a bit more about the tactical officer in this episode, which is unremarkable but watchable.

1.12 DEAR DOCTOR

Dr Phlox writes a letter to a friend sharing his thoughts

TX 23 January 2002
WRITERS Maria Jacquemetton and André Jacquemetton
DIRECTOR James Contner
GUEST CAST David A Kimball (Esaak), Alex Nevil (Menk Man), Chris Rydell (Alien Astronaut), Kellie Waymire (Elizabeth Cutler), Karl Wiedergott (Larr)

DATE UNKNOWN

Phlox is corresponding with Dr Lucas, a human serving on Denobula. He shares his observations of human behaviour, and his growing closeness to Ensign Cutler. He is called on to treat two Valakians found drifting in space. Their planet is suffering an epidemic, and they're looking for a cure. Archer and Phlox agree to go to their planet to try to help. Phlox is a fearful of treating 50 million people. He learns there are two species on the planet, the Valakians and the Menk, who are less advanced and unaffected by the plague. Phlox realises it's a genetic disease, and that the Menk are being exploited by the Valakians. Phlox can't cure the disease, and the Valakians demand Archer gives them warp technology so they can find someone who can. Phlox realises the Menk are on the verge of an enormous evolutionary advance, one that's artificially held in check by the Valakians. He tells Archer he has a cure for the plague, but it will interfere with natural development on the planet. They agree on a compromise – they can ease the symptoms of the disease, which may give the Valakians time to develop their own cure.

QUOTES

- 'Some day, my people are going to come up with some sort of a doctrine, something that tells us what we can and can't do out here, should and shouldn't do. But until somebody tells me that they have drafted that directive, I'm going to have to remind myself that we didn't come out here to play God.' – *Archer decides that a technicality won't stop him from doing Prime Directive stories*

TRIVIA

- No date has been set for when the Prime Directive was established – but we know it hadn't been by 2168, when a crewman on the USS Horizon left a book about gangsters on Sigma Iotia II (*Piece of the Action*). Although, in the same episode, Kirk says subspace radio hadn't been invented, and Archer's Enterprise seems to use one.

RATING

- John Billingsley was condemned by fans at first as being a second Neelix, but this episode shows that he's a talented and versatile actor, and his character has hidden depths and secrets (but thankfully not sinister ones). The plot – a population affected by a terrible plague that's afflicted them for generations which a single Starfleet medical officer can cure in a day or two – isn't original, but it isn't really the point of a genuinely character-driven episode.

1.13 SLEEPING DOGS

DATE UNKNOWN

Archer tries to rescue a stricken Klingon ship

TX 30 January 2002
WRITER Fred Dekker
DIRECTOR Les Landau
GUEST CAST Michelle C Bonilla (Bu'Kah), Stephen Lee (Klingon Captain)

The Enterprise detects a disabled ship in the atmosphere of a gas giant. T'Pol, Reed and Hoshi board the ship and discover it's a Raptor-Class Klingon vessel with an unconscious crew. The Klingons won't want the dishonour of being rescued by humans, but Reed doesn't want the dishonour of leaving them helpless. They are attacked by a Klingon woman, Bu'kah, who steals the shuttlepod and sends a signal to the Klingons saying the Enterprise attacked them. The Away Party are marooned, and the Klingon ship has now sunk too far for the Enterprise to rescue them. They manage to restrain Bu'kah, who refuses any help. Trip thinks he can reinforce the shuttlepod. Hoshi discovers a ship's log that says the Klingons were fighting the Xarantines. The Raptor's hull begins to buckle under the pressure. Hoshi suggests they fire all the torpedoes at once. It's risky, but the shockwave pushes them up into the range of the Enterprise. The crew return to their ship as the Klingon Captain recovers. He threatens Archer, who points out that he doesn't have any torpedoes. The Enterprise leaves as two other Klingon ships start to arrive.

TRIVIA

- Reed's eyes light up when he sees the Klingons have photon torpedoes. He's never even heard the name before.

RATING

- An atmospheric episode where the Klingons are shadowy and vicious, rather than being the Braveheart rejects they often were in the nineties. We know more about the Klingons that the crew does, but the crew soon realise they're in trouble.

1.14 SHADOWS OF P'JEM

DATE UNKNOWN

Archer and T'Pol are kidnapped as tensions between the Andorians and Vulcans rise

TX 6 February 2002
WRITERS Phyllis Strong and Mike Sussman (story by Rick Berman and Brannon Braga)
DIRECTOR Mike Vejar

Forrest tells Archer that the Andorians have destroyed the monastery on P'Jem, and the Vulcans are blaming Archer (see The *Andorian Incident*) and want to reassign T'Pol, who doesn't seem concerned. With two days before she can leave, Archer takes her on a mission to Coridan. Ambushed and captured by rebels, they find themselves tied up together in a small hut. T'Pol comes to appreciate Archer's optimism. The Coridan government contact the Enterprise and tells them not to negotiate with the rebels. They are contacted by Traeg, one of the rebels, who wants weapons in return for the hostages' safe return. The Vulcan ship Ni'Var arrives to collect T'Pol, and its captain

GUEST CAST Vaughn Armstrong (Forrest), Jeffrey Combs (Shran), Steven Dennis (Tholos), Gary Graham (Soval), Gregory Itzin (Sopek), Jeff Kober (Traeg), Stephen Lee (Klingon Captain), Barbara Tarbuck (Chancellor Kalev)

decides to launch a rescue mission. Tucker and Reed take a shuttlepod down first, but are abducted by Shran and Tholos, Andorians they met on P'Jem. Shran is in Archer's debt, and wants to rescue him. Together they reach the rebel compound just as the Vulcan commandos land. T'Pol is injured, and is taken back to the Enterprise. The Vulcans accept that T'Pol should remain on there until she has fully recovered.

TRIVIA

- The three Starfleet senior staff – Williams, Leonard and Forrest – are named for the three stars of the original *Star Trek* (William Shatner, Leonard Nimoy and DeForest Kelley, if you haven't been paying attention).

RATING

- An early follow-up to a successful episode, this is a good story built on good foundations, dealing with exactly the sort of diplomatic hi-jinks and actions with consequences that should be the bread and butter of *Enterprise*.

1.15 SHUTTLEPOD ONE

DATE 9 NOVEMBER 2151

Reed and Trip are trapped in a shuttlepod with no hope of rescue

TX 13 February 2002
WRITERS Rick Berman and Brannon Braga
DIRECTOR David Livingston

Reed and Trip are testing the shuttlepod's targeting scanners well away from the Enterprise. They head for the rendezvous point, where they find wreckage from the ship. This is the result of a collision with a Tesnian ship, and the Enterprise is late because it's taking the Tesnians home, but Trip and Reed assume that it has been destroyed. There is no way for the shuttlepod to reach safety in the ten days life support remaining. Trip tries to find a way to survive, perhaps by reaching the Echo Three subspace amplifier – Reed is more concerned with making a good record of what went wrong and writing goodbye letters. Reed hallucinates being back in Sickbay, seduced by T'Pol. There's disaster when the hull is punctured. They seal the leak, but Trip realises they've been hit by micro singularities and now only have two days of air. They hear a signal from Hoshi, but their communications are damaged, and there's no way to make the new rendezvous. Trip and Reed eject the engine and blow it up – a signal the Enterprise can't miss. The two men are recovered by their ship.

TRIVIA

- It seems to be common Starfleet strategy to eject your engine and fire at it – it's done in *Star Trek: Insurrection*.

RATING

- Another of the episodes that feels like the writers are still desperately trying to figure out Reed. A nice twist on the lifeboat-type show, and a nice contrast between Reed and Trip.

1.16 FUSION

DATE UNKNOWN

The Enterprise encounters a group of Vulcans with emotions – and a dark side

TX 27 February 2002
WRITERS Mike Sussman and Phyllis Strong
(story by Rick Berman and Brannon Braga)
DIRECTOR Rob Hedden
GUEST CAST Vaughn Armstrong (Forrest), John Harrington Bland (Kov), Enrique Murciano (Tolaris), Robert Pine (Tavin)

The Enterprise is exploring the Arachnid Nebula when it meets a Vulcan ship. The crew are civilians, led by Tavin, and the ship needs repairing. Archer is happy to help. The Vulcans are surprisingly jolly, and Tavin explains they are 'V'tosh ka'tur', Vulcans who explore their emotions. T'Pol doesn't like associating with them. She is surprised how intelligent the scientist Tolaris is, though. He suggests she doesn't meditate one night, to see what she dreams. She does so – and dreams of making love to Tolaris. She finds it difficult to deal with her emotions, and Phlox tells her to take things slowly. Starfleet contacts Archer to tell him that the father of one of the Vulcans, Kov, is dying and wants to see his son. Trip convinces Kov to make contact. Tolaris and T'Pol experiment with a mind-meld, but T'Pol becomes very uncomfortable with the intimacy. She has to physically break away, leaving them both in a state of shock. Archer learns of this, and provokes Tolaris, who throws him across the room. Tolaris is a dangerous man. The Vulcans leave, and T'Pol slowly begins to recover.

TRIVIA

- The working title of this episode was *Equilibrium*.

RATING

- More intriguing 'forget everything you know' stuff about the Vulcans, and further hints that T'Pol has a rebellious streak. It cleverly plays with our sympathies – starting off by suggesting that these emotional Vulcans are in the right, before reminding us just how dangerous they could be.

1.17 ROGUE PLANET

DATE UNKNOWN

A jungle planet is stalked by alien hunters

TX 20 March 2002
WRITER Chris Black (story by Chris Black, Rick Berman and Brannon Braga)
DIRECTOR Allan Kroeker
GUEST CAST Stephanie Niznik (Woman), Conor O'Farrell (Buzaan), Eric Pierpoint (Shiraht), Keith Szarabajka (Damrus)

The Enterprise discovers a planet that has broken from its orbit, but which contains pockets of life. There's also an alien ship on the planet. A landing party goes down to the jungle, where they discover an alien camp. They are ambushed by alien hunters, but they are soon talking. These are the Eska, and they've been hunting on this planet for nine generations. Archer sees a mysterious beautiful woman, but everyone else thinks he imagined it. As the hunting party sets off, Archer sees the woman again and she asks for his help. He learns she is a telepathic shapeshifter, and that the Eska are hunting her. The Eska admit they hunt the 'wraiths', and Archer gets Phlox to work on a way to dampen the wraiths' scent. The hunters are thwarted and leave. The woman thanks Archer.

TRIVIA

- Eric Pierpoint auditioned for the role of Ben Sisko.

RATING

- Probably the weakest episode of the season, it's not bad so much as anti-climatic. As a rule of thumb, any episode of *Enterprise* that could work equally well for *Voyager* shouldn't be commissioned, and this has 'unused Chakotay story' written all over it.

1.18 AQUISITION

DATE UNKNOWN

A group of Ferengi ransack the ship

TX 27 March 2002
WRITERS Maria Jacquemetton and André Jacquemetton (story by Rick Berman and Brannon Braga)
DIRECTOR James Whitmore Jr
GUEST CAST Jeffrey Combs (Krem), Clint Howard (Muk), Matt Malloy (Grish), Ethan Phillips (Ulis)

The Enterprise crew is knocked out by four Ferengi, who set about scavenging items from the ship. Trip, who was in the decontamination chamber, is unaffected, and tries to come up with a plan. The Ferengi wake Archer, who realises that they are greedy, and starts to play them off each other as they search for the 'ship's vault' they are sure must be somewhere. Trip revives T'Pol, and the two of them begin playing on the Ferengi paranoia. They lure the four Ferengi into one place, and T'Pol stuns them. The Ferengi are made to put everything back and sent on their way. Archer warns them never to bother a Starfleet vessel again.

TRIVIA

- The first season of *The Next Generation* established that the Federation is only then starting to explore areas of space where the Ferengi dwell – *The Last Outpost* is the first time Starfleet sees them face-to-face. *Enterprise*, set 200 years earlier, gets around the problem by simply never naming the alien race as Ferengi.
- The actors playing the Ferengi span the various generations of the show – Ethan Phillips had already played a Ferengi in *Menage à Troi* before he played Neelix in *Voyager*. Jeffery Combs played Brunt on *Deep Space Nine*, as well as several other major guest parts (he's Shlan in *Enterprise*). Clint Howard was six when he played Balok in *The Corbomite Maneuver*.

RATING

- An episode that starts with the Ferengi being rather sinister, like they were originally designed to be – but which soon reverts to a fun story about outwitting them. Leaving aside the objection that the Ferengi really shouldn't be around this early in *Star Trek* history, it's a fun episode that gives Scott Bakula the chance to be funny for once.

1.19 OASIS

DATE UNKNOWN

Archer investigates a 'haunted' ship

TX 3 April 2002
WRITER Stephen Beck (story by Stephen Beck, Rick Berman and Brannon Braga)
DIRECTOR Jim Charleston
GUEST CAST Rene Auberjonois (Ezral), Tom Bergeron (D'Marr), Claudette Sutherland (Maya), Annie Wersching (Liana), Rudolph Willrich (Kuulan)

In return for some coffee, the alien trader D'Marr tells Archer about a 'haunted ship' that crashed years ago. The Enterprise sets course for that planet, and they discover its dilithium crystals are intact. They soon spot figures who don't register on the sensors. Chasing one, Trip and T'Pol discover a functioning airponics bay, and the crew of the Kantare. They crashed three years ago after being shot down, and rather than draw attention to themselves, they've hidden behind a dampening field. Trip falls for one of the young women, Liana. Meanwhile, the Enterprise crew get suspicious, because there's no evidence the ship was shot at, and the airponics bay couldn't possibly feed all the survivors. Trip discovers the desiccated corpse of one of the crewmen he'd just seen alive. It becomes clear that Liana's father, Ezral, has created holographic versions of the dead crew. He was responsible for the crash – caught in an ion storm, he went to check on his family rather than repair the ship. Trip convinces him that Liana deserves a real life, and they help Ezral repair the ship. Liana looks forward to meeting more real people with some trepidation.

TRIVIA

- Rene Auberjonois played Odo in *Deep Space Nine*, and has also directed episodes.

RATING

- An old-fashioned story, one that could have (and, to some extent, already had) appeared in any previous incarnation of *Star Trek*. Rene Auberjonois is good, but his presence only emphasises that this is nothing new.

1.20 DETAINED

DATE UNKNOWN

Archer and Travis are held in a prison by a race at war with the Suliban

TX 24 April 2002
WRITERS Mike Sussman and Phyllis Strong (story by Rick Berman and Brannon Braga)
DIRECTOR David Livingston
GUEST CAST Dennis Christopher (Danik), David Kagen (Klev), Christopher Shea (Sajen), Dean Stockwell (Grat), Jessica D Stone (Narra)

Travis and Archer wake up in a prison cell, and realise that there are Suliban there. They are taken to Colonel Grat, a civilised man who explains he is a Tandaran, and they trespassed in the Tandaran military zone. He will inform the Enterprise of their location. This signal is received, but it's scrambled, so they can't find the Captain. T'Pol decides to bring the ship to Tandor Prime. Archer is disgusted that women and small children are held at the prison. He's even more shocked to learn that these are civilians – the Suliban who are hostile are members of the Cabal. All Suliban are rounded up by the Tandarans. Archer also learns the Suliban homeworld was destroyed 300 years ago, and the Suliban have become nomadic. Grat learns of Archer's previous dealings with the Suliban, but Archer is disgusted by the internment camp, and won't share any information. Archer wants to free the Suliban, and tells his crew this when they beam a communicator to his cell. Reed is disguised as a Suliban and beams down to the prison with weapons and explosives. He engineers a breakout as Trip arrives in a shuttlepod, destroying the camp's defences. Archer locks Grat in a cell and watches as the Suliban civilians make a break for freedom.

TRIVIA

- Dean Stockwell played Al opposite Scott Bakula in *Quantum Leap*, and the two actors remain good friends.

RATING

- Hints that the Suliban situation is more complicated than we've realised up until now and a fine confrontation between Bakula and Stockwell (without any cute *Quantum Leap* jokes) makes this a great episode.

1.21 VOX SOLA

DATE UNKNOWN

An alien parasite enters the ship

TX 1 May 2002
WRITER Fred Dekker (story by Fred Dekker, Rick Berman and Brannon Braga)
DIRECTOR Roxann Dawson
GUEST CAST Vaughn Armstrong (Kreetassan Captain), Renee Goldsberry (Kelly), Joseph Will (Rostov)

Archer has inadvertently offended the Kreetassans during a 'first contact' meal. As they storm out, a web-like creature detaches from their ship and invades the Enterprise. The life-form is discovered in Cargo Bay Two, where it is growing. It ensnares crewman Rostov, Archer, Trip and a security guard. Phlox suggests they could communicate with the creature, but T'Pol would rather incapacitate it, and they theorise that a burst of radiation would stun it. Reed tries, but it becomes clear that the nervous systems of the crew are now integrated into the creature, and to harm it is to harm them. The trapped crewmen begin to share thoughts. Hoshi and T'Pol irritate each other as they work to communicate with the creature. Travis contacts the Kreetassans who apologise for passing on the creature – and explain that the ultimate taboo of their society is to see someone eat, so inviting them to a meal naturally offended them. They tell the Enterprise where the creature's homeworld is, and Hoshi manages to tell the creature they are taking it home. The crewmen released, they take the creature down to the surface, where it joins a far larger version of itself.

TRIVIA

- Vaughn Armstrong usually plays Admiral Forrest.

RATING

- An episode that doesn't work, mainly because the alien looks a bit silly and the weirdness of the threat never quite comes across. Not a bad episode, but not a terribly exciting one either.

1.22 FALLEN HERO

STARDATE 9 FEBRUARY 2152

A Vulcan ambassador admired by T'Pol is accused of misconduct

TX 8 May 2002
WRITER Alan Cross (story by Chris Black, Rick Berman and Brannon Braga)
DIRECTOR Patrick Norris
GUEST CAST Vaughn Armstrong (Maxwell Forrest), Fionnula Flanagan (V'Lar), J Michael Flynn (Mazarite Official), Dennis Howard (Vulcan Captain), John Rubinstein (Mazarite Captain)

At T'Pol's suggestion, the Enterprise is heading for shore leave on Risa when it receives orders to head to Mazar to retrieve the Vulcan ambassador V'Lar, then transfer her to the Vulcan ship Sh'Raan. T'Pol is clearly looking forward to meeting the ambassador. At Mazar, the Mazarites contact the ship to tell them V'Lar's shuttle is already on its way up. She has been expelled, but no further details are forthcoming. V'Lar is surprisingly friendly. T'Pol knows more than she is letting on, and believes the ambassador to be guilty. A Mazarite ship intercepts the Enterprise and attacks. The Enterprise barely gets away. When V'Lar fails to explain why they want her back, Archer decides to take her back himself. As the Mazarites attack again, V'Lar confesses she was investigating corruption in the Mazarite government and has made many enemies. Archer orders the Enterprise to flee the Mazarites, and Trip pushes the engines to break the Warp 5 barrier. Archer lets the Mazarites on board, claiming V'Lar has been badly burned. Phlox fakes the injuries, but the Mazarites shoot the body to make sure. The Vulcans arrive and fire on the Mazarites. V'Lar is transferred to the Vulcan ship to continue her mission.

TRIVIA

- Fionnula Flanagan played Data's 'mother' in *Inheritance*.

RATING

- Another entry in the ongoing arc about Vulcan society and its hidden depths. This is a fine episode, and Fionnula Flanagan, once again, puts in a memorable guest appearance.

1.23 DESERT CROSSING

DATE 12 FEBRUARY 2152

Archer and Trip end up trapped in the desert after helping an alien leader

TX 8 May 2002
WRITER André Bormanis (story by André Bormanis, Rick Berman and Brannon Braga)
DIRECTOR David Straiton
GUEST CAST Clancy Brown (Zobral), Charles Dennis (Chancellor Trellit), Brandon Karrer (Alien Man)

The Enterprise picks up a distress call from a crippled ship. It's a simple matter to repair it. The charismatic Captain, Zobral, invites Archer and Trip to dinner on his desert planet. They enjoy Zobral's hospitality, and a game of Geskana, a brutal form of Lacrosse. T'Pol is contacted by Trelit, a Chancellor from the far side of the planet. He warns her that Zobral is a terrorist. Archer and Trip make their excuses and leave. Zobral explains he is a freedom fighter, and wants Archer's help – he's heard of Archer from some liberated Suliban. Zobral's camp is attacked, and Archer and Trip flee into the desert. It's a hard slog, particularly for Trip, who becomes delirious. Zobral goes up to the Enterprise, and gives Reed a way of getting down to the surface. Archer and Trip come under attack, but Reed rescues them. Zobral realises now that Archer is not the great warrior he had heard about, and Archer knows he can't get involved in his struggle.

TRIVIA

- Clancy Brown has appeared in memorable roles in many films including *Highlander* (where he played the baddy, the Kurgan), *Flubber*, *The Shawshank Redemption* and *Starship Troopers*.

RATING

- An interesting episode, because unlike a lot of *Star Trek*, it doesn't judge Zobral – at the end of the episode, he may be a terrorist, he may not be. There's already a sub-genre of *Enterprise* episodes about endurance. In previous series, characters marooned on planets tend to have long conversations and come to new understandings. Here, they're simply trying to survive.

1.24 TWO DAYS AND TWO NIGHTS

DATE 18 FEBRUARY 2152

The crew have misadventures on the pleasure planet Risa

TX 15 May 2002
WRITER Chris Black (story by Rick Berman and Brannon Braga)
DIRECTOR Michael Dorn
GUEST CAST Dennis Cockrum (Freebus, James Ingersol (Risan Man), Rudolf Martin (Ravis), Geoff Meed (Dee'Ahn Male), Donna Marie Recco (Dee'Ahn Female), Kellie Waymire (Starfleet Crewman Elizabeth Cutler), Joseph Will (Rostov), Jennifer Williams (Alien Woman), Stephen Wozniak (Latia Male), Dey Young (Keyla)

The Enterprise arrives at Risa, and the crew draw lots to see who can take shore leave. Archer feels guilty when he wins, while T'Pol is happy to stay onboard. Phlox prepares for his annual hibernation. Trip and Reed plan to meet women, Hoshi wants to learn some new languages. Archer just plans to relax, but hits it off with an alien woman, Keyla. He becomes suspicious, and learns she's a Tandaran. Hoshi has a fling with Ravis, an alien with an impossibly complicated language. Trip and Reed meet Dee'Ahn and Latia at a night-club. They flirt, and head off with the 'girls' – who turn out to be shapeshifters who steal all their belongings, even their clothes. Travis is treated by Phlox for an allergic reaction. The crew return to the ship... none of them willing to tell the others what they got up to.

TRIVIA

- The pleasure planet Risa has been seen a number of times over the years – the first time was *Captain's Holiday*.

RATING

- A comedy episode that's not terribly funny, but does genuinely feel like the characters are on holiday. The funniest bit, ironically, is Phlox's hibernation.

1.25 SHOCKWAVE Part I

DATE UNKNOWN

The Enterprise is recalled when the ship accidentally wipes out a whole colony

Reed takes a shuttlepod down to a Paraagan colony, but the atmosphere contains tetrazine and ignites as the shuttle passes through it, killing all 3,600 colonists in a shockwave. An emergency meeting at Starfleet Command orders Archer to bring the Enterprise back to Earth – their mission is over. Archer can't believe he's set Earth's space program

TX 22 May 2002
WRITERS Rick Berman and Brannon Braga
DIRECTOR Allan Kroeker
GUEST CAST Vaughn Armstrong (Forrest), John Fleck (Silik), Stephanie Erb (Receptionist), David Lewis Hays (Tactical Crewman), James Horan ('Future Man'), Matt Winston (Daniels)

back, possibly permanently. He wakes on Earth... the day before the Enterprise launched. He's been brought here by Daniels, who tells him the shockwave wasn't meant to happen according to history – it's a clear act of temporal sabotage. Back in the present, Archer uses information from Daniels to prove they didn't destroy the colony, and that a cloaked Suliban ship did. They have the element of surprise and cripple the Suliban ship. Archer steals data discs from the Suliban that proves his innocence. Silik is ordered to fetch Archer. A swarm of Suliban ships attack and overwhelm the Enterprise before he can get his evidence to the Vulcans. Archer agrees to hand himself over... but finds himself in a devastated city. Daniels is there, shocked – he's brought Archer to his native thirty-first century to protect him from the Suliban, but history has changed, the city shouldn't be devastated. There are no time portals, now – they are trapped here...

QUOTES

- 'As I've told you, the Vulcan Science Directorate has concluded that time travel is impossible.'
  'Well, good for the Vulcan Science Directorate.' – *T'Pol and Archer*

TRIVIA

- The scene of the ruined city that ends the series is deliberately evocative of Ground Zero at the World Trade Centre. Less nobly, Scott Bakula woke up in strange surroundings having travelled through time every week in *Quantum Leap*, and so Daniels' tactic to get him off the Enterprise is strangely familiar.

RATING

- A few of the running stories collide in an episode with both Cold War and Vulcan plots. The crew's reactions to the tragedy at the beginning of the episode really lay the foundation for a story that feels significant.

ENTERPRISE **SEASON TWO**

2.1 SHOCKWAVE Part II

Archer and Daniels attempt to return from the future to defeat the Suliban

TX 18 September 2002
WRITERS Rick Berman and Brannon Braga
DIRECTOR Allan Kroeker
GUEST CAST Keith Allan (Raan), Jim Fitzpatrick (Commander Williams), Vaughn Armstrong (Admiral Forrest), John Fleck (Silik), Gary Graham (Soval), Michael Kosik (Suliban Soldier), Matt Winston (Daniels)

DATE UNKNOWN

Silik leads a Suliban boarding party onto the Enterprise, and doesn't believe the crew's insistence that Archer has just disappeared. Daniels realises that a monument celebrating the foundation of 'the Federation' which Archer helped to found is missing. The whole history of the galaxy has been altered. The Suliban recover the data discs Archer stole from them, and detect a temporal signature that proves Archer has vanished. Silik confines the crew to quarters and takes control of the ship. The Vulcans, angry with Archer and unaware of Suliban involvement, send the D'kyr in pursuit. The Enterprise has docked with the Helix, and Silik can't contact his master from the future – he drugs T'Pol, but she can't help him. The rest of the crew rig a way to communicate with each other. Daniel and Archer find a way to contact the past, but the drugged T'Pol thinks it's an hallucination. Eventually, they get Reed to find a device in Daniels' quarters, but he is captured and beaten. T'Pol and Trip rig a reactor breach, and the Suliban tug the Enterprise away from the Helix. The Enterprise escapes. Silik is still trying to contact his master – and instead opens a time portal that Archer leaps out of. He takes Silik hostage and heads for the Enterprise in a cellship. The Enterprise meets up with the Vulcans, who accept that they didn't destroy the Paragaan colony, but still think the ship should be recalled. T'Pol makes a passionate speech defending Archer, and the Vulcans relent. The Enterprise's mission will continue.

TRIVIA

- We learn that, if time follows the correct path, there will be a statue of Archer erected in the city (which is presumably San Francisco, although this is never specified).

RATING

- An action-packed episode, although not the literally Earth-shattering one we were promised by the first part. Instead, a lot of the interesting plot lines seem to be rather ruthlessly shut down. This is a fast-paced, watchable episode, and let's not turn our noses up at that... but it looked like we were heading for something more radical.

2.2 CARBON CREEK

DATE APRIL 2152

T'Pol tells a story about her ancestors on 1950s Earth

TX 25 September 2002
WRITER Chris Black (Rick Berman, Brannon Braga and Dan O'Shannon)
DIRECTOR James Conter
GUEST CAST J Paul Boehmer (Mestral), Ann Cusack (Maggie), Hank Harris (Jack), Paul Hayes (Businessman), Michael Krawic (Stron), Ron Marasco (Tellus), David Selburg (Vulcan Captain), Clay Wilcox (Billy)

Over dinner, T'Pol tells Archer and Trip about the 'real' first contact between Vulcans and humans, when her second foremother T'Mir and her colleagues ended up on Earth. She was one of four Vulcans studying the launch of Sputnik in October 1957 when their impulse engines failed and they made an emergency landing in which the captain was killed. To survive, they had to visit the nearest human settlement, Carbon Creek. They took up residence, waiting for the rescue ship and took jobs: Stron was a handyman, secretly using his advanced technology to solve plumbing problems, Mestral was a miner and T'Mir worked at a tavern. They were concerned that humans seemed on the brink of nuclear annihilation, and gradually became convinced that their distress signal hadn't reached Vulcan. T'Mir helped a boy, Jack, who couldn't afford a higher education. They used a particle weapon to free trapped miners. As they got used to their new lives, the rescue ship finally signalled its imminent arrival. T'Mir sold an item of Vulcan high technology to a businessman to fund Jack's education: velcro. Mestral decided to stay, and the other two covered for him as they headed home. Trip and Archer don't believe a word of it, but T'Pol heads back to her quarters and secretly checks a family heirloom: the purse T'Mir used in Carbon Creek.

TRIVIA

- Jolene Blalock plays T'Pol's 'second foremother' (presumably her great-grandmother).

RATING

- Charming. A lovely episode where the aliens boldly come to us, with beautifully judged humour that avoids broad farce or heavy-handed satire. There's little in the way of jeopardy – the mine collapse was obviously added when someone got worried that very little actually happens in the episode – but this is classic *Star Trek*.

2.3 MINEFIELD

DATE UNKNOWN

The Enterprise is struck by a Romulan mine

TX 2 October 2002
WRITER John Shiban
DIRECTOR James Contner
GUEST CAST Tim Glenn (Med Tech), Elizabeth Magness (Injured Crewmember)

Archer tries to get to know Reed better, but he only wants to discuss work. T'Pol interrupts to announce the discovery of a new Minshara-Class planet. As the Enterprise enters orbit, though, there's a huge explosion. They've entered a minefield. One mine has stuck to the hull but hasn't exploded, and Reed heads out to defuse it. Archer has a plan in case that doesn't work – detach a section of the hull. A strange craft materialises nearby. It has the power to turn invisible. Hoshi was injured in the explosion, so they can't communicate with it, and it starts firing on them. As the ship moves, the mine rocks – and fires a spike through Reed's leg. Archer heads out to help him. Hoshi translates the language from her sickbed – the planet has been claimed by the Romulan Star Empire. T'Pol warns the Romulans are aggressive. As they work together, Archer and Reed have a chance to talk again... Reed still thinks that fraternising with the other crew is unprofessional, but Archer is impressed that he'd willingly sacrifice himself for his crewmates. As the Romulans lose patience, Archer comes up with a new plan. He cuts Reed free, detaches the hull plating, and the two of them 'surf' away from the explosion on pieces of metal as the mine detonates. The Enterprise makes a swift getaway.

TRIVIA

- In *Balance of Terror*, the first appearance of the Romulans in the original *Star Trek*, we learned that the Earth fought a war with the Romulans 100 years before Kirk's time. This fits in perfectly with the Enterprise – indeed, going strictly by the official *Chronology*, the Romulan Wars should start in 2156 – some time around season six. The war was fought with atomic weapons, and Earth had superior warp drive technology. Earth won the decisive Battle of Cheron and the Neutral Zone was established. *Homefront* stated that the Romulans attacked Earth itself during the war. Crucially, there was no face-to-face contact with the Romulans (Kirk is astonished that they resemble Vulcans). It's implied in *Balance of Terror* that the cloaking device is a recent innovation, but since then it's been established that cloaking technology is constantly improving in the face of better detection methods.

RATING

- Another episode that starts with the characters saying they don't really know Reed, which sounds like a cry for help from the writers – but they neatly subvert expectation by not having Reed loosen up by the end of the story. This stiff-upper-lipped chap is difficult to reconcile with the guy we saw chasing ladyboys on Risa, though. It's a tense episode that gains a bit of resonance from the use of the Romulans. On paper it must have looked like a cheap episode, but pretty much every shot is an effects shot of some kind.

2.4 DEAD STOP

DATE UNKNOWN

The Enterprise is repaired at a sinister unmanned space station

TX 9 October 2002
WRITERS Mike Sussman and Phyllis Strong
DIRECTOR Roxann Dawson
GUEST CAST Roxann Dawson (Voice of the Repair Station – uncredited)

Badly damaged by the Romulan mines, the Enterprise needs repairs and is given the details of a repair station by a Tellarite freighter. The station seems deserted, but reconfigures to accommodate the Enterprise. They dock, and discover it's an automated system. In return for warp plasma, the station will repair everything, even Reed's leg. The station begins repairs and the crew enjoy replicated versions of their favourite meals. Archer can't help but think it's too good to be true. Reed and Trip agree. They don't think the computer is big enough to run the station, and want a better look. The station defences catch them, and beam them back to the Enterprise. Travis is killed in mysterious circumstances in a section of the ship that's being repaired, and the station computer won't explain how. Phlox discovers it's not really Travis, but a replica. Archer and T'Pol follow Trip and Reed's route to the computer core, and discover 40 people connected up to the station. It's using their brains to function, and it's taken Travis. Archer rescues Travis, and Trip delivers the payment of warp plasma... which is booby-trapped. The station is destroyed, and the Enterprise leaves. Unseen, the station starts to reassemble itself.

TRIVIA

- Another episode with no additional credited cast, although director Roxann Dawson (who, of course, played Torres on *Voyager*) is the voice of the repair station.

RATING

- A sinister episode, all the more effective because the station is brightly lit and not remotely spooky. The twist is suitably horrible. It's another small-scale episode, but works.

2.5 A NIGHT IN SICKBAY

DATE UNKNOWN

Porthos is dying after provoking a diplomatic incident

TX 16 October 2002

Archer has somehow offended the Kreetassans when asking for a plasma injector. He's more worried that his dog Porthos, who went down to the Kreetassan homeworld with him, is sick. Phlox prevents the beagle's auto-immune system from collapsing, but can't guarantee he'll pull through. T'Pol establishes that Porthos urinated on a sacred tree, and Archer has to go through a variety of ritual apologies. Archer

WRITERS Rick Berman and Brannon Braga
DIRECTOR David Straiton
GUEST CAST Vaughn Armstrong (Kreetassan Captain)

angrily decides to spend the night in Sickbay with Porthos instead. He tries to sleep, but Phlox keeps him awake by noisily clipping his toenails. Porthos goes into anaphylactic shock. Phlox wonders if Archer's agitation isn't, in part, caused by sexual frustration – he clearly wants T'Pol. Archer dismisses the idea, but dreams about her. Phlox tries an experimental technique on Porthos, a pituitary gland transplant using a Calrissian chameleon as a donor. Talking to Phlox reminds Archer to be more tolerant of alien species, and he performs an elaborate act of contrition that pleases the Kreetassans so much they even give him an extra injector. Porthos recovers.

QUOTES

- 'They're messing us around while Porthos is lying here with one paw in beagle heaven.' – *Archer establishes his priorities*

TRIVIA

- A couple of prop dogs were constructed early in the series to stand in for the real Porthos – there are strict welfare rules governing the use of animals on television, and it's actually quite expensive to have a dog on set all the time, especially when the script only needs him to be asleep in the corner. The props were only meant to be glimpsed, though. Unfortunately, there are some lingering shots in this story, and it's obviously not a real dog.
- The episode was nominated for a 2003 Hugo Award, as was *Carbon Creek*.

RATING

- Almost universally hated by *Star Trek* fans, this is a great episode. True, you can't imagine Kirk or Picard ignoring some dull alien protocol story because their pet was sick, but that's the point: they have to follow Starfleet rules, Archer has a choice and isn't perfect. There's some great interplay between Scott Bakula and John Billingsley, some wonderfully surreal moments, and some great jokes about the sexual tension between Archer and T'Pol.

2.6 MARAUDERS

DATE UNKNOWN

A mining colony is being menaced by Klingons

TX 30 October 2002
WRITER David Wilcox (story by Rick Berman and Brannon Braga)
DIRECTOR Mike Vejar
GUEST CAST Larry Cedar (Tessic), Robertson Dean (Korok), Steven Flynn (Maklii), Bari Hochwald (E'lis), Wayne King Jr (Klingon 1), Peewee Piemonte (Klingon 2), Jesse James Rutherford (Q'Ell)

The Enterprise visits a mining colony hoping to trade for deuterium, but the colonists claim they can't spare any. Archer reaches an agreement with Tessic, the leader, but he wants the Enterprise gone in two days. A Klingon ship arrives, and Tessic panics and asks the crew to hide. The Klingons, led by Korok, seem friendly at first, but become angry when Tessic doesn't have as much deuterium as he demands. When they've gone, Tessic admits to Archer that these marauders have been coming here for five seasons. Archer vows to help them, rigs a trap for the Klingons. T'Pol begins teaching the colonists self-defence. The Klingons arrive, and the Enterprise crew counter-attack, leading them into an area rigged to explode. Korok prefers to retreat than die. A grateful Tessic gives Archer all the deuterium he needs.

TRIVIA

- Deuterium is extremely common in space, and it's odd that a galaxy of spacefaring civilisations would need to land on a planet to mine it, or pay good money for it.

RATING

- An episode without a twist – the crew arrive, are told there are bullies, and fight them off. There's no sense that the Enterprise is outnumbered or outgunned, and they win by outfighting the Klingons, that might is right, whatever the characters say.

2.7 THE SEVENTH

DATE UNKNOWN

T'Pol takes Archer on a top-secret Vulcan mission

T'Pol is given a secret mission by the Vulcans, and surprises Archer by asking him along. She tells him that she is to find a rogue operative, Menos, who became one of the smugglers he was meant to be exposing. He now trades transgenic weapons. Archer brings Travis,

TX 6 November 2002
WRITERS Rick Berman and Brannon Braga
DIRECTOR David Livingston
GUEST CAST Bruce Davison (Menos), Vincent Hammond (Huge Alien), Coleen Maloney (Vulcan Officer), Stephen Mendillo (Vulcan Captain), David Richards (Dockmaster), Richard Wharton (Jossen)

and they head for Pernaia, where the Vulcans say Menos is to be found. They find and apprehend him at an outpost, but can't leave due to snowfall. Trip finds it difficult to cope as Captain in Archer's absence. Menos claims he is innocent, and T'Pol realises she can't trust her memories of their last meeting on Risa – they were altered in a ritual known as Fullara. Menos manages to escape, and when T'Pol catches him again, she wonders about letting him go. Archer tells her that her mission is to bring him back, not assess his guilt. Travis settles the matter by finding weapons-grade bio-toxins in a cloaked compartment of Menos' ship. T'Pol is grateful for Archer's advice.

TRIVIA

- Transgenic weapons have been mentioned a few times on *Star Trek* – presumably they are based on attacking the genetic structure of living matter.

RATING

- A solid episode, but not terribly memorable, and it feels like one of those *Deep Space Nine* episodes where one of the crew went undercover. While the episode seems to want to say something about T'Pol's professional relationship with Archer, it's hard to see what we learn that we didn't already know.

2.8 THE COMMUNICATOR

DATE UNKNOWN

Advanced technology is left on a planet after a covert mission

TX 13 November 2002
WRITER André Bormanis (story by Rick Berman and Brannon Braga)
DIRECTOR James Contner
GUEST CAST Dennis Cockrum (Alien Barkeep), Francis Guinan (Gosis), Tim Kelleher (Pell), Brian Reddy (Temec), Jason Waters (Soldier)

Reed realises he's left his communicator behind on the alien planet the Enterprise has been researching. Hoshi locates it, and Archer and Reed return in disguise to retrieve it before the natives (who are at about a twentieth century-level of technology) discover it. They are arrested, and questioned by Major Pell and General Gosis, who examine the communicator and assume the humans are spies for a rival bloc, the Alliance. When T'Pol signals and asks for 'the Captain', this only increases their suspicion. Reed's disguise starts to peel off, and their origin as aliens is obvious. Archer claims he and Reed are genetically-engineered soldiers. Gosis decides to execute them as traitors, then perform an autopsy. Trip wonders if they could take the Suliban cell ship Archer brought back and use its cloaking device in a rescue attempt. Travis is affected by the radiation, and his right arm becomes invisible. The rescue attempt succeeds, the cell ship dodges enemy fighters, and Archer and Reed are returned to the Enterprise. Archer knows that he's contaminated an alien culture, but T'Pol is impressed that he was willing to die rather than do so.

TRIVIA

- Starfleet have a working cloaking device here, a century before Kirk is sent to retrieve one (*The Enterprise Incident*).

RATING

- An episode that wouldn't be out of place as a Prime Directive episode of *Voyager*, which is a polite way of saying that it's predictable and lifeless, with a comedy subplot that isn't funny. Viewers know Archer isn't going to die, so it's hard to get worked up it. It would have been much more fun to see the effects of the technology falling into the hands of a culture that isn't ready for it.

2.9 SINGULARITY

DATE UNKNOWN

The crew become obsessed with trivial matters

TX 20 November 2002
WRITER Chris Black
DIRECTOR Patrick Norris
GUEST CAST Matthew Kaminsky (Cunningham)

The Enterprise is investigating a black hole in a trinary star system, which gives the crew time to deal with personal matters. Archer struggles to write an introduction to a biography of his father. Trip tries to fix the Captain's chair. Reed is working on a new security protocol to speed up responses in an emergency (which he's dubbed 'Reed Alert'), Hoshi is covering cooking duties as Chef is ill, and Phlox tries to diagnose the cause of Travis' headache. Each becomes more and more obsessed with their task – Archer's one-page introduction hits 19 pages, Trip keeps fitting new features to the chair, Reed agonises about the exact tone of the alarm, Hoshi refuses to feed the crew until she perfects her recipe for oden, and Phlox prepares to cut open Travis' head. T'Pol is unaffected, and realises the radiation from the trinary system is affecting the crew. She can't pilot the ship out of danger on her own, and manages to get Archer to snap out of it long enough to help. Even then, they wouldn't have made it – except that Reed's security protocol covers every eventuality, and the phase cannons are already online. Things return to normal.

TRIVIA

- The episode is *Enterprise's* version of *The Naked Time*, with a weird solar phenomenon causing the crew to behave oddly. The story was repeated early on by *The Next Generation* in *The Naked Now.*

RATING

- Rather that let their hair down, the Enterprise crew put their hair further up. There are some funny moments, the Phlox/Travis plot is deliciously horrific, and the entire cast play their parts beautifully, but you have to admit that watching Sulu attack people with a sword or Tasha seduce Data was much more fun.

2.10 VANISHING POINT

DATE UNKNOWN

A transporter accident turns Hoshi into a ghost

TX 27 November 2002
WRITERS Rick Berman and Brannon Braga
DIRECTOR David Straiton
GUEST CAST Morgan H Margolis (Baird), Gary Riotto (Alien #1), Ric Sarabia (Alien #2), Carly Thomas (Alison), Keone Young (Hoshi's Father)

Hoshi and Trip are examining the ruins of a lost civilisation when a storm moves in. Unwilling to risk a shuttle, Archer beams up Trip, then Hoshi. Hoshi feels strange, but Phlox assures her nothing is wrong. She remains so distracted that Archer has to relieve her of duty. Strange things are happening – the turbolift ignores her, water seems to pass through her when she has a shower. She gradually becomes invisible, and the crew declare her dead. Hoshi tries to find a way to contact them, and discovers a race of aliens who are equally invisible to the crew who are planning to blow up the ship. She goes to the transporter, and rematerialises... only for Reed and Trip inform her that she's only just been to the planet, everything else was just an hallucination. Hoshi decides to stick to shuttlepods from now on.

TRIVIA

- Here, Hoshi and Trip have to beam up one after the other. By *Regeneration*, it's possible for Archer and Reed to beam across to another ship at the same time.

RATING

- ...and it was all a dream. After two seasons, Hoshi hasn't made an impact. Linda Park proves here that she can have a show built round her and do all the funny, scary and sexy stuff, but the story itself is an appalling mish-mash of the dull bits of *The Next Phase, Realm of Fear* and *Coda* with a cop-out ending that primary school teachers wouldn't let their pupils get away with.

2.11 PRECIOUS CARGO

DATE 12 SEPTEMBER 2152

Trip rescues an exotic alien princess

TX 11 December 2002
WRITER David A Goodman (story by Rick Berman and Brannon Braga)
DIRECTOR David Livingston
GUEST CAST Leland Crooke (Firek Plinn), Scott Klace (Firek Goff), Padma Lakshmi (Kaitaama)

Two Retellian pilots need help: they are returning a young woman to her homeworld in suspended animation, and her stasis pod is malfunctioning. Trip helps them, and finds himself intrigued by the woman, who suddenly wakes up. He realises she's a prisoner. One of the pilots, Goff, kidnaps them both. Trip finds a translator and talks to the woman, Kaitaama, who is a member of the royal family of Krios Prime, and treats him with disdain. They take the ship's escape pod and land on a swampy planet. Archer tricks the other pilot, Plinn, into telling them how to find Trip. Kaitaama and Trip bicker, but there is clearly mutual attraction. She kisses him. Before anything else can happen, Archer, T'Pol and Reed show up. The Enterprise takes Kaitaama home. She says protocol will prevent any further contact with Trip... but when she's Queen, she'll be able to change the rules.

TRIVIA

- *The Perfect Mate* featured another beautiful woman from the (same?) Krios system.

- Padma Lakshmi was born in India and moved to the US when she was a teen. She hosted the Italian show *Dominica in Rai*, she's a movie actress who appeared in the Mariah Carey film *Glitter*, she's written cookbooks and presented shows on The Food Network, but is perhaps best known as a model. She had a three-year relationship with novelist Salman Rushdie, who described his book *The Fury* as 'an extended love letter' to her.

RATING

- Not a particularly good episode, and Laksmhi and Trineer lack any real chemistry. It comes across as an attempt to remake *Swept Away* – if so, that's a rather peculiar impulse.

2.12 THE CATWALK

DATE 18 SEPTEMBER 2152

The crew must shelter from a radiation storm

TX 18 December 2002
WRITERS Mike Sussman and Phyllis Strong
DIRECTOR Mike Vejar
GUEST CAST Scott Burkholder (Tagrim), Brian Cousins (Alien Lieutenant), Danny Goldring (Alien Captain), Zach Grenier (Renth), Aaron Lustig (Guri), Elizabeth Magness (Female Crewmember), Sean Smith (Alien Crewman)

Three aliens come aboard and warn the Enterprise of a neutronic wavefront heading their way. They will need to find shelter from the deadly radiation, and Trip suggests that the only places with enough shielding on the ship are the catwalks running along each warp nacelle. The warp engines will have to be taken offline for the duration. The crew relocate to a cramped catwalk, re-routing the controls. Tensions run high, and the aliens don't help as the storm hits. Trip needs to repair a fault. He suits up... and discovers aliens like the ones who warned them on board. They members of the Takret militia, are immune to the radiation, and are looking for the three aliens. They also plan to start the warp engines, which will kill everyone in the catwalk. Archer distracts the invaders while T'Pol and Reed move to regain control of the ship. Archer flies the Enterprise straight at a plasma eddy within the storm, and the Takret flee the ship. After eight days, the crew can return to the rest of the ship. The three aliens apologise for the invasion and leave.

TRIVIA

- The catwalk runs alongside the warp engine itself (presumably there's another one on the other side of the ship).

RATING

- A small-scale show – barely even a bottle show. While there are hints about the claustrophobia and the tensions of being confined in such a small space, it would have been nice to see this really played up. As it is, the Enterprise is a small ship and the psychological pressures would be immense (as they are with submariners in real life). Cramming people even closer together would lead to more than just grumbling about the food and the odd smell. It's a nice change of pace, though.

2.13 DAWN

DATE UNKNOWN

Trip is marooned on a deadly moon with a hostile alien

TX 8 January 2003
WRITER John Shiban
DIRECTOR Roxann Dawson
GUEST CAST Brad Greenquist (Khata'n Zshaar), Gregg Henry (Zho'Kaan)

Trip is testing the autopilot in Shuttlepod One when he is fired upon by an alien ship and makes a crash-landing on a dark moon. He tries to fix the transceiver, but is attacked by an alien, who steals it. The Enterprise is searching for Trip when it's warned off by an Arkonian ship. T'Pol warns Archer that the Vulcans know the Arkonians to be aggressive and territorial. The alien captain admits that he is missing a crewman, Zho'Kaan, and the two agree to pool their resources to search. Trip is captured by Zho'Kaan, and is set to work fixing the transceiver. Without a translator, communication is basic, but Trip learns that the Arkonian's spit can heal wounds. T'Pol has alarming news – at daybreak, the temperature on the moon will rise to 170°. Trip realises he needs to get the transceiver to higher ground, but Zho'Kaan and he fight. They realise their only hope is to co-operate. They manage to signal the Enterprise as the sun starts to rise. Archer mounts a rescue. The Arkonian Captain doesn't seem grateful, but T'Pol thinks he's made a major diplomatic breakthrough. Trip visits Zho'Kaan in Sickbay. Able to communicate at last, they find they have little to say to each other, but Zho'Kaan gives a surly 'thank you' to Trip.

TRIVIA

- The story bears a resemblance to the novel *Enemy Mine*, also made into a film, which is about a human and reptilian alien marooned together on a desolate planet.

RATING

- Didn't we just do the one where Trip gets marooned on a planet with an uncommunicative alien while the Enterprise spares no effort finding him? Another small-scale incident, but the story is efficient enough, and the lack of communication makes it quite interesting. It's also great that Trip and Zho'Kaan aren't buddies by the end.

2.14 STIGMA

DATE UNKNOWN

T'Pol has a deadly disease that she wishes to conceal from the Vulcans

TX 5 February 2003
WRITERS Rick Berman and Brannon Braga
DIRECTOR David Livingston
GUEST CAST Michael Ensign (Oratt), Melinda Page Hamilton (Feezal), Jeffrey Hayenga (Yuris), Bob Morrisey (Strom), Lee Spencer (Vulcan Doctor)

Phlox attends the Interspecies Medical Exchange conference on Dekendi III. He is reunited with one of his wives, Feezal, who helps Trip install a neutron microscope and flirts shamelessly with him. Phlox is the only person who knows T'Pol contracted Pa'nar Syndrome from her mind-meld with Tolaris. Phlox discreetly tries to learn about it from the Vulcan delegation. The Vulcans work out what Phlox is doing, and T'Pol explains that only a few Vulcans can mind-meld, and it is taboo. One of the doctors, Yuris, confides that he is a melder, and passes on what information he has on the condition. He also advises T'Pol that as she didn't consent to the meld, Vulcan society won't be so harsh on her, but she refuses, not wanting to seem to endorse discrimination. Yuris reveals that he is a melder at T'Pol's hearing. Shocked, the other Vulcans allow T'Pol to stay on the Enterprise. T'Pol hopes Yuris' bravery will encourage others to speak out.

TRIVIA

- Paramount instructed the producers of all their television programs to do at least one show about AIDS awareness. *Star Trek* had considered this a number of times in the nineties, always hitting the problem that it would seem extremely pessimistic to depict either the virus or the social prejudice still existing centuries in the future.

RATING

- An obvious AIDS allegory, but one that serves the back story being established for the Vulcans. It's another example of what we know from previous shows being turned on its head: by implication, only a few years before Spock's father was born, his family would be considered social pariahs. It's a strong episode, with T'Pol's silence and taciturn statements of her position saying far, far more than the usual moralising speeches.

2.15 CEASE FIRE

DATE UNKNOWN

Archer is called in to negotiate between the Andorians and Vulcans

TX 12 February 2003
WRITER Chris Black
DIRECTOR David Straiton
GUEST CAST Vaughn Armstrong (Forrest), John Balma (Muroc), Zane Cassidy (Andorian Soldier), Jeffrey Combs (Shran), Gary Graham (Soval), Suzie Plakson (Tarah), Christopher Shea (Telev)

The Andorians call it Weytahm, the Vulcans call it Paan Mokar – a small planet between their two systems that they both claim. Shran has occupied the world and taken hostages, and the Vulcans have sent in a taskforce. Shran wants Archer to chair negotiations, and Vulcan ambassador Soval reluctantly agrees. Archer, T'Pol and Soval head for the planet in a shuttlepod, which is shot down. Trip tries to keep the orbiting Vulcan and Andorian ships from firing on each other. Soval is injured, and Archer discovers that Andorian snipers are trying to kill them – they are led by Tarah, Shran's deputy, who wants war with Vulcan. Soval and Shran sit down together, and agree to a ceasefire and to continue negotiations on Andoria.

QUOTES

- 'What is their fixation with our ears?'
  'I believe they're envious.' – *Soval and T'Pol*

TRIVIA

- The treaty of 2097 that the Vulcans and Andorians signed is twice said to be 'more than a century ago'.

RATING

- An episode that returns to one of the more interesting running plots and characters. It also looks lavish. If the identity of the troublemaker is a bit obvious, that's only because Suzie Plakson proves, once again, to be a memorable presence.

2.16 FUTURE TENSE

DATE UNKNOWN

The Enterprise discovers a mysterious tiny ship complete with human corpse

TX 19 February 2003
WRITERS Mike Sussman and Phyllis Strong
DIRECTOR James Whitmore Jr
GUEST CAST Vaughn Armstrong (Forrest), Cullen Douglas (Suliban Soldier)

The Enterprise finds a mysterious vessel drifting in space. It contains a human body, and Archer wonders if it might be Zefram Cochrane. Trip and Reed investigate, and discover the vessel is far larger on the inside than the outside. The Suliban attack, claiming the ship is theirs, but the Enterprise forces them to retreat. Trip and Reed investigate what looks like the ship's 'black box' while Phlox performs an autopsy on the corpse. The body is the result of generations of interspecies breeding – he's part human, part Vulcan (among other things). As no human has ever bred with a Vulcan, he must be from the future. Archer and T'Pol find schematics for the ship in Daniels' quarters. Archer can see why the Suliban would want to use the vessel to fight their Temporal Cold War. The Enterprise is attacked by a squad of Tholian ships. The Tholians are advanced, but isolationists, and warn Archer that the temporal radiation of the mystery ship is dangerous. Trip and Reed find themselves in a time loop, and Archer decides to get the ship back to Earth and arranges a rendezvous with the nearest Vulcan ship. The Vulcans are attacked by the Tholians, who then turn their attention to the Suliban. Archer activates an emergency beacon on the mystery ship, and plans to destroy it rather than let it fall into enemy hands. In the event, the ship just vanishes – retrieved, presumably, by its owners in the future.

TRIVIA

- The Tholian ships are identical to those seen in *The Tholian Web*. Although they have often been mentioned, this is the first physical evidence of them. Once again we don't see the Tholians themselves, although we do hear the voice of one.

RATING

- Another story about the Temporal Cold War, and another episode that feels a little scrappy and unsatisfying.

2.17 CANAMAR

DATE UNKNOWN

Archer and Tucker are sent to the penal colony of Canamar

TX 26 February 2003
WRITER John Shiban
DIRECTOR Allan Kroeker
GUEST CAST John Hansen (Prisoner), Michael McGrady (Nausicaan), Brian Morri (Enolian Guard), Holmes R Osborne (Enolian Official), Mark Rolston (Kuroda), Sean Whalen (Zoumas)

Archer and Trip are arrested as smugglers by the Enolians and put on a transport ship heading to the penal colony of Canamar. T'Pol quickly convinces the authorities they are innocent, but two of the prisoners, Kuroda and a Nausicaan, hijack the ship. Archer volunteers to help fly the ship for them. The Enterprise learns that the Enolians are keen to destroy the ship rather than let prisoners escape. Kuroda tells Archer he was innocent when first convicted, but learnt criminal skills in prison. He's taking the ship to Tamaal for a rendezvous with another ship. He'll set the transport in a decaying orbit, and everyone but his allies will die. Archer and Trip stall them long enough for Reed and a security team to storm the ship. Kuroda refuses to leave with them, and dies on the transport. Archer wonders how many innocent people are sent to Canamar.

TRIVIA

- The episode was to contain scenes of the transport craft breaking up as it entered the atmosphere. Following the Columbia disaster of 1 February 2003, a number of effects shots were edited out.

RATING

- Straightforward stuff, a prison movie-type story in the vein of *Con Air*, but effective, and there's a nice sense of jeopardy.

2.18 THE CROSSING

DATE UNKNOWN

The crew are possessed by disembodied aliens

TX 2 April 2003
WRITERS Rick Berman and Brannon Braga (story by Rick Berman, Brannon Braga and André Bormanis)
DIRECTOR David Livingston
GUEST CAST Steven Allerick (Cook), Alexander Chance (Crewman #1), Valerie Ianniello (Female Crewman), Matthew Kaminsky (Crewman #2), Joseph Will (Rostov)

The Enterprise is stopped by a vast, luminous spacecraft that draws them inside and shuts down their weapons and engines. Outside, there are thousands of tiny energy beings. Archer is suspicious, although T'Pol says there is nothing to fear. One of the beings takes over Trip and is fascinated to experience the world as a human does. It soon becomes clear that the aliens are hostile – their ship is damaged, and they intend to possess the crew, then use the ship to bring more life-forms to possess. Archer manages to get the ship to escape.

TRIVIA

- As noted, many aliens have taken human form over the years – just as many seem to be friendly as hostile.

RATING

- Fairly standard stuff, livened up by the performances and the fact that even if the audience saw this sort of thing every third week on *Voyager*, it's new to the crew.

2.19 JUDGMENT

DATE UNKNOWN

Archer is tried by the Klingons

TX 9 April 2003
WRITER David A Goodman (story by Taylor Elmore and David A Goodman)
DIRECTOR James L Conway
GUEST CAST Helen Cates (Klingon First Officer), JG Hertzler (Kolos), Danny Kolker (Guard), DJ Lockhart (Cell Guard), Daniel Riordan (Duras), Victor Talmadge (Asahf), Granville Van Dusen (Magistrate) John Vickery (Orak)

Archer is on trial on the Klingon homeworld, accused of conspiring against the Empire. He faces the death penalty, and his defence counsel is aged and ineffective. Archer talks to him, and learns that the military culture is becoming all-pervasive. Archer is accused of conspiring with terrorists; he knows that he helped some refugees. He persuades his lawyer to fight his case, and the two of them demonstrate beyond doubt that Archer is innocent, that the evidence against him is fabricated and that the trial is politically motivated. But it is no good – Archer is sentenced to hard labour on the prison planet Rura Penthe, and his lawyer is sent with him for daring to speak against the system. The Enterprise crew manage to break Archer out, but his lawyer remains, a loyal Klingon to the end.

TRIVIA

- Until now, the Klingon Empire has been presented as aggressive and warlike. It's fascinating to find out that this is a relatively new innovation. Just as humanity has escaped from barbarism in a couple of generations, the Klingon Empire is descending.
- This episode uses props from Kirk and McCoy's trial in *Star Trek VI: The Undiscovered Country.*

RATING

- An OK story, but one that suffers hugely when compared with the scenes from *Star Trek VI: The Undiscovered Country* that provide the look of the episode. This episode also suffers because (ironically, unlike the sixth movie), there's no sense of the political ramifications on Earth of Archer's arrest. But there's a good central dynamic, and if Archer's rescue is accomplished remarkably easily, then at least the episode up to that point has been solid and dramatic.

2.20 HORIZON

DATE 10 JANUARY 2153

Travis returns home to his cargo ship after a tragedy

The Enterprise is monitoring a star close to the position of the Horizon, Travis' family ship, and Travis gets permission to visit them. When he contacts the ship, though, he learns that his father has died. Travis goes

TX 16 April 2003
WRITER André Bormanis
DIRECTOR James A Contner
GUEST CAST Philip Anthony-Rodriguez (Juan), Ken Feinberg (Alien Captain), Nicole Forester (Nora), Corey Mendell Parker (Paul), Adam Paul (Nichols), Joan Pringle (Rianna)

over to the ship, and discovers that the new Captain, his brother Paul, doesn't have the full confidence of the crew. Back on the Enterprise, T'Pol finds that she enjoys the screening of *Frankenstein*, feeling it's a good portrayal of human attitudes to difference. Travis' attempts to help aboard the Horizon are rebuffed. The ship is attacked by raiders, who plant a bomb on the hull. They're going to return soon. Travis wants to put up a fight, but the crew are nervous. Travis upgrades the engines and weapons and fights the raiders off, and Paul proves his bravery.

TRIVIA

- There was a USS Horizon mentioned as an early deep space vessel in *A Piece of the Action*. While it was never seen, by implication it was a Starfleet vessel (and it was referred to as such in *Deep Space Nine*). So it's probably not the same ship.

RATING

- Travis has been practically invisible this season, and here he gets a showcase episode. It's a re-run of *Marauders*, but in space, so it doesn't really feel like it. There's no sense of community on the ship, though, and while some of the family stuff is quite touching, it just doesn't feel like a homecoming – it feels like an exchange trip.

2.21 THE BREACH

DATE UNKNOWN

Phlox must treat a race-enemy of his people

TX 23 April 2003
WRITERS Chris Black and John Shiban (story by Daniel McCarthy)
DIRECTOR Robert Duncan McNeill
GUEST CAST Mark Chaet (Yolen), DC Douglas (Zepht), Laura Putney (Trevix), Henry Stram (Hudak), Jamison Yang (Crewman)

The political situation on a nearby planet has collapsed, and the Denobulans want a party of geologists evacuated. They're deep inside a mountain, and Reed, Trip and Travis are sent on a caving mission to retrieve them. When another ship that's evacuating suffers a radiation leak, an alien is brought to Phlox's Sickbay who objects to being treated by a Denobulan. The Denobulans fought a war centuries ago with his people, and the two cultures still hate each other. Phlox is more tolerant than average, but still loses his temper. The alien refuses treatment, but Phlox manages to persuade him to change his mind after the two discuss their families.

TRIVIA

- There has been some fan speculation that the Denobulans, Phlox's race, are going to be revealed to be the Cardassians going under a different name. There's no real on-screen evidence of that, though.

RATING

- One of those third-form ethical debates that *Star Trek* seems to like so much, but John Billingsley saves the day with a very strong performance that once again demonstrates Phlox has a hidden dark side.

2.22 COGENITOR

DATE UNKNOWN

Trip breaks a taboo when he teaches an alien to read

TX 30 April 2003
WRITER Rick Berman and Brannon Braga
DIRECTOR LeVar Burton
GUEST CAST Andreas Katsulas (Vissian Captain), FJ Rio (Vissian Engineer), Larissa Laskin (Calla), Becky Wahlstrom (Cogenitor), Stacie Renna (Traistana), Laura Interval (Vissian Woman #2)

The Enterprise is studying a star when it detects a Vissian ship far closer than Earth technology could go. The Vissians are advanced and highly intelligent, and extremely friendly. Their Captain and Archer become fast friends and go off together to explore the depths of the star in a Vissian pod. The Vissians have three genders – male, female and cogenitor. The cogenitors are seen as property, but Trip realises the one on the ship is just as intelligent as the men and women. The cogenitor quickly learns to read, and on Archer's return, demands asylum. This causes friction with the Vissians, and Archer is extremely angry with Trip. The cogenitor is returned to its ship. Soon afterwards, they learn it has killed itself.

TRIVIA

- Conner Trineer was very worried when he went to the story office and saw a note on a board: Phlox/Trip/Trisexual, fearing he was about to have an affair with the ship's doctor!

RATING

- Issue-driven storytelling, with a touch of *The Handmaid's Tale*, but an issue without an easy resolution. Trip's motivation for wanting to educate the cogenitor seems entirely innocent (unlike the Reed subplot, which just vanishes about two-thirds of the way through the episode). While our sympathies are always with the cogenitor, we can also see that Trip is causing harm.

2.23 REGENERATION

DATE 1 MARCH 2153

Cyborgs are revived and threaten humanity

TX 7 May 2003
WRITERS Mike Sussman and Phyllis Strong
DIRECTOR David Livingston
GUEST CAST Vaughn Armstrong (Forrest), Jim Fitzpatrick (Williams), Mark Chadwick (Male Tarkalean), Bonita Friedericy (Rooney), Adam Harrington (Researcher), Nicole Randal (Female Tarkalean), Paul Scott (Foster), John Short (Drake), Chris Wynne (Moninger)

Researchers in the Arctic discover alien wreckage and corpses of cyborgs. The cyborgs reactivate, and kill one of the researchers, take another two with them and escape into space on their ship. The Enterprise is told to intercept the ship, which is travelling faster than it was designed to. They find it attacking a Tarkalean freighter. It is clearly being adapted by superior alien technology, and the Enterprise is heavily damaged. The freighter is becoming more advanced by the moment. Archer and Reed beam aboard with explosives. The freighter is destroyed, but it's sent a distress signal. T'Pol assures Archer it won't reach its destination until the twenty-fourth century.

TRIVIA

- The aliens aren't named, but they are Borg and their ship crashed on Earth in *Star Trek: First Contact.*
- This is the first mention of Quadrants in *Enterprise*, and Archer refers to the Delta Quadrant.

RATING

- Should *Enterprise* be doing Borg stories? No. Do they need (once again) to be so coy about naming the aliens? No. Isn't it a bit odd that Borg technology that could carve the Enterprise-D and Voyager up takes so long to get past this Enterprise's polarised hull plating? Yes. But this goes from tension in the Arctic via a tense sabotage plot to a slam-bang action finale. A great episode.

2.24 FIRST FLIGHT

DATE UNKNOWN

Archer learns that an old rival has died

TX 14 May 2003
WRITERS John Shiban and Chris Black
DIRECTOR LeVar Burton
GUEST CAST Vaughn Armstrong (Forrest), Victor Bevine (Flight Controller), Brigid Brannagh (Ruby), Michael Canavan (Vulcan), Keith Carradine (Robinson), John B Moody (Security Officer)

Archer hears that his long-term rival, AG Robinson, has been killed in a mountaineering accident. As the two of them investigate a nebula, Archer tells T'Pol how he and Robinson spent their careers competing, and how the two of them helped to shape the warp program. They had both been up for the job of flying the first Warp 3 test flight. Robinson had won out, but disobeyed orders and one of two test vehicles was destroyed. Archer and one of his engineers, Lieutenant Trip Tucker, were sure the engine worked, but Robinson – covering his own back – said it wasn't. The space program was suspended. Robinson and Archer stole the other prototype and, with Trip's help, launched it on a successful Warp 3 flight. The space program was reinstated, and Archer was assigned Captain of the next generation of starship, the NX-01. Back in the present, T'Pol and Archer discover a new nebula, and name it the Robinson Nebula.

TRIVIA

- At the bar, the officers 'buy drinks' for each other – we don't see any cash change hands, but the implication is that the people of this time still use money. It's established that the New World Economy did away with this in the twenty-second century, but it's still not clear if this was before or after Archer's time.
- We're told why Trip has that nickname – he's Charles Tucker III, it's short for 'triple'.

RATING

- An episode that makes you wish they'd run a few more like it at the beginning of the series. This sketches in some of the back story, and has some good showcase scenes between Bakula and Carradine. There's a nice tone here, and the sense of Starfleet being made up of pioneering, rather cocky test pilots is something that the show could use more of.

2.25 BOUNTY

DATE 21 MARCH 2153

A Tellarite bounty hunter comes after Archer

TX 14 May 2003
WRITERS Hans Tobeason, Mike Sussman and Phyllis Strong (story by Rick Berman and Brannon Braga)
DIRECTOR Roxann Dawson
GUEST CAST Michael Garvey (Captain Goroth), Jordan Lund (Skalaar), Robert O'Reilly (Kago-Darr), Ed O'Ross (Gaavrin), Louis Ortiz (Klingon Warrior)

Archer is kidnapped by Skalaar, a Tellarite bounty hunter who is going to take Archer, an escaped convicted criminal, back to the Klingons. Meanwhile, a virus has triggered T'Pol's Pon farr and Phlox has to fend off her advances. As Skalaar heads to a rendezvous with the Klingon ship, Archer learns it's his last job before he can buy a freighter and get back to a trader's life. They are attacked by another bounty hunter, and Archer helps them survive. It becomes clear the Klingons won't give Skalaar his freighter back, and they don't give him the full reward for Archer. Skalaar gives Archer a lock-pick and Archer manages to fight his way off the Klingon ship. The Enterprise picks him up and makes a getaway.

TRIVIA

- Despite fan objections that only male Vulcans can undergo Pon farr, *Blood Fever* had already established that Vulcan woman can.

RATING

- Archer's (rather easy) escape from prison is followed up, in a story that owes a debt to *Midnight Run*. He's been incredibly lucky – in *Judgment* he met an old lawyer who was a decent man deep down, here he meets a bounty hunter who's practically the same character. It's the fourth time this season Archer has been imprisoned for a crime he didn't commit before escaping.

2.26 THE EXPANSE

DATE 24 APRIL 2153

Earth suffers a devastating attack, and the Enterprise must retaliate

TX 21 May 2003
WRITERS Rick Berman and Brannon Braga
DIRECTOR Allan Kroeker
GUEST CAST Vaughn Armstrong (Forrest), Gary Bullock (Klingon Council Member), Josh Cruze (Captain Ramirez), Dan Desmond (Klingon Chancellor), David Figlioli (Klingon Crewman), John Fleck (Silik), Gary Graham (Soval), James Horan (Humanoid Figure), Daniel Riordan (Duras), L Sidney (Klingon Crewman #2), Bruce Wright (Dr Fer'at)

An alien probe wipes out a 4,000km stretch of Earth's surface, from Venezula to Florida. Seven million people are killed. The Enterprise is recalled to Earth, but intercepted by the Suliban, who tell Archer it was merely a test firing of a Xindi weapon, retroactive revenge for humanity wiping out the Xindi centuries in the future. On Earth, Archer is ordered to the source of the attack, the Delphic Expanse. The Vulcans warn that they should not go there, that all their missions there have ended in madness and death, and order T'Pol to leave the crew. Trip learns his sister was killed. T'Pol refuses to leave the Enterprise, and the ship is fitted with new armaments and heads for the Expanse, prepared to retaliate in kind. Meanwhile, the Klingons are out for Archer's blood, and send Duras to kill him. The Enterprise fights them off and enters the Expanse...

QUOTES

- 'I can't wait to get in there, Captain. Find the people who did this. And tell me we won't be tiptoeing around. None of that non-interference crap T'Pol's always shoving down our throats. Maybe it's a good thing she's leaving.'
  'We'll do what we have to, Trip. Whatever it takes.' – *Tucker and Archer*

TRIVIA

- We see the NX02 is under construction.

RATING

- Wow. *Enterprise* leaps in a new direction, one that's clearly influenced by the attacks on September 11th 2001. This creates a connection and immediacy that not even the films' often rather abstract threats to Earth represented. It's the most visually rich episode of any *Star Trek* episode, and has the rawness and energy of some of the very best and darkest *The Next Generation*. History should warn us that 'radical new directions' for recent *Star Trek* shows soon evaporate, that potential is rarely fully realised, that arcs never quite work, that part twos of stories are almost invariably disappointing, that reset switches can invalidate the best of episodes. But, wow – this doesn't just promise, this delivers. If season three is like this, and builds on this, *Enterprise* is going to be one of the best shows on TV. And hopefully, in among all the gung-ho stuff, we're going to see *Star Trek* do what it can do better than any other show – taking a difficult contemporary issue and sneaking stuff past the network that even shows like *The West Wing* daren't quite say.

A BRIEF HISTORY OF THE *STAR TREK* UNIVERSE

Over the years, a vast amount of detail about the history of the *Star Trek* universe has built up, so much so that there's an official *Star Trek Chronology* book available that keeps track of it all. But this is an overview:

In broad terms, the late twentieth to mid-twenty-first century was a time of chaos. The 1990s saw the Eugenics Wars, when eugenically-bred supermen, like Khan, seized power. They were overthrown, placed in suspended animation and exiled (we first saw Khan in *Space Seed*, he returned in *Star Trek II: The Wrath of Khan*).

Mankind continued to develop space probes, but couldn't solve the problems of greed and selfishness on Earth. World War III, started by the infamous Colonel Green, devastated much of the Earth, killed millions and set off a nuclear winter.

Everything changed when the warp drive was invented by Zefram Cochrane in 2083. A passing Vulcan scoutship detected the first trial run and humanity made contact with an alien race for the first time (we see this in *Star Trek: First Contact*).

Humanity was united by the desire to explore the galaxy. Mars was colonised in 2103; deep space probes were sent out. However, the Vulcans were worried that humanity was a savage species, and kept them in check by limiting their access to the secrets of warp engines. Despite Vulcan pessimism, the twenty-second century saw humanity setting up a united world government, completely abolishing war and poverty within a couple of generations. Colonies were set up throughout the solar system, and humans sent out manned missions and trading ships, albeit ones that were limited to very slow speeds. Limited contact was made with other species, and humanity got at least as far as the next solar system, Alpha Centauri.

- **ENTERPRISE:** In 2151, Earth finally launched the first ship of its Starfleet, the Enterprise NX-01, a ship initially capable of Warp 4.5, but which would soon break the Warp 5 barrier. The Enterprise, led by Captain Jonathan Archer, began a mission to explore – to boldly go where no man has gone before.

  Humanity quickly encountered hostile races like the Klingons, Andorians and Romulans.

  Archer lived at a crucial period in history, and the era was an arena of conflict in a Temporal Cold War between two factions from the future. While little was known at first, one of these factions appeared to be human, the other employed Suliban agents.

  Although we haven't seen it (yet) in *Enterprise*, the Romulan Wars started around Archer's time, with Earth at war with the mysterious Romulans. Earth won, and the Neutral Zone was set up.

  Soon afterwards, in 2161, the United Federation of Planets was established. This united a group of like-minded, democratic planets (including Earth and Vulcan) under one Council and President. Together, the Federation and its Starfleet began to explore the galaxy, expanding gradually and peacefully.

  Around the 2220s, the Federation and Klingons had become sworn enemies, and there were frequent conflicts between the two great powers for the rest of the century.

  In 2245, the NCC-1701 Enterprise was launched, one of the powerful new Constitution-Class starships. The first Captain was Robert April. Spock started his service on the ship under the second captain, Christopher Pike (as seen in the pilot episode, *The Cage*, and the episode *The Menagerie*).

- **STAR TREK:** In 2264, Captain James Tiberius Kirk began his first historic five-year mission as Captain of the Enterprise. The animated **STAR TREK** series is also set during this first five-year mission.
- **STAR TREK: THE MOTION PICTURE:** After years behind a desk, Admiral Kirk returns to command of the Enterprise when Earth is threatened by an enormous alien entity, V'Ger. (Admiral Kirk possibly commanded a second five-year mission after this, as would have been seen in the **STAR TREK II** series).
- **STAR TREK II: THE WRATH OF KHAN / STAR TREK III: THE SEARCH FOR SPOCK / STAR TREK IV: THE VOYAGE HOME:** Around 15 years after the original five-year mission, Spock was killed fighting Khan. However, he was resurrected thanks to the power of the Genesis Planet. Captain Kirk disobeyed orders to recover Spock from there, and was responsible for the destruction of the Enterprise. He was spared a court martial after going back in time to save Earth from an alien probe, but was demoted to Captain – and immediately given command of a new Enterprise, the NCC-1701-A.
- **STAR TREK V: THE FINAL FRONTIER/STAR TREK VI: THE UNDISCOVERED COUNTRY:** Kirk continued as Captain of the Enterprise-A until the ship was decommissioned in the early 2290s. By then, he and Spock had helped to start negotiations between the Federation and Klingons – the great Cold War of the twenty-third century was over.
- **STAR TREK: GENERATIONS:** The baton passed to new generations – the Enterprise-B, even bigger and more powerful than its predecessor, was launched in 2293, and (fittingly, perhaps) Kirk died saving it on its first mission. The USS Excelsior, under Captain Sulu, also continued Kirk's legacy.

  The twenty-fourth century began with new hope and rapid expansion and progress for the Federation. The Klingons and Federation went from an uneasy peace to becoming allies, after the Enterprise-C sacrificed itself saving the Klingon colony of Narendra III from the Romulans. (Seen in *Yesterday's Enterprise.*)

  The late 2340s saw the Federation expand into areas claimed by the Cardassians, and a brief Cardassian War.
- **STAR TREK: THE NEXT GENERATION:** The Enterprise-D was launched in 2364, and began its ongoing mission under Captain Jean-Luc Picard.

  Picard's Enterprise encountered the Borg, a ruthless race of cyborgs (*Q Who?*). One Borg ship almost wiped out the whole Starfleet at the Battle of Wolf 359 in 2366 (as seen in *The Best of Both Worlds Part II*).
- **STAR TREK: DEEP SPACE NINE:** One survivor of that battle, Benjamin Sisko, became the Federation's representative on space station Deep Space Nine, at the edge of the Federation, in 2369.

  Deep Space Nine found itself on the front line of war with the Cardassians and their powerful allies from the Gamma Quadrant, The Dominion. The Dominion War raged across the entire quadrant in the early 2370s, with the Federation forming a temporary alliance with the Klingons and even the Romulans. Eventually, The Dominion was utterly defeated.
- **STAR TREK: GENERATIONS/STAR TREK: FIRST CONTACT/ STAR TREK: INSURRECTION:** The Enterprise-D was destroyed in 2371, but Picard and his crew were assigned to the new Enterprise-E. Worf took up a posting on Deep Space Nine.
- **STAR TREK: VOYAGER:** The USS Voyager was catapulted to the far end of the galaxy in 2371, returning in 2378.

- **STAR TREK: NEMESIS:** Fifteen years after he took command of the Enterprise, Picard and the crew of the Enterprise-E defeated a Reman plot to destroy Earth, at the cost of Data's life. Will Riker finally married Deanna Troi and took up the command of his own ship, the USS Titan. Picard remains Captain of the Enterprise-E.

While we've seen glimpses of the future beyond that, we also know that nothing about that future is set. The human adventure is just beginning... and the sky's the limit.

CHARACTER GUIDE

This section lists the regular characters from the various series and films, as well as characters who make recurring appearances or who are significant parts of the* Star Trek *story.

- **ARCHER, Jonathan *(Scott Bakula)*:** Captain of the first Enterprise. [*Enterprise*]
- **BARCLAY, Reg *(Dwight Schultz)*:** Shy Starfleet engineer who served on the Enterprise, and later on Earth, where he kept in contact with Voyager. [*The Next Generation, Voyager*]
- **BAREIL, Vedek *(Philip Anglim)*:** Influential spiritual figure on Bajor, once in line for Kai. Kira's lover. [*Deep Space Nine*]
- **BASHIR, Julian *(Siddig El Fadil, also credited as Alexander Siddig)*:** Young, idealistic medical officer assigned by Starfleet to serve on Deep Space Nine. [*Deep Space Nine*]
- **B'ETOR *(Gwynyth Walsh)*:** Power-hungry sister of Duras and Lursa. [*The Next Generation, Deep Space Nine, Star Trek: Generations*]
- **CHAKOTAY *(Robert Beltran)*:** American Indian First Officer of Voyager. He had a facial tattoo, and was a member of the Maquis. [*Voyager*]
- **CHAPEL, Christine *(Majel Barrett)*:** Nurse on Kirk's Enterprise, later a doctor in her own right. [*Star Trek*]
- **CHEKOV, Pavel Andreivich *(Walter Koenig)*:** Ensign Navigator on Kirk's Enterprise. Rose to the rank of Commander. [*Star Trek*]
- **COCHRANE, Zefram *(Glenn Corbett, James Cromwell)*:** The human inventor of the warp drive, an explorer, who is renowned as one of the greatest heroes of human history. When the crew of the Enterprise-E travelled back in time and met him, they discovered he was an ordinary man [*Star Trek: First Contact*]. He vanished, and became an inspiration for everyone in Starfleet [*Enterprise*]. Kirk discovered him, still alive, in his time. [*Metamorphosis*]
- **CRUSHER, Beverly *(Gates McFadden)*:** Medical Officer on Picard's Enterprise. Was married to Jack Crusher, a close friend of Picard. [*The Next Generation*]
- **CRUSHER, Wesley *(Wil Wheaton)*:** Son of Beverly Crusher, he went from child prodigy to Starfleet Academy dropout. [*The Next Generation*]
- **DAMAR *(Casey Biggs)*:** Cardassian leader, once Dukat's underling, who defied The Dominion and led his people in open rebellion. [*Deep Space Nine*].
- **DATA *(Brent Spiner)*:** Pale-skinned android Second Officer on Picard's Enterprise. Data longed to understand human emotion. He sacrificed himself to prevent the activation of a Romulan superweapon. [*The Next Generation*]
- **DAX, Jadzia *(Terry Farrell)*** and **DAX Ezri *(Nicole de Boer)*:** Trill science officer of Deep Space Nine. Dax's host Jadzia married Worf and was killed. A new host, Ezri, was found for the symbiont. Previous host were Lela, Tobin, Emony, Audrid, Torias, Joran and Curzon. [*Deep Space Nine*]
- **DECKER, Will *(Steven Collins)*:** Oversaw the refit of the USS Enterprise 1701, after James Kirk's five-year mission. [*Star Trek: The Motion Picture*]
- **DOCTOR, The *(Robert Picardo)*:** An Emergency Medical Hologram who was kept active when the original Medical Officer of Voyager was killed. He quickly developed sentience, and continued to develop. [*Voyager*]
- **DUKAT *(Marc Alaimo)*:** Cardassian, the former commander of the forces that occupied Bajor. Ben Sisko's nemesis, Dukat was obsessed with regaining control of Deep Space Nine. He gradually grew insane, and murdered Jadzia Dax. [*Deep Space Nine*]
- **DURAS *(Patrick Massett)*:** Son of the Klingon who framed Worf's father, and brother of Lursa and B'Etor. Killed by Worf. [*The Next Generation*]
- **EDDINGTON, Michael *(Kenneth Marshall)*:** Federation officer-turned-Maquis, and Sisko's nemesis. Killed by the Jem'Hadar. [*Deep Space Nine*]
- **FEMALE SHAPESHIFTER *(Salome Jens)*:** Founder who introduced Odo to the Great Link. [*Deep Space Nine*]
- **FONTAINE, Vic *(James Darren)*:** Hologramatic crooner created by Bashir. [*Deep Space Nine*]
- **GARAK, Elim *(Andrew Robinson,*** also credited as ***Andrew J Robinson)*:** A Cardassian tailor on Deep Space Nine, Garak had a mysterious past that at the very least involved war crimes and espionage. [*Deep Space Nine*]
- **GOWRON *(Robert O'Reilly)*:** Klingon Chancellor who let corruption slowly weaken the Empire. Killed by Worf and succeeded by Martok. [*The Next Generation, Deep Space Nine*]
- **GUINAN *(Whoopi Goldberg)*:** Mysterious long-lived barkeeper of Ten-Forward on the Enterprise-D. [*The Next Generation*]
- **ILIA *(Persis Khambatta)*:** Deltan navigator who joined the USS Enterprise shortly after Kirk took command from Decker. [*Star Trek: The Motion Picture*]
- **JANEWAY, Kathryn *(Kate Mulgrew)*:** Captain of Voyager [*Voyager*]. She was promoted to Admiral on her return to Earth. [*Star Trek: Nemesis*]
- **KAHLESS *(Robert Herron, Kevin Conway)*:** Legendary Klingon warrior and focal figure of Klingon spiritual worship, prophesied to return. [*Star Trek, The Next Generation*]
- **K'EHLEYR *(Suzie Plakson)*:** Half-human, half-Klingon mother of Worf's son, Alexander. Murdered by Duras. [*The Next Generation*]
- **KES *(Jennifer Lien)*:** Ocampan who joined the Voyager crew. [*Voyager*]
- **KHAN, Noonien Singh *(Ricardo Montalban)*** Genetically engineered super-human from the late twentieth century, exiled to Ceti Alpha V by Kirk. [*Star Trek, Star Trek II: The Wrath of Khan*]
- **KIM, Harry *(Garrett Wang)*:** Operations officer of Voyager. [*Voyager*]
- **KIRA, Nerys *(Nana Visitor)*:** Bajoran First Officer on Deep Space Nine. [*Deep Space Nine*]
- **KIRK, James Tiberius *(William Shatner)*:** The legendary Captain of the original Enterprise and the Enterprise-A. [*Star Trek*]. History records he was killed saving the Enterprise-B on its maiden voyage. [*Star Trek: Generations*]
- **LaFORGE, Geordi *(LeVar Burton)*:** Quickly promoted to Chief Engineer on Picard's Enterprise. Blind, he wore a VISOR to give him vision, and eventually upgraded this to ocular implants. [*The Next Generation*]
- **LEETA *(Chase Masterson)*:** Dabo girl. [*Deep Space Nine*]
- **LORE *(Brent Spiner)*:** Data's evil brother. [*The Next Generation*]
- **LURSA *(Barbara March)*:** Power-hungry sister of Duras and B'Etor. [*The Next Generation, Deep Space Nine, Star Trek: Generations*]
- **MARCUS, David *(Merrit Butrick)*:** Kirk's son by Carol Marcus, killed by the Klingons. [*Star Trek II: The Wrath of Khan, Star Trek III: The Search for Spock*]
- **MARTOK *(JG Hertzler)*:** Klingon General who led the Klingon forces against The Dominion. Succeeded Gowron as Chancellor. [*Deep Space Nine*]
- **MAYWEATHER, Travis *(Anthony Montgomery)*:** Helm officer of Archer's Enterprise. [*Enterprise*]
- **McCOY, Dr Leonard H 'Bones' *(DeForest Kelley)*:** Doctor on Kirk's Enterprise [*Star Trek*]. He was an admiral, and very old, when the Enterprise-D was launched. [*The Next Generation – Encounter at Farpoint*]
- **MORN *(Mark Allen Shepherd)*:** Barfly at Quark's, apparently talkative off-screen. [*Deep Space Nine*]
- **NEELIX *(Ethan Phillips)*:** Talaxian Cook and morale officer on Voyager. [*Voyager*]
- **NOG *(Aron Eisenburg)*:** Ferengi, son of Rom and friend of Jake Sisko, who joined Starfleet and reached the rank of lieutenant. [*Deep Space Nine*]

- **O'BRIEN, Miles Edward *(Colm Meaney)*:** Transporter Chief of the Enterprise-D (among other duties), he was transferred to Deep Space Nine and became Chief of Operations. Married to Keiko. [*The Next Generation, Deep Space Nine*]
- **ODO *(Rene Auberjonois)* :** Shapeshifting constable of Deep Space Nine, a job he also held under the Cardassians. He discovers that his people, the Founders, run the evil Dominion of the Gamma Quadrant. [*Deep Space Nine*].
- **PARIS, Tom *(Robert Duncan McNeill)* :** Helm officer of Voyager. [*Voyager*]
- **PHLOX *(John Billingsley)*:**Denobulan medical officer on the first Enterprise. [*Enterprise*]
- **PICARD, Jean-Luc *(Patrick Stewart)*:** Legendary captain of the Enterprise-D and E. [*The Next Generation, Deep Space Nine, Star Trek: Generations, Star Trek: First Contact, Star Trek: Insurrection, Star Trek: Nemesis*]
- **PORTHOS :** Captain Archer's pet dog. [*Enterprise*]
- **PULASKI, Katherine *(Diana Muldaur)*:** The medical officer of the Enterprise-D for one year. [*The Next Generation*]
- **Q *(John DeLancie)*:** Omnipotent being who has a fascination with humankind, and Picard in particular. [*The Next Generation, Deep Space Nine, Voyager*]
- **QUARK *(Armin Shimerman)*:** Ferengi barkeeper on Deep Space Nine. [*Deep Space Nine*]
- **RAND, Janice *(Grace Lee Whitney)*:** Yeoman on Kirk's Enterprise [*Star Trek*] she rose to the position of Transporter Chief [*Star Trek: The Motion Picture*]. She later served as communications officer on Sulu's Excelsior. [*Star Trek VI: The Undiscovered Country, Voyager*]
- **REED, Malcolm *(Dominic Keating)*:** Security officer of Archer's Enterprise. [*Enterprise*]
- **RIKER, William T *(Jonathan Frakes)*:** First officer of Picard's Enterprise, his trusted 'Number One'. Riker eventually married his old flame, Deanna Troi. [*The Next Generation*]
- **RO, Laren *(Michelle Forbes)*:** Rebellious Bajoran officer who served on Picard's Enterprise. [*The Next Generation*]
- **ROM *(Max Grodenchik)*:** Quark's brother and father of Nog. Rom succeeded Zek as Grand Nagus. [*Deep Space Nine*]
- **ROZHENKO, Alexander *(Jon Steuer, Brian Bonsall, James Sloyan)*:** Worf's son, by K'Ehleyr. After his mother's death, Alexander was brought up by Worf's human adopted parents, the Rozhenkos. [*The Next Generation, Deep Space Nine*]
- **SAAVIK *(Kirstie Alley, Robin Curtis)*:** Vulcan protegé of Spock. It was originally intended that Saavik was half-Romulan, half-Vulcan, but this was never mentioned on-screen. It's possible Saavik bore Spock's child. [*Star Trek II: The Wrath of Khan, Star Trek III: The Search for Spock, Star Trek IV: The Voyage Home*]
- **SAREK *(Mark Lenard)*:** Spock's father, a revered Vulcan ambassador and one of the architects of the Federation for over a century. [*Star Trek – Journey to Babel, Star Trek III – IV and VI, The Next Generation*]
- **SATO, Hoshi *(Linda Park)*:** Communications Officer of Archer's Enterprise. [*Enterprise*]
- **SCOTT, Montgomery 'Scotty' *(James Doohan)*:** Scottish engineer of Kirk's Enterprise [*Star Trek, Star Trek I – VII*]. He survived into the twenty-fourth century. [*The Next Generation*]
- **SELA *(Denise Crosby)*:** Daughter of Tasha Yar and a Romulan, thanks to a temporal paradox. [*The Next Generation*]
- **SESKA *(Martha Hackett)*:** Cardassian agent, disguised as a Bajoran, aboard Voyager. [*Voyager*]
- **SEVEN OF NINE *(Jeri Ryan)*:** Borg, originally a human girl, Annika Hansen, before she was assimilated. Seven was rescued by Voyager. [*Voyager*].
- **SISKO, Benjamin *(Avery Brooks)*:** Commander of Deep Space Nine. His wife Jennifer, was killed by the Borg at the Battle of Wolf 359. He has a son, Jake. The Bajoran prophets and Wormhole aliens named him Emissary, the central figure of their religion. He died fulfilling their prophecies. [*Deep Space Nine*].
- **SISKO, Jake *(Cirroc Lofton)*:** The son of Ben Sisko, he grows up on Deep Space Nine after his father is posted there, and becomes a writer. [*Deep Space Nine*]
- **SOONG, Dr Noonien *(Brent Spiner)*:** Brilliant scientist and creator of the positronic brain, Soong is known to have created four androids – B-4, Lore, Data and an android of his dead wife. [*The Next Generation*]
- **SPOCK, Mr *(Leonard Nimoy)*:** The half-Vulcan, half-human science officer of Kirk's Enterprise (although he was serving on the ship before Kirk did – *The Cage*) [*Star Trek*]. He later became a Federation Ambassador. [*The Next Generation*]
- **SPOT *(Spot, Brandy and Monster)*:** Data's cat. [*The Next Generation*]
- **SULU, Hikaru *(George Takei)*:** Helmsman of Kirk's Enterprise [*Star Trek*], Sulu eventually got his own command, the USS Excelsior [*Star Trek VI: The Undiscovered Country*]. One of his officers there was a young Tuvok [*Voyager*]. His daughter Demora served on the Enterprise-B [*Star Trek: Generations*].
- **TORRES, B'Elanna *(Roxann Biggs-Dawson,* also credited as *Roxann Dawson)*:** Maquis Chief Engineer of Voyager. [*Voyager*]
- **T'POL *(Jolene Blalock)*:** Vulcan science officer of Archer's Enterprise. [*Enterprise*]
- **TROI, Deanna *(Marina Sirtis)*:** Half-Betazoid, half-human counselor on Picard's Enterprise. Deanna is an empath who had a relationship with Will Riker when they were younger, and who eventually married him. [*The Next Generation*]
- **TROI, Lwaxana *(Majel Barrett)*:** Deanna Troi's pushy Betazoid mother. [*The Next Generation, Deep Space Nine*]
- **TUCKER, Charles 'Trip' *(Connor Trinner)*:** Texan First Officer and Chief Engineer of Archer's Enterprise. [*Enterprise*]
- **TUVOK *(Tim Russ)*:** Vulcan Security Chief of Voyager. [*Voyager*]
- **UHURA *(Nichelle Nichols)*:** Communications Officer of Kirk's Enterprise [*Star Trek*]. Her first name was never given on screen. It was 'Upenda' in the original writers' guidelines, but it's officially 'Nyota', according to Paramount.
- **VASH *(Jennifer Hetrick)*:** Picard's archaelogist lover. [*The Next Generation, Deep Space Nine*]
- **WEYOUN *(Jeffrey Combs)*:** Cloned Vorta and devoted servant of the Founders, Weyoun led Dominion activities in the Alpha Quadrant and died for his masters on several occasions. [*Deep Space Nine*]
- **WINN, Kai *(Louise Fletcher)*:** Manipulative, power-seeking Bajoran religious leader who eventually sided with Dukat and the Pah-wraiths, leading to her demise. [*Deep Space Nine*]
- **WORF *(Michael Dorn)*:** Klingon Security Officer of the Enterprise-D, then Strategic Operations Officer of Deep Space Nine. Worf became Federation Ambassador to the Klingon Empire, but then returned to be Picard's Security Chief. [*The Next Generation, Deep Space Nine*]. His grandfather was a Klingon lawyer [*Star Trek VI: The Undiscovered Country*]. Worf was raised by human adoptive parents, the Rozhenkos, and married Dax.
- **YAR, Natasha 'Tasha' *(Denise Crosby)*:** Security Chief on the Enterprise-D, killed in action (*Skin of Evil*). She survived in a parallel timeline (*Yesterday's Enterprise*) and, to cut a long story short, had a daughter called Sela [*The Next Generation*].
- **YATES, Kasidy *(Penny Johnson)*:** Freighter captain who became Sisko's second wife. [*Deep Space Nine*]
- **ZEK *(Wallace Shawn)*:** Ferengi Grand Nagus who was supported in his business dealings by his lover, Quark's mother, Ishka. Appointed Rom as his successor on his retirement. [*Deep Space Nine*]
- **ZIMMERMAN, Dr Lewis *(Robert Picardo)*:** Model for the Starfleet Emergency Medical Hologram. [*Deep Space Nine*]
- **ZIYAL, Tora *(Melanie Smith)*:** Daughter of Dukat who found friendship with Kira and the station personnel during the Cardassian occupation of Deep Space Nine. [*Deep Space Nine*]

GLOSSARY

***Star Trek** is somewhat notorious for its 'technobabble' – seemingly meaningless technical jargon. While it's essentially all made up, it is consistent – much of the 'science' of **Star Trek** has been worked out in some detail by the people behind the scenes – there are even a couple of official **Star Trek Technical Manuals** that go into great detail about exactly how the transporters, phasers and warp engines work. There are many terms that are commonly used, but aren't always fully-explained in the series themselves. Here, we'll try to give a quick explanation of the main terms:*

- **ANDORIANS:** Blue-skinned, with antennae. The Andorians are warlike, and in Archer's time they fought wars with the **Vulcans**. By Kirk's time they had joined the **Federation**.
- **AWAY TEAM:** The small group that's sent over from a **starship** to planets or ships that need investigating. It's always the senior officers that go, although occasionally a **redshirt** or two goes with them.
- **BADLANDS:** An area of space near Deep Space Nine that's full of electromagnetic storms. The **Maquis** use it to hide from the **Federation**. It was here that Voyager was catapulted into the Delta **Quadrant**.
- **BAJORANS:** Natives of Bajor, devastated by generations of **Cardassian** occupation, which ended just before *Deep Space Nine* starts. Deep Space Nine orbits Bajor, and the Bajoran **Wormhole** is a crucial strategic point. Ensign Ro was Bajoran, as were many characters in *Deep Space Nine*, including Kira Nerys. They look human, except for knobbly ridges on the bridge of their nose.
- **BETAZOIDS:** A matriarchal race of empaths (which means they can 'read' people's emotions) who resemble humans with especially dark eyes. They come from the idyllic planet Betazed. Counsellor Deanna Troi is half-Betazoid, half-human.
- **BORG:** A race of cyborgs (half-human, half-robot creatures) from a distant part of our galaxy, first seen in *The Next Generation*. The Borg exist to assimilate other races – converting them into part of the Borg Collective and stealing their knowledge. The Borg are numerous, highly advanced and utterly ruthless. In many ways, they are organised like social insects – they have a 'hive mind', in which different Borg perform set functions. A typical Borg is a drone, and they are ruled by the Borg Queen.

  It took almost the entire **Starfleet** to stop one Borg Cube at the Battle of Wolf 359 (*The Best of Both Worlds*), and there were many casualties, including Deep Space Nine commander Sisko's wife. Just before Wolf 359, they converted Picard into a spokesman for their cause, Locutus – although Picard was soon rescued, it was an event that traumatised him. The **Federation** dreads the Borg, but has gained valuable knowledge about them from Voyager, which encountered them on their home turf, and even gained a reformed Borg crewmember, Seven of Nine.
- **CARDASSIAN:** Grey-skinned humanoids with reptilian features. The Cardassians are a proud, cultured, devious and aggressive race from Cardassia Prime. The Cardassian Union is an area of space that borders the Federation and is near **Bajor**, ruled by the High Council. Senior Cardassians are known as Guls. Their feared secret police are the Obsidian Order. They occupied Bajor for many years, and set up a giant space station they called Terok Nor. When they abandoned the planet, **Starfleet** took over the station and renamed it Deep Space Nine.
- **CHANGELINGS:** see **Dominion**.
- **CLASS-M PLANETS:** Planets like Earth, capable of supporting human life. A term used since the original series, it was only in *Enterprise* that we discover what 'M' stood for – it's a **Vulcan** term, and stands for the Vulcan word Minshara. Other classes of planets have been established. Class-Y planets are extremely dangerous (Demon).
- **CLOAKING DEVICE:** A technology developed by the **Romulans** that makes their ships invisible. The **Klingons** have traded with the Romulans for the technology, but the **Federation** has never developed it – although the USS Defiant in *Deep Space Nine* has a cloaking device loaned by the Romulans to help in the fight against the **Dominion**.
- **DEMILITARISED ZONE:** See **Maquis**.
- **DILITHIUM CRYSTALS:** See **Warp**.
- **DISRUPTORS:** See **Phasers**.
- **DOMINION:** An aggressive empire from the Gamma **Quadrant**, their equivalent of the **Federation**. The Dominion is ruled by the Founders, Odo's people, the shapeshifters who are normally all merged together in the Great Link. For millennia, other species were suspicious of the shapeshifters, and this made them extremely xenophobic in return. Administration in the Dominion is carried out by the Vorta, humanoid with bat-like ears and piercing blue eyes. The troops are the Jem'Hadar, humanoid rhinos who are specially-bred, and controlled by the Vorta using the drug ketracel white. The Dominion allied itself with the **Cardassians** and launched an invasion of the Alpha Quadrant. It took the combined might of the Federation, **Klingons** and **Romulans** to defeat them in a lengthy campaign known as the Dominion War.
- **ENTERPRISE:** See **Starships**.
- **FEDERATION:** The United Federation of Planets, the good guys in *Star Trek* – a democratic, diverse alliance of (by *The Next Generation*) about 150 planets, including Earth, **Vulcan** and **Betazed**. The Federation is vast – with the fastest starship, it would take seven years to fly from one end of Federation space to the other. The planets are united under the Federation Code of Justice, its Charter, which pledges the Federation 'to seek out new life and new civilisations, to boldly go where no one has gone before'. They are ruled by an elected President and a Council. Federation headquarters is in San Francisco, while the President seems to be based in Paris. Earth is an important member, but by no means the dominating power. The Federation **Starfleet** is the organisation that includes the crews of the Enterprise and (most of) the crews of Deep Space Nine and Voyager.
- **FERENGI:** Squat, big-eared, pointy-toothed capitalists, the Ferengi are traders, merchants and conmen who are always looking to acquire wealth. They are ruled by the Ferengi Commerce Authority, led by the Grand Nagus and live their lives by the Rules of Acquisition, snappy business mottos like 'Never allow family to stand in the way of opportunity.' They can be vicious, and have been known to wield whips and fly powerful Marauder starships, but they tend to be cowardly. They treat Ferengi women as inferiors.
- **FOUNDERS:** See **Dominion**.
- **GALAXY CLASS:** See **Starships**.
- **HIROGEN:** Tall, powerful hunters from the Delta **Quadrant** who have advanced armour and weapons. Their entire society is based on the glory of killing prey.
- **HOLODECKS:** By the time of *The Next Generation*, these are chambers that can be programmed to create ultra-convincing replicas of other environments. They create actual, solid, objects, albeit ones that can't exist outside the holodeck. These are primarily used for recreation (Quark ran a holodeck brothel on Deep Space Nine), but also for training purposes. By the time of Voyager, characters have immersed themselves in holonovels, interactive adventures. Voyager's Emergency Medical Hologram (or EMH) was so sophisticated that he was sentient, and gradually overcame many of the limitations of his programming.
- **HYPOSPRAY:** A futuristic medical instrument like a syringe that doesn't use a needle and can work through clothing.
- **IMPULSE DRIVE:** Engines used when a spaceship is travelling slower than the speed of light, within solar systems, rather than in deep space. 'Full impulse' is normally about a quarter of the speed of light – although it can be pushed faster. In Kirk's time, the impulse engines were described as 'rocket engines', but this was probably a misnomer – even Archer's Enterprise 100 years earlier was using nuclear fusion.

- **JEFFERIES TUBES:** The maintenance ducts that prove useful places to crawl through when you need to get around a Federation ship unseen. (The name is an in-joke: Matt Jefferies was a designer on the original show.)
- **JEM'HADAR:** See **Dominion**.
- **KAZON:** Tall, with large foreheads, the Kazon are raiders from the Delta **Quadrant**. They have no central authority, just various scattered clans, run by a Maje. They lack advanced technology. There are about 18 clans at any given time – we know about the Hobii, Mostral, Nistrim, Ogla, Oglamar, Pommar and Relora clans.
- **KLINGONS:** The arch enemies of the **Federation** at the time of the original series, by the end of Kirk's time the two powers had entered into a détente (*Star Trek VI: The Undiscovered Country*), and by the time of *The Next Generation*, they were uneasy allies. The *Klingon Empire* is roughly as powerful as the Federation, and is ruled from the Klingon homeworld, Qo'noS. The Klingons are a race of warriors, naturally aggressive, devious and unruly, with strict and elaborate codes of honour and clan structures to keep their urges in check. They are ruled by an Chancellor and a High Council. The first Emperor was Kahless, who killed his tyrant brother with a bat'leth, the traditional Klingon sword (which looks remarkably like a giant bicycle repair tool). Klingons at the time of Kirk's five-year mission looked like swarthy humans, but at every other time they have had darker skin, elaborate ridged foreheads and sharp teeth. The reason why they changed appearance so radically is the subject of much fan speculation. In real life, it's easily explained – the makers could afford better make-up. In the series, the problem has only been addressed obliquely – Worf suggested in *Trials and Tribble-ations* that it was 'not something we talk about'.
- **MAQUIS:** At the end of the **Cardassian** War, a treaty was signed between the **Federation** and the Cardassians that allowed both powers to remain in the area of disputed space between their two territories. Knowing the Cardassians violated this treaty, one group of human colonists in the demilitarised zone, the Maquis, secretly armed themselves and fought Cardassian oppression. The Federation authorities considered them terrorists, and treated even expressions of sympathy with the Maquis as suspicious. Many of the crew of Voyager were Maquis.
- **MIRROR UNIVERSE:** First seen in *Mirror, Mirror*, the Mirror Universe is a parallel universe like our own, but where humanity is barbaric, decadent and warlike, and where there are vicious versions of familiar characters. Kirk persuaded the Mirror Spock to try to convert humanity's Empire to the ways of peace. Starting with *Crossover*, the crew of Deep Space Nine had a number of encounters with the Mirror Universe, and it was discovered that Spock's pacifism weakened the Empire, allowing the **Klingons** and **Cardassians** to enslave humanity.
- **NCC:** The first part of the registration number of every **Starfleet** ship. Kirk's Enterprise was the NCC-1701, the replacement ship seen in the later movies was the NCC-1701-A. Picard has commanded the NCC-1701-D and (since *Star Trek: First Contact*) the NCC-1701-E. To distinguish them, shorthand is used – the ship seen throughout *The Next Generation* is the Enterprise-D. The Enterprise-B was seen in *Star Trek: Generations*, the Enterprise-C in *Yesterday's Enterprise*. In *Enterprise*, Captain Archer's ship is the NX-01-NX, being the designation for an experimental vessel (the Excelsior was NX-2000 in *Star Trek III: The Search for Spock*, but had graduated to being the NCC-2000 by *Star Trek VI: The Undiscovered Country*). What NCC stands for has never been established – it's based on a pre-1950 American registration system for aircraft (NC being standard aircraft, NX being experimental ones and NR being racing planes). Fans have settled on 'Naval Construction Contract'. It seems that the numbers are assigned in the order of the ships entering service – as noted, Archer's Enterprise, the first Starfleet vessel is NX-01, while Voyager, launched 220 years later, is NCC-74656. The USS Relativity, from the twenty-ninth century, was the NCV-474439-G.

  Non-Starfleet ships also have registry numbers – the **Vulcans** use a NSP prefix, the **Klingons** IKS, and there's an SS prefix, which seems to be used by human ships that aren't part of **Starfleet**.
- **NEUTRAL ZONE:** A buffer zone in space between the **Federation** and the **Romulans**, which no ship from either side can enter, for any reason, without breaking the peace treaty between the two powers. The area on either side of this no-man's land in space is heavily patrolled , and it's frequently a flashpoint and source of tension. It was set up after the Romulan Wars in the twenty-second century (after Archer's Enterprise was launched, but a century before Kirk's time).
- **OCAMPA:** Pixie-like race from the Delta **Quadrant**, Kes' people. They had a natural lifespan of just nine years, but are fast learners. Many are telepathic and have other psychic powers. Ocampan women can bear children once, when they reach a time called the elogium.
- **PHASERS:** Energy weapons that range from pistols through artillery pieces to massive phaser banks on starships. The phaser fires a powerful beam of light which can be subtly controlled to cause a range of effects from stunning to disintegrating an opponent. Ships' phasers are usually aimed by the computers, which can get a lock on a target and still hit it if it moves.

  The **Klingons** and **Romulans** use disruptors, not phasers, but there seems little practical difference between the two technologies.
- **PHOTON TORPEDOES:** Powerful missiles that contain small amounts of antimatter fired at **warp** speed at an enemy target. The torpedo itself is advanced, capable of being programmed to seek a specific target or being set as a mine. Later ships can also fire torpedoes in spread patterns. They generally more destructive than **phasers**, and can be used when a **starship** is at **warp**. By the time of the **Dominion** War, **Starfleet** has developed an even more powerful weapon, the quantum torpedo.
- **PRIME DIRECTIVE:** The most important law of the **Federation**, it prevents any member of **Starfleet** from interfering in the natural development of any society. This means no Starfleet mission can involve itself in a planet's internal conflicts or supply advanced technology to it. Starfleet General Order 1 requires a Captain to sacrifice his own ship rather than violate the Prime Directive, if necessary. There have been a variety of interpretations of the law over the years, and it frequently appears to be a rule more observed in the breach. Starfleet Captains often agonise whether their plans violate the Prime Directive.

  In the future, when the Federation develops time travel, there is also a Temporal Prime Directive that prevents interference in established history.
- **Q CONTINUUM:** The Q are a race of omnipotent beings who dwell in the Q Continuum. They are mischievous and malevolent, and one of them, simply called Q, has a special fascination for mankind, and Picard in particular. This fascination takes the form of setting various tests, often rather surreal ones. They can change form, but generally mimic the races they come into contact with.
- **QUADRANTS:** Our galaxy, which is roughly disc-shaped, is divided into four vast quadrants. Most of the **Federation** falls in the Alpha Quadrant, but the galaxy is so big that not even half of this 'home' quadrant has been mapped, let alone explored. The **Cardassian** Union borders the furthest borders of Federation space – at maximum warp, it would take a ship years to reach Earth from here (a fact conveniently forgotten by some writers of *Deep Space Nine* who've needed to get characters to Earth in a matter of days). Some of the Federation falls in the Beta Quadrant (Earth straddles the meridian between the two), but this is where both the **Klingon** and **Romulan** empires are found, and so little exploration by Federation scientists has been possible (colloqually, 'the Alpha Quadrant' is used to describe Earth's bit of the galaxy, Federation, Klingons, Romulans and all). The Gamma Quadrant is the most distant from Earth, and was completely unknown until the **Bajoran Wormhole** opened. It is the home of the **Dominion**, who fought a devastating war with the Federation. The Delta Quadrant is also inaccessible and was completely unknown until USS Voyager was marooned there, so far from the Alpha Quadrant that it would take 70 years to return. As they made their way home, they proved the Federation's theory that the **Borg** came from this part of space.

- **QUANTUM SINGULARITY:** A very small black hole.
- **RANKS: Starfleet** uses a system that's a simplified version of naval ranks. The career path for a Starfleet officer runs from Cadet (while at Starfleet Academy), Ensign, Lieutenant, Lieutenant Commander, Commander, Captain, Commodore (which seems to have fallen out of use by The Next Generation) to Admiral.

  Within those ranks, there seems to be a degree of differentiation – for example, there are 'Junior Grade' Lieutenants and 'Fleet Captains'. Seniority is recognised – long-serving Captains and those of important Starfleet ships (like the *Enterprise*) can overrule other Captains, and even stand their ground with Admirals.

  Almost everyone who serves on a Starfleet ship has been through the Academy and is an officer. In Kirk's time there was the rank of Yeoman, but this seems to have fallen into disuse. Some specialists don't seem to be officers and have the title Chief, as in 'Transporter Chief'. Captains have the ability to promote their crew, and to assign 'Acting' rank, so Picard was able to make Wesley Crusher an 'Acting Ensign', and Janeway was able to assign ranks to the Maquis who joined her crew.
- **REDSHIRT:** A fan term meaning a disposable character. As stand-up comedians have noted, when Kirk, Spock and McCoy beam down to a planet, they often take a member of the security team who we've never seen before, who dies a horrible death in the first act. In the original series they were often the only one wearing a red shirt.
- **REPLICATORS:** Dispensing machines that can instantly create a wide variety of materials, including food. They can be programmed to create almost anything, barring some rare materials, although connoisseurs claim that replicated food isn't as good as the real thing.
- **ROMULANS:** Warlike isolationists who were once part of **Vulcan** society but renounced the way of logic. Their ships were the first with **cloaking devices**, and include the small Bird of Prey craft and the powerful Warbirds. The Romulan Star Empire borders the **Federation**, and the two are separated by the **Neutral Zone**. The Empire is run from Romulus, by a Senate of proconsuls lead by a Praetor. The twin planet, Remus, is home to the Remans, a bat-like oppressed minority.
- **RUNABOUTS:** Small **starships** used by the **Starfleet** personnel of Deep Space Nine that are larger and faster than a shuttle, but far smaller than ships like the Enterprise and Voyager.
- **SAUCER SECTION:** The bit of the Enterprise that looks like a disc. The main bit below that is the engineering hull. The rockets that stick out the back are the nacelles. The saucer section has the bridge and all the living quarters in it, and can be detached in emergencies – we first see this in *Encounter at Farpoint*, and it saves the crew in *Star Trek: Generations*.
- **SECTOR:** A relatively small area of space, one containing only a handful of star systems. There are hundreds of sectors in the **Federation**. Sector 001 contains Earth's solar system.
- **SHIELDS:** Forcefields that protect a **starship**. There are two types: deflectors, which sweep space debris out of the way of a ship (travelling so fast, even a grain of dust could punch a hole in the hull) – the dish on the front of the Enterprise is the deflector dish; and shields, more powerful forcefields that absorb attacks. Starships are usually heavily shielded – even the lowest power shields can protect against atomic explosions – but this means their opponents have to use powerful weapons. Even a ship like the Enterprise will start to see its shields collapse after a few direct hits on the same spot from **photon torpedoes**, **phasers** or similar weapons. If the opponent manages to get past the shields, then they can target the engine room, Bridge or other vital areas, and will almost certainly win the battle. **Transporters** normally can't work through shields. Shields aren't kept on most of the time – when trouble rears its head, the captain has to order 'raise shields' or 'shields up'. Smaller shields, containment fields, have a vast number of uses, such as security barriers and storing dangerous materials. In the event of a hull breach, emergency containment fields activate to keep the air inside the ship. Captain Archer's original Enterprise doesn't have shields, but can 'polarise the hull plating', a more primitive method of protection.
- **SHUTTLES: Starships** carry shuttles for journeys that, for a variety of reasons, can't be carried out with **transporters**. These are tiny ships that are kept in a shuttlebay. The bigger the ship, the more shuttles it tends to carry – Kirk's Enterprise had, according to most sources, between two and six shuttles. The Enterprise-D had 25 as well as 12 two-man shuttlepods. There are a variety of different types of shuttles for various purposes, capable of different speeds and ranges.
- **SPECIES 8472:** A three-legged, two-armed race with long faces and greyish, scaled bodies. A hostile race that preys on all species, including the **Borg** (who gave them their name). They come from another dimension, fluidic space. They infect other races with their cells, which rapidly take over their host. The species uses organic technology. They appear to be telepathic. Their weapons can destroy Borg Cubes and even whole planets.
- **STARBASE:** Bases dotted around the **Federation** – some are space stations, others are based on the surface of planets. They have better medical and engineering facilities than starships. If the Enterprise needs repairs or specialist medical treatment, they head for the nearest Starbase. In Kirk's era, there were 17 Starbases (although Starbase 200 was mentioned in *The Alternative Factor*), by Picard's time there are about 500 (although Starbase 718 was mentioned in The Neutral Zone) The Federation also has a few Deep Space stations at the frontiers of exploration – Deep Space Nine, of course, being the most famous, but DS3 (*Inheritance, Interface*), DS4 (*The Chase, Suspicions*) and DS5 (*Parallels, Star Trek: First Contact*) have also been mentioned.
- **STARDATES:** Ordinary timekeeping doesn't work when travelling faster than light at **warp** speeds, so 'stardates' are used instead in *Star Trek*.

  In the original series, stardates were four digit numbers, followed by a decimal place. Fans in the seventies tried to work out the system used to calculate them, coming up with a number of elaborate theories, but Gene Roddenberry and DC Fontana both confirmed that they were just meaningless numbers that progressed roughly as the series did. *Where No Man Has Gone Before*, the first filmed, had a stardate of 1312.4, *Turnabout Intruder*, the last, was set on stardate 5928.5, *Star Trek VI: The Undiscovered Country*, the last recorded voyage of Kirk's Enterprise, took place on stardate 9523.1.

  The Next Generation had an elaborate five-digit system, with the first episode having a stardate of 41153.7. The first number was always 4 (which was said at first to stand for the twenty-fourth century), the second was the number of the season of *The Next Generation* the story was set in, with the last three digits progressing as the season does. So *Best of Both Worlds* part 1, the last episode of the third season, has a stardate of 43989.1, and part two, the first of the fourth season, starts at stardate 44001.4. There were a couple of unfortunate side effects – firstly, all the season cliffhangers apparently took place on New Year's Eve, secondly, the series and its successors ran more than ten years, and so they passed 49999.9. Stardates since then (the fifth series of *Deep Space Nine*, the second series of *Voyager* and *Star Trek: First Contact*) have had stardates beginning with 5. *Star Trek: Nemesis* has a stardate of 56844.9.

  Under both systems, the intention is that each single digit represents a day, each thousand digits is a year – so stardate 2001.4 would be exactly a year and a day after stardate 1000.4 (and likewise stardates 42001.4 and 41000.4 in *The Next Generation*). Pedants might note that this doesn't work, because there aren't a thousand days in a year.

  At the time *Enterprise* is set, the mid-twenty-second century, the stardate system has not yet been adopted.
- **STARFLEET:** The **Federation's starships** and their crews. Starfleet isn't a military organisation, but one of exploration and diplomacy – although, they wear uniforms, carry rank and the ships are often heavily armed. Officers in Starfleet have graduated from the Starfleet Academy in San Francisco after an intensive four-year course that reportedly includes everything from **warp** theory and **shuttle** piloting to creative writing and cookery. Starships report to Starfleet Command.

Before *Enterprise*, it was assumed that Starfleet had always been an arm of the Federation – but Archer captained his Enterprise before the Federation was founded and worked for Starfleet.

- **STARSHIPS:** Ships capable of travelling the vast distances between stars (as opposed to the far shorter distances within solar systems). In Kirk's time, it seems to be shorthand for the type of ship his USS Enterprise is: large, long-range and capable of meeting any challenge. While most **Federation** ships share common design elements, they come in all shapes and sizes, with some having very specific roles, others being jacks-of-all-trades.

  Each Federation starship is of a particular type, or class, of ship. The class is named after the first ship of the type to be commissioned. Kirk's USS Enterprise is Constitution-class. The USS Excelsior and the USS Enterprise-B (larger than Kirk's Enterprise, smaller than Picard's) are both Excelsior-class. *The Next Generation*'s USS Enterprise-D is Galaxy-class. The USS Enterprise-E is one of only two of the largest known **Starfleet** vessels, Sovereign-class starships, (the other being the USS Sovereign).

  According to the original writers', and Kirk in *Tomorrow is Yesterday*, there were 12 Constitution-class starships in his day. More starships than that are accounted for in the run of the original series, although as they're clearly rather accident-prone perhaps some are replacements for lost ships. We see the USS Enterprise (lost in *Star Trek III: The Search for Spock*), USS Constellation (lost in *The Doomsday Machine*), USS Intrepid (lost in *The Immunity Syndrome*), USS Exeter (Lost in *The Omega Glory*), USS Defiant (lost in *The Tholian Web*), USS Farragut (Half the crew killed when Kirk served on it in *Obsession*), USS Excalibur, USS Hood, USS Lexington and USS Potemkin (all from *The Ultimate Computer*, all seriously damaged in that story) and USS Yorktown (mentioned in *Obsession*). In *Court Martial* a status board also refers to the USS Essex, USS Constitution, USS Republic and two ships that aren't named, the NCC-1685 and NCC-1718.

  Star Trek VI: The Undiscovered Country also has the USS Eagle, USS Endeavor and USS Kongo, but that's set decades later, when we can presume Starfleet has built more ships. The replacement USS Enterprise-A (first seen at the end of *Star Trek IV: The Voyage Home*) also falls into this category.

  It was originally stated in *The Next Generation* writers' guidelines that the Federation had six Galaxy-class ships – the first two to be launched being the USS Galaxy (mentioned in *Tears of the Prophets* and *Star Trek: Nemesis*) and the USS Enterprise-D (lost in *Star Trek: Generations*), with Enterprise's 'sister ship' being the USS Yamato (lost in *Contagion*). Over the years, we've also seen the USS Odyssey (lost in *The Jem'Hadar*), USS Magellan and USS Trinculo (seen in *Sacrifice of Angels*), USS Venture (seen or referred to in *The Way of the Warrior*, *Sacrifice of Angels* and *Tears of the Prophets*) and the USS Challenger, commanded by Geordi in an alternative future (*Timeless*).

  In Kirk's day, there was a Constitution-class ship called USS Defiant, but the USS Defiant used on Deep Space Nine was a new (Defiant-class) ship. The runabouts are officially Danube-class.

  The USS Voyager is Intrepid-class.

  There are any number of classes of ship, including Constellation (like Picard's old ship, the USS Stargazer) and Ambassador (like the Enterprise-C and the USS Excalibur seen in the *New Frontier* novels). A common type of smaller ship used in both Kirk and Picard's time (like the USS Reliant in *Star Trek II: The Wrath of Khan*) is Miranda-class. One of the oldest is Daedalus-class. By the tenty-ninth century, Starfleet will operate Wells-class starships like the USS Relativity that are capable of time travel.
- **SUBSPACE:** While never exactly defined, subspace is a dimension or continuum that maps onto normal space but where faster-than-light travel is possible. Ships travelling at **warp** and all communications signals travel through subspace.
- **TALAXIANS:** Neelix's people. They fought a war with the *Haakonians*, during which *Rinax*, the Talaxian moon, was destroyed, killing hundreds of thousands of people.
- **TETRYON:** A (made-up) subatomic particle that's only stable in **subspace**.
- **TRACTOR BEAM:** An energy beam that's used to tow or repel objects like smaller ships. If powerful enough, tractor beams can fix a hostile ship in place or prevent it from escaping.
- **TRANSPORTERS:** Teleportation devices that allow people and objects to be *'beamed'* from one location to another. At a prototype stage at the time *Enterprise* is set, they're still quite limited and prone to malfunction in *Star Trek*. By the time of *The Next Generation*, the technology has been refined and transporters are far more flexible – people can be beamed straight from the surface of a planet to Sickbay or the Bridge, for example, they don't have to go via the transporter room. Transporters need a good signal – like radio waves, they don't always work in some atmospheric conditions (like especially violent storms), or through some materials (like dense rock or particular metals). The transporter can't be used when a ship is travelling at **warp** speed or when its shields are up (unless the writers forget!)
- **TRICORDER:** A handheld multi-purpose scientific instrument and recording device carried by **Away Teams**. There are specialised medical tricorders.
- **TRILL:** Trills are a symbiotic species from the planet Trill. A humanoid host (that looks human with discreet giraffe-like markings on their faces and bodies) combines with an immortal worm-like symbiont. Dax in *Deep Space Nine* is a Trill.
- **USS:** Officially, what USS stands for has never been spelt out in the series – it's clearly not United States Ship, as in the current US Navy (and as with the real USS Enterprise, a US Navy aircraft carrier). According to Captain Pike in The Cage, the 'USS' stands for 'United Space Ship'. But that was in an unbroadcast pilot, before a lot of the details of the show were fixed. Fans now prefer 'United Star Ship'.
- **VIDIIANS:** A once-beautiful race from the Delta **Quadrant**, ravaged by the Phage, a disfiguring disease. They have become surgeons and medics, but to survive they abduct other species and harvest their organs.
- **VORTA:** See **Dominion**.
- **VULCANS:** A pointy-eared, green-blooded race that has dedicated itself to logic, rather than emotions. Mr Spock was half-Vulcan (his mother was human). *Voyager's* Tuvok and *Enterprise's* T'Pol are fully Vulcan. There are a couple of common misconceptions about Vulcans – they do have emotions, they just suppress them via meditation and training. And there's no such thing as 'the Vulcan death grip' – they can render people unconscious by touching their neck in a special way, but it's never fatal. Vulcans are also notable for only mating once every seven years – at which time they revert to their savage nature. The Vulcans call this time the Pon farr. They have the ability to link their minds to other beings to facilitate communication or to discover information – this is known as the mind meld. According to Spock in *This Side of Paradise*, he does have a first name, but it's unpronouncable for humans (According to the 1970s book *The Officers' Manual*, Spock's first name is Xtmprszntwlfd). The Vulcans come from the planet Vulcan, which is close to Earth. They were the first aliens the human race made official contact with (*Star Trek: First Contact*), and at first they held humanity back from exploring space, worried that they were not ready (*Enterprise*). By Kirk's time, Vulcans and humans are both important members of the **Federation**.
- **WARP DRIVE:** The powerful engines that allow **starships** to travel many times faster than the speed of light. They work by colliding matter and antimatter together in the warp core (a process somehow involving warp plasma and regulated by rare and fragile dilithium crystals) to create a fantastic amount of energy which is then channelled through power transfer conduits to the field coils in the nacelles (the two 'rockets' that stick out the back of the Enterprise). These create a warp field, a bubble which allows a ship to fly faster than Einstein would approve of by putting the ship in **subspace**. Failure of this process at any stage can be catastrophic. Most feared is a warp core breach, when the antimatter in the engines gets out of its containment field – this would instantly destroy a starship (and everything else in the area). Warp engines produce a warp signature that allows a ship to be tracked.

The speed of a starship is measured as a warp factor. In the original series, it was held that the speed was light speed multiplied by the cube of the warp factor, so Warp 3 was nine times and Warp 4 64 times the speed of light. The production teams from *The Next Generation* on have agreed Warp 1 is the speed of light, then the scale increases exponentially to Warp 10, infinite speed.

A typical speed for a **Federation** ship on routine business is about Warp 6 (392 times the speed of light – or just over a light year a day, so it takes a few days to travel between solar systems).

Maximum warp is the fastest a ship can travel – this varies from ship to ship, with Archer's Enterprise capable of about Warp 5 at first, Kirk's Enterprise about Warp 8 (it varies from episode to episode – it's Warp 6 in *Spock's Brain*, Warp 9 in *The Paradise Syndrome*, and, with external help, the ship manages to get to Warp 11 in *The Changeling* and Warp 14 in *That Which Survives*), and Picard's capable of Warp 9.6 for short periods. Cheekily, the makers of *All Good Things* broke their own rule and showed the future Enterprise seen in that story moving at Warp 13. Warp 9 is faster than most ships can manage, but at that speed it would still take 66 years to travel from one end of the galaxy to the other.

In Kirk's time, the Federation was experimenting with the much faster transwarp, but – as Scotty predicted – couldn't get it to work. The **Borg** have transwarp drive, and can cross the galaxy in days.

- **WORMHOLE:** An idea adapted from real science, a wormhole is, essentially, a tunnel in space that leads straight to a distant part of the galaxy. Deep Space Nine is located near the Bajoran wormhole which leads to a point in the Gamma **Quadrant** – without this short-cut, it would take the fastest **Federation** ship 60 years to make the same journey. Wormholes are usually short-lived and unpredictable – the Bajoran Wormhole is permanent, giving the planet Bajor (and Deep Space Nine, which orbits Bajor) enormous strategic importance.

INDEX

This index doesn't list every mention of regular characters, actors or concepts (like 'Kirk', 'Patrick Stewart' or 'Enterprise'), but does refer to all significant mentions of them. Main story entries are marked in **bold**. The episode titles specify which series they belong to – *Star Trek* (ST), the animated series (ANI), *Star Trek II* (ST2), *The Next Generation* (TNG), *Deep Space Nine* (DS9), *Voyager* (VOY) and *Enterprise* (ENT).

C

D

H

M

Q

R

S

T

U

V

W

X

Y

Z